THE JUNIOR LEAGUE
CENTENNIAL
COOKBOOK

PHOTO BY
PRICE STUDIOS INC.
11 WEST 42 ST.
N.Y.C.

THE JUNIOR LEAGUE
CENTENNIAL
COOKBOOK

Over 750 of the Most Treasured Recipes

from 200 Junior Leagues

by

The Association of Junior Leagues International Inc.

An Ellen Rolfes Book

MAIN STREET BOOKS / DOUBLEDAY
NEW YORK LONDON TORONTO SYDNEY AUCKLAND

To the spirit of voluntarism, and to all those individuals who do indeed change the world through their acts of caring

Food Editor: Ellen Brown
Contributing Writers: Mary Loveless
                            Betsey Steeger

THE ASSOCIATION OF JUNIOR LEAGUES INTERNATIONAL INC.
The Association of Junior Leagues International Inc. is an organization of women committed to promoting voluntarism, developing the potential of women and improving the community through the effective action and leadership of trained volunteers. Its purpose is exclusively educational and charitable.

The Association of Junior Leagues International Inc. reaches out to women of all races, religions, and national origins who demonstrate an interest in and commitment to voluntarism.

Junior League is a registered trademark of The Association of Junior Leagues International Inc. It is in use in four countries: United States, Canada, Mexico, and Great Britain. Reg. U. S. Pat. & Tm. Off.

Photographs appearing on pages 1, 56, 91, 125, 149, 189, and 293 courtesy of The Association of Junior Leagues International Inc.

Photographs appearing on the half-title and title pages, on page 228 and on page 258 courtesy of the Junior League of the City of New York.

A MAIN STREET BOOK
PUBLISHED BY DOUBLEDAY
a division of Bantam Doubleday Dell Publishing Group, Inc.
1540 Broadway, New York, New York 10036

MAIN STREET BOOKS, DOUBLEDAY, and the portrayal of a building with a tree are trademarks of Doubleday, a division of Bantam Doubleday Dell Publishing Group, Inc.

Library of Congress Cataloging-in-Publication Data

ISBN 0-385-47731-7
Copyright © 1996 by The Association of Junior Leagues International Inc.
All Rights Reserved
Printed in the United States of America
4 5 6 7 8 9 10
Book Design: Barbara Cohen Aronica

CONTENTS

INTRODUCTION

This book is a celebration of a journey—a journey of women, a journey of partnership, a journey of courage. It is a celebration of the Junior League as it approaches its one hundredth anniversary.

The history of this remarkable organization can perhaps best be summed up in its slogan: *The Junior League—Where a Woman Can Change the World.* Little did a compassionate nineteen-year-old named Mary Harriman know, when she persuaded a group of young women in 1901 in New York City to found an organization committed to "improving the conditions that surround us," that she had identified a path that would provide women volunteers and their communities opportunities to indeed grow and change. At the end of a century of continuous growth, the Junior League today numbers approximately 200,000 volunteers in nearly 300 Junior Leagues in four countries: the United States, Canada, Mexico, and Great Britain. All these women join in a shared commitment to "promote voluntarism, develop the potential of women and improve the community."

While we can't possibly capture in these pages the accomplishments of hundreds of thousands of women who have volunteered in the past and who volunteer today, we hope to give you a taste of who they were and are, what they have done and what they do—and perhaps some of the reasons why.

In the chapter openings, you will find messages about our values and our vision. As you prepare your favorite recipes from this book, we hope you will pause for a moment to reflect on the unique persons and programs highlighted throughout the book. The Volunteers of Distinction are women who, in the supportive Junior League atmosphere, took risks and developed the leadership abilities necessary to spearhead social change in their communities. Take a moment to think about their character,

vision, commitment. The Programs of Distinction demonstrate the impact individual Junior Leagues have made in their communities and beyond. Stop awhile to savor how the scope of the programs convey intelligent planning . . . how the attention to detail suggests passion and follow-through . . . how the outcomes speak to caring.

A good way to experience the variety and richness of the Junior Leagues' contributions to their communities is in this "best of the Junior Leagues" community cookbook. It is difficult to overstate how successful the Junior League cookbooks have been in raising funds for their communities. Sales have been so strong that in many bookstores, Junior League cookbooks are an unofficial category and have their own display section. Since Junior Leagues began publishing cookbooks in the 1950s, more than eighteen million cookbooks have been sold. In any given year, the Junior Leagues in aggregate may publish as many as 200 cookbooks that raise several million dollars. The proceeds fund programs ranging from shelters for runaway youth, homeless families, and battered spouses to food banks, mobile health vans, organ donation, downtown revitalization, the arts, historical preservation . . . to the promotion of voluntarism itself. The Junior League cookbooks—from which we present here only a few choice samplings—preserve a community's culture and heritage and provide a source of deep pride for its inhabitants.

In 1901, one woman's dream to improve her community set in motion a chain reaction that has reverberated down through a hundred years. It has been an incredible journey—and a journey that continues toward the next hundred years. We are so pleased to have you with us at our centennial feast.

—Holly Sloan, Executive Director

Chronological List of Member Junior Leagues (by year of founding or, from 1921 on, year of acceptance into the Association)

City of New York, New York	1901	Tacoma, Washington	1921	Akron, Ohio	1926
Boston, Massachusetts	1907	Birmingham, Alabama	1922	Boise, Idaho	1926
Brooklyn, New York	1910	Dallas, Texas	1922	Charlotte, North Carolina	1926
Portland, Oregon	1910	Indianapolis, Indiana	1922	Houston, Texas	1926
Baltimore, Maryland	1912	Kingston, New York	1922	Los Angeles, California	1926
Chicago, Illinois	1912	Little Rock, Arkansas	1922	Miami, Florida	1926
Cleveland, Ohio	1912	Memphis, Tennessee	1922	Montgomery, Alabama	1926
Montreal, Quebec	1912	Nashville, Tennessee	1922	Pasadena, California	1926
Philadelphia, Pennsylvania	1912	Orange County, New York	1922	Savannah, Georgia	1926
San Francisco, California	1912	Pittsburgh, Pennsylvania	1922	Toronto, Ontario	1926
Oranges & Short Hills, New Jersey	1913	Portland, Maine	1922	Asheville, North Carolina	1927
Washington, DC	1913	Springfield, Massachusetts	1922	Fairmont, West Virginia	1927
Detroit, Michigan	1914	Charleston, South Carolina	1923	Greensboro, North Carolina	1927
Kansas City, Missouri	1914	Charleston, West Virginia	1923	Richmond, Virginia	1927
St. Louis, Missouri	1914	Columbus, Ohio	1923	Winnipeg, Manitoba	1927
Atlanta, Georgia	1916	Elizabeth-Plainfield, New Jersey	1923	Flint, Michigan	1928
Milwaukee, Wisconsin	1916	Greater New Haven, Connecticut	1923	Oklahoma City, Oklahoma	1928
Racine, Wisconsin	1916	Greater Waterbury, Connecticut	1923	Roanoke Valley, Virginia	1928
Albany, New York	1917	Honolulu, Hawaii	1923	Tampa, Florida	1928
Chattanooga, Tennessee	1917	Minneapolis, Minnesota	1923	Augusta, Georgia	1929
St. Paul, Minnesota	1917	Stamford-Norwalk, Connecticut	1923	Harrisburg, Pennsylvania	1929
Greater Utica, New York	1918	Tulsa, Oklahoma	1923	Lynchburg, Virginia	1929
Wilmington, Delaware	1918	Winston-Salem, North Carolina	1923	San Diego, California	1929
Buffalo, New York	1919	Colorado Springs, Colorado	1924	Troy, New York	1929
Denver, Colorado	1919	Evanston–North Shore, Illinois	1924	Williamsport, Pennsylvania	1929
Omaha, Nebraska	1919	Jacksonville, Florida	1924	Fort Worth, Texas	1930
Poughkeepsie, New York	1919	Lancaster, Pennsylvania	1924	Mexico City, Mexico	1930
Cincinnati, Ohio	1920	Lexington, Kentucky	1924	Raleigh, North Carolina	1930
Dayton, Ohio	1920	New Orleans, Louisiana	1924	Rockford, Illinois	1930
Eastern Fairfield County, Connecticut	1920	Reading, Pennsylvania	1924	Des Moines, Iowa	1931
Duluth, Minnesota	1921	San Antonio, Texas	1924	Greater Elmira–Corning, New York	1931
Greater Princeton, New Jersey	1921	Seattle, Washington	1924	Greater Vancouver, British Columbia	1931
Hartford, Connecticut	1921	Columbia, South Carolina	1925	Mobile, Alabama	1931
Knoxville, Tennessee	1921	El Paso, Texas	1925	St. Petersburg, Florida	1931
Lincoln, Nebraska	1921	Erie, Pennsylvania	1925	Binghamton, New York	1932
Louisville, Kentucky	1921	Grand Rapids, Michigan	1925	Schenectady, New York	1932
Montclair-Newark, New Jersey	1921	Norfolk–Virginia Beach, Virginia	1925	Youngstown, Ohio	1932
Rhode Island, Rhode Island	1921	Parkersburg, West Virginia	1925	Bergen County, New Jersey	1933
St. Joseph, Missouri	1921	Santa Barbara, California	1925	Berkshire County, Massachusetts	1933
Sioux City, Iowa	1921	Spokane, Washington	1925	Halifax, Nova Scotia	1933
Syracuse, New York	1921	Wichita, Kansas	1925	Huntington, West Virginia	1933
		Worcester, Massachusetts	1925		

THE JUNIOR LEAGUE
CENTENNIAL
COOKBOOK

A CELEBRATION OF WOMEN

For the past hundred years, the volunteer women of the Junior League have sought to meet their communities' needs. In these pages, we celebrate their remarkable journey as they pursue a shared vision of a world in which all people work together to create safe, healthy, and productive communities.

These caring women have brought to their communities a woman's way of volunteering—a way tempered in the homefires of family building that emphasizes sharing, "taking turns," and working toward consensual solutions. It is a way of working that approaches community problems not from special interests but from a holistic view that values all partners and forges a common path toward the better future we all desire.

League suffragists march for "Votes for Women."
Early 1900s.

There are hundreds of thousands of these women— the ones who traveled the road in the past, the many who make the journey today and, as the Junior League continues to grow, the many more who will blaze the trail into the future. It is a story of courage and commitment that began with one woman, Mary Harriman, and a small group of 85 women in one city, New York. Now, almost a hundred years later, it embraces approximately 200,000 women in nearly 300 communities throughout the United States, Canada, Mexico, and Great Britain.

Junior League volunteers come from varying backgrounds and interests, ranging from the professional to the homemaker to the public official, from the pediatric surgeon to the disc jockey to the priest, and include such luminaries as:

- *Sandra Day O'Connor,* the first woman to serve on the U.S. Supreme Court

- Four U.S. First Ladies: *Eleanor Roosevelt,* who helped establish the first Junior League in New York City, *Betty Ford, Nancy Reagan,* and *Barbara Bush*

- The Honorable *Florence Bird,* former Canadian Senator and chair, Royal Commission on the Status of Women

- Pulitzer Prize-winning author *Eudora Welty;* and

- *Shirley Temple Black,* child actress and former U.S. Ambassador to the United Nations and Czechoslovakia.

What is truly extraordinary is that these women *chose* to associate with each other around a shared vision. In their connectedness, each individual and each community gets stronger, the world gets better.

The Junior League is a historical body on a historical continuum. We pause at the hundred-year mark to salute the women of the Junior League— as individuals and as an international association of volunteers—to celebrate their accomplishments and wish them well as they move forward into the twenty-first century.

PARTY FOOD, APPETIZERS AND BEVERAGES

PARTY FOOD: DIPS, SPREADS & HORS D'OEUVRES

ARTICHOKE PHYLLO FLOWERS

8 to 10 tablespoons butter

2 shallots, minced

1 (19-ounce) package frozen artichoke hearts, thawed and diced

2 cloves garlic, minced

8 ounces ricotta cheese

1 egg, beaten

½ cup half-and-half

½ cup grated Parmesan cheese

2 tablespoons snipped chives

Salt and pepper

9 sheets phyllo pastry, thawed if frozen

To make filling: In a medium skillet, melt 2 tablespoons of the butter over medium heat. Add the shallots and sauté for 1 minute. Add the diced artichokes and sauté for 5 to 6 minutes or until lightly browned, adding the garlic for the last 2 minutes. Set aside to cool. In a bowl soften the ricotta, then beat in the egg and half-and-half until blended. Add the Parmesan, chives, and artichoke mixture. Salt and pepper to taste; mix well. Set the filling aside.

To assemble: Melt the remaining 6 to 8 tablespoons butter in a small pan. Heat the oven to 350 degrees. Unroll the phyllo and cover with waxed paper and then with a damp towel to keep it from drying out. Lay 1 sheet of phyllo dough on a flat surface and lightly brush with melted butter. Repeat 2 more times. Cut into 5 strips lengthwise and 4 strips widthwise to make twenty 3-inch squares. Lay 1 square on a work surface and place another square on top of it at opposite angles. Press the squares into the cups of a mini muffin pan. Repeat until all the cups are filled with phyllo squares. Spoon the filling equally into the cups. Bake for 15 to 20 minutes or until the filling feels set and phyllo is lightly golden. Cool 5 minutes. Gently ease out of the pan with the tip of a knife.

MAKES 60

Feast of Eden, Monterey, CA

HOT ARTICHOKE DIP

1 cup mayonnaise
1 cup freshly grated Parmesan
    cheese
1 (8½-ounce) can water-packed
    artichoke hearts, drained and
    chopped coarse
1 (7-ounce) can chopped green
    chiles

Preheat the oven to 375 degrees.

Combine the mayonnaise, Parmesan, artichoke hearts, and chiles and pour the mixture into a shallow baking dish. Bake 10 to 15 minutes or until bubbly and heated through. Serve with tortilla chips.

MAKES 2 CUPS   *The Seattle Classic,* Seattle, WA

MUCHO GUSTO DIP

3 ripe avocados
3 tablespoons lemon juice
Salt and pepper
1 cup sour cream
1 package taco seasoning mix
2 (15-ounce) cans refried bean
1 (4½-ounce) can ripe olives,
    drained and chopped
1 (4-ounce) can chopped green
    chiles
3 ripe tomatoes, chopped coarse
½ cup chopped scallions
1½ cups grated Cheddar cheese
Tortilla chips

Cut the avocados in half lengthwise and remove the pits. Scoop out the meat with a spoon, place in a small bowl, and mash with a fork. Stir in the lemon juice; add salt and pepper to taste.

In another small bowl, combine the sour cream and taco seasoning mix. Stir to blend well.

Spread the refried beans in an even layer on a large round platter or shallow casserole dish. Spread the mashed avocado on top of the beans. Cover with the sour cream. Scatter the chopped olives, chiles, tomatoes, and scallions over the sour cream. Top with the grated cheese.

Serve with tortilla chips for dipping.

SERVES 12   *Celebrate Miami,* Miami, FL

GUACAMOLE DIP

2 large avocados
1 tablespoon lemon juice
¼ cup chopped onion
1 small tomato, seeded and chopped
    fine
Salt to taste
¼ cup sour cream
½ to 1 tablespoon crushed red
    pepper flakes or chopped jalapeño
    pepper
Chopped fresh cilantro to taste
Tortilla chips

Cut the avocados in half lengthwise and remove the pits. Scoop out the meat with a spoon, place in a small bowl, and mash with a fork. Add the lemon juice, onion, tomato, and salt. Stir in the sour cream, red pepper, and cilantro. Serve with tortilla chips warmed in a 200 degree oven.

SERVES 6   *Buen Provecho,* Mexico City

SPINACH-FILLED MUSHROOMS

16-20 small (2-inch) mushrooms,
    wiped and trimmed
1 cup finely chopped onion
3 tablespoons butter
1 (10-ounce) package frozen
    chopped spinach, cooked, drained,
    and squeezed
½ cup grated Swiss cheese
Grated Parmesan cheese

Preheat the oven to 300 degrees. Butter a shallow baking pan large enough to hold the mushroom caps in 1 layer.

Remove stems from the mushrooms. Chop the stems fine and sauté with the onion in butter about 5 minutes or until the onion is tender but not brown. Add the spinach and stir to mix thoroughly. Add the Swiss cheese, stirring lightly. Remove from the heat.

Fill the mushroom caps with the mixture. Sprinkle with Parmesan and arrange in the prepared pan. Bake uncovered for 15 to 20 minutes. Serve warm.

SERVES 6 TO 8   *Utah Dining Car,* Ogden, UT

TZATZIKI

This easy and refreshing dip is of Greek-Turkish origin. Try it as a garnish with baked potatoes.

4 cucumbers
3 cloves garlic, peeled and minced
1 tablespoon olive oil
Salt and pepper to taste
2 cups yogurt, or yogurt and sour
    cream mixed

Peel and seed the cucumbers, and put through a fine grater (not a blender). Allow to drain in a colander until the juices have stopped running.

In a small bowl, mash the garlic with the olive oil, salt, and pepper. Stir in the cucumbers and yogurt. Chill, covered, for 1 hour or more. Serve as a dip with crackers or raw vegetables.

SERVES 6–8   *Discover Dayton,* Dayton, OH

ASPARAGUS ROLLS

Both the appearance and the taste are beautiful . . . truly a superb hors d'oeuvre. Remember that they must be made in advance.

25 fresh asparagus spears
Salt to taste
25 thin slices white bread
8 ounces cream cheese, softened
3 ounces blue cheese, softened
1 egg
3 sticks (¾ pound) butter, melted

In a large skillet, bring enough water to boil to barely cover asparagus. Trim the spears to the same length as the bread slices and place in the skillet. Sprinkle with salt and cover tightly. Boil gently until the lower parts of the stalks are barely fork-tender—about 3 to 5 minutes, depending on the age of the asparagus. Drain immediately and rinse in cold water until the cooking process has ended.

Remove crusts from the bread and flatten the slices with a rolling pin. Combine cheeses and egg in a mixing bowl and beat with an electric mixer until blended. Spread the mixture evenly over the bread slices. Place an asparagus spear on the edge of each one and roll up. Dip in melted butter to coat all sides. Place seam side down on a cookie sheet and chill for 24 hours, or freeze until ready to bake.

Preheat the oven to 400 degrees. Cut the rolls into thirds and bake for 10 minutes or until lightly browned. Bake the frozen rolls without thawing for 15 minutes or until brown. Serve immediately.

MAKES 75   *Private Collection 2,* Palo Alto, CA

WRAPPED ASPARAGUS

Serve this as a delicious but slightly messy finger food or on lettuce leaves as a first course.

36 asparagus spears of medium
    thickness (about 1 pound)
36 slices prosciutto (4 inches long)
4 ounces blue cheese, crumbled

BALSAMIC VINAIGRETTE
½ cup balsamic vinegar
½ cup vegetable oil
½ cup olive oil
½ teaspoon salt
½ teaspoon pepper
½ teaspoon lemon juice
2 teaspoons minced fresh basil, or ½
    teaspoon dried

Trim asparagus to 4-5 inches and peel the thick ends with a potato peeler. Arrange the stalks in 1 layer in container. Cover tightly with plastic wrap. Microwave on high for 4½ minutes. Prick plastic to release steam. Remove from oven and plunge the asparagus into ice water. Drain and dry.

Wrap each asparagus stalk in a slice of prosciutto. Arrange the asparagus on a large, flat platter with a lip around the edge. Sprinkle the blue cheese over the wrapped asparagus.

Mix the vinaigrette ingredients in a jar with a tight-fitting lid and shake to mix. When ready to serve, drizzle over the top of the asparagus, using just enough to coat lightly. Reserve the remaining dressing for another use.

MAKES 3 DOZEN; SERVES 4 AS A FIRST COURSE
Saint Louis Days, Saint Louis Nights Cookbook, Saint Louis, MO

DIXIE CAVIAR

Try this dip with corn chips, or as a salad served on a bed of lettuce or in a hollowed-out tomato.

4 cups frozen or canned black-eyed
    peas
1 (16-ounce) can white hominy,
    drained (optional)
2 medium tomatoes, chopped
1 cup Italian salad dressing
1 cup chopped green pepper
½ cup chopped onion
4 scallions, sliced
1 or 2 jalapeño peppers, seeded and
    chopped
1 or 2 cloves garlic, minced
¼ cup sour cream or plain yogurt
Chopped fresh cilantro or parsley to
    taste
Tortilla chips or crackers

If using frozen black-eyed peas, cook according to package directions; drain. If using canned peas, rinse and drain. In a large bowl, combine the drained peas, hominy, tomatoes, salad dressing, green pepper, onion, scallions, jalapeño peppers, and garlic. Cover and chill for 1 to 2 days.

Drain the mixture, reserving the liquid. Partially chop in a food processor by pulsing twice. Do not purée. Return enough of the liquid to the mixture to make a nice dipping consistency. Top with sour cream and cilantro. Serve cold with tortilla chips or crackers.

MAKES 10 CUPS   *Heart & Soul,* Memphis, TN

SPICY CAYENNE TOASTS WITH SUN-DRIED TOMATO SPREAD

Sensational, yet so simple.

SUN-DRIED TOMATO SPREAD
1½ ounces sun-dried tomatoes
¼ cup olive oil
2 cloves garlic, minced
2 tablespoons minced parsley
5 basil leaves, chopped
1 scallion, chopped
1 teaspoon freshly ground black
  pepper
½ teaspoon salt
Pinch of sugar
4 ounces goat cheese, crumbled

CAYENNE TOASTS
½ cup olive oil
2 teaspoons ground red pepper
  (cayenne)
1 teaspoon salt
1 teaspoon sugar
½ teaspoon paprika
1½ teaspoons garlic powder
1 loaf French bread baguette, sliced
  into ¼-inch slices

Prepare the sun-dried tomato spread: To rehydrate sun-dried tomatoes, place them in boiling water for 5 minutes. Drain. Place the tomatoes and remaining ingredients, except goat cheese, in a container and refrigerate for 4 hours. Process in a food processor until smooth.

Prepare the cayenne toasts: Preheat the oven to 200 degrees. In the container of a blender or food processor, or in a jar with a tight-fitting lid, combine the olive oil and seasonings, mixing well. Lay the bread slices on a cookie sheet. Brush one side lightly with the flavored oil. Bake 1 hour or until crisp. Cool. (The toasts may be prepared ahead of time and frozen.)

To serve, spread some of the tomato mixture on the toasts and sprinkle with goat cheese.

SERVES 8–10   *California Sizzles,* Pasadena, CA

FRESH CORN SALSA

Excellent served with chips, broiled or grilled fish or chicken.

4 ears fresh corn, shucked
1 cup diced zucchini squash
3 tablespoons olive oil
3 medium tomatoes, diced
1 serrano chile, seeded and minced
1 medium onion, diced
½ cup chopped cilantro
2 tablespoons lime juice
2 teaspoons liquid smoke
½ teaspoon ground cumin
1 (8-ounce) can tomato sauce

Boil the corn for 2 or 3 minutes; when cool enough to handle, cut off the cob. In a skillet, sauté the squash in olive oil until the skin is bright green but the squash is still crisp. Remove from the heat.

In a serving bowl, combine the tomatoes, chile, onion, cilantro, lime juice, liquid smoke, cumin, and tomato sauce. Stir in the corn kernels and zucchini. Mix well, cover, and refrigerate for 1 hour or more. Serve cold.

MAKES 4 CUPS   *Some Like It Hot,* McAllen, TX

PAPAYA SALSA

This salsa is a refreshing complement to the smoky, salty flavor of grilled seafood.

3 cups diced ripe papaya
1 cup diced tomato
1 cup diced red bell pepper
1½ cups diced red onion
½ jalapeño pepper, seeded and
  chopped fine
2 teaspoons ground cumin
2 tablespoons extra-virgin olive oil
2½ tablespoons red wine vinegar
6 tablespoons freshly squeezed lime
  juice
2 tablespoons freshly squeezed
  lemon juice
1 teaspoon freshly ground black
  pepper
Dash Tabasco
1 cup loosely packed and coarsely
  chopped cilantro

Combine all ingredients in a large porcelain or glass bowl. Toss thoroughly. Cover and let stand for 1 or 2 hours. Serve chilled or at room temperature.

NOTE: Salsa will keep in the refrigerator for up to 1 week.

MAKES 1 QUART · *Another Taste of Aloha,* Honolulu, HI

NUTS AND BOLTS

2 small boxes Cheez-Its
3 cans mixed nuts (3-4 cups)
8 ounces shelled pecans
1 quart popcorn (best freshly
  popped)
2 packages sesame chips
2 cans coconut chips
1 small box pretzel sticks
2 sticks (½ pound) margarine
½ teaspoon garlic salt or 1 clove
  garlic, crushed
1 teaspoon salt
1 teaspoon curry powder
Dash Tabasco
1 tablespoon Worcestershire sauce

Preheat the oven to 250 degrees.

Mix the Cheez-Its, nuts, popcorn, chips, and pretzel sticks in a large roasting pan. Melt the margarine in a small pan and stir in the seasonings. Sprinkle over the mixture in the roasting pan. Bake for 1 hour, stirring 2 or 3 times. Cool on absorbent paper and store in cans or jars.

SERVES 12 OR MORE · *Cincinnati Celebrates,* Cincinnati, OH

SPICED NUTS

1 cup sugar
1 tablespoon vanilla extract
1 tablespoon ground cinnamon
5 tablespoons water
2 cups whole nut meats

Combine the sugar, vanilla, cinnamon, and water in a saucepan. Bring to a boil and cook over low heat for 5 minutes. Add the nuts and stir until coated. Spread on a baking sheet to cool.

MAKES 2 1/4 CUPS   *From Market to Mealtime,* Fayetteville, AR

SPICED PECANS

1 egg white, slightly beaten
2 tablespoons cold water
½ cup sugar
¼ teaspoon ground cloves
¼ teaspoon ground allspice
¼ teaspoon ground cinnamon
½ teaspoon salt
4 cups pecan halves

Preheat the oven to 250 degrees. Coat 2 baking sheets lightly with vegetable oil cooking spray. Combine the egg white, water, sugar, and seasonings, mixing well. Set aside for 15 minutes. Add the pecans and mix. Spread evenly on the prepared baking sheets. Bake 1 hour. Immediately loosen the pecans from the sheets with a spatula. Store in an airtight container.

MAKES 4 CUPS   *Atlanta Cooknotes,* Atlanta, GA

PIMIENTO CHEESE

2 pounds sharp Cheddar cheese,
  grated coarsely
3 hard-boiled eggs, grated coarse
1 large onion, grated coarse
2 (7-ounce) cans whole pimientos,
  chopped coarse, with their juice
2 cups mayonnaise
3 tablespoons prepared mustard
3 tablespoons Worcestershire sauce
2 teaspoons salt
½ teaspoon freshly ground black
  pepper
½ teaspoon paprika
½ teaspoon onion salt
½ teaspoon garlic salt
½ teaspoon celery salt

Stir all ingredients in your largest mixing bowl until just well mixed. Do not mash or pack down—the mixture should be coarse and loose. It will become firmer when chilled. Use to stuff celery, for sandwiches, and on Melba rounds. It keeps well when refrigerated—about 3 weeks. Do not freeze.

MAKES 2 QUARTS   *The Dallas Junior League Cookbook,* Dallas, TX

JALAPEÑO CHEESE SPREAD

The number of jalapeños can be adjusted depending on the stamina of your guests.

1 small onion, quartered
2 fresh jalapeños, seeded
2 (3-ounce) packages cream cheese
Juice of 1 lemon
1 tablespoon Worcestershire sauce
4 ounces sharp Cheddar cheese, grated
4 ounces longhorn Cheddar cheese, grated
4 ounces pimiento cheese spread
¼ cup chopped pecans
1 teaspoon paprika
Parsley

Finely chop the onion and jalapeños in a food processor. Add the cream cheese, lemon juice, and Worcestershire. Process until well blended. In a medium bowl, combine the cheeses, pecans, and paprika. Stir until thoroughly blended. Add the jalapeño mixture. Mix well. Shape on a serving plate. Garnish with parsley.

Serve with crackers or chips.

MAKES 3 CUPS   *Necessities & Temptations*, Austin, TX

CROWD PLEASIN' CHUTNEY SPREAD

2 (8-ounce) packages light cream cheese, softened
3 tablespoons curry powder
1 teaspoon salt
1 (5-ounce) jar ginger chutney
2 bunches scallions, sliced
10 strips bacon, cooked, drained well, and crumbled
¼ cup finely chopped smoked almonds or sesame seeds

In a small bowl, combine the cream cheese, curry powder, and salt. Stir with a spoon until thoroughly mixed. Spread the cheese mixture on the bottom of a 10-inch quiche dish. Purée the chutney in a food processor or blender. Spread the chutney on top of the cheese mixture. Spread the scallions evenly over the chutney layer. Sprinkle the bacon and almonds on top. Serve with melba toast or wheat crackers.

NOTE: May be prepared a day ahead.

SERVES 8   *Savor the Brandywine Valley*, Wilmington, DE

BREAK THE BARRIERS, INC.
JUNIOR LEAGUE OF FRESNO, CALIFORNIA

The Junior League of Fresno, California, provided critical help—financial and volunteer—for the Break the Barriers, Inc., center in Fresno. BTB is a unique sports-art center seeking to unite both able-bodied and disabled children and adults in a family atmosphere in order to enhance both their physical and mental potentials. The primary goal of the center is to build self-esteem of each individual while he or she learns a sport or art from a professional.

WALNUT STILTON TORTA

This appetizer is heaven for cheese and nut lovers. Prepare a few days in advance for an even richer flavor.

2 (8-ounce) packages cream cheese, softened

2 sticks (½ pound) unsalted butter, softened

¼ cup port wine

⅓ pound Stilton cheese, crumbled

½ cup coarsely chopped walnuts, lightly toasted

Toasted walnut halves and red seedless grapes for garnish

Lightly butter a 5-cup decorative ring mold, fluted mold, or several small ramekins or bowls. In a large mixing bowl, blend the cream cheese and butter until light and fluffy. Mix in the port. Spread 1½ cups of this mixture into the mold. Press in half the Stilton and half the walnuts. Add another 1½ cups of the cream cheese mixture, then the remaining Stilton and walnuts. Finish with the remaining cream cheese. Press with the back of a spoon to remove any air pockets. Cover with plastic wrap and refrigerate until firm.

To unmold, wrap a hot towel around the mold. Run a knife around the edge and invert the torta onto a serving platter. Garnish around the base with walnut halves and grapes. Let stand 30 minutes at room temperature before serving. Serve with water crackers or sliced baguettes.

SERVES 10 OR MORE *Delicious Decisions,* San Diego, CA

PESTO LAYERED TORTA

This torte is layered green and white. Choose a mold that will show it off to its best advantage.

4 tablespoons (½ stick) unsalted butter, softened

2 (8-ounce) packages cream cheese, softened

¾ cup pesto (purchase or use your favorite recipe)

Oil a deep 3-cup mold—a slightly tapered bowl works fine. Dampen a length of cheesecloth and lay it in the mold, allowing it to overhang.

Beat the butter and cheese together until thoroughly mixed. Divide the cheese into sixths. Put one portion into the bottom of the mold, spreading carefully to cover. Use about 2 tablespoons of pesto to form the second layer. Continue to layer cheese and pesto, using 2 to 4 tablespoons pesto as necessary. Lay the mixture around the edges first to form clean layers; end with a cheese layer. Cover with the overhanging cheesecloth and refrigerate for several hours.

To unmold, invert onto a serving plate; remove cloth. Garnish as desired. Serve with crackers.

SERVES 8–10 *Lagniappe on the Neches,* Beaumont, TX

FRENCH HERB CHEESE

8 ounces cream cheese, softened

4 tablespoons (½ stick) butter, softened

3 cloves garlic, minced

¼ teaspoon seasoned salt

2 tablespoons chopped fresh parsley

2 tablespoons chopped fresh chives

Coarsely ground black pepper

Tabasco to taste

Combine the cream cheese and butter in a bowl or the container of a food processor. Add the garlic, seasoned salt, parsley, chives, 1 teaspoon of pepper, and a dash of Tabasco. Mix by hand or in the processor until well blended.

Transfer to a serving bowl and sprinkle with additional coarse black pepper. Cover and let stand at room temperature for 1 hour to allow flavors to blend. Serve with crackers.

SERVES 8–10 *Lagniappe on the Neches,* Beaumont, TX

MUSHROOM WALNUT TERRINE

4 tablespoons (½ stick) butter
4 cups chopped fresh mushrooms
    (10 ounces)
½ cup chopped scallions (white part
    only)
¼ teaspoon dried thyme
1 teaspoon salt
⅓ cup sherry
8 ounces cream cheese, softened
1 cup finely chopped walnuts,
    toasted
¼ cup chopped fresh parsley
Dash hot pepper sauce
¼ cup finely chopped fresh chives
Crackers

In a large heavy skillet, melt the butter over moderate heat. Add the mushrooms, scallions, and thyme. Cook, stirring, until the scallions are transparent, about 5 to 8 minutes. Add the salt and sherry and cook until the liquid is almost evaporated. Remove from the heat and cool.

Mix the cream cheese and the cooled mushroom mixture in a large bowl. Stir to blend thoroughly. Stir in the walnuts, parsley, and hot pepper sauce. Transfer to a serving dish and chill, covered, for at least 2 hours. Sprinkle the top with chives and serve with crackers.

SERVES 8–10   *Women of Great Taste,* Wichita, KS

CURRIED CHEESE

1 (8-ounce) package plus 1
    (3-ounce) package cream cheese,
    softened
2 teaspoons sour cream
1½ teaspoons curry powder
½ cup bacon bits (purchased)
½ cup chopped peanuts
½ cup chopped scallions
½ cup raisins
Peach, mango, or apricot chutney

Blend cream cheese and sour cream until smooth. Add curry and blend well. Add bacon bits, peanuts, scallions, and raisins. Mix well. Spread into serving dish or form into shape of choice and top with chutney. Serve with crackers.

SERVES 6–8   *Gourmet L.A.,* Los Angeles, CA

FRENCH BREAD SPREAD

8 tablespoons (1 stick) butter,
    softened
½ cup mayonnaise
½ cup grated Cheddar cheese
¼ cup chopped fresh chives
1 small can sliced black olives,
    drained
½ teaspoon garlic salt
½ teaspoon freshly ground black
    pepper
1 loaf French bread, about 18 inches
    long

In a mixing bowl, combine the butter and mayonnaise and stir with a wooden spoon until well combined. Stir in the grated cheese, chives, black olives, garlic, salt, and pepper.

Preheat the broiler. Slice the bread 1 inch thick and spread one side of each slice thickly with the butter mixture. Lay the slices spread side up on a cookie sheet. Slide under the broiler only until the edges are brown. Serve warm.

SERVES 8–10   *The Wild, Wild West,* Odessa, TX

HERBED CHEESE SPREAD

1 (8-ounce) tub whipped sweet
  butter
2 (8-ounce) packages cream cheese,
  softened
1½ teaspoons fresh marjoram leaves
  or ½ teaspoon dried
1½ teaspoons chopped fresh oregano
  or ½ teaspoon dried
½ teaspoon garlic powder
2 teaspoons chopped fresh basil or
  ½ teaspoon dried
1½ teaspoons chopped fresh dill
  weed or ½ teaspoon dried
½ teaspoon freshly ground black
  pepper
1½ teaspoons fresh thyme leaves or
  ½ teaspoon dried

In a small bowl, blend the butter and cream cheese together with a wooden spoon. Blend in the marjoram, oregano, garlic powder, basil, dill weed, pepper, and thyme. Refrigerate for at least 1 hour to allow the flavors to blend. Serve with crackers or on endive leaves.

SERVES 12–15   *Stirring Performances,* Winston-Salem, NC

MEXICAN KITCHEN DIP

1 tablespoon butter
3 tablespoons chopped green pepper
1 large onion, chopped
2 cloves garlic, chopped
1 teaspoon chili powder
½ teaspoon cumin seed
5 fresh tomatoes, chopped
¾ pound Cheddar cheese, grated
Salt to taste
½ teaspoon dried red pepper
  (cayenne)
1 egg, well beaten with a little milk

Melt the butter in a saucepan and cook the green pepper, onion, and garlic for about 3 minutes. Add the chili powder, cumin seed, and tomatoes. Simmer for 20 minutes. Add the cheese slowly. Stir in the salt and cayenne pepper. When the cheese has melted, stir in the egg. Serve hot with tortilla chips.

SERVES 6–8   *Amarillo Junior League Cookbook,* Amarillo, TX

TRILBY

A popular, delicious cheese and egg spread.

1 pound mild Cheddar cheese,
   crumbled by hand
2 medium onions, minced, or 4-6
   scallions with green part, chopped
   finely
6 hard-cooked eggs, chopped
2 sprigs parsley, chopped
Salt and pepper to taste
Dash paprika
1 cup mayonnaise, or as needed
Parsley for garnish

In a large bowl, combine the cheese, onion, chopped egg, salt, pepper, and paprika. Mix well. Add 1 cup of mayonnaise. Mash together, adding more mayonnaise if necessary to form a cohesive ball. Divide into 2 balls. Chill, covered, for 1 hour to allow flavors to blend. Garnish with parsley. Serve with crackers or party-size bread slices.

MAKES 2 CHEESE BALLS   *Nutbread and Nostalgia,* South Bend, IN

BLACK BEAN NACHO DIP

1 medium onion, chopped
2 garlic cloves, chopped
2 tablespoons olive oil
2 tablespoons chili powder
2 (15-ounce) cans black beans
1 teaspoon cumin seeds
Ground red pepper (cayenne) to
   taste
10 ounces Monterey Jack cheese,
   grated
Salt to taste

GARNISH
2 ripe tomatoes, chopped
3 tablespoons chopped fresh cilantro
2 tablespoons jalapeño pepper
1 cup sour cream

Preheat the oven to 450 degrees. Lightly coat a shallow ceramic casserole with vegetable oil cooking spray.

In a medium saucepan, sauté the onion and garlic in the oil until clear. Sprinkle with chili powder and cook 1 minute longer. Add 1 can of drained beans and 1 can of undrained beans. Cook until the mixture thickens.

Mash the beans until the mixture is half smooth and half chunky. Add the cumin seeds. Season to taste with salt and cayenne. Spoon the mixture into the prepared casserole, top with the grated cheese, and bake for 10 minutes or until the cheese melts. Remove from the oven and spread the casserole with sour cream. Top with tomatoes, cilantro, and jalapeño slices.

SERVES 20   *Making Waves in the Kitchen,* Indian River, CA

TEXAS TORTILLAS

1 (8-ounce) package cream cheese, softened
1 (8-ounce) carton sour cream
5 scallions with tops, chopped fine, or 1 small onion, minced
3 jalapeño peppers, seeded and chopped fine, or a 4-ounce can chopped green chiles
2 tablespoons chopped black olives (optional)
½ cup sharp Cheddar cheese, shredded (optional)
1 (12-count) package large flour tortillas
Picante sauce (purchased)

Place the cream cheese, sour cream, scallions, jalapeños, olives, and cheese in a food processor. Process until smooth. Spread the mixture on flour tortillas and roll up. Wrap the tortillas in damp paper towels and place in plastic storage bags. Chill. To serve, cut tortillas into 1-inch pieces. Place on a tray with a bowl of picante sauce and toothpicks.

VARIATION: A bit of lime juice and garlic powder give this a different flavor.

MAKES 5 DOZEN   *Hearts & Flowers*, Waco, TX

TORTILLA TUCKS

Make these the day before you plan to serve them.

10 (6-inch) flour tortillas
2 (8-ounce) packages cream cheese, softened
9 ounces Cheddar cheese, shredded
2 cups bottled salsa
5-6 scallions, chopped
1 (16-ounce) can black olives, drained and chopped
1 ripe avocado, peeled and pitted, sliced thin

Spread each tortilla with a layer of cream cheese. Sprinkle with Cheddar cheese, salsa, scallions, and olives. Top with some avocado slices. Roll up as tightly as possible and place seam side down on a flat dish. Cover with plastic wrap; refrigerate from 8 to 24 hours. To serve, slice into 1-inch rounds.

SERVES 6–8   *For Goodness Taste*, Rochester, NY

CRIPPLED CHILDREN'S WORKSHOP
JUNIOR LEAGUE OF EASTERN FAIRFIELD COUNTY, CT.

In 1939, the Junior League of Eastern Fairfield County, Connecticut, the Connecticut Society for Crippled Children, and the Bridgeport Visiting Nurses Association began the Crippled Children's Workshop. It was the first facility in Connecticut to serve individuals with physical disabilities, and grew to the point it could be turned over to the community in 1943. It has recently opened outreach centers in Stamford and Fairfield, Connecticut.

FETA-TOMATO CROSTINI

3 (6-inch) French bread rolls, split
2 tablespoons olive oil
1 (7-ounce) package feta cheese,
  crumbled
1-2 teaspoons garlic powder
3 small ripe tomatoes, chopped
1½ tablespoons balsamic vinegar
2 tablespoons chopped fresh mint
Lettuce leaves

Brush the cut side of each roll with olive oil; place on a baking sheet. Broil 6 inches from the heat (with electric oven door partially opened) for 2 minutes or until lightly browned. Place some of the cheese on each roll; sprinkle lightly with garlic powder. Place the tomatoes over the cheese; drizzle with balsamic vinegar and sprinkle with mint. Serve on lettuce leaves and garnish, if desired, with fresh mint sprigs. Serve immediately.

SERVES 6   *Very Virginia,* Hampton Roads, VA

SPINACH-FETA TRIANGLES

2 (10-ounce) packages frozen
  chopped spinach, thawed
½ cup finely chopped onion
3 tablespoons olive oil
Grated nutmeg to taste
Salt and pepper to taste
3 tablespoons dried dill
⅓ cup ricotta cheese
¼ cup feta cheese, crumbled
1 pound phyllo pastry, thawed if
  frozen (see Note)
2 sticks (½ pound) butter, melted

Make the filling: Drain the thawed spinach and squeeze dry. Sauté the onion in the olive oil until soft and golden. Add the spinach and cook over low heat, stirring frequently, until the mixture is dry. Season with nutmeg, salt, and pepper. Add the dill. Cool completely. Add the ricotta cheese, then the feta cheese. Taste and correct seasoning.

Assemble the triangles: Unroll the phyllo; cover with waxed paper and then with a damp towel to keep it from drying out. Place 1 sheet of phyllo on a flat surface and brush with melted butter. Top with a second sheet and butter again. Keep the unused phyllo covered until ready to use. Cut the buttered phyllo sheets crosswise into fifths. Place a rounded teaspoon of the filling about an inch from the end of the first strip. Form a triangle by folding the right-hand corner across the filling to the opposite side. Continue folding, as if folding a flag, until the strip is used. Do not fold too tightly, as the filling will expand with baking. Place the stuffed triangle seam side down on a buttered baking sheet. Brush the top with butter. Continue with the remaining phyllo dough.

Filled phyllo triangles can be kept in the refrigerator, unbaked, for 24 hours or frozen immediately. If freezing, place on an unbuttered baking sheet, freeze overnight, and transfer to a plastic bag until needed.

Bake freshly made triangles in the upper third of a preheated 350 degree oven for about 25 minutes. Bake frozen triangles, unthawed, on a buttered baking sheet at 250 degrees for 45 minutes or until the filling is hot. Serve warm or at room temperature.

NOTE: Defrost phyllo pastry in its original wrapper in the refrigerator for at least 2 days.

MAKES 60   *Out of Our League Too Appetizers,* Greensboro, NC

PESTO HOTS

½ cup lightly packed fresh basil
  leaves, slivered
½ cup freshly grated Parmesan
  cheese
1 garlic clove, minced
6 tablespoons mayonnaise
1 French bread baguette, sliced into
  ¼-inch-thick rounds

Preheat the broiler. Stir together the basil, cheese, garlic, and mayonnaise. Arrange the bread slices on a cookie sheet. Place the cookie sheet under the broiler and toast the bread on one side. Remove from the oven, turn the bread slices over, and spread each slice with a generous teaspoonful of the pesto mixture. Return to the broiler. Cook until bubbly and lightly browned.

SERVES 10–12   *More Than a Tea Party,* Boston, MA

PESTO AND CREAM CHEESE ON SUN-DRIED TOMATOES

Pesto may be purchased or homemade.

PESTO
2 cups fresh basil leaves, lightly
  packed
4 cloves garlic, peeled
½ cup pine nuts
¾ to 1 cup olive oil
¾ cup freshly grated Parmesan
  cheese
Salt and pepper to taste (optional)

CHEESE FILLING
1 cup sun-dried tomatoes in olive
  oil, drained, chopped medium
  fine in a food processor or by
  hand
2 (8-ounce) packages cream cheese
  or 16 ounces Neufchâtel cheese,
  softened and sliced ½ inch thick

Fresh basil, rosemary sprigs or pine
  nuts for garnish
Crackers, deli bread slices, or bread
  sticks

To prepare the pesto: Whirl the basil and garlic in a food processor or blender until coarsely chopped. Add the pine nuts; process off and on for 15 seconds. With the processor on, slowly add the olive oil. Stir in the cheese. Taste for seasoning; if desired, add salt and pepper. (yields approximately 4 ounces. Excess pesto may be covered and refrigerated or frozen.)

Spread the tomatoes onto a rimmed serving platter, preferably one with a rimmed center and surrounding compartment for crackers. Cover carefully with cream cheese. (It is helpful to place slices of cheese side by side over tomatoes and then spread carefully with a knife.) Spread the desired amount of pesto over the cheese. The more pesto used, the more pungent the flavor. Cover with plastic wrap placed directly on the pesto. Refrigerate at least 1 hour.

Garnish with a sprig of fresh basil or rosemary; scatter pine nuts on top. Serve with simple crackers (such as water crackers), deli bread or bread sticks.

SERVES 8–10   *Rogue River Rendezvous,* Jackson County, OR

PESTO-STUFFED CHERRY TOMATOES

2 cups (1 pint) cherry tomatoes

1 (3-ounce) package cream cheese, softened

2 tablespoons fresh lemon juice

¼ cup grated Parmesan cheese

¼ cup finely chopped pine nuts or sunflower seeds

¾ cup finely chopped fresh parsley

¼ cup finely chopped watercress

1½ teaspoons dried basil leaves

2 cloves garlic, crushed

Cut tops off cherry tomatoes. Scoop out pulp. Drain tomatoes upside down on paper toweling while preparing filling. Beat the cream cheese with the lemon juice in a medium bowl until smooth. Stir in remaining ingredients. Fill cherry tomatoes with cheese mixture. Chill.

SERVES 6–8

Appetizers, Butte, MT

PITA CHEESE CRISPS

⅔ cup grated Romano or Parmesan cheese

4 cups grated Cheddar cheese

12 tablespoons (1½ sticks) unsalted butter, softened

1 clove garlic, minced

¾ teaspoon Worcestershire sauce

1 teaspoon paprika

¼ teaspoon ground red pepper (cayenne)

6 large pita breads

Preheat the oven to 350 degrees. In a large mixing bowl or food processor, combine the cheeses, butter, garlic, Worcestershire sauce, paprika, and cayenne pepper. Split the pita breads into 2 flat disks. Spread with cheese mixture and cut into small wedges with a serrated knife. Place the wedges ½ inch apart on an ungreased cookie sheet. Bake for 10 to 12 minutes and serve warm.

NOTE: These may be made ahead and frozen before baking.

MAKES ABOUT 60 WEDGES

Stirring Performances, Winston-Salem, NC

PITA BREAD CHEESE WEDGES

8 tablespoons (1 stick) butter, softened

6 pita breads

¾ cup grated Parmesan cheese

Split each bread into 2 flat disks and then each disk into quarters. Brush butter on the rough side of the bread and sprinkle with cheese. Place on baking sheet and broil 5 inches from the source of heat until lightly toasted.

MAKES 48 TRIANGLES

Nuggets: Recipes Good as Gold, Colorado Springs, CO

CHEESE STRAWS

1 scant cup all-purpose flour
½ teaspoon baking powder
1 teaspoon salt
Dash of ground red pepper
   (cayenne)
1 cup grated sharp Cheddar cheese
5⅓ tablespoons butter
2-3 teaspoons water

Mix the flour, baking powder, salt, cayenne, and cheese. Add the butter and rub in until the mixture resembles coarse meal. Sprinkle in enough water to make a stiff dough. Roll out about ⅛ inch thick and cut in 3 × ¼-inch strips. Bake on a cookie sheet at 400 degrees for 10 minutes, or until slightly brown.

MAKES 5 DOZEN   *Company's Coming: Foods for Entertaining,*
Kansas City, MO

FOUR-CHEESE PUFFS

1 pound loaf unsliced white bread
8 tablespoons (1 stick) butter
¼ cup grated mozzarella cheese
¼ cup grated sharp Cheddar cheese
¼ cup grated Swiss cheese
1 (3-ounce) package cream cheese,
   softened
½ teaspoon dry mustard
⅛ teaspoon ground red pepper
   (cayenne)
Pinch of salt
2 egg whites

Trim and discard the crusts from the top, bottom, and sides of the loaf. Cut the bread into 1-inch cubes. Set aside. In a saucepan, combine the butter and cheeses. Stir over moderate heat until melted. Add the mustard, cayenne, and salt. Remove from the heat. Beat the eggs until stiff. Fold into the cheese mixture. Using a fondue fork or skewer, spear the bread cubes one at a time and dip into the mixture until well coated.

   Arrange the cubes on a baking sheet. Freeze immediately until firm, preferably overnight. Remove the puffs from the baking sheet and store in plastic bags in the freezer until ready to use. At serving time, place the frozen cubes on a baking sheet and bake at 400 degrees for 10 minutes, until nicely browned.

MAKES 50 PUFFS   *Gatherings,* Milwaukee, WI

BRIE CRISPS

Use your leftover Brie to make these lovely wafers.

4 ounces Brie cheese, rind removed,
   at room temperature
8 tablespoons (1 stick) butter, at
   room temperature
⅔ cup all-purpose flour
2 generous dashes ground red
   pepper (cayenne), or to taste
⅛ teaspoon salt
Paprika

Combine the cheese and butter in a food processor and mix until creamy. Add the flour, cayenne, and salt and blend until the dough almost forms a ball in the food processor. Shape into a 2-inch-thick cylinder and wrap tightly in plastic wrap. Refrigerate overnight. Slice the dough into ¼-inch rounds, place 2 inches apart on a cookie sheet, and bake at 400 degrees for 10 to 12 minutes or until the edges are brown. Cool on a rack. Sprinkle with paprika.

SERVES 8–10   *Beyond Parsley,* Kansas City, MO

AUTUMN BRIE

1 small McIntosh or Cortland apple
⅓ cup golden raisins
1 cup apple cider
1 (4-inch) round Brie cheese
Chopped pecans for garnish

Preheat the oven to 350 degrees. Core and chop the apple. Place in a saucepan with the raisins and cider and boil gently until the apples are tender but not mushy (approximately ½ to 2 minutes). Put the Brie in an ovenproof dish slightly larger than the Brie. Strain the liquid from the apple/raisin mixture and put drained apple and raisins on top of the Brie. Garnish with chopped pecans and bake for 15 to 20 minutes.

Serve with sliced French bread.

SERVES 4
Maine Ingredients, Portland, ME

JOSEFINAS

8 Mexican hard rolls (see Note)
1 cup drained canned green chiles
2 sticks (½ pound) butter, softened
1 clove garlic, minced
1 cup mayonnaise
8 ounces Monterey Jack cheese, grated

Preheat the broiler. Slice the rolls crosswise into ½-inch-thick slices and arrange on a baking sheet. Slide the pan under the broiler and toast the bread until golden on one side.

Rinse the seeds off the chiles, drain well, and chop. Mix with the butter and garlic. Spread the chili mixture on the untoasted side of the bread slices. Mix the mayonnaise and cheese; spread on the bread. Broil until the cheese is brown and puffy. Serve at once.

NOTE: One thin loaf of French bread may be substituted for the rolls.

MAKES 30
Fiesta, Corpus Christi, TX

APACHE CHEESE BREAD

Use this dip to start your fiesta.

1 (9-inch) Apache loaf of bread, or any hard, round loaf
16 ounces sharp Cheddar cheese, grated
1 (8-ounce) package cream cheese, softened
1 (8-ounce) carton sour cream
½ cup minced scallions
1 teaspoon Worcestershire sauce
2 (4½ ounce) cans chopped green chiles
1 cup chopped ham

Preheat the oven to 350 degrees.

Cut the top off the bread, reserving the top, and scoop out the inside. Combine the remaining ingredients and mix well. This will be a very stiff mixture. Fill the bread shell with the cheese mixture, replace the top, and place on a cookie sheet. Bake for 1 hour and 10 minutes. Serve as a dip with tortilla chips or torn pieces of the inside of the loaf.

MAKES 6 CUPS
Celebrations on the Bayou, Monroe, LA

CROUTONS WITH THREE CHEESES AND SUN-DRIED TOMATOES

1 French bread baguette, cut into
   ¼-inch slices
2-3 tablespoons olive oil
¼ pound goat cheese with herbs
¼ pound ricotta cheese
¼ pound mozzarella cheese,
   shredded
1 large garlic clove, minced
White pepper to taste
18 sun-dried tomatoes, drained and
   halved

Preheat the oven to 300 degrees. Arrange the bread slices on a baking sheet. Brush the tops with olive oil. Bake until the croutons are golden brown, about 2 minutes. Remove from the oven and set aside. Increase the oven temperature to 350 degrees.

Blend the cheeses and garlic in a bowl. Season with pepper. Mound 1 teaspoon of the cheese mixture on each crouton. Top with a sun-dried tomato half. Cover with an additional teaspoon of the cheese mixture.

Bake until the cheese begins to melt. Serve immediately.

MAKES ABOUT 36   *One Magnificent Cookbook,* Chicago, IL

THE GREAT CRAB CAPER

1 pound crabmeat
2 cups mayonnaise
1 tablespoon horseradish
2 tablespoons capers, rinsed and
   drained
1 teaspoon grated lemon rind
½ teaspoon garlic powder
2 dashes Tabasco
1 teaspoon Worcestershire sauce

Preheat the oven to 350 degrees. Pick over the crabmeat to remove any bits of shell and cartilage. In a mixing bowl, combine the mayonnaise, horseradish, capers, lemon rind, garlic powder, Tabasco, and Worcestershire. Mix well and fold in the crabmeat. Transfer to a greased 2-quart casserole. Bake uncovered for 20-30 minutes or until bubbly. Serve with assorted crackers.

MAKES 3 CUPS   *Maine Ingredients,* Portland, ME

PARTY PERFECT CRABMEAT

2 pounds lump crabmeat
½ cup finely chopped scallions
2 teaspoons butter
2 tablespoons yogurt, or as needed
2 tablespoons mayonnaise
¼ teaspoon salt
Pepper to taste (may use red, black,
   and/or white)
2 teaspoons lemon juice

Pick over the crabmeat to remove any bits of shell and cartilage. Lightly spray a 4½ cup decorative mold with vegetable oil cooking spray.

In a nonstick skillet, sauté the scallions in the butter until slightly limp. Remove from the heat and allow to cool. In a small mixing bowl, stir together the 2 tablespoons of yogurt, the mayonnaise, salt, pepper, and lemon juice; blend in the cooled scallions. Add more yogurt if you want a creamier sauce. Toss the crabmeat and sauce together gently until the crab is thoroughly moistened. Pack into the prepared mold, cover with plastic wrap, and refrigerate for at least 3 hours. Unmold onto a serving plate and serve with crackers.

MAKES 4 CUPS   *River Road Recipes: A Healthy Collection,*
Baton Rouge, LA

CHESAPEAKE CRAB DIP

3 (8-ounce) packages cream cheese
1 clove garlic, minced
½ cup mayonnaise
2 teaspoons dry mustard
Seasoned salt to taste
1 pound backfin crabmeat, picked
    over well
¼ cup dry white wine
¼ cup dry sherry

Heat the cream cheese gently in a heavy saucepan; when soft, stir to blend and add the garlic, mayonnaise, mustard, and seasoned salt. Fold in the crabmeat. The mixture may be briefly set aside at this point. Before serving, add the white wine and sherry. Pour into a chafing dish, allowing time to warm. Serve with melba toast rounds or bite-size pastry shells.

MAKES 3 CUPS

Tidewater on the Half-Shell,
Norfolk–Virginia Beach, VA

KNOCK-YOUR-SOCKS-OFF HOT CRAB DIP

½ cup dry white wine
4 ounces cream cheese, at room
    temperature
1 (16-ounce) can water-packed
    artichoke hearts, drained and
    chopped finely
1 cup mayonnaise
1 egg
1 pound fresh crabmeat or 2
    (8-ounce) cans crabmeat, drained
    and picked over well
2 ounces blue cheese, crumbled fine
Slices black olives for garnish
    (optional)

Preheat the oven to 350 degrees. In a saucepan over low heat, combine the white wine and cream cheese and simmer until the cheese is creamy. Remove from the heat and blend thoroughly with a wire whisk.

Stir in the artichoke hearts, mayonnaise, egg, crabmeat, and blue cheese. Pour into an 8 × 8-inch ovenproof baking dish and bake for 30 minutes. Garnish with black olives if desired.

Serve with crackers.

MAKES 4 CUPS

From Portland's Palate, Portland, OR

CRABMEAT SPREAD

12 ounces cream cheese, softened
1 tablespoon Worcestershire sauce
1 tablespoon lemon juice
2 tablespoons mayonnaise
1 small onion, grated
Dash of garlic salt
½ pound cooked crabmeat, picked
    over and flaked
6 ounces chili sauce
Chopped fresh parsley

In a bowl combine the cream cheese, Worcestershire sauce, lemon juice, mayonnaise, onion, garlic salt, and crabmeat. Mix well. Spread in a shallow serving dish. Pour the chili sauce over the crab mixture. Garnish with parsley and refrigerate until ready to serve. Accompany with crackers.

SERVES 15

Winning at the Table, Las Vegas, NV

CANAPÉ LORENZO

This lavish hors d'oeuvre descends from Lorenzo Delmonico, who founded the American restaurant industry before the Civil War. It is an ideal appetizer for formal dinners or dressy buffet events.

1 pound lump crabmeat, picked
   over to remove bits of shell and
   cartilage
2 sticks (½-pound) plus 5
   tablespoons butter, at room
   temperature
¼ cup finely diced onion
1 tablespoon flour
2 cups light cream
Pinch of salt
¼ teaspoon ground red pepper
   (cayenne)
¼ teaspoon ground white pepper
¼ teaspoon grated nutmeg
1 cup freshly grated Parmesan
   cheese
40 (2-inch) toast rounds or 20
   (4-inch) toast rounds sliced in half
½ teaspoon paprika

Preheat the oven to 400 degrees. In a small skillet sauté the crabmeat in 3 tablespoons of the butter until lightly browned. Set aside. In a saucepan, sauté the chopped onion in 2 tablespoons of butter for 3 to 5 minutes, until transparent but not browned. Add the flour to the cooked onions and gradually stir in the cream. Add the salt, cayenne, white pepper, and nutmeg. Simmer over a very low flame, stirring until thickened. Remove from the heat and add the crab sauté.

Work together with fingers the remaining ½ pound of butter and the grated Parmesan. Spread the crab mixture on each side of the toast rounds, and then spread a dollop of the Parmesan butter over each canapé. Put the assembled canapés on a greased cookie sheet. Dust with a little paprika and lightly brown in oven.

NOTE: Make half the amount of butter and Parmesan mixture and use less on each canapé to produce a wonderful canapé, which is less rich.

MAKES APPROXIMATELY 30–40 PIECES

Hunt to Harbor: An Epicurean Tour, Baltimore, MD

CRUSTY CRAB POINTS

6 ounces crabmeat, picked over well
8 tablespoons (1 stick) butter,
   softened
1 (5-ounce) jar sharp Cheddar
   cheese spread
½ teaspoon mayonnaise
½ teaspoon seasoned salt
½ teaspoon garlic powder
3 English muffins, halved

If using canned crabmeat, drain. Combine the crabmeat, butter, cheese spread, mayonnaise, and seasonings and beat with an electric mixer. Spread on the English muffin halves. Freeze for 1 to 1½ hours. Cut each muffin half into 6 wedges. Refreeze in plastic bags until ready to serve. Broil until golden brown and bubbly, about 5 minutes. Serve immediately.

NOTE: The filling is also good on party rye. Or leave the English muffin halves uncut and serve as open-face sandwiches.

MAKES 3 DOZEN

Honest to Goodness, Springfield, IL

TEXAS CRABGRASS

8 tablespoons (1 stick) butter,
  melted
½ cup chopped onion
1 (10-ounce) package frozen
  chopped spinach
½ pound fresh crabmeat or 1
  (7-ounce) can crabmeat, drained
  and picked over
¾ cup grated Parmesan cheese

In a small skillet, melt the butter and sauté the onions for 4 to 5 minutes. In a saucepan, bring the spinach to a boil; cook for 1 minute, drain well, and add to the butter mixture. Add the crabmeat and cheese. Heat and serve in a chafing dish with crackers or melba toast rounds.

SERVES 8 *Company's Coming—Foods for Entertaining*, Kansas City, MO

JUNIOR LEAGUE SEAFOOD DIP

1 round loaf of French or Italian
  bread
1 cup grated Cheddar cheese
1 cup chopped onion
1 cup tiny shrimp or crabmeat,
  coarsely chopped
1 cup mayonnaise
Cubed French or Italian bread

Preheat the oven to 350 degrees. Slice off the top of the bread and hollow out the center to form a bowl. Cut the bread from the center into cubes and set aside.

Mix the grated cheese, onion, shrimp, and mayonnaise by hand or in a food processor until just blended. Transfer to the hollowed bread, place on a cookie sheet, and bake for 20 minutes until bubbly. Serve with crackers and the reserved bread cubes.

NOTE: The dip can also be baked in a buttered casserole and served with bread or crackers.

SERVES 6-8 *Without Reservations*, Pittsburgh, PA

SEAFOOD ELEGANTE

3 sticks (¾ pound) unsalted butter
1 tablespoon curry powder, or to
  taste
1 cup finely chopped yellow onion
2 cups peeled and grated Granny
  Smith apples
2½ teaspoons salt
1 tablespoon sugar
½ cup all-purpose flour
1 cup chicken broth
2½ cups half-and-half
3 pounds peeled and deveined small
  shrimp
2 cups fresh backfin crabmeat,
  picked over well
3 tablespoons fresh lemon juice

Melt 1½ sticks of butter in a heavy saucepan. Add the curry powder and cook for 1 minute over medium heat. Add the onion, apple, salt, and sugar; cook 8 to 10 minutes or until the onions are soft. Gradually add the flour and cook for 2 to 3 minutes, stirring constantly. Slowly add the broth and half-and-half, stirring constantly until mixture is thick. Remove from the heat and set aside.

In a heavy skillet, melt the remaining 1½ sticks of butter. Add the shrimp and crab; cook until the shrimp are just pink, stirring constantly. Do not overcook. Add the seafood mixture and lemon juice to the cream sauce; heat thoroughly. Serve in a chafing dish. The dip may be prepared 1 to 2 days ahead or frozen.

SERVES 20 *Thymes Remembered*, Tallahassee, FL

SPICY SHRIMP SPREAD

Great with crackers or as a stuffing for tomatoes or mushrooms.

1 (8-ounce) package cream cheese, at room temperature
2 tablespoons chopped onion
2 tablespoons sour cream
1 tablespoon creamed horseradish
¼ teaspoon salt
Dash pepper
8 ounces cooked shrimp, chopped

Preheat the oven to 375 degrees. Butter a shallow baking dish.

In a mixing bowl, combine the cream cheese, onion, sour cream, horseradish, salt, and pepper. Stir until thoroughly blended, then fold in the shrimp.

Transfer to the prepared dish and bake for 20 minutes, or until bubbly. Serve hot or cold.

MAKES 2 CUPS   *¡Delicioso!,* Corpus Christi, TX

SHRIMP AND WATER CHESTNUT DIP

Especially delicious when using both shrimp and crab. Serve on your favorite crackers.

1 small can cocktail-size shrimp
1 (6-ounce) box frozen Alaskan king crab (optional)
½ cup mayonnaise
1 can water chestnuts, drained and chopped fine
1 teaspoon prepared mustard
1 tablespoon chopped scallion
1 teaspoon Worcestershire sauce
2 dashes Tabasco
Chopped parsley

Drain the shrimp. Defrost the crab if using, squeeze out the excess liquid, and cut into small pieces.

In a mixing bowl, combine the mayonnaise, water chestnuts, mustard, scallion, Worcestershire, and Tabasco; stir well and fold in the shrimp and crab. Transfer to a serving dish, sprinkle with parsley, and cover with plastic wrap. Chill for at least 1 hour before serving.

MAKES 2 CUPS   *Sunflower Sampler,* Wichita, KS

DEVILED SHRIMP

These shrimp are beautiful served in a large bowl over cracked ice with long bamboo skewers. Or arrange the drained marinated shrimp on a platter and put the reserved marinade in a small bowl for dipping.

2 pounds medium to large raw
   shrimp
1 lemon, sliced thin
1 medium red onion, sliced thin
1 cup pitted black olives, well
   drained
2 tablespoons chopped pimiento
¼ cup vegetable oil
2 cloves garlic, minced
1 tablespoon dry mustard
1 tablespoon salt
½ cup lemon juice
1 tablespoon red wine vinegar
1 bay leaf, crumbled
Dash of ground red pepper
   (cayenne)
Chopped parsley to taste

Shell and devein the shrimp. Bring 1 quart of salted water to a boil, add the shrimp, and cook for a scant 3 minutes. Drain at once, rinse in cold water, drain again, and set aside.

In a bowl, combine the lemon slices, onion, black olives, and pimiento; toss well. In a separate bowl, or in a jar with a tight-fitting lid, combine the oil, garlic, dry mustard, salt, lemon juice, wine vinegar, bay leaf, cayenne, and parsley. Whisk or shake vigorously and add to the bowl with the lemon mixture. Arrange the shrimp on a serving dish and pour the marinade over them. Cover and chill no longer than 3 hours. Serve with toothpicks or bamboo skewers.

SERVES 8–10   *San Francisco à la Carte,* San Francisco, CA

DILLED GRILLED PRAWNS

24 prawns or jumbo shrimp
¼ cup dry vermouth
¼ cup olive oil
2 tablespoons chopped fresh parsley
2 tablespoons chopped scallion
2 tablespoons chopped fresh dill or 2
   teaspoons dried dill
1 tablespoon Dijon mustard
1 medium clove garlic, minced
1 bay leaf
Freshly ground pepper to taste

Cover 24 bamboo skewers with hot water and soak 30 minutes or more. Peel and devein the prawns. Thread each prawn on a skewer and place in a shallow baking dish.

Combine all the other ingredients in a small bowl and whisk together. Pour the marinade over the prawns, cover, and refrigerate at least 1 hour or overnight.

Preheat a grill. Remove the prawns from the marinade. Grill 1 to 2 minutes per side, or until barely opaque throughout. Serve hot or at room temperature.

MAKES 24 APPETIZERS   *Simply Classic,* Seattle, WA

SHRIMP STUFFED WITH FETA AND DILL

4 ounces cream cheese, softened
4 ounces feta cheese
2 tablespoons lemon juice
2 tablespoons snipped fresh dill or 2
  teaspoons dried dill
Pinch of salt
Pinch of ground red pepper
  (cayenne)
⅛ teaspoon coarsely ground black
  pepper
1½ pounds large shrimp
Parsley and additional fresh dill
  sprigs for garnish

In a food processor fitted with the metal blade or in a blender, mix the cream cheese and feta and blend until smooth. Add the lemon juice, dill, salt, cayenne, and black pepper. Blend the mixture until well combined. Cover and chill for 1 hour or until firm.

Shell the shrimp, leaving the tail and first joint of the shell intact. Cut a deep slit down the length of the outside curve of each shrimp and devein. Place the shrimp in a large saucepan of rapidly boiling salted water and cover with a lid for about 60 to 90 seconds, or until they turn pink and are cooked inside. Drain the shrimp in a colander, refresh under cold running water, and pat dry.

Transfer the cheese mixture to a pastry bag and pipe some cheese stuffing into the slit of each shrimp. Arrange on a platter and chill for 1 hour or until the filling is firm. Garnish with parsley and fresh dill sprigs.

MAKES 25 TO 30   *Pinch of Salt Lake,* Salt Lake City, UT

TOM'S SHRIMP TACO

Very colorful and pretty on an hors-d'oeuvre table.

1 (8-ounce) package cream cheese,
  softened
¼ cup heavy cream
½ bottle chili sauce
1 (4-ounce) can cooked tiny shrimp,
  drained, rinsed, and patted dry
6 scallions, chopped
¾ cup chopped green bell pepper
1 (3–4-ounce) can pitted black
  olives, drained, patted dry, and
  sliced
1 (8-ounce) package grated
  mozzarella cheese

Mix the cream cheese and the heavy cream. Pat down on a platter in an even layer. Spread with the remaining ingredients in the order that they appear above. Chill at least 1 hour before serving. Serve with tortilla chips.

NOTE: This can be made a day ahead provided the shrimp and olives are well drained and patted dry.

SERVES 8   *Off the Hook,* Stamford-Norwalk, CT

SALMON TARTLETS

PHYLLO TARTLET SHELLS
1 large egg white
2 tablespoons olive oil
¼ teaspoon salt
8 sheets phyllo, thawed if frozen

SMOKED SALMON FILLING
2 (8-ounce) packages low-fat cream
   cheese
6 ounces thinly sliced smoked
   salmon
2 scallions, chopped
4 teaspoons horseradish, drained

GARNISH
1 cup shredded cucumber

Phyllo Tartlets:

Heat the oven to 325 degrees. Lightly coat 2 mini muffin pans with vegetable oil cooking spray.

Whisk together the egg white, oil, and salt in a small bowl. Lay 1 sheet of phyllo on a work surface (keep the rest covered with waxed paper and a damp towel). Lightly brush it with the egg white mixture. Lay a second phyllo sheet on top of the first and brush again. Repeat with a third sheet. Top with fourth sheet of phyllo, but do not brush with egg white mixture. Work as quickly as possible to prevent the phyllo from drying out.

Cut the layered dough into 4 strips lengthwise and 6 strips crosswise for a total of 24 squares. Press the squares into the prepared muffin cups and bake for 8 to 12 minutes or until golden and crisp. Cool on a rack.

Repeat the procedure with the remaining phyllo and egg white mixture. The tartlets can be stored in a closed container at room temperature for up to one week or frozen for 2 months.

Salmon Filling:

Combine the cream cheese and smoked salmon in a food processor and process until fairly smooth. Add the scallions and horseradish and pulse until just combined. Or mince the salmon with a knife and combine with the cream cheese, scallions, and horseradish. The filling can be made ahead and refrigerated for up to 2 days.

Assembly:

Within 2 hours of serving, spoon 1 heaping teaspoon of filling into each tartlet shell and garnish with shredded cucumber.

MAKES 48   *Gold'n Delicious,* Spokane, WA

SMOKED SALMON PÂTÉ

The nice smoky taste of the salmon provides the flavoring for this spread.

¼ pound thinly sliced smoked
   salmon
2 (8-ounce) packages cream cheese,
   softened
6 teaspoons minced onion
¼ cup chopped fresh dill
3 tablespoons lemon juice
Tabasco to taste
Additional chopped dill and dill
   sprigs for garnish

Chop the smoked salmon. Combine in a bowl with the cream cheese, onion, dill, lemon juice, and Tabasco, mixing thoroughly with a wooden spoon or your hands to blend. Transfer to an attractive serving bowl; cover and refrigerate for at least 2 hours.

To serve, sprinkle with additional chopped dill and garnish with dill sprigs. Spread on crackers or pumpernickel bread.

SERVES 8–10   *Off the Hook,* Stamford-Norwalk, CT

ANCHOVY-FILLED MUSHROOMS

24 medium or 40 small mushrooms
¼ cup olive oil
1 (2-ounce) can flat anchovy fillets, drained
1 garlic clove, minced
1 teaspoon fresh lemon juice
¾ cup (or less) fresh soft bread crumbs
¼ cup minced parsley
Freshly ground black pepper to taste

Heat the oven to 350 degrees. Wipe the mushrooms; remove and chop the stems. Heat 3 tablespoons of the oil in a small skillet and sauté the chopped stems for 3 minutes. Chop the anchovies; mix with the garlic. Add to the skillet along with the lemon juice, bread crumbs, parsley, and pepper. Stir to mix.

Fill the mushroom caps with the mixture. Place in a shallow baking dish. Drizzle the remaining tablespoon of oil over the mushrooms. Bake for 15 minutes or until heated through.

SERVES 10–12   *Soupçon II,* Chicago, IL

ESCARGOT CROUSTADES

½ cup dry white wine
½ cup chicken broth
3 tablespoons minced shallots
½ teaspoon dried thyme
1 small bay leaf
1 teaspoon cornstarch, dissolved in 2 teaspoons water
1 cup heavy cream
2 garlic cloves, minced
1 (7-ounce) can large snails, rinsed and patted dry (about 15 snails)
1 tablespoon butter
2 tablespoons minced parsley
Salt and pepper to taste
15 croustades (see below)

Combine the wine, broth, shallots, thyme, and bay leaf in a skillet and reduce the liquid over high heat to 3 tablespoons. Add the cornstarch, cream, and garlic and boil until reduced to ⅓ cup. Stir in the snails, butter, parsley, and salt and pepper. Remove the bay leaf. May be prepared ahead to this point earlier in the day. Keep covered and refrigerated. Reheat before proceeding. Fill each croustade with a snail and some of the sauce. Serve hot, garnished with a sprig of parsley.

CROUSTADES

1 loaf unsliced firm-textured white bread
8 tablespoons (1 stick) butter, or as needed

Preheat the oven to 350 degrees. Remove crusts and slice the bread into 1-inch cubes. Hollow out the centers with the tip of a paring knife, leaving walls ½ inch thick. Melt the butter and brush the bread cases inside and out. Place on an ungreased baking sheet and bake for 10 to 12 minutes or until golden.

MAKES 15   *Capital Beginnings,* Ottawa, ON

OYSTER AND SCALLION DIP

8 tablespoons (1 stick) butter
3 bunches scallions, white and green
   parts, sliced thin
Minced garlic to taste
1 quart shucked oysters, drained and
   chopped fine
Salt and pepper to taste
4 slices toast, crushed into crumbs

Melt the butter in a skillet or heavy saucepan. Add the scallions and garlic and sauté over very low heat for 8 to 10 minutes, until soft. Add the oysters, bring to a boil over medium-high heat, and simmer about 1 minute. Season with salt and pepper. Before serving, heat the mixture and add the crumbs. Serve in a chafing dish with your favorite crackers.

SERVES 12

Magic, Birmingham, AL

TORTILLA PINWHEELS

These easy-to-make pinwheels are perfect when you need something wonderful in a hurry.

1 (8-ounce) package cream cheese,
   softened
1 (7-ounce) can chopped green
   chiles, drained
1 (4-ounce) can chopped ripe olives
4-6 dashes hot pepper sauce
½ teaspoon garlic powder or 4 fresh
   garlic cloves, minced
8 to 10 flour tortillas
5 to 6 ounces thinly sliced chicken,
   turkey, or other luncheon meat

In a bowl, combine the cream cheese with the green chiles, ripe olives, hot pepper sauce, and garlic. Mix well. Spread some of the mixture on each flour tortilla. Cover with sliced chicken. Roll up tightly. Wrap in plastic wrap and chill in the refrigerator at least 2 hours. When ready to serve, remove the plastic wrap and slice the tortillas in 1-inch pieces. Serve chilled or at room temperature.

MAKES 60–70

Seasoned with Sun, El Paso, TX

COCONUT CHICKEN NUGGETS

4-5 whole boneless, skinless, chicken
   breasts (about 2½ pounds)
Vegetable oil for deep frying
3 eggs
½ cup milk
¾ cup all-purpose flour
1 (7-ounce) package shredded
   coconut
Chinese plum sauce

Heat 1 inch of oil in a deep fryer or large skillet to 350 degrees. Cut the chicken into 1-inch pieces. Beat the eggs in a bowl; add the milk, flour, and coconut to make a batter.

Dip the chicken pieces in the batter to coat. Fry in the hot oil in batches without crowding, turning often, until golden brown, about 5 minutes. Serve with plum sauce for dipping.

NOTE: These appetizers can be made ahead and frozen. When ready to serve, reheat in a 350 degree oven for 10 minutes.

MAKES ABOUT 4 DOZEN   *Family & Company,* Binghamton, NY

CURRIED CHICKEN ROUNDS

1 (5-ounce) can boned chicken,
    undrained
½ cup grated Swiss cheese
1 (8-ounce) can water chestnuts,
    drained and chopped fine
2 tablespoons finely chopped
    scallions
¼ cup mayonnaise
1 teaspoon lemon juice
¼ teaspoon curry powder
Dash of pepper
1 (8-ounce) tube flaky-style
    refrigerator rolls
3 tablespoons chutney

Heat the oven to 400 degrees. In a bowl, mix the chicken, cheese, water chestnuts, scallions, mayonnaise, lemon juice, curry powder, and pepper. Separate each refrigerator roll into 3 layers. Place on an ungreased baking sheet, spoon on ½ tablespoon of the chicken mixture, and top with ¼ teaspoon chutney. Bake for 10 minutes or until brown. Serve hot.

MAKES 36

Drumsticks Along the Mohawk, Schenectady, NY

CHICKEN PILLOWS

Everyone wants just one more of these flaky, tender bites—they're irresistible.

2 whole chicken breasts, skinned,
    boned, and halved (about 1
    pound)
3 tablespoons lemon juice
2 tablespoons olive oil or vegetable
    oil
1 teaspoon finely chopped garlic
1 teaspoon dried oregano
8 tablespoons (1 stick) butter
½ pound phyllo or strudel leaves

Cut the chicken into 1-inch cubes. Combine the lemon juice, oil, garlic, and oregano in a small bowl. Mix well. Add the chicken and turn to coat with the marinade. Cover and refrigerate overnight.

Preheat the oven to 400 degrees. Melt the butter over low heat. Unwrap the phyllo or strudel leaves and place on a sheet of wax paper. (Keep unused phyllo covered with another sheet of wax paper and a damp tea towel at all times to prevent drying.) Cut the leaves in half lengthwise with scissors. You will have two sets of long strips, about 6 inches wide. Take one strip, fold it in half crosswise, and brush with melted butter.

Place two pieces of chicken at the short end and roll up in the pastry to the midpoint. Fold the edges of pastry in, like a package, and continue rolling. Brush all over with butter and place seam side down on a cookie sheet. Repeat with the remaining chicken and phyllo strips. (The pastries may be frozen at this point.)

Bake for 15 minutes or until golden (20 minutes if frozen). Serve hot.

MAKES 2 DOZEN

A Matter of Taste, Morristown, NJ

SKEWERED SESAME CHICKEN WITH CHILI DIP

SESAME CHICKEN

2 tablespoons rice wine vinegar

2 tablespoons dark Asian sesame oil

1 tablespoon freshly chopped garlic

2 tablespoons soy sauce

1 large whole boneless, skinless
   chicken breast (about 1⅓ pounds)

¼ cup white sesame seeds

¼ cup black sesame seeds

2 teaspoons cornstarch

3 tablespoons all-purpose flour

Peanut oil

48 snow peas

CHILI DIP

1 tablespoon rice wine vinegar

2 tablespoons chili paste with garlic

1 tablespoon soy sauce

1 teaspoon sesame oil

1 tablespoon minced fresh gingeroot

¾ cup mayonnaise

1 tablespoon sugar

Dash of Tabasco

1 red bell pepper, hollowed out

Kale leaves, for garnish

To prepare the chicken: Cut the meat into 48 bite-sized chunks. Mix the rice wine vinegar, sesame oil, garlic, and soy sauce, and pour over the chicken. Cover and refrigerate overnight.

When ready to cook, mix the sesame seeds, cornstarch, and flour. Dip the marinated chicken in the sesame seed mixture. Place on tray and let stand 10 minutes. Heat ¼ inch of peanut oil in sauté pan and brown the chicken on all sides in batches, without crowding. Drain on paper towels.

Remove the tips, tails, and strings from the snow peas. Place in a saucepan with a few tablespoons of boiling water; cover and steam for 1 minute over high heat. Cool in ice water and pat dry. Wrap each pea pod around a chicken piece and fasten with wooden skewers.

To prepare the chili dip; combine all ingredients, blending well. Fill the red pepper shell. To assemble, line a tray with kale. Place the pepper with chili dip in the center. Arrange the skewered chicken pieces around the pepper.

SERVES 12   *Bountiful Arbor,* Ann Arbor, MI

HAM ROLLS WITH MUSHROOMS

1 pound mushrooms, wiped clean
   and trimmed

⅓ cup minced shallots

4 tablespoons (½ stick) butter

2 (3-ounce) packages cream cheese,
   softened

2 teaspoons Dijon mustard

Pinch of ground red pepper
   (cayenne)

Lemon juice to taste

Salt and pepper to taste

1 pound baked ham, sliced thin

1 bunch watercress, cleaned and
   chopped

Chop the mushrooms fine and squeeze them in a tea towel, a handful at a time, to remove the moisture. In a skillet, cook the shallots in the butter over moderate heat, stirring until translucent. Add the mushrooms and cook them, stirring, until the liquid is evaporated. Remove the skillet from the heat and stir in the cream cheese, mustard, cayenne, and lemon juice; add salt and pepper to taste. Transfer the mixture to a bowl and let it cool.

Lay the ham slices flat on a work surface and spread about 2 tablespoons of the mushroom mixture on each slice. Sprinkle each slice with 1 tablespoon of chopped watercress. Roll up the ham. Chill the rolls, covered, for at least 1 hour. Cut each roll crosswise into 4 sections and arrange them on a serving tray.

MAKES ABOUT 6 DOZEN   *Scarsdale Entertains,* Central Westchester, NY

PUFF PASTRY PROSCIUTTO PINWHEELS

Impressive and not hard to make!

1 sheet frozen puff pastry
   (approximately 1 pound), thawed
3 tablespoons honey mustard
¼ pound thinly sliced prosciutto,
   chopped
1 cup grated Parmesan cheese
1 egg

Place the puff pastry on a lightly floured surface and roll out to a 12 × 18-inch rectangle; spread mustard on top of the pastry. Arrange the prosciutto evenly to cover all the pastry; sprinkle with cheese. Lightly press the cheese into the prosciutto with a rolling pin. Starting at one long edge, roll up the pastry like a jelly roll just to the middle of the dough (approximately 3 times); roll up the other side in the same way. Where the 2 rolls meet in the center, use a small amount of water to seal.

Cut the rolls into ½-inch slices, using a serrated knife. Place the slices on a cookie sheet lined with parchment; flatten slightly with a spatula. Refrigerate at least 15 minutes or until ready to bake.

Preheat the oven to 400 degrees. Beat the egg with 2 tablespoons of water; brush each pinwheel with egg wash. Bake 10 minutes, until lightly golden. Turn the pinwheels over; bake 5 minutes more. Serve warm.

MAKES 2 DOZEN   *The Bountiful Arbor,* Ann Arbor, MI

SAUSAGE ROLLS

These are nice for morning parties.

2 cups all-purpose flour
½ teaspoon salt
3 teaspoons baking powder
5 tablespoons shortening
⅔ cup milk
1 pound well-seasoned bulk sausage

Mix the flour, salt, and baking powder; cut in the shortening until the mixture resembles coarse crumbs; add the milk all at once and mix with a fork until a dough is formed. Divide the dough into 2 parts; roll one part into a rectangle ¼ inch thick. Spread with half the sausage. Roll up starting with a long end, as for jelly roll; repeat with the remaining dough.

Wrap the rolls in waxed paper and chill in the refrigerator. When ready to serve, slice into rounds ⅓ or ¼ inch thick and place on a lightly greased baking sheet. Bake in a 400 degree oven for 5 to 10 minutes or until lightly browned.

SERVES 10–12   *A Cook's Tour of Shreveport,* Shreveport, LA

HARVEST POPCORN

5⅓ tablespoons butter
1 teaspoon dried dill
1 teaspoon lemon pepper
1 teaspoon Worcestershire sauce
½ teaspoon garlic powder
½ teaspoon onion powder
¼ teaspoon salt
2 quarts freshly popped popcorn
2 cups canned shoestring potatoes
1 cup mixed nuts

Melt the butter in a small saucepan and add the dill, lemon pepper, Worcestershire, garlic powder, onion powder, and salt. Turn the freshly popped corn into a large bowl; add the shoestring potatoes and nuts. Toss with the seasoned butter and serve right away.

MAKES 11 CUPS   *Cornsilk,* Sioux City, IA

DOLMADES (GREEK STUFFED GRAPE LEAVES)

1 pound ground lamb or beef chuck
⅓ cup raw rice
1 egg
2 tablespoons chopped parsley
2 tablespoons chopped mint leaves
1 large onion, chopped fine
½ cup chopped celery
4 tablespoons (½ stick) butter
3 cups chicken broth, or as needed
Salt and pepper to taste
1 (10-ounce) jar grape leaves in
   brine

Mix the ground meat, rice, egg, parsley, and mint in a large bowl. Sauté the onion and celery in the butter until translucent, about 5 minutes. Cool slightly and add to the meat mixture. Add ½ cup of the chicken broth and season to taste with salt and pepper.

Carefully unroll the grape leaves, rinse in cold water and boil in a large pot of water for 5 minutes; drain well. Spread out 1 leaf at a time on a work surface. Cut out and discard the stem end and the hard part of the center rib. Place 1 tablespoon of the meat mixture on the longest point of each grape leaf; fold over once; fold edges toward center and roll again to complete each little package.

Place the stuffed leaves, seam side down, in layers in a large deep pan. Add the remaining 2½ cups of chicken broth, cover and simmer for 1 hour. Serve hot or cold.

MAKES ABOUT 40   *Little Rock Cooks,* Little Rock, AR

PATRIOT'S PÂTÉ

1 pound chicken livers, well rinsed
½ pound bacon, diced
1 large onion, chopped
4 garlic cloves, chopped
4 bay leaves
1 teaspoon salt
¼ teaspoon ground red pepper
   (cayenne)
2 tablespoons Worcestershire sauce
¼ teaspoon grated nutmeg
½ teaspoon prepared mustard
⅛ teaspoon ground cloves

Place the livers in a large saucepan with the bacon. Add the onion, garlic, bay leaves, salt, red pepper, Worcestershire sauce, and enough water to cover. Bring to a boil, reduce the heat, and simmer, covered, for 20 minutes.

Drain the livers, discarding the liquid and the bay leaves. Place the solid ingredients in the bowl of a food processor. Add to this mixture the nutmeg, mustard, and cloves. Process until smooth. Transfer the liver mixture to a crock, decorative mold, or individual ramekins. Refrigerate covered until ready to use. Serve with cornichons and grainy mustard as accompaniments.

NOTE: The pâté can be kept in the refrigerator for 1 week or frozen for up to 1 month.

SERVES 8–10   *More Than a Tea Party,* Boston, MA

APPETIZERS

LONE STAR FONDUE

A bread pot filled with ham and cheese fondue.

1 round, firm loaf of bread (8–10 inches in diameter)
2 tablespoons vegetable oil
1 tablespoon butter, melted
½ cup sour cream
8 ounces sharp Cheddar cheese, grated
1 (8-ounce) package cream cheese, softened
1 cup diced cooked ham (3 ounces)
½ cup chopped scallions
1 (4-ounce) can green chiles, drained and chopped
1 teaspoon Worcestershire sauce

Preheat the oven to 350 degrees. Slice off the top of the bread and set aside. Hollow out the inside with a small paring knife, leaving a half-inch shell. Cut the removed bread into 1-inch cubes. You should have about 4 cups. In a large skillet, combine the oil and butter. Add the bread cubes and stir until thoroughly coated. Place on a cookie sheet. Bake for 10 to 15 minutes turning occasionally, until golden brown. Remove from the oven and reserve.

To prepare the fondue: In a large bowl combine the sour cream, Cheddar, and cream cheese. Stir in the ham, scallions, chiles, and Worcestershire sauce. Spoon the mixture into the hollowed bread, filling it. Replace the top of bread. Wrap the filled loaf with several layers of heavy-duty aluminum foil. Set the loaf on a cookie sheet. Bake at 350 degrees for 1 hour and 10 minutes or until the cheese filling is melted and heated through. To serve, remove the wrapping and put the loaf on a serving dish with the bread cubes placed around it for dipping.

MAKES 4 CUPS FONDUE   *The Wild, Wild West,* Odessa, TX

CHEESY ITALIAN SUPPER PIE

Pastry for 2-crust pie (page 338)
5 eggs
2 cups ricotta cheese
1 cup grated Parmesan cheese
¼ cup chopped onion
2 tablespoons snipped parsley
Salt
¼ teaspoon ground black pepper
2 cloves garlic, minced
1 teaspoon dried oregano, crushed
1 teaspoon dried marjoram, crushed
2 tablespoons olive oil
1 (10½-ounce) can tomato purée
⅔ cup pitted sliced ripe olives
8 ounces sliced mozzarella cheese
½ cup sliced fresh mushrooms
1 cup sliced green pepper

Preheat the oven to 425 degrees. Prepare the pastry. Roll out one half and line a 10-inch pie plate. Trim edge. In a large bowl, beat eggs. Stir in the ricotta cheese, Parmesan cheese, onion, parsley, ½ teaspoon of salt, and the pepper. Set aside. Put in the garlic, oregano, marjoram, ⅛ teaspoon of salt, and the olive oil in a saucepan and heat for 1 minute. Stir in the tomato purée and olives. Spread half the egg mixture in the pie shell. Top with half the mozzarella cheese, half the tomato mixture, half the mushrooms, and half the green pepper. Repeat the layers. Roll out the top crust and place over the filling. Cut slits in the center for steam to escape. Seal and flute the edges. Cover the edges with foil and bake for 20 minutes. Uncover the edges and bake 25 to 30 minutes more, or until golden brown.

SERVES 6–8   *Pride of Peoria,* Peoria, IL

SAVANNAH QUICHE

1 (9-inch) pie shell
2 ripe tomatoes
Salt and pepper to taste
½ cup all-purpose flour
2 tablespoons vegetable oil
1 cup chopped onion
3 slices Provolone cheese, broken
   into bite-size pieces
1½ cups light cream
2 eggs, beaten
¾ cup grated Swiss cheese

Bake the pie shell in a 425 degree oven for 5 to 7 minutes. Peel and slice the tomatoes ¾ inch thick. Sprinkle with salt and pepper and dip in flour. Heat the oil in a skillet and sauté the tomatoes 3 to 4 minutes on each side. Remove with a spatula and drain.

Place the tomatoes and onion on the bottom of the pie crust. Scatter the Provolone on top. Mix the cream and eggs together. Pour into the pie shell. Sprinkle Swiss cheese on top. Bake at 375 degrees for 35 to 40 minutes. Cool on a rack for 10 minutes before cutting into wedges.

SERVES 8–10 AS AN APPETIZER, 6 AS AN ENTREE

300 Years of Caroline Cooking, Greenville, SC

MARINATED MUSHROOMS

1½ pounds small mushrooms
1½ cups white or wine vinegar
1 cup Italian dressing
1 teaspoon dried oregano

Wipe and trim the mushrooms. In a nonaluminum saucepan, combine the vinegar and 1½ cups of water; heat to boiling. Add the mushrooms and boil for 2 minutes. Drain; reserve ½ cup of the cooking liquid. Cool the mushrooms for 1 hour. Mix the 1½ cup of reserved cooking liquid with the Italian dressing and oregano. Pour over the cooked mushrooms. They can be eaten immediately, but the flavor gets better after 12 hours. They can be kept for 7 to 10 days.

SERVES 20

Treat Yourself to the Best, Wheeling, WV

CAPONATA

½ cup olive oil
2 small eggplants, peeled and diced
2 onions, sliced thin
1 cup diced celery
2 cups chopped fresh Italian
   tomatoes or a (16-ounce) can
   Italian tomatoes, undrained
2 tablespoons capers, drained
1 tablespoon pine nuts
8 black Italian olives, pitted and
   chopped
2 tablespoons sugar
¼ cup red wine vinegar
½ teaspoon salt
Pinch of ground black pepper

Heat the oil in a large nonreactive skillet; fry the eggplant, stirring occasionally, until soft and lightly browned, about 8 minutes. Remove the eggplant from the pan with a slotted spoon and reserve. Add the onion and celery to the frying pan and sauté until soft and slightly golden, about 5 minutes. Purée the tomatoes or force them through a sieve. Add to the onions and celery and simmer for 15 to 20 minutes. Add the capers, pine nuts, olives, sugar, wine vinegar, salt, pepper, and the reserved eggplant. Cover the skillet and allow mixture to simmer for about 20 minutes, stirring occasionally.

Allow the caponata to cool, then chill in the refrigerator. Serve with thinly sliced French bread as a first course or as a hors d'oeuvre.

SERVES 8

California Treasure, Fresno, CA

SPINACH-STUFFED CREPES

The secret to creating a pretty presentation with these bundles is a very soft cream cheese filling spread lightly on very thin crepes.

SPINACH CREPE BATTER

¼ pound spinach, thoroughly washed and drained

1 cup all-purpose flour

Pinch of salt

1 egg

⅔ cup milk

Butter or oil, for cooking

FILLING

1 (8-ounce) package cream cheese, softened

Salt and freshly ground pepper to taste

¼ cup chopped chives

8 long chives, to garnish

For the batter: In a saucepan, cook spinach with a little water for 3 to 5 minutes and push through a strainer to make a thin purée. Mix the flour and salt in a bowl. Beat in the egg and milk. Add the spinach purée. Allow the batter to stand for 10-20 minutes.

For the filling: Season the cream cheese with salt and pepper and add the chopped chives. Mix and set aside. Melt a teaspoon of butter in a crepe pan and use the batter to make 8 small, thin crepes. Put about 2 tablespoons of cheese filling in each crepe and roll up. Tie with chive bows and serve.

MAKES 8

Above and Beyond Pastry, Kansas City, MO

FELLINI'S LINGUINE

5 tablespoons olive oil

5 tablespoons (½ stick) unsalted butter

1 tablespoon flour

1 cup chicken broth

1 garlic clove, minced

2 teaspoons dried parsley

2 teaspoons lemon juice

Salt

Freshly ground black pepper

1 (14-ounce) can artichoke hearts, drained and quartered

3 tablespoons Parmesan cheese

2 teaspoons capers

1 pound hot cooked and drained linguine

Prosciutto or ham for garnish

Melt 4 tablespoons each of the oil and butter. Add the flour and stir until smooth, about 2-3 minutes. Gradually add the broth, stirring until thickened, about 1 minute. Add the garlic, parsley, lemon juice, and salt and pepper to taste; cook 5 minutes, stirring constantly. Add the artichokes, 2 tablespoons of Parmesan, and capers. Cover the sauce and simmer about 10 minutes.

Heat the remaining 1 tablespoon each of butter and oil in pan. Add the remaining 1 tablespoon of Parmesan and the linguine. Toss lightly. Arrange the pasta on a platter and pour the sauce over. Garnish with prosciutto or ham.

SERVES 4–6

Simply Simpático, Albuquerque, NM

FARFALLE IN LIGHT HERB BROTH

Serve this colorful dish with a chilled white wine for a delightful summer dinner.

20 medium to large asparagus stalks
1 pound uncooked farfalle pasta
6 tablespoons cornstarch
1 (14-ounce) can chicken broth
½ teaspoon finely chopped garlic
¼ cup virgin olive oil
4 ounces thinly sliced prosciutto
5 ounces sun-dried tomatoes in olive oil
2 tablespoons sliced basil
2 tablespoons coarsely chopped parsley
1 tablespoon chopped fresh dill
Freshly ground black pepper to taste
Grated Parmesan cheese to taste

Peel the asparagus and snap off the tough ends. Blanch in boiling water for 20 seconds; drain and cool. Slice diagonally into 1-inch pieces; set aside. Cook the pasta in a large pot of boiling water until tender but still firm; drain. Blend the cornstarch with ¼ cup of the chicken broth in a small bowl. Put the remaining broth in a saucepan and bring to a boil. Whisk in the cornstarch mixture. Cook until thickened, stirring constantly; remove from the heat.

Sauté the garlic in the olive oil in a large heavy saucepan. Add the prosciutto, tomatoes, basil, parsley, dill, pepper, and the reserved asparagus. Sauté for 30 seconds. Stir in the thickened chicken broth. Bring to a simmer. Add the pasta. Simmer until heated through. Serve immediately; sprinkle with the cheese.

N O T E : Farfalle is the Italian word for butterfly. It is often referred to as bowtie pasta.

S E R V E S 4   *I'll Taste Manhattan,* New York, NY

ZESTY LINGUINE WITH VODKA AND ROSY TOMATO SAUCE

2 tablespoons olive oil
3 tablespoons butter
1 small onion, chopped
1 clove garlic, minced
1 (28-ounce) can Italian plum tomatoes
1 tablespoon chopped fresh basil
⅛ teaspoon dried red pepper flakes or ⅛ teaspoon ground red pepper (cayenne)
½ cup vodka
½ cup heavy cream
3 tablespoons grated Parmesan cheese
12 ounces fresh linguine
Freshly ground black pepper
Chopped parsley

Combine the olive oil and butter in a medium skillet and sauté the onion for about 5 minutes. Add the garlic and sauté another minute. Add the tomatoes, basil, red pepper, and vodka. Simmer about 15 minutes until the sauce is reduced. Add the cream and simmer until thickened, about 5 minutes more. Add the Parmesan and blend well.

Cook the pasta according to package directions. Layer some of the sauce on a heated serving platter, top with the pasta, then add more sauce. Garnish with black pepper and parsley.

S E R V E S 4   *Settings,* Philadelphia, PA

FETTUCCINE IN BASIL CREAM

This is a very attractive pasta dish. For a colorful addition, consider a cup or two of fresh asparagus tips and/or a quarter pound of lobster or crabmeat.

3 tablespoons olive oil
3 tablespoons butter
1-2 cloves garlic, minced
3-4 tomatoes, peeled, seeded, and
   chopped
½ cup dry white wine
½ cup finely chopped fresh basil
   leaves
½ cup heavy cream
Salt and white pepper to taste
1 pound fettuccine (fresh is best!)
Freshly grated Parmesan cheese

Heat the oil and butter in a heavy saucepan over medium heat. Gently sauté the garlic for a minute, then add the tomatoes, wine, and basil. Simmer 5-10 minutes or until the sauce has thickened. Add the heavy cream and simmer another 2-3 minutes. Add salt and white pepper to taste.

In a large kettle, cook the fettuccine in boiling salted water according to package directions. When it has reached the al dente stage, drain immediately. Add the sauce to the hot fettuccine, toss, and serve immediately on warm plates. Add a leaf or two of basil to each serving for a pretty touch. Pass a bowl of freshly grated Parmesan cheese.

SERVES 4–6   *Private Collection 2,* Palo Alto, CA

OREGANATA PASTA

1 (6-ounce) jar marinated artichoke
   hearts, drained and coarsely
   chopped, liquid reserved
½ pound fresh mushrooms, sliced
1 tablespoon grated onion
1 garlic clove, minced
1 (15-ounce) can tomato sauce
1 cup dry white wine
1 (2¼-ounce) can sliced ripe olives,
   drained
2 teaspoons dried basil
2 teaspoons dried oregano
1 teaspoon salt
½ teaspoon fennel seed
¼ teaspoon freshly ground black
   pepper
1 pound spaghetti or other pasta
Freshly grated Parmesan cheese

In a large sauté pan over medium heat, heat the artichoke marinade until bubbly. Add the mushrooms, onion, and garlic to the marinade and sauté over high heat for 5 minutes. Add the artichokes, tomato sauce, wine, olives, and seasonings. Simmer the sauce uncovered for 20 minutes.

Meanwhile, cook the pasta according to package directions. Pour the sauce over the pasta, sprinkle with Parmesan, and serve.

SERVES 4–6   *Portland's Palate,* Portland, OR

MOREL AND ASPARAGUS RISOTTO

Morels are delicious in season, but this dish may be made just as easily with other mushrooms. Arborio is the rice of choice for risotto.

15 medium stalks asparagus
6 ounces (6-8 slices) bacon, chopped
  (pancetta if available)
2 medium onions, chopped
12 ounces fresh morels, cleaned and
  sliced
4 tablespoons (½ stick) unsalted
  butter
1½ cups uncooked arborio rice
3-4 cups hot chicken broth
⅔ cup grated Parmesan cheese
Salt and freshly ground pepper to
  taste

Peel the asparagus, snap off the tough stem ends, and cut the stalks into 1-inch pieces. Parboil the asparagus in boiling water for 2 minutes; drain. Cook the bacon in a skillet until light brown. Add the onions. Sauté over low heat until the onions are tender, 8 to 10 minutes.

Cook the morels in the butter in a sauté pan until tender, about 3 minutes. Add the morels to the onion mixture. Add the rice and stir until thoroughly coated. Add 1 cup of the hot broth, stirring until the liquid is absorbed. Continue adding hot broth in ½-cup amounts, stirring until the rice absorbs the broth before adding more. Cook until the rice is tender, about 25 minutes; the mixture will be creamy and thick. Stir in the asparagus, Parmesan, salt, and pepper; toss lightly. Serve immediately.

SERVES 6   *I'll Taste Manhattan*, New York, NY

ESCABECHE

1 Spanish onion or 2 medium white
  onions, sliced thin
2 cloves garlic, peeled
2 bay leaves
1 cup red wine vinegar
Salt
10 black peppercorns
1 cup small stuffed Spanish olives
1 cup olive oil
3 pounds halibut or sole fillets
Boston lettuce leaves or avocado
  halves

Prepare the marinade: Combine the onion, garlic, bay leaves, vinegar, 1 tablespoon of salt and the peppercorns in a saucepan; cover and simmer until the onions are tender, about 20 minutes. Cool the marinade and add the olives and ¾ cup of the olive oil.

Meanwhile, cut the fillets into 1½- to 2-inch-wide pieces and sprinkle lightly with salt. Heat the remaining ¼ cup of olive oil in a large skillet and sauté the fish for about 1 mintue on each side, or until barely done. If all the fish does not fit in one layer, sauté in batches adding more olive oil as needed. Transfer the fish to a glass or ceramic bowl or dish. Pour the marinade over the fish, cover, and chill for at least 24 hours. Remove the bay leaves and garlic.

Serve the escabeche on Boston lettuce leaves or in avocado halves with a generous portion of olives, onion, and marinade.

SERVES 8   *New York Entertains*, New York, NY

CALIFORNIA PIZZA

Unbelievably good—just like California weather.

PIZZA DOUGH

1 cup lukewarm water (110 degrees)

2 (1-ounce) packages active dry yeast

3½ cups unbleached all-purpose flour, or as needed

1 teaspoon coarse salt

1 teaspoon sugar

1 tablespoon olive oil

PESTO

½ cup olive oil

2 cups tightly packed fresh basil leaves

2 cloves garlic, chopped

3 tablespoons pine nuts

½ cup freshly grated Parmesan cheese

THE PIZZA

1 onion, sliced thin

1 red bell pepper, seeded and sliced into strips

1 green bell pepper, seeded and sliced into strips

2 tablespoons olive oil

½ pound garlic and fennel sausage or sweet Italian sausage links

2 teaspoons cornmeal

3 ounces goat cheese

10 ounces mozzarella cheese, coarsely grated

2 tablespoons freshly grated Parmesan cheese

Prepare the dough: Dissolve the yeast in 1 cup of lukewarm water and set aside. Mix the flour and salt in a bowl. Make a well in the center; pour in the dissolved yeast and the olive oil. Blend in the flour with a fork, working toward the outside of the well. As the dough becomes stiff, incorporate additional flour by hand. Use only enough flour to make a soft but manageable dough. Gather the dough into a ball and knead for 8 to 10 minutes on a floured board. Place in an oil-coated bowl, cover with a damp cloth, and let rise in a warm, draft-free place until doubled in size, approximately 2 hours.

Meanwhile, prepare the pesto: In a blender or food processor, combine the olive oil, basil, garlic, and pine nuts. Process until the consistency is uniform. Stir in the cheese. Set aside.

Make the pizza: Sauté the onion and pepper in 1 tablespoon of the olive oil and 1 tablespoon of water in a large skillet over medium heat. Stir frequently until the peppers are soft. Drain and set aside. In the same skillet, brown the sausage, breaking it into pieces as it cooks. Drain off excess fat. Chop coarsely and set aside.

Preheat the oven to 400 degrees. Spread the remaining tablespoon of olive oil evenly over a 12-inch pizza pan. Sprinkle with cornmeal. Punch down the pizza dough, flatten lightly with a rolling pin, turn and flatten gently with the fingers. Place the dough in the pan and spread to edges with the fingertips. Bake 5 minutes.

Spread the pesto over the dough. Crumble the goat cheese evenly over the pesto. Add the onions and peppers, sausage, mozzarella, and Parmesan. Bake 10 minutes or until the crust is slightly brown and cheese is bubbly.

MAKES ONE 12-INCH PIZZA

Delicious Decisions, San Diego, CA

SEVICHE

The raw fish is "cooked" in the acidic action of the citrus juice in this Latin American specialty.

4 pounds very fresh fish fillets, cut into bite-size pieces (flounder, halibut, or red snapper)
2 cups lemon or lime juice, or as needed
1 bay leaf
2 medium onions, chopped fine
4 medium tomatoes, chopped
¼ cup olive oil
½ cup chopped cilantro
3 tablespoons chopped parsley
20 stuffed olives, sliced
2 serrano chiles or to taste, chopped and seeded
1 teaspoon dried oregano
½ teaspoon dried thyme
Salt and pepper to taste
½ cup ketchup
Hot sauce to taste

Arrange the fish in one layer in a large shallow glass or stainless-steel container. Pour in enough lemon juice to cover the fish completely. Add the bay leaf, cover tightly, and refrigerate for 4 to 5 hours, or until the fish is opaque rather than transparent. Drain and discard the bay leaf.

Combine the onions, tomatoes, olive oil, cilantro, parsley, olives, chiles, seasonings, ketchup, and hot sauce. Mix well and toss with the fish. Transfer to a serving bowl, cover, and chill for several hours. Serve with tortilla chips or crackers.

SERVES 12   *Buen Provecho,* Mexico City

SPECIAL SHRIMP SEA ISLAND

5 pounds shrimp, cooked (see page 43), shelled, and deveined
10 mild white onions, sliced into rings
2 cups olive oil
1½ cups cider vinegar
1 large jar capers, undrained
Salt, sugar, Tabasco and Worcestershire sauce to taste

In a deep flat pan, make a layer of shrimp, then a layer of onions, continuing to alternate layers until both ingredients are used up.

Combine the oil, vinegar, capers and juice, salt, sugar, Tabasco, and Worcestershire. Pour over the shrimp, cover tightly, and marinate at least 12 hours in the refrigerator.

Drain and serve with toothpicks as an appetizer.

SERVES 25   *Gator Country Cooks,* Gainesville, FL

SHRIMP AND PASTA EN PAPILLOTE

These delightful appetizers should be served in their wrappers as the first course at a sit-down dinner.

1 pound angel hair pasta, cooked
  and drained
48 medium shrimp, shelled and
  deveined
8 tablespoons (1 stick) butter
1 red bell pepper, chopped fine
½ pound mushrooms, sliced
½ cup diced scallions
½ cup chopped parsley
3 tablespoons soy sauce
2 teaspoons Worcestershire sauce
2 teaspoons garlic salt
½ teaspoon powdered ginger
Dash of Tabasco
1 cup chicken broth
16 fresh snow peas, strings removed,
  cut lengthwise into slivers

Preheat the oven to 375 degrees. Cut 8 squares of aluminum foil, approximately 12 × 12 inches, or use 8 sheets of oiled cooking parchment. Divide the pasta evenly among the squares, mounding it in the center. Place 6 shrimp on top of each mound of pasta.

Melt the butter over moderate heat in a large skillet and add the pepper, mushrooms, scallions, parsley, and seasonings. Stir for 2 minutes. Add the chicken broth and stir for another 3 minutes. Divide the mixture evenly and pour over each pasta portion. Top with slivered snow peas.

With each foil square, bring two opposite sides together over the top and fold down until almost touching shrimp. Seal the two open ends, forming a square package. If you are using parchment, gather the edges to enclose the food loosely; tie the neck tightly with string or a wire twist.

Put the packages on a large baking sheet and bake for 15 to 20 minutes; the parchment will puff and brown. Remove from the oven and place on individual plates. To serve, cut an X in top of the packages and lift the edges away, or let diners break open their packages at the table.

SERVES 8

Dining by Fireflies: Unexpected Pleasures of the New South, Charlotte, NC

SWEET MUSTARD SHRIMP

An elegant first course that can be prepared in advance.

½ cup Dijon mustard
2 teaspoons dry mustard
1 teaspoon toasted mustard seeds
1-2 tablespoons fresh lemon juice
6 tablespoons sugar
½ cup cider vinegar
½ cup vegetable oil
1 teaspoon ground cinnamon
2 tablespoons dried dill
2 tablespoons finely chopped red
  onion
2 pounds medium shrimp

Combine the Dijon mustard, dry mustard, mustard seeds, lemon juice, sugar, and cider vinegar in a bowl. Whisk in the oil. Stir in the cinnamon, dill, and onion. Chill, tightly covered. (The marinade may be made in advance and kept in the refrigerator for up to a week.)

Steam the shrimp, or cook according to the directions on page 43. Peel and devein. Combine with the marinade and refrigerate for 2 hours to overnight. Serve over a bed of greens.

VARIATION: Serve the shrimp on wooden skewers as a wonderful hors d'oeuvre.

SERVES 10–12

I'll Taste Manhattan, New York, NY

MARINATED SHRIMP AND AVOCADOS

2 pounds shrimp, cooked (see
  below), shelled, and deveined
2 avocados, pitted, peeled and cut
  into chunks
2 small onions, sliced thin

MARINADE
1 cup vegetable oil
1 cup wine vinegar
½ cup lemon juice
1 tablespoon salt
¼ teaspoon ground black pepper
2 teaspoons sugar
1 teaspoon dried thyme
1 teaspoon dry mustard
2 teaspoons dried oregano
½ teaspoon garlic powder

Place the shrimp, avocados, and onions in a shallow bowl. Pour the marinade over, cover, and refrigerate overnight. Drain and serve. For an appetizer, spoon on crackers. For salad, serve on lettuce leaves.

To make the marinade, combine the oil, vinegar, lemon juice, and seasonings with ½ cup of water. Whisk by hand or process in a blender until thickened.

SERVES 24 AS APPETIZER, 8 AS SALAD

The Bounty of East Texas, Longview, TX

SEASONED PRAWNS

On the West Coast, large shrimp are called prawns. Although suggested in this recipe and in many others, deveining is really an optional cosmetic procedure.

MARINADE
⅓ cup white vinegar
2 tablespoons vegetable oil
4 teaspoons capers, with some juice
1 teaspoon celery seed
½ teaspoon salt
⅛ teaspoon Tabasco

COURT BOUILLON
¼ cup chopped celery tops
2 tablespoons mixed pickling spices
1½ teaspoons salt
1 pound large raw prawns

½ onion, sliced thin and separated
  into rings
3–4 bay leaves

Combine the marinade ingredients; set aside.

To cook the shrimp, first make a court bouillon: In a 3-quart saucepan, bring 2 quarts of water to a boil. Add the celery tops, pickling spices, and 1½ teaspoons of salt. Drop in the prawns; boil 1–2 minutes, or until they turn pink. Do not overcook. Remove from the heat, drain, and cool. Shell and devein the prawns, and brush off most of the pickling spices and clinging pieces of celery.

In a glass or ceramic bowl, layer the prawns with the onion slices and bay leaves. Pour the marinade over the prawns. Refrigerate for 24 hours or longer. Stir once or twice during this time to thoroughly marinate all the ingredients. Drain off the marinade and discard the bay leaves. Serve the prawns in a glass bowl.

NOTE: To serve as a first course, include some onion slices with each portion.

SERVES 4–6   *California Fresh,* Oakland–East Bay, CA

CARIBBEAN SHRIMP WITH ISLAND SALSA

SHRIMP

½ cup dark rum

2 tablespoons lemon juice

2 tablespoons pickling spices

1 tablespoon whole black peppercorns

1 teaspoon crushed red pepper flakes

1 teaspoon salt

40 medium shrimp, shelled and deveined

ISLAND SALSA

5 Roma tomatoes, peeled, seeded, and diced

1 papaya, peeled, seeded, and diced

1 small red onion, diced

½ cup sliced black olives

2 tablespoons finely chopped fresh mint

Zest and juice of 2 limes

2 tablespoons dark brown sugar

Dash of cumin

Dash of chili powder

Dash of crushed red pepper flakes

Dash of salt

2 shakes of Worcestershire sauce

Shrimp: In a large pan combine the rum, lemon juice, pickling spices, peppercorns, red pepper flakes, and salt with ½ cup of water. Place over medium high heat until the liquid begins to steam. Add the shrimp and stir until they are light pink and opaque, just firm to the touch. Remove with a slotted spoon to a bowl of crushed ice. Toss with the ice to quickly stop the cooking. Chill the shrimp with the ice until ready to serve. Drain and arrange on a serving platter with Island Salsa.

Island Salsa: Combine the tomatoes, papaya, and onion in a bowl. Place the mixture in a food processor or blender to purée. Return the purée to the bowl. Add the remaining ingredients and stir to blend well. Set aside for 1 hour or more. The salsa is best when served at room temperature.

SERVES 10–12

Celebrate!, Sacramento, CA

SOUTH OF THE BORDER SHRIMP

2 pounds large shrimp, shelled and deveined, with tails left intact

¾ cup olive oil

¼ cup white wine vinegar

2-3 tablespoons fresh lemon juice

2 large cloves garlic, minced

½ teaspoon crushed red pepper flakes

Salt and ground black pepper to taste

½ cup finely chopped cilantro

2 jalapeño peppers, seeded and minced

1 large lemon, sliced

1 large red onion, sliced

Bring a large pot of water to a boil. Add the shrimp and cook until pink, about 3 minutes. Drain and transfer to a large bowl of ice water until shrimp are cooled. Drain and place the shrimp in a large bowl.

In a medium-size bowl, whisk together the oil, vinegar, lemon juice, garlic, red pepper flakes, salt and black pepper. Stir in the cilantro and jalapeños. Pour some of the marinade over the shrimp, gently tossing to coat. In a large shallow dish, layer the shrimp, lemon slices, and onion. Pour the remaining marinade over the shrimp. Cover and refrigerate at least 6 hours.

SERVES 6–8

California Sizzles, Pasadena, CA

CRABMEAT IN LIMES

3 large limes
¾ cup safflower oil
2 cloves garlic, minced
1 teaspoon grated fresh ginger
½ cup lime juice
⅓ cup dry white wine
⅓ cup chopped chives
1 teaspoon salt
¾ teaspoon ground black pepper
1 pound fresh crabmeat, picked over
  to remove bits of shell and
  cartilage
½ cup grated carrot

Cut the limes in half lengthwise. Squeeze enough juice from the limes to measure ½ cup. Remove the pulp from the lime shells. Set the shells aside.

In a large skillet, heat 2 tablespoons of the oil. Add the garlic and ginger. Sauté for 1 or 2 minutes, until golden. Add the remaining oil, the lime juice, wine, chives, salt and pepper. Stir to combine. Add the crabmeat and cook, stirring frequently, for 5 minutes. Spoon the crabmeat mixture into 6 lime shells and garnish with grated carrot. Serve immediately.

VARIATION: Cooked lobster, shrimp, or monkfish may be substituted for the crabmeat.

SERVES 6   *Settings,* Philadelphia, PA

CRAB STRUDEL

1 tablespoon lemon juice
½ pound crabmeat, picked over to
  remove bits of shell and cartilage
2 tablespoons minced scallion
3 tablespoons butter, or as needed
2 tablespoons chopped parsley
2 drops Tabasco
Dash of salt and ground black
  pepper
½ pound Brie cheese, cut into
  small, thin pieces
6 sheets frozen phyllo dough,
  thawed

Preheat the oven to 375 degrees. Sprinkle the lemon juice over the crabmeat. Sauté the scallion in 1 tablespoon of the butter. Add the crabmeat and heat through. Add the parsley, Tabasco, salt, and pepper. Mix well. Place the Brie slices over the top of the crabmeat mixture; allow to melt. Gently mix together.

Unroll the phyllo onto a work surface; keep the unused portion covered with waxed paper and a damp towel. Melt the remaining 2 tablespoons of butter. Brush one sheet of phyllo lightly with butter; cover with another sheet and brush with butter.

Spread ⅓ of the crab mixture along the short end. Roll, tucking ends under; brush with butter. Place seam side down on a cookie sheet. Repeat for the remaining phyllo and crabmeat. Bake for 20-25 minutes. To serve, slice each roll into 12 pieces.

VARIATION: Use feta cheese and spinach in place of Brie and crab.

SERVES 15   *A Cleveland Collection,* Cleveland, OH

CAPE FEAR CRAB CAKES WITH LEMON DILL SAUCE

CRAB CAKES
3 tablespoons butter
1 scallion chopped fine
1 clove garlic, minced
2 tablespoons red bell pepper, chopped fine
Ground red pepper to taste (cayenne)
3 tablespoons heavy cream
1 tablespoon Dijon mustard
1 egg, beaten
1 teaspoon minced fresh basil
1 teaspoon minced fresh parsley
1 cup fine dry bread crumbs
1 pound fresh lump crabmeat, picked over to remove bits of shell and cartilage
¼ cup Parmesan cheese
2 tablespoons vegetable oil

LEMON DILL SAUCE
¾ cup mayonnaise
½ cup buttermilk
2 tablespoons fresh dill chopped
1 tablespoon minced fresh parsley
2 teaspoons fresh lemon juice
1 tablespoon grated lemon peel
1 clove garlic, minced

Melt 1 tablespoon of the butter in a large skillet and sauté the scallion, garlic, and red bell pepper until wilted, about 2 minutes. Add the ground red pepper, cream, and mustard. Cool slightly. Add the egg, basil, parsley, ½ cup of the bread crumbs, and the crabmeat. Mix lightly. Mold into 16 2-inch-wide patties.

Combine the remaining ½ cup of bread crumbs and the Parmesan cheese in a shallow dish. Roll the patties in the crumb and cheese mixture. Chill for at least 1 hour (The crab cakes can be made early in the day and refrigerated, covered, up to this point.)

Combine the oil and the remaining 2 tablespoons of butter over moderate heat in a large skillet. Sauté the crab cakes 3 minutes on each side. Serve with lemon dill sauce.

Lemon Dill Sauce: Combine all ingredients in medium bowl. Chill until the mixture thickens.

MAKES 16

Dining by Fireflies: Unexpected Pleasures of the New South, Charlotte, NC

WASTECAP PORTLAND
JUNIOR LEAGUE OF PORTLAND, MAINE

From February to May of 1991 the Junior League of Portland, Maine, coordinated and funded a pilot program called WasteCap Portland, involving five small businesses from the Old Port district of Portland. In June, 1991, the program was expanded to include retail stores, restaurants, and office management companies. Teams of trained business members, community volunteers, and environmental specialists—coordinated and funded by the Junior League—visit companies and assess opportunities for waste reduction and recycling.

GEODUCK FRITTERS

The geoduck, a specialty of the Northwest, is a clam whose shell can measure up to eight inches, with a neck equally long. If the geoduck is unavailable, substitute minced clams.

BATTER

1 cup all-purpose flour
2 tablespoons peanut oil
1 egg
¼ cup beer
½ teaspoon salt
½ teaspoon sugar

GEODUCK MIXTURE

1 tablespoon chopped onion
2 tablespoons butter
½ teaspoon curry powder
1 cup chopped geoduck, drained
½ cup peeled and grated sweet
   potato
¼ cup peeled and grated carrot

Peanut oil for deep frying

Batter: Combine the flour, oil, egg, beer, salt, and sugar in a small bowl. Beat with a hand-held mixer until smooth. If possible, the batter should be made 5 hours in advance and kept at room temperature.

Geoduck mixture: Sauté the onion in the butter until brown, then stir in the curry and geoduck. Add the sweet potato and carrot, stir 1 minute, and remove from the heat. Chill immediately to keep crisp.

To make the fritters, pour 2 to 4 inches of oil into a deep heavy pan and heat to 375 degrees. Blend the geoduck mixture into the batter at the last minute. Drop the fritter mixture into the hot oil, 6 to 8 fritters at a time. Fry about 2 minutes, until golden brown. Drain on paper towels. Keep warm in a 200 degree oven until all the batter is used.

SERVES 8 AS AN HORS D'OEUVRE, 4 AS A MAIN COURSE   *The Seattle Classic,* Seattle, WA

CHINESE CHICKEN WINGS

½ cup soy sauce
1 cup pineapple juice
⅓ cup packed brown sugar
1 teaspoon garlic salt
½ teaspoon ground black pepper
1 teaspoon ground dried ginger
2-3 pounds chicken wingettes (wing
   tips removed)

Combine the soysauce, pineapple juice, brown sugar, and seasonings in a bowl and stir to make marinade. Place the chicken in a large baking dish and pour the marinade over the chicken. Cover and refrigerate for 24 hours, turning occasionally.

Arrange the wings in a single layer. Heat the oven to 350 degrees. Bake the chicken wings, turning once, until they are golden brown, about 45 minutes.

SERVES 6   *Udderly Delicious,* Racine, WI

ASIAN CHICKEN WINGS

Great taste—worth the messy fingers!

3 pounds chicken wings
⅓ cup soy sauce
2 tablespoons vegetable oil
2 tablespoons chili sauce
½ cup honey
1 teaspoon salt
½ teaspoon grated fresh ginger
¼ teaspoon garlic powder
¼ teaspoon ground red pepper
  (cayenne), optional

Wash the chicken wings and pat dry. Remove and discard the wing tips. Separate each wing into 2 pieces by bending the 2 parts backward, then cutting through at the joint with a sharp knife. Place in an airtight container. Mix the remaining ingredients and pour the marinade over the chicken wings. Cover and refrigerate overnight, turning occasionally.

Preheat the oven to 375 degrees. Arrange the chicken wings on a foil-lined pan. Brush with marinade and bake 25 minutes. Turn the wings, brush with marinade, and bake 25 minutes longer.

MAKES ABOUT 36   *Great Beginnings, Grand Finales,* South Bend, IN

PICNIC SANDWICH

1 (1-pound) loaf frozen bread dough
4 ounces thinly sliced cooked ham
4 ounces thinly sliced cotto salami
4 ounces thinly sliced pickle and
  pimiento loaf, or other luncheon
  meat
8 ounces ricotta cheese
6 ounces provolone or Monterey
  Jack cheese, shredded coarsely
1 medium onion, chopped
½ cup chopped green bell pepper
½ cup chopped red bell pepper
1 teaspoon dried oregano
1 egg beaten with 1 tablespoon
  water (optional)
Sesame seeds or poppy seeds
  (optional)

Let the dough thaw to room temperature. Preheat the oven to 350 degrees. Cut the meats into ¼-inch-wide strips. Mix the meats, cheeses, onion, chopped peppers, and oregano.

On a lightly floured surface, roll the dough to a 10 × 14-inch rectangle. Place the dough on a lightly greased baking sheet. Spread the filling over the center third of the dough. Bring the edges to the center and seal.

Turn the dough seam side down. Make slits on top of the loaf. If desired, brush with egg wash and sprinkle with sesame or poppy seeds. Place in oven immediately and bake for 25 minutes or until golden brown. Cool on a rack to ensure a crispy bottom.

MAKES 1 LOAF   *Great Beginnings, Grand Finales,* South Bend, IN

SPINACH PEPPERONI FRITTATAS

1 (10-ounce) package frozen
   spinach, thawed
1½ cups ricotta cheese
¾ cup freshly grated Parmesan
   cheese
2 eggs
1½ tablespoons Worcestershire sauce
1 teaspoon dried basil
½ teaspoon salt
½ teaspoon garlic powder
½ teaspoon ground black pepper
½ small onion, chopped fine
8 ounces pepperoni, cut into 36
   slices

Preheat the oven to 375 degrees. Squeeze excess moisture from the spinach. Mix the spinach, cheeses, eggs, Worcestershire sauce, basil, salt, garlic powder, pepper, and onion in a large bowl, stirring until blended well.

Grease 36 mini muffin cups or spray the cups with vegetable oil cooking spray. Place 1 slice of pepperoni in each cup. Top with enough spinach mixture to fill each cup. Bake for 25 minutes. Serve hot, or allow to cool and remove from cups for freezing.

N O T E : If frozen, thaw and reheat at 350 degrees for 10 minutes.

M A K E S 3 6   *Savor the Brandywine Valley,* Wilmington, DE

PEPPERONI BREAD

Hearty bread that's very easy to prepare.

1 loaf frozen bread dough
1 egg
1 teaspoon snipped parsley
1 teaspoon dried oregano
1 teaspoon salt
¼ teaspoon ground black pepper
1 (8- to 10-inch) stick of pepperoni,
   skinned and sliced thin
1 cup grated mozzarella cheese
1 cup cooked or canned
   mushrooms, drained (optional)
Sesame seeds

Thaw the dough according to package directions. Spread the thawed dough into a large rectangle on a greased jelly roll pan or baking sheet with a rim. Make an egg wash by mixing the egg and seasonings. Brush half the egg wash on the dough almost to the edges.

Layer the pepperoni slices, 3 or 4 to a row, down the center third of the bread. Sprinkle with cheese and optional mushrooms. Fold one third of the dough over the filling, then the other third over. Flip the dough over so the seam side is underneath.

Brush the loaf with the remaining egg wash. Sprinkle with sesame seeds. Bake in a preheated 350 degree oven for 25 minutes or until golden brown.

M A K E S 1 L O A F   *Applehood & Motherpie,* Rochester, NY

NEW YORK JUNIOR LEAGUE HOSPITAL VOLUNTEERS
THE JUNIOR LEAGUE OF NEW YORK CITY

Begun during World War I, the New York Junior League Hospital Volunteers started the first system of volunteer help in a New York City hospital outpatient department at Bellevue's Children's Clinic. Since then, the League has helped pioneer other projects at Bellevue, including the famed physical rehabilitation program initiated by Dr. Howard Rusk. Today, through five committees at work in New York City hospitals, the NYJL continues its tradition of helping children cope with hospitalization and family separation by serving as teachers, friends, and playmates.

BEVERAGES

WAIKIKI WORKOUT

1 cup orange juice
1 banana
1 kiwifruit
1 tablespoon honey
2 or 3 ice cubes

Pour the juice in a blender. Add the banana, kiwi, and honey; blend until smooth. Add ice and blend until thick. Serve.

SERVES 1   *Another Taste of Aloha,* Honolulu, HI

WATERMELON PARTY PUNCH

Great fun for a children's party!

1 large watermelon, approximately
    25 pounds
1 (12-ounce) can frozen limeade or
    lemonade, thawed
¼ cup grenadine syrup
1 or 2 (32-ounce) bottles lemon–lime
    carbonated beverage, chilled
3-4 scoops pineapple sherbet

Select a melon with a flat base. The day before serving, make sawtooth cuts to remove an 8-inch oval section from the top and set aside. Scoop out the pulp, remove the seeds, and purée the melon in a blender. Strain and pour into the melon shell. Stir in the undiluted lemonade or limeade, 2 cups of water, and the syrup. Cover with the reserved lid and refrigerate overnight.

Before serving, stir in a carbonated beverage until the melon is ¾ full. Add the sherbet. Use a skewer to poke holes in the melon large enough for drinking straws. Serve with the lid on.

VARIATION: Spike with vodka for an adult party.

MAKES ABOUT 1 GALLON   *L'Apéritifs,* Butte, MT

HOT SPICED PERCOLATOR PUNCH

2¼ cups pineapple juice
2 cups cranberry juice
1 tablespoon whole cloves
1 tablespoon whole allspice
3 cinnamon sticks (broken)
¼ teaspoon salt
½ cup packed brown sugar

Pour the juices and 1¾ cups of water into an 8-cup percolator. Place the remaining ingredients in the percolator basket. Perk for 10 minutes or until the spices permeate. Serve hot.

VARIATION: This is also good spiked with Bourbon.

SERVES 8–10   *Pear Tree,* Knoxville, TN

BACK PORCH LEMONADE

1 cup sugar
1⅓ cups fresh lemon juice
1 tablespoon lemon zest, grated fine
Lemon slices and fresh mint leaves
    for garnish

Combine the sugar and 1 cup of water in a small saucepan over medium heat and bring to a boil. Reduce the heat and simmer 5-6 minutes, stirring occasionally. Remove from heat and cool the syrup completely.

Combine the syrup with the lemon juice and zest; add 8 cups of cold water. Garnish and serve over ice.

MAKES ABOUT 2 ½ QUARTS

Georgia on My Menu, Cobb–Marietta, GA

CALIFORNIA CAPPUCCINO

The perfect ending.

1 cup heavy cream
½ cup crème de cacao
3 tablespoons Tía María liqueur
3 tablespoons dark rum
8 cups hot coffee
8 tablespoons caffè d'Vita
    cappuccino mix
Powdered non-dairy creamer
    (optional)
Grated nutmeg
8 cinnamon sticks, optional

Whip the cream several hours in advance; refrigerate until ready to use. Combine the crème de cacao, Tía María, and rum in a glass measuring cup; set aside.

Heat 12-ounce mugs or cups with hot tap water for a few minutes. Pour out the hot water and pour in 10 ounces of hot coffee. Add 1 tablespoon of cappuccino mix to each and stir well. For a creamier consistency, stir in powdered coffee creamer to taste. Add 1¾ tablespoons of the liqueur mixture to each; stir well.

Top with dollops of whipped cream and sprinkle with nutmeg. Garnish with a swizzle stick of cinnamon. Serve immediately.

SERVES 8   *R.S.V.P.,* Orange County, CA

CAFÉ AU LAIT

FOR 2
1½ tablespoons sugar
1 cup hot milk
1 cup hot coffee

FOR 30
¾ cup sugar
15 cups hot milk
15 cups hot black coffee

Caramelize the sugar by placing it in a heavy dry skillet over low heat until it melts. Continue cooking over low heat until it becomes a thick, clear, golden-brown liquid. Remove the caramel from the heat. Add the hot milk slowly and carefully to avoid being burned.

Fill coffee cups by simultaneously pouring equal amounts of the hot coffee and hot milk. Sweeten with sugar if desired.

SERVES 2 OR 30   *Talk About Good II,* Lafayette, LA

ELLA'S DELTA MINT TEA

7 tea bags
12 sprigs mint
Zest of 3 lemons
8 cups boiling water
Juice of 7 lemons
2 cups sugar

In a large earthenware pitcher, steep the tea, mint, and lemon zest in boiling water for 12 minutes. Remove with a slotted spoon.

Add the lemon juice and sugar to the hot tea and stir until the sugar is dissolved. Strain. Combine with 8 cups of cold water. Serve over ice.

MAKES 1 GALLON   *Southern Sideboards,* Jackson, MS

SPICED ICED TEA

5 tea bags
4 cups boiling water
2 cinnamon sticks
1½ cups sugar
1½ cups pineapple juice
1 cup juice from spiced pickled
   peaches
Juice of 3 lemons
Juice of 3 oranges
Orange or lemon slices
Fresh mint leaves

Pour the boiling water over the tea bags and cinnamon sticks. Steep 15 to 20 minutes. Strain into a gallon container. Add the sugar and stir to dissolve thoroughly. Add the fruit juices and 8 cups of cold water. Refrigerate until serving time. Garnish with orange slices and mint leaves. Serve over ice.

MAKES 3–4 QUARTS   *The Carolina Collection,* Fayetteville, NC

SALEM COLLEGE ICED TEA

The best iced tea in the world, and one reason loyal alumnae enjoy returning at commencement time.

4 sprigs fresh mint
8-12 whole cloves
1 ounce loose tea
Juice of 8 lemons
Juice of 6 oranges
1 (46-ounce) can pineapple juice
2 cups sugar

Add the mint and cloves to 8 cups of water; bring to a boil. Simmer for 10–15 minutes. Remove from the heat. Add the tea and allow to steep for 10 to 15 minutes. Strain, and while still hot, add the fruit juices and sugar. Stir to dissolve and allow to cool. Serve over ice.

MAKES ABOUT 1 GALLON   *Heritage of Hospitality,* Winston-Salem, NC

ALMOND TEA

If you prefer hot tea, simply add all the water before steeping the tea bags.

3 tea bags
1 cup sugar
1 teaspoon vanilla extract
1½ teaspoons almond extract
Juice of 3 lemons, or 6 tablespoons
    concentrated lemon juice

In a saucepan, bring 2 cups of water to a boil. Reduce the heat to a simmer, and add the tea bags, and steep for 5 minutes. Remove the tea bags. Add the sugar, extracts, and lemon juice. Simmer and stir until the sugar is dissolved. Remove from the heat. Add 6 cups of cold water and chill. Serve over ice.

MAKES ABOUT 2 QUARTS   *Hearts & Flowers,* Waco, TX

TEXAS ICED TEA

½ teaspoon ground cloves
½ teaspoon ground cinnamon
Dash of grated nutmeg
4 tablespoons loose tea
1 (6-ounce) can frozen lemonade
1 (6-ounce) can frozen orange juice

Put the spices in 2 quarts of water in a saucepan and bring to a strong boil. Add the tea and remove from the heat. Steep for 5 minutes. Strain.

Add the fruit juices plus 4 juice cans of water to the tea. Pour over ice in tall glasses. If serving from a pitcher, add lemon and orange slices for color.

MAKES 2 QUARTS   *Texas Tables,* Dallas, TX

CHAMPAGNE PUNCH

This punch is beautiful in a large silver bowl with a fancy ice block floating in it. Half the preparation can be done the day before.

1½ cups confectioners' sugar
½ cup Triple Sec or other orange-
    flavored liqueur
½ cup Cognac
½ cup maraschino cherry juice
Maraschino cherries (optional)
2 bottles chilled Champagne
1 orange, sliced
1 lemon, sliced
1 quart pineapple sherbet

Combine the sugar, liqueur, Cognac, cherry juice and cherries, if desired. Pour into a punch bowl. Just before serving, add the chilled Champagne, orange and lemon slices, and the sherbet. Stir to mix.

MAKES 3 QUARTS   *Holiday Flavors and Favors,* Greensboro, NC

ORCHID ISLAND SEA-BREEZE PUNCH

2 cups chilled cranberry juice
1 cup chilled grapefruit juice
1 cup chilled vodka
Juice of 1 lime
1 tablespoon superfine sugar
1 liter bottle chilled sparkling wine
Lime slices to garnish
Grapefruit slices to garnish

In 2-quart pitcher or punch bowl, combine the cranberry juice, grapefruit juice, vodka, lime juice, and sugar. Stir until the sugar is dissolved. Add the sparkling wine. Pour over crushed ice and garnish with lime and grapefruit slices.

SERVES 12   *Making Waves in the Kitchen,* Indian River, FL

WASSAIL

2¾ cups plus 1 tablespoon sugar
⅓ cup instant tea
½ teaspoon ground cinnamon
¼ teaspoon ground cloves

Combine the ingredients in a jar. Use 2 tablespoons of mix per cup of boiling hot water, or serve in a punch bowl and float thin slices of lemon.

SERVES 10   *Tested, Tried & True,* Flint, MI

SUSTAINER SLUSH

1½ to 3½ cups Bourbon whiskey (as desired)
1 (12-ounce) can frozen lemonade concentrate
2 tablespoons frozen orange juice concentrate
Mint sprigs or maraschino cherries

In an electric blender, combine the Bourbon, lemonade and orange juice concentrates, and 4½ cups water. Place in the freezer for 1 to 3 hours until the mixture freezes. Just before serving, mix in the blender. Pour into cocktail glasses. Add a sprig of mint and/or cherry to garnish.

SERVES 6–8   *A Slice of Paradise,* West Palm Beach, FL

AL'S HOLIDAY MILK PUNCH

1 cup crushed ice
1 pint vanilla ice cream
5 ounces milk
2½ ounces Bourbon whiskey
1 ounce rum
¾ ounce brandy
¾ ounce cognac
4½ teaspoons sugar

In a blender, combine the crushed ice and vanilla ice cream. Add the milk, liquors, and sugar. Blend until well mixed.

SERVES 6   *Lagniappe on the Neches,* Beaumont, TX

BLACK-EYED SUSAN

Shaved ice
1 ounce vodka
1 ounce rum
¾ ounce Triple Sec or other
   orange-flavored liqueur
Lime wedge
Pineapple juice
Orange juice

Fill a 12-ounce glass with shaved ice. Add the vodka, rum, and Triple Sec. Squeeze in the lime wedge and drop into the glass. Fill with equal parts pineapple and orange juice.

SERVES 1   *Hunt to Harbor—An Epicurean Tour,* Baltimore, MD

SANDY'S MINT JULEP

MINT SYRUP
2 cups sugar
4 cups mint sprigs

MINT JULEP
1½ ounces mint syrup per serving
2 ounces Bourbon whiskey per
   serving
Crushed ice
Mint sprigs

To make mint syrup, boil 4 cups of water and the sugar over medium heat for 10 minutes. Add the mint sprigs and simmer for 30 minutes. Set aside overnight. Strain.

To make a mint julep, measure the mint syrup and Bourbon into a silver julep cup. Fill with crushed ice. Add a straw and garnish with mint sprigs. To frost the cup, dry the outside and refrigerate at least one hour, or freeze. Remove from the freezer 30 minutes before serving.

SERVES 25–30   *Atlanta Cooknotes,* Atlanta, GA

BRANDY ICE

6 scoops vanilla ice cream
6 ounces brandy
3 ounces white crème de cacao
1½ ounces white crème de menthe
   (optional)
8 ice cubes

Place all ingredients in a blender and blend quickly.

SERVES 4–6   *The Cotton Country Collection,* Monroe, LA

A Celebration of Community

There is a tension in society between what our communities are really like and what we want them to be like. We yearn for a sense of connectedness with other people and a sense of oneness and harmony with our environment—yet reality often finds us separated and jarred by conflicting boundaries of religion, ethnicity, politics, class, or race.

For a hundred years, it has been the mission of the Junior League—and organizations like the Junior League—to create communities in which all people can come together and feel supported by one another, experiencing a sense of well-being and discovering opportunities to build productive lives. In these pages, we celebrate this journey toward true community.

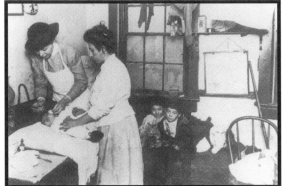

A League volunteer helps a mother care for her baby in an urban settlement house. Early 1900s.

It is an incredibly difficult journey and one that requires a resolute heart. Since its beginnings in 1901 in the settlement houses in New York City, where Junior League volunteers sought to ease the burdens of overcrowded, unhealthy tenements through educational and nutritional programs for families, the Junior League has sustained its commitment. It has taken on critical social issues and addressed them through varied initiatives that creatively and intentionally link people and resources, creating wholeness where there had been none before.

Time magazine, in an article on voluntary organizations, cited the Junior League as "a powerful force for social change." That force is felt when a battered child is nursed back to health in a League-sponsored crisis center. It resonates across a community when the Junior League becomes involved in a downtown revitalization coalition, breathing new life into historic structures and sparking an upsurge of economic opportunities for all citizens. It reverberates when a public awareness campaign against domestic violence is staged by League advocates on the steps of state capitols—or members testify before U.S. Congressional committees on funding for the homeless, or a campaign to promote the early immunization of children is embraced by Junior Leagues in four countries.

While the Junior League has been known historically for its role as community convener, today that role is taking on a new meaning, a new sense of urgency, as communities experience shortages of funds and shrinking volunteer time. As the Junior League moves into its second hundred years, we reach out in our celebration to new partners across the whole spectrum of community life, with the intent of fostering an all-embracing spirit of good will and cooperation.

SALADS

CLEOPATRA SALAD

CROUTONS
1 cup small bread cubes
1 tablespoon butter, melted
1 tablespoon Parmesan cheese

Toss the bread cubes with the butter and Parmesan cheese, in a skillet. Toast over moderate heat, stirring frequently until golden brown. Cool.

DRESSING
1 egg (optional; see Note)
⅓ cup olive oil
¼ cup lemon juice
1 teaspoon Worcestershire sauce
1 clove garlic, crushed
¾ teaspoon salt
¼ teaspoon ground black pepper

Beat the egg in a small bowl. Add the olive oil, lemon juice, Worcestershire sauce, garlic, salt, and pepper; beat until blended. Set aside.

SALAD
½ head romaine lettuce, rinsed and spun dry
½ head iceberg lettuce, rinsed and spun dry
2 cups seedless grapes, stemmed, rinsed, and dried
4-6 ounces blue cheese

Tear the lettuces into large pieces. Arrange the greens, grapes, croutons, and blue cheese in a large salad bowl. Pour the dressing over the salad. Toss lightly before serving.

NOTE: The egg yolk may be omitted if you fear the possibility of salmonella.

SERVES 6

Sunsational, Orlando, FL

FREE SHOTS FOR KIDS
JUNIOR LEAGUE OF AKRON, OHIO

On one Saturday each May, the Junior League of Akron, Ohio, administers its Free Shots for Kids program in three area malls. Started in 1993 and scheduled to run at least through 1996, the program was formed in an effort to increase the low immunization rate in Summit county. In 1993, 874 children received 1,580 vaccinations; in 1994, 1,036 children received 2,035 doses of vaccines, with similar increases expected each year. An Immunization Coalition has been formed among the Junior League, Akron's Children's Hospital, the local health departments, and the Ohio Health Department.

A Pretty Green Salad

DRESSING
¾ teaspoon dry mustard
¾ teaspoon salt
½ teaspoon celery seed
1 teaspoon sugar (optional)
½ tablespoon minced onion
¼ cup wine vinegar
½ cup olive oil

SALAD
½ pound fresh spinach, washed
   thoroughly and spun dry
½ small head purple cabbage
Dried fruit bits
Slivered almonds, toasted

Combine all the dressing ingredients, mixing well. Set aside until needed.

In a large bowl, tear the spinach and cabbage into bite-sized pieces. Add the dried fruit and slivered almonds. Toss to mix. Top with dressing.

SERVES 6   *The Wild, Wild West,* Odessa, TX

Greek Salad

Healthy, elegant and delicious, too!

DRESSING
¼ cup plus 1 tablespoon olive oil
¼ cup red wine vinegar
½ teaspoon dried oregano
½ teaspoon salt
¼ teaspoon ground black pepper

SALAD
2 heads romaine lettuce, rinsed and
   spun dry
3 large ripe tomatoes, cut up
1 cucumber, sliced
1 medium green bell pepper, diced
1 small onion, sliced
8 pitted ripe olives
⅔ cup crumbled feta cheese

Prepare the dressing ahead: combine the olive oil and vinegar; add the oregano, salt, and pepper. Whisk until blended.

Tear the greens into large pieces. Place in a salad bowl and add the tomatoes, cucumber, green pepper, onion, and olives. Toss with the dressing and feta cheese just before serving.

SERVES 6   *River Feast,* Cincinnati, OH

MARDI GRAS SALAD

MARDI GRAS DRESSING
2 teaspoons chopped onion, or 2
    teaspoons onion juice
½ cup cider vinegar
1 teaspoon sugar, or to taste
1 teaspoon dry mustard
1 teaspoon salt
⅔ cup vegetable oil

MARDI GRAS SALAD
1 head lettuce, shredded
1 (10-ounce) bag spinach leaves,
    stemmed and shredded
10 slices bacon, fried, drained, and
    crumbled
1 red onion, slivered
1½ cups mandarin orange sections
1 (8-ounce) package mushrooms,
    sliced

Make the dressing: Put the onion, cider vinegar, sugar, dry mustard, and salt in a blender. Start on low speed and slowly add the oil. The dressing can be made ahead of time and refrigerated in the blender container.

Line a salad bowl with the lettuce and spinach. Add the crumbled bacon, onion, orange sections, and mushrooms. Mix and toss the ingredients. Briefly blend the dressing before tossing with the salad. Serve at once.

SERVES 8–10   *Celebrations on the Bayou,* Monroe, LA

ORANGE AND ROMAINE TOSS

A colorful combination of fruits and greens.

1 head romaine lettuce, rinsed and
    spun dry
3 kiwifruit, peeled and sliced
1 (11-ounce) can mandarin orange
    sections, drained
1 large red onion, sliced
½ cup olive oil
¼ cup lime juice
3 tablespoons red wine vinegar
3 tablespoons orange marmalade
Salt and freshly ground black pepper
    to taste
Croutons (preferably homemade; see
    page 62)
⅓ cup halved pecans
3 ounces blue cheese, crumbled

Tear the lettuce into bite-size pieces and place in a salad bowl with the kiwifruit, orange sections, and onion. Combine the olive oil, lime juice, vinegar, marmalade, salt, and pepper. Mix well. Toss the salad with the dressing just before serving. Top with croutons, nuts, and blue cheese.

SERVES 6–8   *Family and Company,* Binghamton, NY

CRUNCHY ROMAINE TOSS

SWEET AND SOUR DRESSING
1 cup vegetable oil
½ cup sugar
½ cup wine vinegar
1 tablespoon soy sauce
Salt and pepper to taste

SALAD
¼ cup unsalted butter
1 cup walnuts, chopped
1 package ramen noodles, uncooked
    and broken up (discard flavor
    packet)
1 head romaine lettuce, washed,
    spun dry, and broken into pieces
1 bunch broccoli, chopped coarse
4 scallions, chopped
1 cup Sweet and Sour Dressing

To prepare the dressing, blend all ingredients.

In a small saucepan, melt the butter and brown the walnuts and noodles; cool on paper towels. Line a salad bowl with the romaine. Add the noodles and walnuts, broccoli, and scallions. Pour enough sweet and sour dressing over to coat the ingredients and toss well. Reserve remaining dressing for another use.

SERVES 10–12

Come on In!, Jackson, MS

WILLAMETTE VALLEY SALAD

2 heads mixed salad greens, torn
    into pieces
2-3 avocados, pitted, peeled, and
    sliced
⅓ pound good-quality blue cheese
1 cup Oregon hazelnuts, toasted and
    chopped (see Note)

DIJON DRESSING
⅓ cup red wine vinegar
⅔ cup olive oil
2 tablespoons Dijon mustard
Sea salt
Freshly ground black pepper

Place the salad greens in a serving bowl and chill.

Make the dressing: In a small bowl, whisk the vinegar, oil, mustard, salt, and pepper. Set aside.

Just before serving, arrange the avocado slices on the greens. Add the dressing and toss lightly. Crumble the cheese over the top. Sprinkle with nuts and serve.

NOTE: To toast nuts: Place hazelnuts in a single layer on a cookie sheet in a 350 degree oven. Toast for 5-10 minutes, watching closely. Shake cookie sheet occasionally. As the nuts begin to brown they cook very quickly. Allow to cool and chop nuts by hand.

SERVES 6–8

From Portland's Palate, Portland, OR

CENTER STAGE SALAD

This is a delightful salad with many varia-tions. Try adding crumbled bacon or sub-stituting Stilton or Maytag blue cheese for the Roquefort.

2 heads Boston lettuce, rinsed and
    spun dry
4 to 6 ounces Roquefort cheese,
    crumbled
½ red onion, sliced thin
3 scallions, sliced thin
Cayenne nuts (below)
Center Stage vinaigrette (below)

Tear the lettuce into serving-size pieces and place in a bowl. Chill. When ready to serve, add the cheese, onion, scallions, and nuts. Toss with the vinaigrette dressing.

CAYENNE NUTS
⅓ cup sugar
4 tablespoons (½ stick) unsalted
    butter
¼ cup fresh orange juice
1½ teaspoons salt
1¼ teaspoons ground cinnamon
¼ to ½ teaspoon ground red pepper
    (cayenne)
¼ teaspoon ground mace
1 pound pecan halves

Position a rack in the center of the oven and heat the oven to 250 degrees. Line a jelly roll pan with aluminum foil. Combine the sugar, butter, orange juice, salt, cinnamon, cayenne, and mace in a heavy skillet and place over low heat until the butter melts and the sugar is dissolved. Increase the heat to medium. Add the nuts and toss until coated. Spread in a single layer on the prepared pan. Bake 1 hour, stirring every 15 minutes.

Remove the pan to a rack and separate the nuts with a fork. Cool completely. Store in an airtight container up to 5 days. The nuts can be frozen for 1 month. Bring to room temperature before serving. If sticky, heat on a foil-lined pan at 250 degrees until crisp, about 20 minutes.

CENTER STAGE VINAIGRETTE
½ cup olive oil
3 tablespoons raspberry vinegar
1 tablespoon minced shallots
¼ teaspoon salt
⅛ teaspoon ground white pepper

Combine all ingredients and blend well.

SERVES 8   *California Heritage Continues,* Pasadena, CA

SALAD WITH WARM BRIE DRESSING

CROUTONS

5 slices whole wheat or multi-grain
  bread
2 tablespoons butter
1 clove garlic

SALAD

1 head romaine lettuce
1 bunch watercress

WARM BRIE DRESSING

½ cup vegetable oil
¼ cup chopped onion
1 tablespoon minced garlic
⅓ cup tarragon vinegar
1 tablespoon lemon juice
1 tablespoon Dijon mustard
7 ounces Brie cheese

Remove crusts from the bread and cut into cubes. Melt the butter in a heavy skillet. Put the garlic through a garlic press and add to the butter. Stir. Fry the bread cubes in the garlic butter until golden. Remove from the skillet and drain on paper towels.

Wash and dry the romaine lettuce. Slice vertically through the center spine of each leaf. Then slice each piece horizontally into 1½-inch strips. Wash, dry, and remove the tough stems from the watercress. Toss with the romaine and arrange on individual plates.

Heat the oil in a heavy skillet and sauté the onion and garlic over medium heat until limp and slightly golden, about 4 minutes. Remove from heat and add the vinegar, lemon juice, and mustard. Combine well. Remove and discard the thin layer of rind from the Brie. Cut the cheese into chunks. Return the skillet to the heat and add the Brie; stir with a wooden spoon until melted. Pour the dressing over the greens and top with croutons. Serve immediately while still warm.

SERVES 6   *A Matter of Taste,* Morristown, NJ

SWISS GRAPE SALAD

**MUSTARD VINAIGRETTE
DRESSING**

¼ cup cider vinegar
½ cup vegetable oil
2 teaspoons Dijon mustard
1 to 2 tablespoons brown sugar
1 teaspoon seasoned salt
¼ teaspoon ground black pepper
2 tablespoons sliced scallion

SALAD

6 cups lightly packed fresh spinach
  leaves, rinsed, dried, and tough
  stems removed
6 ounces Swiss cheese, cut into
  matchstick strips
6 ounces Cheddar cheese, cut into
  matchstick strips
2 cups seedless grapes, stemmed,
  rinsed, and dried
4 slices bacon, cooked crisp,
  drained, and crumbled

Make the dressing: In a small bowl, whisk together the vinegar, oil, mustard, brown sugar, salt, and pepper. Blend thoroughly. Stir in the scallion. Cover and chill several hours or overnight. Just before serving, mix dressing thoroughly.

To make the salad: Arrange the spinach, cheeses, and grapes on a platter or individual serving plates. Spoon the dressing over the salad and sprinkle with the crumbled bacon.

SERVES 4   *Amber Waves,* Omaha, NE

SPINACH SALAD WITH CURRY GINGER VINAIGRETTE

SALAD

2 bunches spinach leaves, thoroughly washed, dried, and stems removed

1 head romaine lettuce, rinsed and dried

2 cups thinly sliced red onion

Curry Ginger Vinaigrette (see below)

2 large red apples, unpeeled and sliced thin lengthwise

½ cup raisins

¾ cup dry-roasted pecans

Tear the spinach and romaine into bit-sized pieces. Add the onion, toss with the vinaigrette and place on individual serving plates. Toss the apple slices gently in vinaigrette and arrange in a fanlike design on top of the greens. Sprinkle with raisins and pecans. Serve immediately.

CURRY GINGER VINAIGRETTE

¼ cup white wine vinegar

¼ cup ginger jelly, or 1 tablespoon minced fresh gingerroot

2 tablespoons curry powder

¼ teaspoon Tabasco

Salt and ground black pepper to taste

¾ cup olive oil

Combine the vinegar, jelly, curry powder, Tabasco, salt, and pepper in a small bowl. Slowly whisk in the oil until the mixture is emulsified. Cover and chill until ready to use.

SERVES 6–8   *Celebrate!*, Sacramento, CA

WEDDING SPINACH SALAD WITH YOGURT DRESSING

½ pound spinach, thoroughly washed and dried, stems removed

½ small cucumber, sliced thin

2 fresh peaches, sliced

3 fresh plums, sliced

2 tablespoons sliced scallion

YOGURT DRESSING

1 cup lemon lowfat yogurt

1 tablespoon fresh lemon juice

⅓ teaspoon dried dill weed or 1 teaspoon chopped fresh dill weed

Tear the spinach into bite-size pieces. Place in a bowl with the cucumber, peaches, plums, and scallion.

Combine the yogurt, lemon juice, 1 tablespoon of water, and the dill in a small bowl and whisk until smooth. Add to the salad and toss.

SERVES 4–6   *Feast of Eden*, Monterey, CA

SPINACH-STRAWBERRY SALAD

1 pound fresh spinach, thoroughly
  washed, dried, and torn into bite-
  size pieces
1 tablespoon chopped fresh dill or 1
  teaspoon dried dill weed
1 teaspoon sesame seeds, toasted
  (see page 65)
1 pint strawberries, washed, hulled,
  and sliced in half
Sesame Dressing (page 65), or
  vinaigrette dressing (page 58)

Place the spinach in a large bowl and sprinkle with the dill and sesame seeds. Add the strawberries. Pour the dressing over and toss gently.

N O T E : This looks lovely in a glass bowl.

S E R V E S 4 – 6   *Udderly Delicious,* Racine, WI

SPINACH SALAD WITH WALNUTS AND GORGONZOLA

8 ounces fresh spinach, thoroughly
  washed and dried
10 slices bacon, cooked until crisp,
  drained, and crumbled
½ cup crumbled Gorgonzola cheese
¼ to ½ cup coarsely chopped
  walnuts, toasted
¼ cup vegetable oil
¼ cup olive oil
⅓ cup white wine vinegar
1 tablespoon mayonnaise
1 tablespoon snipped fresh basil or 1
  teaspoon crushed dried basil
1 or 2 cloves garlic, minced
Pinch of sugar (optional)
Salt and freshly ground black pepper

Remove tough stems from the spinach; tear the large leaves into bite-size pieces. Place in a salad bowl. Add the bacon, Gorgonzola, and walnuts.

In a small bowl, whisk together the vegetable oil, olive oil, vinegar, mayonnaise, basil, garlic, sugar, salt, and pepper. Pour over the spinach mixture and toss.

N O T E : Let this salad stand at room temperature for 10 to 15 minutes after tossing. It tastes best if not served ice cold.

S E R V E S 6   *Heart & Soul,* Memphis, TN

NEW START FURNISHINGS
JUNIOR LEAGUE OF BALTIMORE, MARYLAND

New Start Furnishings, a project of the Junior League of Baltimore, Maryland, provides good quality used or new furniture and household goods to families and individuals moving from shelters into permanent housing. Since 1992, NSF has provided such basic items as beds, mattresses, pots, pans, linens, and soap to over 500 families and individuals, reducing the cost of setting up a household and helping to prevent them from slipping back into homelessness.

SPINACH AND BEAN SPROUT SALAD

SALAD
1 (10-ounce) package fresh spinach
1 cup bean sprouts
1 (8-ounce) can water chestnuts, drained and sliced thin

SESAME DRESSING
½ cup vegetable oil
¼ cup soy sauce or tamari
3 tablespoons lemon juice
¾ tablespoon grated onion
1½ tablespoons toasted sesame seeds (see Note)
½ teaspoon sugar
Freshly ground black pepper
¼ teaspoon garlic powder

Salad: Wash the spinach well in cold water and remove the stems. Wrap in a dry kitchen towel and place in the refrigerator to crisp for 4 to 6 hours. Combine with the bean sprouts and water chestnuts in a bowl and toss. If using canned bean sprouts, drain well, rinse with cool water, and chill.

Dressing: Combine the oil, soy sauce, lemon juice, onion, sesame seeds, and seasonings in a bowl and whisk until slightly thickened. Let stand 1 hour at room temperature to blend flavors. At serving time, toss with the salad, using only enough dressing to coat the spinach leaves lightly.

NOTE: To toast sesame seeds, place in a dry flat pan over medium heat until browned. Watch carefully, as they brown quickly.

SERVES 6–8 *The Stenciled Strawberry Cookbook,* Albany, NY

WATERCRESS, PEAR, AND BLUE CHEESE SALAD

A spectacular salad!

1 small head Boston lettuce, rinsed, dried, and torn into pieces
1 bunch watercress, rinsed, dried, and stalks removed
2 ripe pears, cored and sliced
½ cup crumbled blue cheese
½ cup walnut halves

CREAMY TARRAGON DRESSING
1 teaspoon salt
½ teaspoon freshly ground black pepper
¼ teaspoon sugar (optional)
½ teaspoon dry mustard
Juice of ½ lemon
1 clove garlic, minced
5 tablespoons tarragon vinegar
½ cup vegetable oil
2 tablespoons extra virgin olive oil
1 egg, slightly beaten (optional; see Note)
¼ cup light cream

Divide the greens among 4 salad plates and chill. Meanwhile, prepare the dressing: Combine all the ingredients in a jar and shake vigorously to blend. When ready to serve, arrange the pear slices over the chilled greens. Top with blue cheese and walnuts and drizzle with a spoonful or two of dressing. Put the remaining dressing in a bowl and pass separately.

NOTE: Omit the raw egg if you want to avoid the possibility of salmonella contamination.

SERVES 4 *Thymes Remembered,* Tallahassee, FL

CELERY ROOT SALAD

1 cup julienned strips of celery root
2 Belgian endives, washed and sliced
   lengthwise into matchstick strips
Grated zest of ½ orange
Grated zest of ½ lemon
½ cup pitted black olives
½ cup chopped parsley
2 bunches watercress, washed, dried,
   and tough stems removed
½ cup olive oil
⅓ cup freshly squeezed lemon juice
1 clove garlic, peeled and halved
Salt and freshly ground pepper

Put the celery root, endive, orange and lemon zest, olives, and parsley in a salad bowl, with watercress covering all. Cover the salad with plastic wrap and chill in the refrigerator.

Meanwhile, mix the oil, lemon juice, garlic, and salt and pepper to taste. Let stand at room temperature for 1 to 2 hours. To serve, remove the garlic and toss the dressing with the salad.

SERVES 6   *New York Entertains,* New York, NY

GORGONZOLA AND PECAN CRUNCH SALAD WITH HAZELNUT VINAIGRETTE

SALAD
7 cups mixed lettuces (e.g., red leaf,
   green leaf, Bibb, butter)
6 ounces Gorgonzola cheese,
   crumbled

Wash and dry the mixed lettuces. Tear into bite-size pieces. Chill.

Combine a handful of lettuces with 1 ounce of Gorgonzola cheese per person and place on individual salad plates. To serve, sprinkle Pecan Crunch on each salad and drizzle with Hazelnut Vinaigrette.

PECAN CRUNCH
⅔ cup pecans, chopped coarse
2 tablespoons butter
1 tablespoon sugar
½ teaspoon salt
Freshly ground black pepper to taste
¼ teaspoon ground red pepper
   (cayenne)

Combine the pecans with the butter, sugar, salt, and black and red pepper in a small heavy pan. Cook over low heat, stirring occasionally, until the sugar caramelizes. Place the mixture in a small paper bag to cool. Shake occasionally to break up pieces. (The pecan crunch can be stored in an airtight container up to a week or frozen up to a month.)

HAZELNUT VINAIGRETTE
1 teaspoon Dijon mustard
1 teaspoon grated orange zest
2 teaspoons honey
2 tablespoons red wine vinegar
¼ cup orange juice
¼ cup hazelnut oil
¼ cup light olive oil

Combine the mustard, orange zest, honey, vinegar, and orange juice in a medium bowl. Whisk in the oils until well blended. (The vinaigrette can be refrigerated for up to 2 days.)

SERVES 6   *Dining by Fireflies: Unexpected Pleasures of the New South,* Charlotte, NC

GORGONZOLA AND WALNUT SALAD

WALNUT VINAIGRETTE DRESSING
1 tablespoon Dijon mustard
3 tablespoons white wine vinegar
1 tablespoon fresh lemon juice
½ cup walnut oil
¼ teaspoon salt
¼ teaspoon freshly ground black pepper

Put all the ingredients in a jar. Cover securely and shake until slightly thickened, creamy, and well combined. Set aside.

SALAD
1 large head romaine lettuce, rinsed, dried, and torn into bite-sized pieces
½ pound Gorgonzola or other blue-veined cheese, crumbled
1 cup coarsely chopped walnuts
1 Red Delicious apple

In a salad bowl, combine the lettuce, cheese, and walnuts. Slice the unpeeled apple into the salad. Add enough dressing to just coat the leaves. Toss and serve.
SERVES 6–8
California Fresh, Lafayette, CA

COLD ASPARAGUS WITH PECANS

1⅓ pounds fresh asparagus, as young and tender as possible, or 2 (10-ounce) packages frozen asparagus
¾ cup finely chopped pecans
2 tablespoons vegetable oil
¼ cup cider vinegar
¼ cup soy sauce
1 teaspoon sugar (optional)
Ground black pepper to taste

Trim the asparagus and cook in boiling water for 6 or 7 minutes, or until barely tender and still bright green. Drain and rinse under cold water. Drain again. Arrange in 1 or 2 layers in an oblong serving dish. Mix the pecans with the oil, vinegar, soy sauce, and sugar. Pour over the asparagus, lifting the stalks so that the mixture penetrates to the bottom. Sprinkle with pepper. Serve chilled. The dish may be marinated up to 36 hours ahead.
SERVES 6–8
Magic, Birmingham, AL

LYNCHBURG SHELTERED INDUSTRIES
JUNIOR LEAGUE OF LYNCHBURG, VIRGINIA

Lynchburg Sheltered Industries, a project of the Junior League of Lynchburg, Virginia, provides employment training and long-term employment for handicapped citizens. Most training is accomplished through actual production work on jobs subcontracted with area businesses. In addition to instruction in work-related skills, persons may receive individualized academic instruction, which may include handling money, using city transportation and improving academics and self-help skills.

MARINATED ASPARAGUS SALAD

24 fresh asparagus spears, trimmed
½ cup olive oil
½ cup light vegetable oil
¼ cup coarsely chopped fresh
    parsley
¼ cup fresh lime juice (1–2 large
    limes)
1 tablespoon sugar
2 tablespoons spicy brown mustard
⅓ cup chopped yellow bell pepper
½ small mild onion, sliced in rings
Red leaf lettuce

The night before, or 3 or 4 hours before serving: In a steamer or large skillet, steam asparagus just until tender; drain. Refresh under cold water to stop cooking and retain color. Place in a shallow serving dish. In a medium bowl, combine the oils, parsley, lime juice, sugar, and mustard; set aside. Layer the chopped bell pepper and onion slices on top of the asparagus; pour the marinade over the vegetables. Cover with plastic wrap; refrigerate 3 to 4 hours or overnight.

When ready to serve: Line salad plates with lettuce, red edges to outside of plates. Place the marinated vegetables diagonally in the center of each plate.

SERVES 4   *Tampa Treasures,* Tampa, FL

ZESTY BEET SALAD

A unique blend of textures and flavors.

2 pounds beets
2 cups vinegar
1 large onion, diced
2 tablespoons sugar
1 teaspoon salt
Freshly ground black pepper to taste
2 bay leaves
3 hard-boiled eggs, chopped fine
4 ounces anchovy fillets, chopped
Leaf lettuce

DRESSING
1 cup mayonnaise
1 teaspoon onion juice (optional)
2 tablespoons minced green pepper
½ cup chili sauce
¼ cup sour cream
1 tablespoon grated horseradish

Preheat the oven to 350 degrees. Cut tops off beets, leaving on 1 inch of stem; wash and place in a casserole dish with ¼ cup of water. Cover and bake for 40 minutes. Let cool. Slip off the skins of the beets. Combine the vinegar, onion, sugar, salt, pepper, and bay leaves. marinate the beets in this mixture for several hours.

Meanwhile, combine all the dressing ingredients and refrigerate. When ready to serve, drain the beets and chop coarse. Combine with the eggs, anchovies, and dressing. Serve on lettuce leaves.

SERVES 6   *Capital Beginnings,* Ottawa, ON

BROCCOLI SALAD I

Even George Bush would like this!

SALAD

1 head of broccoli (or a
  combination of broccoli and
  cauliflower)
1 medium Spanish onion, sliced thin
1 cup Michigan cherries
1 cup sunflower seeds
8-10 slices bacon, cooked crisp,
  drained, and crumbled

DRESSING

1 cup mayonnaise
1 tablespoon sugar
2 tablespoons vinegar

Separate the broccoli and/or cauliflower into florets; cut the tender part of the stalks into thin slices. Blanch by immersing in rapidly boiling water and removing immediately. Cool and chill. Combine the dressing ingredients and mix with the broccoli, onion, dried cherries, and sunflower seeds. Toss with the bacon just before serving.

SERVES 12   *The Bountiful Arbor,* Ann Arbor, MI

BROCCOLI SALAD II

½ cup mayonnaise
1½ teaspoons sugar
1 tablespoon vinegar
1 bunch broccoli (florets and tender
  stalks)
½ sweet onion, chopped
½ pound bacon, fried, drained, and
  crumbled
½ cup grated Cheddar cheese

Make the salad dressing by combining the mayonnaise, sugar, and vinegar. The dressing can be used immediately, but is best if allowed to sit for 3 or 4 hours.

Chop the broccoli into bite-sized pieces. Add the onion, bacon, and cheese. Toss with the salad dressing.

SERVES 4–6   *Utah Dining Car,* Ogden, UT

FERNSIDE: CENTER FOR GRIEVING CHILDREN
JUNIOR LEAGUE OF CINCINNATI, OHIO

The Junior League of Cincinnati provided the initial and ongoing funding and volunteer support for Fernside: Center for Grieving Children, the second grieving center for children in the U.S. The primary mission of Fernside is to provide peer support groups in a loving and non-judgmental environment, for children and teens who are grieving the death of an immediate family member, to help them understand and effectively cope with their grief and eventually rebuild their lives. Since its founding in 1986, Fernside has grown from serving 16 children in two groups to 750 people in 42 groups and 12 parent support groups per month.

HEARTS OF PALM SWAMP CABBAGE

Swamp cabbage is a Florida tradition. Serve it with fish and hush puppies.

2 raw hearts of sabal palm, trimmed and sliced
1 onion, chopped
1 slice bacon or fatback
½ cup milk
½ cup water
¼ cup Bourbon or blended whiskey
Salt and pepper to taste

Combine all ingredients. Simmer, adding more liquid if necessary, for 30 to 40 minutes or until the palm is very soft. Remove the bacon before serving.

SERVES 6

Heart of the Palms, Palm Beach, FL

MARINATED VEGETABLE SALAD WITH DIJON DRESSING

1 cup cauliflower florets
1 cup broccoli florets
3 ounces green beans, trimmed
⅓ red bell pepper, cut into strips
12 ounces canned hearts of palm, drained, cut into ½-inch diagonal slices
5 ounces fresh spinach, thoroughly washed, stems removed, patted dry

DRESSING
⅓ cup extra virgin olive oil
3 tablespoons red wine vinegar
¾ tablespoon Dijon mustard
¼ teaspoon salt
¾ teaspoon freshly ground black pepper
¼ teaspoon dried oregano
¼ teaspoon minced garlic

In a large pan bring 1½ quarts of water to a boil. Drop the cauliflower and broccoli into the boiling water. Cook 4 minutes. Remove the florets with a slotted spoon. Drain and rinse under water. Drain again.

Return the water to a boil and add the green beans. Cook 2 minutes. Remove, drain, rinse with cold water. Drain again. Combine the cauliflower, broccoli, green beans, bell pepper, and hearts of palm in a bowl.

Put the dressing ingredients into a container with a tight-fitting lid and shake well. Pour the dressing over the vegetables and toss to mix. Refrigerate for 2 to 3 hours. Prepare a bed of spinach on a serving platter. Spoon the vegetables over.

SERVES 4

One Magnificent Cookbook, Chicago, IL

STUFFED TOMATO SALAD

½ cup chopped ripe olives
½ cup chopped green stuffed olives
2 teaspoons sweet pickle relish
¼ cup chopped green bell pepper
1 cup chopped celery
Mayonnaise, enough to hold stuffing
　together
1 tomato per serving
Lettuce
Paprika

Peel and hollow out 1 tomato per serving. Invert to drain; chill for 30 minutes or longer.

Mix the olives, relish, green pepper, and celery with enough mayonnaise to hold together. Place tomatoes on bed of lettuce on individual serving plates and fill to overflowing with stuffing. Place a dab of mayonnaise on top and sprinkle with paprika.

SERVES 4–6　　　　　　　　*Gator Country Cooks,* Gainesville, FL

FIRE AND ICE

2 large red onions, cut into ¼-inch
　slices
6 large firm tomatoes, peeled and
　quartered
1 bell pepper, cored and cut into
　strips
¾ cup cider vinegar
1½ teaspoons celery seed
1½ teaspoons mustard seed
½ teaspoon salt
2 tablespoons sugar
½ teaspoon cracked black pepper

Place the onions, tomatoes, and bell pepper strips in a bowl. In a small saucepan, bring the vinegar, ¼ cup of water, and the seasonings to a boil. Boil for 1 minute only. While still hot, pour over the vegetables. Chill.

SERVES 6　　　　　　*The Cotton Country Collection,* Monroe, LA

STAY-CRISP SLAW

1 large cabbage, cored and grated
　fine
1 bell pepper, seeded, cored, and
　chopped fine
1 medium onion, chopped fine
½ to 1 cup finely chopped celery

DRESSING
1 cup vinegar
¾ cup sugar
1 teaspoon turmeric
½ teaspoon white mustard seed
1 teaspoon salt
Dash of pepper

Grate the cabbage into a large bowl. Place the dressing ingredients in a saucepan and bring to a boil. While it is still boiling hot, pour it over the cabbage and mix until the cabbage is thoroughly moistened. Place in the refrigerator for several hours until crisp. Then add the chopped pepper, onion, and celery; store in a covered container. The slaw stays crisp indefinitely.

SERVES 8–10　　　　　　*Huntsville Heritage,* Huntsville, AL

WATERMELON POPPY SEED DRESSING

1¾ cups cubed watermelon
½ teaspoon unflavored gelatin
½ teaspoon dry mustard
2 teaspoons poppy seeds
2 tablespoons honey
1½ teaspoons white wine vinegar

Process the watermelon in a blender until smooth; combine with the gelatin in a saucepan. Let stand 1 minute. Cook over low heat, stirring until thick. Remove from the heat and add the remaining ingredients. Blend well. Cover and chill for 8 hours. Serve with fruit or salad greens.

MAKES 1 ½ CUPS   *Udderly Delicious,* Racine, WI

SALVATORE'S ITALIAN SALAD DRESSING

This is very strong, flavorful, and delicious!

½ cup olive oil
2 tablespoons minced onion
1 tablespoon freshly grated
   Parmesan cheese
1 teaspoon salt
¾ teaspoon Worcestershire sauce
¾ teaspoon dry mustard
¾ teaspoon teaspoon dried basil
¾ teaspoon dried oregano
¾ teaspoon sugar
¾ teaspoon ground black pepper
¼ cup red wine vinegar
1 tablespoon lemon juice

In a blender or food processor, combine the olive oil, onion, Parmesan, salt, Worcestershire, mustard, basil, oregano, sugar, and pepper. Blend for 30 seconds. Add the vinegar and lemon juice and blend for 30 seconds. Chill. Serve with mixed salad greens, hearts of palm, tomatoes, and avocado.

MAKES 1 CUP   *Celebrations on the Bayou,* Monroe, LA

WHITE BEAN SALAD

The rosemary adds a wonderful flavor!

1 (16-ounce) can navy beans,
   drained and rinsed
1 (2-ounce) jar pimientos, drained
   and chopped
1 clove garlic, minced
½ teaspoon ground black pepper
1 tablespoon olive oil
2 tablespoons red wine vinegar
2 tablespoons capers
1½ teaspoons chopped fresh
   rosemary, or ½ teaspoon dried
Lettuce leaves

Combine the navy beans, pimiento, garlic, pepper, olive oil, vinegar, capers, and rosemary in a bowl; mix well. Spoon onto lettuce-lined platter. Serve at room temperature.

SERVES 6   *The Best of Wheeling,* Wheeling, WV

MOLDED GAZPACHO SALAD WITH AVOCADO CREAM

GAZPACHO SALAD
2 envelopes unflavored gelatin
4½ cups tomato juice
¼ cup wine vinegar
1 clove garlic, crushed
2 teaspoons salt
¼ teaspoon ground black pepper
Dash of ground red pepper
    (cayenne)
2 large tomatoes, peeled, chopped,
    and drained
½ cup finely chopped scallions
¾ cup finely chopped green bell
    pepper
¾ cup peeled, finely chopped
    cucumber, drained
¼ cup finely chopped pimiento
Parsley

Soften the gelatin in 1 cup of tomato juice for 5 minutes. Pour into a small saucepan and heat until the mixture simmers and the gelatin is dissolved. Remove from the heat. Combine in a bowl with the remaining tomato juice, the vinegar, garlic, salt, and black and red pepper. Chill until the mixture begins to set.

Fold in the tomatoes, scallion, green pepper, cucumber, and pimiento. Pour into an oiled 6-cup ring mold. Chill about 3 hours or until firm. Unmold the salad, garnish with parsley, and serve with Avocado Cream.

AVOCADO CREAM
⅓ cup mashed avocado
½ cup sour cream
½ teaspoon salt
Dash of ground red pepper
    (cayenne)

Combine all the ingredients and blend well. This recipe is particularly popular with men.

SERVES 6–8   *Flavors*, San Antonio, TX

TOMATO ASPIC

1 (35-ounce) can tomatoes, drained
1 cucumber, peeled
1 medium onion
½ bunch celery
¼ green bell pepper
4 tablespoons vinegar
1 package unflavored gelatin
2 cups boiling water
Ground red pepper (cayenne) to
    taste
Salt
Grated Cheddar cheese

Put the tomatoes in a mixing bowl. Mash fine with a wooden spoon. Dice the cucumber, onion, celery, and green pepper fine, add to the tomatoes; season with 2 tablespoons of the vinegar, the cayenne and plenty of salt.

Soften the gelatin in ¼ cup of cold water for 3 to 5 minutes and add 2 cups of boiling water, or a combination of water and tomato juice. Stir to dissolve thoroughly. Add the remaining 2 tablespoons of vinegar, and salt and pepper to taste. Chill until the mixture begins to set.

Fold the vegetable mixture into the gelatin; transfer to an oiled 6-cup mold. Chill until firm. Turn out on a bed of lettuce, sprinkle with grated cheese, and serve with mayonnaise.

SERVES 4–6   *Junior League of Dallas Cookbook*, Dallas, TX

ALICE'S HOT POTATO SALAD

The potatoes can be prepared ahead of time and the hot dressing added just before serving.

15 medium-sized red-skinned
    potatoes, unpeeled
1 pound bacon, cut in small pieces
4 bunches scallions, chopped
Salt and pepper to taste
Celery salt and celery seed to taste
¾ cup vinegar
¼ cup sugar
3 eggs, well beaten

Boil the potatoes in their skins in a covered saucepan until tender, but do not let them become mushy. Cool. Dice the potatoes (with skins on) and place in a large bowl.

Fry the bacon until crisp, reserving ¾ cup of the drippings. To the potatoes, add the bacon, scallions, salt, pepper, celery salt, and celery seed.

When ready to serve, combine the vinegar, sugar, ¾ cup of water, and the eggs in a saucepan; bring to a boil. Heat the reserved bacon drippings in a separate pan. Pour both over the potatoes and stir gently. Serve warm.

SERVES 10–12   *Nutbread and Nostalgia,* South Bend, IN

CLAY'S POTATO SALAD

5 medium potatoes
6 or 7 slices bacon
½ cup diced onion
¾ cup diced celery
5 hard-boiled eggs, chopped
Pinch of sugar
1 teaspoon seasoned salt
Pepper to taste
Mayonnaise

Boil the potatoes in their jackets in a covered saucepan until tender but not mushy. When cool enough to handle, remove skins and dice the potatoes into a bowl. Fry the bacon in a skillet until crisp; remove with a spatula to drain on paper towels. Pour the hot bacon drippings over the potatoes. When cool, add the remaining ingredients with enough mayonnaise to bind together. Stir gently until mixed. Crumble the bacon on top, or blend it in if you desire.

SERVES 4–6   *The Blue Denim Gourmet,* Odessa, TX

PARMESAN POTATO SALAD

4 cups cooked potages, sliced
4 hard-boiled eggs, chopped
½ cup chopped celery
¼ cup chopped onion
¼ cup chopped green bell pepper
Salt to taste
8 slices bacon, fried, drained, and
    crumbled
¾ to 1 cup grated Parmesan cheese
Mayonnaise to moisten

Combine all the ingredients in a bowl; mix lightly. Chill. Sprinkle with additional cheese if desired.

SERVES 6   *The Carolina Collection,* Fayetteville, NC

DOCKSIDE POTATO SALAD

5 or 6 medium-sized red-skinned
   potatoes
Salt
¼ cup finely chopped onion
¼ cup finely chopped celery,
   including some leaves
1 dill pickle, chopped
⅓ cup chopped fresh parsley, or 2
   tablespoons dried
6 strips bacon, cooked crisp and
   crumbled
Freshly ground black pepper
1 teaspoon vinegar
¼ cup vegetable oil
1 to 1¼ cups mayonnaise

Cook the potatoes in their jackets in a covered saucepan of boiling salted water until tender, about 30 minutes. Cool completely and chill in the refrigerator. Peel and cut into thin bite-size pieces. Place in a large bowl.

Add the onion, celery, pickle, parsley, and bacon. Sprinkle salt, pepper, vinegar, and oil over all. Gently turn the ingredients over with a wooden spoon until well mixed. Add the mayonnaise and turn again until well moistened. Cover tightly and refrigerate for several hours before serving.

SERVES 6–8   *Tidewater On the Halfshell,* Norfolk-Virginia Beach, VA

SPICY BROWN RICE AND BLACK-EYED PEA SALAD

2 (16-ounce) cans black-eyed peas,
   drained
½ cup chopped onion
½ pound lean cooked ham steak,
   trimmed and cut into ¼-inch
   cubes
1 clove garlic, minced
3 tablespoons white wine vinegar
3 tablespoons pickled jalapeño
   peppers, seeded (if desired) and
   minced
⅓ cup vegetable oil
3 tablespoons fresh lemon juice
1½ cups chopped scallions
Salt and ground black pepper to
   taste
1½ cups uncooked brown rice

Combine the black-eyed peas, onion, ham, and garlic in a small skillet and cook, covered, over low heat for 10 to 15 minutes or until the onions are translucent. Keep covered and warm.

In a small bowl, whisk together the vinegar and jalapeño peppers. Add the oil in a stream and keep whisking until the dressing emulsifies. Combine the black-eyed pea mixture with the dressing. Stir in the lemon juice, scallions, salt, and pepper and allow to marinate at least 1 hour, stirring occasionally.

Cook the rice according to package directions. Spoon the black-eyed pea mixture on top of the hot rice to serve.

SERVES 8   *Sensational Seasonings: A Taste & Tour of Arkansas,*
Fort Smith, AR

INDONESIAN RICE SALAD

2 cups cooked, cooled brown rice
½ cup raisins
2 scallions, chopped
¼ cup toasted sesame seeds
½ cup thinly sliced water chestnuts
1 cup fresh mung bean sprouts
¼ cup dry-roasted cashews
1 large green bell pepper, chopped
1 stalk celery, chopped
Chopped fresh parsley to taste

DRESSING
¾ cup orange juice
½ cup safflower oil
1 tablespoon dark Asian sesame oil
3 to 4 tablespoons tamari sauce or
   soy sauce
2 tablespoons dry sherry
Juice of 1 lemon
1 or 2 cloves garlic, minced
½ to 1 teaspoon minced fresh
   gingerroot
Salt and pepper to taste

Plum sauce for topping

Combine the salad ingredients in a serving bowl. Combine the dressing ingredients in a mixing bowl and whisk until blended. Toss together and top with plum sauce.

N O T E : To toast sesame seeds, place them in a dry flat skillet over medium heat for 2 minutes, or place in a pie pan and heat in a 350 degree oven, stirring often, for 10 to 15 minutes until golden.

V A R I A T I O N : Add any or all of the following: ½ cup thinly sliced bamboo shoots, fresh raw snow peas, fresh pineapple chunks, toasted unsweetened coconut.

S E R V E S 4 – 6   *Posh Pantry,* Kankakee, IL

ARMENIAN CRACKED WHEAT SALAD (TABBOULEH)

1 cup bulgur (cracked wheat)
2 cups boiling water
⅓ cup plus 2 tablespoons fresh
   lemon juice
1 cup chopped scallions
1 cup chopped fresh tomatoes, or
   halved cherry tomatoes
1 cup chopped peeled cucumber
1 cup minced parsley
3-4 tablespoons chopped fresh mint
   or 3 tablespoons crumbled dry
   mint
1 teaspoon salt
¼ teaspoon dried thyme
⅛ teaspoon ground black pepper
¼ cup olive oil
Romaine lettuce leaves for garnish

Combine the bulgur, boiling water, and 2 tablespoons of lemon juice in a large mixing bowl. Let stand for 1 hour; then drain thoroughly by placing in a colander and shaking until all the liquid is removed.

   Place the drained bulgur in a salad bowl; add the scallions, tomatoes, cucumber, parsley, mint, salt, thyme, pepper, oil, and ⅓ cup of lemon juice. Stir to blend. Cover and chill thoroughly for several hours or overnight. Serve on a bed of romaine lettuce.

S E R V E S 4 – 6   *California Treasure,* Fresno, CA

MEXICAN FIESTA SALAD WITH CILANTRO DRESSING

This colorful salad makes a great entree. Prepare the beans and dressing the day before and marinate overnight.

BEANS

½ cup dried black beans, rinsed and picked over
2 tablespoons olive oil
2 tablespoons white wine vinegar
½ teaspoon salt

CILANTRO DRESSING

3 to 5 jalapeño peppers, seeded
¼ cup white wine vinegar
1 clove garlic
1 teaspoon salt
⅔ cup olive oil
½ cup packed fresh cilantro leaves and stems

SALAD

½ cup chopped red onion
2 cups thinly sliced iceberg lettuce
1½ cups seeded and chopped tomatoes
1 cup corn kernels
½ cup chopped green bell pepper
1 cup shredded Monterey Jack cheese
1 ripe avocado
4 slices lean bacon, cooked, drained, and crumbled
Cilantro sprig for garnish

Cover the beans with 2 inches of cold water in a large pot, bring to a boil, and continue boiling for 3 minutes. Remove from the heat and let the beans soak for 10 minutes. Drain the beans and cover with 2 inches cold water. Bring to a boil and simmer for 45 minutes, or until just tender. Drain and refresh under cold water. Transfer the beans to a bowl and add the oil, vinegar, and salt. Cover and chill for 2 hours. (The beans can be cooked up to 24 hours in advance and kept chilled.)

While the beans are chilling, make the cilantro dressing: In a blender, purée the jalapeños with the vinegar, garlic, and salt. Continue processing and add the oil in a steady stream, blending until emulsified. Add the cilantro and blend until finely chopped.

To assemble the salad: Drain the beans and toss with the chopped red onion. In the bottom of a 2-quart soufflé dish or a bowl, arrange the lettuce; top it with the beans, reserving 2 tablespoons, and layer the chopped tomatoes on top, reserving 1 tablespoon. In a small bowl toss together the corn and bell pepper; top the tomatoes with the corn, reserving 1 tablespoon; and top the corn with the cheese. (The salad may be prepared up to this point 8 hours in advance and kept covered and chilled.) Halve the avocado lengthwise, reserving one half; peel the remaining half and cut it into 6 slices. Arrange the avocado slices like the spokes of a wheel on top of the cheese. Fill in the spaces between the avocado alternately with reserved beans, tomatoes, corn, and the bacon. Garnish the salad with a cilantro sprig and serve with cilantro dressing.

SERVES 4   *Hearts & Flours,* Waco, TX

THAI NOODLE SALAD

SALAD

1 pound thin spaghetti, cooked according to package directions

1 cup shredded carrots

1 cucumber, peeled, halved lengthwise, seeded, and sliced thin

⅓ cup chopped scallions

1 red or green bell pepper, cut into fine julienne strips

THAI SALAD DRESSING

¼ cup peanut butter

1½ tablespoons vegetable or peanut oil

2 tablespoons soy sauce

2 cloves garlic, minced

1 teaspoon sugar

1 teaspoon grated fresh gingerroot

2 tablespoons sherry

1 teaspoon dark Asian sesame oil

2 tablespoons lemon juice

1 scallion, sliced

½ teaspoon chili powder

¼ cup chicken broth

⅓ cup chopped roasted peanuts, for garnish

Assemble the salad: Combine the pasta with the vegetables in a large bowl and toss to combine.

Make the dressing: Place all the dressing ingredients in a good processor or blender and blend until smooth.

Add the dressing to the pasta and toss. Sprinkle with coarsely chopped peanuts.

SERVES 6 *Without Reservations*, Pittsburgh, PA

JOIN THE P.A.R.T.Y.: PARTICIPATE IN READING THROUGHOUT THE YEAR JUNIOR LEAGUE OF COLUMBUS, OHIO

The Junior League of Columbus, Ohio, formed a task force with the input and expertise of educators from the Columbus Public Schools, the Ohio Department of Education, Ohio State University and Capital University. The resulting program, Join the P.A.R.T.Y.: Participate in Reading Throughout the Year, addresses the unmet needs of reluctant readers, those middle school students who have the ability to read but who are at risk due to their reluctance to become readers and writers. Each student is paired with a Junior League volunteer who acts as his or her reading partner or literacy advocate, and they meet face-to-face once a month and keep in touch weekly by phone.

TEXAS PASTA SALAD

1 pound pasta (wagon-wheel shaped
   or fusilli), cooked and drained
⅔ cup cider vinegar
¼ cup safflower oil
¾ cup chopped celery
¾ cup chopped green bell pepper
8 scallions, chopped
1 (2-ounce) jar chopped pimientos,
   drained
4 dashes Worcestershire sauce
4 dashes Tabasco
2 tablespoons chopped green chiles
1 teaspoon salt
1½ teaspoons ground black pepper
2 cups black-eyed peas, cooked and
   drained
6 ounces ripe olives, chopped and
   drained
2 ounces green olives, chopped and
   drained
1 cup mayonnaise
2 tablespoons picante salsa

In a large bowl, mix all the ingredients. Cover and chill at least 24 hours.

S E R V E 1 2

South of the Fork, Dallas, TX

SUMMER PASTA SALAD

1 tablespoon plus 1 teaspoon
   vegetable oil
12 ounces Italian sausages
5 ripe tomatoes, peeled and chopped
1 cup lightly packed fresh basil
   leaves or 2 tablespoons dried basil
1 large clove garlic, minced, or
   garlic powder to taste
1 tablespoon salt
1 pound vermicelli or linguine
1 pound mozzarella cheese, cut into
   small pieces
Steamed broccoli florets and/or
   sautéed sliced mushrooms
   (optional)
Freshly ground pepper to taste

In a heavy skillet, heat 1 teaspoon of oil over medium heat. Add the sausages and cook 3 to 4 minutes, until browned on both sides. Reduce the heat, cover, and continue cooking for 8 minutes. Remove and cool on a plate. Slice into ½-inch rounds and set aside.

Bring a large pot of water (at least 7 or 8 quarts) to a boil. Put the tomatoes, basil, and garlic together in a small bowl. When the water is at a rolling boil, add the salt and tablespoon of oil. Cook the pasta just until tender but still firm. Drain the pasta; quickly return to the still-warm pot. Immediately stir in the mozzarella. (Heat from the pasta will melt the cheese cubes slightly.) Add tomato mixture; mix well.

At this time, add the sausage, along with broccoli and/or mushrooms if desired. Season to taste with salt and pepper. Serve at room temperature.

S E R V E S 4 – 6

A Brooklyn Tradition, Brooklyn, NY

MACEDONIA DI FRUTTA

This one is always a part of the dinner conversation.

1 cup bite-size pieces of apple
1 cup melon balls
1 cup seedless grapes
1 cup cut-up fresh peaches
1 cup cut-up fresh pears
1 cup pitted Bing cherries
1 cup sugar
1 cup liqueur of choice: amaretto, Drambuie, Grand Marinier, curaçao, crème de menthe, Cognac, or cherry brandy

Combine the fruit in a large bowl and mix gently. Sprinkle the sugar over the fruit and pour the liqueur over all. Mix thoroughly but carefully to avoid bruising the fruit. Cover and refrigerate at least 2 hours. Mix again before serving.

N O T E : Use any combination and number of fresh fruits in season. Allow ¾ cup fruit and 2 tablespoons each of sugar and liqueur for each serving.

S E R V E S 8   *R.S.V.P.,* Orange County, CA

BERRY SUMMER SALAD

2 bunches fresh spinach, thoroughly washed, dried, and torn
2 pints fresh strawberries, cleaned, hulled and halved

DRESSING
½ cup vegetable oil
¼ cup cider vinegar
⅓ cup sugar
2 tablespoons sesame seeds
1 tablespoon poppy seeds
1½ teaspoons minced onion
¼ teaspoon Worcestershire sauce
¼ teaspoon paprika

Place the spinach and strawberries in a bowl; do not mix. Place dressing ingredients in a blender or food processor and blend until thoroughly mixed and thickened. Do not overmix. Just before serving, toss the salad gently with only enough dressing to coat the spinach and berries.

S E R V E S 6 – 8   *Savor the Flavor of Oregon*, Eugene, OR

"CHARLIE THE TUNA" SALAD

1½ pound ahi (tuna) steaks, 1¼
  inches thick
Salt and freshly ground pepper
Garlic powder
Olive oil
½ cup mayonnaise
3½ ounces capers
1 tablespoon lemon juice
1 teaspoon dill weed

Season the fish with salt, pepper, and garlic powder. Brush a light coating of olive oil on each steak so that it will not stick to the grill. Grill over hot coals until well browned on the outside but still pink on the inside, about 6 minutes per side. Do not overcook. Cool and chop against the grain into ¼-inch chunks.

Combine the mayonnaise with the capers, lemon juice, and dill weed and gently mix with the fish. The tuna should remain in chunks. Chill before serving. Serve as a salad or with bread, crackers, or chips.

SERVES 4–6 *Another Taste of Aloha*, Honolulu, HI

WARM SCALLOP SALAD WITH SAFFRON VINAIGRETTE

6 cups baby greens (arugula, chervil,
  chickweed, dandelion, and/or oak
  leaf, all available at specialty
  stores)
3 tablespoons light olive oil, plus
  extra for salad
Salt and pepper

SAFFRON VINAIGRETTE
2 large pinches saffron threads
¼ cup white wine vinegar
½ cup light olive oil
2 tablespoons finely chopped shallots
Salt and pepper to taste

24 large fresh sea scallops, sliced in
  half crosswise

Arrange the greens evenly among 8 salad plates. Dress the greens with a sprinkle of oil, salt, and freshly ground pepper.

Make the vinaigrette: Over gentle heat, infuse the saffron in the vinegar and ¼ cup of water. Simmer until the liquid is reduced by half. Add this to the ½ cup of oil with the shallots and season with salt and pepper.

In a large nonstick skillet, briskly cook the scallops in 3 tablespoons of olive oil, approximately 45 seconds each side, or until golden and just cooked through. Put aside and cover to keep warm. Deglaze the pan with the vinaigrette dressing, adding a bit of water. Place 6 scallop rounds on each plate around the greens. Top with hot vinaigrette.

SERVES 8 *Settings*, Philadelphia, PA

VINTAGE, INC.
JUNIOR LEAGUE OF PITTSBURGH, PENNSYLVANIA

In 1973, the Junior League of Pittsburgh joined efforts with several churches and ministries to consolidate their activities in order to reach a large, diverse group of senior adults, and formed Vintage, Inc. Vintage raises the quality of life for senior adults by using and developing their potential, helping the elderly to help themselves. Programs in the areas of education, socialization and recreation, nutrition, counseling, and voluntarism are available at Vintage's three senior centers, a small personal care boarding home, and two sites for adult day care.

BRAZILIAN SHRIMP SALAD

Cilantro, also known as Chinese parsley, is spicy yet refreshing. It is used often in Chinese and Mexican dishes.

1 pound medium shrimp, cooked, shelled, and deveined
1 stalk celery, cut into julienne strips (1 cup)
1 small green bell pepper, julienned (1 cup)
1 medium carrot, julienned (1 cup)
½ cup chopped fresh cilantro
¾ cup vegetable oil
3 tablespoons lime juice
2 teaspoons sugar
¾ teaspoon grated lime peel
¼ teaspoon crushed red pepper flakes
¾ teaspoon ground cumin
2 bunches fresh spinach, well washed and dried, torn
3 bananas, sliced
¾ cup chopped unsalted peanuts
½ cup shredded unsweetened coconut

Combine the shrimp, celery, green pepper, carrots, and cilantro in a bowl. In another bowl, whisk together the vegetable oil, lime juice, sugar, lime peel, red pepper flakes, and cumin. Pour over the shrimp mixture and toss together well. Cover and chill.

Arrange the spinach leaves on 6 salad plates. Place some of the shrimp mixture on the spinach. Arrange the banana slices around the shrimp and sprinkle with the peanuts and shredded coconut. Spoon over any remaining dressing.

SERVES 6   *San Francisco Encore,* San Francisco, CA

CRAWFISH OR SHRIMP SALAD

1 pound cooked shrimp or crawfish tails
4 hard-boiled eggs
2 stalks celery, chopped
6 midget gherkins, chopped
6 green olives, chopped (optional)
1 cup mayonnaise
1 tablespoon dry mustard
1 teaspoon salt
½ teaspoon ground red pepper (cayenne)
1 teaspoon Worcestershire sauce
½ teaspoon onion salt

In a large bowl, combine all ingredients in the order listed and blend well. Correct the seasoning and serve on bed of lettuce or in tomatoes or avocados.

SERVES 4–6   *Talk About Good II,* Lafayette, LA

SHRIMP SALAD GUADALAJARA

1 medium red onion
1 red bell pepper
1 green bell pepper
3 medium tomatoes, peeled and
   seeded
1½ pounds medium raw shrimp,
   shelled and deveined
½ cup pitted ripe black olives,
   drained
½ cup stuffed green olives
Jalapeño dressing (below)
2 lemons

JALAPEÑO DRESSING
1 clove garlic
3 fresh or canned jalapeño chiles,
   seeded and minced
½ cup olive oil
⅓ cup lemon juice
1 teaspoon ground cumin
1 bay leaf
Salt and freshly ground black pepper

Slice the onion, red and green peppers, and tomatoes in julienne strips. Place the shrimp in boiling water and cook just until they turn pink, about 2 minutes. Drain. Cut the black and green olives in half. Combine all ingredients, except the lemons, in a serving bowl and toss with the dressing. Slice the lemons thin and use for garnish.

Mince the garlic and chile peppers and combine with other ingredients. Mix well. Remove the bay leaf before using.

SERVES 6–8   *California Heritage Continues,* Pasadena, CA

SHRIMP SALAD WITH SNOW PEAS AND WATER CHESTNUTS

½ pound snow peas, strings
   removed
¾ pound cooked shrimp, shelled
   and deveined
1 cup sliced canned water chestnuts,
   drained
2 tablespoons light soy sauce
1 tablespoon rice vinegar
2 tablespoons honey
Juice of 1 lemon
½ cup light vegetable oil

Bring a large pot of water to the boil. Blanch the snow peas in rapidly boiling water for 30 seconds. Drain and refresh under cold water. Drain again. Arrange the shrimp, snow peas, and water chestnuts in a serving dish. Combine all remaining ingredients for the dressing and pour it over the salad. Toss well and serve.

SERVES 4–6   *Off the Hook,* Stamford–Norwalk, CT

SALADE NIÇOISE

STEP ONE

2 cups olive oil

½ cup tarragon vinegar

¼ cup fresh lemon juice

2 cloves garlic, crushed

1 tablespoon dry mustard

1 teaspoon sugar

1 tablespoon salt

Freshly ground black pepper

STEP TWO

2 pounds new potatoes, freshly
  boiled and sliced

2 cups freshly cooked green beans

1 (14-ounce) can artichoke hearts,
  drained

STEP THREE

Salad greens

3 (7-ounce) cans tuna, drained and
  marinated in 1 tablespoon lemon
  juice

1 pint cherry tomatoes

1 cup pitted ripe olives (optional)

6 hard-boiled eggs, quartered

½ cup canned or bottled red pepper
  strips

1 large green bell pepper, cut into
  rings (optional)

1 (2-ounce) can anchovies (optional)

2 tablespoons capers

¼ cup chopped fresh parsley

Step One: Blend the olive oil, vinegar, lemon juice, garlic, mustard, sugar, salt, and pepper in a blender. Set the dressing aside.

Step Two: Combine the potatoes, green beans, and artichoke hearts. Marinate with the dressing for at least 2 hours. Stir occasionally.

Step Three: When ready to serve, line a salad bowl with greens. Drain the marinated vegetables and keep the dressing for later use. Place the drained vegetables on the greens. Put the tuna in the middle of the bowl and arrange the tomatoes, olives, eggs, red and green peppers, anchovies, and capers around it. Sprinkle a little of the salad dressing over the salad and garnish with the parsley. Pass the salad dressing at the table if more is needed.

SERVES 6–8   *A Taste of Oregon*, Eugene, OR

GROWING UP GREAT
JUNIOR LEAGUE OF NORFOLK-VIRGINIA BEACH

Growing Up Great, a 1994 Association of Junior Leagues International/BMW Merit Award winner and project of the Junior League of Norfolk-Virginia Beach, Virginia, is a maternal and child health program, the aim of which is to improve prenatal, infant and early childhood health care through a variety of educational and awareness initiatives. The project was designed to reach every new parent and every parent of young children in the community with at least one program component. At the halfway mark of the three-year commitment, the program had provided direct services to 10,200 people, reached 160,000 with printed brochures and 1,413,578 via a media campaign.

FORT WILLIAMS CHICKEN SALAD

1 (9-ounce) package frozen French-
  cut green beans or frozen snow peas
3 cups shredded cooked boneless
  chicken breast (about 1½ pounds)
3 cups cooked spiral-shaped pasta
1 cup fresh blueberries
¾ cup thinly sliced celery
¼ cup thinly sliced scallions
2 tablespoons finely chopped fresh
  oregano, or 2 teaspoons dried
½ cup plus 2 tablespoons plain low-
  fat mayonnaise
3 tablespoons blueberry vinegar
½ teaspoon salt
½ teaspoon coarsely ground black
  pepper

Thaw and chop the green beans, place between paper towels, and squeeze until barely moist. Combine the beans and the chicken, pasta, blueberries, celery, scallions, and oregano in a large bowl.

In another bowl, combine the yogurt, mayonnaise, blueberry vinegar, salt, and pepper and stir well. Pour over the chicken mixture and toss gently. Cover and chill for 2 hours. Serve over lettuce if desired.

SERVES 6   *Maine Ingredients,* Portland, ME

ASIAN CHICKEN SALAD

Rice sticks are thin rice-flour noodles that fry and expand very quickly. They are usually sold coiled in nests and wrapped in cellophane; they are available in Asian markets and some supermarkets.

2 tablespoons slivered almonds
2 tablespoons sesame seeds
3 whole chicken breasts, cooked,
  skinned, boned, and shredded
4 scallions, chopped
2 ounces rice sticks
1 large head lettuce, chopped

DRESSING
½ cup vegetable oil
6 tablespoons cider vinegar
¼ cup sugar
1½ teaspoons salt
1 teaspoon ground black pepper

In a preheated 300 degree oven, toast the almonds and sesame seeds, stirring occasionally, until lightly browned. In a large bowl, toss the shredded chicken with the sesame seeds, almonds, and scallions. Cover and refrigerate. Just before serving, fry the rice sticks according to package directions. Add the fried rice sticks and lettuce to the chicken mixture. Toss with dressing.

Combine the oil, vinegar, sugar, salt, and pepper. Blend well and pour over the chicken mixture, using just enough dressing to coat lightly.

SERVES 8   *Winning at the Table,* Las Vegas, NV

NORTH SHORE CHICKEN SALAD

DRESSING
2 large cloves garlic, minced
1 tablespoon Dijon mustard
½ teaspoon salt
¼ teaspoon sugar
¼ teaspoon freshly ground black
    pepper
¼ cup rice wine vinegar
⅓ cup vegetable oil

SALAD
4 cups freshly cooked wild rice
    (cooked in chicken stock)
Juice of ½ lemon
1 whole chicken breast, cooked and
    cubed
3 scallions, including tops, sliced
½ red bell pepper, diced
2 ounces snow pea pods, cut into 1-
    inch pieces
1 or 2 ripe avocados, cut into
    medium-size pieces
1 cup toasted pecan halves
Lettuce leaves

Combine all the dressing ingredients in a food processor; blend thoroughly. (Or mix all the ingredients together well in a bowl.)

Toss the warm rice with the lemon juice in a medium bowl; cool. Add the cubed chicken, scallions, bell pepper, and pea pods, toss with the dressing. Cover; refrigerate for 2 to 4 hours. Just before serving, add the avocados and pecans; toss gently. Transfer to a salad bowl; garnish with lettuce leaves.

SERVES 6   *Celebrated Seasons*, Minneapolis, MN

CHUTNEY CHICKEN SALAD

Unusual.

1 cup raisins
1 cup salted peanuts
1 cup mango chutney
1 cup coconut flakes
2 bananas, sliced
1 teaspoon lemon juice
Salt and pepper to taste
1½ cups mayonnaise
2 to 3 pounds cooked and cubed
    chicken

Soak the raisins in warm water 15 minutes. Drain and combine with the remaining ingredients. Chill 6 hours.

SERVES 8   *Fare by the Sea*, Sarasota, FL

SAN JUAN SUMMER SALAD

MANGO CHUTNEY DRESSING
¾ cup vegetable oil
½ cup mango chutney
¼ cup white wine vinegar
3 medium cloves garlic, minced
1 tablespoon Dijon mustard
1 tablespoon soy sauce
1 tablespoon dark Asian sesame oil
¾ teaspoon Tabasco or to taste

SALAD
3 cups cooked chicken breast, cut
   into ½-inch pieces
3 cups cantaloupe, cut into ½-inch
   pieces
1 cup thinly sliced celery
½ cup thinly sliced scallions
⅓ cup roasted, salted cashews
Lettuce leaves

Make the dressing: Combine the oil, chutney, vinegar, garlic, mustard, soy sauce, sesame oil, and Tabasco in a processor or blender. Purée until smooth. This can be prepared 1 day ahead. Cover and refrigerate.

In a large bowl, combine the chicken, cantaloupe, and celery. Reserve 1 tablespoon of the scallions and add the remainder to the salad. (You can prepare it up to this point 4 hours ahead. Cover and refrigerate.) Before serving, add the cashews to the salad. Toss with enough dressing to coat. Arrange lettuce leaves on 6 plates. Mound the salad on the lettuce. Sprinkle reserved scallions on top and serve.

NOTE: Cantaloupes, once ripe, should be stored in the refrigerator. These melons absorb other food odors, so wrap them in plastic.

SERVES 6   *Simply Classic,* Seattle, WA

TORTELLINI CHICKEN SALAD WITH SUN-DRIED TOMATOES

4 ounces cheese tortellini or other
   pasta, cooked, drained, and cooled
4 ounces grilled chicken, diced
2 frozen artichoke hearts, thawed
   and sliced
1 ounce fresh spinach, torn into
   pieces
12 sun-dried tomatoes, either
   marinated or, if dried, plumped in
   water
2 ounces feta cheese
3 slices red onion
Mixed greens (optional)

VINAIGRETTE DRESSING
2 cloves garlic
1 teaspoon dried oregano
1 tablespoon tomato paste
6 tablespoons balsamic vinegar
Salt and pepper to taste
½ cup olive oil

In a serving bowl, combine the tortellini, diced chicken, artichoke hearts, spinach, tomatoes, feta cheese, and onion. Toss together.

To make the vinaigrette, purée the garlic, oregano, tomato paste, vinegar, salt, and pepper in a blender or food processor; then, with the machine running, gradually add the oil to make a smooth emulsion. To serve, combine enough dressing with the salad ingredients to moisten them and toss to coat well. Serve over mixed greens if desired.

SERVES 2   *A Slice of Paradise,* Palm Beach, FL

CHINESE CHICKEN AND WALNUT SALAD

DRESSING

1 cup corn oil or walnut oil
½ cup hoisin sauce
½ cup soy sauce
½ cup red wine vinegar
1 tablespoon chopped garlic
1 tablespoon freshly grated
    gingerroot
½ cup sesame seeds

SALAD

1 bunch spinach, thoroughly washed
½ bunch napa or Chinese cabbage,
    rinsed
2 cups cooked and shredded chicken
4 carrots, peeled and cut into
    julienne strips
1½ cups coarsely chopped walnuts
1 red bell pepper, seeded and cut
    into julienne strips
4 scallions, sliced thinly lengthwise

Combine the oil, hoisin sauce, soy sauce, vinegar, garlic, ginger, and sesame seeds; blend well. Refrigerate.

Remove stems from the spinach. Slice the spinach into ½-inch strips. Core the cabbage and slice into ½-inch pieces. Dry and crisp the greens in the refrigerator.

Just before serving, combine the greens with the chicken, carrots, walnuts, bell pepper, and scallions in a large bowl. Toss well. Add dressing to taste and retoss. The reserved dressing may be stored in a covered glass container in the refrigerator.

VARIATIONS: Consider substituting beef and toasted almonds or shrimp and toasted pine nuts for the chicken and walnuts.

SERVES 6–8   *Delicious Decisions*, San Diego, CA

COLD BEEF SALAD

2 cups julienne strips of rare roast
    beef
½ cup sliced celery
⅓ cup chopped sour pickle
¼ cup chopped scallions
¼ cup capers, drained
Lettuce leaves

SPICY DIJON DRESSING

½ cup salad oil
3 tablespoons vinegar
1 tablespoon Dijon mustard
½ clove garlic
Dash of hot pepper sauce
Salt and pepper to taste

In a serving bowl, combine the beef, celery, pickle, scallions, and capers. Toss together, cover, and chill.

Combine the dressing ingredients in a jar with a tight-fitting lid. Shake well and let stand at room temperature, for at least 1 hour, for flavors to blend. When ready to serve, remove and discard the garlic. Toss the dressing with the salad over lettuce leaves.

SERVES 4   *Heritage of Hospitality*, Winston-Salem, NC

STEAK SUPPER SALAD

This is a sophisticated, attractive salad for a light supper. Serve with warm crusty French bread and a red wine. Perfect for a gourmet picnic.

SALAD
1 flank steak, 1½ to 2 pounds
¼ cup olive oil
½ cup red wine vinegar
Freshly ground black pepper
2 pounds new potatoes
1 pound fresh asparagus
1 pound fresh green beans, trimmed
1 large red bell pepper, cut into
    julienne strips
Romaine and leaf lettuce

MUSTARD VINAIGRETTE
1 tablespoon Champagne mustard
1 teaspoon Pommery mustard
¼ cup white wine vinegar
Salt and pepper to taste
½ cup olive oil

Marinate steak in the olive oil mixed with vinegar and pepper for 3 to 4 hours or overnight. Pan-fry the steak over high heat until medium rare. Cool. Cut the steak into julienne strips.

Boil potatoes until just tender. Do not overcook. Cool and slice.

Snap off the tough ends of the asparagus and cook the stalks in a pot of boiling water until tender crisp. Remove with a spatula and plunge into cold water. Drain. Repeat the cooking process with the green beans in the same pot of water. Cut the asparagus and beans into 2-inch diagonal pieces.

Combine the beef, vegetables, bell pepper, and dressing. Toss well. Serve on a generous bed of romaine and leaf lettuce. Toss together before serving.

Make the vinaigrette: Combine the mustards, vinegar, salt, and pepper. Mix well. Drizzle oil into the mixture, whisking until well blended.

SERVES 6   *Second Round Tea-Time at the Masters,* Augusta, GA

BEEF AND MUSHROOM VINAIGRETTE

A good summertime entree.

1 large white Bermuda or Vidalia
    onion
15 large mushrooms
Salt
Lemon juice
1 to 1½ pounds medium-rare beef
    tenderloin sliced thin
¼ cup red wine vinegar
1 teaspoon prepared brown mustard
Pinch of marjoram
Pinch of chervil
Ground black pepper
½ cup vegetable oil
Watercress sprigs for garnish

Slice the onion thin and separate into rings. Drop the mushrooms into boiling water with pinch of salt and a few drops of lemon juice. Remove immediately with a slotted spoon. Blot dry; slice lengthwise. Do the same with the onions.

Arrange the mushrooms, meat, and onions on a platter. Blend the vinegar into the mustard; stir in the herbs, salt, and pepper to taste. Gradually blend in the oil. Pour over the meat, mushrooms and onion. Chill for several hours, basting occasionally. Garnish with watercress.

SERVES 4–6   *Mountain Elegance,* Asheville, NC

MINNESOTA WILD RICE AND BEEF SALAD

2 cups julienne strips of rare roast
   beef
1½ to 2 cups cooked wild rice
2 to 3 tablespoons slivered almonds
1 small onion, minced
2 to 3 tablespoons chopped green
   bell pepper
1 cup sour cream
1½ to 2 tablespoons Dijon mustard
2 to 3 tablespoons wine vinegar
Pinch of sugar
Dried chervil
Lettuce leaves

Mix the beef, rice, almonds, onion, and green pepper in a bowl. In the other bowl, season the sour cream to taste with mustard, vinegar, very little sugar, and ½ teaspoon or more dried chervil.

Toss the meat and rice mixture with the sour cream dressing and refrigerate for an hour or so. Serve on lettuce leaves.

SERVES 6   *Thyme for All Seasons,* Duluth, MN

ROAST BEEF SALAD WITH PESTO VINAIGRETTE

¼ cup pine nuts
½ cup olive oil
1 clove garlic
1 cup lightly packed fresh basil
   leaves
1 ounce Parmesan cheese, freshly
   grated (⅓ cup)
¾ teaspoon salt
¼ cup red wine vinegar
1 pound rare roast beef, in julienne
   strips
2 heads Boston lettuce, cored,
   rinsed, and dried
8 radicchio leaves, rinsed and dried

Heat the oven to 300 degrees. Put 2 tablespoons of the pine nuts in a pie pan and toast in the oven, stirring occasionally, for 8 to 10 minutes. Set aside.

Combine the oil and garlic in a food processor and blend until the garlic is fine. Add the basil and the remaining 2 tablespoons of pine nuts, the cheese, and the salt. Process until fairly smooth. Stir in the vinegar and ¼ cup of water. Set the pesto vinaigrette aside.

Cut the beef into strips. Tear the lettuce into pieces. Shred the radicchio.

Line a serving platter or 4 individual plates with the greens. Top with the roast beef and sprinkle with the toasted nuts. Drizzle some of the pesto vinaigrette over the salad before serving.

SERVES 4   *Making Waves in the Kitchen,* Indian River, FL

A CELEBRATION OF DIVERSITY

In successful communities that work for everyone, people are mutually supportive. They both accept responsibility for being part of the community and are provided with the supports they need to play productive roles.

The Junior League believes that if we are to help create communities that work for everyone, we need to involve everyone. We recognize that the business of building communities requires a tremendous openness and an embrace of diverse life styles, diverse beliefs, diverse thinking. And so, in our hundredth year, we celebrate our journey toward communities that are inclusive and caring.

The leap to the next century of our own history as well as the history of the human race is teaching the Junior League important lessons. Perhaps the most important is that we must create within our own organization the kind of environment we are seeking to create externally. In the early 1970s, the Junior League fully realized that we, too, were unnecessarily and unhelpfully separate, that we needed to accept responsibility as everyone else does for the barriers, the discriminatory practices,

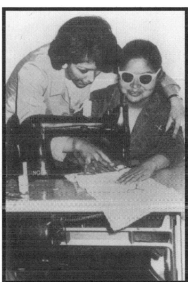

Junior League members establish Mexico City's Center for the Blind, now internationally renowned, in 1930, and run it for 23 years before transferring it to the community in 1953.

systems, and attitudes, that had developed both within our own organization and within society.

The Junior League set out on a journey of embracing diversity and developing a policy of open membership—and has been on that journey ever since. Our approach is both strategic and multidimensional. We continually develop and implement a range of activities designed to promote multicultural development that include dialogues on diversity, multicultural institutes, written resources, and consultations with trained personnel. Junior Leagues are committed to reaching out to women of all races, religions and national origins who are interested in and committed to voluntarism.

The Junior League believes that the depth of separation that has been created in our society requires all organizations to "walk the talk" with rigor and vigilance. Happily, we have learned that once you start on this journey, which is long-term and lifelong, you never want to go back. The personal growth that results from valuing many cultures—the freeing of the spirit, the richness of experience, the largeness of vision—is both humbling and ennobling. We celebrate this journey.

SOUPS & STEWS

CHEDDAR CHOWDER

3½ cups chicken broth
½ cup chopped onion
1 clove garlic, minced
2 stalks celery, sliced
3 carrots, peeled and sliced
1 large potato, peeled and cubed
4 tablespoons (½ stick) butter
¼ cup all-purpose flour
2 cups milk
1 tablespoon Dijon mustard
¼ teaspoon freshly ground black
   pepper
¼ teaspoon paprika
2 tablespoons chopped pimiento
2 cups grated mild Cheddar cheese
   (8 ounces) (see Note)
1 (17-ounce) can corn kernels,
   drained

Combine the chicken broth, onion, garlic, celery, carrots, and potato cubes in a 3-quart saucepan. Bring to a boil. Cover. Reduce the heat and simmer until the vegetables are tender, approximately 20 minutes.

While the vegetables are cooking, melt the butter in a separate saucepan. Add the flour, whisking until smooth. Cook the roux for 1 minute, stirring. Gradually add the milk to the roux. Cook over medium heat, stirring until thick and bubbly.

Add the mustard, pepper, paprika, pimiento, and cheese to the white sauce. Stir until the cheese melts. Gradually add the cheese sauce and corn to the vegetable mixture. Heat, stirring until hot.

NOTE: You can substitute 1 cup of Monterey Jack and 1 cup of mild Cheddar, or use 2 cups of sharp Cheddar cheese.

SERVES 6–8   *Even More Special,* Durham, NC

CANADIAN CHEESE SOUP

½ cup grated carrots
½ cup finely chopped celery
1 cup boiling water
2 tablespoons chopped onion
4 tablespoons (½ stick) butter
6 tablespoons all-purpose flour
2 cups milk
2 cups chicken broth
½ pound sharp Cheddar cheese,
   diced (1½ cups)
Parsley

Add the carrots and celery to the boiling water in a small pan, cover, and simmer until very tender, about 10 minutes. Set aside.

In a medium saucepan, sauté the onion in the butter for 5 minutes until soft but not brown. Add the flour to the onion and butter and blend well. Cook for 2 or 3 minutes, add the milk and chicken broth, and cook until thickened, stirring constantly.

Add the cheese and stir until blended. Add the cooked vegetables, with their liquid, to the cheese mixture. Heat thoroughly. Garnish with minced parsley. Serve with bread sticks.

SERVES 4–6   *Aw Shucks: Another Junior League Cookbook,*
Fort Wayne, IN

BUTTERNUT APPLE SOUP

Absolutely delicious!

2 onions, chopped
3 tablespoons butter
2 cups diced butternut squash
1 Granny Smith apple, peeled and
    chopped
3 tablespoons all-purpose flour
1 to 2 teaspoons curry powder
Pinch of grated nutmeg
3 cups chicken broth
1½ cups milk
Grated rind and juice of 1 orange
Salt, pepper, and a pinch of sugar to
    taste
Chopped parsley and heavy cream
    for garnish

In a large saucepan, sauté the onions in butter about 5 minutes, until soft. Add the squash and apple. Sauté until the butter is absorbed, about 3 minutes, stirring occasionally. Add the flour, curry powder, and nutmeg. Cook for 2 minutes. Add chicken broth, milk, and the orange rind and juice. Simmer slowly uncovered for 15 to 20 minutes until the vegetables are tender.

Purée the soup in a blender or food processor. Add salt, pepper, and sugar. Serve hot, topped with a dollop of cream and a sprinkling of parsley.

NOTE: This soup improves with keeping. Prepare a day or two in advance if time allows. Keep refrigerated.

SERVES 6   *Capital Beginnings,* Ottawa, ON

CARROT GINGER SOUP

*Wonderfully fragrant, beautiful and ap-
petizing.*

¾ cup minced onion
¼ cup peeled and minced fresh
    gingerroot
4 tablespoons (½ stick) plus 3
    tablespoons unsalted butter
6 cups chicken broth
10 to 12 medium carrots, peeled and
    sliced
1 teaspoon sugar
1½ cups half-and-half
¼ cup all-purpose flour
½ teaspoon ground cinnamon
Salt and pepper
Paper-thin carrot slices for garnish

In a Dutch oven, sauté the onion and gingerroot in 4 tablespoons of the butter for 5 to 7 minutes or until the onion in softened. Add the broth, carrots, and sugar. Cover and simmer for 35 minutes. Purée the mixture in a blender or food processor and strain. Return to the Dutch oven and stir in the half-and-half. Cook over low heat for 4 minutes.

In a large saucepan, melt the remaining 3 tablespoons of butter and stir in the flour. Cook over medium heat until bubbly. Slowly add the carrot mixture to the butter-flour mixture, stirring constantly until well blended. Season with cinnamon, salt, and pepper to taste. Garnish with carrot slices and serve warm.

SERVES 6   *Sassafras! The Ozarks Cookbook,* Springfield, MO

CAULIFLOWER SOUP

4 tablespoons (½ stick) butter
1 large white onion, peeled and
    minced
1 clove garlic, peeled and minced
1 large head cauliflower, trimmed
    and chopped
4½ cups chicken broth
Salt and pepper to taste
¼ cup half-and-half
Minced fresh parsley
Croutons

Heat the butter in a large heavy saucepan. Add the onion and garlic and sauté slowly for 6 to 8 minutes until soft. Add the cauliflower and chicken broth. Bring to a boil. Cover, and simmer for 40 minutes. Sieve the soup or purée in a blender. Return the soup to the pan and season to taste.

Reheat the soup prior to serving and add the half-and-half during the last few minutes. Do not boil. Garnish with fresh parsley and croutons.

SERVES 4–6   *Some Like It South*, Pensacola, FL

CORN CHOWDER

1 cup peeled and diced potatoes
1 cup peeled and diced carrots
6 slices bacon
⅓ cup chopped onion
¼ cup all-purpose flour
1 teaspoon salt
Dash of pepper
3 cups milk
1 cup half-and-half
2 cups cooked fresh corn, cut from
    the cob
Chopped parsley

Combine the potatoes, carrots, and ½ cup of water in a small saucepan. Bring to a boil, lower the heat, and cook until tender, about 15 minutes. In a skillet, cook the bacon until crisp. Reserve drippings. Crumble the bacon and set a side.

In a large saucepan, sauté the onion in 3 tablespoons of bacon drippings for 5 minutes. Blend in the flour, salt, and pepper. Gradually stir in the milk and half-and-half. Add the potatoes, carrots, and their liquid. Cook and stir until smooth and slightly thickened. Add the corn and heat through. Adjust seasonings. Serve in bowls with bacon and parsley garnish.

SERVES 4–6   *Soupçon I,* Chicago, IL

NEW DIRECTIONS
JUNIOR LEAGUE OF TORONTO, ONTARIO, CANADA

Founded in 1983 by the Junior League of Toronto, New Directions is a support service for the displaced homemaker who has lost her major source of income through divorce, separation, disability or death of a spouse and is not eligible for government assistance. New Directions provides peer support, counseling, resources, and referrals, and the over 130 volunteers and staff work to assist women in rebuilding their lives by restoring self-esteem and working toward self-sufficiency.

PUMPKIN WILD RICE SOUP

1 cup chopped onion
2 tablespoons butter
4 cups chicken broth
1 (16-ounce) can pumpkin (see Note)
1⅓ cups cooked wild rice
⅛ teaspoon white pepper
1 cup heavy cream
Snipped fresh chives or parsley

Sauté the onion in the butter in a large saucepan for 5 minutes. Stir in the broth and pumpkin. Heat, stirring occasionally, over low heat for 10 to 15 minutes. Stir in the wild rice and pepper. Continue to heat for another 10 minutes. Stir in the cream and heat through; do not boil. Garnish with chives or parsley and serve immediately.

N O T E : Two cups of cooked buttercup or butternut squash can be substituted for the pumpkin.

S E R V E S 8   *Celebrated Seasons,* Minneapolis, MN

BAYOU BISQUE

1 cup chopped onion
1 whole clove garlic, peeled
2 tablespoons butter
2 cups chicken broth
1 teaspoon salt
½ teaspoon grated nutmeg
½ teaspoon ground allspice
½ teaspoon ground coriander
¼ teaspoon pepper
2 cups light cream
1½ cups canned pumpkin
1 (8-ounce) can tomatoes, well-
    drained and chopped

In a medium saucepan, sauté the onion and garlic in butter for 8 to 10 minutes, until golden brown. Remove the garlic and discard. Stir in the chicken broth, salt, nutmeg, allspice, coriander, and pepper. Bring to a boil, reduce the heat, cover and simmer for 15 minutes.

Combine the light cream and pumpkin, mixing until smooth. When the broth has simmered 15 minutes, stir in the pumpkin mixture and the tomatoes. Heat gently until very hot (do not boil) and serve.

S E R V E S 6   *Clusters of Culinary Creations,* Kankakee, IL

COLD PURÉE OF PUMPKIN SOUP

1 onion, chopped
2 tablespoons chopped leeks
2 tablespoons butter
2 cups chicken broth
2 cups unsweetened canned pumpkin
    or puréed cooked fresh pumpkin
½ teaspoon sugar
½ teaspoon ground mace
¼ teaspoon grated nutmeg
½ teaspoon salt
Freshly ground white pepper
Light cream
½ cup heavy cream, salted and
    whipped

Sauté the onion and leeks in the butter for 5 minutes, until transparent. Mix in the chicken broth and pumpkin and heat thoroughly. Purée the mixture in a blender, then push through a strainer or food mill. Add the sugar, mace, nutmeg, salt, and pepper to taste. Chill.

Before serving, adjust the seasonings if necessary and thin to the desired consistency with light cream. Serve garnished with salted whipped cream.

S E R V E S 6   *New York Entertains,* New York, NY

BAKED POTATO SOUP

1 cup sliced celery
¾ cup chopped onion
2 tablespoons butter
2 tablespoons all-purpose flour
2 cups half-and-half
1 tablespoon chopped fresh parsley
1 chicken bouillon cube or 1
　teaspoon chicken granules
½ teaspoon salt
¼ teaspoon pepper
4 large baking potatoes, baked and
　cubed
For garnish: grated Cheddar cheese,
　sour cream, chopped fresh chives,
　bacon bits

In a large saucepan, sauté the celery and onion in butter for 8 to 10 minutes, until tender. Blend the flour with ¼ cup of the half-and-half. Add to the celery and onions, blending well. Add ½ cup of water, the parsley, bouillon, salt, and pepper. Simmer until heated. Do not boil. Stir in the potatoes. Add the remaining half-and-half and heat through without boiling. Serve with a choice of garnishes.

To microwave: Sauté celery and onions in butter on high for 3 to 4 minutes, stirring once. Stir flour into vegetables. Add ¼ cup half-and-half, ½ cup water, parsley, bouillon, salt, and pepper. Cover and cook on high 3 minutes. Add remaining half-and-half. Cook on high for 3 minutes and stir. Stir in potatoes. Reduce power to medium and continue cooking until heated through. Do not boil.

SERVES 2–4　　*Perennials: A Southern Celebration of Food and Flavors,* Gainesville, GA

VICHYSSOISE

6 medium potatoes, peeled and
　cubed
2 medium onions, cut fine
3 cups heavy cream
4 cups chicken broth
Salt and pepper to taste
Snipped chives

Cook the potatoes and onions, covered, in a small amount of water for about 40 minutes or until they form a soft mush. Press through a fine sieve. Cool. Mix in the cream, broth, salt, and pepper. Chill well. Serve sprinkled with snipped chives.

SERVES 6　　*Junior League of Dallas Cookbook,* Dallas, TX

THE ONE AND ONLY ONION SOUP

14-18 medium onions (about 2
　pounds)
¼ cup olive oil or peanut oil
4 tablespoons (½ stick) unsalted
　butter
Salt and pepper
2 level tablespoons sugar
8 cups beef broth
8 slices French bread
8 heaping tablespoons freshly grated
　Parmesan cheese

Peel and slice the onions, cutting on the bias to avoid rings, and saute slowly in the oil, stirring frequently, for 15 to 20 minutes. When the onion gets clear and tender (never burnt or crisp), add the butter. Add salt and pepper to taste and, for the secret ingredient, add the sugar.

　Heat the beef broth in a saucepan and combine with the onions. Trim slices of bread to fit ovenproof earthenware cups or individual casseroles and toast slightly. Put a slice of bread into each cup. Fill with soup and a heaping tablespoon of Parmesan cheese. Place covers (if available) on cups and put in a 375 degree oven for 20 minutes. Serve sizzling.

SERVES 8　　*300 Years of Carolina Cooking,* Greenville, SC

JUDY'S MUSHROOM BARLEY SOUP

Great to have on a back burner on a Sunday afternoon as family members come in from outdoor activities.

¼ cup vegetable oil
2 pounds beef short ribs
1 cup chopped onions
1 cup sliced carrots
2 (16-ounce) cans whole tomatoes, crushed, with liquid
1 tablespoon salt, or to taste
Marjoram and thyme to taste
¼ teaspoon ground black pepper
½ cup barley, rinsed
1 pound fresh mushrooms, sliced
½ cup chopped parsley

Heat the oil in a large heavy kettle. Add the meat and brown. Add the onions and carrots. Sauté for 5 minutes. Add the crushed tomatoes, seasonings, and barley, and 7 cups of water. Bring to a boil, lower the heat, and simmer, covered, for 1½ to 2 hours, until the meat is almost falling off the bones.

Remove the meat and bones from the soup and cut the meat into 1-inch pieces. Add the meat and mushrooms to the soup. Cook for 5 more minutes or until mushrooms are tender. Stir in the parsley and serve hot.

SERVES 6–8

Thyme for All Seasons, Duluth, MN

SHERRIED WILD RICE SOUP

This delicious soup can be prepared the day before serving.

1 cup wild rice
Salt
4 tablespoons (½ stick) butter
1 medium onion, chopped fine
2 cups sliced mushrooms
½ cup thinly sliced celery
¼ cup all-purpose flour
5¼ cups chicken broth
½ teaspoon curry powder
½ teaspoon dry mustard
½ teaspoon dried chervil
¼ teaspoon ground white pepper
2 cups half-and-half
⅔ cup dry sherry
Minced fresh parsley, minced chives, or thinly sliced mushrooms

Rinse the wild rice until the water runs clear. Heat 4 cups of water and 1 tablespoon of salt to boiling. Add the rice and cover. Simmer for about 45 minutes or until rice is tender. Drain off excess water.

In a heavy saucepan, melt the butter, stir in the onion, and cook 5 minutes or until golden. Stir in the mushrooms and celery and cook 4 minutes. Mix the flour and gradually blend in the chicken broth, stirring constantly until slightly thickened.

Stir in the wild rice, ½ teaspoon salt, the curry powder, dry mustard, chervil, and white pepper. Lower the heat and stir in the half-and-half and sherry. Heat to simmering, stirring occasionally. Do not boil. Garnish with parsley, chives or mushroom slices.

SERVES 6–8

Creme de Colorado, Denver, CO

CREAM OF MUSHROOM SOUP

1½ pounds fresh mushrooms, wiped
    and trimmed
9 tablespoons butter
2 finely chopped shallots
6 tablespoons all-purpose flour
6 cups chicken broth
2 egg yolks
¾ cup heavy cream
Salt
White pepper

Separate the mushroom caps and stems. Slice half the caps about ⅛ inch thick. Coarsely chop the remaining caps and all the stems. In a skillet, melt 2 tablespoons of the butter. Add the sliced mushrooms to the butter and sauté for 2 minutes or until lightly colored. Transfer to a bowl and set aside. In the same skillet, melt 2 more tablespoons of butter and cook the remaining stems and caps with the shallots for 2 minutes. Set aside in the skillet.

In a heavy saucepan, melt the remaining 5 tablespoons of butter over moderate heat. Remove the pan from the heat and stir in the flour. Return to the stove and cook over low heat, stirring constantly, for 1 to 2 minutes. Do not let the roux brown. Remove the pan from the heat and allow to cool for a few seconds. Gradually add the chicken stock, stirring constantly with a wire whisk. Return to the heat and stir until the cream soup base comes to a boil, thickens and is perfectly smooth. Add the chopped mushrooms and shallots. Simmer, stirring occasionally, for 15 minutes.

Purée the soup through a food mill into a mixing bowl, then back through a fine sieve to the saucepan. With a wire whisk, blend the egg yolks and cream together in a bowl. Whisk some of the hot soup into the egg-cream mixture, 2 tablespoons at a time, until ½ cup has been added. Then reverse the process and slowly whisk the now warm egg-cream mixture into the soup. Bring to a boil and boil for 30 seconds, stirring constantly. Remove the pan from the heat. Taste and season with salt and white pepper. Add reserved sliced mushrooms and serve in a tureen.

NOTE: Sherry may be added to taste if desired.

SERVES 4–6   *Little Rock Cooks,* Little Rock, AR

WILD MUSHROOM SOUP

5 tablespoons butter
1 small onion, minced
2 large shallots, minced
¾ pound fresh wild mushrooms,
    chopped fine
1 tablespoon all-purpose flour
1 (10½-ounce) can beef consommé
1 (13¾-ounce) can beef broth
3 bay leaves
Salt and pepper to taste
½ cup heavy cream
Chopped parsley

Melt the butter in a heavy saucepan and add the onion and shallots. Stir in the mushrooms and cook 5 to 7 minutes, until quite soft. Sprinkle in the flour, stirring constantly. Gradually stir in the consommé and broth; add the bay leaves. Season to taste with salt and pepper. Heat and stir until hot. Add the cream just before serving. Garnish with parsley.

SERVES 6–8   *Settings,* Philadelphia, PA

MUSHROOM BISQUE

8 tablespoons (1 stick) butter
1 pound fresh mushrooms, wiped, trimmed, and sliced
2 shallots, minced
4 cups chicken broth
6 tablespoons all-purpose flour
3 cups milk
1 cup heavy cream
2 tablespoons sherry
1½ teaspoons salt
9 or 10 drops hot pepper sauce
Ground white pepper to taste
1 (7-ounce) box wild and long grain rice, cooked (optional)
Chopped parsley for garnish

Melt 2 tablespoons of butter in a skillet. Add the mushrooms and shallots. Sauté 5 minutes. Place the mushrooms, shallots, and chicken broth in a blender and blend until smooth. Melt the remaining 6 tablespoons of butter in a saucepan and stir in the flour. In another saucepan, bring the milk to a boil. Add the hot milk all at once to the butter-flour mixture, stirring vigorously with a whisk until smooth. Add the heavy cream, mushroom mixture, sherry, salt and hot pepper sauce. Season with pepper. If desired, add the cooked rice. Garnish with parsley. The bisque will keep in the refrigerator up to 1 week. Reheat and serve.

MAKES ABOUT 2½ QUARTS

Gulfshore Delights, Fort Meyers, FL

RED BELL PEPPER SOUP

4 medium red bell peppers, cored and chopped
2 leeks, thoroughly cleaned and chopped (white portion only)
1 medium onion, chopped
3 tablespoons butter
2 cups chicken broth
2 cups heavy cream
Salt and pepper to taste

In a heavy saucepan, sauté the peppers, leeks, and onion in 1 tablespoon of butter until softened, about 10 minutes. Add the broth and cream. Increase the heat and simmer until the liquid is reduced by one-third, about 30 minutes. Purée in a blender. Return the mixture to the saucepan and simmer for 15 minutes. Remove from the heat. Stir in the remaining 2 tablespoons of butter; season with salt and pepper. Serve hot.

SERVES 6   *Second Round Tea-Time at the Masters,* Augusta, GA

SPINACH YOGURT SOUP

A light and easy favorite that can be garnished with lemon rounds for a festive touch.

10 ounces fresh spinach
1 large onion, chopped coarse
2 cups plain yogurt
¾ cup chicken broth

Rinse the spinach thoroughly and drain. Remove the stems and tough center veins in the larger leaves. Combine the spinach, onion, and 1 cup of water in a stockpot. Bring to a boil, cover, and cook for 5 minutes or until the spinach is wilted and the onion is tender. Drain.

Purée the mixture in a food processor. Add the yogurt. Process until blended. Return the spinach mixture to the stockpot. Stir in the chicken broth. Cook until heated through, stirring constantly. Ladle into soup bowls. NOTE: The soup can be stored in the refrigerator for one or two days and can be served hot or cold. An excellent addition to a ''make ahead'' picnic.

SERVES 4   *I'll Taste Manhattan,* New York, NY

SPINACH SOUP PROVOLONE

1 (10-ounce) package frozen
    chopped spinach, thawed but not
    drained
¼ cup finely chopped onion
8 tablespoons (1 stick) butter
4 tablespoons all-purpose flour
4 cups milk
1½ teaspoon salt or to taste
½ to ¾ cup grated provolone
    cheese
Crumbled bacon

Purée the spinach in a food processor and set aside. Sauté the onion in the butter in a heavy saucepan for 5 minutes, until translucent. Add the flour, stirring constantly for 2 minutes. Gradually stir in the milk and cook until smooth and thickened. Add the puréed spinach and salt. Heat thoroughly. Serve topped with a generous sprinkling of grated cheese and crumbled bacon.

N O T E : Spinach soup with a difference—the provolone is essential. For a smashing buffet presentation, serve the soup in a large hollowed-out hubbard or banana squash.

S E R V E S   6   *Beyond Parsley,* Kansas City, MO

GAZPACHO

A Florida favorite.

1 cucumber, peeled and cut into
    chunks
½ green bell pepper, seeded and cut
    into chunks
1 small onion, cut into chunks
2 tomatoes, peeled
½ ripe avocado, peeled
4 cups tomato juice
3 tablespoons olive oil
2 tablespoons wine vinegar
½ teaspoon dried oregano
Salt to taste

Using the steel blade of a food processor, coarsely chop the cucumber. Transfer to a bowl. Process the green pepper and onion until finely chopped. Add to the cucumber. Cut the tomatoes into ¼-inch cubes. Cut the avocado into ½-inch cubes. Add the tomatoes and avocado to the cucumber along with the tomato juice, oil, vinegar, oregano, and salt. Chill at least 2 hours.

S E R V E S   8   *Far by the Sea,* Sarasota, FL

BRIGHT BEGINNINGS, INC.
JUNIOR LEAGUE OF WASHINGTON, DC

Bright Beginnings, a project created by the Junior League of Washington, DC, provides high-quality services to preschool children of homeless families. It is a safe, nuturing, caring environment designed to promote self-confidence and self-esteem, and offering an educational curriculum meeting the special needs of homeless preschoolers. Programs are tailored to meet the children's personal needs, and when children are well-cared for during the day, homeless parents have the opportunity to seek jobs, training, and permanent housing.

SUMMER TOMATO SOUP

12 large, very ripe tomatoes, peeled
  and chopped
6 scallions, chopped
1 tablespoon salt, or to taste
1 teaspoon sugar
½ teaspoon marjoram
½ teaspoon dried thyme
2 teaspoons grated lime peel
2 tablespoons lime juice
1½ cups sour cream
1 teaspoon curry powder
Minced parsley

Put the tomatoes, scallions, salt, sugar, marjoram, thyme, lime peel and lime juice into a blender container. Blend until the mixture is puréed. Add the sour cream and curry powder. Chill. Garnish with minced parsley.

SERVES 6–8

Soup & Bread, Butte, MT

TOMATO DILL SOUP IN PUFF PASTRY

An impressive beginning for a special dinner.

3 tablespoons butter
2 yellow onions, sliced
2 pounds very ripe tomatoes or 32
  ounces canned tomatoes, drained
2 cloves garlic, chopped
1 teaspoon salt
½ teaspoon sugar
¼ teaspoon ground white pepper
3 tablespoons tomato paste
¼ cup flour
1½ cups half-and-half
1½ cups heavy cream
2 tablespoons chopped fresh dill
2 (8-ounce) packages frozen puff
  pastry, defrosted according to
  directions
2 egg yolks, beaten

Melt the butter in a heavy nonreactive saucepan and sauté the onions for 8 to 10 minutes, until they are soft. Add the tomatoes, garlic, 1½ cups water, the salt, sugar, and pepper. Cover and cook slowly until the tomatoes are very soft, about 20 minutes. Stir in the tomato paste. Dissolve the flour in ½ cup of water. Add 2½ cups more water and stir until smooth. Add this mixture to the tomatoes and bring to a boil, stirring constantly. Strain the soup and add the half-and-half, cream, and dill. Ladle the warm soup into 8 straight-sided soup bowls, filling them two-thirds to three-quarters full.

Preheat the oven to 400 degrees. Cut rounds from the defrosted puff pastry 1 inch larger than the diameter of the soup bowls. Paint around the edge of the bowls with the beaten egg yolk. Then place a pastry round over the top of each bowl, slightly stretching it and pressing to secure. Cut out miniature hearts, stars, etc., from the remaining dough and affix them to the pastry tops with the egg yolk. Place the bowls on a cookie sheet and bake uncovered about 15 minutes or until lightly browned. Serve immediately.

SERVES 8

California Heritage Continues, Pasadena, CA

TOMATO BISQUE

1 medium onion, sliced thin
1 tablespoon butter
2 pounds ripe tomatoes, peeled, seeded, and chopped
1 bay leaf
1 heaping tablespoon brown sugar
2 teaspoons finely chopped fresh basil or 1 teaspoon dried basil
2 whole cloves
1 teaspoon salt
½ teaspoon ground black pepper
2 cups light cream
1 cup milk
2 tablespoons chopped chives
6 large croutons, buttered

In a heavy saucepan, sauté the onion in the butter for 5 minutes. Add the chopped tomatoes, bay leaf, brown sugar, basil, cloves, salt, and pepper. Simmer, stirring occasionally, until the tomatoes are thoroughly cooked, about 25 minutes. Remove the bay leaf and cloves and transfer the mixture to a blender or food processor to purée. Strain. Add the cream and milk and heat through. Sprinkle with chopped chives. Serve topped with toasted buttered croutons.

SERVES 6

Colorado Cache, Denver, CO

BLACK BEAN SOUP

2 cups dried black beans
1 large ham bone
¼ cup vegetable oil
½ cup chopped onion
2 stalks celery, cut up
½ cup chopped celery leaves
2 medium-sized carrots, chopped
4 whole cloves
10 peppercorns
2 bay leaves
8 grains mustard seed
2 teaspoons salt
2 small cloves garlic
Dash of ground red pepper (cayenne)
⅓ cup Marsala or sherry
Thin lemon slices
Hard-boiled egg slices

Wash and pick over the beans. Put them in a soup kettle with 2 quarts of cold water and the ham bone water and bring to a boil. Meanwhile, heat the oil in a skillet. Add the onion, celery, celery leaves, and carrots; sauté for 8 to 10 minutes, until they just begin to brown. Add to the beans.

Tie the cloves, peppercorns (gently bruised), bay leaves, and mustard seed in cheesecloth. Add to the beans along with the salt and garlic. Cover and simmer until the beans are tender, about 4 hours. Add a little more water if it cooks away too much. At the end of cooking time, remove the ham bone and cheesecloth bag and purée the soup in a blender. Reheat to boiling and taste for seasoning. Add the cayenne and stir in the Marsala.

When serving, place a thin slice of lemon and a slice of hard-boiled egg in each soup plate or bowl and pour hot soup over them.

SERVES 12

Home Cookin', Wichita Falls, TX

TIFFANY'S BEAN POT SOUP

This soup probably was the best-known item served at Tiffany's Saloon in Cerrillos, New Mexico. The saloon, operating in the territorial period, was one block east of the hotel where Governor Lew Wallace finished writing his famous Ben-Hur. *Tiffany's burned to the ground on March 15, 1977. This recipe was made public by the restaurant.*

2 cups dried pinto beans, rinsed and
   picked over
1 pound ham, cubed
1 (22-ounce) can tomato juice
4 cups chicken broth
3 onions, chopped
¼ cup chopped green bell pepper
3 cloves garlic, minced
3 tablespoons chopped parsley
¼ cup packed brown sugar
1 tablespoon chili powder
1 teaspoon salt
1 teaspoon crushed bay leaves
1 teaspoon dried oregano
½ teaspoon cumin seeds, ground
½ teaspoon rosemary leaves,
   crushed
½ teaspoon celery seed
½ teaspoon ground thyme
½ teaspoon ground marjoram
½ teaspoon dried basil
¼ teaspoon curry powder
4 whole cloves
1 cup sherry

Soak the beans in water overnight in a large Dutch oven. Drain and return to the pot. Add 4 cups of fresh water and the remaining ingredients except for the sherry. Bring to a boil, cover, and cook slowly until the beans are tender, about 3 hours. Stir in the sherry. Serve in generous soup bowls topped with chopped scallions, if desired.

SERVES 8–10
Simply Simpático, Albuquerque, NM

GATEWAY CHILDREN'S SHELTER
JUNIOR LEAGUE OF CLEARWATER-DUNEDIN, FLORIDA

Gateway Children's Shelter, Inc., grew out of the need for a daycare component in Clearwater, Florida's, homeless services network. The Junior League of Clearwater–Dunedin researched the problem, developed a plan, and raised the money necessary. The center, which opened in December of 1991, provides a stable environment and a quality preschool experience for children who need both so much. The Junior League set up a scholarship fund that guarantees the continuation of the program.

NARCISSA TITMAN'S CURRIED GREEN PEA SOUP

1 small onion, peeled
1 small carrot, peeled
1 stalk celery
1 medium potato, peeled
2 cups chicken broth
1 (10-ounce) package frozen peas,
   thawed
1 clove garlic, peeled and minced
1 teaspoon salt
1 teaspoon curry powder
1 cup light cream

Roughly chop the onion, carrot, celery, and potato. Put 1 cup of the chicken broth, the chopped vegetables, peas, garlic, and seasonings in a saucepan. Bring to a boil. Reduce the heat, cover, and simmer for 15 minutes. Put into a blender and purée. While the motor is running, add the remaining cup of chicken broth and the cream. Serve hot or cold.

SERVES 4–6

A Brooklyn Tradition, Brooklyn, NY

ERWTENSOEP (DUTCH SPLIT PEA SOUP)

1 pound dried split peas
1 shank or butt end of smoked ham
   (1½ to 2 pounds)
1 pig's knuckle, smoked if possible
3 large onions, chopped coarse
1 leek, thoroughly cleaned, halved
   lengthwise, and sliced crosswise
2 celery ribs, chopped coarse
2 carrots, chopped coarse
1 potato, chopped coarse
2 teaspoons thyme
Salt
Freshly ground pepper
4 knockwurst, sliced
1 tablespoon hickory smoked salt,
   optional
¼ cup chopped parsley

If the peas require soaking, soak overnight covered in water. Drain before starting the soup. Combine the ham and pig's knuckle with the peas and 3 quarts of water in a large Dutch oven or heavy pot. Bring to a boil, reduce the heat, and cook 30 to 40 minutes, skimming frequently.

Add the onions, leek, celery, carrots, and potato. Add the thyme and season well with salt and pepper. Simmer slowly, uncovered, for about 5 hours or until very thick, stirring occasionally.

Remove the pig's knuckle and discard. Remove the ham, cut into pieces, and return the soup with the sliced knockwurst 30 minutes before serving. Add the optional smoked salt and stir in the parsley. Serve with whole-grain bread and sweet butter.

SERVES 8

New York Entertains, New York, NY

Collard Greens Soup (Verzada)

½ cup Great Northern beans, rinsed
  and picked over
1 small ham bone
1 small ham hock
½ pound beef short ribs
1 bay leaf
1 teaspoon salt
½ onion, peeled and chopped
½ green bell pepper, chopped
1 blood sausage (morzilla)
3 tablespoons bacon drippings
2 potatoes, peeled and diced
1 bunch fresh collard greens, or 2
  packages frozen, chopped fine

Soak the beans overnight in water to cover. Drain. Put the ham bone, ham hock, short ribs, bay leaf, and salt in a large pot. Add 2 quarts of fresh water. Bring to a boil, removing foam with a skimmer. Lower the heat and simmer, partially covered for 30 minutes. Add the beans, cover, and cook until tender, about 1½ hours.

In a skillet, sauté the onion, green pepper, and sausage (cut in 3 pieces) in the bacon drippings until the onion is soft. Add the potatoes, collard greens, and 1 cup of the boiling soup. Cook uncovered for 10 minutes. Transfer the vegetable-sausage mixture to the soup pot. Cover and simmer until potatoes and greens are done. Serve hot.

SERVES 4–6   *The Gasparilla Cookbook,* Tampa, FL

Irena Kirshman's Minestrone

2 cups beef broth (see Note)
3 slices bacon, cut in small pieces
½ small green cabbage, shredded
1 onion, chopped
1 clove garlic, crushed
2 carrots, diced
2 stalks celery, chopped
Salt and pepper to taste
½ (10-ounce) package frozen
  chopped spinach
½ (10-ounce) package frozen green
  peas
1 (10-ounce) can navy beans,
  drained and rinsed
⅓ cup thin pasta or macaroni
¼ teaspoon dried marjoram
¼ teaspoon dried thyme
¼ teaspoon dried basil
1 cup freshly grated Parmesan
  cheese

Bring the broth and 2 cups of water to a simmer in a large heavy pot. Add the bacon, cabbage, onion, garlic, carrots, and celery. Season with salt and pepper to taste. Simmer uncovered until the vegetables are almost tender, about 15 minutes.

Cut the frozen spinach into small pieces and add to the broth along with the peas, beans, macaroni, and herbs. Simmer about 8 minutes or until macaroni is tender. Taste for seasoning. Serve hot, sprinkled generously with Parmesan cheese.

NOTE: In Milan, this soup is prepared with only half the above quantity of liquid and is so thick it is not so much a soup as a bowl of vegetables. If you prefer it this way, don't prepare anything to follow, because it is very filling.

SERVES 8–10   *Heritage of Hospitality,* Winston-Salem, NC

MINESTRONE

¼ pound lean salt pork, diced
4 cups rich beef broth
1 cup cubed potatoes
1 cup carrot chunks
1 cup cubed turnips
¾ cup uncooked rice
1 cup sliced onion
½ cup lima beans
½ cup green peas
¼ small head of cabbage, shredded
¼ pound fresh spinach, shredded
1 leek (white part only), halved
   lengthwise, washed, sliced
   crosswise
½ cup celery chunks
4 medium tomatoes, diced, or 3
   cups canned tomatoes
2 tablespoons tomato paste
2 tablespoons chopped parsley
½ teaspoon ground sage
½ teaspoon ground black pepper
Salt to taste
Grated Parmesan cheese

Cook the salt pork in just enough water to cover in a large covered kettle for 30 minutes. Add the beef broth and return to a boil. Add the potatoes, carrots, turnips, and rice. Cover and cook for 10 minutes. Add all the remaining ingredients except the Parmesan cheese. Slowly bring to a boil and cook uncovered 1 hour, or until the soup is very thick and the vegetables are tender. Sprinkle with Parmesan cheese and serve as a main dish.

NOTE: The soup may be thinned with chicken broth.

SERVES 12   *I've Got a Cook in Kalamazoo*, Kalamazoo, MI

LEEK CHOWDER

6 tablespoons butter
3 cups fresh mushrooms, wiped and
   trimmed, sliced
3 large leeks, trimmed, halved
   lengthwise, washed, and cut into
   2-inch pieces
10 ounces fresh asparagus cut into
   2-inch lengths, blanched, or
   10-ounce package frozen
   asparagus, thawed and drained
3 tablespoons all-purpose flour
½ teaspoon salt
¼ teaspoon pepper
2 cups chicken broth
2 cups light cream
1 (12-ounce) can white corn kernels
Dash of saffron threads, crushed

Melt the butter in a large heavy saucepan. Add the mushrooms, leeks, and asparagus; cook over medium heat, stirring frequently, for 5 to 6 minutes, until tender but not browned.

Stir in the flour, salt, and pepper. Gradually add the chicken broth and light cream. Cook until thickened and bubbly. Reduce the heat and add the corn and saffron. Heat, but do not boil.

SERVES 6–8   *Utah Dining Car*, Ogden, UT

TURKEY SOUP

TURKEY STOCK

Bones and carcass from leftover turkey
8 peppercorns
1 bay leaf
1 teaspoon dried thyme
6 whole cloves
6 sprigs parsley
1 medium onion, diced
3 ribs celery, diced
1 carrot, diced

Break the carcass into small pieces and put in a stockpot or large kettle with all the remaining ingredients. Add 4 quarts of cold water and bring to a boil. Reduce the heat at once and simmer uncovered for 2½ to 3 hours, or until reduced by half. Strain. Cool uncovered and refrigerate until ready to use. Remove fat. The heated broth may be served as is, used as turkey stock, or used as the base for turkey soup.

TURKEY SOUP

3 large onions, chopped fine
3 ribs celery, chopped fine
2 carrots, peeled and chopped
2 sticks (½ pound) butter
1½ cups all-purpose flour
3 quarts turkey stock
2 cups light cream
Salt and pepper
¼ cup finely diced cooked turkey
¼ cup cooked rice

Cook the onions, celery, and carrots in a little water in a saucepan for 20 minutes or until tender. Set aside. In a large heavy pan, melt the butter and thoroughly blend in the flour over low heat. Heat the turkey stock and cream. Add very gradually to the butter-flour mixture, stirring with a whisk until lumps disappear. Add the reserved vegetables, the water in which they were cooked, and the seasonings. Stir and cook over low heat 10 minutes. Taste and correct the seasoning. Add the turkey and rice. Serve in large bowls. Makes 3 quarts of soup.

SERVES 12-16   *Houston Junior League Cookbook,* Houston, TX

PENDER ISLAND CLAM CHOWDER

This soup is indigenous to the Pacific Northwest and is fun to make.

48 unshucked large clams (butter
    clams or quahogs)
8 slices bacon, diced
2 large onions, diced
3 medium potatoes, diced
2 cups clam broth
4 cups milk
Salt and pepper

If the clams have been dug at the seashore, soak them overnight in a bucket of seawater to cover. Scrub them well and discard any that float or have broken shells. Drain. Place the clams in a kettle with a tight lid. Add 1 cup of water and steam the clams over medium-high heat for 5 to 10 minutes, until the shells open. Remove the clams from the shells. Reserve the broth. Cut them into small pieces, removing the black tip on the neck. The clams may be forced through the coarse blade of a food grinder if desired.

Cook the bacon until crisp and drain on paper towels. Cook the onions in the bacon fat until they are transparent and set them aside. Fry the potatoes in the bacon fat until they are slightly brown and set them aside. Place the bacon, onions, and potatoes in the kettle and pour in the clam broth, adding water if necessary to make 2 cups. Bring to a boil, reduce the heat, and add the clams and milk. Slowly return the soup to the boiling point but do not boil. Add salt and pepper to taste and serve immediately.

SERVES 4-6   *A League of Cooks,* Greater Vancouver, BC

CHICAGO FISH CHOWDER

2 pounds haddock or cod fillets, cut into 2-inch chunks
2 cups peeled and diced new potatoes
8 tablespoons (1 stick) butter
¼ cup chopped celery leaves
3 bay leaves
4 whole cloves
2½ teaspoons salt
¼ teaspoon ground white pepper
1 clove garlic, minced
1 cup dry vermouth
2 cups boiling fish stock
2 cups half-and-half
1½ teaspoons chopped fresh dill for garnish

Preheat the oven to 350 degrees. In a large casserole combine the fish, potatoes, and butter. Add the celery leaves, bay leaves, and cloves tied in a cheesecloth bag. Season with the salt, pepper, and garlic; add the vermouth. Cover, place in the oven, and bake for 50 to 60 minutes, until the fish flakes and the potatoes are tender.

Remove from the oven. Discard the spice bag. Pour the boiling fish stock over all. In a small saucepan heat, but do not boil, the half-and-half. Add it to the chowder. Sprinkle dill on top and serve immediately.

SERVES 6

One Magnificent Cookbook, Chicago, IL

SALMON CHOWDER

4 large potatoes, peeled and diced
4 carrots, peeled and diced
2 large white onions, peeled and diced
½ pound bacon, diced, cooked and drained
1 teaspoon ground red pepper (cayenne)
1 teaspoon freshly ground black pepper
1 pound salmon fillets or steaks, bones and skin removed, in bite-sized pieces
2 cups heavy cream
1 (17-ounce) can creamed-style corn
4 tablespoons (½ stick) unsalted butter
1½ teaspoons salt
Chopped fresh parsley for garnish

In a covered pot, boil potatoes, carrots, and onions in 1½ quarts of water for 20 minutes. Add the bacon and boil 10 more minutes. Add the ground red and black pepper and boil 10 more minutes. Add the salmon, reduce the heat, and simmer 20 minutes. Add the cream, corn, butter, and salt; continue to simmer until well blended and heated through. Do not boil. Garnish with parsley and serve.

SERVES 8–10

Come on In!, Jackson, MS

SEAFOOD CHEDDAR BISQUE

¼ pound uncooked scallops,
  chopped

¼ pound uncooked shrimp, shelled,
  deveined, and chopped

¼ pound cooked crabmeat, picked
  over and shredded

2 scallions, white part only, chopped

1 stalk celery, chopped

2 tablespoons chopped parsley

1½ tablespoons chopped pimiento

2½ cups rich fish stock or bottled
  clam juice

1 cup plus 2 tablespoons bottled
  clam juice

3 tablespoons butter

5 tablespoons flour

3 tablespoons dry vermouth

¼ cup half-and-half

¾ cup heavy cream

1 teaspoon dill weed

¾ teaspoon dried thyme

½ teaspoon seafood seasoning
  (optional)

½ teaspoon ground white pepper

½ teaspoon grated nutmeg

Salt

1½ cups grated Cheddar cheese

4 Shrimp for garnish

Fresh dill for garnish

In the container of a blender, combine the scallops, shrimp, crabmeat, scallions, celery, parsley, and pimiento with the fish stock and clam juice and blend until smooth.

Melt the butter in a small heavy saucepan over low heat. Stir in the flour and then the vermouth. Gradually whisk in the half-and-half. Stir into the seafood mixture. Blend in the cream, dill, thyme, seafood seasoning, pepper, and the nutmeg. Season to taste with salt. Add the cheese and stir until melted. Simmer 10 minutes. Serve hot garnished with 1 whole shrimp and a sprig of dill.

SERVES 4

Celebrate!, Sacramento, CA

DeKALB RAPE CRISIS CENTER
JUNIOR LEAGUE OF DeKALB COUNTY, GEORGIA

The DeKalb Rape Crisis Center was begun by the Junior League of DeKalb County, Georgia, to address the needs of sexual assault victims and their families. Volunteers staff a 24-hour crisis line, provide counseling and referral services, and support rape survivors by accompanying them to the hospital or courtroom. The center includes a Speaker's Bureau, educating the community on the issue of violence against women. The Junior League continues to support the center, which became an independent nonprofit in 1993, with financial contributions and volunteers.

SAN JUAN'S SEAFOOD CHOWDER

CHOWDER

1 yellow onion, peeled and chopped
1 cup chopped leeks, white part
    only
½ cup chopped celery
4 tablespoons (½ stick) butter
2 cups bottled clam juice
2½ cups dry white wine
3 cloves garlic, minced
1 bay leaf
½ teaspoon dried thyme
¼ teaspoon freshly ground pepper
Dash of Tabasco
½ cup chopped parsley
1 pound scallops
10 freshly shucked steamer clams
1 pound fillets of sole, cut into 1½-
    inch squares
1 pound medium shrimp, shelled
    and deveined
1 cup heavy cream, scalded
Croutons for garnish

CROUTONS

½ French bread baguette
8 tablespoons (1 stick) butter

Sauté onion, leeks, and celery in the butter in a large heavy saucepan until tender. Add the clam juice, wine, garlic, bay leaf, thyme, pepper, Tabasco, and parsley. Bring to a boil, reduce the heat, and simmer uncovered for about 5 minutes.

Add the scallops and clams and cook over medium-low heat for 3 minutes. Add the sole and shrimp and cook until the shrimp just turn pink. Remove the bay leaf and stir in the cream. Heat but do not boil. Serve garnished with croutons.

Slice the bread into ¼-inch slices. Melt the butter in a skillet and sauté the bread in batches over moderate heat until golden brown, turning as needed. Drain on paper towels.

Serve the soup in wide bowls and garnish with croutons.

SERVES 8–10 *The Seattle Classic,* Seattle, WA

CRAB SOUP

1 tablespoon butter
1 teaspoon grated onion
2 tomatoes, chopped
½ cup thinly sliced mushrooms
1 teaspoon minced fresh chives
1 pound lump crabmeat, picked over
    to remove bits of shell and cartilage
Salt to taste
Ground red pepper (cayenne) to taste
1½ cups half-and-half
1 jigger (3 tablespoons) brandy
1 cup hot cooked rice
2 tablespoons chopped fresh parsley

Melt the butter in saucepan. Add the onion and sauté over medium heat for 2 to 3 minutes, until transparent. Add the tomatoes, mushrooms, and chives. Bring to a boil and cook 1 minute. Add the crabmeat and heat through. Season with salt and cayenne and cook another minute. Add the half-and-half and brandy. Heat thoroughly. Place 2 tablespoons of hot cooked rice into each of 4 soup bowls and ladle the soup over the rice. Garnish with parsley.

SERVES 4 *Making Waves in the Kitchen,* Indian River, FL

OYSTER-ARTICHOKE SOUP

This soup improves with age. Make it at least 8 hours before serving; refrigerate and reheat to serve. It will keep well for 2 to 3 days.

8 tablespoons (1 stick) butter
2 bunches scallions
2 cloves garlic
3 cans (8-10 count) artichoke hearts
3 tablespoons flour
4 (10½-ounce) cans chicken broth
1 teaspoon crushed red pepper flakes
1 teaspoon anise seed
1 teaspoon salt
1 tablespoon Worcestershire sauce
1 quart shucked oysters

In a 4-quart heavy pot, melt butter and sauté chopped scallions and garlic until soft. Wash and drain artichokes. Cut each into 4 pieces and add to onions. Sprinkle with flour and stir to coat well. Do not brown. Add chicken broth, red pepper, anise seed, salt, and Worcestershire. Simmer for about 15 minutes. While mixture cooks, drain oysters, reserve the liquor, and check oysters for shells. To chop oysters, put in blender and without removing hand from switch, turn motor on and off twice. Add oysters and oyster liquid to pot. Simmer for about 10 minutes. Do not boil.

SERVES 8   *The Cotton Country Collection,* Monroe, LA

ARTICHOKE AND SCALLOP CHOWDER

3 tablespoons butter
1 cup finely chopped red onion
2 tablespoons freshly squeezed lemon juice
3 cups bottled clam juice
3 cups heavy cream
1½ cups canned or frozen artichoke hearts, diced
2½ pounds bay scallops
¼ teaspoon salt
¼ teaspoon ground white pepper
⅛ teaspoon ground red pepper (cayenne)
1 tablespoon snipped fresh chives

In a large heavy pot, melt the butter over medium heat. Add the onion and cook just until translucent, about 3 minutes. Add the lemon juice and simmer until evaporated. Add the clam juice, cream, artichokes, and scallops. Heat to scalding and simmer gently about 4 minutes. Do not boil. Season with salt, white pepper, and cayenne. Ladle the soup into heated bowls and garnish with snipped chives. Serve immediately.

SERVES 8   *Simply Classic,* Seattle, WA

TORTILLA SOUP I

1 medium onion, chopped

1 jalapeño pepper, seeded (if
desired) and chopped

2 cloves garlic, minced

2 pounds beef chuck, cut in small
cubes (optional)

2 tablespoons oil

1 (14½-ounce) can tomatoes

1 (5-ounce) can tomatoes and green
chiles

1 (10¾-ounce) can tomato soup

1 (10½-ounce) can beef broth

1 (10¾-ounce) can chicken broth

1 teaspoon ground cumin

1 teaspoon chili powder

1 teaspoon salt

½ teaspoon lemon-pepper seasoning

2 teaspoons Worcestershire sauce

3 tablespoons Tabasco (or to taste)

4 corn tortillas, cut into 1-inch
squares

¼ cup grated Cheddar cheese

Sauté the onion, jalapeño, garlic, and beef (if using) in the oil in a large kettle for 5 minutes, or until the meat loses its color. Add the tomatoes and tomato soup, 1½ soup cans of water, the broth, and the seasonings. Bring to a boil, lower the heat, and simmer uncovered for 50 minutes. Add the tortillas and cook an additional 10 minutes. Pour into mugs and sprinkle with cheese.

SERVES 6–8   *Flavors,* San Antonio, TX

TORTILLA SOUP II

1 tablespoon vegetable oil

12 corn tortillas, cut into small
squares or strips

1 tomato, diced

1 thin slice onion

½ clove garlic, minced

1 sprig epazote

Salt to taste

6 cups chicken broth

Manchego or mozzarella cheese,
grated

Avocado, diced (optional)

Chile sauce (optional)

Pasilla chile (optional)

Heat the oil in a heavy saucepan and fry the tortilla strips until lightly browned. Drain on paper towels. In the same pan, fry the tomato, onion, and garlic until the tomato starts to look slightly dry. Add the epazote, salt, and chicken broth. Bring to a boil, lower the heat, and simmer uncovered about ½ hour. Add the tortillas and serve immediately, sprinkled with cheese. You may also garnish with diced avocado, chile sauce, or a pasilla chile browned in oil.

SERVES 4–6   *Buen Provecho,* Mexico City

ITALIAN SAUSAGE SOUP

½ pound sweet Italian sausage links
½ pound hot Italian sausage links
2 cloves garlic, minced
1 cup chopped onion
2 carrots, peeled and diced
¾ pound zucchini, diced
1 green bell pepper, diced
½ cup dry white wine
5 cups chicken broth
1 pound fresh or canned Italian
    plum tomatoes, peeled and
    chopped
2 teaspoons dried basil
1 teaspoon dried oregano
Freshly ground black pepper
½ cup pastini (tiny Italian soup
    pasta)
Freshly grated Romano cheese

Brown the sausage links in a large heavy saucepan and drain off all but 1 tablespoon of fat. Cut the sausages into 1-inch pieces; return to the pan. Add the garlic and onion. Sauté for 5 minutes, until onion is transparent. Stir in the carrots, zucchini, green pepper, wine, broth, tomatoes, basil, oregano, and ground black pepper. Bring to a boil. Add the pastini and cook 20 minutes. Serve with Romano cheese and crusty French or Italian bread.

SERVES 6–8   *A Cleveland Collection,* Cleveland, OH

FOREST HILLS ZUCCHINI SOUP

1 pound Italian sausage links, mild
    or hot, cut into 1-inch pieces
½ pound ground beef chuck
2 cups sliced celery (½ inch thick)
1½ cups coarsely chopped onion
2 pounds zucchini, sliced ½ inch
    thick
2 (28-ounce) cans tomatoes in sauce
2 teaspoons salt
1 teaspoon Italian seasoning
1 teaspoon dried oregano
½ teaspoon dried basil
½ teaspoon garlic powder
2 green bell peppers, cut into
    ½-inch dice
Shredded mozzarella cheese
Grated Parmesan cheese

Brown the sausage and ground beef in a large Dutch oven. Drain off all but 2 teaspoons of fat. Add the celery and onion. Cook 10 minutes, stirring often. Add the zucchini, tomatoes, and seasonings. Cover and simmer for 20 minutes. Add the green pepper. Cover and cook 10 minutes.

Ladle the soup into bowls at serving time. Sprinkle generously with mozzarella and Parmesan cheese. Brown under broiler if desired.

MAKES 3–4 QUARTS   *Applehood & Motherpie,* Rochester, NY

HUNGARIAN GOULASH SOUP WITH SPAETZLE

1 onion, chopped
1 clove garlic, minced
2 tablespoons lard or vegetable oil
1 tablespoon sweet Hungarian
  paprika
2 pounds beef chuck steak, cut into
  ½-inch cubes
1 tablespoon caraway seeds
2 teaspoons salt
½ teaspoon ground black pepper
3 potatoes, peeled and diced
1 carrot, peeled and diced
1 parsnip, peeled and diced
1 tomato, seeded and chopped
½ green bell pepper, seeded and
  minced
¼ cup minced parsley

SPAETZLE
½ cup all-purpose flour
1 egg
⅛ teaspoon salt

In a Dutch oven, sauté the onion and garlic in the lard for 5 minutes or until soft. Stir in the paprika and then the cubed beef. Add ½ cup of water. Bring to a boil over moderate heat and cook for 5 minutes. Stir in the caraway seed mixed with ¼ cup of water and cook the mixture until the liquid has evaporated. Add 10 cups of water, the salt and pepper. Bring to a boil. Reduce the heat and simmer, partially covered, for 1½ hours or until the meat is almost tender. Add the potatoes, carrot, parsnip, tomato, and green pepper and simmer another 30 minutes. Meanwhile, make the spaetzle dough.

To prepare the spaetzle, mix the flour with the egg, salt, and about 2 tablespoons of water to form a soft dough. Cover and set aside for 30 minutes. Pinch the dough into pieces the size of peas and drop into the simmering soup, lifting the spaetzle from the bottom of the pan. Add the parsley and simmer 5 minutes longer or until spaetzle is cooked. Add salt and pepper to taste.

SERVES 6   *Superlatives,* Oklahoma City, OK

EGGPLANT SUPPER SOUP

2 tablespoons olive oil
2 tablespoons butter
1 medium onion, chopped
1 pound lean ground chuck
1 medium eggplant, peeled and cubed
1 clove garlic, crushed
1 cup finely sliced carrots
1 cup chopped celery
2 (16-ounce) cans whole tomatoes
3½ cups beef broth
½ teaspoon grated nutmeg
1 teaspoon sugar
1 teaspoon salt
½ teaspoon ground black pepper
½ cup macaroni
2 tablespoons minced fresh parsley
Parmesan cheese for garnish

Heat the oil and butter in 6-8 quart Dutch oven. Add the onion and sauté until lightly browned, about 8 minutes. Add the meat and cook, stirring, until it begins to brown. Add the eggplant, garlic, carrots, celery, tomatoes (break up whole pieces), broth, nutmeg, sugar, salt, and pepper. Bring to a boil, reduce the heat, cover, and simmer 2½ hours.

Ten to fifteen minutes before serving, add the macaroni and parsley to the soup and simmer until the macaroni is tender. Serve hot with Parmesan cheese sprinkled on top.

SERVES 12   *Stirring Performances,* Winston-Salem, NC

STRAWBERRY SOUP

A lovely soup to begin an elegant dinner.

1 quart fresh strawberries, cleaned
   and hulled, or 1 (16-ounce)
   package frozen whole
   strawberries, thawed and drained
1 cup sour cream
1 cup light cream
¼ cup sugar
2 tablespoons light rum or 1
   teaspoon rum flavoring

Purée the strawberries in a blender or food processor. Add the sour cream, light cream, sugar, and rum. Continue blending until smooth. Chill several hours or overnight. Garnish with fresh strawberry slices.

S E R V E S   6 – 8   *Pinch of Salt Lake,* Salt Lake City, UT

ICED FRUIT AND WINE SOUP

What could be more decadent? Keep in mind that this must be made ahead of time.

⅓ cup sugar
1 cup port wine
2 tablespoons fresh lemon juice
1 stick cinnamon
4 cups puréed strawberries or
   raspberries
¼ cup sour cream
Pinch of salt
½ cup heavy cream
Fresh mint sprigs for garnish

In a medium saucepan, stir together the sugar, port, lemon juice, and cinnamon stick with 2 cups of water. Bring to a boil, reduce the heat, and simmer, uncovered, for 10 minutes. Stir in the puréed fruit. Simmer 5 minutes longer. Discard the cinnamon stick and let cool.

Whisk in the sour cream, salt, and heavy cream. Cover and chill for 4 hours or overnight. Garnish each serving with a sprig of fresh mint.

V A R I A T I O N : In summertime, try substituting peaches for the berries and Riesling wine or Champagne for the port. Do not add Champagne or Riesling until you are ready to whisk in the sour cream, salt, and heavy cream.

S E R V E S   4 – 6   *Capital Beginnings,* Ottawa, ON

TOTS OF TEENS
JUNIOR LEAGUE OF FAYETTEVILLE, NORTH CAROLINA

Tots of Teens, a project funded and staffed by the Junior League of Fayetteville, North Carolina, assists teenage mothers in high school complete their education. The Junior League pays the daycare costs for the children of the teen mothers, and in return, the girls agree to attend school regularly, delay a pregnancy, and attend monthly meetings sponsored by the League that address issues of birth control, child care, nutrition, and parenting skills. Tots of Teens has served approximately ten high school girls each year since 1989, and every student who has successfully completed the program has graduated from high school.

WILD BERRY SUMMER SOUP

This soup can be prepared several days prior to serving.

1 cup blueberries
1 cup raspberries
4 cups strawberries, hulled
½ cup port wine
1 teaspoon minced fresh gingerroot
¼ cup light cream
1 tablespoon chopped fresh mint
2 tablespoons sugar
1 to 2 tablespoons raspberry vinegar
  or white wine vinegar
Fresh mint sprigs
Lemon zest
Orange zest

Put the blueberries in a blender or the bowl of a food processor fitted with the steel blade. Blend until smooth; strain. Set aside. Process the raspberries and then strawberries. Strain and set aside.

In a 1-quart saucepan, bring the wine and ginger to boiling. Reduce the heat and simmer 5 minutes. Add the cream; return to boiling and cook 1 minute longer, stirring constantly. Remove the pan from the heat.

In a blender or food processor, combine the strained blueberries, raspberries, and strawberries with the chopped mint, sugar, and vinegar. Process until combined. Add the cream mixture. Process again until well combined.

Pour the soup into a container, cover, and refrigerate until thoroughly chilled. To serve, ladle chilled soup into thoroughly chilled bowls. Garnish with mint, lemon and orange zest.

SERVES 6   *Maine Ingredients,* Portland, ME

LOUISIANA RED BEANS AND RICE

1 pound red beans (see Note), rinsed
  and picked over
1 (8-ounce) ham hock
3 cups chopped onion
1 bunch scallions, chopped
2 cloves garlic, minced
1 tablespoon salt
1 cup chopped green bell pepper
1 cup minced parsley
1 teaspoon ground red pepper
  (cayenne)
1 teaspoon ground black pepper
⅛ teaspoon Tabasco
1 tablespoon Worcestershire sauce
1 (8-ounce) can tomato sauce
¼ teaspoon dried oregano
¼ teaspoon dried thyme

Put the beans and ham hock in a large soup kettle, add 2 quarts of water, bring to a boil, and reduce the heat. Cook slowly uncovered for 45 minutes. Add all the other ingredients and cook slowly for 1 hour or until the beans are tender and the liquid is thick. Serve over steamed rice.

NOTE: These are not red kidney beans but a smaller bean, often used in Mexican cooking. If unavailable, substitute pink, pinto, or kidney beans. The original recipe called for soaking the beans overnight, which is no longer necessary because of today's processing methods.

SERVES 12   *Fiesta,* Corpus Christi, TX

GUMBO YA YA (CHICKEN AND ANDOUILLE SAUSAGE GUMBO)

1 (5-pound) chicken, cut into 10
    pieces
Salt and freshly ground black pepper
Ground red pepper (cayenne)
Garlic powder
2½ cups all-purpose flour
1 cup vegetable oil
2 cups chopped onion
2 cups chopped green bell pepper
1½ cups chopped celery
6 cups chicken broth
1 pound andouille sausage or
    kielbasa, diced
1½ teaspoons minced fresh garlic
Steamed white rice

Arrange the chicken on a baking sheet and season evenly with salt, black and red pepper, and garlic powder. Let stand 30 minutes at room temperature. Combine the chicken pieces and flour in a large paper bag and shake until the chicken is well coated.

Heat the oil in a large skillet over medium-high heat. Add the chicken (reserve the remaining flour) and brown on both sides. Remove with a slotted spoon and drain on paper towels; set aside.

Loosen any brown bits on the bottom of the skillet. Using a whisk, add 1 cup of the reserved flour and stir constantly until the roux is very dark brown. Do not brown. Remove from the heat and add the onion, green pepper, and celery, stirring to blend thoroughly and prevent burning. Transfer to a large saucepan. Stir in the broth and bring to a boil over medium-high heat. Reduce the heat, add the sausage and garlic, and simmer 45 minutes, stirring occasionally.

Remove the chicken and cut the meat from the bones into small pieces. Return the chicken to the saucepan and heat thoroughly. Season with salt and pepper and serve immediately over steamed rice in individual soup bowls.

VARIATION: Oysters may be added for the last 5 minutes of cooking.

SERVES 8   *Talk About Good II,* Lafayette, LA

CRAWFISH FILÉ GUMBO

1 cup vegetable oil
1 cup all-purpose flour
1 cup chopped celery
1 cup chopped onion
1 (6-ounce) can tomato paste
2 tablespoons butter
1 (10-ounce) can Rotel tomatoes
1 pound crawfish tails
1 pound crabmeat (claw is better),
    picked over well
½ cup chopped scallions (green tops
    only)
½ cup chopped bell pepper
½ cup chopped parsley
Crushed garlic, salt, and ground
    black pepper to taste
Hot cooked rice
Filé powder

Heat the oil in a large heavy pot. Add the flour and stir constantly over medium-high heat, without burning, to make a dark roux. Add the celery and onions; sauté 30 minutes. Add 4 quarts of water.

Brown the tomato paste in the butter in a small pan. Cook until it loses its bright red color. Stir in ½ to ¾ can Rotel tomatoes. Add this mixture to the other pot and simmer 1 hour.

Add the crawfish, crabmeat, scallion tops, bell pepper, and parsley. Season with garlic, salt, and black pepper and simmer about 20 to 30 minutes.

This is a thin gumbo. If it needs to be thickened, add a little cornstarch dissolved in water. Serve on rice and let each person add filé to his or her own taste.

SERVES 12   *River Road Recipes: A Second Helping,* Baton Rouge, LA

LOUISIANA SHRIMP AND CORN GUMBO

5 tablespoons olive oil

5 tablespoons all-purpose flour

2 onions, chopped fine

1 green bell pepper, chopped fine

4 shallots, chopped fine

2 tablespoons minced fresh parsley

Salt to taste

Ground black pepper to taste

⅛ teaspoon ground red pepper
  (cayenne)

1 teaspoon Cajun vegetable seasoning

3 dashes hot red pepper sauce

3 dashes Worcestershire sauce

1 tablespoon chopped fresh basil or
  1 teaspoon dried

1 (16-ounce) can undrained
  tomatoes, chopped

1 pound frozen corn kernels

3 cups chicken broth

2 pounds small or medium shrimp,
  peeled

In a Dutch oven over medium heat, heat the olive oil and stir in the flour. Cook, stirring constantly, until the mixture turns dark brown. Do not burn. When the roux is brown, add the onions, bell pepper, shallots, and parsley. Sauté on low heat for 10 minutes. Add salt, black and red pepper, Cajun vegetable seasoning, hot pepper sauce, Worcestershire, and basil. Simmer 5 more minutes. Add the tomatoes, corn, and broth. Cover and simmer over low heat for 1 to 1½ hours, adding shrimp during last 15 minutes of cooking time.

NOTE: This soup may be prepared ahead of time and slowly warmed to serving temperature.

MAKES ABOUT 2½ QUARTS   *Celebrations on the Bayou,* Monroe, LA

CHICKEN, SAUSAGE, AND OYSTER GUMBO

1 (3-pound) chicken, cut into pieces

¼ cup all-purpose flour

¼ cup vegetable oil

1½ cups chopped yellow onion

1½ cups chopped celery

½ cup chopped green bell pepper

½ cup chopped scallions

3 cloves garlic, minced

¼ cup chopped fresh parsley

1 bay leaf

½ teaspoon dried thyme

¾ pound hard sausage (preferably
  andouille), sliced

Salt

Ground black pepper

Ground red pepper (cayenne)

Worcestershire sauce

1 cup shucked oysters, with liquid

3 cups hot steamed rice

3 teaspoons filé powder

Cook the chicken in 4 cups of water until tender, skimming off the fat and foam frequently. Reserve the broth and remove the meat from the bones.

In a Dutch oven, heat the oil and gradually add flour, stirring constantly until a dark-brown roux is formed. Add the onion, celery, green pepper, scallions, garlic, parsley, bay leaf, and thyme. Cook until tender, stirring often. Slowly add the reserved broth, stirring constantly. Add the chicken meat.

In a skillet, fry the sausage; drain; add to the gumbo. Cover and simmer 1 hour, stirring occasionally. Add salt, black pepper, cayenne, and Worcestershire sauce to taste. Add the oysters with their liquid and heat just until edges curl. Serve over rice and sprinkle ½ teaspoon filé powder over each serving.

SERVES 6   *Jambalaya,* New Orleans, LA

SEAFOOD STEW MANHATTAN STYLE

It's the tomatoes that give this a Manhattan aura.

3 tablespoons butter
1 medium onion, peeled
2 ribs celery
1 clove garlic, peeled
1 (16-ounce) can crushed plum
    tomatoes in purée, or 1 can whole
    plum tomatoes
2 cups chicken broth, or 1 cup
    bottled clam juice plus 1 cup
    water
1 teaspoon dried thyme
1 bay leaf, broken in half
¼ teaspoon crushed dried red
    pepper flakes
1 pound firm, nonoily fish such as
    cod, haddock, halibut, or
    monkfish
12 to 16 mussels
½ cup chopped Italian parsley
1 tablespoon chopped fresh tarragon
    or 1 teaspoon dried
Salt and ground black pepper to
    taste

Melt the butter in a heavy 4-quart pot. Chop the onion and the celery and mince the garlic. Cook the vegetables in the butter over medium heat until softened, about 3 minutes. Add the tomatoes and the chicken stock or clam juice and water. Add the thyme, bay leaf, and red pepper flakes. Bring to a boil and simmer partially covered for 10 minutes.

Cut the fish into 1½-inch cubes. Scrub the mussels and pull off their beards. Stir the parsley and tarragon into the stew and add the fish, stirring in gently. Arrange the mussels on the top. Cover and cook on low heat until the mussels have steamed open and the fish is opaque, about 5 minutes. Discard the bay leaf and season the stew with salt and pepper. Serve in shallow bowls with toasted French bread.

SERVES 4   *Off the Hook,* Stamford-Norwalk, CT

LOBSTERMAN'S STEW

4 (1½-pound) lobsters, cooked
10 tablespoons butter
½ cup finely chopped onion
10 cloves garlic, minced
Ground black pepper to taste
2 cups plus 2 tablespoons Madeira
6 cups heavy cream
3 cups light cream

Scoop the green tomalley (liver) from the lobster bodies. Set aside. Remove the lobster meat from the shells. Set the shells aside.

In a large saucepan, melt 6 tablespoons of the butter over medium heat. Add the tomalley, onion, garlic, black pepper, and 2 tablespoons of Madeira; sauté until the onion is soft. Add the remaining 4 tablespoons of butter, the heavy cream, light cream, and the remaining 2 cups of Madeira. Stir to combine ingredients. Add the lobster meat.

Tie the lobster shells in a cheesecloth bag and let soak in the stew. Simmer the stew on low heat for 3 to 5 hours or longer if time allows. The longer it simmers, the more flavorful it will be. Before serving remove the cheesecloth bag, squeeze dry, and discard.

SERVES 4   *Maine Ingredients,* Portland, ME

BACK BAY SEAFOOD GUMBO

5 tablespoons bacon drippings

6 tablespoons all-purpose flour

2 onions, chopped

1½ cups chopped celery

2 cloves garlic, minced

1 (28-ounce) can tomatoes, chopped

1 (8-ounce) can tomato sauce

1 tablespoon salt

1 teaspoon ground black pepper

1 tablespoon parsley flakes

2 teaspoons Creole seasoning, or to
   taste

10 drops hot pepper sauce

1 (16-ounce) package frozen cut okra

3 pounds raw medium shrimp,
   peeled and deveined

1 pound crabmeat, picked over well

4 gumbo (blue) crabs (optional)

1 pint oysters (optional)

3 tablespoons Worcestershire sauce,
   or to taste

Hot cooked rice

Make a roux by combining the bacon drippings and flour in a large heavy kettle and stirring constantly over medium heat for 30 minutes or until very dark.

Add the onion, celery, and garlic; sauté for 5 minutes. Add the tomatoes, tomato sauce, 6 cups of water, the salt, pepper, parsley, and seasonings. Simmer 1 hour. Add the okra and cook over low heat for 1 hour. Add the shrimp, crabmeat, crabs, and oysters if desired and cook 20 minutes. Add Worcestershire and stir well. Serve over rice.

SERVES 10   *Celebrations on the Bayou,* Monroe, LA

WINTER WOOLLY SOUP

This robust soup is best made a day ahead and gently reheated. It freezes well.

Meaty bone from a roasted leg of
   lamb

6 carrots, peeled and sliced

3 potatoes, peeled and cubed

2 white turnips, peeled and cubed

2 stalks celery, sliced

2 onions, peeled and chopped

1¼ cups dried split peas

2 teaspoons salt

1 teaspoon freshly ground black
   pepper

½ teaspoon dried rosemary

½ teaspoon dried thyme

1 bay leaf

1 cup or more cubed cooked lamb

Put the bone in a large soup kettle, add 4 quarts of water, and bring to a boil over medium-high heat. Lower the heat, cover, and simmer for 1 hour.

Add the carrots, potatoes, turnips, celery, onions, split peas, salt, pepper, rosemary, thyme, and bay leaf. Simmer for 1 more hour. Remove and discard the bone and the bay leaf. Taste and adjust the seasoning. Add the cubed cooked lamb and continue simmering just until the lamb is heated through. Serve hot.

SERVES 8–10   *R.S.V.P.,* Portland, ME

COUNTRY STEW

This may be a country stew, but oh how the city folks will love it!

2 whole chickens (2½ pounds each)
1 tablespoon salt
2 medium onions, chopped
¼ pound raw country ham or bacon, cut in bite-sized pieces
1 (28-ounce) can tomatoes
1 (8½-ounce) can corn kernels
1 (10-ounce) package frozen lima beans
1 (10-ounce) package frozen okra
1¼ teaspoon Tabasco, or to taste
¼ teaspoon dried thyme
½ teaspoon salt
⅛ teaspoon ground black pepper
3 tablespoons butter
¼ cup flour
1 small green bell pepper, chopped fine

Put the chickens, breast side down, in a large kettle with a lid and add the giblets (except for the livers). Add enough water to barely cover. Add the salt and onion. Bring to a boil, skim off foam, and reduce the heat. Cover and simmer 45 minutes or until the chicken is tender. Fifteen minutes before the end of cooking time, add the livers.

Remove the chicken and giblets from broth. When cool enough to handle, remove the meat from the bones. Return the meat to the broth. Add the ham, tomatoes, corn, limas, okra, Tabasco, thyme, salt, and pepper. Simmer 1 hour, partially covered, stirring occasionally.

Melt the butter in saucepan, blend in the flour, and heat, stirring constantly until bubbles form and the mixture browns. Add the roux gradually to the stew and cook over medium heat, stirring, until slightly thickened. Add the chopped green pepper and simmer 10 minutes longer. Serve very hot on cornbread squares or with corn sticks.

SERVES 12–14   *Cotton Country Cooking,* Decatur, AL

CALDILLO (MEXICAN STEW)

2 to 3 tablespoons lard or vegetable shortening
1 pork chop, boned and cubed
3 pounds cubed beef
1½ cup diced onions
3 cups green chile strips
1 cup beef broth
1 cup chicken broth
2 tablespoons salt
1 tablespoon ground black pepper
2 tablespoons garlic powder
2 teaspoons ground cumin
1 tablespoon chili powder
2 pounds potatoes, peeled and cubed
Flour tortillas

In a large heavy kettle, melt the lard over medium heat and brown the meat, in batches if necessary to avoid overcrowding. Add the onions and cook until clear, 3 to 5 minutes.

Add the chile strips, the beef and chicken broth, salt, pepper, garlic powder, cumin, chili powder, and potatoes. Add enough water to make soupy. Cook partially covered for 3 hours on medium heat. Serve with warm buttered flour tortillas.

SERVES 6–8   *The Wild, Wild West,* Odessa, TX

MARJORIE PURNELL'S CADILLAC STEW

6 strips bacon
½ cup diced salt pork
⅔ cup all-purpose flour
Salt and ground black pepper to
    taste
3 pound lean beef, cut into 1-inch
    cubes (eye of round or sirloin can
    be used)
¼ cup brandy
12 small onions, peeled and left
    whole
6 carrots, diced
4 whole cloves and 1 bay leaf, tied
    in a cheesecloth bag
Pinch of marjoram
½ teaspoon thyme
2 tablespoons chopped parsley
12 mushrooms, sliced
1 cup beef bouillon
½ cup dry red wine

Heat the oven to 300 degrees. In a heavy skillet, fry the bacon and salt pork until crisp. Drain and crumble the bacon and put into a large casserole. Discard the salt pork.

Combine the flour, salt, and pepper in a bowl and dredge the beef cubes. Brown in the fat remaining in the skillet over medium high heat; work in batches if necessary to avoid overcrowding. Transfer the beef cubes to the casserole, pour warmed brandy over them, and flame.

Add more fat, if necessary, to the skillet and sauté the onions and carrots with the cloves, bay leaf, marjoram, thyme, and parsley for 10 minutes. Add the mushrooms and sauté 5 more minutes. Transfer to the casserole and pour the bouillon and red wine over all. Cover and bake for 3 hours. Remove the cheesecloth bag before serving.

SERVES 8   *The Dallas Junior League Cookbook,* Dallas, TX

GARBANZO SOUP

1 small onion, chopped
1 clove garlic, minced
1 celery stalk, sliced
1 teaspoon virgin olive oil
1 cup canned Italian plum tomatoes,
    with liquid
1 carrot, sliced
½ small red bell pepper, diced
½ teaspoon dried basil or 1½
    teaspoons fresh
1 cup canned chick-peas
    (garbanzos), drained and rinsed
4 cups chicken broth
Salt and pepper to taste

In a large saucepan, sauté onion, garlic, and celery for 5 minutes in the heated oil. Add the remaining ingredients. Bring to a boil, reduce the heat, and simmer covered for 20 minutes.

SERVES 6   *Dessert Treasures,* Phoenix, AZ

TAMPA-STYLE BLACK BEAN CHILI

There is no controversy over whether to serve this chili with or without beans—the beans make the chili!

1½ pounds dried black beans, rinsed and picked over, or 6 (15-ounce) cans black beans
2 tablespoons vegetable oil
1 large onion, chopped
8 garlic cloves, minced
2 to 4 pounds ground beef
2 (28-ounce) cans tomatoes
2 large green bell peppers, chopped
3 tablespoons chili powder, or to taste
3 tablespoons ground cumin, or to taste
8 to 10 dried chili peppers, or to taste
6 to 12 ounces beer
Sour cream for garnish
Diced tomatoes for garnish
Chopped cilantro or parsley for garnish

About 6½ hours before serving, soak and cook the dried beans according to package directions; drain. (Or drain the canned beans, reserving some of the liquid to thin the chili, if desired.)

Heat the oil in a large heavy kettle. Add the onion and garlic; cook until soft. Add the ground beef; cook and stir until brown. Drain liquid. Add the tomatoes, green peppers, chili powder, cumin, and chili peppers. Cook over low heat 10 minutes.

Add the drained beans with some bean liquid, if desired. Simmer over low heat about 3 hours, stirring frequently. If chili is getting too thick, add up to 12 ounces of beer during cooking. Serve garnished with sour cream, diced tomatoes, and chopped cilantro or parsley.

SERVES 12   *Tampa Treasures,* Tampa, FL

GREEN CHILE SOUP

1 onion, chopped
6 tablespoons unsalted butter
12 ounces green chile, chopped
56 ounces canned plum tomatoes, drained and chopped
12 ounces cream cheese
29 ounces chicken broth
3 cups half-and-half or 2 cups milk
2 tablespoons plus 2 teaspoons lemon juice
Ground red pepper (cayenne)

Sauté the onions in the butter in a saucepan until soft. Add the chiles and tomatoes. Cook 8 to 10 minutes or until the liquid is gone. Stir in the cream cheese until melted, but do not boil. Stir in the chicken broth, half-and-half, and lemon juice. Serve warm or at room temperature; sprinkle each serving with a dash of cayenne.

SERVES 12–16   *Desert Treasures,* Phoenix, AZ

FIREHOUSE CHILI

2 tablespoons vegetable oil

1½ pounds ground chuck or very lean ground beef

1 large onion, chopped

1 clove garlic, crushed

Salt to taste

¼ teaspoon ground red pepper (cayenne)

¼ teaspoon dried oregano

¼ teaspoon ground cumin

1½ to 2 tablespoons chili powder, or to taste

2 (10-ounce) cans Rotel tomatoes, undrained

1 (8-ounce) can tomato sauce

2 (16-ounce) cans red kidney beans, undrained

Heat the oil in a large skillet. Add the meat, stirring to break up lumps, and cook until brown. Add the onion and garlic and cook until onion is limp. Drain off the fat and place the meat in a Dutch oven. Add salt, cayenne, oregano, cumin, and chili powder. Break up the tomatoes and add along with the tomato sauce and kidney beans. Mix well and bring to a simmer. Taste for seasoning and correct if necessary.

Simmer for ½ hour uncovered and 1½ hours covered. If the mixture becomes too thick, add a little tomato juice.

SERVES 6–8   *Magic,* Birmingham, AL

CHILI BLANCO

2 cups dried Great Northern beans, rinsed and picked over

3 whole chicken breasts, skinned

2 tablespoons olive oil

2 cups finely chopped onion

2 large cloves garlic, minced

2 (4-ounce) cans chopped chiles

1 serrano or jalapeño chile, cored, seeded, and minced

2 teaspoons ground cumin

1 tablespoon minced fresh oregano, or 1½ teaspoons dried

¼ teaspoon ground cloves

¼ teaspoon ground red pepper (cayenne)

3 cups canned chicken broth

Salt to taste

2 cups grated Monterey Jack cheese

Diced tomatoes, additional grated cheese, chopped scallions, and chopped cilantro for garnish

Place the beans in a large heavy pot and cover with plenty of water. Soak for 1 hour. Meanwhile, put chicken breasts in a large skillet; cover with 3½ cups water. Bring to a boil, cover, and simmer 30 minutes. Remove the chicken from the pan, reserving the liquid, and let cool. When the chicken is cool, remove the bones and shred the meat.

Drain the beans, rinse and set aside. In the same pot, heat the oil over medium heat. Add the onion and cook, stirring, for 10 minutes. Add the garlic, chiles, cumin, oregano, cloves, and cayenne and cook 2 more minutes. Add the beans, broth, and reserved chicken cooking liquid. Bring to a boil, cover, and simmer, stirring occasionally, until the beans are tender, about 2 hours. Add salt to taste and adjust seasoning.

Before serving, add shredded chicken and cheese. Stir until the cheese is melted and the chicken is heated through. Garnish, if desired, with diced tomatoes, grated cheese, chopped scallions, and chopped cilantro.

SERVES 4–8   *A River Runs Backward,* Jacksonville, FL

A Celebration of the Volunteer

On a path of community service that began a hundred years ago, the Junior League celebrates the individual member, for it is she who rediscovers the time-tested values of voluntarism and community responsibility. She transforms these values in the light of her own insights and recharges them with her energy and spirit for future generations.

One Junior League volunteer put it this way: "We believe in the intrinsic value of voluntarism, that it makes a difference, that it changes society. It not only changes the people who are the recipients of the volunteer action, but it actually changes the hearts of the volunteers. By giving, you become a better person. When you volunteer, you receive so much more than you ever give."

The Junior League has historically provided an avenue for women to express their deep passion and caring for their communities. Caring comes in many forms. It is impossible to quantify the impact of the countless numbers of one-on-one interactions that Junior League members have had with low-birthweight babies, babies born with AIDS, underserved children eager to learn and develop them-

Through Project Reach Out, a Tulsa League volunteer shares a warm moment with a senior in a nursing home, 1983.

selves, elderly citizens alone, inmates who lack job skills training, or teens in want of adult guidance. It is impossible to document the effect of advocates who speak out in public forums for the homeless, abused and neglected children, foster families, education reform, safer environments, or domestic violence prevention.

While the spirit of voluntarism begins with one helping one, it often takes on a boldness of its own—attracting others, building a strength-on-strength, person-by-person momentum that can and does swell into a vital community force. But underlying that force remains the individual act of caring, the single act of kindness that is eternal.

As Gandhi observed, "Each one of us is setting an example for someone else, and each one of us has a responsibility to shape the future as we wish it to be." Without the caring of the individual, the Junior League as an organization has no meaning—and the concept of community has no meaning. In these pages, we celebrate the volunteer, for we cannot exist without those very individuals who are the soul of our organization.

Vegetables & Side Dishes

Vegetable Timbales with Red Pepper Purée

2 tablespoons butter plus additional
  as needed
1 medium zucchini, cut into ¼-inch
  pieces
1 small onion, chopped
4 cups packed fresh spinach leaves
  or (10-ounce) package frozen
  spinach, thawed and squeezed dry
¾ cup half-and-half
½ teaspoon salt
Dash of grated nutmeg
Dash of ground red pepper
  (cayenne)
3 large eggs
2 tablespoons grated Parmesan
  cheese

Red Pepper Purée
5 red bell peppers
1 teaspoon salt

In a large skillet, melt 2 tablespoons butter over medium heat. Add the zucchini and onion. Sauté about 3 minutes or until the onion is translucent and zucchini is tender. Add the spinach and sauté until wilted. Remove from the heat and cool slightly.

Preheat the oven to 350 degrees. In a food processor, combine the spinach mixture, half-and-half, salt, nutmeg, and red pepper. Process until smooth. Add the eggs and cheese and blend well. Coat the insides of eight 2½-inch muffin tins or custard cups with softened butter. Spoon in the timbale mixture to within ¼ inch of the rims. Place the filled tins in a roasting pan. Pour boiling water into the pan to a depth of 1 inch. Bake for about 30 minutes, or until a knife inserted into a timbale comes out clean. Remove from the oven, let stand 10 minutes, and unmold onto plates which have been spread with red pepper purée.

Roast and peel the peppers: Place the whole peppers on the rack of a broiler pan 6 inches from the heat. Broil them on all sides until they darken and blister. Remove from the heat and let cool in a sealed plastic or paper bag for 15 minutes. Peel and remove cores and seeds. Purée with salt in a food processor until smooth.

SERVES 8   *Capital Beginnings,* Ottawa, ON

AMY'S SEVEN VEGETABLE CASSEROLE

A vegetable gardener's delight.

4 small or 2 medium zucchini,
   sliced crosswise ¼ inch thick
1 large carrot, sliced very thin
   crosswise
1 large stalk celery, destringed, cut
   diagonally ¼ inch thick
½ each large red and large green
   bell pepper, cut into ½-inch
   pieces
1 banana pepper, chopped fine
   (optional)
1 large tomato, peeled and diced
½ small onion, chopped coarse
½ cup chicken broth
1½ cups grated sharp Cheddar
   cheese
Salt to taste

Preheat the oven to 350 degrees. Combine the vegetables, chicken broth, and ¾ cup of the cheese in a mixing bowl. Season with salt if desired. Place in an ungreased casserole. Cover and bake for 1 to 1½ hours. Fork-test the carrots for tenderness. Top with the remaining ¾ cup of cheese for the last 15 minutes of baking. Serve in small individual bowls or drain well with a slotted spoon.

N O T E : The casserole can be assembled up to 5 days ahead, covered, and refrigerated. Bring to room temperature and bake before serving.

S E R V E S   4 – 6   *Clock Wise Cuisine,* Detroit, MI

ACORN SQUASH WITH APPLESAUCE

2 acorn squash
2 teaspoons lemon juice
¼ cup raisins
1½ cups applesauce
¼ cup packed brown sugar
3 tablespoons chopped walnuts
Butter

Preheat the oven to 400 degrees. Scrub the squash, halve lengthwise, and scoop out the seeds. Mix together the lemon juice, raisins, applesauce, brown sugar, and walnuts. Spoon the mixture into the squash halves and dot with butter. Place in a baking dish with ½ inch of hot water in the bottom. Cover and bake for 30 minutes; remove the cover and bake for an additional 30 minutes.

S E R V E S   4   *A League of Cooks,* Greater Vancouver, BC

COMMUNITY HARVEST
JUNIOR LEAGUE OF FORT MYERS, FLORIDA

Community Harvest was kicked off by the Junior League of Fort Myers, Florida, in 1991. Junior League members pick up donated food weekly from area restaurants and food suppliers, and deliver it to the community's soup kitchens. Last year, 17,000 pounds of meat, rice, and vegetables; 2,500 loaves of bread; 415 dozen donuts; 248 cases of soft drinks; and 90 gallons of soup were donated and distributed. One of the recipients, the Southwest Florida Addiction Center, estimated that the program saves them over $2,500 a year in bakery products alone.

Asparagus Tomato Stir-Fry

1 teaspoon cornstarch dissolved in 1
   tablespoon water
2 teaspoons soy sauce
1 teaspoon salt
1 pound asparagus
1 tablespoon vegetable oil
4 scallions
1½ cups fresh mushrooms, sliced
2 small tomatoes, cut into thin
   wedges

Stir the soy sauce and salt into the dissolved cornstarch and set aside. Snap off and discard the woody bases from the asparagus. Slice the asparagus crosswise on the bias into 1½-inch lengths. Bias-slice the scallions into 1-inch lengths.

Preheat a wok or large skillet over high heat and add the oil. Stir-fry the scallions and asparagus for 3 to 4 minutes. Add the mushrooms and stir-fry 1 minute more. Add the soy sauce mixture to the vegetables. Cook and stir until thickened and bubbly. Add the tomatoes and heat through. Serve at once.

SERVES 6   *Udderly Delicious,* Racine, WI

Como's Cabbage

Mrs. Perry Como chooses this recipe because she and her husband enjoy its sweet-and-sour flavor.

4 tablespoons (½ stick) butter
1 large Bermuda onion, chopped
   fine
2 large tart green apples, peeled,
   quartered, and cut into thin slices
   or chopped
1 cabbage, about 2 pounds,
   quartered and cut into thin slices
   or chopped
⅓ cup packed light brown sugar
½ cup vinegar
Salt and pepper to taste

Melt the butter in a large heavy pot. Add the onion and sauté over medium heat until transparent, stirring constantly to prevent burning. Add the apples, cabbage, and 1 cup of water. Cook uncovered over low heat for 1 hour, stirring frequently. Add the sugar and vinegar and simmer 5-10 minutes. Season with salt and pepper.

SERVES 6–8   *Palm Beach Entertains,* Palm Beach, FL

Zesty Carrot Sticks

A welcome change from raw carrots. The longer they marinate, the better they are.

1 pound carrots, peeled and cut into
   strips
½ cup vegetable oil
½ cup white wine vinegar
1 teaspoon sugar
4 cloves garlic, coarsely chopped
1½ teaspoons dried oregano
Parsley

Combine the carrots with 1 cup of water in a saucepan and cook until tender. Drain. Mix the oil, vinegar, sugar, garlic, and oregano. Pour over the carrots and refrigerate in a tightly covered container for several hours or overnight. When ready to serve, drain and garnish with parsley.

SERVES 8   *Fare by the Sea,* Sarasota, FL

CARROTS À LA CHAMPAGNE

Carrots that are tenderly dressed with Champagne and dill.

2 pounds carrots
4 tablespoons (½ stick) butter
½ cup beef broth
1 cup very dry Champagne
2 tablespoons freshly squeezed lemon juice
1½ tablespoons minced fresh dill weed or 1½ teaspoons dried
Thin slices of lemon and sprigs of fresh dill for garnish

Clean and scrape the carrots. Slice by hand or in a food processor into thin rounds. Melt the butter in a saucepan. Sauté the carrots until they just begin to brown. Add the beef broth and Champagne. Cover and cook over medium heat until just tender but still firm. Remove the cover, turn up the heat to high, and cook until most of the liquid is cooked away. Remove from the heat. Add the lemon juice and dill. Toss well and serve. Garnish individual servings or vegetable bowl with thin slices of lemon and sprigs of fresh dill weed.

SERVES 6–8   *A Matter of Taste*, Morristown, NJ

GLAZED CARROTS AND PARSNIPS

A colorful vegetable for a dinner party.

10 medium carrots
5 medium parsnips
2 cups apple juice
5 tablespoons butter
5 tablespoons honey
2 tablespoons lemon juice
1 tablespoon chopped fresh mint leaves or 1 teaspoon dried
Pinch of grated nutmeg
Pinch of ground black pepper

Peel the vegetables and cut into 3-inch julienne strips. Cook in a saucepan with the apple juice and 2 cups of water until tender. Drain and discard the liquid. Add the butter, honey, lemon juice, mint, nutmeg, and pepper. Cook, uncovered for 3 minutes over medium heat, stirring to glaze.

SERVES 6–8   *Jubilation*, Toronto, ON

JOANNA'S GREEN CORN CAKES

These may be made with buttermilk, but only Yankees desecrate them with syrup.

6 small ears of fresh corn
½ teaspoon salt
1 teaspoon baking soda
1 cup all-purpose flour
2 egg yolks
1 cup sour milk or buttermilk

Place a cast-iron griddle over medium-low heat while you make the batter.

Husk the corn, cut the kernels off the cobs, and process the kernels briefly in a blender or food processor. Transfer to a mixing bowl and beat in the egg yolks and sour milk.

Stir the flour, salt, and baking soda together and mix quickly with the corn. Use about 1 tablespoon for each pancake and pour onto the hot griddle. Cook until golden brown on both sides. Serve with butter.

MAKES 10–15 CAKES   *Nashville Seasons*, Nashville, TN

CORN MAQUE CHOUX

¾ cup chopped onion
¾ cup bacon fat
10 ears fresh corn, kernels cut from cob
4 Creole or Rotel tomatoes, peeled and chopped
⅓ cup minced green bell pepper
1 teaspoon salt
1 teaspoon black pepper

In a skillet, sauté the onion in the bacon fat until transparent, about 5 minutes. Add the corn and cook 10 minutes, stirring constantly. Add the tomatoes and green pepper and cook 5 minutes or until very soft. Add salt and pepper. Serve as a vegetable or use in a baked stuffed green pepper or tomato.

SERVES 8   *Plantation Cookbook*, New Orleans, LA

IMAM BAYELDI (BAKED EGGPLANT)

"The Emperor swooned." Ancient tradition in the Middle East holds that when the Imam first tasted this dish, he fainted with ecstasy!

1 medium eggplant
1 teaspoon salt
2 tablespoons olive oil or vegetable oil, or as needed
2 medium onions, sliced very thin
3 cloves garlic, minced
½ cup finely chopped parsley
1 cup tomato sauce
Salt and pepper to taste

Rinse the eggplant; cut off and discard the stem end. Divide the eggplant into 8 equal pieces by cutting lengthwise in half, crosswise in half, then each piece in half. Sprinkle the cut sides with salt; let stand 2 hours in a colander to drain off excess moisture. Rinse with cold water and pat dry with paper towels. Heat the oven to 350 degrees. Put the oil in a medium skillet over medium-high heat and brown the eggplant on all sides. Transfer to a 2-quart baking dish; arrange the pieces skin side down. In the same skillet brown the onions in oil over medium heat. Stir in the garlic, parsley, tomato sauce, salt, and pepper; bring to a boil. Remove from the heat. Evenly cover the eggplant pieces with the mixture. Cover and bake for ½ hour.

SERVES 4–6   *Discover Dayton*, Dayton, OH

EGGPLANT PARMIGIANA

1 cup milk
1 egg, slightly beaten
1 cup all-purpose flour
2 medium eggplants, peeled and cut into ½-inch slices
1 (29-ounce) can tomato sauce
1 (12-ounce) can tomato paste
1 (16-ounce) can tomatoes, drained
¼ cup Burgundy wine
1 teaspoon dried whole oregano
½ teaspoon dried whole basil
¼ teaspoon dried whole thyme
¼ teaspoon garlic salt
10 to 16 slices mozzarella cheese
Grated Parmesan cheese

Heat the oven to 350 degrees. Lightly oil a 13 × 9 × 2-inch baking dish, combine the milk, egg, and 1 tablespoon of vegetable oil; gradually add the flour, beating until smooth. Heat 3 or 4 tablespoons of oil in a heavy skillet over medium-high heat. Dip the eggplant slices, a few at a time, into the batter and fry in hot oil until golden. Drain well on paper towels; set aside. In a medium saucepan, combine the tomato sauce and paste, the drained tomatoes, wine, and spices, mixing well. Simmer the sauce 10 minutes. Arrange half the eggplant slices in the prepared baking dish. Top with half the mozzarella slices. Spoon half the tomato mixture over the cheese. Repeat the layers. Top with a sprinkling of Parmesan cheese. Bake uncovered for 30 to 40 minutes or until the sauce is bubbly. Allow to stand at room temperature for 15 minutes; cut into squares to serve.

SERVES 6–8   *Sooner Sampler*, Norman, OK

HARICOTS VERTS IN PLUM TOMATOES

An elegant presentation for a special dinner party.

4 plum tomatoes
48 haricots, or very thin green beans
¾ cup olive oil
⅓ cup red wine vinegar
1 tablespoon Dijon mustard
Salt and freshly ground pepper to taste

Slice off the top and bottom of each tomato. Remove the pulp with a spoon to create hollow cylinders; set aside. Trim the stem ends of the green beans. Steam the beans in a saucepan for 3 to 5 minutes or just until tender; do not overcook. Place 12 green beans, or as many as will fit, in each tomato; arrange the tomatoes on a serving plate. Combine the olive oil, vinegar, mustard, salt, and pepper in a bowl or blender container; whisk or process until smooth. Drizzle 1 teaspoon of the vinaigrette over each tomato.

SERVES 4   *I'll Taste Manhattan,* New York, NY

GREEN BEANS IN DILL SAUCE

1½ pounds fresh green beans, rinsed and dried, stem ends removed
2 tablespoons sugar
⅓ cup cider vinegar
⅔ cup olive oil
¾ cup thinly sliced scallions, tops included
3 tablespoons chopped parsley
3 tablespoons minced fresh dill or 1½ teaspoons dried
½ cup coarsely chopped walnuts
Salt and ground black pepper
Dill sprigs for garnish

To cook the green beans by the Paul Meyers method: Place 2 tablespoons of sugar in a heavy medium saucepan. At the same time, bring 2 cups of water to a boil in another saucepan. Turn the heat on to high in the pan with the sugar. Watch the sugar carefully, and when it just begins to melt and bubble, place the beans in the pan, then immediately pour the boiling water over the vegetables. Work with caution to avoid being scalded. Cover the pan and cook until tender, about 3 to 5 minutes. Drain and run cool water over the beans to stop the cooking process. Drain again thoroughly.

Blend the vinegar and oil into an emulsion by pouring the vinegar into food processor or blender, then adding oil in a slow thin stream. Whirl the emulsion for 1 minute; stir in the scallions, parsley, dill, and walnuts. Toss the mixture with the beans while they are still warm; season with salt and freshly ground pepper to taste. Chill for a few hours. Bring the beans to room temperature and garnish with sprigs of fresh dill before serving.

SERVES 8   *California Treasure,* Fresno, CA

BAKED LEEKS AND GARDEN FRESH TOMATOES

4 leeks
4 tablespoons (½ stick) butter
4 ripe tomatoes
Salt and pepper to taste
2 to 3 tablespoons chopped fresh
   basil
1½ teaspoons cornstarch
½ cup heavy cream

Preheat the oven to 375 degrees. Trim off roots and the green part of the leeks. Wash the white stalks thoroughly to remove all grit; cut into 1-inch pieces.

Melt the butter in an ovenproof skillet, add the leeks, and bake for 10 minutes. Cut the tomatoes in half horizontally; sprinkle with salt, pepper, and basil. Put the tomatoes cut side down on the leeks and reduce the oven temperature to 350 degrees. Bake 5 minutes, then turn the tomatoes over and bake 5 minutes longer. Remove from the oven.

Mix the cornstarch with the cream and whisk until smooth. Remove the tomatoes to a hot platter and stir the cream mixture into the leeks. Place the skillet over medium heat and cook until the sauce thickens slightly. Use a spatula to spread the resulting leek sauce over the tomatoes.

SERVES 4

Maine Ingredients, Portland, ME

ST. ANTHONY HOTEL'S FAMOUS SPINACH PUDDING

This is a very old recipe, tried and proven many times.

1 (10-ounce) package fresh spinach
½ cup chopped celery
¼ cup chopped parsley
1 small clove garlic, minced, or ¼
   cup finely chopped onion
3 eggs
1 cup freshly made fine white bread
   crumbs, plus additional as needed
4 tablespoons (½ stick) butter,
   softened, plus additional as needed
Salt and pepper to taste

Remove the stems from the spinach and wash thoroughly. In the water that clings to the leaves, cook the spinach until just tender. Press the spinach in a colander, reserving the liquid, to get it completely dry. Put the spinach, celery, parsley, and garlic or onion through a grinder or purée in a food processor. This yields approximately 1 cup of spinach mixture.

Mix the spinach with the eggs, 1 cup of bread crumbs, 4 tablespoons of butter, the salt, and pepper. Cut several thicknesses of cheesecloth approximately 8 × 18 inches. Spread the cheesecloth with additional butter, then sprinkle with enough bread crumbs to cover the butter. Spoon the spinach on the cheesecloth lengthwise along a short end. Gently roll the cheesecloth around the spinach. Tie both ends and also the center if necessary. In a skillet or saucepan, bring the reserved spinach liquid and enough water to cover the spinach roll to a boil. Add the spinach roll and boil for 30 minutes. Cool. The spinach roll may be frozen at this point. When ready to use, slice, place in a buttered casserole, cover, and heat at 350 degrees about 10 minutes.

SERVES 12

Flavors, San Antonio, TX

SKILLET SPINACH

2 tablespoons butter
1 tablespoon flour
1 tablespoon grated onion
2 cups frozen or cooked fresh
   spinach
3 eggs
½ cup grated Cheddar cheese
Salt and pepper to taste

In a skillet, melt the butter; stir in the flour and onion. Cook the mixture over moderate heat, stirring for 5 minutes or until it is lightly browned. Add frozen spinach, broken into chunks and cook it over moderate heat for 5 minutes or until it is thawed. If using cooked fresh spinach, heat and stir until thoroughly hot. Beat the eggs lightly and stir in. Add the cheese, salt, and pepper and cook for 5 minutes longer or until the eggs are set and cheese is melted.

S E R V E S 3–4   *Home Cookin'*, Wichita Falls, TX

SWEET AND SOUR SQUASH

This is a tasty substitute for the ubiquitous tossed green salad at summer barbecues.

4 small zucchini
4 small yellow squash
½ cup chopped celery (optional)
1 red onion, chopped fine (optional)
1 red bell pepper, seeded and
   chopped (optional)
1 cup sherry wine vinegar
½ cup sugar
⅓ cup olive oil
1 teaspoon salt
1 teaspoon freshly ground black
   pepper

Slice the zucchini and yellow squash paper-thin into a large shallow bowl. Add the celery, red onion, and bell pepper, if you wish. Combine the remaining ingredients in a saucepan. Bring to a boil and stir to dissolve the sugar. Pour the dressing over the vegetables while still hot. Cover and marinate at room temperature or chill overnight. Drain and serve.

N O T E : If you have just plucked the squash from the vine, you may wish to marinate it only an hour at room temperature to preserve the fresh quality, but overnight will please you, too.

S E R V E S 8   *Private Collection 2*, Palo Alto, CA

STUFFED BAKED TOMATOES

8 medium tomatoes
Salt
¼ cup olive oil
6 scallions, chopped
1 (10-ounce) package frozen
   chopped spinach, thawed and
   squeezed dry
⅓ cup chopped fresh parsley
½ teaspoon dried basil
½ teaspoon dried thyme
6 tablespoons crumbled feta cheese

Slice the tops off the tomatoes. Scoop out the pulp and reserve. Lightly salt the inside of the tomatoes and invert on paper towels to drain.

Sauté the scallions and chopped tomato pulp in the olive oil in a medium skillet for 3 to 4 minutes. Add the spinach, parsley, basil, and thyme. Cook over medium high heat until the liquid evaporates, stirring frequently. Stir in 3 tablespoons of the feta cheese.

Stuff the tomato shells with the spinach mixture. Place in a greased baking dish. Sprinkle the remaining cheese over top. The tomatoes may be refrigerated at this point until ready to heat. Before serving, place in a preheated 375 degree oven for 10 to 15 minutes, until heated through. Do not let the skins split.

S E R V E S 6–8   *Mountain Measures—A Second Serving*, Charleston, WV

Fresh Tomato Tart

Basic pastry dough (page 338)
8 ounces mozzarella cheese, shredded
2 tablespoons chopped fresh basil
4 or 5 ripe tomatoes, in ½-inch slices
½ teaspoon salt
¼ teaspoon pepper
1 tablespoon extra virgin olive oil
Chopped fresh basil for garnish

Preheat the oven to 400 degrees. Line a 10-inch loose-bottom tart pan with pastry dough. Cover the bottom of the pastry with cheese and sprinkle with basil. Arrange the tomato slices to cover the cheese as evenly as possible. Sprinkle the tomatoes with salt and pepper and drizzle with oil. Bake 30 to 40 minutes. Garnish with chopped basil. Slice in wedges and serve warm or at room temperature.

SERVES 8–10

Come on In!, Jackson, MS

Vera Cruz tomatoes

4 tomatoes
Salt
3 strips bacon
¼ cup chopped onion
8 ounces fresh spinach, rinsed and dried, coarse stems removed
¼ cup sour cream
½ shredded mozzarella cheese

Cut a thin slice from the top of each tomato and scoop out the insides with a teaspoon. Sprinkle the shells with salt and invert on paper towels to drain while you prepare the stuffing.

In a large skillet, fry the bacon until crisp; drain on paper towels and crumble. Pour off all but 2 tablespoons of fat. Cook the onions in the bacon drippings for 5 minutes. Snip the spinach into medium-size pieces, stir into the skillet, and cook for 3 to 5 minutes, until wilted. Remove from the heat and allow to cool. Meanwhile, heat the oven to 375 degrees.

Add the sour cream and bacon to the spinach; stir well to combine. Fill the tomatoes with the mixture and place in a greased 8-inch baking dish or pie plate. Bake for 20 to 30 minutes, until tender. Top with the shredded cheese and bake 2 to 3 minutes more.

SERVES 4

Cookbook, Grand Rapids, MI

World's Best Turnip Greens

5 or 6 strips bacon
1 small onion, chopped
2 tablespoons chopped green pepper
1 teaspoon sugar
1 teaspoon salt
1 tablespoon vinegar
Dash of Tabasco
3 pounds turnip greens, well washed, coarse stems removed
1 hard-boiled egg, chopped

Cut the bacon into small pieces and cook in a large Dutch oven until crisp. Remove with a slotted spoon and drain on paper towels. Sauté the onion and green pepper in the bacon drippings for 5 to 8 minutes, until soft. Add the sugar, salt, vinegar, Tabasco, and greens. Cook over medium heat for 15 minutes, until the greens are wilted. Reduce the heat and continue cooking for 30 minutes or until tender. Garnish with reserved bacon and chopped egg.

SERVES 4

Magic, Birmingham, AL

ZUCCHINI MILANO

A zesty dish from an old family restaurant in Milan. This was so popular that the recipe was printed and made available for the asking, but only if your I.D. showed that you were not from Milan.

7 or 8 medium zucchini, cut into
  ¼-inch slices
2 teaspoons salt
8 slices bacon, diced
1 large onion, chopped
1 large clove garlic, minced
4 slices light or dark bread, diced
2 cups shredded mozzarella or
  Cheddar cheese
1 teaspoon Italian seasoning (or
  combination of oregano,
  marjoram, and basil to make 1
  teaspoon)
Dash of freshly ground black pepper
1 (15-ounce) can tomato sauce
¼ cup grated Parmesan cheese

Preheat the oven to 350 degrees. Lightly oil a 13 × 9-inch ovenproof dish.

In a large saucepan, cook the zucchini in 1 cup of boiling water with 1 teaspoon of salt until barely tender, about 3 to 5 minutes. Drain. In a skillet, cook the bacon until crisp; remove from the pan with a slotted spoon. Drain and put in a bowl. Add the onion and garlic to the skillet and sauté 5 to 6 minutes, until tender. Drain. Add to the bacon.

Stir the onion-bacon mixture into the drained zucchini; add the bread, cheese, Italian seasoning, remaining teaspoon of salt, pepper, and tomato sauce. Toss lightly until well coated. Spoon the zucchini into the prepared dish. Sprinkle with Parmesan cheese. Bake 20 minutes or until bubbly.

SERVES 10–12   *Tennessee Tables,* Knoxville, TN

MINTED ZUCCHINI

2 pounds zucchini
2 tablespoons olive oil
1 tablespoon butter
1 teaspoon salt
½ teaspoon ground black pepper
½ cup chopped fresh mint
¼ teaspoon sugar
Fresh mint sprigs for garnish

Cut the zucchini into eighths lengthwise to form sticks. Cut the sticks in half crosswise. Heat the oil and butter in a large skillet or wok. Add the zucchini and cook over medium-high heat, for 3 to 5 minutes. Add the salt, pepper, chopped mint, and sugar. Sauté for 3 to 5 minutes more. Do not overcook. Garnish with fresh mint sprigs.

SERVES 4   *Gourmet L.A.,* Los Angeles, CA

ZUCCHINI PANCAKES

2 eggs
3 tablespoons all-purpose flour, as
  needed
2 tablespoons Parmesan cheese
1 tablespoon sherry
1 teaspoon chopped chives
1 teaspoon chopped fresh parsley or
  ¼ teaspoon dried
Garlic salt
Salt and ground black pepper
2 cups grated zucchini

Heat in cast-iron skillet or griddle over moderate heat. In a mixing bowl, beat the eggs lightly and add the flour, cheese, sherry, chives, parsley, and seasonings. Stir to blend; fold in the grated zucchini. If the mixture is too thin, add more flour. Fry like pancakes over moderate heat until brown on both sides.

SERVES 4   *Thru the Grapevine,* Greater Elmira–Corning, NY

BAKED ZUCCHINI

1½ pounds zucchini, scrubbed and
  trimmed
1 onion, chopped
1½ tablespoons butter
½ teaspoon poppy seeds
½ teaspoon garlic salt
½ teaspoon ground black pepper
Grated Parmesan cheese

Preheat the oven to 375 degrees. Lightly butter a medium-size baking dish.

Slice the squash into ¼-inch-thick rounds. Boil gently in salted water with the onion for 7 to 10 minutes, until tender. Drain in a colander. Add the butter, poppy seeds, and seasonings, mix together, and place in the prepared baking dish. Sprinkle all over with Parmesan cheese. Bake uncovered for 30 minutes.

SERVES 6   *Recipe Jubilee,* Mobile, AL

CINNAMON APPLES

2 cups sugar
4 or 5 cinnamon sticks
8-10 medium apples

In a large saucepan, combine the sugar, the cinnamon sticks, and 1 cup of water. If desired add a few drops of red food coloring. Bring to a boil. Peel and core the apples. Cook them in the syrup, turning as needed, for 15 to 20 minutes or until tender. Remove from the syrup with a slotted spoon and cool to room temperature. These are especially good chilled and stuffed with cream cheese.

SERVES 8 TO 10   *From Market to Mealtime,* Fayetteville, NC

NASSAU GRITS

This is an excellent dish with fried fish.

1 pound sliced bacon
2 green bell peppers, chopped fine
2 medium onions, chopped fine
1 (28-ounce) can whole tomatoes, chopped
1½ cups finely ground ham
1½ cups white hominy grits

In a nonreactive skillet, cook the bacon until crisp; drain on paper towels. Pour off all but 2 or 3 tablespoons of the drippings. Cook the peppers and onions in the same skillet for 7 to 8 minutes, until soft. Add the tomatoes and simmer uncovered for 30 minutes. Stir in the ham.

In a separate saucepan, cook the grits according to package directions. When the grits are cooked, add the ham mixture and stir well. Serve hot with bacon crumbled on top.

SERVES 12   *Some Like It South,* Pensacola, FL

GRITS SOUFFLÉ

1 cup cooked grits
3 tablespoons hot milk
2 tablespoons finely chopped onion
3 egg yolks
½ cup grated Cheddar cheese
3 egg whites, beaten stiff

Heat the oven to 350 degrees. Combine the grits, hot milk, and onion in a bowl; stir until blended. Beat the egg yolks until thick and lemon colored. Stir the yolks and cheese into the grits mixture. Fold in the egg whites. Pour the mixture into an ungreased 1-quart casserole. Place the dish in a roasting pan and pour boiling water to a depth of 1 inch into the roasting pan. Bake in the preheated oven 1 hour without opening the oven door.

SERVES 4   *A Taste of Tampa,* Tampa, FL

EASY BAKED POLENTA

A perfect accompaniment to lamb, pork, or game.

1½ cups yellow cornmeal
1 large Spanish onion, sliced
½ cup plus 2 tablespoons olive oil
¼ cup grated Parmesan cheese
½ cup chopped Italian parsley
2 eggs, lightly beaten
1 pound ripe plum tomatoes, chopped coarse
1 small onion, chopped
1 medium clove garlic, minced
1 cup vegetable stock or chicken broth
½ cup firmly packed chopped fresh spinach
¼ cup slivered almonds, toasted
½ teaspoon salt
⅛ teaspoon ground black pepper

Preheat the oven to 350 degrees. In a 3-quart saucepan, gradually stir the cornmeal into 1 quart of boiling salted water. Cook, stirring constantly with a wire whisk, for 4 minutes. Reduce the heat to low. Cook 10 minutes, stirring occasionally, to make the polenta.

In an ovenproof 10-inch skillet, sauté the sliced onion in ¼ cup of olive oil for 5 minutes or until translucent. Stir into the hot polenta. Add the Parmesan, parsley, and eggs and stir to combine.

Pour 2 tablespoons of oil into the skillet; spread the polenta evenly in the skillet. Top with 2 tablespoons of oil. Bake uncovered for 1 hour or until golden.

Meanwhile, in a saucepan, heat the remaining 2 tablespoons of oil. Add the tomatoes, chopped onion, and garlic. Cook, stirring occasionally, until the onion is tender. Add the remaining ingredients. Simmer 10 minutes. Serve the sauce with the polenta.

SERVES 6–8   *The Beautiful Arbor,* Ann Arbor, MI

CORNMEAL MUSH BREAD

A cross between cornbread and a corn souf-flé. The outside will be crunchy with a moist inside.

1 (8½-ounce) can cream-style corn
1 cup sour cream
1 cup self-rising cornmeal (see Note)
½ teaspoon salt
2 eggs
½ cup vegetable oil

Preheat the oven to 350 degrees. Grease a medium-size cast-iron skillet and place in the oven to heat while you prepare the batter.

In a mixing bowl, combine the corn, sour cream, cornmeal, salt, and eggs. Stir well. Add the vegetable oil and stir until blended. Pour the batter into the heated skillet and bake 25 to 30 minutes, until the top is golden brown.

N O T E : If self-rising cornmeal is not available, use regular cornmeal plus ½ teaspoon salt and 1 level teaspoon baking powder.

S E R V E S 4 – 6   *Encore! Nashville,* Nashville, TN

BLACK BEANS CILANTRO

Wonderful as a side dish, or serve with flour tortillas and fresh salad as a distinctive main course.

1 pound dried black beans, rinsed
  and picked over
2 quarts chicken broth
¼ cup olive oil
1 onion, chopped
5 cloves garlic, chopped
2 fresh hot chiles, seeded and chopped
¼ cup chopped fresh parsley
½ cup chopped fresh cilantro

Put the beans in a large stockpot and add the chicken broth. Bring to a boil over the heat, and simmer, covered, without stirring, until the stock starts to turn black, approximately 2 hours. Add the onion, garlic, chiles, parsley, and cilantro. Continue to simmer another 30 minutes, until the beans are tender and the liquid is slightly thick. Serve with a combination of sour cream, grated Monterey Jack and Cheddar cheese, salsa, and chopped cilantro.

S E R V E S 6   *Feast of Eden,* Monterey, CA

HOPPIN' JOHN

A traditional New Year's Day feast is Hoppin' John served with collard greens: the peas for plenty of pocket change and the greens for folding money all through the year.

½ pound slab bacon or ham hock
1 cup dried black-eyed peas, rinsed
  and picked over
1 teaspoon salt
½ teaspoon ground black pepper
⅛ teaspoon ground red pepper
  (cayenne)
1 cup raw rice
Chopped onion

Cut the bacon into ¼-inch cubes and fry in a skillet, stirring, until browned. Remove with a slotted spoon and drain on paper towels. Set aside.

In a saucepan, combine the peas with 4 cups of cold water, the salt, black pepper, and red pepper. Add 2 to 3 tablespoons of the bacon drippings. Bring to a boil, lower the heat, and simmer, covered, for about 1 hour and 15 minutes, or until tender but not mushy. Approximately 1 cup of liquid should remain; boil uncovered to reduce the liquid if necessary.

When the peas are almost ready, cook the rice according to package directions. Stir into the peas, heat for 2 or 3 minutes, and serve garnished with the bacon and chopped onion.

S E R V E S 4 – 6   *Atlanta Cooknotes,* Atlanta, GA

REAL CAJUN RED BEANS AND RICE

1 pound dried red beans, picked over and rinsed
½ pound salt pork
3 cups chopped onion
1 bunch scallions, chopped
1 cup chopped parsley
1 cup chopped green bell pepper
2 large cloves garlic, crushed
1 tablespoon salt
1 teaspoon ground red pepper (cayenne), or to taste
1 teaspoon ground black pepper
3 generous dashes Tabasco, or to taste
1 tablespoon Worcestershire sauce
¼ teaspoon dried oregano
¼ teaspoon dried thyme
1 (8-ounce) can tomato sauce
1 pound bulk sausage made into 8 to 10 tiny patties (optional)
2 cups raw rice, cooked according to package directions

Soak the beans overnight in water to cover. Drain just before using.

Put the drained beans, salt pork, and 2 quarts of water in a stockpot. Cover, bring to a boil, lower the heat, and simmer for 45 minutes.

Add the vegetables, seasonings, and tomato sauce. Cook slowly for another hour, stirring occasionally. Add the sausage for extra body if desired. Cook 45 minutes more. The dish may be prepared in advance up to this point.

Before serving bring to a boil, lower the heat, and simmer gently 30 to 40 minutes. Serve over boiled rice.

SERVES 6   *A Cook's Tour,* Shreveport, LA

SOUTH LOUISIANA RED BEANS

Cornbread goes well with red beans.

1 pound dried red kidney beans, picked over and rinsed
1 pound pepperoni, sliced
1 large onion, chopped
1 clove garlic, chopped
Ham bone with generous amount of meat
1 bay leaf
Dash of ground red pepper (cayenne)
Cumin powder to taste

Cover the beans with cold water and soak overnight. Drain.

In a large heavy kettle, cook the pepperoni, onion, and garlic over medium heat until slightly browned. Add the drained beans, the ham bone, bay leaf, red pepper, and cumin. Pour in enough cold water to cover.

Bring to a boil, lower the heat, and simmer, covered, for about 2½ hours. Remove ham bone and bay leaf before serving.

SERVES 8   *River Road Recipes,* Baton Rouge, LA

OLD SETTLER'S BAKED BEANS

Great for picnics and cookouts.

½ **pound sliced bacon, cut into
pieces**
1 **onion, chopped coarse**
1 **pound ground beef**
1 **(15-ounce) can red kidney beans,
drained**
1 **(15-ounce) can pork and beans**
1 **(15-ounce) can butter beans,
drained**
¼ **cup packed light brown sugar**
¼ **cup granulated sugar**
¼ **cup ketchup**
¼ **cup bottled barbecue sauce**
2 **tablespoons prepared mustard**
1 **teaspoon salt**
2 **tablespoons molasses**
½ **teaspoon ground black pepper**
½ **teaspoon chili powder**

Preheat the oven to 350 degrees. Lightly grease a 4-quart baking dish. Fry the bacon in a medium-sized skillet until crisp. Remove from the pan and drain. Sauté the onion in the bacon drippings. Remove from the pan and drain. Brown the beef and drain well.

In a large bowl, combine all the ingredients and stir well. Turn into the prepared baking dish. Cover and bake 1 hour.

SERVES 6–8   *Sassafras! The Ozarks Cookbook,* Springfield, MO

RAVE REVIEW BAKED BEANS

1 **pound loose sausage or ground
beef**
1 **onion, chopped**
1 **bell pepper, chopped**
2 **(16-ounce) cans pork and beans**
½ **cup packed light brown sugar**
¼ **cup molasses**
1 **teaspoon dry mustard**
2 **teaspoons Worcestershire sauce**
½ **cup ketchup**
Ground black pepper to taste

Preheat the oven to 325 degrees. Lightly grease a medium-size casserole.

Brown the meat in a skillet, stirring to break into bite-sized pieces; remove from the skillet. Brown the onion and bell pepper in the meat drippings. Drain the meat, onion, and pepper well. Stir together the pork and beans, brown sugar, molasses, mustard, Worcestershire, ketchup, and black pepper. Mix in the meat, onion and bell pepper. Pour into the prepared casserole. Bake uncovered for about an hour or until the liquid is slightly thickened and the meat is tender.

SERVES 6–8   *Rave Reviews,* North Little Rock, AR

POTATOES WITH SHIITAKES AND BRIE

Great with grilled sausages and a mixed green salad.

6 new potatoes, scrubbed
1 teaspoon unsalted butter
8 ounces shiitake mushrooms, wiped and trimmed
1 small whole round Brie cheese
Salt and freshly ground black pepper to taste
1 cup heavy cream
1 clove garlic, minced
1 teaspoon dried thyme
3 tablespoons grated Parmesan cheese
¼ cup fine dry bread crumbs

Slice the unpeeled potatoes ⅛ inch thick. Cover with cold water in a bowl. Let stand for 30 minutes, changing the water twice. Drain the slices and pat dry.

Preheat the oven to 425 degrees. Coat a 10-inch baking dish with the unsalted butter. Remove the stems from the mushrooms and discard. Slice the caps thin. Remove the rind from the cheese and cut the cheese into cubes. (This is more easily done with cold firm cheese.) Layer one-third of the potato slices in the buttered baking dish. Layer half the mushrooms and Brie, sprinkling the layers with salt and pepper. Repeat the layers with the remaining potatoes, mushrooms, and Brie. Combine the cream, garlic, and thyme in a small bowl; mix well and pour over the layers, pressing the layers into the liquid.

Cover the casserole with foil and bake for 30 minutes. Remove the foil. Sprinkle with a mixture of the Parmesan cheese and bread crumbs. Bake uncovered for 30 minutes longer or until the top is golden brown and crusty.

SERVES 6   *I'll Taste Manhattan,* New York, NY

POTATO AND CARROT CASSEROLE

4 tablespoons (½ stick) butter
6 to 7 cups potatoes, peeled and cut into ⅛-inch slices
2 cups carrots, cut into ⅛-inch slices and lightly steamed until crisp-tender
Vegetable seasoning salt
Freshly ground pepper
1 cup grated Swiss cheese
1¼ cups heavy cream

Preheat the oven to 300 degrees. Grease a medium-size flameproof baking dish.

Layer the potatoes and carrots in the baking dish, seasoning each layer. Sprinkle each layer with cheese and dot with butter. Pour the cream over the potatoes and carrots. Slowly bring the casserole to almost simmering on top of the stove. Cover and place in the middle of the oven. Bake uncovered for 1 to 1¼ hours, never letting the cream bubble. The dish is ready when the cream has been absorbed and the top is lightly browned.

SERVES 6   *Pride of Peoria,* Peoria, IL

NEW POTATOES AND HERBED SHALLOT BUTTER

1¼ pounds small new potatoes
1 tablespoon butter
⅓ cup finely chopped shallots
2 cloves garlic, minced
½ teaspoon dried tarragon
1 teaspoon snipped chives
1 teaspoon chopped fresh parsley or ½ teaspoon dried
¼ teaspoon salt
⅛ teaspoon freshly ground pepper

Cook the potatoes in boiling water, covered, until just tender, about 15 minutes. Melt the butter in a large skillet. Add the shallots and garlic and sauté over low heat until softened, about 5 minutes. Add the cooked potatoes to the skillet and stir well. Season with the tarragon, chives, parsley, salt, and pepper and cook, stirring, until the potatoes are heated through.

SERVES 6   *Gold'n Delicious,* Spokane, WA

WHITE CHEDDAR PARSNIPS AND POTATOES

2 pounds parsnips
2 pounds potatoes
⅓ cup heavy cream or as needed
3 to 4 tablespoons butter, or to
    taste, plus additional for topping
Salt and freshly ground pepper
Freshly grated nutmeg
1 pound white Cheddar cheese,
    grated

Peel the parsnips and potatoes and cut into small pieces. Combine in a deep saucepan, cover with water, and cook until tender, about 20 minutes.

Meanwhile, preheat the oven to 350 degrees. Butter a 13 × 9-inch baking dish.

Drain the potatoes and parsnips well and whip with cream and butter to the consistency of mashed potatoes. Season with salt, pepper, and nutmeg.

Spread the bottom of the prepared dish with half the potato-parsnip mixture and top with half of the grated cheese. Repeat, finishing with remaining cheese on top. Dot with butter. Bake uncovered for 15 to 20 minutes or until hot.

VARIATION: As an alternative presentation, transfer the purée to a pastry bag fitted with a large star tip and pipe individual portions onto a baking sheet. Sprinkle with grated cheese and bake until the cheese melts.

SERVES 8–10   *Above and Beyond Parsley,* Kansas City, MO

BUCK'S TATERS

Great for cookouts.

6 baking potatoes
4 onions, sliced thin
Seasoned salt
Freshly ground pepper to taste
6 tablespoons butter

Preheat the oven to 400 degrees.

Peel the potatoes. Make crosswise slices in the potatoes about ¼ inch apart, being careful not to cut all the way through. About every second slice in each potato, insert a slice of onion. Sprinkle with seasoned salt and pepper. Place 1 tablespoon of butter on top and wrap each potato in foil. Bake for 1 hour.

SERVES 6   *To Market, to Market,* Owensboro, KY

TWICE BAKED POTATOES

4 large baking potatoes, scrubbed
8 tablespoons (1 stick) butter
2 teaspoons salt
¼ teaspoon ground black pepper
⅛ teaspoon ground red pepper
    (cayenne)
¼ cup milk, or as needed
2 egg yolks, beaten
1 cup shredded sharp Cheddar
    cheese

Preheat the oven to 400 degrees. Bake the potatoes on a rack for 1 hour or until soft. Allow them to cool slightly.

Cut the potatoes in half, scoop out the pulp, and place in a mixing bowl, setting the skins aside. Add the butter, salt, and black and red pepper. Mash well, adding enough milk to make a fairly stiff mixture. Add the beaten egg yolks and stir well.

Spoon the mixture into the potato skins and top with shredded cheese. Place on a cookie sheet and bake for 20 minutes, until well browned.

SERVES 8   *Hearts & Flours,* Waco, TX

GRATIN DAUPHINOIS

4 tablespoons (½ stick) butter
2 pounds potatoes, peeled
2 cups milk
1½ cups heavy cream
1 large or 2 small cloves garlic, minced
¾ teaspoon salt
½ teaspoon freshly ground white pepper
2 to 4 ounces grated Swiss cheese

Heat the oven to 400 degrees. Coat a 2- or 3-quart baking dish with 1 tablespoon of the butter.

Slice the potatoes ⅛ inch thick and place in a large saucepan. Add the milk, cream, garlic, salt, and pepper. Bring to a boil over moderate heat, stirring to prevent scorching. Remove the pan from the heat. Pour the potato mixture into the prepared baking dish. Sprinkle grated cheese on top and dot with the remaining 3 tablespoons of butter. To avoid spills on the oven floor, set the baking dish on a rimmed cookie sheet. Place in the oven and bake uncovered for 30 minutes. Reduce the heat to 350 degrees and continue baking 30 minutes. The potatoes are done when they are nicely browned and the tip of a knife pierces the potatoes easily. Allow the dish to stand 15 to 20 minutes before serving.

SERVES 8 *Second Round Tea-Time at the Masters*, Augusta, GA

GREEK POTATOES

4 to 6 medium-sized potatoes
2 tablespoons butter
2 tablespoons olive oil
1 tablespoon lemon juice
1 teaspoon dried oregano
1 teaspoon dried parsley flakes
1 teaspoon salt
¼ teaspoon freshly ground pepper

Peel the potatoes and cut into 1- to 1½-inch wedges. Heat the butter and oil in a large skillet. Add the potatoes and lemon juice. Sauté to an even brown, turning potatoes to brown on all sides. Cover the skillet and continue to cook until the potatoes are tender, approximately 20 minutes. Uncover the skillet, sprinkle the potatoes with the seasonings, mix, and serve.

SERVES 6 *Hunt to Harbor—An Epicurean Tour*, Baltimore, MD

SWEET POTATO SOUFFLÉ

1 tablespoon butter
1 pound sweet potatoes, boiled and peeled (4 medium)
1½ cups light cream
¼ cup sugar, or more to taste
1 teaspoon vanilla extract
½ cup sherry
Juice of 1 orange
Grated rind of 1 orange
Salt to taste
4 egg yolks, well beaten
4 egg whites, beaten stiff

Preheat the oven to 400 degrees. Butter a shallow 2-quart baking dish.

Press the sweet potatoes through a sieve or purée in a blender. In a mixing bowl, combine the purée with the butter, cream, sugar, vanilla, wine, orange juice, grated rind, and salt. When cool, stir the egg yolks, then lightly fold in the egg whites. Transfer to the baking dish and bake for about 40 minutes or until firm.

SERVES 8 *Texas Tables*, Dallas, TX

SWEET POTATO CASSEROLE

8 sweet potatoes
8 tablespoons (1 stick) butter
2 eggs, beaten
¼ cup tablespoons sherry
¼ teaspoons grated nutmeg
Salt and pepper to taste
½ cup chopped pecans
Marshmallows

Preheat the oven to 350 degrees. Lightly oil a rectangular baking dish.

Boil, peel, and mash the sweet potatoes. Add 6 tablespoons of the butter, the eggs and sherry. Whip the potatoes until fluffy. Add the nutmeg, salt, and pepper; fold in the pecans. Melt the remaining 2 tablespoons of butter. Transfer the potatoes to the prepared baking dish and pour the butter over the top. Bake for 15 minutes or until hot. Top generously with marshmallows and broil until the tops are brown.

SERVES 8–10

Southern Accent, Pine Bluff, AR

BARLEY AND PINE NUT PILAF

Excellent with game or poultry. Try as a stuffing for game hens or an accompaniment to grilled butterflied leg of lamb.

1 cup pearl barley
6 tablespoons butter
3 ounces (⅓ cup) pine nuts
1 cup chopped scallions
½ cup chopped fresh parsley or 2½
    tablespoons dried
¼ teaspoon salt
¼ teaspoon ground black pepper
1⅓ cups chicken broth

Preheat the oven to 350 degrees. Rinse the barley in cold water and drain.

In a medium skillet, heat the butter and brown the pine nuts. (Be careful—they burn easily.) Remove with a slotted spoon and reserve. Sauté the scallions and barley until the barley is lightly toasted. Remove from the heat. Stir in the nuts, parsley, salt, and pepper. Spoon into an ungreased 2-quart casserole.

Heat the broth to boiling and pour over the barley mixture. Stir to blend well. Bake uncovered, for 1 hour and 10 minutes.

SERVES 6

Private Collection I, Palo Alto, CA

SOS CHILDREN'S VILLAGE OF FLORIDA, INC.
JUNIOR LEAGUE OF GREATER FT. LAUDERDALE, FLORIDA

SOS Children's Village of Florida, a project of the Junior League of Fort Lauderdale, is a residential child care program which provides a stable, nurturing home and family for foster children who do not have a realistic opportunity to return to their own family or be placed in an adoptive home. The goal of SOS CVF is to remove the children from the revolving doors of temporary foster care and give them a permanent home in small, family-like groups.

NUTTY RICE

2 sticks (½ pound) butter
4 scallions, chopped
1 clove garlic, minced
1 pound mushrooms, wiped, trimmed, and sliced
2 cups raw long-grain brown rice
½ teaspoon dried thyme
¼ teaspoon turmeric
Vegetable seasoning salt
Freshly ground black pepper
1½ cups chopped pecans
5 cups boiling vegetable stock or chicken broth

Preheat the oven to 400 degrees. Melt the butter in a large skillet. Sauté the scallions, garlic, and mushrooms for 5 minutes or until the scallions turn golden. Add the rice and stir until all the grains are coated with butter. Season with thyme, turmeric, vegetable seasoning, and pepper. Stir in the pecans.

Turn into a 3-quart casserole. Pour the boiling stock over the rice. Cover and bake for 1 hour 20 minutes or until the liquid has been absorbed.

NOTE: You can refrigerate or freeze this before baking. Return the casserole to room temperature and bake as directed.

SERVES 14–16   *Pride of Peoria*, Peoria, IL

PECAN PILAF

Excellent with any meat; a complete meal with a baked fruit dish.

8 tablespoons (1 stick) butter
1 cup coarsely chopped pecans
½ cup chopped onion
2 cups raw long-grain white rice
4 cups chicken broth
1 teaspoon salt
½ teaspoon dried thyme
⅛ teaspoon ground black pepper
2 tablespoons chopped parsley

In a large skillet, melt 3 tablespoons of the butter. Add the pecans and sauté 10 minutes or until lightly browned. Remove the pecans; cover and set aside.

In the same skillet, melt the remaining 5 tablespoons of butter. Add the onion and sauté 6 to 8 minutes, until tender. Add the rice; stir to thoroughly coat grains. Add the broth, salt, thyme, and pepper. Cover; simmer 18 minutes or until the rice is tender and all the liquid is absorbed. Remove from the heat; stir in the pecans and parsley.

NOTE: To prepare ahead of time. Before adding nuts and parsley, cover and refrigerate up to 24 hours. To heat, add an extra ¾ cup water to the cooked rice in a skillet. Cover; heat 5 to 8 minutes until hot. Stir in nuts and parsley.

SERVES 8   *Perennials: A Celebration of Foods & Flavors*, Gainesville, GA

FAMILY VISITATION CENTER
JUNIOR LEAGUE OF JACKSONVILLE, FLORIDA

The Junior League of Jacksonville, Florida, responding to a request from the county's juvenile court judges, entered into a coalition with Health and Rehabilitative Services and the Children's Home Society and opened the Family Visitation Center in January of 1993. The quiet, safe, neutral home-like setting enables foster children and their families to visit in a supervised environment as frequently as once a week. Parenting classes and parent support groups are offered by CHS during non-visitation hours, and approximately 150–200 family visits take place each month.

RICE PILAF WITH MINCED VEGETABLES

1 cup raw long-grain white rice
½ teaspoon salt
¼ teaspoon ground white pepper
2 stalks celery, minced very fine
1 large carrot, minced very fine
2 tablespoons snipped fresh chives
4 tablespoons (½ stick) butter

In a 1-quart saucepan, bring 2 cups of water to a boil; add the rice, salt, and pepper. Cover and cook over low heat for 20 minutes or until the rice has absorbed the liquid. While the rice cooks, combine the celery, carrot, and chives and mince again. In a skillet, sauté the cooked rice in the butter over medium heat until golden, breaking up lumps with a spatula or spoon. Remove the rice from the heat and fold in the raw minced vegetables.

NOTE: The rice can be sautéed right after cooking or cooked in advance and chilled until needed. Mincing the vegetables is the key to success with this recipe. The carrots and celery are never fully cooked, only lightly steamed when folded into the hot rice. Minced fine, the vegetable pieces will be small enough to require only the briefest exposure to heat to lose their raw texture.

SERVES 4–6   *California Fresh,* Oakland–East Bay, CA

RICE INDIENNE

Curried rice with a sweet topping.

3 tablespoons butter
2 teaspoons curry powder
1 cup raw white rice
2 cups chicken broth
⅔ cup seedless raisins
⅓ cup chopped scallions
⅓ cup chopped green pepper
⅓ cup chopped celery
2 tablespoons chutney
2 tablespoons chopped pimiento
2 tablespoons chopped almonds
1 tablespoon cider vinegar
1 tablespoon brown sugar
Salt to taste

In a saucepan, combine 2 tablespoons of the butter, the curry powder and the rice. Cook over low heat for 5 minutes, stirring occasionally. Add the chicken broth and heat to boiling. Stir, cover, and cook over low heat until the liquid is absorbed, about 15 minutes. While the rice is cooking, combine the raisins, scallions, green pepper, celery, and remaining tablespoons of butter in a saucepan and cook over low heat until the vegetables are just tender. Add the chutney, pimiento, almonds, vinegar, brown sugar, and salt to the vegetable mixture. Stir until well blended. Place the rice on a serving platter and spoon the vegetable mixture over top.

SERVES 4   *Capital Classics,* Washington, D.C.

SAVANNAH RED RICE

¼ pound sliced bacon
½ cup chopped onion
½ chopped celery
¼ chopped green bell pepper
2 cups raw white rice
2 (16-ounce) cans tomatoes, with
    their juice, puréed in a blender
1 tablespoon salt
¼ teaspoon ground black pepper
1 teaspoon sugar
⅛ teaspoon Tabasco, or to taste

In a large frying pan, cook the bacon until crisp; remove from the pan. Crumble and reserve. Sauté the onion, celery, and green pepper in the bacon drippings until tender. Add the rice, tomatoes, crumbled bacon, and seasonings. Cook on top of the stove for 10 minutes. Meanwhile, heat the oven to 350 degrees and grease a large casserole dish. Pour the rice mixture into the prepared dish, cover tightly, and bake for 1 hour.

SERVES 8

Savannah Style, Savannah, GA

DIRTY RICE

A must for every Cajun's table! This delectable dish is even better when prepared a day ahead. It also freezes well.

1 pound giblets (wild fowl, chicken,
    or turkey), chopped fine
2 cups raw white rice
½ pound loose pork sausage
1 cup chopped onion
½ cup chopped bell pepper
½ cup chopped celery
2 cloves garlic, chopped
½ cup chopped fresh parsley
1 cup scallion tops
Salt and pepper to taste

Boil the giblets in a saucepan of salted water to cover until very tender. Drain, reserving the liquid, and set the giblets aside. Return the liquid to the saucepan, adding more water if necessary to make 4 cups. Add the rice, bring to a boil, and cook, covered, over low heat for 20 minutes or until tender. Set aside and keep warm.

In a deep heavy skillet start the pork sausage on low heat; as soon as the fat begins to cook out, add the onion, bell pepper, celery, and garlic. Continue cooking on low heat, stirring occasionally, until all the vegetables are soft. Add the cooked rice, giblets, parsley, scallion tops, salt, and pepper and stir all together lightly but thoroughly. If possible, add some drippings from the fowl or meat which you are serving. Do not let parsley and scallion tops become scorched.

SERVES 10–12

Pirate's Pantry, Lake Charles, LA

WILD RICE MEDLEY WITH TOASTED PINE NUTS, DRIED APRICOTS, AND GOLDEN RAISINS

3 cups chicken broth
½ cup wild rice
½ cup basmati rice
½ cup kashi (see Note)
1 cup toasted pine nuts
1 cup dried apricots, chopped
½ cup golden raisins
1 cup finely chopped celery

Combine the chicken broth, both rices, and the kashi in medium saucepan. Cover and bring to a boil over high heat. Reduce the heat and simmer until rice is just cooked through, 20 to 30 minutes. Strain off any remaining liquid. Add the pine nuts, apricots, raisins, and celery to the cooked rice. Mix well and serve.

NOTE: Kashi is a five-grain mixture found in the cereal section of health food stores. If it's not readily available, white rice can be substituted.

SERVES 6

Dining by Fireflies: Unexpected Flavors of the New South,
Charlotte, NC

SHERRIED WILD RICE

Something special!

1 cup wild rice
8 tablespoons (1 stick) butter
½ cup slivered almonds
2 tablespoons finely chopped onion
8 ounces fresh mushrooms, wiped, trimmed, and sliced
1 teaspoon salt
2 tablespoons sherry
3 cups boiling chicken broth

Pour 1½ quarts of boiling water over the rice and let it stand for 30 minutes. Drain. Pour another 1½ quarts of boiling water over the rice. Allow the rice to cool completely in the water; drain well.

Preheat the oven to 325 degrees. In a skillet, melt the butter and stir in the rice, almonds, onion, mushrooms, and salt. Sauté over medium heat for 5 minutes, being careful not to let the almonds or onions brown. Stir in the sherry. Turn into a 2½-quart casserole. Pour the boiling chicken broth over the rice. Bake uncovered for 1 hour and 15 minutes. Uncover and bake for 35 to 40 minutes, or until the liquid is absorbed.

SERVES 8

Nuggets: Recipes Good as Gold, Colorado Springs, CO

SEVEN VEGETABLE COUSCOUS

2 cups cabbage chunks
1 medium onion, chopped
2 medium turnips or white potatoes, peeled and cubed
1 (10-ounce) sweet potato or butternut squash, peeled and cubed
2 parsnips or carrots, peeled and cut into sticks
2 tablespoons olive oil
1 cup canned crushed tomatoes in tomato purée
½ teaspoon ground cumin
½ teaspoon ground coriander
1 teaspoon turmeric
½ teaspoon salt
1 (19-ounce) can chick-peas, drained
¼ teaspoon ground ginger
¼ teaspoon ground cinnamon
1 cup couscous
½ cup slivered almonds
⅓ cup raisins

In a 2-quart glass measure or casserole suitable for microwaving, layer vegetables in the following order: cabbage, onion, turnips, sweet potato and parsnips. Drizzle with ¼ cup of water and olive oil; cover with vented plastic wrap or a lid. Microwave on high for 10 minutes. Stir the vegetables, cover, and microwave on high for 5 to 7 minutes or until the vegetables are tender.

Combine the tomatoes with the cumin, coriander, ½ teaspoon of turmeric, and the salt. Stir the mixture into the vegetables. Stir in the chick-peas. Cover and microwave on high for 3 minutes. Set aside.

Combine 2 cups of water, ½ teaspoon turmeric, the ginger and cinnamon in a 4-cup glass measure. Cover with vented plastic wrap and microwave on high for 6 minutes or until boiling. Stir in the couscous. Cover and microwave on high for 2 minutes. Let stand 5 minutes. Serve the vegetables over the couscous. Garnish with almonds and raisins.

SERVES 6–8

Women of Great Taste, Wichita, KS

A CELEBRATION OF LEADERSHIP

Leadership development is an important part of the Junior League experience. Throughout our hundred-year history, we, as an organization, have provided avenues for women to acquire leadership skills.

While it is true that the Junior League is a place where women can learn to manage large numbers of people and organizations with sizable budgets (the larger Leagues, for example, have memberships of more than 2,000 volunteers, own their headquarters, and have budgets in the millions), we have recognized that leadership that simply "manages" cannot achieve our mission of promoting voluntarism and building communities. Rather, the Junior League focuses on providing opportunities for members to acquire the kinds of skills that are necessary to effect profound and systemic community change—in other words, the difficult jobs. We strive to develop women who—

• have vision, and are able to help others envision a better world so that they can plan insightfully and take bold actions to reach their vision

• can work effectively within the creative but often painful tension that exists between reality and vision—between the world the way it really is and the world the way we would like it to be

• know their reality and are nonjudgmental and curious about others' realities

• have clarified their own values and lead by example

The Chair of the Association's Public Issues Committee testifies before a Congressional subcommittee on child welfare legislation, 1980.

• who are committed to their own personal growth and the growth of others

Over the decades, the Junior League has been grateful to have received recognition for its leadership from many of its colleagues in each of the four countries in which Junior Leagues are located: the United States, Canada, Mexico, and Great Britain. But perhaps the one that best sums up the Junior League concept of leadership is the U.S. President's Voluntary Action Award, which honors our organization for "mobilizing volunteers."

That will continue to be our goal as we move in celebration into our next hundred years: to "mobilize volunteers" who are curious, reflective, open, flexible, trusting and trustworthy, honest, vulnerable, and courageous.

MEATS

No Peekie Roast Beefie

**Standing aged prime rib roast—
well-marbleized**
Salt and freshly ground pepper
Parsley sprigs for garnish

Allow the rib roast to stand at room temperature for 1 hour. Preheat the oven to 375 degrees. Season the meat and place in a shallow roasting pan. Do not cover or add water. Cook in oven just 1 hour. Turn off the heat, but do not open the oven door at any time until ready to serve.

Regardless of the length of time the roast has been in the oven, 30 to 40 minutes before serving turn the oven back on to 325 degrees and finish cooking. Remove to a serving platter and garnish with parsley. The meat will be very brown and crisp on the outside, beautifully pink all the way through—medium rare and very juicy.

Marigolds to Munch On, Peoria, IL

Garlic-Roasted Châteaubriand with Cognac Mustard Sauce

**2 beef tenderloins (2½ pounds
each), Châteaubriand cut,
trimmed of fat and sinew**
3 medium garlic cloves, slivered
2½ tablespoons extra virgin olive oil
1½ tablespoons unsalted butter

Cognac Mustard Sauce
**8 tablespoons (1 stick) plus 1½
tablespoons unsalted butter**
4 medium shallots, minced
2 cups beef broth
2 tablespoons Cognac
2 tablespoons Dijon mustard
3 tablespoons minced fresh parsley
**Salt and freshly ground pepper to
taste**

With a small sharp knife, make several ¾-inch-deep slits in the meat. Insert garlic slivers into the slits. Brush the meat with 2 tablespoons of the oil. Set aside.

Preheat the oven to 450 degrees. In a large skillet, heat the remaining ½ tablespoon oil over medium-high heat. Brown the meat quickly on all sides. Remove the meat to a rack in a roasting pan. Set the skillet aside. Roast the meat to the desired doneness, about 20 minutes for medium-rare.

For the sauce, melt 1½ tablespoons of butter in reserved skillet. Add the shallots and sauté until softened, about 4 minutes. Remove the tenderloins from the roasting pan to a warm platter. Set aside, covered loosely with foil. Skim the fat from the pan. Over high heat, stir in the beef broth, scraping up browned bits. Add the shallots. Bring to a boil and cook until reduced by half. Add the Cognac and boil 1 minute. Reduce the heat to low. Whisk in the mustard. Cut the stick of butter into 8 pieces and whisk in 1 piece at a time. Stir until the butter is melted. Add the parsley and season with salt and freshly ground pepper. Carve the meat into ½-inch slices. Spoon sauce over and serve immediately.

SERVES 8

One Magnificent Cookbook, Chicago, IL

BEEF TENDERLOIN WITH MUSTARD PEPPERCORN SAUCE

MUSTARD PEPPERCORN SAUCE
1 tablespoon sugar
2 tablespoons tarragon vinegar or
  white wine vinegar
¼ cup Dijon mustard
½ teaspoon salt
2 eggs yolks
2 tablespoons green peppercorns,
  rinsed and drained
1 tablespoon unsalted butter
½ cup heavy cream

½ teaspoon salt
½ teaspoon ground cinnamon
½ teaspoon ground cumin
2 tablespoons green peppercorns,
  rinsed and drained
1 (3–4 pound) beef tenderloin,
  trimmed of fat and sinew
1-2 tablespoons vegetable oil
 Mustard peppercorn sauce

Make the sauce: In the top of a double-boiler, combine the sugar, vinegar, mustard, salt, egg yolks, and peppercorns. Whisk over hot water until thickened, about 5 minutes. Remove from the heat and stir in the butter. Allow to cool. Whip the cream until stiff and gently fold into the mustard sauce. Cover and refrigerate until serving time. The sauce may be made up to 1 week in advance.

Roast the beef: preheat the oven to 350 degrees. Mix together the salt, cinnamon, cumin, and peppercorns and spread evenly over both sides of the tenderloin. In a large skillet, heat the oil over medium-high heat. Sear the meat quickly on both sides and then transfer to a rack in a roasting pan. Roast for 40 to 55 minutes for rare. The meat will be very rare at 125 degrees on a meat thermometer and medium rare at 135°. Let the meat stand for 10 minutes before carving. Serve with the sauce.

SERVES 4–6   *California Heritage Collection,* Pasadena, CA

FILET DE BOEUF AU POIVRE

1 small whole beef tenderloin,
  approximately 4 pounds, trimmed
  of fat and sinew
¼ cup brandy
1 tablespoon coarsely ground black
  pepper
1 scallion, minced fine
2 cloves garlic, minced fine
Salt to taste

Tie the thin tail end of the beef under to make a roast approximately the same thickness for whole length. Combine the brandy, pepper, scallion, and garlic in a small bowl. Rub over the roast, sprinkle with salt, and let stand at room temperature for at least 1 hour.

Preheat the oven to 400 degrees. Roast the beef for 35 to 45 minutes or until a meat thermometer reads 125 degrees for rare. Remove from the oven. Let rest for 15 to 20 minutes before carving.

SERVES 6   *Savor the Brandywine Valley,* Wilmington, DE

PARENTING POWER
JUNIOR LEAGUE OF TAMPA, FLORIDA

Parenting Power is a current project of the Junior League of Tampa in collaboration with the Maternal Child Health Coalition. The goal of the program is to provide parenting classes which will increase early intervention, prevent infant mortality, and reduce the number of infants who "fail to thrive." Junior League volunteers provide meals, coordinate an incentive program, and facilitate interaction during the seven-week parenting skills sessions.

FILET OF BEEF

5 pounds beef filet, trimmed of fat
  and sinew
1½ cups dry red wine
1½ tablespoons Worcestershire sauce
Juice of 2 lemons
Freshly ground black pepper

Combine the wine, Worcestershire, lemon juice, and pepper in a nonreactive pan large enough to hold the meat. Add the filet and marinate at room temperature for several hours.

Preheat the oven to 500 degrees. Drain off the marinade, put the meat in a roasting pan, and roast it for 5 minutes per pound. Then turn the oven off. Do not open the oven door for 2 hours.

This beef is best served at room temperature, sliced very thin. If this is not practical, prepare the meat the day before serving. Chill and slice cold, then let stand until it reaches room temperature.

SERVES 8   *Southern Championship Blue Ribbon Recipes,* Montgomery, AL

FILET FROID

4 tablespoons (½ stick) butter
2 carrots, chopped
1 cup chopped celery
1 cup chopped onion
2 cloves garlic, minced
1 small (2-pound) beef tenderloin,
  trimmed of fat and sinew, at
  room temperature
½ pound thick-sliced bacon, cut
  into 2-inch pieces
1 cup sour cream
1 tablespoon grated onion
1 tablespoon chopped chives
Salt and freshly ground black pepper
  to taste
Watercress for garnish

Preheat the oven to 500 degrees. Heat the butter in a medium skillet and sauté the carrots, celery, onion, and 1 clove of garlic for 10 minutes or until soft. Spoon into a roasting pan. Place the tenderloin on the vegetables. Bake a total of 20 minutes for rare or 30 minutes for medium. Let cool in the pan 1 hour.

Place the tenderloin on a dish. Transfer the vegetables and juices in the roasting pan to a sieve set over a bowl and press with the back of a wooden spoon to extract the juices. Reserve the juices.

In the skillet, fry the bacon for 2 or 3 minutes while stirring. Add the remaining clove of garlic and continue cooking until the bacon is crisp. Remove the bacon and drain on paper towels. In a bowl, combine the sour cream, onion, chives, salt, pepper, and 2 teaspoons of the strained meat juices. Stir the bacon into the sour cream just before serving. Slice the tenderloin and arrange on a serving platter with garnish. Serve with the sauce.

SERVES 4–6   *Sassafras! The Ozarks Cookbook,* Springfield, MO

CARL BELL'S MARINADE

⅓ cup barbecue sauce
½ cup soy sauce
¼ cup vegetable oil
¼ cup white wine
2 to 3 teaspoons garlic powder
½ teaspoon seasoned flavor
  enhancer

Combine all ingredients and store the marinade in a glass jar in the refrigerator. Use as needed for beef or chicken.

MAKES 1 ⅓ CUPS   *Women of Great Taste,* Wichita, KS

VALLEY CHÂTEAUBRIAND

Salt and freshly ground black pepper
  to taste
1 tenderloin beefsteak, about 2
  pounds, trimmed of fat and sinew
3 tablespoons butter
½ pound fresh mushrooms, wiped,
  trimmed, and sliced
1 tablespoon chopped chives
1 tablespoon chopped fresh parsley
2 small shallots, chopped
1 teaspoon Worcestershire sauce
½ cup dry sherry
2 tablespoons brandy

Salt and pepper the meat as desired. Grill to desired doneness. Melt the butter in a skillet over medium-high heat and sauté the sliced mushrooms 4 minutes. Add the chives, parsley, and shallots and simmer for 5 minutes. Add salt and pepper to taste and the Worcestershire; stir to combine. Blend in the sherry and bring to a simmer. Add the brandy just before serving and thin sauce with more sherry if desired. Spoon the sauce over grilled meat.

SERVES 4   *Thymes Remembered,* Tallahassee, FL

BESS'S BEEF TENDERLOIN WITH BORDELAISE SAUCE

1 large beef tenderloin (4 to 6
  pounds), trimmed of fat and
  sinew
6 tablespoons butter, softened
2 cloves garlic, halved
Onion salt
Seasoned pepper

BORDELAISE SAUCE
4 tablespoons (½ stick) butter
2 shallots, chopped
2 cloves garlic, chopped
2 onions, sliced thin
4 carrots, sliced thin
2 sprigs parsley
2 whole cloves
12 whole black peppercorns
1 bay leaf
¼ cup flour
2 (10½ ounce) cans beef bouillon
1 teaspoon salt
¼ teaspoon ground black pepper
½ cup dry red wine
2 tablespoons snipped parsley

Preheat the oven to 400 degrees. Rub the tenderloin with the garlic and then with 2 tablespoons of softened butter. Heavily shake the seasonings on all sides of the meat until well coated. Heat the remaining 4 tablespoons of butter in a large skillet until smoking hot. Brown the meat on all sides, rolling it over often, until well seared. Transfer to a shallow roasting pan and roast uncovered to the desired degree of doneness. Roast 20 minutes for rare, 25 to 30 minutes for medium. Do *not* cook tenderloin well done.

To prepare the Bordelaise sauce, melt the butter in a large skillet. Sauté the shallots, garlic, onions, carrots, parsley sprigs, cloves, peppercorns, and bay leaf until onion is golden and tender, 6 to 8 minutes. Reduce the heat to low and add the flour. Stir constantly until the flour is light brown and thickened. Add the beef bouillon and simmer until slightly thickened and smooth, stirring often. Pour through a food mill or large strainer. Mash as much as possible. Add the salt, pepper, wine, and snipped parsley. Chill until ready to used. Reheat slowly in a double boiler.

SERVES 8–10   *Superlatives,* Oklahoma City, OK

BAKED STEAK

A very special recipe that's almost too good to be true!

**3-inch-thick boneless sirloin steak
  (3–4 pounds)**
3 tablespoons butter, melted
1 cup bottled chili sauce
3 tablespoons Worcestershire sauce
¼ cup chopped onion

MUSHROOM SAUCE:
**1 pound mushrooms, wiped,
  trimmed, and sliced**
2 tablespoons butter
1 tablespoon Worcestershire sauce
¼ cup bottled chili sauce
1 cup heavy cream

Preheat the oven to 450 degrees. Put the steak in an ovenproof skillet and sear on all sides over high heat or under the broiler. Combine the butter, chili sauce, Worcestershire and onion. Pour over the steak; bake uncovered 45 minutes for rare.

While the steak is baking, sauté the mushrooms in the butter about 2 minutes, until lightly browned. Add the Worcestershire, chili sauce, and cream. Cook over medium heat until slightly thickened, about 15 minutes. After baking, let the steak stand 2 minutes, then slice. Serve with the mushroom sauce.

SERVES 6–8

For Goodness Taste, Rochester, NY

FLANK STEAK WITH MUSTARD CAPER SAUCE

Yes! The once lowly flank steak has come into its own. You will be delighted with this recipe for its ease of preparation and yet quite sophisticated flavors.

4 tablespoons (½ stick) butter
1 tablespoon vegetable oil
1 flank steak, about 1½ pounds
3 tablespoons dry vermouth
1 tablespoon Dijon mustard
¼ teaspoon Worcestershire sauce
1½ tablespoon capers
Watercress

In a large heavy skillet, melt 1 tablespoon of the butter with the oil over medium heat. Place the meat in the pan and brown, turning once, about 5 to 6 minutes, depending on the thickness and temperature of the steak. It should be pink in the center when done. Transfer to a carving board and cover with foil to keep warm.

In the same pan, over low heat, melt the remaining 3 tablespoons butter in the pan drippings. With a flat whisk, briskly stir in the vermouth, mustard, Worcestershire, and capers. Set aside to keep warm.

Cut the meat in thin slices across the grain at a 45 degree angle. Spoon sauce over all and garnish with watercress.

SERVES 4

Private Collection 2, Palo Alto, CA

MARINATED GRILLED FLANK STEAK

Juice of 1 lemon
½ cup soy sauce
¼ cup (or more) dry red wine
3 tablespoons vegetable oil
2 tablespoons Worcestershire sauce
1 large clove garlic, sliced
Ground black pepper to taste
Chopped scallions or chives
   (optional)
Chopped dill weed (optional)
Celery seed (optional)
1 flank steak, about 1½ pounds,
   trimmed

Make a marinade by combining the lemon juice, soy sauce, wine, oil, Worcestershire, garlic, pepper, and if desired the scallions, dill, and celery seed.

Place the steak in a dish or a zipper-lock plastic bag, pour the marinade over, cover or seal tightly, and let stand in the refrigerator for at least 2 or up to 12 hours, turning once or twice.

Remove from the marinade and broil the meat over hot coals for 4 minutes on each side for rare meat. Slice the meat on the diagonal across the grain and serve.

SERVES 4–6   *Magic,* Birmingham, AL

AUSTIN FAJITAS

1½ to 2 pounds skirt steak or lean
   flank steak, or 6 chicken breast
   halves boned and skinned

MARINADE
¼ cup vegetable oil
2 tablespoons lemon juice
2 tablespoons soy sauce
2 tablespoons chopped scallions
1 clove garlic, minced
1 teaspoon coarsely ground black
   pepper
1 teaspoon celery salt
1 teaspoon jalapeño juice (optional)

FAJITAS
Warm flour tortillas
Garnishes (salsa, refried beans,
   guacamole, grilled sliced onions,
   grated cheese, chili con queso)

Remove all fat from the steak and wipe the meat with paper towels. Combine the marinade ingredients and mix well. Place the steak and the marinade in a shallow dish. Let stand at cool room temperature or in the refrigerator for at least 6 hours, turning frequently. Drain off the liquid. Broil over hot coals to the desired degree of doneness. Cut the steak diagonally in thin slices.

Provide guests with warm tortillas, sliced steak, and bowls of garnishes to make their favorite rolled and stuffed fajitas.

SERVES 4   *Necessities and Temptations,* Austin, TX

BROILED FLANK STEAK

In the Southwest, outdoor cooking is a favorite and delicious way to prepare a meal because it keeps the heat out of the kitchen. Try this recipe for your next barbecue.

1 flank steak, 2 to 3 pounds
¼ cup soy sauce
3 tablespoons honey
2 tablespoons vinegar
½ teaspoon garlic salt
1½ teaspoon ground ginger
½ cup vegetable oil
1 onion, chopped fine
½ cup beer

Score the meat on both sides in a crisscross pattern, making cuts about 1 inch apart and ⅛ inch deep. Place the meat in a large shallow casserole. Combine the remaining ingredients in a blender or food processor. Blend well and pour over the meat. Cover and marinate in the refrigerator at least 6 hours, preferably overnight. During the marinating process turn the meat several times. Grill over hot coals or broil 4 minutes on each side for rare meat. Slice on the diagonal to serve.

SERVES 6–8

Winning at the Table, Las Vegas, NV

MEDALLIONS OF BEEF WITH WILD MUSHROOM CABERNET SAUCE

4 thick filet mignon medallions, 4 to 5 ounces each
Salt and pepper
2 tablespoons olive oil
2 cups chopped wild mushrooms: morels, shiitake, and chanterelles
2 shallots, minced
2 teaspoons minced garlic
2 teaspoons chopped dried thyme
4 to 5 tablespoons butter
2 cups Cabernet Sauvignon or other full-bodied wine
1 cup rich beef broth or glace de viande

Lightly season the medallions with salt and pepper. Heat the oil in a heavy skillet. When it begins to smoke, add the medallions and cook over high heat to the desired degree of doneness, about 3 to 4 minutes per side for rare. Remove medallions from the skillet to a warm oven.

Reduce the heat to medium high. In the same skillet sauté the mushrooms, shallots, garlic, and thyme in 2 tablespoons of the butter about 2 minutes, until lightly browned. Pour the Cabernet into the skillet and bring to a boil. Boil until reduced by half. Add the beef broth and return to a boil. Boil until reduced to 1 cup. Remove the skillet from heat and whisk in the remaining 2 or 3 tablespoons of butter. Finish with salt and pepper to taste. Pour the sauce over the medallions, and serve.

SERVES 4

Celebrate!, Sacramento, CA

CANCER PATIENT SUPPORT PROGRAM
JUNIOR LEAGUE OF WINSTON-SALEM, NORTH CAROLINA

The Cancer Patient Support Program began in 1980 as a result of a collaboration among the Junior League of Winston-Salem, North Carolina, and several other agencies, foundations, and organizations. With both inpatient and outpatient components, the CPSP is a support service for cancer patients and their families, providing a library, support groups, psychological services, and other programs. In 1993, the Cancer Patient Support Program had 24,730 patient contacts.

ROAST BARBECUE

Double or triple this for an après ski or theater party.

3 pounds chuck roast
2 tablespoons shortening
1 large onion, chopped
2 tablespoons vinegar
2 tablespoons lemon juice
¾ cup water
½ cup chopped celery
2 cups ketchup
3 tablespoons Worcestershire sauce
2 tablespoons brown sugar
1 tablespoon prepared mustard
2 tablespoons chili powder
½ teaspoon ground black pepper

Trim the meat of fat and brown in hot shortening in a Dutch oven. Mix the remaining ingredients and pour over the meat. Bring to a boil, cover, and reduce the heat to low. As soon as the meat is tender enough (approximately 2 to 3 hours), use 2 forks and shred or pull the meat apart. Continue cooking until the meat is very tender. (Cooking time frequently varies from 3 to 6 hours.) Serve on buns.

SERVES 12   *Applehood & Motherpie,* Rochester, NY

POT ROAST CARIBE

A prize-winning recipe that's a takeoff on traditional Mexican mole sauces.

3 pounds beef chuck roast
2 tablespoons cooking oil
2 cloves garlic, crushed
1 cup chopped onion
1 teaspoon salt
1 (15-ounce) can tomato sauce
1 (4-ounce) can chopped green chiles
2 tablespoons sugar
1 tablespoon cocoa powder
1 tablespoon chili powder
1 teaspoon ground cumin
1 teaspoon ground coriander
½ teaspoon ground cinnamon
¼ teaspoon dried oregano
1 tablespoon flour
1 teaspoon grated orange rind
½ cup ground almonds
8 small onions, peeled
3 medium yellow crookneck squash,
    cut into 1½-inch chunks
¼ cup slivered almonds, lightly toasted
Parsley and cherry tomatoes for
    garnish

In a large Dutch oven, brown the meat in hot oil on all sides. Remove the meat to a plate. In the same oil, cook the garlic and chopped onion about 5 minutes or until the onion is lightly browned. Stir in the salt, tomato sauce, and chiles.

In a small bowl combine the sugar, cocoa, chili powder, cumin, coriander, cinnamon, oregano, and flour. Stir into the tomato mixture in the pan along with the orange rind and ground almonds. Mix well. Return the meat to the pan and cook, tightly covered, over low heat for 2 hours or until the meat is tender.

Add the peeled whole onions and squash to the sauce around the meat; cover and continue to cook about ½ hour or until the vegetables are fork tender. To serve, place the meat in the center of a platter; spoon some of the sauce over. Arrange the vegetables around the roast and sprinkle with toasted almonds. Garnish with parsley and cherry tomatoes.

SERVES 6–8   *Simply Simpático,* Albuquerque, NM

BEEF ROLL, ITALIAN STYLE

4 slices round steak, ¼ inch thick
(about 2 pounds)
½ teaspoon salt
⅛ teaspoon ground black pepper
2 tablespoons olive oil

FILLING
1½ cups fine dry bread crumbs
1 clove garlic, minced
2 tablespoons grated onion
¼ cup chopped parsley
3 tablespoons grated Parmesan
cheese
½ cup finely diced mozzarella
cheese
6 thin slices salami, chopped

SAUCE
1 (16-ounce) can stewed tomatoes
1 (10½-ounce) can condensed beef
consommé, undiluted
2 carrots, peeled and sliced thin
1 (10-ounce) package frozen lima
beans, partially thawed
¼ cup spicy ketchup

Flatten the slices of meat with the edge of a saucer to an even thinness. Sprinkle lightly with salt and pepper.

To prepare the filling, toss together all ingredients; set aside ½ cup for sauce.

Spread about ½ cup filling over each steak slice. Roll up tightly jelly-role fashion. Tie each end securely with twine. Heat the oil in a large skillet and brown the rolls well on all sides. Place in a casserole.

To prepare the sauce, combine all the ingredients, plus the ½ cup of reserved filling, in a medium saucepan. Bring to a boil; stir occasionally to break up the tomatoes.

Pour the sauce over the meat rolls. Bake uncovered for 1½ to 2 hours or until tender. To serve, remove the twine and cut each roll in half. Arrange on a platter and pour sauce over rolls.

SERVES 4–6   *Clusters of Culinary Creations,* Kankakee, IL

POT ROAST BRAISED IN WINE

5 pounds boned and rolled chuck or
rump roast
Flour for dredging
4 tablespoons (½ stick) butter
½ cup chopped onion
½ cup chopped leeks or scallions
½ cup chopped carrots
1 clove garlic, crushed
2 cups dry red wine
Salt to taste
8 crushed peppercorns
1 bay leaf
¼ teaspoon dried marjoram
¼ teaspoon dried thyme
2 tablespoons Cognac, warmed

Preheat the oven to 325 degrees. Dredge the roast with flour. Heat the butter in a Dutch oven, add the meat, and brown on all sides, over medium high heat. Add the onion, leeks, and carrots and sauté until browned. Add the garlic and cook 1 minute. Stir in the wine and seasonings. Add the cognac and ignite. Cover and bake 4 hours, turning the roast several times. If necessary, add more wine.

Transfer the meat to a warm platter and keep hot. Strain the sauce, correct the seasoning, and pour over the beef.

SERVES 6–8   *Marigolds to Munch On,* Peoria, IL

DILL POT ROAST

3 to 3½ pounds boneless rump,
   arm, or chuck roast
1 teaspoon salt
¼ teaspoon ground black pepper
1 teaspoon dill seed
1 tablespoon wine vinegar
3 tablespoons flour
1 teaspoon dill weed
1 cup sour cream

Preheat the oven to very low (200 degrees). Season the beef with salt, pepper, and dill seed. Place in an ovenproof dish; add the vinegar mixed with ¼ cup of water. Cover and bake for 5 hours, turning several times. Remove the meat. To the liquid in the pan, add the flour and dill weed. Cook and stir to thicken. Add the sour cream. Spoon sauce over sliced beef.

SERVES 6–8

Beyond Parsley, Kansas City, MO

NEW ORLEANS GRILLADES

1½ pounds lean round steak, ½ inch
   thick
2–3 tablespoons beef or chicken
   broth or wine
1 tablespoon vegetable oil
2 tablespoons flour
2 onions, chopped
1 large clove garlic, crushed
1 medium green bell pepper,
   chopped
1 large stalk celery, chopped
1 (16-ounce) can whole peeled
   tomatoes, chopped, liquid
   reserved
Hot water plus reserved tomato
   liquid to measure 1½ cups
2 bay leaves, crumbled
¼ teaspoon dried thyme
2 tablespoons chopped fresh parsley
¼ teaspoon salt
¼ teaspoon celery seed

Pound the steak with a meat mallet and flatten to ¼-inch thickness. Trim off the fat and cut the meat into 6 squares. Brown the meat in a nonstick skillet. Add broth or wine as needed to prevent sticking. Remove the meat, drain on paper towels, and blot the pan with a paper towel to remove any fat.

Heat the oil in the skillet; blend in the flour and stir until brown. Add the onions, garlic, bell pepper, and celery, stirring frequently until the vegetables soften. Add a little tomato liquid or broth if needed.

Transfer to a Crock-Pot or flameproof casserole and add the 1½ cups of liquid, the bay leaves, thyme, parsley, salt, and celery seed. Stir until well mixed. Add the browned steak, cover, and slow-cook all day or cook on top of the stove until the meat falls apart.

SERVES 6   *River Road Recipes: A Healthy Collection,* Baton Rouge, LA

MABODOFU

Tofu with hot peppers and meat sauce.

2 teaspoons vegetable oil
1 clove garlic, minced
¼ cup chopped scallions
½ teaspoon minced hot red peppers
¼ pound mushrooms, trimmed and
    sliced
1 pound ground beef
½ cup water or vegetable stock
1½ teaspoons sake or white wine
2½ teaspoons soy sauce
½ teaspoon salt
1½ teaspoons dark Asian sesame oil
1 block tofu, cut into pieces ½ inch
    thick by 1¼ inches square
2½ teaspoons cornstarch
Chopped scallions

Heat a wok or skillet; coat with oil. Add the garlic, scallions, and red peppers; stir-fry on high heat for 15 seconds. Reduce the heat to medium, add the mushrooms, and sauté 1 minute. Add the beef and cook until browned, stirring to break up lumps; drain off fat. Add water or stock, sake, soy sauce, salt, and sesame oil; bring to a boil and cook 30 seconds. Add the tofu. Dissolve the cornstarch in 2 tablespoons of water; add to the wok. Simmer until thick. Serve hot with steamed rice, garnished with chopped scallions.

SERVES 3–4

A Brooklyn Tradition, Brooklyn, NY

ITALIAN SPAGHETTI SAUCE WITH MEATBALLS

SAUCE
3 tablespoons vegetable oil
¾ cup chopped onion
1 clove garlic, minced
2 (6-ounce) cans tomato paste
1 tablespoon sugar
1½ teaspoons salt
½ teaspoon freshly ground pepper
1½ teaspoons dried oregano
1 bay leaf
4 cups canned tomato sauce

MEATBALLS
1 slice firm white bread
1 pound ground beef
2 eggs
½ cup grated Parmesan cheese
2 tablespoons chopped parsley
1 clove garlic, minced
1 teaspoon dried oregano
1 teaspoon salt
Dash of ground black pepper
2 tablespoons olive oil

Make the sauce: Heat the oil in a heavy nonaluminum pan; add the onion and sauté for 5 minutes, until translucent. Add the garlic and cook for 1 minute. Stir in the tomato paste, 1 cup of water, the sugar, salt, pepper, oregano, bay leaf, and tomato sauce. Simmer uncovered for 30 minutes.

While the sauce is simmering, make the meatballs: Soak the bread in water for 2 or 3 minutes. Drain and squeeze partially dry. Place the bread in a mixing bowl with the ground beef, eggs, Parmesan cheese, parsley, garlic, oregano, salt and pepper. Mix gently with the hands until the ingredients are evenly combined. Form into about 20 small balls. Heat the olive oil in a skillet, add the meatballs without crowding, and brown on all sides over medium high heat.

Remove the bay leaf from the sauce and add the meatballs. Simmer 30 minutes longer. Serve over hot pasta.

SERVES 6

Thyme for All Seasons, Duluth, MN

SOUTH OF THE BORDER LASAGNE

This is a great dish for casual entertaining and can easily be doubled to serve a large crowd.

2 pounds ground chuck
1 onion, chopped
1 clove garlic, minced
2 tablespoons chili powder
3 cups tomato sauce
1 teaspoon sugar
1 tablespoon salt
½ cup sliced black olives
1 (4-ounce) can chopped green
   chiles
12 corn tortillas
Vegetable oil
2 cups small curd cottage cheese
1 egg, beaten
8 ounces Monterey Jack cheese,
   grated
1 cup grated Cheddar cheese

TOPPINGS
½ cup chopped scallions
½ cup sour cream
½ cup sliced black olives

In a large heavy skillet, brown the meat over medium-high heat, stirring to break up lumps. Push to one side of the pan, drain off any fat, and add the onion. Sauté 5 minutes, until translucent; add the garlic and cook 1 minute longer. Sprinkle the chili powder over the meat and onions and mix well. Add the tomato sauce, sugar, salt, olives, and chiles. Simmer uncovered for 15 minutes.

While the mixture simmers, heat the oven to 350 degrees. Oil a 13 × 9-inch baking dish. In a small skillet, heat 1 to 2 tablespoons of oil and soften the tortillas by placing them one by one in the hot oil until soft and pliable. Beat together the cottage cheese and egg; set aside.

Place a third of the meat mixture in the prepared baking dish. Top with a layer of half the Monterey Jack cheese. Spoon on half the cottage cheese and cover with half the tortillas. Repeat the process, ending with the meat sauce on top. Cover with grated Cheddar cheese and bake for 30 minutes, until bubbly.

Allow the lasagne to stand at room temperature for 15 minutes before cutting into squares. Place the toppings in small bowls and let guests serve themselves.

SERVES 8–10   *Necessities and Temptations,* Austin, TX

SOJOURN WOMEN'S CENTER TRANSITIONAL HOUSING
JUNIOR LEAGUE OF SPRINGFIELD, ILLINOIS

The Sojourn Women's Center Transitional Housing Project used Junior League of Springfield, Illinois, funds and volunteers to rent and upgrade several apartments for use by women attempting to separate from abusive partners. Transitional housing clients were required to have a service plan which insured independent living skills such as financial management, parenting, and home maintenance. Since the transitional housing program became active 19 families have used this housing option to establish independent living.

HELEN CAPORAL'S FABULOUS SPAGHETTI SAUCE

MEATBALLS

2 pounds ground beef

2 eggs

1 small onion, chopped

3 cloves garlic, minced

1 teaspoon dried oregano

¼ pound Romano or Parmesan
  cheese, grated

Salt

Ground black pepper

2 slices firm white bread

2 pounds Italian sausage links

SPAGHETTI SAUCE

8 (8-ounce) cans tomato sauce

2 teaspoons dried oregano

¼ teaspoon ground red pepper
  (cayenne)

½ gallon Chianti or other dry red
  wine

1 foot-long pepperoni, sliced

Romano cheese, cut into small
  chunks

½ pound fresh mushrooms, sliced
  and sautéed, or 1 (8-ounce) can
  sliced mushrooms

Start this recipe early in the day. To prepare the meatballs, combine the ground beef, eggs, and chopped onion in a mixing bowl with the garlic, oregano, grated cheese, and salt and pepper to taste. Soak the bread in a small amount of water. Stir the bread with a fork and add to the meat mixture. Mix gently with the hands to combine the ingredients. Shape into small meatballs. Set aside. (The meatballs and sausage can be fried a day ahead and refrigerated.)

To prepare the spaghetti sauce, combine the tomato sauce, oregano, ground red pepper, and half the red wine in a nonaluminum kettle or stockpot. Add the meatballs, sausage, and pepperoni pieces, bring to a boil, and lower the heat. Simmer uncovered, continuing to add red wine throughout the day until the sauce is very dark red in color. The sauce will have lost some of its tomato flavor. About 15 minutes before serving, add the mushrooms and small chunks of Romano cheese. Serve over hot spaghetti.

Heat 1 tablespoon of oil in a skillet and brown the meatballs on all sides over medium-high heat, in batches if necessary to avoid crowding. Cut the sausages into bite-size pieces and brown in the same skillet.

SERVES 12

Superlatives, Oklahoma City, OK

COASTAL CHILDREN'S ADVOCACY CENTER
JUNIOR LEAGUE OF SAVANNAH, GEORGIA

The Coastal Children's Advocacy Center was established in 1992 with volunteer and financial support from the Junior League of Savannah, Georgia. CCAC is a safe place where abused children can talk about their experiences and begin the healing process. The center, whose motto is "It's okay to tell," provides crisis counseling for victimized children and their non-offending family members, information and referrals, case management, and follow-up services. The center has served more than 500 children, the majority between 2 and 7 years of age.

FLAUTAS

PORK SAUCE

3 to 4 pounds boneless lean pork roast, loin end

4 (10-ounce) cans tomatoes with green chiles

2 (10½-ounce) cans beef broth

2 medium onions, chopped

1 teaspoon cumin

3 cloves garlic, minced

1 tablespoon dried oregano

3 tablespoons chili powder

Salt and ground black pepper to taste

FILLING

1 pound ground beef

1 onion, chopped

1 teaspoon garlic salt

Salt and ground black pepper to taste

½ teaspoon ground cumin

1 to 2 tablespoons vegetable oil

24 corn tortillas

½ pound Monterey Jack cheese, grated

Garnish: sour cream, lettuce, guacamole

Make the pork sauce: Trim the fat from the roast and place the meat in a large kettle. Add the tomatoes, broth, onions, and seasonings. Simmer, covered, over the lowest possible heat for about 6 hours. Break the meat up with a fork and mix well in the sauce. This sauce freezes well and makes a great topping for tamales.

Make the filling: In a heavy skillet, brown the meat and add the onion and seasonings. Add ½ cup of water and cook until the water is absorbed.

To make the flautas, lightly oil two 9 × 12 baking pans. Preheat the oven to 350 degrees. In a separate small skillet, heat the oil and soften the tortillas by dipping them one at a time in the hot oil until they are soft and pliable. Drain on paper towels. Spread a tablespoonful of the ground meat mixture on a tortilla, add some grated cheese, roll up and place seam side down in the prepared pans. Repeat using the rest of the tortillas and filling. Spoon pork sauce over the entire dish and top with the remaining cheese. Bake uncovered for about 30 minutes or until the cheese is melted and bubbly. Garnish with sour cream, chopped lettuce, and guacamole.

MAKES 24   *The Bounty of East Texas*, Longview, TX

PROJECT LEAD
JUNIOR LEAGUE OF FORT WAYNE, INDIANA

The Junior League of Fort Wayne, Indiana, founded Project LEAD (Leadership, Experience, and Development) in 1982 to establish ongoing leadership training programs in local high schools. Teams of student volunteers participated in training including adult mentors who provided support and guidance to the young people as they worked together to complete volunteer projects benefiting the community. Hundreds of Fort Wayne youth participated in LEAD, and other programs have developed as a result.

CORNISH PASTIES

Takes time, but ohhh so good. Pronounced to rhyme with "nasty," these meat turnovers from England are anything but!

FILLING

2 pounds beef (top round or sirloin) cut into ½-inch cubes

1½ to 2 cups ½-inch diced raw potatoes

1½ cups ½-inch diced raw rutabaga

1 medium onion, chopped coarse

2 large carrots, diced fine

Salt and pepper to taste

SUET PASTRY

3 cups all-purpose flour, plus additional for work surface

1 tablespoon salt

1 cup ground suet, at room temperature, plus additional for filling pasties

1 cup ice water, or less

Make the filling: Mix all the ingredients together in a large bowl and set aside.

Make the suet pastry: Using the hands, mix the flour, salt, and 1 cup of suet together until the suet is incorporated with the flour. Add ice water by the tablespoon until the mixture sticks together. Shape into 9 balls. On a well-floured surface, roll each ball into a circle as thin as a pie crust.

Preheat the oven to 425 degrees. Spray a cookie sheet with vegetable oil cooking spray. As each circle is rolled out, place ¾ packed cup of filling on one half of the circle. Place a generous teaspoon of suet on top of the filling. Fold the dough over to form a half circle shape. Dampen the edges and fold the pastry edge toward the inside for a tight seal. Seal further with the tines of a fork. Make a 1½-inch vent in top of each pasty. Place the pasties on the prepared cookie sheet. Bake for 30 minutes or until brown. Turn the oven down to 325 degrees and bake another 30 minutes. The pasties are ready to be eaten, or you may cook on a rack and freeze them. Thaw for 3 hours—not in the microwave. To reheat, bake 1 pasty 15 minutes at 350 degrees or 4 pasties for 30 minutes.

MAKES 9   *Clock Wise Cuisine,* Detroit, MI

LEMON BARBECUED MEAT LOAVES

1½ pound ground chuck

4 slices dried bread, cubed

¼ cup lemon juice

¼ cup minced onion

1 egg, slightly beaten

2 teaspoons seasoned salt

½ cup ketchup

⅓ cup packed brown sugar

1 teaspoon dry mustard

¼ teaspoon ground allspice

¼ teaspoon ground cloves

6 thin lemon slices

Preheat the oven to 350 degrees. In a bowl, combine the ground chuck, bread cubes, lemon juice, onion, egg, and salt. Mix well and shape into 6 individual loaves. Arrange on a greased 9 × 13-inch baking dish. Bake 15 minutes.

Meanwhile, in a small bowl, combine the ketchup, brown sugar, mustard, allspice, and cloves. Cover the loaves with the sauce and top each with a lemon slice. Bake 30 minutes longer, basting occasionally with sauce from the pan.

SERVES 6   *Virginia Hospitality,* Hampton Roads, VA

NATCHITOCHES MEAT PIES

*These celebrated deep-fried turnovers are
named for their city of origin, Natchitoches
(pronounced NACK-i-tosh), Louisiana.
They are a real treat served for lunch with
a green salad.*

PASTRY

4 cups all-purpose flour
2 teaspoons baking powder
¼ teaspoon salt
½ cup lard or solid vegetable
  shortening, melted
¾ cup milk
2 whole eggs

MEAT FILLING

1½ pounds ground pork loin
1½ pounds ground lean beef
1½ tablespoons flour
2 medium white onions, chopped
  fine
4 cloves garlic, minced
1 cup chopped scallions
¼ cup chopped fresh parsley
Salt
Freshly ground black pepper
Ground red pepper (cayenne)

In a heavy skillet over medium high heat, cook the pork and beef together, stirring to break up lumps, until the texture is mealy and the meat has lost its raw color. Cook for 2 to 3 minutes and stir in the scallions and parsley. Remove from the heat and season highly with salt, red and black pepper. Cook the filling before placing on pastry rounds. Be sure that the same amount of meat and gravy goes into each pie.

Place the flour, baking powder, and salt in a bowl. Beat together the melted shortening, milk, and eggs. Stir these into the flour, mixing thoroughly. Form the dough into a ball. Cover with a towel and let stand for 15 to 20 minutes before rolling out.

Roll out a portion of the dough on a lightly floured board. Cut into rounds the size of a saucer. Place a generous tablespoon of the meat mixture on one side of the pastry round. Dampen the edges. Fold the pastry over the filling and seal the edges with a floured fork. Gather pastry scraps and reroll once. Continue making pastries until all the dough and filling are used.

Heat 2 to 3 inches of oil in a deep heavy pan to 375 degrees. Add the meat pies a few at a time. Cook without crowding, turning occasionally, for 7 or 8 minutes, until golden brown. Drain on paper towels and serve hot.

To freeze: wrap pies individually or freeze until firm on cookie sheets, then place frozen pies in a plastic bag. To serve: let frozen pies defrost and fry in deep hot shortening until golden brown.

MAKES ABOUT 24 PIES   *A Cook's Tour,* Shreveport, LA

ASIAN MARINATED RACK OF LAMB

1 (8-ounce) jar hoisin sauce
½ cup honey
¼ cup dark Asian sesame oil
¼ cup dry sherry
¼ cup sesame seeds
¼ cup Asian fermented black beans,
  rinsed (optional)
2 teaspoons orange zest
1 teaspoon curry powder
2 racks of lamb (16 chops total),
  frenched and trimmed

For the marinade, combine and blend in a food processor the hoisin sauce, honey, sesame oil, sherry, sesame seeds, black beans, orange zest, and curry powder. Pour the marinade over the lamb in a large pan and marinate for several hours or overnight (up to 24 hours if desired).

Pour off the marinade. Allow the meat to come to room temperature while you heat the oven to 450 degrees.

Roast the lamb about 30 minutes, or until a meat thermometer registers between 140 and 145 degrees for medium rare. To serve, carve rack into individual chops. Serve 2 chops per person.

SERVES 8   *Simply Classic,* Seattle, WA

LAMB NOISETTES WITH ROSEMARY

The noisette, or eye of the loin chop, makes an elegant main dish for a formal luncheon.

6 lamb noisettes
Peanut oil
½ teaspoon powdered rosemary
Salt

Brush both sides of the chops with oil. Sprinkle them with the rosemary. Cook to your taste under the broiler or pan-broil them in a large heavy frying pan that has been sprinkled with a very thin layer of salt and heated before putting in the chops.

SERVES 6   *The Dallas Junior League Cookbook,* Dallas, TX

ROAST LAMB WITH TWO SAUCES

RED WINE BLACK BEAN SAUCE
1 cup dried black beans, picked over and rinsed
2 tablespoons chopped onion
2 tablespoons minced shallots
½ cup heavy cream
1 bay leaf
Pinch of thyme
Pinch of oregano
3 cups chicken broth, or as needed
⅓ cup Madeira or port
⅓ cup of red wine
2 tablespoons butter, softened

LAMB FILET
2-3 pounds lamb tenderloin
Salt
2 teaspoons crushed black and white peppers, combined
3 tablespoons vegetable oil

BASIL SAUCE
3 tablespoons butter
1 tablespoon flour
1 cup chicken broth
1 clove garlic, minced
1 bunch fresh basil, washed, dried, and stems removed

The night before, start the red wine black bean sauce: Place the beans in a medium pot; cover with water, and soak overnight.

The next day, drain the beans and put them back into the pot. Add the onions, shallots, cream, bay leaf, thyme, oregano; pour in enough chicken broth to cover. Bring to a boil, reduce the heat, cover, and simmer until the beans are very tender. Purée in a blender or food processor, adding a little chicken broth if the sauce is too thick. Strain through a fine sieve. Pour the wines into the pot; bring to a boil. Add the bean purée and simmer 5 minutes; keep the sauce hot.

Preheat the oven to 375 degrees. Salt the lamb on all sides; roll in crushed pepper to coat. Heat a large heavy skillet until very hot. Add the oil; brown the lamb on all sides. Transfer the lamb to a shallow baking pan; place in the oven and bake 8 minutes for rare, 12 to 15 minutes for well done. Remove from the oven; cover and let stand 10 minutes to seal in juices before serving.

While the lamb bakes, make the basil sauce: In a small saucepan over medium heat, melt the butter; whisk in the flour until well combined. Gradually add the chicken broth; whisk until thickened. Remove from the heat; add the garlic and basil. Purée in a blender or food processor. Strain through a fine sieve; keep hot.

Just before serving, whisk the 2 tablespoons of softened butter into black bean sauce; stir until the butter melts. Carefully ladle some of the sauce onto each of 4 or 6 serving plates, just to cover the bottom of the plate. Slice the lamb into medallions; arrange in a fan shape on the sauce. Make a thin line of basil sauce around the lamb. Using a toothpick, swirl the sauce decoratively.

SERVES 4–6   *Tampa Treasures,* Tampa, FL

LAMB MERLOT

½ cup soy sauce

½ cup dark Asian sesame oil

¼ cup chopped celery leaves

2 cloves garlic, minced

1 tablespoon dried thyme

1 teaspoon dried rosemary

½ teaspoon dried oregano

1 teaspoon dry mustard

1 leg of lamb (5-6 pounds), trimmed
of fat (see Note)

1 cup Merlot or other full-bodied
dry red wine

Make a marinade by combining the soy sauce, sesame oil, celery leaves, garlic, thyme, rosemary, oregano, and mustard. Blend well. Pour the marinade over the lamb and refrigerate overnight, turning the meat at least once the next morning to coat well.

Preheat the oven to 350 degrees. Drain the lamb, reserving the marinade, and place on a rack in a roasting pan. Roast 12 to 15 minutes per pound (or until 147 to 150 degrees on a meat thermometer). The lamb should be slightly pink on the inside.

Let the lamb stand at room temperature for 15 minutes before carving. Meanwhile, combine the reserved marinade and Merlot in a small saucepan and bring to a boil. Reduce the heat and simmer for several minutes to blend flavors. Serve separately.

NOTE: Three boned and trimmed racks of lamb may be substituted for the leg. Roast the marinated racks in a 450 degree oven for 20 to 25 minutes, basting frequently. A rack usually contains 8 ribs. Three racks serves 10 to 12 generously.

SERVES 8–10   *California Fresh*, Oakland–East Bay, CA

AGNEAU À LA MOUTARDE

For those who like the taste of fresh pepper.

1 leg of lamb (4-5 pounds),
butterflied

MARINADE

1 (8-ounce) jar Dijon mustard

½ cup olive oil

1 clove garlic, minced

2 teaspoons dried rosemary

1 teaspoon crushed bay leaves

½ cup honey

¼ cup freshly ground black pepper

1 small onion, minced

GARNISH

Fresh rosemary

Herb blossoms

Carefully trim all fat and sinew from the lamb. Open the meat on a work surface, cut side down, and make small slits at 2-inch intervals with a paring knife. Mix together all the marinade ingredients. Spread generously on all surfaces of the lamb. Cover tightly and marinate for at least 24 hours, preferably 2 days.

Preheat the oven to 350 degrees and prepare a barbecue grill for cooking. Drain the lamb, reserving the marinade. Bake the lamb for 20 to 30 minutes. Remove from the oven and finish cooking on the grill. (Grilling time will vary according to the thickness of the lamb. It should be charred on the outside but still pink on the inside.)

Transfer the lamb to a platter and cut into thin slices. Warm the marinade and pour some down the center of the slices. Garnish with fresh rosemary and herb blossoms. Serve with additional marinade.

SERVES 8   *A Matter of Taste*, Morristown, NJ

GRECIAN STUFFED LEG OF LAMB WITH LAMB SAUCE

6 to 7 pounds leg of lamb
½ teaspoon thyme
1 beaten egg
¼ cup milk
1 garlic clove, crushed
¼ teaspoon salt
Freshly ground black pepper
½ cup chopped parsley
¼ cup chopped pine nuts or almonds
1½ cups dried bread cubes
½ pound ground cooked ham

LAMB SAUCE
Leg of lamb bones
2-3 tablespoons vegetable oil
1 medium carrot, chopped fine
1 medium onion, chopped fine
2-3 tablespoons all-purpose flour
1 cup good red wine (preferably
   Burgundy)
2 cups chicken broth
1 celery stalk with leaves, chopped fine
1 garlic clove, mashed
1 teaspoon dried thyme
1 bay leaf, broken into 3 or 4 bits
Salt and pepper to taste
1 tablespoon chopped parsley

Remove the bone from the lamb or have your butcher do it. Make sure the cavity is enlarged. Trim away as much fat as possible. Rub the lamb all over with the thyme. Prepare the stuffing by combining the egg, milk, garlic, salt, pepper, parsley, nuts, bread crumbs, and ham. Spoon the stuffing into the cavity, sew or skewer it shut, and tie the lamb at 1-inch intervals. Place on a rack in a shallow roasting pan. Roast it at 325 degrees for 1½ to 2 hours or until done to your taste. Serve with lamb sauce (below).

Have your butcher saw the bones into 2½-inch chunks. In a heavy dutch oven, brown the bones in the oil with the carrot and onion for several minutes. Sprinkle with the flour and continue to brown for a few minutes more, stirring occasionally; be very careful that the flour does not burn. Remove from the heat; add the wine and broth, stirring well. Return the pot to the heat and bring to a simmer for several minutes, skimming off any scum if necessary as it forms. Add the celery, garlic, thyme, and bay leaf. Cover partially and simmer gently for 2 hours, skimming if necessary. Add additional broth and/or wine if the liquid evaporates below the level of the ingredients. Strain the sauce into another saucepan, using the back of a wooden spoon to press out the vegetable juices. The sauce should be velvet smooth. Degrease if necessary and season to taste with salt and pepper. Add the parsley just before serving.

NOTE: The flavor improves dramatically if the sauce is made a couple of days in advance and refrigerated. The degreasing is easier when the sauce is chilled.

MAKES ABOUT 2 CUPS   *A League of Cooks*, British Columbia

LAMB WITH HERB-HAZELNUT CRUST

A showstopper that gets more raves than Broadway.

1 cup hazelnuts, skinned (see Note)
8 tablespoons (1 stick) unsalted
   butter, softened
1 cup fine dry bread crumbs
3 cloves garlic, chopped fine
3 tablespoons chopped fresh
   rosemary
1 (6 to 7-pound) leg of lamb,
   trimmed of fat
Salt and freshly ground pepper to
   taste

Preheat the oven to 350 degrees. Process the hazelnuts in a food processor until coarsely chopped. Cream the butter in a bowl. Add the hazelnuts, bread crumbs, garlic, and rosemary; mix well. Season the lamb with salt and pepper; place it in a roasting pan. Pat the hazelnut mixture evenly over the lamb, allowing some to drop into the pan. Roast for 1¼ to 1½ hours or until meat thermometer registers 130 degrees for medium rare. Use the pan juices to make a flavorful gravy.

NOTE: To skin the hazelnuts, soak them in cold water for 1 minute. Drain and place on a baking sheet. Roast in a 400-degree oven for 5 to 7 minutes. Wrap the nuts immediately in a kitchen towel and rub vigorously until most of the skins are removed.

SERVES 10   *I'll Take Manhattan*, New York, NY

BUTTERFLIED LEG OF LAMB

Plan on starting this well in advance. It's best when marinated for at least 24 hours.

1 leg of lamb, butterflied and trimmed of fat (allow ½ pound bone-in weight for each person)

MARINADE
½ cup vegetable oil
¼ cup red wine vinegar
½ cup chopped onion
2 cloves garlic, minced
1 bay leaf
½ teaspoon dried basil or 1 teaspoon chopped fresh basil
½ teaspoon dried oregano or 1 teaspoon minced fresh oregano
2 teaspoons Dijon mustard
Salt and pepper to taste

Combine the ingredients for the marinade. Put the lamb into a large glass baking dish or a zipper-lock plastic storage bag and add the marinade. Seal tightly. Refrigerate the meat for 24 hours minimum or up to 2 days, turning it over occasionally.

When ready to cook, remove the lamb from the marinade and let stand at room temperature for ½ hour. Prepare a charcoal or gas-fired grill or preheat the broiler.

Grill the lamb on a barbecue grill for 15 minutes per side, basting frequently with the marinade, until done as desired. (For well done, allow 20 minutes per side.) If done in the oven, broil 4 inches from heat for 10 minutes per side. Then reduce the heat to 425 degrees and finish cooking in the oven for another 15 minutes or to the desired doneness. Lamb is best when pink inside and crusty outside. Serve any remaining marinade, heated, over lamb.

SERVES 10–12   *Treat Yourself to the Best,* Wheeling, WV

GRILLED LEG OF LAMB WITH ONIONS

1 leg of lamb, 4 to 6 pounds, boned and butterflied
6 medium-size onions, peeled and left whole
1 cup peanut oil
2 cups dry red wine
6 cloves garlic, chopped coarse
2 teaspoons cracked peppercorns
2 teaspoons salt
Juice of 1 lemon
1 teaspoon dried tarragon
½ teaspoon dried basil

Remove as much fat and sinew as possible from the lamb before marinating. Opening the meat flat, place it in a pan large enough to accommodate the meat, marinade, and onions. Prick the onion's all over with tines of a fork to allow marinade absorption. Place in the pan with the meat.

Make a marinade by combining the oil, red wine, garlic, peppercorns, salt, lemon juice, and herbs. Pour over the meat and onions. Marinate at least 6 hours in a cool place or overnight in the refrigerator. Turn often. The lamb should be grilled in the same manner as a steak. For rare, cook 8 minutes on each side. Onions should be placed on grill before the meat in order to brown well.

SERVES 4–6   *The Cotton Country Collection,* Monroe, LA

APRICOT-STUFFED PORK TENDERLOIN

½ cup dried apricots, chopped
2 tablespoons finely chopped onion
3 tablespoons butter, plus additional
as needed
1½ cups soft white bread crumbs
1 teaspoon dried parsley
¼ teaspoon salt
¼ teaspoon dried thyme
2 pork tenderloins (approximately ¾
pound each)
Ground black pepper to taste

Preheat the oven to 325 degrees. Cover the apricots with cold water and heat until boiling. Cover and reduce the heat. Simmer until tender 5 to 10 minutes. Drain.

Sauté the onion in 3 tablespoons of butter until soft, about 5 minutes. Add the crumbs, parsley, salt, and thyme. Toss lightly to combine; mix in the cooled apricots.

Slit the tenderloins lengthwise, not quite through. Lay the tenderloins flat and spread each one with half the apricot mixture. Roll lengthwise, jelly roll fashion. Tie to secure. (If preferred, place stuffing between two tenderloins and tie securely.) Place on rack in a small pan and spread with butter or margarine. Sprinkle with salt and pepper. Bake for 1 to 1¼ hours, basting occasionally. Garnish with spiced crabapples and watercress or parsley.

SERVES 4

Jubilation, Toronto

MARINATED PORK TENDERLOIN

MARINADE
8 Brazil nuts, shelled
2 tablespoons coriander seeds
¼ teaspoon freshly ground black
pepper
1 clove garlic
1 tablespoon brown sugar
1 teaspoon salt
¼ cup soy sauce
¼ cup olive oil
½ small onion

MEAT
3 pounds pork tenderloin

Combine the marinade ingredients in a food processor or blender and process until the nuts are chopped. Place the pork in a zipper-lock plastic bag and pour the marinade over. Refrigerate, turning occasionally, for 2 to 24 hours. Just before cooking, remove the pork from the marinade. Grill or broil for 20 to 25 minutes, turning so that all sides are brown and the pork is cooked but not dry. Slice into medallions and serve.

SERVES 6

Gold'n Delicious, Spokane, WA

PORK TENDERLOIN WITH CINNAMON

2 pounds pork tenderloin
¼ cup soy sauce
1½ teaspoons ground cinnamon
¼ cup sugar
¼ teaspoon salt
2 tablespoons sherry
1 teaspoon powdered ginger
2 teaspoons dry mustard
2 teaspoons lemon juice

Preheat the oven to 325 degrees. Place the pork in a roasting pan. Combine the soy sauce, cinnamon, sugar, salt, sherry, ginger, mustard, and lemon juice. Stir well and pour over the meat.

Bake for 45 minutes or until the internal temperature of the meat registers 145 degrees on a meat thermometer. Baste frequently with the sauce. Slice and serve hot with the pan juices.

SERVES 4–6

Virginia Seasons, Richmond, VA

ILLINI PORK MEDALLIONS

2 tablespoons vegetable oil

2 large pork tenderloins (1¼ pounds
   each)

4 tablespoons (½ stick) butter, melted

1 medium onion, sliced

½ cup thinly sliced celery

¼ pound fresh mushrooms, wiped,
   trimmed, and sliced

1 tablespoon flour

½ cup beef broth

½ cup white wine

1 teaspoon salt

¼ teaspoon freshly ground black
   pepper

Hot cooked rice

GARNISH

Spiced crab apples

Orange slices

Preheat the oven to 325 degrees. Heat the oil in a heavy skillet and brown the meat quickly on all sides. Remove to a plate. Melt the butter in the same skillet and sauté the onion, celery, and mushrooms for five minutes, until tender. Combine the flour and broth and stir into the vegetables. Stir in the wine and bring to a boil.

Arrange the tenderloins in a 13 × 9-inch baking pan and sprinkle with salt and pepper. Pour the vegetable mixture over all. Cover and bake for 1½ hours at 325 degrees. Cook to an internal temperature of 180 degrees for fresh pork. Remove pork from pan and cut into ½-inch-thick slices. Arrange on a platter and serve with rice.

SERVES 6   *Honest to Goodness,* Springfield, IL

PORK MEDALLIONS WITH CURRANTS AND SCOTCH

⅓ cup currants

½ cup Scotch whisky

2 pork tenderloins, about ¾ to 1
   pound each, visible fat removed

Salt and ground black pepper

2 tablespoons butter

3 tablespoons Dijon mustard

3 tablespoons brown sugar

½ cup chicken broth

1 teaspoon dried thyme

Combine the currants and Scotch in a bowl. Set aside. Cut the tenderloins into ¾-inch fillets. Season with salt and pepper. Heat the butter in a heavy-bottomed skillet over medium-high heat. Brown the fillets quickly, allowing about 1 minute per side. Reduce the heat and cook an additional 5 to 6 minutes per side.

Remove the fillets and keep warm. Pour off any accumulated fat. Drain the currants, reserving the Scotch. Add the Scotch to the drippings in the skillet, stirring to scrape up the crusty bits on the bottom. Stir in the mustard, sugar, broth, and thyme. Whisk until smooth. Bring the mixture to a boil and continue to boil to thicken slightly. Reduce the heat and add the currants and fillets. Cover the pan and heat the fillets in the sauce for 2-3 minutes. Serve immediately.

SERVES 6-8

Sensational Seasons: A Taste & Tour of Arkansas, Fort Smith, AR

MARINATED PORK TENDERLOIN WITH MUSTARD SAUCE

MEAT
3 pork tenderloins, ¾ pound each
½ cup soy sauce
½ cup Bourbon whiskey
¼ cup packed brown sugar

MUSTARD SAUCE
½ cup sour cream
½ cup mayonnaise
1 tablespoon dry mustard
1 tablespoon chopped scallions or
  onions
1½ tablespoons white wine vinegar

To prepare the meat: In a shallow dish, blend the soy sauce, Bourbon, and brown sugar. Add the meat, turning to coat with the liquid, and marinate in the refrigerator for several hours.

While the meat is marinating, prepare sauce: In a medium bowl, mix the sour cream, mayonnaise, mustard, scallions, and vinegar. Let stand at room temperature at least 4 hours.

Preheat the oven to 325 degrees. Bake the meat in the marinade for 45 minutes, basting frequently. Serve with the sauce.

SERVES 4   *South of the Fork,* Dallas, TX

MICHIGAN CROWN ROAST OF PORK WITH WILD RICE STUFFING

Spectacular company meal!

WILD RICE STUFFING
1 cup wild rice
1 teaspoon salt
¼ teaspoon dried thyme
1 bay leaf
2 sprigs parsley, chopped
4 tablespoons (½ stick) butter
½ pound mushrooms, sautéed
1 small onion, chopped
2 ribs celery, chopped
½ cup pine nuts or pecans
  (optional)
½ cup dried cherries

1 crown roast of pork, 6 to 7
  pounds (2 ribs per person),
  backbone removed and rib ends
  frenched
Salt, pepper, and minced garlic, to
  taste
Whole spiced crabapples, 1 for each
  rib

To prepare the stuffing, place the wild rice in a saucepan, cover with cold water, and bring to a boil. Remove from the heat and skim. Drain in a colander. Return to the saucepan and add 3 cups of water, the salt, thyme, bay leaf, and chopped parsley. Bring to a boil, reduce the heat to a simmer, cover, and cook about 30 minutes, or until tender. Remove from the heat and drain. Add the butter and blend. Add the sautéed mushrooms, onion, celery, nuts, and dried cherries.

Preheat the oven to 325 degrees. Place the roast with the rib ends up on a rack in a shallow pan. Cover each rib end with foil so the bones will not char; season with salt, pepper, and garlic salt. Roast about 30 minutes per pound, or until a meat thermometer registers 185 degrees. Halfway through the roasting time, fill the cavity with wild rice stuffing. When the roast is done, place it on a heated platter. Remove the foil from the tips of the ribs and place a spiced crabapple on the end of each rib. To serve, slice downward between the ribs and remove the chops one at a time. Serve each person 2 chops and a spoonful of stuffing.

SERVES 6-8   *The Bountiful Arbor,* Ann Arbor, MI

BEGINNER'S PIG ROAST

PEOPLE

Friendly butcher
Friend with electric spit big enough for pig
Friend who knows how to butcher pig
Oneself

EQUIPMENT

Electric spit and electric outlet
4 large pieces of sheet metal on angle iron to surround pit
Extension cord
Garden hose and water outlet
14-gauge galvanized wire pliers and cutters
3 pairs welding gloves
2 pairs vise grips (optional for holding sheet metal)
Sledgehammer
Shovel and mattock
Wheelbarrow
Garden rake
Large pile of dry cherry wood
Little bit of kerosene
Matches
2 really sharp knives
2 pairs new white work gloves
Pickup truck to transport spit
Station wagon to transport pig
Large folding banquet table
Newspaper and plastic cover to cover table
Garbage bags
Phillips and regular screwdrivers
Splitting maul
Concrete block
Grass seed
Lots of cold beer
Sleeping bag for night before
Boombox or tape players (cassette, preferably)
Change of clothes
Lawn chairs for cookers
Fifth of Scotch
Repertoire of lies and dirty jokes

Order one pig one month before "pig roast day" from friendly butcher; 1 pound per person, minimum 50 pounds. Ask friendly butcher to fill pig's stomach with kielbasa or chicken and to place one clove of garlic in each ham and shoulder. Dig pit 12 to 18 inches deep to fit pig and spit one week before roast day; dig supplemental pit, 2 feet × 2 feet × 12 inches, nearby. Gather all equipment for pig roast.

Get up early. Hook up water hose. Two hours before roasting begins, fill main pit with wood to 12 inches above ground and start fire. While one friend watches fire, go pick up pig from friendly butcher who opens store early for you. Put pig on spit rod. Wire pig tightly to spit rod. Put spit rod on spit after flames are gone and fire is all coals. Throw switch on motor. Start fire in supplemental pit so will have coals as needed.

Watch pig cook. Drink cold beer and supplement with Scotch as needed. Roast pig 1 hour for each 10 pounds, minimum of 5 hours. Sheet metal keeps heat on pig. May be longer without. To see if pig is done, cut one shoulder and one ham to bone. If all white, is done. If not, keep roasting until done. One hour before you want to eat, take pig off spit and put on banquet table. Use clean gloves to remove skin. Have smart friend butcher pig. Slice large portions as smart friend butchers. Serve pig while hot. Make sure it doesn't rain. As pig cooks it may slip on spit. Rewire. One day after roast, fill pit with concrete blocks so you don't have to re-dig pit next year. Cover blocks with dirt. Plant grass seed.

HINT: Serve with fresh corn on the cob, fresh sliced tomatoes and scallions, and fresh green beans.

SERVES MANY   *Treat Yourself to the Best,* Wheeling, WV

CROWN ROAST OF PORK WITH MACADAMIA NUT STUFFING

ROAST

1 tablespoon salt

Dash of ground black pepper

1½ tablespoons lemon juice

2 tablespoons chopped parsley

1 clove garlic, minced

1 tablespoon olive oil

½ teaspoon dried basil

2 tablespoons finely chopped onion

1 crown roast of pork, 6 to 7
   pounds, backbone removed and
   rib ends frenched

MACADAMIA NUT STUFFING

8 tablespoons (1 stick) butter, plus
   additional for basting

1½ cloves garlic, chopped

1 cup chopped onion

1½ cups chopped celery

3 cups diced fresh pineapple

1½ cups peeled and diced tart apple

1½ cups peeled and sliced papaya

¾ teaspoon ground black pepper

1½ teaspoons salt

1½ cups chopped macadamia nuts

7 to 8 cups diced bread, crusts
   removed

GARNISHES

Watercress or parsley wedges

Papaya and pineapple wedges

Preheat the oven to 350 degrees.

To prepare the roast: Mix the salt, pepper, lemon juice, parsley, garlic, olive oil, basil, and onion into a paste. Cut 6 or 8 slits on the inside of the roast and place some of the paste in each slit. Rub the outside of the roast with more of the paste. Place the roast rib ends up in a large roasting pan and set aside.

To prepare the stuffing: Melt 8 tablespoons of butter and sauté the garlic, onion, and celery for 5 minutes. Add the fruits and seasoning, and simmer until heated through. Toss lightly with the nuts and bread. Place the stuffing inside the crown, saving any extra stuffing to heat and serve separately.

Roast the meat covered, allowing 30 minutes per pound, until a meat thermometer registers 175 degrees. Baste with melted butter every 20 minutes. Uncover during the last hour to brown. Place the roast on heated serving platter and garnish.

SERVES 12   *The Seattle Classic,* Seattle, WA

WOMEN'S HEALTH AWARENESS PROJECT JUNIOR LEAGUE OF PEORIA, ILLINOIS

The Junior League of Peoria, Illinois, initiated the Women's Health Awareness Project to focus on women's health issues, with special emphasis on breast health education, nutrition, and fitness. This project was also originated to create an awareness and support of the Susan G. Komen Breast Cancer Foundation, a national foundation developed in memory of a Junior League of Peoria member who died at the age of 36 from breast cancer. An offshoot of this project was the organization of the "Race for the Cure" to raise money for breast cancer research.

CROWN ROAST OF PORK WITH CRANBERRY STUFFING AND MUSTARD SAUCE BALCHAN

1 crown roast of pork,
approximately 18 chops, backbone
removed and rib ends frenched
Cranberry stuffing (below)
Orange slices or spiced peaches and
watercress sprigs for garnish
Mustard sauce Balchan (below)

CRANBERRY STUFFING
8 tablespoons (1 stick) butter
4 cups cooked wild rice
2 cups raw cranberries, chopped
coarsely
3½ tablespoons sugar
2 tablespoons grated onion
1 teaspoon salt
½ teaspoon dried marjoram
1 clove garlic, minced fine
½ teaspoon ground black pepper
½ teaspoon ground mace
½ teaspoon dried thyme
½ teaspoon dried dill weed

MUSTARD SAUCE BALCHAN
4 tablespoons pan drippings or 4
tablespoons (½ stick) butter
¼ cup all-purpose flour
1 cup dry white wine
½ cup chicken broth
¼ cup heavy cream
3 tablespoons Dijon mustard
2 tablespoons dry mustard
Salt and ground black pepper to
taste

Preheat the oven to 350 degrees. Cover each rib end of the roast with foil to prevent burning in the oven. Wrap foil around the bottom of the roast so the stuffing will not leak through. Place the roast in a large roasting pan with the rib ends up. Roast 20 minutes per pound. One hour before the roast has completed cooking, fill the middle of the crown with cranberry stuffing, piling it quite high. Extra stuffing can be put in a buttered baking dish, covered, and heated 30 minutes. Return the roast to the oven and roast an additional 1 hour. If the stuffing becomes too brown, cover it with foil. Place roast on a platter, remove the foil tips, and decorate with paper frills. Garnish with orange slices or spiced peaches and watercress sprigs. Pass the mustard sauce separately.

To prepare the stuffing: In a large saucepan, melt the butter and add the wild rice, cranberries, sugar, onion, salt, and spices. Cook over medium-low heat for 10 to 15 minutes or until heated thoroughly. Stir the mixture often. Allow the stuffing to cool.

To prepare the sauce: In a medium saucepan, blend the pan drippings with the flour. Cook the roux over low heat for 3 minutes. Stir in the white wine and cook until thickened, approximately 3 minutes. Add the chicken broth and cream and cook an additional 5 minutes. Stir in the Dijon mustard and dry mustard. Season with salt and pepper to taste.

NOTE: The roast can be kept warm in a 200 degree oven while the mustard sauce is prepared.

SERVES 8–10 *The California Heritage Cookbook,* Pasadena, CA

PORK ROAST AND APPLES

1 loin or center rib pork roast, 4 to 5 pounds
1 teaspoon salt
⅛ teaspoon ground black pepper
1¼ teaspoons ground ginger
¾ teaspoon grated nutmeg
¾ teaspoon ground cinnamon
¼ cup honey
1 tablespoon lemon juice
¼ teaspoon ground cinnamon
2 medium apples peeled, cored, and cut in wedges

Preheat the oven to 325 degrees. Rub the outside of the roast with a mixture of the salt, pepper, 1 teaspoon of the ginger, ½ teaspoon nutmeg, and ½ teaspoon cinnamon. Place the roast fat side up in a shallow roasting pan. Insert a meat thermometer if desired, and roast until the meat reaches an internal temperature of 170 degrees, about 2½ hours. When the meat is ready, transfer to a serving dish. In a medium skillet, combine the honey, ½ cup water, the lemon juice, and the remaining spices. Bring to a boil and add the apple wedges. Simmer covered for 8-10 minutes, until the apples are just tender and slightly translucent. Serve with the roast.

SERVES 8

Cornsilk, Sioux City, IA

FESTIVE PORK ROAST

1 (5-pound) boneless rolled pork roast
4 teaspoon cornstarch

MARINADE
1½ cups dry red wine
⅔ cup packed brown sugar
½ cup vinegar
½ cup ketchup
¼ cup vegetable oil
3 tablespoons soy sauce
4 cloves garlic, minced
2 teaspoons curry powder or to taste
1 teaspoon ground ginger
½ teaspoon freshly ground black pepper

Place the meat in a large zipper-lock plastic bag. Combine all the marinade ingredients in a bowl and add ½ cup of water. Stir to combine, then pour the marinade over the meat, close the bag, and set it in a shallow dish. Marinate in the refrigerator for 6 to 8 hours or overnight, turning occasionally.

Preheat the oven to 325 degrees. Drain meat, reserving 2½ cups marinade. Pat the meat dry and place on a rack in a shallow roasting pan. Roast for 2½ hours or until a meat thermometer registers 170 degrees.

Blend the cornstarch into the reserved marinade; cook, stirring, until thickened and bubbly. Brush the roast frequently with the sauce during the last 15 minutes of cooking. Heat the remaining sauce and pass with the meat.

SERVES 12

Beyond Parsley, Kansas City, MO

TOTAL COLLABORATION
JUNIOR LEAGUE OF ST. LOUIS, MISSOURI

The TOTAL (Teen Opportunities to Achieve in Life) Collaboration created by the Junior League of St. Louis combines two programs. TOTAL Team is an after school program designed to provide middle school students of both genders with a solid foundation for making well-informed choices in life, centering around strengthening self-esteem, receiving life options training, and participating in community service. TOTAL Partners is a comprehensive program for pregnant and parenting high school students. Both TOTAL programs encourage teens to stay in school and work to establish and achieve positive life goals.

PORK ROAST CASSIS

1 boneless rolled pork roast, 4-5
   pounds

MARINADE
½ cup glace de viande, or 2
   tablespoons beef extract dissolved
   in ½ cup water
½ cup sherry
2 cloves garlic, minced
1 tablespoon dry mustard
1 teaspoon ground ginger
1 teaspoon dried thyme, crushed

CASSIS SAUCE
1 (10-ounce) jar currant jelly
1½ teaspoons cornstarch
1 tablespoon soy sauce
2 tablespoons crème de cassis
   liqueur
3 tablespoons sherry

Put the meat in a large zipper-lock plastic bag. Combine all the marinade ingredients. Pour the marinade over the meat, seal the bag, and refrigerate for 24 hours.

Preheat the oven to 325 degrees. Remove the meat from the marinade; roast for 2½ to 3 hours or until the internal temperature is 160 degrees.

Make the sauce: Heat the currant jelly in a small saucepan until melted. Dissolve the cornstarch in the soy sauce. Add the cassis, sherry, and soy sauce to the saucepan. Heat until the sauce is lightly thickened. Serve over the pork roast.

VARIATION: Add ½ cup of dried currants to the sauce.

SERVES 8-10   *A Cleveland Collection,* Cleveland, OH

PORK LOIN WITH CHERRY ALMOND SAUCE

1 boned and tied pork loin roast, 4
   to 6 pounds
1 (12-ounce) jar cherry preserves
¼ cup light corn syrup
¼ cup red wine vinegar
¼ teaspoon salt
¼ teaspoon grated nutmeg
¼ teaspoon ground cloves
¼ teaspoon ground cinnamon
⅛ teaspoon ground black pepper
¼ cup slivered blanched almonds

Preheat the oven to 325 degrees. Put the pork on a rack in a shallow roasting pan. Place in the oven and roast uncovered about 3 hours.

Meanwhile, combine the cherry preserves, corn syrup, vinegar, salt, and spices. Bring to a boil and boil 1 minute. Add the almonds.

Baste the meat with the sauce several times during the last 30 minutes of roasting time. Serve the remaining sauce with the meat.

SERVES 8   *Clusters of Culinary Creations,* Kankakee, IL

PORK CHOPS À LA ROGUE

An appropriate main course for an elegant dinner.

8 loin pork chops, cut 1 inch thick
½ teaspoon vegetable oil
Salt and ground black pepper to
 taste
6 fresh pears, peeled, halved, and
 cored
3 tablespoons orange juice
¼ cup packed brown sugar
¼ teaspoon ground cinnamon
⅓ cup dry sherry
6 teaspoons butter
1 teaspoon cornstarch

Preheat the oven to 350 degrees. In a skillet over medium heat, brown the pork chops in oil. Place the chops in a shallow pan; sprinkle with salt and pepper. Arrange the pear halves rounded side down on and around the chops. Sprinkle with the orange juice, then with the brown sugar and cinnamon. Pour the sherry over all.

Put a teaspoon of butter in the hollow of each pear. Cover and bake 20 minutes. Continue baking uncovered for an additional 20 minutes. Remove from the oven and place the pears and pork chops on a warm serving dish. Dissolve the cornstarch in 1 tablespoon of water, add to the juices in the pan, and cook until the mixture thickens. Pour the sauce over the chops and pears.

SERVES 6–8   *Rogue River Rendezvous,* Jackson County, OR

PORK CHOPS ARDENNAISE

12 slices thick bacon, cut into strips
 or small squares
¾ cup white wine
3 scallions, chopped fine
4 or 5 loin pork chops
Salt and freshly ground pepper to
 taste
2 tablespoons flour
4 tablespoons (½ stick) butter
½ cup heavy cream
1 teaspoon Dijon mustard
1 tablespoon chopped parsley

Place the bacon in a bowl and cover with the wine and onions. Let stand for 30 minutes. Drain and reserve the wine.

Lightly season the chops with salt and pepper and dredge in flour. Heat the butter in a heavy skillet and cook the chops over moderate heat for 6 or 7 minutes per side. Add the bacon and onions. Continue cooking for 2 to 3 minutes. Add the cream and the reserved wine and simmer for 10 to 12 minutes. Remove the chops to a warm serving platter. Boil the sauce until slightly reduced; add the mustard and parsley. Adjust the seasonings and spoon the sauce over chops.

SERVES 3–4   *Traditions,* Little Rock, AR

SPARERIBS

4 pounds spareribs
1 cup vinegar
½ cup lemon juice
1 teaspoon salt
1 teaspoon ground black pepper
1 bottle A-1 sauce
1 bottle Worcestershire sauce
½ bottle lemon juice

Make a basting sauce of the vinegar, lemon juice, salt, pepper, and 1 cup of water. Prepare a charcoal fire and place the ribs on a rack about 4 inches from the coals. Baste the ribs over a low fire every 10 minutes for 40 minutes.

Combine the A-1 and Worcestershire sauce with the ½ bottle of lemon juice. Cook the ribs for 20 minutes longer, basting frequently with the sauce.

SERVES 6   *Recipe Jubilee,* Mobile, AL

SUPERB SPARERIBS

3 pounds spareribs
1 teaspoon salt
¼ teaspoon sugar
⅛ teaspoon turmeric
⅛ teaspoon paprika
⅛ teaspoon celery salt
⅛ teaspoon ground black pepper

MARINADE
1 cup ketchup
½ cup minced green bell pepper
½ cup minced onion
⅓ cup cider vinegar
¼ cup packed dark brown sugar
1 tablespoon Worcestershire sauce
1½ teaspoons minced garlic
1 teaspoon dry mustard
½ teaspoon Tabasco
½ teaspoon salt
¼ teaspoon dried basil
¼ teaspoon ground black pepper

Place the ribs on a flat surface. Combine the salt, sugar, turmeric, paprika, celery salt, and pepper. Rub the ribs on both sides with the mixture and place in a large deep bowl.

Make the marinade: Combine all ingredients and add ¾ cup of water. Mix well, spoon over the ribs, and marinate overnight, turning occasionally.

Arrange the ribs on a rack in a smoker and smoke according to the manufacturer's instructions for 4 to 6 hours.

SERVES 4   *Magic,* Birmingham, AL

DRUNKEN AUNT'S BEAN CURD

This quick and easy Asian stir-fry combines lean ground pork and firm tofu. Serve with steamed rice.

¼ cup vegetable oil
3 small cloves garlic, minced
7 scallions, chopped
1 tablespoon chopped fresh
    gingerroot
½ pound lean ground pork
2 squares firm tofu (bean curd),
    diced
2 tablespoons hot bean paste
1½ tablespoons soy sauce
1 tablespoon rice wine or sherry
1½ teaspoons cornstarch mixed with
    1 tablespoon water

Heat the oil in a wok or large skillet. Stir-fry the garlic, scallions, and ginger until fragrant, about 1 minute. Add the pork and cook, stirring to separate into small pieces, until the pork changes color. Add the tofu, 1 cup of water, the bean paste, soy sauce, and wine or sherry. Cover and steam for 3 minutes. Stir in the cornstarch mixture and cook until thickened. Transfer to a serving platter. Serve immediately.

SERVES 4   *San Francisco Encore,* San Francisco, CA

STUFFED CHILES IN NUT SAUCE

NOGADA SAUCE

5 slices firm white bread, crusts
  removed
Cold milk
4 cups heavy cream
4½ cups shelled pecans or walnuts
Salt to taste

STUFFED CHILES

16 poblano chiles
3½ pounds tomatoes, chopped
1 medium onion, chopped
Chopped parsley to taste
1 cinnamon stick
2 tablespoons vegetable oil
3½ pounds ground meat (beef and
  pork)
1½ cups raisins
1½ cups shelled almonds, peeled
Pinch of sugar
½ cup green olives, pitted and
  halved (optional)
Pomegranate seeds or canned
  cherries, chopped, for garnish
Parsley sprigs for garnish

Prepare the nogada sauce: Soak the bread in a small amount of cold milk. Liquefy in a blender the cream, nuts, salt, and milk-soaked bread. The sauce should be quite thick, so more cream may be added if needed. Refrigerate until well chilled.

Peel the chiles: Place them directly over a gas flame or under the broiler until they char and blister, turning from time to time. Put them in a plastic bag and seal it for 10 to 20 minutes to loosen the skins. Slit each peeled chile along one side and carefully remove the seed and veins; leave the stem end intact.

In a large heavy saucepan, fry the tomatoes, onion, parsley, and cinnamon stick in the oil until the onions are soft. Add the meat, raisins, almonds, sugar, and olives. Cook, stirring occasionally, for 20 minutes or until browned. Remove the cinnamon stick.

Stuff the chiles with the meat mixture until they are well filled. Arrange the warm chiles on a serving platter and pour over the chilled mogada sauce. Garnish with pomegranate seeds and parsley sprigs. Serve right away.

SERVES 8   *Buen Provecho,* Mexico City

SPAGHETTI ALLA CARBONARA

This recipe is a house specialty at the Las Vegas Hilton's Italian restaurant, Leonardo's. For a more elaborate fare, it makes a wonderful accompaniment to a shrimp entree.

¾ pound spaghetti
½ cup chicken broth
2 tablespoons dry white wine
1 garlic clove, minced
8 tablespoons (1 stick) butter
4 slices bacon, cooked and crumbled
Salt and freshly ground pepper to taste
¾ cup freshly grated Parmesan cheese
2 egg yolks

Cook the spaghetti in a large pot of boiling salted water until it is tender but still firm. Drain and keep warm. (Do not rinse spaghetti.)

In a large skillet, combine the chicken broth, wine, garlic, butter, and bacon. Bring the mixture to a boil. Season with salt and pepper. Add the warm spaghetti and toss well. Finally add the Parmesan cheese and egg yolks. Toss again and serve on warm plates.

SERVES 2–4   *Winning at the Table,* Las Vegas, NV

STUFFED HAM

1 ready-to-eat ham, shank portion,
  bone in (about 10 pounds)
Paprika

DRESSING
1 medium box soda crackers
⅓ jar India relish or chow chow
  pickle
6 hard-boiled eggs, mashed
½ cup vinegar
½ cup packed brown sugar
½ teaspoon ground cloves
2 tablespoons prepared mustard
Salt
Ground black pepper
Celery seed

Have the butcher cut the bone out of the ham, replace it and tie the ham. Place the ham on a rack in a roasting pan and bake about 18 minutes a pound, untill a meat thermometer registers 160 degrees.

Combine the dressing ingredients in a bowl, moistening with enough water to make a stiff but cohesive mixture. While the ham is hot, remove the bone and stuff the cavity with the dressing, saving enough to pat over the outside of the ham. Sprinkle generously with paprika. Slice and serve.

MAKES 18–20 SERVINGS   *Huntsville Heritage,* Huntsville, AL

SALSICCE CON PEPERONI E PASTA

8 links Italian sweet or hot sausage
2 tablespoons olive oil
2 large onions, sliced into rings
2 red bell peppers, sliced into strips
2 green bell peppers, sliced into strips
1 large clove garlic, minced
1 (28-ounce) can chopped Italian
  plum tomatoes
1 teaspoon dried oregano
1 pound pasta (linguine, fettuccine,
  etc.), cooked and drained

Place the sausage links in a large skillet and add ½ cup of water. Cover and cook over medium heat until lightly browned on all sides, approximately 20 minutes. In a separate skillet, heat the olive oil. Add the onions, red peppers, green peppers, and garlic. Cook and stir over medium heat until the vegetables are slightly limp, approximately 5 minutes. Add the tomatoes with their juice and the oregano. Cook another 5 minutes. Remove from the heat. When the sausages are cooked, drain off excess grease and add the links to the pepper mixture. Serve over the hot pasta.

SERVES 4–6   *Pinch of Salt Lake,* Salt Lake City, UT

SAUSAGE GRITS

*Great for brunch. And it can be assembled
the night before and baked in the morning.*

1 pound bulk pork sausage
2 cups shredded Cheddar cheese
3 tablespoons butter
3 cups hot cooked grits
3 eggs, beaten
1½ cups milk

Preheat the oven to 350 degrees. Lightly coat a 13 × 9-inch baking pan with vegetable oil cooking spray.

In a heavy skillet, cook the sausage, stirring frequently, until brown. Spoon into the prepared baking pan.

Add the cheese and butter to the hot grits and stir until melted. In a small bowl, combine the eggs and milk. Stir into the grits.

Pour the grits mixture over the sausage. Bake uncovered for 1 hour. Serve hot.

SERVES 8   *A Slice of Paradise,* West Palm Beach, FL

RED BEANS AND RICE

1 ham bone
¼ teaspoon Tabasco
1 teaspoon Worcestershire sauce
1 pound red beans, washed and
    picked over
1 cup chopped celery
1 cup chopped onion
1½ cloves garlic, minced
3 tablespoons vegetable oil
½ pound ham, cubed
¼ pound hot sausage, diced
2 bay leaves
Salt and freshly ground pepper to
    taste
¼ cup chopped parsley
2 cups cooked rice

In a large pot or Dutch oven, combine the ham bone with 4 cups of water, the Tabasco, Worcestershire, and beans. Bring to a boil, lower the heat, and cook, uncovered, over a low flame. In a small skillet, sauté the celery, onion, and garlic in the oil until transparent. In another pan sauté the ham and sausage until lightly browned; drain. Add the cooked meats and the onion mixture to the beans. Add the bay leaves, salt, and pepper and continue to cook over a low flame until the beans are soft and creamy, approximately 2½ hours. Remove the bay leaves and add the parsley before serving. For additional thickness, uncover and cook longer. Serve over hot fluffy rice.

SERVES 8   *The Plantation Cookbook,* New Orleans, LA

"GATOR" MEAT BALLS

Need to come South for a 'gator!

5¼ pounds alligator meat
1½ pounds onions, peeled
2 bunches scallions, trimmed
2 bunches parsley, washed
1 whole head garlic, peeled
¼ bunch celery, cleaned
1 cup vegetable oil
2¼ pounds cold mashed potatoes
2½ pounds cracker meal, plus
    additional as needed
8 eggs
6 tablespoons Creole seasoning
¼ cup salt
2 tablespoons black pepper
Fat for deep frying

Put the meat through a meat grinder together with the onions, scallions, parsley, garlic, and celery. Or chop coarse in a food processor, working in batches.

Heat the oil in a large heavy kettle and add the meat mixture. Cook, stirring, for 30 minutes. Add the potatoes, cracker meal, eggs, and seasonings. Mix well and chill at least 1 hour.

Shape into 1-ounce balls. Roll in cracker meal and fry in deep fat.

MAKES ABOUT 208 BALLS   *Pirate's Pantry,* Lake Charles, LA

PASTA DELLA MADRE DI DIAVOLO

1 pound penne pasta
⅓ cup olive oil
2 tablespoons crushed garlic
2 scallions, chopped fine
1 bay leaf
5 sprigs fresh thyme
1½ cups diced hot coppacola (pork shoulder butt)
1 cup seeded and finely chopped fresh jalapeño peppers
⅓ cup dry red wine
1 pound raw shrimp, shelled and deveined, tails intact
½ cup grated Parmesan or Pecorino cheese
Salt and ground black pepper
¼ cup chopped parsley

Cook the penne in a large pot of boiling salted water until it is tender but still firm. Drain and set aside.

Heat the olive oil over medium heat in a large saucepan. Add the garlic, scallions, bay leaf, and thyme. Reduce the heat and simmer for a few minutes. Add the dried coppacola and simmer for approximately 4 minutes. Add the peppers and red wine. Continue to simmer for another 2 or 3 minutes, stirring frequently. Add the shrimp and cook until the shrimp turn pink.

Add the boiled penne to the saucepan, mix, and cover. This allows the pasta to absorb the liquids. Transfer the mixture to a large serving dish; mix in the Parmesan cheese and freshly ground pepper. Sprinkle with chopped parsley and serve.

SERVES 4–6

Feast of Eden, Monterey, CA

VEAL SCALLOPS IN MUSTARD-CREAM SAUCE

4 tablespoons (½ stick) butter
2 tablespoons vegetable oil
4 scallions, chopped
1¾ pounds veal scallops or cutlets, sliced ¼ inch thick and pounded thin
Freshly ground pepper to taste
⅓ cup dry white wine
3 tablespoons Dijon mustard
½ cup heavy cream
1 large tomato, peeled, seeded, and chopped
Chopped fresh parsley

Melt the butter with the oil in a large skillet. Add the scallions and cook for 4 or 5 minutes over low heat. Remove with a slotted spoon and reserve. Increase the heat to moderately high and add the veal, in batches if necessary. Cook 1 to 2 minutes per side. Remove the veal, season with pepper, and keep warm.

Return the scallions to the pan, add the wine, and bring to a boil. Cook until the mixture is reduced to ¼ cup. Whisk in the mustard and cream; boil for 2 minutes. Place the veal on a serving dish. Spoon the sauce over the veal. Garnish with tomatoes and parsley.

SERVES 4–6

A Cleveland Collection, Cleveland, OH

VEAL SCALLOPS WITH SHALLOTS AND APPLES

¾ cup freshly grated Parmesan
  cheese

¼ cup all-purpose flour

Salt and freshly ground pepper

1 pound veal scallops or cutlets,
  sliced ¼ inch thick and pounded
  thin

4 tablespoons olive oil or butter

2 green apples, peeled, cored, and
  sliced

4 shallots, cut in wedges, or 1 onion
  cut in wedges and halved

1 cup chicken broth

Mix the grated cheese and the flour. Salt and pepper the veal and dredge in the cheese and flour mixture. Heat the oil in a large skillet over medium heat. Cook veal for 2 minutes on each side or until brown. Remove the veal from the pan and keep warm.

Add the apples and shallots to the pan. sauté for 3 minutes; add the broth and simmer for 5 minutes. Return the veal to the pan and heat 1 minute longer. Transfer the veal in its sauce to a heated platter and serve.

S E R V E S 4   *Some Like It Hot,* McAllen, TX

GRILLADES

4 pounds beef or veal rounds, ½
  inch thick

½ cup bacon drippings

½ cup all-purpose flour

1 cup chopped onions

2 cups chopped scallions

¾ cup chopped celery

1½ cups chopped green bell pepper

2 cloves garlic, minced

2 cups chopped tomatoes

½ teaspoon dried tarragon
  (optional)

⅔ teaspoon dried thyme

1 cup red wine

1 tablespoon salt

½ teaspoon black pepper

3 bay leaves

½ teaspoon Tabasco

2 tablespoons Worcestershire sauce

3 tablespoons chopped parlsey

Remove all fat from the meat. Cut the meat into serving-size pieces and pound to ¼-inch thickness. In a Dutch oven, working in batches to avoid crowding, brown the meat well in 4 tablespoons of the bacon grease. As the meat browns, remove it to a warm plate. Add the remaining 4 tablespoons of bacon grease and the flour to the drippings in the pan. Stir and cook to make a dark brown roux. Add the onions, scallions, celery, green pepper, and garlic, and sauté until limp. Add the tomatoes, tarragon, and thyme and cook for 3 minutes. Add the wine and 1 cup of water. Stir well for several minutes. Return the meat to the pan and add the salt, pepper, bay leaves, Tabasco, and Worcestershire sauce.

Lower the heat, stir, and continue cooking. If veal rounds are used, simmer covered approximately 1 hour. If beef rounds are used, simmer covered approximately 2 hours. Remove the bay leaves. Stir in the parsley. Remove from the heat, allow to cool and let the grillades set for several hours or overnight in the refrigerator. More liquid may be added. Grillades should be very tender. Serve over grits or rice.

S E R V E S 8   *The Plantation Cookbook,* New Orleans, LA

VEAL WITH SEAFOOD

Heavenly.

1½ pounds veal scallops or cutlets, sliced ¼ inch thick and pounded thin
1 teaspoon salt
1 teaspoon ground white pepper
3 tablespoons all-purpose flour
6 tablespoons butter
1 tablespoon olive oil
2 tablespoons chopped scallion
½ cup dry white wine
1 cup heavy cream
½ pound mushrooms, wiped, trimmed and sliced
1 tablespoon lemon juice
2 tablespoons chopped parsley
¼ pound shrimp, peeled, deveined, and steamed
½ pound crabmeat, picked over well

Pat the veal dry with paper towels. Combine the salt, pepper, and flour in a shallow dish. Dredge the veal in the flour, shaking off the excess.

In a large heavy skillet, melt 3 tablespoons of the butter with the oil. When hot, sauté the scallops for 2 minutes on each side. Remove to a heated platter and keep warm.

Reduce the heat and sauté the scallion for 1 minute; remove from the pan. Add the wine and deglaze the pan over high heat until the liquid is reduced by half, about 2 minutes. Reduce the heat to low. Add the cream and simmer for 4 minutes. Add the mushrooms and cook for 3 minutes. Add the lemon juice and 1 tablespoon of the parsley; cook 1 minute. Pour the sauce over veal.

In a separate pan, melt the remaining 3 tablespoons of butter and toss the shrimp and crabmeat until warm, about 2 minutes. Spoon on top of the veal and sprinkle with remaining parsley.

SERVES 6   *Gulfshore Delights,* Fort Myers, FL

VEAL SCALOPPINE MARSALA

Good with buttered thin spaghetti.

1½ pounds baby beef or milk-fed veal scallops (eye of round or sirloin), sliced ¼ inch thick
½ cup all-purpose flour
⅓ cup grated Parmesan cheese
1 teaspoon salt
4 tablespoons (½ stick) butter
¼ pound fresh mushrooms, wiped, trimmed, and sliced
2 scallions with tops, chopped
½ cup consommé or beef broth
1 to 2 tablespoons lemon juice
¼ cup dry Marsala wine
Chopped parsley

Cut the meat into 3 or 4-inch pieces. Pound very thin between sheets of wax paper. In a shallow dish, combine the flour, grated cheese, and salt. Dredge the meat in the flour mixture, shaking off as much as possible.

Heat 2 tablespoons of the butter in a large skillet and brown each scallop for about 1 minute on each side, in batches if necessary. Remove to a plate and keep warm. Add the remaining 2 tablespoons of butter to the skillet and sauté the mushrooms and scallions for 2 minutes. Add the consommé, lemon juice, and Marsala. Stir well. Return the meat to the skillet and simmer for about 3 minutes. (If veal is used, simmer only 1 minute.)

To serve, pour the pan juices over the meat and sprinkle with parsley.

SERVES 6   *Houston Junior League Cookbook,* Houston, TX

VEAL MARSALA

Very quick and absolutely delicious!

1 pound veal scallops or cutlets,
    sliced ¼ inch thick and pounded
    thin
Salt and freshly ground pepper
All-purpose flour for dredging
8 tablespoons (1 stick) butter
¼ cup olive oil
1 tablespoon chopped fresh garlic
1 cup sliced fresh mushrooms
½ cup dry Marsala wine
1 cup chicken broth
¼ cup fresh lemon juice
1 tablespoon sugar (optional)
¼ cup chopped fresh parsley
Lemon slices and parsley for garnish

Season the meat on both sides with salt and pepper. Lightly dredge in flour and shake off the excess.

Melt the butter with the olive oil in a skillet over medium-high heat. Sauté the meat quickly, without browning, 1 to 2 minutes on each side, and transfer to a serving platter. Sauté the garlic and mushrooms in the same skillet and spoon over the meat. Add the Marsala, chicken broth, lemon juice, sugar, and parsley to the skillet and bring to a quick boil, reducing the liquid slightly. Pour over the meat. Garnish with sliced lemons and parsley.

SERVES 4   *Thymes Remembered,* Tallahassee, FL

ROAST VEAL DIJON

A prominent San Francisco family's revered cook of many years prepared this often for the loveliest of dinner parties. It is easy and foolproof, but be sure to use only the finest white veal.

1 small, boned rolled leg of veal (3
    to 4 pounds)
8 tablespoons (1 stick) butter,
    melted
1 (8-ounce) jar Dijon wine mustard
1 (10½-ounce) can consommé
¼ cup sherry
Chopped parsley

Preheat the oven to 300 degrees. Place the meat in a shallow roasting pan. Blend the melted butter and mustard and pour over the meat, covering all sides. Roast 4 hours. During the last hour, baste every 20 minutes with a mixture of consommé and sherry.

The meat will carve more easily if you wait 20 to 30 minutes after removing it from the oven, keeping it warm on the back of the stove with a loose cover of foil. Make a gravy of the pan juices, thickening, if necessary, with arrowroot or flour. Pass the gravy separately with chopped parsley sprinkled on top.

NOTE: Carrot soufflé and fresh asparagus spears with Hollandaise are just right with this.

SERVES 4–6   *Private Collection 1,* Palo Alto, CA

VEAL POJARSKI

SAUCE STROGANOFF
4 tablespoons (½ stick) butter
1 medium onion, sliced
¼ cup tomato paste
Pinch of thyme
¼ bay leaf
1 tablespoon flour
1 cup boiling chicken or veal broth,
    or as needed
¾ cup sour cream, at room
    temperature
¼ cup sautéed mushrooms
Salt and freshly ground pepper

VEAL PATTIES
1 pound lean veal, ground
8 tablespoons (1 stick) butter,
    softened
¾ cup fine fresh bread crumbs
½ cup half-and-half
Salt and freshly ground pepper
1 tablespoon olive oil

Make the sauce: Melt the butter in a heavy saucepan and sauté the onion for 4 to 5 minutes. Add the tomato paste, thyme, and bay leaf. Simmer on low heat for a few minutes. Stir in the flour, mix well, and add the boiling broth (more if the mixture seems too thick). Cook uncovered for 30 minutes. Strain, then blend in the sour cream and mushrooms. Season to taste with salt and pepper. Keep warm while you prepare the veal patties.

Preheat the oven to 375 degrees. In a mixing bowl, combine the veal, 6 tablespoons of butter, the bread crumbs, half-and-half, and salt and pepper to taste. Mix well. Cover and refrigerate for 10 minutes. Form into 8 to 12 cutlets or patties. In an ovenproof skillet, heat the remaining 2 tablespoons of butter with the olive oil. Brown the patties quickly on one side. Turn them over and finish cooking in the oven for 8 minutes. Serve with Stroganoff sauce.

SERVES 4–6   *Virginia Hospitality*, Hampton Roads, VA

CROCK-POT VENISON

1 boneless venison roast, 3-4 pounds
½ plus ⅓ cup vinegar
2 tablespoons plus 1 teaspoon salt
7 garlic cloves, chopped
Flour
2 tablespoons vegetable oil
1 large onion, sliced
3 tablespoons brown sugar
1½ teaspoons dry mustard
3 tablespoons Worcestershire sauce
1 (14-ounce) can tomatoes

Put the roast in a deep bowl. Make a marinade using ½ cup of the vinegar, 2 tablespoons of the salt, and 4 cloves of chopped garlic. Pour the marinade over the roast, adding enough water to cover the venison. Cover and refrigerate overnight.

Remove the venison from the marinade and pat dry. Sprinkle the meat with the remaining teaspoon of salt and dredge with flour. Heat the oil in a heavy skillet and brown the roast on all sides.

Transfer the roast to a Crock-Pot and add the sliced onion. In a bowl, mix the brown sugar, mustard, 3 tablespoons of flour, and the Worcestershire to a paste. Stir in the tomatoes, the remaining ⅓ cup of vinegar, and 3 cloves of chopped garlic. Cook on the low setting for 8 to 10 hours, until tender.

SERVES 6   *To Market, to Market*, Owensboro, KY

MARINATED VENISON STEAK

½ cup dry white wine
⅓ cup olive oil
3 tablespoons soy sauce
½ teaspoon ground cumin
1 large garlic clove, crushed
2 large or 4 small young venison
   steaks

Combine the wine, olive oil, soy sauce, cumin, and garlic and pour the marinade over 2 large or 4 small venison steaks in a shallow bowl. Marinate the steaks at room temperature for 2 to 3 hours, turning occasionally. Drain the steaks and broil to medium rare over charcoal. (Overcooking will make the meat tough.) Brush with marinade while steaks are broiling.

SERVES 4

Quail County, Albany, GA

CHICKEN-FRIED VENISON

An absolutely fabulous way to prepare venison!

Venison back strap
4 cups milk
2 teaspoons garlic salt
Salt and pepper to taste
2 cups all-purpose flour
Oil for deep frying

Remove all silver membrane from the venison. Slice the meat into ½-inch-thick slices, across the grain. Pound each slice on both sides with a meat mallet. Mix the milk and garlic salt in a bowl with the meat; cover and refrigerate overnight.

Remove the meat from the marinade and pat dry. Salt and pepper both sides, and shake a few pieces at a time in a small brown paper sack with the flour. Fry a few at a time in a deep fat fryer at 365 degrees until golden brown. Drain on paper towels and serve immediately with cream gravy and biscuits. For breakfast, serve with scrambled eggs; for dinner, mashed potatoes.

SERVES 4

¡Delicioso!, Corpus Christi, TX

LIVER YOU'LL LOVE

MARINADE
½ cup vegetable oil
1½ tablespoons lemon juice
¼ teaspoon salt
⅛ teaspoon paprika
1 small bay leaf

1 pound beef or calf's liver sliced ½
   inch thick
3 tablespoons bacon fat
1 onion, chopped
½ to 1 green bell pepper, chopped
3 tablespoons flour
1 can condensed beef broth
¼ cup red wine
1 teaspoon soy sauce
Salt and ground black pepper to
   taste

Combine all ingredients in a shallow bowl and stir.

Marinate the liver for ½ hour, turning from time to time. Sauté the liver in the bacon fat for 3 to 4 minutes on each side, until no longer red. Remove to a plate and keep warm. Add the onion and green pepper to the pan drippings and cook for 5 to 8 minutes. Stir in the flour. Gradually add the broth and wine, stirring until thickened. Add the soy sauce, salt, and pepper.

Return the liver to the pan and heat in the sauce. Serve with rice.

SERVES 4

A Taste of Tampa, Tampa, FL

A CELEBRATION OF COURAGE

To care for the well-being of others takes courage. In these pages we celebrate the courage of volunteers like the members of the Junior League who rejoice in the very magnitude of the word "community," who see beyond their own small circle of family and acquaintances to the larger world around them. They refuse to look the other way at community inequities or injustices or to say, "That's their problem."

Over its hundred-year history, the Junior League can take credit for many firsts in service innovation and advocacy. In these pages we celebrate the special strength it takes to break new ground.

For example, Leagues have been enormously insightful over the years about spotting gaps in social services and coming forward

More than 400 League members assemble planes, make parachutes, and serve as flying instructors in the armed forces during World War II.

with fresh, new ideas to do it better. One of the first innovations of the founding New York City League at the turn of the century was to recognize that new immigrants were often fearful of established institutions like schools—and so in collaboration with the school system it began a widely replicated visiting-teachers program that brought services directly to the immigrants' homes. Fast-forward to the 1980s and you find the Junior League creating the first U.S. public awareness campaign about the special problems and service needs of women addicted to alcohol.

In the 1920s, the Junior League spearheaded the development of children's theater. Over the years, formal stage presentations have evolved into traveling puppet shows that today bring important social messages to children in their schools: messages, for example, about the needs of the physically challenged or the importance of substance abuse prevention.

Leagues have always been a strong voice in many local, state, and national forums to better conditions for women and children. From the 1930s, when Virginia Junior Leagues undertook a comprehensive state needs assessment to formulate a child welfare program and lobby for state funds, to the 1980s, when a League initiated the Court Appointed Special Advocate (CASA) program to protect children from falling through the cracks in the court system, League members have courageously spoken out on behalf of those who cannot speak for themselves.

Just to survive as an organization for a hundred years takes a kind of courage. It requires a courageous heart, for example, to rigorously examine your own organizational practices to ensure that you are being inclusive of the widest possible range of people in your membership—and that you are truly listening and valuing all perspectives in your community. The journey is always outward, and it is for the brave.

FISH & SEAFOOD

BAKED CATFISH

8 skinned catfish fillets
1 cup fine dry bread crumbs
1 cup grated Parmesan cheese
¾ cup chopped fresh parsley
½ teaspoon dried oregano
¼ teaspoon dried basil
1 teaspoon paprika
2 teaspoons salt
1 teaspoon ground black pepper
2 sticks (½ pound) butter, melted
Lemon wedges
Parsley sprigs

Preheat the oven to 375 degrees. Lightly coat a 13 × 9-inch baking dish with vegetable oil cooking spray.

Pat the fish dry with paper toweling. Combine the dry ingredients in a shallow bowl and stir well. Dip the catfish in the melted butter and roll in the bread crumb mixture. Arrange the fillets in the prepared baking dish. Bake uncovered for 20 to 30 minutes or until the fish flakes easily when tested with a fork. Garnish with lemon wedges and parsley sprigs.

VARIATION: Cornflake crumbs may be substituted for bread crumbs. Bass fillets may be substituted for the catfish.

SERVES 8   *To Market, to Market,* Owensboro, KY

BRONZED SWORDFISH WITH TROPICAL FRUIT–BLACK BEAN SALSA

TROPICAL FRUIT–BLACK BEAN
SALSA
1 small pineapple, peeled, cored, and diced
2 kiwifruit, peeled and diced
1 mango, peeled and diced
1 papaya, peeled and diced
1 cup cooked black beans, rinsed thoroughly
¼ poblano or Anaheim pepper, diced
½ cup rice wine vinegar
¼ cup dark rum
2 tablespoons sugar
Juice of 2 limes
1 bunch cilantro, chopped
Salt to taste

4 (7-ounce) swordfish steaks
2 sticks (½ pound) butter, melted
½ cup blackening spice

Combine all the salsa ingredients and set aside.

Heat a large cast-iron skillet over high heat until very hot. Dip the swordfish steaks in butter. Place on platter. Sprinkle liberally with blackening spice on one side only. Place the steaks in the pan, spice side down, and cook for about 2 minutes on each side or until cooked through. Top with salsa.

SERVES 4   *The Bountiful Arbor,* Ann Arbor, MI

GINGER-LIME-CILANTRO SWORDFISH

GINGER-LIME-CILANTRO SAUCE
1 teaspoon chopped shallot
1 cup dry white wine
1 tablespoon grated fresh gingerroot
½ cup heavy cream
12 tablespoons (1½ sticks) unsalted
 butter
Juice of 2 limes
1 tablespoon chopped fresh cilantro
Salt and ground black pepper to
 taste

4 swordfish steaks
Olive oil
Salt and ground black pepper to
 taste

Make the sauce: Combine the shallot, wine, and grated ginger in a medium saucepan. Simmer until reduced to ¼ cup. Add the cream, butter, lime juice, cilantro, and salt and pepper. Whisk and simmer for 3 to 4 minutes to thicken. Hold over very low heat until ready to serve.

Rub the swordfish with olive oil. Grill 4 to 5 inches from the heat source for 4 minutes on each side for 1-inch-thick steaks. Sprinkle with salt and pepper and serve hot surrounded by cream sauce.

SERVES 4
Above and Beyond Parsley, Kansas City, MO

GRILLED NANTUCKET SWORDFISH AND DILLY DIJON SAUCE

DILLY DIJON SAUCE
1 cup Dijon mustard
⅓ cup sour cream
⅓ cup sugar
⅓ cup white wine vinegar
1 cup olive oil
¼ cup fresh dill weed or 2
 tablespoons dried
Salt and ground black pepper to
 taste

1½ cups mayonnaise
½ cup olive oil
2 teaspoons minced garlic
2 teaspoons minced fresh parsley
1 cup sour cream
4 pounds fresh swordfish steaks

Make the sauce: In a blender or food processor, combine the mustard, sour cream, sugar, and vinegar. Gradually add the olive oil while the machine is running. Transfer the sauce to a covered container; fold in the dill and refrigerate until ready to serve.

Mix the mayonnaise, olive oil, garlic, parsley, and sour cream in a large shallow baking dish. Add the swordfish and marinate, refrigerated, at least 2 hours, turning the fish several times. Grill 4 to 5 inches from the heat source for 1-inch-thick steaks, turning once, until the fish flakes easily when tested with a fork. Serve with the sauce.

SERVES 8
For Goodness Taste, Rochester NY

PACIFIC ALBACORE WITH SALSA

SALSA
1 cup chopped ripe tomatoes
4 ounces chopped green chiles
¼ cup finely chopped onion
1 clove garlic, minced
1 teaspoon lime juice
1 tablespoon chopped cilantro

ALBACORE
1½ pounds fresh albacore, cut into 6
   small steaks
2 tablespoons unsalted butter,
   softened
¼ pound Monterey Jack cheese,
   grated
¼ pound Cheddar cheese, grated

Preheat the oven to 325 degrees. Combine the salsa ingredients and mix well. (Salsa can be prepared ahead and refrigerated, allowing the flavors to mellow.) Place the fish in a well-buttered baking dish. Cover with salsa and bake 20 minutes. Remove from the oven; sprinkle cheese over the top and bake an additional 10 minutes.

SERVES 6   *Delicious Decisions,* San Diego, CA

GRILLED TUNA WITH PINEAPPLE SALSA

½ cup olive oil
¼ cup lemon juice
4 scallions, chopped, including tops
4 tuna steaks, 1 inch thick

PINEAPPLE SALSA
1 small fresh pineapple, cut into
   small cubes
1 small red onion, diced
1 medium red bell pepper, cored,
   seeded, and diced
1 medium yellow or orange pepper,
   cored, seeded, and diced
½ to ¾ teaspoon finely minced
   jalapeño or serrano chile pepper
1 teaspoon ground coriander
1 teaspoon ground cumin
2 tablespoons lime juice
1 clove garlic, minced

Combine the oil, lemon juice, and scallions. Pour over the tuna steaks in a flat pan and marinate for several hours before grilling tuna. Meanwhile, prepare pineapple salsa by combining all the salsa ingredients. Set aside. When ready to cook, place the tuna steaks directly on a hot oiled grill. Cook for 4 minutes on each side, turning once. Do not overcook. Serve with salsa on top or passed in a bowl.

SERVES 4   *Without Reservations,* Pittsburgh, PA

MARINATED GRILLED TUNA WITH TOMATO-BASIL SAUCE

The tomato-basil sauce can double as a lovely fresh summer pasta sauce.

6 fresh tuna steaks, about 6 ounces
   each (see Note)
Freshly ground pepper to taste
6 tablespoons olive oil
2 tablespoons lemon juice
2 tablespoons chopped fresh oregano
   or 1 tablespoon dried

TOMATO-BASIL SAUCE
1½ tablespoons butter
1½ tablespoons olive oil
3 tablespoons finely chopped shallots
2 tablespoons red wine
1 tablespoon sherry wine vinegar
1 pound plum tomatoes, peeled,
   seeded, and diced
1½ tablespoons chopped fresh basil
Salt and freshly ground pepper to
   taste
6 small sprigs fresh oregano and 6
   small fresh basil leaves for garnish

Sprinkle the tuna steaks on both sides with pepper. Combine the oil, lemon juice, and oregano in a shallow glass dish just large enough to hold the tuna in a single layer and stir to blend. Add the tuna, turning to coat both sides. Set aside at room temperature and let marinate for 1 hour, turning once or twice.

Build a charcoal fire or preheat a gas grill or broiler. When the grill or oven is ready, cook the fish for about 4 to 5 minutes on each side for medium rare.

Meanwhile make the sauce: In a medium skillet, melt the butter with the olive oil over medium heat. Add the shallots and cook until softened, about 3 minutes. Add the wine and vinegar and cook over high heat for about 1 minute, stirring constantly. Reduce the heat to medium low. Add the diced tomatoes and simmer for 5 to 6 minutes, or until most of the liquid has evaporated. Stir in the basil, season with salt and pepper, and simmer for 30 seconds. Keep warm.

Serve the fish immediately with the warm sauce and garnish.

NOTE: If swordfish is substituted, increase cooking time by 5 to 6 minutes per side. The sauce can be made a few hours before serving and reheated.

SERVES 6   *The Bountiful Arbor,* Ann Arbor, MI

SEARED SHUTOME (OR BLUEFISH) WITH MAUI ONIONS AND KULA TOMATOES

1 medium Maui onion, peeled and
   diced fine (see Note)
2 tablespoons butter
2 Kula tomatoes, peeled, seeded,
   and diced fine
1 sprig fresh thyme
Salt and freshly ground black pepper
   to taste
8 (3-ounce) slices shutome, cut ½
   inch thick
¼ cup virgin olive oil
8 small fresh thyme sprigs for
   garnish

Sauté the onion in the butter until tender. Add the tomatoes and thyme. Season and simmer over low heat for 3 minutes. Adjust the seasoning and reserve. Season the shutome medallions and rub them with olive oil. Sear in a very hot pan for about 1½ minutes, leaving the fish underdone inside. Top each fish medallion with the onion and tomato mixture. Garnish with fresh thyme and serve.

NOTE: A Texas onion or a Vidalia sweet onion can be substituted.

SERVES 4   *Another Taste of Aloha,* Honolulu, HI

CRUNCHY FRIED FISH

2 pounds fish fillets (flounder,
    snapper, or sole)
Salt and pepper
1 cup all-purpose flour
2 teaspoons baking powder
1 egg yolk
1 cup lukewarm water
1 tablespoon vegetable oil
1 egg white, stiffly beaten
Vegetable oil for frying

Pat the fillets dry with paper toweling and sprinkle with salt and pepper to taste. Combine the flour, baking powder, and 1 teaspoon of salt in bowl; drop the egg yolk in the center. Add the water and oil; stir well. Fold the egg white into the batter. Dip the fillets in the batter; fry in ¼ inch of oil heated to 375 degrees until golden on both sides. Drain on paper towels.

SERVES 6   *Peachtree Bouquet,* DeKalb County

RED SNAPPER VERACRUZ

2 limes
1¾ to 2 pounds red snapper fillets
Salt
5 tablespoons olive oil
Chopped fresh cilantro for garnish

SAUCE VERACRUZ
½ cup chopped onion
3 cloves garlic, crushed
¼ cup olive oil
3 large tomatoes, peeled, seeded,
    and chopped
1 large bay leaf
½ teaspoon oregano
12 pitted green olives, cut in half
2 tablespoons capers
2 jalapeño peppers, seeded and cut
    into strips
½ teaspoon salt
¼ teaspoon freshly ground pepper
1 tablespoon chopped fresh cilantro
1 tablespoon lime juice

Preheat the oven to 325 degrees. Squeeze lime juice over the fish and set aside until ready to cook.

To make the sauce, sauté the onion and garlic in the oil until soft. Stir in the remaining ingredients. Season to taste. Cook over medium heat for 10 minutes or until some of the liquid has evaporated.

Sprinkle the fillets lightly with salt and sear on both sides in the oil. Drain and remove to an ovenproof casserole or platter. Cover with the sauce and bake for 10 to 15 minutes. Garnish with chopped cilantro and serve.

SERVES 8   *The Star of Texas Cookbook,* Houston, TX

CHAMPAGNE SNAPPER

1 cup Champagne or dry white wine
1 tablespoon butter
1 bay leaf
¼ cup finely chopped fresh parsley
1 tablespoon chopped onion
1 tablespoon finely chopped celery
2 tablespoons cream
4 snapper fillets (see Note)
1 teaspoon salt
½ teaspoon freshly ground pepper
⅓ cup sliced mushrooms
2 tablespoons freshly grated
 Parmesan cheese

Preheat the oven to 350 degrees. Butter a 13 × 9-inch baking dish.

Combine the Champagne, butter, bay leaf, parsley, onion, and celery in a saucepan. Bring to a boil, reduce heat, and simmer until reduced by half. Remove the bay leaf and add the cream. Take the pan off the stove. Dry the fish with paper toweling and sprinkle with salt and pepper. Arrange in one layer in the baking dish. Add the mushrooms to the sauce and pour the sauce over the fillets. Sprinkle with cheese. Bake uncovered for 25 to 30 minutes, or until the top is browned.

NOTE: Sole or cod may be substituted for snapper.

SERVES 4   *Sunny Side Up*, Fort Lauderdale, FL

RED SNAPPER AND TOASTED PECAN BUTTER

4 fresh or frozen red snapper fillets,
 about 6 ounces each
½ cup all-purpose flour
4 teaspoons paprika
2 teaspoons garlic powder
1½ teaspoons salt
¼ teaspoon crumbled dried thyme
¼ teaspoon plus ⅛ teaspoon ground
 red pepper (cayenne)
½ cup milk
¼ cup peanut oil
⅔ cups pecans
⅛ teaspoon white pepper
4 tablespoons (½ stick) butter
2 tablespoons finely snipped parsley
1 tablespoon fresh lemon juice

Thaw the fish, if frozen. In a medium bowl, combine the flour, paprika, garlic powder, salt, thyme, and ¼ teaspoon of red pepper. Dip each fillet in milk, then in the flour mixture.

In a 12-inch skillet, heat the peanut oil over medium heat. Add the fillets and cook for 6 minutes, turning once, until golden brown. Remove the fillets and keep warm.

For pecan butter, toss the pecans with the white pepper and the remaining ⅛ teaspoon of red pepper. In an 8-inch skillet, melt the butter, add the seasoned pecans; and cook about 3 minutes, or until lightly browned. Remove from the heat. Stir in the parsley and lemon juice.

Transfer the red snapper fillets to dinner plates. Spoon pecan butter over the fillets and serve immediately.

SERVES 4   *Heart & Soul*, Memphis, TN

THE LITERACY COUNCIL OF SOUTHWEST LOUISIANA, INC.
THE JUNIOR LEAGUE OF LAKE CHARLES, LOUISIANA

The Literacy Council of Southwest Louisiana, Inc., was begun by the Junior League of Lake Charles in 1987. The Literary Council is devoted to ensuring that adults in the area have the opportunity to acquire the basic skills of reading and writing. Volunteers are trained in the successful Laubach method of one-on-one tutoring, and the program has been successful in training approximately 90 to 185 tutors and students each year.

REDFISH SPECIAL

4 thin redfish fillets
1 teaspoon lemon pepper seasoning
All-purpose flour
5 tablespoons unsalted butter
6 tablespoons fresh lemon juice
½ teaspoon garlic salt
1 teaspoon Worcestershire sauce

Preheat the broiler. Sprinkle both sides of each redfish fillet with lemon pepper and dust with flour. Sauté the fillets in 3 tablespoons of butter for 5 minutes, turning once. Arrange the sautéed fillets in a separate ovenproof pan, add the lemon juice and dot with 2 tablespoons of butter. Pour the butter from the sauté pan over the fish and add the garlic salt and Worcestershire. Broil 3 minutes without turning. Serve immediately.

SERVES 4

Come on In!, Jackson, MS

SHRIMP-STUFFED SOLE

6 serving-size pieces fillet of sole
3 tablespoons butter
3 tablespoons flour
1 cup light cream
½ cup milk
1 cup shredded Gruyère cheese
1 tablespoon sherry
3 dashes Tabasco (optional)
1½ cups cooked, shelled, deveined shrimp
½ teaspoon salt
½ teaspoon freshly ground pepper
2 teaspoons parsley flakes

Butter a medium-size rectangular baking dish. Preheat the oven to 350 degrees.

Pat the fillets dry with paper toweling. In a saucepan, melt the butter over medium heat; stir in the flour, cooking until well blended and bubbly. Remove from the heat and gradually stir in the cream, then the milk. Cook over medium heat until the sauce thickens and comes to a boil. Add the shredded cheese, stirring until melted. Blend in the sherry and Tabasco.

Chop the shrimp, reserving 6 to 12 whole shrimp for garnish. In a mixing bowl, combine the chopped shrimp, salt, pepper, and parsley flakes. Blend in 3 tablespoons of the cheese sauce. Spoon some of the shrimp mixture evenly across the center of each fillet. Fold the ends of each fillet over the stuffing.

Place the fillets seam side down in the prepared baking dish. Pour the remaining sauce evenly over the top of the fillets. Bake uncovered for 30 minutes, or until the fish flakes easily and the sauce is lightly browned.

SERVES 6

A Taste of Oregon, Eugene, OR

KIDSFIRST ANNIVERSARY PROJECT
JUNIOR LEAGUE OF SOUTH BEND, INDIANA

To celebrate its 50th anniversary, the Junior League of South Bend, Indiana, began two child-serving projects under the umbrella name Kidsfirst. First, they collaborated with several agencies to create the Children's Center, a "kid friendly" environment for child victims of physical and sexual abuse. The Junior League set up a training outline, goals and objectives, and procedures manual for the center, along with doing the renovation work and providing many of their volunteers and volunteer coordinator.

Second, they designed a hands-on Children's Museum for the South Bend community. The League provided funding to build the museum, and is providing volunteers to staff it.

FILLET OF SOLE IN PACKETS

4 to 6 stalks celery, cut into ¼-inch
dice

2 leeks, white portion only,
thoroughly washed, cut into ¼-
inch dice

4 medium carrots, cut into ¼-inch
dice

3 or more tablespoons butter

Salt and freshly ground pepper to
taste

2 pounds fillets of sole

2 ripe tomatoes, sliced

1 lemon, sliced

4 bay leaves

¾ teaspoon fresh thyme or ½
teaspoon dried

Place 4 squares (12 × 12 inches each) of cooking parchment or aluminum foil on a work surface. Preheat the oven to 450 degrees.

In a medium skillet, sauté the celery, leeks, and carrots in 3 or more tablespoons butter for 5 minutes, or until tender. Season with salt and pepper.

On each parchment square, layer ¼ of the ingredients in the following order: sautéed vegetables, sole fillets, salt and pepper, tomato slices, lemon slices, bay leaf, thyme. Fold the packets securely, tucking the edges under, and place on a baking sheet. Bake 20 minutes. Slit packages before serving, or allow guests to open their own.

SERVES 4   *California Fresh,* Oakland–East Bay, CA

GRILLED HALIBUT WITH GINGER BUTTER

GINGER BUTTER

2 scallions, chopped fine

1 tablespoon minced, peeled fresh
gingerroot

8 tablespoons (1 stick) butter, at
room temperature

Salt and freshly ground pepper to
taste

Juice of 1 lemon

2 tablespoons dark Asian sesame oil

2 tablespoons soy sauce

2 tablespoons lemon juice or rice
wine vinegar

2 tablespoons chopped fresh parsley

½ teaspoons dried thyme

2 scallions, chopped

Dash of ground red pepper
(cayenne)

4 halibut steaks, 1½ inches thick

Make the ginger butter: Beat together the scallions, ginger, butter, salt, pepper, and lemon juice, or process in a food processor. Let stand at room temperature until ready to use.

Make a marinade by combining the sesame oil, soy sauce, lemon juice, parsley, thyme, scallions, and red pepper in a shallow glass dish. Add the halibut steaks, turning once to coat thoroughly. Cover and refrigerate from 1 to 4 hours.

Grill the fish over hot coals for 10 minutes for each inch of thickness, turning midway through the cooking time. The fish should be firm to the touch. Or, if you wish, broil the fish 6 inches from the source of heat for the same length of time. Remove the fish to a warm platter. Top each warm steak with a generous dollop of ginger butter.

SERVES 4   *California Sizzles,* Pasadena, CA

SAUTÉED HALIBUT WITH NECTARINE SALSA

NECTARINE SALSA
4 ripe nectarines, peeled and diced
½ red bell pepper, diced
1 cup finely chopped scallions
½ cup finely chopped fresh chives
1 tablespoon chopped cilantro
Juice of 2 limes

1½ pounds halibut fillets
1 ripe nectarine, peeled and puréed
3 tablespoons flour
2 tablespoons peanut oil

Combine all the salsa ingredients in a bowl and set aside.

Place the halibut fillets in a shallow glass dish, cover with purée, and marinate for 1 hour. Remove from the marinade and coat the fillets lightly with flour. Heat the oil in a saucepan and sauté the fillets about 3 minutes per side. Arrange on serving plates pooled with 4 or 5 tablespoons of the nectarine salsa.

SERVES 4

Feast of Eden, Monterey, CA

TROUT, RUSSIAN STYLE

6 to 9 trout, filleted
½ teaspoon salt
¼ teaspoon ground white pepper
2 eggs, well beaten
¼ cup milk
1½ cups toasted bread crumbs, pulverized
2 tablespoons corn or peanut oil
8 tablespoons (1 stick) butter, softened.
2 eggs, hard cooked, chopped fine
⅓ cup finely chopped fresh parsley
2 tablespoons finely chopped pimiento
2 lemons, sliced thin

Sprinkle the trout fillets with salt and pepper. Mix the beaten eggs and milk. Dip the fillets in the mixture and roll gently in bread crumbs. Heat oil in a stovetop grill or large heavy skillet to medium heat. (If using an electric fry pan, heat to 300 degrees.) Pour in just enough oil to keep the fish from sticking.

Make a paste of the butter, hard-cooked eggs, parsley, and pimiento. Cook the trout on the grill until golden in color, about 5 to 6 minutes on each side. Place on a heated platter. Spread the butter paste over each piece and top each with 2 or 3 slices of lemon. Serve immediately.

SERVES 6–9

The Gasparilla Cookbook, Tampa, FL

COURT APPOINTED SPECIAL ADVOCATES (CASA)
JUNIOR LEAGUE OF KNOXVILLE, TENNESSEE

The Court Appointed Special Advocates (CASA) program of the Junior League of Knoxville, Tennessee, ensures that children involved in the Juvenile Court System have a "voice in court." A volunteer follows each case and ensures that the children and family receive the necessary services while involved in the court system. A CASA volunteer serves as an advocate for a neglected or abused child by providing the court with information obtained through personal interview and investigation of records, following through with each case.

FISH STEW

1 cup vegetable oil
1 cup all-purpose flour
3 large onions, chopped
1 cup chopped celery
3 cloves garlic, chopped
1 (36-ounce) can tomatoes
2 (6-ounce) cans tomato paste
4 pounds fish (cat, goo, large sac-a-lait, redfish)
Salt and pepper to taste
2 tablespoons chopped scallion tops
2 tablespoons chopped parsley
Hot cooked rice

Heat the oil in a deep heavy kettle, stir in the flour, and cook over medium heat until the roux turns reddish brown (be careful not to burn it). Add the onions, celery, and garlic; cook until soft. Add the tomatoes and tomato paste. Bring to a boil, lower the heat, and cook slowly for 5 minutes. Add 2½ quarts of water, return to a boil, lower the heat, and simmer uncovered for 1 hour.

Cut the fish into 1-inch chunks and add to the court-bouillon. Cook just until done—no longer than 15 minutes. Season to taste and add the scallion tops and parsley about 5 minutes before serving. Serve over rice in soup plates.

SERVES 10–12 *Talk About Good I,* Lafayette, LA

SHAD AND ROE

1 shad, filleted
Juice of ½ lemon
Seasoned salt
Paprika
2 tablespoons butter
2 pairs shad roe
4 strips bacon

Preheat the oven to 400 degrees. Drizzle the shad fillets with lemon juice and sprinkle with seasoned salt and paprika. Dot with butter. Sprinkle the roe with seasoned salt. Let the bacon soften for a few minutes so that you may wrap it completely around the roe. Secure the bacon with toothpicks.

Place the fillets and roe in a greased baking pan and bake for 10 minutes. Remove from the oven, baste the fillets with the pan juices, and slide under the broiler until the fillets are lightly browned. Carefully remove the fish from the pan to a platter and continue broiling the roe until the bacon is crisp, turning once when needed.

NOTE: The bacon-wrapped roe may be cooked separately in a frying pan with a small amount of cooking oil.

SERVES 4–6 *Savannah Style,* Savannah, GA

SALMON BAKED IN WINE AND TARRAGON

4 salmon steaks
2 tablespoons butter, softened
⅛ teaspoon salt
¼ teaspoon ground white pepper
2 tablespoons lemon juice
¼ cup white wine
½ teaspoon dried tarragon

Preheat the oven to 450 degrees. Coat a baking dish with vegetable oil cooking spray.

Arrange the salmon in the prepared dish and rub with butter. Mix the salt, pepper, lemon juice, wine, and tarragon; pour over the fish. Bake uncovered until the fish flakes easily when tested with a fork, allowing 10 minutes of cooking time per inch of thickness. Serve hot.

SERVES 4 *Very Virginia,* Newport News, VA

SALMON STEAKS WITH PISTACHIO BUTTER

PISTACHIO BUTTER

12 tablespoons (1½ sticks) unsalted
    butter, softened
3 tablespoons minced shelled
    pistachio nuts
Grated zest of ½ lime

6 salmon steaks, 6 to 7 ounces each
¼ cup extra virgin olive oil
¼ cup freshly squeezed lime juice
1 teaspoon dried basil
2 limes, sliced, for garnish

Make the pistachio butter: Cream the butter in a bowl with the back of a wooden spoon or in a food processor fitted with the steel blade. Mix in the nuts and lime zest. To store, spoon the butter into a crock, cover and chill until needed. Remove butter from the refrigerator 45 minutes before you use it.

Preheat the broiler. Line a shallow broiler pan with aluminum foil and spray with vegetable oil cooking spray. Arrange the salmon steaks in the pan. Mix together the oil, lime juice, and basil. Brush the top of the steaks with the oil mixture.

Broil the steaks 4 to 6 inches from the heat source for 3 to 5 minutes. Turn the steaks over with a spatula. Brush the fish with the oil mixture and continue broiling until the fish flakes easily when tested with a fork, 4 to 5 minutes. Using a spatula, transfer the steaks to individual plates. Garnish with lime slices and a dollop of pistachio butter. Serve immediately.

SERVES 6

Some Like It Hot, McAllen, TX

BARBECUED SALMON, DELANO STYLE

1 (5- to 8-pound) whole salmon,
    scaled and filleted
2 sticks (½ pound) butter
1 to 2 bunches scallions, chopped
4 lemons, sliced
2 to 4 tablespoons soy sauce
1½ cups dry vermouth or dry white
    wine

Prepare coals on a barbecue. The salmon will have additional flavor if hickory or alderwood chips previously soaked in water are added to the coals. Lay the salmon in a tray of heavy-duty aluminum foil with sides crimped to a depth of at least 1 inch. Place ¼-inch-thick slices of butter over the salmon. Cover the butter with scallions, cover the scallions with lemon slices, and lightly sprinkle on the soy sauce. Pour vermouth over all.

Lay the foil tray of salmon on the grill over the coals. Cover the fish with a foil tent larger than the tray, so the smoke can circulate around the fish, or cover the barbecue. Cook salmon until a milky white substance appears and the fish flakes when pressed with a fork. *Do not overcook.* Serve with Delano sauce (below).

DELANO SAUCE

1¼ cups tightly packed watercress
    leaves with blossoms, if available
Dash of Tabasco
1¼ cups tightly packed spinach
    leaves
¾ cup mayonnaise
¼ cup capers
2 teaspoons minced chives

Combine all ingredients in a food processor or blender and process until puréed. Transfer to a sauceboat and serve with salmon.

SERVES 8–12

The Seattle Classic, Seattle, WA

BOURBON BASTED SALMON

1½ pounds salmon fillets
¼ cup packed brown sugar
3 tablespoons Bourbon whiskey
3 tablespoons chopped scallions
2 tablespoons soy sauce
2 tablespoons vegetable oil

Place the salmon skin side down in a shallow baking dish. Remove all bones. A whole salmon fillet has a small row of bones near the top. Working with the grain of the salmon, use tweezers to pull out each bone. In a small bowl, combine all the other ingredients. Pour over the salmon and marinate in the refrigerator for at least 1 hour.

Brush the inside of a fish grilling basket with vegetable oil. Remove the salmon from the marinade, reserving marinade. Place the salmon in the basket and close securely. Grill the salmon in the basket over hot coals, turning once, until opaque throughout, about 7 minutes per side. Baste with reserved marinade while cooking. Serve hot or cold. N O T E : Salmon can alternately be cooked directly on an oiled grill, turning once, about 7 minutes per side.

S E R V E S 4   *Simply Classic,* Seattle, WA

SALMON WITH WOVEN PASTRY CRUST

Spinach and leeks nestled under the salmon provide wonderful flavor and color.

1 clove garlic, crushed
1 large shallot, chopped fine
2 tablespoons Pernod
2 tablespoons unsalted butter
1 cup chopped cooked spinach, drained
1 large leek washed thoroughly and cut into julienne strips
1 tablespoon lemon juice
2 sheets puff pastry
1 egg yolk, beaten
1 (3- to 4-pound) salmon fillet, skinned

Sauté the garlic, shallot, and Pernod in the butter in a medium sauté pan for 1 minute. Add the spinach and leeks. Sauté for 1 minute. Stir in the lemon juice. Set aside to cool.

Spread one sheet of the puff pastry on a work surface. Brush the pastry with egg yolk. Spread the cooled spinach mixture evenly over the center of the pastry. Place the salmon fillet on the spinach. Brush the top of the remaining pastry sheet with egg yolk. Cut into ¾-inch-wide strips. Place one strip of the pastry diagonally across the fish, with the egg side down. Add strips parallel to the first strip and ¾ inch apart. Repeat the process with strips in the opposite direction. Crimp the edges to the bottom pastry with a fork. Trim away the excess pastry, leaving a 1-inch border. Place on a baking sheet. Chill until time to bake.

Preheat the oven to 300 degrees. Bake for 15 to 20 minutes or until the pastry is puffed and golden brown.

S E R V E S 1 0   *I'll Taste Manhattan,* New York, NY

MARINATED SALMON SEARED IN PEPPER

¼ cup soy sauce
2 cloves garlic, minced
3 tablespoons lemon juice
1 teaspoon grated lemon peel
1 teaspoon sugar
2 (12-ounce) center-cut salmon
  fillets, skinned and halved
3 tablespoons coarsely cracked black
  pepper
¼ cup olive oil

Combine the soy sauce, garlic, lemon juice, lemon peel, and sugar in a sealable plastic bag. Add the salmon; seal and refrigerate for 1 hour, turning occasionally. Remove the salmon and pat dry; discard the marinade.

Press pepper into each piece of salmon, coating it thoroughly. Heat the oil in a skillet until hot but not smoking. Sauté the salmon for 2 to 3 minutes on each side until it flakes easily when tested with a fork. Transfer the salmon to paper towels; drain for 30 seconds and serve immediately.

SERVES 4   *Sensational Seasons: A Taste and Tour of Arkansas,*
                                                          Fort Smith, AR

SALMON OVER COALS

BEER SAUCE
1 pound butter
1 (12-ounce) can beer
4 lemons

CUCUMBER-DILL SAUCE
1 cucumber, peeled and seeded
Salt
1 cup sour cream
1 teaspoon chopped chives
1 teaspoon ground white pepper

8 salmon fillets, cleaned, dried, and
  ready to cook

To prepare the beer sauce, melt the butter and stir in 1 can of beer. Squeeze the 4 lemons; reserve 1 tablespoon of the juice and add the remaining juice to the butter-beer mixture. Set aside.

To prepare the cucumber-dill sauce, shred the cucumber with a coarse grater. Sprinkle with salt and let stand at room temperature for 1 hour. Drain thoroughly. Combine with the sour cream, the 1 tablespoon of lemon juice, chives, and white pepper. Chill.

Prepare a charcoal grill that has a good hot fire with evenly distributed coals. Dip each salmon fillet in beer sauce and place on the oiled grill rack. Baste the fillets frequently with beer sauce when cooking. Cook 7 to 10 minutes per side, depending on thickness. The fish is done when it flakes easily when tested with a fork. Remove from the grill and serve immediately with cucumber-dill sauce.

SERVES 8   *Posh Pantry,* Kankakee, IL

SALMON WITH GINGER BUTTER

3 tablespoons dry sherry
2 tablespoons soy sauce
1 tablespoon dark Asian sesame oil
1 tablespoon minced fresh gingerroot
2 tablespoons minced fresh parsley
2 pounds salmon fillets
2 tablespoons butter, cut into small
  pieces
⅛ teaspoon salt
⅛ teaspoon freshly ground black
  pepper
1 lemon, cut into wedges

Combine the sherry, soy sauce, sesame oil and ginger. Brush the fillets with the sherry mixture and sprinkle with parsley. Dot butter evenly across the surface. Season with salt and pepper. This may be prepared several hours ahead and refrigerated.

Broil or grill the salmon without turning until the fish turns pink and flakes easily, approximately 10 to 15 minutes. Serve with lemon wedges.

SERVES 4   *Gold'n Delicious,* Spokane, WA

CRISP SCALLOP AND SALMON CAKES

Café des Artistes is an elegant, romantic, and long-time-favorite restaurant located near Manhattan's West Side. At the café, these are served as a warm luncheon dish with farmhouse potatoes and tomato-basil sauce. They are also delicious chilled, sliced, and served with a green salad.

1 cup chopped onion
9 tablespoons unsalted butter, softened
1 cup white wine
12 ounces fresh salmon
4 ounces bay scallops
1 whole jalapeño pepper, seeded (optional)
1 large egg
1 tablespoon fresh lemon juice
1 tablespoon Cognac
Salt and freshly ground white pepper to taste
1 cup heavy cream
¼ cup chopped fresh dill
2 cups fine dry bread crumbs
¼ cup vegetable oil

Sauté the onion in 1 tablespoon of the butter in a sauté pan until tender, about 5 minutes. Add the wine. Cook until the liquid has completely evaporated.

Set aside. Purée 4 ounces of the salmon, the scallops, and the jalapeño pepper in a food processor. Add the egg, lemon juice, and Cognac; process until smooth. Chill.

Cream the remaining 8 tablespoons of butter with salt and white pepper in a bowl. Add the seafood purée and mix well. Add the cream. Mix at low speed just until blended. Chop the remaining 8 ounces of salmon. Add to the puréed mixture with the sautéed onion and dill. Mix well. Correct the seasoning if necessary. Chill until time to cook.

Shape the chilled mixture into 8 patties; coat with bread crumbs. Heat the oil in a heavy sauté pan over medium heat and fry half the patties until golden brown on one side. Turn the patties over and reduce the heat slightly. Cook, uncovered, until golden brown and cooked through. Repeat with the remaining patties.

SERVES 8   *I'll Taste Manhattan,* New York, NY

FETTUCCINE WITH SMOKED SALMON AND BLACK PEPPER SAUCE

1 bunch watercress, stemmed
1 medium red onion, peeled and quartered
1 tablespoon unsalted butter
2 cups heavy cream
2 teaspoons coarsely ground black pepper
12 ounces fettuccine
Salt to taste
4 ounces smoked salmon cut into ⅜-inch pieces
Grated zest of 1 medium lemon

Chop the watercress fine with the metal blade of a food processor, about 5 seconds. Reserve. Chop the onion coarse, about 5 pulses. Cook the onion in butter in a skillet over low heat until softened, about 5 minutes. Set aside.

Simmer the cream and pepper in a skillet over medium heat until reduced to 1½ cups, about 7 minutes. Keep warm.

Cook the fettuccine in boiling salted water until tender but still firm, about 7 minutes. Drain, reserving ¼ cup of the water. Toss the fettuccine, reserved water, reduced cream mixture, and salt in a serving bowl. Top with the watercress, onion, salmon, and lemon zest.

SERVES 4–6   *California Sizzles,* Pasadena, CA

PENNE, PEPPER, AND SALMON IN GARLIC SAUCE

A delightful luncheon dish. Half portions can be served as appetizers.

½ cup heavy cream

4 cloves garlic, lightly crushed

¼ cup fresh lemon juice

¾ cup olive oil

2 tablespoons minced fresh dill

2 tablespoons minced fresh parsley

Salt and pepper to taste

1 pound penne or other tubular pasta

6 ounces thinly sliced smoked salmon, cut into 2 × ⅓-inch strips

1 large red bell pepper, cut into julienne strips

1 small red onion, sliced thin

4 dill sprigs

Bring the cream to a boil in a saucepan over moderate heat. Add the garlic and simmer for 15 minutes or until the garlic is softened and the cream is reduced to about ¼ cup. Purée the mixture in a food processor or blender until very smooth. Add the lemon juice and blend well. Add the oil in a slow stream with the motor running, blending until emulsified. Blend in the dill, parsley, salt, and pepper. Set the sauce aside.

Cook the penne in large pot of boiling salted water until tender. Drain and transfer to a large bowl. Set aside 16 smoked salmon strips for garnish. Toss the penne with the pepper strips and onion and remaining smoked salmon. Add the sauce and toss gently.

Divide the mixture among 4 plates and garnish each serving with 4 strips of reserved salmon and a dill sprig. Serve warm or at room temperature.

SERVES 4 *Savor the Brandywine Valley,* Wilmington, DE

SMOKED SALMON QUICHE

4 eggs

2 egg yolks

2 cups heavy cream

½ cup grated Parmesan cheese

½ teaspoon salt

½ teaspoon ground white pepper

⅛ teaspoon grated nutmeg

½ pound sliced smoked salmon, cut into pieces

1 (9-inch) pastry crust (page 338),

Heat the oven to 425 degrees. Partially bake the pastry shell for 5 to 7 minutes. Remove from the oven and lower the heat to 400 degrees.

Beat together the eggs, egg yolks, cream, cheese, and seasonings. Reserve one piece of salmon; arrange the rest in the pastry shell and pour the custard mixture over. Place the reserved piece of smoked salmon on top and bake in for 30 minutes, or until a knife inserted between the center and the rim comes out clean. Let stand for 10 minutes; cut into wedges to serve.

SERVES 6–8 *A League of Cooks,* Greater Vancouver, BC

SIMPLY SUPERB SCALLOPS

1½ pounds sea scallops, cut in half horizontally

4 tablespoons (½ stick) butter, melted

3 tablespoons fine dry bread crumbs

⅛ teaspoon garlic salt

⅛ teaspoon dry mustard

½ teaspoon paprika

2 tablespoons dry sherry

Lemon slices

Heat the broiler. Rinse the scallops and pat dry. Pour 4 tablespoons of melted butter into the broiler pan. Add the scallops; turn to coat. Combine the bread crumbs and seasonings; sprinkle over the scallops. Drizzle with the remaining tablespoon of butter. Brown the scallops under the broiler for 5 to 7 minutes. Turn off the broiler and let the scallops heat 3 minutes longer. Sprinkle with sherry. Serve hot, garnished with lemon slices.

SERVES 4 *Celebrated Seasons,* Minneapolis, MN

LIME AND GINGER SCALLOP SAUTÉ

LIME-GINGER BUTTER

4 tablespoons (½ stick) unsalted
   butter, at room temperature
2 teaspoons grated lime zest
1 tablespoon minced peeled fresh
   gingerroot
1 teaspoon salt
Freshly ground pepper to taste

⅓ cup walnut halves
1 pound sea scallops, patted dry
1 tablespoon olive oil
1 tablespoon unsalted butter
3 tablespoons fresh lime juice
Chopped parsley for garnish

Make the lime-ginger butter: Combine the butter, lime zest, ginger, salt, and pepper in bowl; mix well. Shape into a 2½-inch roll. Wrap in plastic wrap and chill until firm.

Spread the walnuts on a baking sheet. Toast at 350 degrees for 3 to 5 minutes or until golden brown. Sauté the scallops in heated olive oil and butter in a skillet over high heat for 2 minutes or until golden brown; drain the skillet. Stir in the lime juice and cook for 1 minute; reduce heat. Add lime-ginger butter 1 tablespoon at a time. Cook just until the sauce thickens. Stir in the walnuts; garnish with parsley.

SERVES 4   *The Best of Wheeling*, Wheeling, WV

SHRIMP AND SCALLOP LINGUINE

1 tablespoon butter
1 tablespoon olive oil
½ red bell pepper, chopped
½ green bell pepper, chopped
1 small zucchini, sliced
1 pound bay shrimp
1 pound scallops
2 tablespoons white wine
3 cups heavy cream
1 pound fresh linguine or spinach
   linguine
Salt and pepper to taste
Juice of 1 lemon
1 cup grated Parmesan cheese

Heat the butter and olive oil in a large heavy saucepan and sauté the red and green peppers and the zucchini for 3 minutes. Add the shrimp and scallops; cook and stir just until the seafood is opaque, approximately 3 minutes. Remove the solids with a slotted spoon to a bowl; set aside.

Add the wine and cream to the juices remaining in the pan. Increase the heat to medium high; cook until the cream bubbles and begins to thicken.

Bring a large pot of salted water to a boil and add the pasta. Cook for 4 to 5 minutes, until tender but still firm. Drain and keep hot.

Add the shrimp, scallops, vegetables, salt, pepper, and lemon juice to the cream mixture; cook and stir until hot. Remove from the heat and fold in the cheese.

Serve the sauce over the pasta.

SERVES 4   *Savor the Flavor of Oregon*, Eugene, OR

Shore Scallops with Avocado Butter

Avocado Butter
8 tablespoons (1 stick) butter, at
  room temperature
Salt and freshly ground pepper
½ medium-size very ripe avocado,
  peeled, pitted, and chopped

8 tablespoons (1 stick) salted butter
2 teaspoons chopped fresh thyme
3 scallions, sliced thin
1 clove garlic, minced
½ pound mushrooms, wiped,
  trimmed, and sliced
½ red bell pepper, cut into julienne
  strips
¼ cup diced green bell pepper
1¼ pounds fresh scallops, rinsed
2 tablespoons freshly squeezed
  lemon juice
¼ cup dry white wine
2 cups hot cooked rice

Make the avocado butter: Cream the butter until fluffy; add the salt and pepper. Fold in the avocado and mix well. Set aside.

In a large saucepan, melt 4 tablespoons of butter. Add the thyme, scallions and garlic. Cook until the scallions are transparent. Add the mushrooms and both peppers and sauté until the peppers are crisp-tender. Remove from the heat and set aside.

In a bowl, combine the scallops and lemon juice. Set aside. In a saucepan, melt the remaining 4 tablespoons of butter. Add the scallops and cook until opaque, about 3 minutes. Add the reserved vegetables. Stir in the wine and cook uncovered for several minutes, until wine reduces. Serve the scallops, vegetables, and sauce over hot rice. Top with a dollop of avocado butter.

Serves 4

One Magnificent Cookbook, Chicago, IL

Maine Seafood Bake

3 pounds fresh seafood (any
  combination of scallops, haddock,
  raw shrimp, and/or cooked
  lobster meat)
20 buttered crackers, crushed
6 tablespoons butter
⅓ cup sherry
2 tablespoons lemon juice
1 teaspoon salt
½ teaspoon freshly ground pepper
½ teaspoon onion powder
½ teaspoons garlic powder
Paprika
2 tablespoons dried parsley flakes

Preheat the oven to 400 degrees. If using shrimp, peel and devein them. Cut the larger seafood into bite-sized pieces. In a 2-quart oven-proof casserole, arrange the seafood and sprinkle with cracker crumbs. In a small saucepan, melt the butter; add the sherry and lemon juice and heat for 2 minutes. Pour the butter mixture evenly over the seafood. Season with salt, pepper, onion and garlic powder. Lightly sprinkle with paprika and parsley. Bake uncovered for 30 minutes.

Serves 6

Maine Ingredients, Portland, ME

OYSTER AND PECAN STUFFING

3 loaves French bread
1½ cups finely chopped scallions
1½ cups finely chopped white
   onions
4 cups finely chopped green bell
   pepper
3 teaspoons minced garlic
12 tablespoons (1½ sticks) butter
5 cups finely chopped celery
2 pounds ground meat
3 or 4 dozen oysters, drained,
   reserving liquid
1 cup chopped pecans
1 cup chopped fresh parsley
Salt and pepper to taste
Ground red pepper (cayenne) to
   taste
1 bay leaf
½ teaspoon dried thyme
2 eggs, beaten

Slice the bread, arrange on a baking sheet, and place in a 250 degree oven until thoroughly dried. Put the dried bread in a plastic bag and use a rolling pin to roll into fine crumbs.

Sauté the scallions, white onions, green pepper, and garlic in 1 stick of the butter in a large skillet until transparent. Add the celery and sauté for an 2 additional minutes. In a separate skillet, fry the ground meat until lightly browned; drain off fat. Chop the oysters, if large. Mix the meat, oysters, and sautéed vegetables together, and add the bread crumbs. Add oyster liquid by the spoonful until the stuffing has reached the desired consistency. Stir in the pecans, parsley, salt, pepper, cayenne, bay leaf, and thyme. Combine the eggs with the remaining ½ stick of softened butter and mix into the stuffing.

MAKES ENOUGH STUFFING FOR A 12- TO 14-POUND TURKEY

The Plantation Cookbook, New Orleans, LA

OYSTERS MOSCA

1 large onion, chopped
8 tablespoons (1 stick) butter
3 cloves garlic, minced
2 tablespoons chopped fresh parsley
½ teaspoon dried thyme
¾ teaspoon dried oregano
⅛ teaspoon ground red pepper
   (cayenne)
Salt and ground black pepper to
   taste
4 dozen oysters, drained, reserving
   liquid
1 cup fine dry bread crumbs
2 slices bacon, fried and crumbled
10 almonds, crushed
Grated Parmesan cheese

Preheat the oven to 350 degrees. In a large skillet, sauté the onion in the butter until translucent, about 5 minutes. Add the garlic, parsley, seasonings, and oysters. Cook until oysters curl at the edges; then add the reserved oyster liquid. Fold in the bread crumbs, bacon, and almonds. Spoon into a casserole or individual ramekins. Sprinkle with cheese. Bake uncovered for 15 to 20 minutes.

SERVES 4

Southern Sideboards, Jackson, MS

VERMICELLI WITH CLAM SAUCE

3 cloves garlic, cut in half
⅔ cup olive oil
1 cup bottled clam juice
¼ teaspoon salt
Freshly ground pepper to taste
½ teaspoon dried oregano
3 (7½-ounce) cans minced clams
½ cup chopped fresh parsley
½ cup chopped scallions, with tops
1 pound freshly cooked vermicelli
Freshly grated Parmesan cheese
Fresh clams in the shell, if available

Sauté the garlic in the oil, mashing it as it cooks. Add the clam juice, salt, pepper, and oregano and simmer for 5 minutes. Add the minced clams and their juice and cook uncovered so the liquid will reduce. Add the parsley and scallions and cook 10 minute longer.

Toss half the sauce with the hot vermicelli and ½ cup of Parmesan cheese. Pour the remaining sauce on top and arrange freshly steamed clams around the sides of the dish. Serve with additional grated Parmesan.

SERVES 4–6   *Heritage of Hospitality,* Winston-Salem, NC

BAHAMIAN CONCH FRITTERS

1½ pounds conch
1 medium onion, chopped fine
2 tablespoons finely chopped green
  bell pepper
1 medium tomato, chopped fine
3 tablespoons finely chopped, tender
  celery parts and leaves
½ cup evaporated milk mixed with
  ½ cup water
2 tablespoons butter, softened
1 teaspoon salt
1 egg, well beaten
2 teaspoons baking powder
1 cup all-purpose flour
Vegetable oil

Grind the conch in a meat grinder and place in a large bowl. Add the onion, green pepper, tomato, celery, milk, butter, salt, and egg. Stir to combine. Mix the baking powder and flour together and stir into the wet ingredients.

Heat oil for deep frying to 375 degrees. Drop the batter by generous tablespoonfuls into the hot oil. Fry a few at a time until brown. Drain on paper toweling; keep warm in a 200 degree oven until all the batter has been used. Serve hot.

MAKES ABOUT 40 FRITTERS   *Heart of the Palms,* West Palm Beach, FL

VIRGINIA CRAB IMPERIAL

2 eggs, well beaten
¼ teaspoon dry mustard
Dash of ground white pepper
2 pounds backfin crabmeat, picked
  over to remove bits of shell and
  cartilage
4 tablespoons chopped pimiento
2¼ cups mayonnaise
½ cup Parmesan cheese

Preheat the oven to 350 degrees. Beat the eggs with the mustard and pepper. Combine with the crabmeat, pimiento, and 2 cups of the mayonnaise. Spoon the mixture into a 2-quart casserole dish and spread ¼ cup mayonnaise over the top. Sprinkle with cheese. Bake uncovered for about 20 minutes, until brown and bubbly.

SERVES 8   *Virginia Hospitality,* Hampton Roads, VA

MARYLAND STEAMED BLUE CRABS

1 cup beer
1 cup vinegar
3 dozen live Maryland blue crabs
1 cup Old Bay seasoning or crab
  boil
Cider vinegar, melted butter, and
  crab seasoning for serving

Plunge the crabs into hot water for 1 minute to kill them. Anyone who has ever chased an unruly crab will appreciate the importance of this step. Fit a large crab pot with a rack. Pour the beer and vinegar into the bottom of the pan, just level with the bottom of the rack. If more liquid is needed, add it until the level is reached.

Make layers of 6 crabs and 6 tablespoons of crab seasoning. Repeat until all the crabs are in the pot. Bring to a boil uncovered. Reduce the heat, cover, and simmer for 20 minutes. Serve hot on a table covered with a layer of newspaper. Eat the crab pieces plain or dip them in cider vinegar or melted butter. Extra crab seasoning may be sprinkled on crabs if desired.

SERVES 8–10 — *Of Tide and Thyme,* Annapolis, MD

CRAB SOUFFLÉ SANDWICHES

4 tablespoons (½ stick) butter
⅓ cup all-purpose flour
¼ cup mayonnaise
1 cup sliced mushrooms, sautéed in
  butter
2 cups half-and-half
6 eggs, separated
3 tablespoons dry sherry
½ teaspoon Worcestershire sauce
Salt
Freshly ground white pepper to taste
⅛ teaspoon ground red pepper
  (cayenne)
2½ cups lump or backfin crabmeat,
  picked over to remove bits of
  shell and cartilage
12 thin slices firm white bread,
  trimmed and buttered on one side
½ teaspoon cream of tartar
1 cup freshly grated Parmesan
  cheese

Melt the butter in a large heavy saucepan until foamy. Add the flour, blend, and cook for 3 minutes. Stir in the mayonnaise. Drain the sautéed mushrooms and set the mushrooms aside. Add enough half-and-half to the mushroom juices to make 2 cups. Gradually stir into the flour mixture, cook and stir until the sauce is thickened. Remove from the heat.

In a bowl, beat the egg yolks and sherry together. Stir in half the cream mixture, then add this back to the remaining cream sauce. Return the pan to the heat and stir for 3 minutes. Do not boil. Add the Worcestershire sauce, ¾ teaspoon of salt, the white and red peppers, mushrooms, and crab.

Cut the buttered bread slices in half diagonally. Place 12 half slices 2 inches apart on a large baking sheet and spread with half the cooled crab mixture. Cover with the other half of the bread and the rest of the crab mixture, making a two-layer, open-faced sandwich. Chill.

Half an hour before serving time, preheat the oven to 375 degrees. Beat the egg whites with ½ teaspoon of salt until foamy. Add the cream of tartar and beat until stiff but not dry. Spread on the top and sides of each sandwich, covering each thoroughly. Sprinkle with Parmesan cheese. Bake for 15 to 20 minutes, until lightly browned.

SERVES 12 — *Savor the Flavor of Oregon,* Eugene, OR

DEVILED CRAB

4 tablespoons (½ stick) butter
1 medium onion, chopped fine
2 large mushrooms, chopped
½ green bell pepper, chopped
¼ teaspoon salt
⅛ teaspoon freshly ground pepper
½ teaspoon dry mustard
1 tablespoon Worcestershire sauce
Dash of Tabasco
1 tablespoon flour
1 cup hot milk
1 cup hot clam juice or broth
2 egg yolks, well beaten
1 pound lump crab meat, picked
   over well to remove bits of shell
   and cartilage

Melt the butter in the top part of a double boiler over direct heat. Add the onion, mushrooms, and green pepper and sauté for 5 minutes. Stir in the salt, pepper, mustard, Worcestershire, Tabasco, and flour. Whisk in the hot milk, hot clam juice, and well beaten egg yolks. Cook in the double boiler over hot water for 10 minutes or until thickened, stirring constantly. Add the crabmeat and cook for 5 minutes more. Remove from heat and place in individual casseroles or crab shells. Serve hot.

SERVES 6 *Out of Our League,* Greensboro, NC

MUSHROOM-CRUST CRAB QUICHE

5 tablespoons butter
½ pound mushrooms, wiped,
   trimmed, and chopped fine
½ cup crushed crackers (about 16)
1¼ teaspoons dried tarragon leaves
¾ cup chopped scallions
¾ cup shredded Monterey Jack
   cheese
¾ cup shredded Swiss cheese
¾ cup small-curd cottage cheese
¼ cup ricotta cheese
3 eggs, beaten
¼ teaspoon ground red pepper
   (cayenne)
2 tablespoons sherry
6 ounces crabmeat, picked over well

Preheat the oven to 350 degrees. Melt 3 tablespoons of the butter in a skillet. Add the mushrooms and sauté until tender. Remove from the heat. Stir in the crushed crackers and 1 teaspoon of tarragon. Press into an oiled 9-inch pie pan. Bake for 15 minutes.

Melt the remaining 2 tablespoons of butter, add the scallions, and sauté until tender. Spread the scallions over the cooked mushroom crust. Blend together the shredded Jack and Swiss cheeses, the cottage cheese, ricotta, and beaten eggs. Season with the remaining ¼ teaspoon of tarragon, the cayenne and sherry. Fold in the crabmeat. Pour the mixture over the onions and bake for about 40 minutes or until firm. Allow to sit for 5 minutes before serving.

SERVES 4–6 *Gourmet L.A.,* Los Angeles, CA

MARINATED CRAB

Heavenly.

¼ cup vegetable oil
3 tablespoons tarragon vinegar
1¼ teaspoons salt
¾ teaspoon freshly ground pepper
⅛ teaspoon dried thyme
¼ teaspoon dried basil
1 tablespoon minced fresh parsley
1¼ cups chopped onion
2 tablespoons lemon juice
1 pound lump crabmeat, picked over
  to remove bits of shell and cartilage

Combine all ingredients except crabmeat; mix well. Pour over the crabmeat in a ceramic bowl and marinate, covered, for at least 4 hours in the refrigerator.

NOTE: Although crabmeat is very perishable, it will keep up to 5 days in the marinade. Never marinate in aluminum pans.

SERVES 4–6   *Encore! Nashville,* Nashville, TN

CRAB-STUFFED POTATOES

6 medium baking potatoes
8 tablespoons (1 stick) butter
½ cup light cream
1 teaspoon salt
⅛ teaspoon ground white pepper
3½ teaspoons grated onion
1 cup grated sharp Cheddar cheese
½ pound fresh lump crabmeat,
  picked over well
½ teaspoon paprika

Scrub the potatoes and bake for 30 minutes in 450 degree oven. Pierce the potatoes with a fork and turn over. Bake for another 20 to 30 minutes. Remove from the oven and cool briefly.

Cut each potato in half lengthwise and carefully scoop potato from the skins into a medium-sized mixing bowl. Add the butter, cream, salt, pepper, and onion. Whip with an electric mixer until smooth. Fold in the cheese and crabmeat.

Fill each potato skin with the mixture, mounding slightly. Sprinkle with paprika. Arrange on a baking sheet and bake for 15 minutes.

SERVES 6   *Rare Collection,* Galveston, TX

BEST MARYLAND CRAB CAKES

4 slices white bread with crusts
  trimmed or ½ cup fine dry bread
  crumbs
½ teaspoon dry mustard
½ teaspoon Old Bay seasoning
1 egg
½ cup mayonnaise
½ teaspoon lemon juice
½ teaspoon Worcestershire sauce
1 pound lump or backfin crabmeat,
  picked over to remove bits of
  shell and cartilage
Vegetable oil for frying

Tear the bread into pieces and process in a food processor to form fine crumbs. Toss the bread crumbs with the mustard and Old Bay seasoning and set aside.

Beat the egg in a mixing bowl and blend in the mayonnaise, lemon juice, and Worcestershire sauce. Gently fold in the crabmeat along with half the seasoned bread crumbs.

Divide the mixture into 8 to 10 portions and shape each into a flat patty about 1 inch thick. Coat the patties with the remaining bread crumbs and refrigerate for at least 2 hours.

Heat 2 tablespoons of oil in a heavy skillet and fry the patties in batches for 2 to 3 minutes on each side, or until golden brown. Add more oil as necessary between batches. Drain on paper towels and serve hot.

SERVES 4–6   *Of Tide and Thyme,* Annapolis, MD

DUNGENESS CRAB CAKES

CRAB CAKES

3 cups fine fresh bread crumbs

2 large eggs, beaten

2 tablespoons mayonnaise

2 tablespoons minced onion

2 tablespoons minced celery

2 tablespoons minced red bell
  pepper

1 tablespoon minced fresh parsley

1 medium clove garlic, minced

½ teaspoon dried mustard

¼ teaspoon ground red pepper
  (cayenne)

1 pound Dungeness crabmeat

2 tablespoons olive oil

Orange Sauce or Pineapple Salsa
  (see below)

Mix together 1 cup of the bread crumbs, the eggs, mayonnaise, onion, celery, bell pepper, parsley, garlic, and seasonings. Stir in the crabmeat. Chill the mixture at least 2 hours or up to overnight. Shape the crab mixture into 12 small cakes. Evenly coat each cake with the remaining bread crumbs. (You may not need to use all of the bread crumbs.)

Heat the oil in a large skillet over medium heat. Fry the cakes until brown and crisp, about 5 minutes per side. To serve crab cakes, place a large spoonful of orange sauce on each plate and top with 2 crab cakes. Drizzle extra sauce over the cakes. Alternately, serve hot cakes with pineapple salsa on the side.

ORANGE SAUCE

2 large shallots, minced

¼ cup white wine

1 cup orange juice, reduced by
  boiling to 2 tablespoons

4 tablespoons (½ stick) butter, cut
  into bits

2 tablespoons plain yogurt

2 tablespoons cream

¼ teaspoon Tabasco

In a nonreactive pan, heat the shallots, wine, and reduced orange juice together until the liquid is further reduced to 2 tablespoons. Gradually whisk in the butter, stirring well after each addition. Remove from the heat and stir in the yogurt, cream, and Tabasco.

PINEAPPLE SALSA

2 cups diced pineapple

¼ cup diced red bell pepper

¼ cup diced green bell pepper

¼ cup diced red onion

½ jalapeño pepper, minced

2 tablespoons minced cilantro leaves

1 tablespoon lime juice

1 tablespoon thinly sliced scallion

Combine all the ingredients in a medium-sized bowl. Stir well, cover, and refrigerate 2 to 4 hours. Bring to room temperature before serving.

SERVES 6   *Simply Classic,* Seattle, WA

BARBARA MIKULSKI'S CRAB CAKES

1 egg, beaten
½ cup mayonnaise
½ teaspoon Worcestershire sauce
1 tablespoon dried parsley flakes
1 teaspoon Old Bay seasoning or
    seafood seasoning
½ teaspoon salt
½ teaspoon ground black pepper
½ teaspoon dry mustard
6 finely crumbled saltines
1 pound lump or backfin crabmeat,
    picked over well
4 tablespoons (½ stick) butter

In a mixing bowl, combine the egg, mayonnaise, Worchestershire sauce, parsley, and seasonings. Stir in the cracker crumbs and gently fold in the crabmeat.

Form the mixture into 12 small or 6 large cakes. Chill until ready to cook.

Heat the butter in a heavy skillet and brown the crab cakes, in batches if necessary, for 3 to 5 minutes on each side.

SERVES 6   *Hunt to Harbor–An Epicurean Tour*, Baltimore, MD

ANGELIC SHRIMP AND LOBSTER

3 tablespoons butter
3 cloves garlic, chopped
2 shallots, chopped fine
1 cup white wine
1 cup chicken broth
Freshly ground black pepper to taste
Dash of crushed red pepper flakes
1 pound medium to large shrimp,
    peeled and deveined
1 pound cooked lobster meat,
    chopped
1 cup light cream (milk may be
    substituted)
1 pound angel hair pasta
¼ cup chopped fresh parsley

In a large skillet, over medium heat, melt the butter and sauté the garlic and shallots for 2 minutes. Add the wine, chicken broth, and black and red pepper. Bring to a boil over medium-high heat and cook until the liquid starts to reduce. Add the shrimp and cook approximately 5 minutes, until opaque. Add the lobster just to heat through. Reduce the heat to a simmer, add the cream, and turn the heat off after 1 to 2 minutes.

Meanwhile, cook the angel hair pasta according to package directions. Remove the seafood from the sauce with a slotted spoon and set aside. Toss the pasta with the sauce. Place the seafood on top of the pasta. Sprinkle with parsley and serve immediately.

SERVES 4–6   *Maine Ingredients*, Portland, ME

ERC RESOURCE & REFERRAL
JUNIOR LEAGUE OF TOPEKA, KANSAS

Everywoman's Resource Center was established in 1978 as the result of a cooperative effort of several women's organizations spear-headed by the Junior League of Topeka, Kansas. Its mission was to meet the special needs of women in changing society. Today the Center serves women, men, teens and children and specializes in resource and referral for securing child care, employment, affordable housing and resolution to crisis situations.

PASTA WITH LOBSTER AND SHRIMP

2 tablespoons salt
1 bay leaf
2 slices lemon
2 slices onion
1 stalk celery with leaves
3 peppercorns
2 sprigs parsley
1 medium-sized live lobster
1 pound shelled and cleaned shrimp
   or 2 pounds shrimp in shells

In a kettle, bring about 6 quarts of water to a boil with 2 tablespoons of salt. Add the bay leaf, lemon and onion slices, celery, peppercorns, and parsley. Plunge the lobster head first into the boiling water. Cover, return to a boil, and cook for 5 to 6 minutes per pound from the time the water begins boiling again.

Remove the lobster and skim off any scum from the broth. Add the shrimp and simmer for about 4 minutes, until they turn pink. Remove the shrimp and reserve one cup of broth. Remove the meat from the lobster and cut into uniform chunks. Reserve the tomalley for the sauce. Combine the shrimp and lobster meat, cover, and keep warm while you make the sauce.

SAUCE
6 tablespoons butter
2 tablespoons minced onion
6 tablespoons all-purpose flour
1 cup reserved fish broth
1 cup chicken broth
1½ cups light cream
½ cup dry white wine
¼ cup grated Parmesan cheese
1 tablespoon sharp mustard
3-4 drops hot pepper sauce
3 tablespoons brandy
1 teaspoon salt
Ground white pepper to taste

Melt the butter in a large heavy pan. Add the minced onion and cook 2 to 3 minutes; do not brown. Stir in the flour. Gradually add the reserved fish and chicken broth, the cream and white wine. Cook and stir over low heat until smooth and thickened, about 10 minutes. Stir in the cheese, mustard, hot sauce, brandy, and salt and continue to cook over low heat another 10 minutes, stirring frequently. Add the lobster and shrimp, mixing gently. Stir in the reserved tomalley. Simmer gently until heated through.

SPAGHETTI
1 tablespoon salt
1 tablespoon oil
1 pound spaghetti
3 tablespoons butter
3 tablespoons grated Parmesan
   cheese

Add salt and oil to a large pot of water. Bring to a boil. Add the spaghetti, stirring vigorously. Cook about 8 minutes, or until tender. Drain thoroughly. Return to the pot with the butter and Parmesan cheese. Toss over low heat until the pasta is coated with butter and cheese. Lift out onto a warm platter and ladle the hot sauce over the spaghetti.

SERVES 4-6

R.S.V.P., Portland, ME

DILLED LOBSTER ROLLS

1 pound lobster meat
1 small cucumber, peeled and diced
½ cup shredded carrots
½ cup mayonnaise
2 tablespoons Dijon mustard
1 teaspoon dried dill, or to taste
Freshly ground pepper to taste
4 rolls, lightly toasted
Paprika for garnish

In a medium bowl, gently toss the lobster, cucumber, and carrots. In a small bowl, mix the mayonnaise, mustard, dill, and pepper. Toss the mayonnaise mixture with the lobster. Serve in rolls. Sprinkle lightly with paprika.

SERVES 4

Maine Ingredients, Portland ME

LOBSTER MEDALLIONS IN GARLIC-CHIVE BUTTER SAUCE

2 (10-ounce) lobster tails
8 tablespoons (1 stick) butter
2 tablespoons heavy cream
2 tablespoons lemon juice
1 tablespoon chopped fresh chives, plus additional for garnish
1 clove garlic, minced fine

Bring 2 quarts of water to boil, add the lobster tails, cover, reduce the heat, and simmer 12 minutes. Drain and rinse with cold water. Slit the shells and remove the meat. Chill, then cut into ½-inch slices. Set aside while preparing the sauce.

Melt the butter in a heavy saucepan. Add the cream and cook over low heat for 1 minute. Stir in the lemon juice, chives, and garlic and remove from the heat. Arrange the lobster medallions on 4 plates and spoon sauce over the top. Garnish with chives.

SERVES 4

Making Waves in the Kitchen, Indian River, FL

LOBSTER WITH CHAMPAGNE DIPPING SAUCE

1 bottle dry champagne
1 cup chopped fresh parsley
1 small bunch fresh thyme
1 bay leaf
4 shallots, chopped
12 tablespoons (1½ sticks) unsalted butter
Salt and pepper to taste
4 live lobsters, 1½ to 2 pounds each

To make the sauce, pour the Champagne into a medium saucepan and add the parsley, thyme, bay leaf, and shallots. Cook over medium heat until just 1 cup of liquid remains, about 25–30 minutes. Strain the liquid and discard the herbs. Slowly whisk in the butter, one tablespoon at a time, over low heat. When all the butter has been added, season the sauce with salt and pepper to taste. Keep the mixture warm while preparing the lobsters.

In a large pot, bring to a boil enough salted water to cover the lobsters. Remove the rubber bands that hold the claws shut. Plunge the lobsters in, head first. Cover and bring the water to a boil again. Cook the lobsters for 10 to 12 minutes from the time the water returns to a boil. Serve lobster accompanied with Champagne dipping sauce.

SERVES 4

Maine Ingredients, Portland, ME

CRAWFISH ÉTOUFFÉE I

8 tablespoons (1 stick) butter
1 tablespoon flour
1 onion, chopped fine
1 bell pepper, chopped fine
1 stalk celery, chopped fine
Crawfish fat, if available
1 pound peeled crawfish tails
1 teaspoon salt
1 teaspoon ground black pepper
¼ teaspoon ground red pepper
   (cayenne)
Dash of Tabasco
2 tablespoons chopped scallion tops
2 tablespoons minced parsley
Hot cooked rice

In a heavy saucepan, melt the butter and stir in the flour until smooth. Sauté the vegetables slowly in the butter and flour mixture for 30 to 45 minutes. If crawfish fat is available, add it now and simmer 15 minutes. Add the crawfish tails and seasonings and cook, covered, over low heat for 15 minutes. Add ¼ to ½ cup hot water to obtain the desired thickness of gravy. Add the scallion tops and parsley. Cook 5 minutes longer and serve over hot rice.

SERVES 4 *Lagniappe on the Neches,* Beaumont, TX

CRAWFISH ÉTOUFFÉE II

¼ cup vegetable oil
4 tablespoons (½ stick) margarine
1 cup all-purpose flour
2 bunches scallions
3 bell peppers
1 stalk celery
1 (16-ounce) can tomatoes
1 tablespoon garlic powder
2 teaspoons salt
1 tablespoon lemon juice
1 tablespoon ground black pepper
1 teaspoon ground red pepper
   (cayenne)
¼ cup chopped fresh parsley
3 tablespoons Worcestershire sauce
6 cups hot water or homemade
   seafood stock
3 pounds peeled crawfish tails,
   lightly rinsed and drained
3 cups uncooked rice

Heat the oil and margarine in a Dutch oven. Add the flour and make a roux by cooking and stirring over low heat for about 20 minutes, until the mixture is a light reddish brown. Chop the scallions and reserve the tops. In a food processor or blender, chop the peppers, celery, and tomatoes. Add to the roux. Add the chopped white part of the scallions, the garlic powder, salt, lemon juice, black and red peppers, parsley, and Worcestershire. Cover and cook for 15 to 20 minutes, stirring frequently. Add the water and cook slowly for at least an hour. Add crawfish tails and reserved chopped scallion tops and cook about 15 minutes. Meanwhile, cook the rice. Serve the crawfish over the hot rice.

CRAWFISH PIE: Use 3 (9-inch) unbaked pie crusts. Pour filling over bottom crust and cover with top crusts. Cut slits in top. Bake on a cookie sheet at 350 degrees for 15 minutes, until golden brown. Pies will be considerably higher in fat content.

SERVES 12 *River Road Recipes: A Healthy Collection,* Baton Rouge, LA

CRAWFISH CARDINAL

5 tablespoons butter
¼ cup minced onion
1 clove garlic, minced
5 tablespoons all-purpose flour
1 tablespoon tomato paste
1¼ cups chicken broth or 1 cup
　　clam juice and ¼ cup water
1 teaspoon salt
Pinch of dried thyme
¼ teaspoon grated nutmeg
½ teaspoon Tabasco
1 bay leaf
1 cup light cream
2 tablespoons lemon juice
2 tablespoons brandy
1 pound peeled crawfish tails

Heat the oven to 350 degrees. In a large skillet, melt the butter and sauté the onion and garlic until tender but not brown. Blend in the flour. Add the tomato paste and cook 2 minutes. Gradually stir in the liquid. Add the salt, thyme, nutmeg, Tabasco, and bay leaf. Mix well. Stir in the cream, lemon juice, and brandy. Add the crawfish. Remove the bay leaf. Spoon into 6 individual ramekins and bake until bubbly, approximately 10 minutes.

SERVES 6　　　　　　　　　　　　　　　　*Jambalaya,* New Orleans, LA

NEW ORLEANS EGGPLANT

2 medium eggplants
1 large onion
½ green bell pepper
½ bunch scallions
2 cloves garlic
2 tablespoons bacon drippings or
　　vegetable oil
2 tablespoons minced parsley
3 or 4 slices bread, soaked in water
1 pound shrimp, boiled, peeled, and
　　chopped
1 small piece of ham, ground
1 or 2 eggs
Salt and pepper to taste
Fine dry bread crumbs
2 tablespoons butter

Boil eggplants in a large pot of water until fork tender. Cool. Chop the onion, pepper, and scallions fine; sauté in the bacon drippings with garlic for 5 minutes, until wilted.

Slice the eggplants in half lengthwise. Scoop out the eggplant pulp carefully so as not to damage the skin. Add the pulp to the onion mixture and simmer uncovered for 20 minutes. Stir in the parsley and simmer about 5 minutes. Remove from the heat. Squeeze the bread dry and mix in well. Add the chopped shrimp and ground ham. Blend in 1 or 2 eggs to bind; season with salt and pepper to taste. Stir in a few bread crumbs if needed. Stuff the shells, sprinkle with bread crumbs, and dot with butter. Bake at 350 degrees for 15 minutes.

SERVES 4　　　　　　　　*The Cotton Country Collection,* Monroe, LA

BARBECUE SHRIMP

1 pound butter

4 cloves garlic crushed

3 bay leaves

1 tablespoon dried oregano

1 teaspoon dried rosemary

1 teaspoon barbecue spice

Salt and freshly ground pepper to
taste

½ cup Chardonnay or other white
wine

5 pounds large unshelled shrimp
(15–20 count per pound)

Melt the butter in a large heavy saucepan. Add the garlic, bay leaves, oregano, rosemary, barbecue spice, salt, pepper, and wine. Bring to a simmer and stir in the shrimp. Cover and cook for 15 minutes. Remove the cover and cook 15 minutes longer. Let the shrimp stand in the sauce for 10 minutes before serving. Serve with hot New Orleans French bread to dip in the sauce.

SERVES 10

Tell Me More, Lafayette, LA

CAJUN SHRIMP

1 bunch scallions

6 tablespoons butter, softened

1 clove garlic, minced

2 teaspoons lime juice

2 teaspoons peanut butter

3 tablespoons dry sherry

1 teaspoon Old Bay seasoning or
Beau Monde seasoning

1½ pounds uncooked large shrimp
(20 count), shelled, deveined, and
butterflied

20 small dried Japanese red pepper
pods (see Note)

⅓ cup minced fresh parsley

3 to 4 cups hot cooked white rice

½ cup dry roasted peanuts, chopped
coarse

Cut the scallions into fine slivers 2 inches long. Place in a small bowl of ice water to develop curl; set aside. In another small bowl, combine 3 tablespoons of the butter, the garlic, lime juice, and peanut butter. Add the sherry and Old Bay seasoning; mix until smooth. Set the sauce aside.

Melt the remaining 3 tablespoons of butter in a large heavy skillet. Heat until almost ready to turn golden. Add the shrimp and sauté for 2 to 3 minutes, until they begin to turn pink. Pour the sauce over and add the red peppers, continuing to stir for 2 to 3 minutes more. Add 2 tablespoons of the parsley and sauté for 1 minute longer, until the shrimp are cooked thoroughly but not overly cooked. Turn off the heat while preparing to serve.

Drain the onion curls. Place the hot rice in a large shallow heated serving dish. Add the remaining parsley and toss. Place the shrimp, peppers, and any pan juices over the rice; garnish with onion curls and chopped peanuts. Warn guests not to eat pepper pods unless they have cast-iron mouths!

NOTE: Pepper pods release just enough heat to enhance flavor, yet this unusual combination of ingredients will not overpower the delicate flavor of the shrimp.

SERVES 4–6

Pinch of Salt Lake, Salt Lake City, UT

ASIAN CHARCOAL-BROILED SHRIMP

Everyone loves these!

2 pounds jumbo shrimp
⅓ cup vegetable oil
⅓ cup sherry
3 tablespoons plus 1 teaspoon soy
   sauce
1 clove garlic, minced
2 bay leaves
2 teaspoons Worcestershire sauce
Lemon juice
Dash of hot pepper sauce
8 tablespoons (1 stick) butter

Wash the shrimp and drain. With a sharp knife, cut down the back of each shrimp and remove the intestinal vein, leaving the shell on. This is the secret to the absorption of the marinade. Combine the oil, sherry, 3 tablespoons of soy sauce, the garlic, bay leaves, Worcestershire sauce, a dash of lemon juice, and the hot pepper sauce in a container large enough to hold the shrimp. Add the shrimp to the marinade and refrigerate the mixture for 3 to 4 hours, turning the shrimp occasionally. Drain and reserve the marinade.

Arrange the shrimp in a wire grilling basket with closely placed grids. Grill over a bed of coal for 8 to 10 minutes, turning and basting often with the marinade.

Melt the butter and combine with 2 tablespoons of lemon juice and 1 teaspoon of soy sauce to make a sauce. Serve the shrimp in their shells with sauce for dipping.

SERVES 4–6   *Sensational Seasonings: A Taste and Tour of Arkansas,* Fort Smith, AR

SHRIMP WITH FETA SAUCE

½ cup minced onion
1½ tablespoons butter
1½ tablespoons vegetable oil
½ cup dry white wine
4 ripe tomatoes, peeled, seeded, and
   chopped
1 small clove garlic, minced
½ teaspoon salt
¼ teaspoon freshly ground pepper
¾ teaspoon dried oregano
4 ounces feta cheese, crumbled
1 pound large uncooked shrimp,
   shelled and deveined
Cooked spinach noodles
½ cup chopped fresh parsley

In a heavy skillet, sauté the onion in the butter and oil until soft. Add the wine, tomatoes, garlic, salt, pepper, and oregano. Simmer until the sauce is slightly thickened. Stir in the feta cheese and simmer for 10 to 15 minutes longer.

Just before serving, add the shrimp to the simmering sauce and cook 5 minutes or until shrimp are just tender. Be careful not to overcook. Serve over spinach noodles and garnish heavily with parsley for color. Crusty French bread and a crisp green salad complete the meal.

SERVES 4–6   *Palm Country Cuisine,* Greater Lakeland, FL

SAFFRON SHRIMP

20 large shrimp (about 1¾ pounds),
    shelled and deveined
¾ teaspoon salt
¼ teaspoon ground black pepper
½ tablespoon leaf saffron or ¼
    teaspoon powdered saffron
1 large shallot, chopped
2 cloves garlic, chopped
1 tablespoon chopped parsley
Juice of 2 lemons
3 tablespoons olive oil
½ teaspoon fresh thyme or ¼
    teaspoon dried thyme
8 tablespoons (1 stick) butter
Cooked rice

Rinse the shrimp and drain on paper towels. Combine the salt, pepper, saffron, shallot, parsley, and garlic in a bowl. Add the lemon juice, olive oil, and thyme. Place the shrimp in the marinade. Cover and let stand 30 minutes or more in the refrigerator, turning several times.

Preheat the broiler. Melt the butter and set aside. Place the shrimp on a rack in a foil-lined broiler pan. Broil 3 inches from the heat for 2 to 3 minutes per side until pink. Let the marinade drip into the pan beneath. Arrange the shrimp on a warm platter containing a bed of steamed rice. Pour the pan dripping and extra marinade into the pan with butter. Heat the sauce to boiling and serve with the shrimp.

SERVES 4–6   *A Taste of Tampa,* Tampa, FL

SCAMPI FINES HERBES (TROPICANA HOTEL)

This quick-to-prepare main dish is featured in the Rhapsody Room. Serve the scampi with rice pilaf or linguine.

1 tablespoon finely chopped shallot
1½ teaspoons minced garlic
½ cup clarified butter
12 large raw shrimp, shelled and
    deveined
2 tablespoons brandy
¼ teaspoon dried oregano
¼ teaspoon dried basil
½ teaspoon fresh minced parsley
¼ cup dry white wine
¾ cup diced fresh or canned
    tomatoes, drained
Salt and freshly ground pepper to
    taste

In a large skillet over medium heat, sauté the shallot and garlic in the clarified butter for 2 minutes or until transparent but not brown. Add the shrimp and cook for 3 or 4 minutes or until the shrimp turn pink. Slowly pour the brandy into the skillet and cook for 30 seconds. (If your skillet is very hot, the brandy may ignite. Therefore, add it very carefully to avoid being burned.) Add the herbs, wine, and tomatoes and simmer 5 minutes. Season to taste with salt and pepper.

SERVES 2   *Winning at the Table,* Las Vegas, NV

GARLIC-LIME MARINATED SHRIMP

This marinade is also fantastic for chicken.

3 pounds large shrimp, shelled and
  deveined, tails left on
3 cloves garlic, crushed
1½ teaspoons salt
½ cup packed brown sugar
3 tablespoons grainy mustard
¼ cup cider vinegar
Juice of 1 lime
Juice of ½ large lemon
6 tablespoons olive oil
Freshly ground black pepper to taste

The night before preparation, place the shrimp in a shallow bowl. Mix the garlic, salt, brown sugar, mustard, vinegar, and lime and lemon juices; blend well. Whisk in the oil; add the pepper and pour over the shrimp. Cover and refrigerate overnight, turning once. When ready to cook, bring the shrimp to room temperature. Grill over hot coals or under broiler for 2 to 3 minutes per side.

SERVES 6   *Tampa Treasures,* Tampa, FL

SHRIMP AND CHEESE GRITS

1 cup hominy grits
½ teaspoon salt
4 tablespoons (½ stick) butter
1 cup grated sharp Cheddar cheese
½ cup grated Parmesan cheese
Pinch of white pepper
Pinch of ground red pepper
  (cayenne)
Grated nutmeg to taste
1½ pounds shrimp, shelled and
  deveined
6 slices bacon
Peanut oil
2 cups sliced mushrooms
1¼ cups sliced scallions
2 cloves garlic, minced
4 teaspoons lemon juice
Hot pepper sauce
3 tablespoons chopped fresh parsley
Salt and ground black pepper to
  taste

Bring 4 cups of water to a boil and slowly stir in the grits. Reduce the heat and continue cooking, stirring frequently, for about 20 minutes or until the grits are thick and tender. Stir in the salt and butter. Add the cheeses and white pepper, cayenne, and nutmeg. Stir to combine thoroughly; adjust seasonings to taste. Set aside.

Wash the shrimp and pat dry. Dice the bacon and cook in a large skillet until just crisp. Drain the bacon on paper toweling and reserve. Add enough oil to the bacon fat to make a thin layer. When hot, add the shrimp. Cook and stir; add the mushrooms, scallions, and garlic when the shrimp start to color. Add the hot sauce, parsley, salt, and pepper.

Divide the cheese grits among 4 warm plates. Spoon the shrimp over and serve immediately.

SERVES 4   *Sweet Home Alabama,* Huntsville, AL

SASSY SOUTHERN TIER SHRIMP

Begin with our best, as we did, for your family and company.

½ cup olive oil
¼ cup grapefruit juice
¼ cup tequila
2 cloves garlic, minced
1 teaspoon ground cumin
½ teaspoon salt
½ teaspoon sugar
½ teaspoon bottled hot pepper
   sauce
1 pound shrimp, shelled and
   deveined

AVOCADO SAUCE
2 small ripe avocados, peeled and
   mashed
1 small tomato, chopped
¼ cup chopped green chiles,
   drained
¼ cup minced onion
¼ cup sour cream
2 tablespoon chopped fresh cilantro
½ teaspoon salt

In a large bowl, combine the oil, grapefruit juice, tequila, garlic, cumin, salt, sugar, and hot sauce until well blended. Add the shrimp; toss to coat well. Cover and refrigerate at least 2 hours, turning occasionally. Broil or grill 4 inches from the source of heat for 4 to 5 minutes, turning once and brushing frequently with the marinade. Serve with avocado sauce as dip.

In a small bowl, combine all ingredients until well blended. Cover and refrigerate until served.

MAKES 16–20 SERVINGS

Family & Company, Binghamton, NY

GARLIC BROILED SHRIMP

The mother-in-law of one of our testers pronounced this "Pure heaven!"

2 pounds large fresh shrimp, shelled
   and deveined (Note)
8 tablespoons (1 stick) butter,
   melted
½ cup olive oil
¼ cup chopped fresh parsley
1 tablespoon chopped scallion
3 cloves garlic, minced
1½ tablespoons fresh lemon juice
Freshly ground black pepper

Rinse the shrimp and drain on paper toweling. Combine the butter, olive oil, parsley, scallion, garlic, and lemon juice in a large shallow dish. Add the shrimp, tossing to coat. Cover and marinate in the refrigerator at least 30 minutes, stirring occasionally.

Preheat the broiler. Place the shrimp on broiler pan and broil 4 inches from heat source for 3 to 4 minutes. Turn and broil for another 3 minutes or until done. Top with a few turns of the pepper mill and serve with the pan drippings over pasta or rice.

NOTE: I prefer to use shrimp that have been peeled but with the tails left on and split (or butterflied) up the back. You can ask your fish market to do this for you.

SERVES 4–6

Off the Hook, Stamford–Norwalk, CT

BLACK SHRIMP

3 sticks (¾ pound) butter, melted
8 tablespoons (½ cup) ground black
 pepper
1 large bottle Wishbone Italian
 dressing
1 teaspoon salt
5 pounds fresh shrimp in the shell

Combine the butter, pepper, dressing, and salt in a long, shallow baking dish or the bottom of a roasting pan. Add the shrimp and bake at 350 degrees for 45 minutes, stirring once or twice. Serve this with a tossed green salad and French bread to dip up the sauce. Let each peel his or her own—messy but fun.
SERVES 8 *Cooking Through Rose-Colored Glasses,* Tyler, TX

SPICY SHRIMP SPAGHETTI

¼ cup olive oil
½ pound fresh shrimp, shelled and
 deveined
½ cup chopped onion
2 cloves garlic, crushed
2 teaspoons Cajun seafood seasoning
1 (16-ounce) can tomatoes,
 undrained and diced
Salt and freshly ground pepper to
 taste
1 teaspoon dried basil
8 ounces spaghetti, cooked
1 small can black olives, drained
Freshly grated Parmesan cheese

Place the olive oil in a skillet and heat until hot. Add the shrimp, onion, garlic, and 1 teaspoon of the Cajun seasoning. Sauté until the shrimp is pink. Remove the shrimp and onion with a slotted spoon. Set aside.

Add the tomatoes, remaining Cajun seasoning, salt, pepper, and basil to the juices in the pan. Bring to a boil, then turn down the heat and simmer uncovered for 5 minutes. Return the shrimp to the pan and cook 2 minutes. Pour the mixture over the spaghetti and toss well. Garnish with black olives and Parmesan cheese.
SERVES 4 *The Wild, Wild West,* Odessa, TX

PINE ISLAND SHRIMP

This sauce is great!

8 tablespoons (1 stick) butter
1 cup sliced fresh mushrooms
¼ cup finely minced onion
Dash of garlic powder
3 tablespoons all-purpose flour
¼ cup white wine
1 cup chicken broth
1 cup sour cream
1 tablespoon chopped parsley
2 pounds medium shrimp, cooked,
 shelled, and deveined
Rice or pasta

Melt the butter in a heavy saucepan and sauté the mushrooms and onion for 2 to 3 minutes. Add the garlic powder and stir in the flour. Gradually blend in the wine and chicken broth; cook and stir until the sauce thickens. Lower the heat and add the sour cream. Do not boil. Add parsley and shrimp just before serving. Serve over rice or pasta.
SERVES 6 *Thymes Remembered,* Tallahassee, FL

BLACK AND RED PEPPERED SHRIMP

4 tablespoons (½ stick) butter
3 cloves garlic, peeled and minced
1 teaspoon crushed red pepper flakes
1 teaspoon freshly ground black
  pepper
½ teaspoon salt
1 pound medium raw shrimp in
  shells
1 lemon, sliced thin

Preheat the oven to 400 degrees. In a large cast-iron skillet, melt the butter over medium heat. Add the garlic and sauté 2 to 3 minutes, until tender but not brown. Stir in the red pepper flakes, ground black pepper, and salt. Add the shrimp and lemon slices. Toss to coat thoroughly. Place the shrimp mixture in a casserole dish and bake for 15 minutes, stirring occasionally. Serve with crusty French or sourdough bread to soak up the drippings.

SERVES 4   *California Sizzles,* Pasadena, CA

TIPSY MARINATED SHRIMP

Large, succulent shrimp, perfect for a seaside barbecue.

½ cup Bourbon whiskey
½ cup soy sauce
½ cup Dijon mustard
½ cup packed brown sugar
1 teaspoon salt
2 tablespoons Worcestershire sauce
½ cup finely chopped onion
2 pounds large shrimp, shelled and
  deveined

Combine all ingredients except shrimp in a shallow bowl. Whisk until blended. Marinate the shrimp in the bowl for ½ hour, no longer. Thread the shrimp on skewers and grill over hot coals until lightly browned. Baste with marinade several times while browning.

SERVES 4   *A Matter of Taste,* Morristown, NJ

BASIC SHRIMP CREOLE

6 tablespoons bacon drippings
4 medium onions, chopped fine
4 to 6 bell peppers, chopped fine
3 tablespoons all-purpose flour
1 (20-ounce) can tomatoes
2 (6-ounce) cans tomato paste
1 (32-ounce) can tomato juice
Salt to taste
Ground red pepper (cayenne) to
  taste
1 tablespoon filé powder
3½ pounds boiled and shelled small
  shrimp

Heat the bacon drippings in a large heavy nonreactive skillet. Sauté the onions and peppers for 8 to 10 minutes or until tender. Remove with a slotted spoon to a bowl. To the grease remaining in the skillet, add the flour and let it brown. Add the sautéed onions and peppers, the tomatoes, tomato paste, juice, and seasonings. Bring to a boil and let simmer uncovered for 1½ to 2 hours. Add the shrimp just before serving over boiled rice.

SERVES 6–8   *A Cook's Tour,* Shreveport, LA

SHRIMP CREOLE

2½ pounds raw unshelled shrimp
1½ tablespoons bacon drippings
1½ tablespoons all-purpose flour
½ cup finely chopped onion
½ cup finely chopped green bell
  pepper
⅓ cup finely chopped celery
1 (8-ounce) can tomato sauce
1 (16-ounce) can Italian plum
  tomatoes with basil, reserving
  liquid
1 clove garlic, minced
3 dashes Tabasco
2 tablespoons Worcestershire sauce
1 teaspoon sugar
2 teaspoons salt
¼ teaspoon ground black pepper
2 tablespoons chopped fresh parsley
¾ cup chopped scallions
2 cups steamed rice

Shell and devein the shrimp. In a large pot, heat the bacon drippings and add the flour. Stir until the roux is golden brown. Add the onion, green pepper, and celery; cook until tender. Pour in the tomato sauce, tomatoes, and liquid. Blend well. Add the garlic, Tabasco, Worcestershire sauce, sugar, salt, and pepper. Simmer uncovered for 30 minutes, stirring occasionally. Add the shrimp, parsley, and scallions; cook 40 minutes. Serve over rice.

SERVES 4

Jambalaya, New Orleans, LA

MOBILE SHRIMP CREOLE

2 tablespoons all-purpose flour
2 tablespoons shortening
2 onions, chopped fine
2 cloves garlic, chopped fine
1 large bell pepper, chopped fine
2 teaspoons finely chopped parsley
1 (16-ounce) can tomatoes
⅛ teaspoon ground red pepper
  (cayenne)
1 teaspoon salt
2 bay leaves
⅓ teaspoon celery seed
¼ teaspoon powdered thyme
2 pounds raw shrimp, shelled and
  deveined
2 teaspoons Worcestershire sauce

Make a good rich roux by browning the flour in the shortening, preferably in an old fashioned iron pot, but a heavy new pot will do if the cover fits tightly. Into this, add the onions, garlic, bell pepper, and parsley. Stir until the onions are soft. Add the tomatoes and their juice. Season with red pepper, salt, bay leaves, celery seed, and thyme. Add the shrimp, cover the pot and simmer for 1 hour. Half an hour before serving, add the Worcestershire sauce. Do not add water, as the juice from the tomatoes and shrimp is enough. Serve with rice.

SERVES 4

One of a Kind, Mobile, AL

RED BELL PEPPER SHRIMP

3 tablespoons bacon drippings

5 tablespoons all-purpose flour

1 cup half-and-half

1 cup fish stock or bottled clam broth

⅓ cup dry sherry

1 large red bell pepper, roasted (see page 126)

½ teaspoon paprika

⅛ teaspoon ground red pepper (cayenne)

1 teaspoon salt

Ground black pepper to taste

1 pound shrimp, shelled and deveined

In a large skillet, heat the bacon drippings. Add the flour. Cook 3 minutes over medium-high heat, stirring constantly. Whisk in the half-and-half, fish stock, and sherry. Cook until thickened. Purée the bell pepper in a blender or food processor. Add to the sauce. Add the paprika, cayenne, salt, black pepper, and shrimp. Cook 10 to 12 minutes. Serve over hot buttered pasta.

SERVES 4   *Second Round Tea-Time at the Masters,* Augusta, GA

CRAB SMOTHERED SHRIMP

2 dozen raw jumbo shrimp, shelled and deveined

8 tablespoons (1 stick) plus 2 tablespoons butter

½ cup minced celery

1 small onion, minced

½ cup minced green bell pepper

1 tablespoon chopped parsley

1 pound fresh lump crabmeat, picked over to remove bits of shell and cartilage

1 teaspoon salt

1 teaspoon Worcestershire sauce

¼ teaspoon dried thyme

Dash of Tabasco

½ cup seasoned bread crumbs

1 egg, beaten

1 cup light cream

Paprika

Preheat the oven to 400 degrees. Split the shrimp lengthwise so they can be opened flat, but do not cut all the way through. Spread the shrimp flat in a 9 × 13-inch shallow baking dish and set aside. In a medium skillet, melt 2 tablespoons of butter. Sauté the celery, onion, and green pepper until the onion is transparent. Remove from the heat. Add the parsley. Toss this mixture with the crabmeat. Add the seasonings, bread crumbs, egg, and cream. Toss gently but thoroughly. Mound some of the crab mixture on each of the shrimp. Melt 1 stick of butter and pour over all. Sprinkle the top with paprika and bake uncovered for 20 minutes.

NOTE: For a heart healthy recipe, omit the salt and substitute corn oil margarine for the butter (it doesn't really change the taste), surimi for the crabmeat, ¼ cup cholesterol-free egg substitute for the whole egg, and evaporated skim milk for the cream.

SERVES 4–6   *Rare Collection,* Galveston, TX

SHRIMP SCAMPI

2 sticks (½ pound) butter
2 cloves garlic, chopped fine, or 1
   teaspoon garlic powder
2 tablespoons parsley, chopped fine
¼ cup dry white wine or vermouth
Fresh lemon juice to taste
Salt and ground black pepper to taste
2 pounds raw shrimp, shelled and
   deveined
5 cups hot cooked rice

Melt the butter in a large skillet or sauté pan; add the garlic, parsley, wine, lemon juice, salt, and pepper. Simmer for about 3 minutes. Add the shrimp and cook 4 minutes more. Serve over hot rice.

SERVES 4–5 *Treasures of the Smokies*, Johnson City, TN

SHRIMP ÉTOUFFÉE

Straight from the Louisiana bayou comes this marvelous mixture to be served over its own herbed rice.

1 medium onion, chopped fine
2 finely chopped scallions and green
   tops
3 or 4 cloves garlic, minced
¼ cup finely chopped celery
8 tablespoons (1 stick) butter
2 tablespoons all-purpose flour
1 (10½-ounce) can tomato purée
2 bay leaves
1 teaspoon Worcestershire sauce
4 drops Tabasco
1 teaspoon salt
½ teaspoon sugar
½ teaspoon crushed thyme
⅛ teaspoon ground black pepper
1 pound raw shrimp, shelled and
   deveined
2 hard-boiled eggs, quartered

HERBED RICE
3 tablespoons butter
1 cup finely chopped onion
1 cup raw white rice
½ teaspoon dried marjoram
½ teaspoon dried summer savory
1 teaspoon dried rosemary
½ teaspoon salt
2 cups chicken broth

In a large skillet, sauté the onion, scallions, garlic, and celery in butter until tender. Add the flour; cook and stir until lightly browned. Add 2½ cups of water, the tomato purée, bay leaves, Worcestershire, Tabasco, salt, sugar, thyme, and pepper. Simmer uncovered, stirring occasionally, for 25 minutes or until the sauce has almost reached the desired consistency. Add the shrimp and continue cooking for 15 minutes. Garnish with quartered hard-boiled eggs. Serve over herbed rice.

Melt the butter in a medium saucepan. Add the onion and rice. Cook and stir over low heat until the onion begins to brown. Add the marjoram, savory, rosemary, salt, and chicken broth. Bring to a boil and stir, then turn the heat as low as possible, cover, and cook for 14 minutes. Remove the saucepan from the heat, but leave the lid on for 10 minutes or until ready to serve.

SERVES 6 *Cotton Country Cooking*, Morgan County, AL

A CELEBRATION OF THE PAST

The Junior League's history can be viewed through many lenses. It can be seen from the perspective of women's social history, a small group of homogeneous women evolving into a robust organization of 200,000 women of diverse backgrounds, employment, and interests. It can be charted through its changing governance issues, occasioned by the organization's remarkable growth from a single League in 1901 to today's complex organization of approximately 300 Leagues joined in association in four countries: the United States, Canada, Mexico, and Great Britain.

But since the Junior League has always focused on "promoting voluntarism, developing the potential of women and improving the community," on this brief page we highlight some of the inspired community achievements that have marked the organization's history and earned it the right to take a bow as it prepares to celebrate one hundred years of service.

The Junior League was founded in 1901 by teenagers— 18- and 19-year-old women (hence the name "Junior") who became swept up in the reform zeal of the progressive era at the turn of the century. Moved by the suffering they saw around them among the waves of new immigrants, they took action. Where they saw hunger and disease, they provided nutrition and children's dental care programs. Where they saw a child neglected or alone, they provided placement in foster homes and set about establishing orphanages. Where they saw lack of opportunity, they created educational and cultural programs. Where they saw fear of public institutions, they brought care to the immigrants' homes. Where they saw blighted neighborhoods, they created parks and playgrounds. Virtually every program addressed the needs of children, families, and working women.

Members celebrate the 10th annual conference of The Association of Junior Leagues at the Hotel Plaza in New York City, 1930.

As the organization grew, the energy and idealism of its spirited young founders continued to spark the creativity of Junior League activities. In the schools, League action has ranged from advocating free lunches in 1910 to systemic reform in middle schools in the 1990s. In hospitals and clinics, Leagues helped those afflicted with polio, cancer, and epilepsy, spearheaded the promotion of organ donation, and in Mexico City established the most complete, internationally recognized center for the blind in the Spanish-speaking world. In the legislatures, Leagues worked to develop services and set standards in areas like welfare and adoption. Leagues pioneered in educational TV and nonviolent programming, children's museums, child care centers, literacy, diagnostic testing, environmental issues, and vocational training for women in prisons.

If you live in a Junior League community, it is likely there are many agencies and services you are unaware were initiated by the Junior League.

POULTRY

MESQUITE GRILLED CHICKEN WITH NEW POTATO SKEWERS

MARINADE
½ cup soy sauce
Juice of 1 lemon
¼ to ½ cup olive oil
1 tablespoon oregano
1 teaspoon garlic powder
1 teaspoon coarse ground black
  pepper

12 boneless chicken breast halves
6 to 9 mesquite chips
36 small new potatoes
Vegetable oil
3 red onions, quartered

Combine the marinade ingredients; mix well. Pour over the chicken and let stand for 1 hour. Meanwhile, soak the mesquite chips in water. Prepare a grill for a moderately hot fire.

Rub each potato with vegetable oil. Thread 3 or 4 potatoes on each of 8 to 10 skewers; interspersed with onion quarters. When the fire is ready, place mesquite chips on the coals. Put the potatoes on the grill and cook for 15 minutes, basting with marinade as they cook. Place the chicken breasts on the grill for 20 to 30 minutes, depending on the size of the breasts. Turn every 10 minutes; baste chicken frequently while cooking. When the chicken and potatoes are browned and tender, remove to a platter and serve.

SERVES 8   *Celebrations on the Bayou,* Monroe, LA

SOUTHWESTERN GRILLED CHICKEN

2 medium tomatoes, quartered
2 cups chopped onion
½ cup chopped red bell pepper
4 garlic cloves
¼ cup packed fresh cilantro leaves
⅔ cup soy sauce
6 tablespoons vegetable oil
2 tablespoons fresh lime juice
1½ teaspoons ground black pepper
4 to 5 large whole chicken breasts,
  split, rib bones removed (boneless
  breasts can also be used)
Chopped fresh parsley, for garnish

Place the tomatoes, onion, pepper, garlic, cilantro, soy sauce, oil, lime juice, and black pepper in a blender or food processor and process for 30 seconds. Pour the marinade over the chicken breasts and marinate, covered and refrigerated, for at least 4 hours, turning frequently.

Remove the chicken from the marinade and grill over medium coals for 20 to 30 minutes, turning frequently and basting with the marinade. Sprinkle the breasts with parsley before serving. Serve with black beans.

SERVES 8–10   *California Heritage Continues,* Pasadena, CA

POLYNESIAN CHICKEN KEBABS

1 small can mandarin oranges or
  pineapple chunks or both
1½ pounds skinless boneless chicken
  breast halves
½ cup soy sauce
¼ cup Madeira or sherry
3 tablespoons applesauce
1 clove garlic, minced
2 teaspoons maple syrup
¼ teaspoon ground ginger

Drain the oranges or pineapple chunks. Cut the chicken into cubes. Combine the soy sauce, Madeira, applesauce, garlic, maple syrup, and ginger with ¼ cup of water and pour over the chicken. Marinate for at least 2 hours in the refrigerator.

Preheat the broiler or barbecue grill. Meanwhile, soak bamboo skewers in cold water for ½ hour or more.

Remove the chicken from the marinade and drain. Pour the marinade into a saucepan and boil for 5 minutes. Thread the chicken cubes, alternating with orange or pineapple segments, on the bamboo skewers. Broil or grill for a few minutes on each side, turning to cook evenly. Brush several times with the marinade. Serve immediately.

SERVES 6–8   *Capital Beginnings,* Ottawa, ON

HERB GRILLED CHICKEN

2 to 2½ pounds chicken parts
¾ cup safflower oil
¾ cup lemon juice
2 teaspoons seasoned salt
2 teaspoons paprika
2 teaspoons dried basil
2 teaspoons dried thyme
½ teaspoon garlic powder

Wash the chicken and put in a heavy plastic zipper-lock bag. Combine the remaining ingredients and pour over the chicken. Seal the bag. Marinate in the refrigerator several hours or overnight. Broil or grill the chicken 4 inches from heat sources for 15 to 20 minutes per side or until done. Baste often with the marinade.

NOTE: To shorten marinating time place the chicken and marinade mixture in an 8 × 12-inch baking dish. Microwave, covered, on high for 10 minutes. Grill 8 to 10 minutes per side.

SERVES 4   *Udderly Delicious,* Racine, WI

SAMOAN CHICKEN WITH LIME CREAM SAUCE

2 whole chicken breasts, halved,
  skinned, and boned
4 thin slices prosciutto
¼ papaya, diced
5 tablespoons flaked coconut
½ teaspoon dried thyme
1 teaspoon curry powder
2 tablespoons butter
3 tablespoons vegetable oil
Juice of 1 lime
1 cup heavy cream
1 tablespoon lime zest
1 tablespoon butter

Preheat the oven to 375 degrees. Flatten the chicken breasts with a mallet. Layer prosciutto and papaya on each breast. Roll and secure ends with a toothpick. Coat the rolled breasts with a mixture of coconut, thyme and curry.

In an ovenproof skillet, heat the butter and oil together. When hot, add the chicken breasts, seam side down. Sear and turn to brown the other sides. Transfer to the oven and bake uncovered for 15 minutes.

Remove the skillet from the oven and strain the fat from the pan, retaining the browned coconut for the sauce. Put the chicken breasts in a serving dish and cover to keep warm. On high heat, pour the lime juice into the pan and stir briefly to deglaze. Add the cream and bring to a boil over high heat. Reduce the heat and simmer for 10 minutes or until reduced and thickened. Add the lime zest and butter. Stir for 1 to 2 minutes. Remove from the heat and pour over chicken.

SERVES 4   *Celebrate!,* Sacramento, CA

FLORENTINE CHICKEN BREASTS WITH MUSTARD SAUCE

CHICKEN
½ pound ricotta cheese
½ pound fresh spinach leaves,
  washed and spun dry
½ cup broccoli florets
Salt and freshly ground black pepper
  to taste
Pinch of dried thyme
Pinch of dried tarragon
4 whole chicken breasts, boned, skin
  left on
4 tablespoons (½ stick) butter

MUSTARD SAUCE
¼ cup white wine
2 cups heavy cream
1 to 2 tablespoons Dijon mustard

Preheat oven to 350 degrees. In a food processor, combine the ricotta, spinach, broccoli, salt, pepper, thyme, and tarragon. Pulse a few times to chop.

Place the chicken breasts on a work surface, skin side up. Starting at the top, gently pull the skin away from the meat without tearing it. Work your hand slowly between the skin and the meat, leaving the sides still attached. Stuff each breast with enough of the ricotta-spinach mixture to form a compact pouch. Fold the sides of the breast underneath. Place the chicken breasts in a shallow roasting pan. Top each with a tablespoon of butter and bake for 1 hour or until the top is golden.

To prepare the sauce: Remove the chicken from the roasting pan and move the pan to the top of the stove. Cover the chicken loosely with foil to keep it warm. Deglaze the very hot pan with the white wine, stirring. Add the cream, stirring over medium-high heat; add mustard to taste. Continue stirring until the sauce thickens, about 10 minutes. Serve the sauce over the chicken breasts.

SERVES 4   *More Than a Tea Party,* Boston, MA

STUFFED CHICKEN BREASTS O'BRIEN

4 whole chicken breasts, boned, but
  with skin intact
½ pound fresh spinach washed,
  dried, and chopped fine
½ pound ricotta cheese
4 ounces mozzarella cheese, grated
½ teaspoon salt
Pinch of ground black pepper
½ teaspoon garlic powder
¼ teaspoon dried thyme
½ teaspoon dried tarragon
Softened butter

Preheat the oven to 350 degrees. Butter a shallow baking dish large enough to hold the chicken breasts in one layer.

Place the chicken breasts on a work surface, skin side up. Starting at the top, gently pull the skin away from the meat to form a pocket, leaving the sides still attached.

Combine the spinach, cheeses, and seasonings. Divide into 4 portions. Place 1 portion of filling under the skin of each breast. Smooth the skin over the filling, tucking the ends under. Rub each breast with butter and place in the buttered baking dish. Bake, covered, for 45 minutes to 1 hour. Serve sliced, hot or cold.

SERVES 4   *Mountain Measures—A Second Serving,* Charleston, WV

LILLY PULITZER'S BAKED CHICKEN

1 cup juice from lemons, limes, or
  sour oranges
1 teaspoon salt
1 teaspoon freshly ground black
  pepper
1½ cups dry white wine
6 cloves garlic, crushed
1 teaspoon dried basil
3 broiler chickens, quartered
2 sticks (½ pound) butter, melted
3 cups crumbled potato chips

In a large bowl, combine the juice, salt, pepper, wine, garlic, and basil. Add the chicken pieces, cover, and marinate in the refrigerator for 4 hours, turning occasionally. Remove the chicken pieces and pat dry.

Preheat the oven to 400 degrees. Dip each chicken piece into the melted butter and then roll in the crumbled chips. Arrange the chicken in a large shallow baking dish and bake uncovered for 1 hour.

SERVES 6–8   *Palm Beach Entertains,* West Palm Beach, FL

COUNTRY CAPTAIN

When General George Patton was en route through Columbus, Georgia, he wired ahead, "If you can't give me a party and have Country Captain, put some in a bucket and bring it to the train."

1 frying chicken, 2 to 3 pounds, cut
  into serving pieces
Salt and ground white pepper
Flour for dredging
2 tablespoons butter
2 tablespoons vegetable oil
2 onions, chopped fine
2 green bell peppers, chopped
1 or 2 garlic cloves, crushed
2 teaspoons curry powder
2 (16-ounce) cans tomatoes
1 teaspoon chopped parsley, plus
  additional for garnish
½ teaspoon dried thyme
Ground black pepper
Hot cooked rice
¼ cup dried currants
½ cup toasted slivered almonds

Preheat the oven to 350 degrees. Season the chicken pieces well with salt and pepper; dredge in flour, shaking off the excess. Heat the butter and oil together in a large heavy skillet and brown the chicken pieces on all sides. Remove the chicken pieces to a shallow roasting pan and cover lightly with foil to keep warm.

Pour off most of the fat from the skillet. Add the onions, green peppers, and garlic. Cook over low heat, stirring constantly, until the vegetables are wilted. Season with salt, white pepper, and the curry powder. Add the tomatoes, chopped parsley, thyme, and ground black pepper to taste. Bring the sauce to a boil, stirring, and pour over the chicken. If it does not cover the chicken, rinse out the skillet with a cup or more of water and pour over the chicken. Bake covered for about 45 minutes.

When ready to serve, place the chicken in the middle of a platter and pile 2 cups of cooked rice around it. Mix the currants with the sauce and pour some over the rice. Scatter almonds over the top. Extra sauce should be put in a gravy boat. Garnish with parsley.

SERVES 4   *A Southern Collection,* Columbus, GA

CHICKEN IN SHERRY SAUCE

2 broilers, halved
1 teaspoon salt
½ teaspoon ground black pepper
3 tablespoons butter, softened
1 large onion, chopped
4 carrots, sliced into thin rounds
½ green bell pepper, chopped
2 tablespoons bacon drippings
2 (10½-ounce) cans consommé
2 teaspoons curry powder
1½ to 2 cups sherry
Hot cooked brown or wild rice

Preheat the broiler. Salt and pepper the chicken pieces and rub with butter. Place skin side up in a broiler pan and broil until brown. Transfer to a roasting pan and reduce the oven heat to 350 degrees.

Sauté the onion, carrots, and green pepper in the bacon drippings. When brown, add the consommé and curry powder. Simmer 10 minutes. Pour the sauce over the chicken. Cover and bake for 1½ hours. Add the sherry for the last ½ hour of baking. Serve on rice.

SERVES 4   *The Gasparilla Cookbook,* Tampa, FL

NORWEGIAN STUFFED CHICKEN

Colorful vegetables and cheese form a creamy stuffing.

¾ pound fresh spinach, stems
   removed, torn into small pieces
1½ cups shredded Jarlsberg cheese
½ cup fresh bread crumbs
½ cup shredded carrots
½ cup sliced scallions
2 tablespoons snipped fresh dill
½ teaspoon salt
⅛ teaspoon pepper
1 egg, well beaten
¼ cup plus 2 tablespoons chopped
   parsley
3 whole chicken breasts, split
4 tablespoons (½ stick) butter,
   melted
2 tablespoons lemon juice

Preheat the oven to 375 degrees. Combine the spinach, cheese, bread crumbs, carrots, scallions, dill, salt, pepper, egg, and ¼ cup of chopped parsley in a bowl. Place the chicken breast halves on a work surface. Gently pull the skin away from the meat without tearing it. Start at the top and work your hand slowly between the skin and the meat, leaving the sides still attached. Stuff the spinach mixture between the breast meat and skin.

Place the chicken breasts, skin side up, in a shallow baking dish. Combine the butter, lemon juice, and remaining 2 tablespoons of parsley. Drizzle over the chicken. Bake until tender, approximately 45 minutes. Baste frequently with pan drippings.

SERVES 6   *Capital Classics,* Washington, D.C.

CHICKEN BREASTS IN PHYLLO

1½ cups mayonnaise

1 cup chopped scallions

⅓ cup lemon juice

2 cloves garlic, minced

2 teaspoons dried tarragon

12 chicken breast halves, boned and
skinned

Salt and pepper

24 sheets phyllo dough (about 1
pound)

20 tablespoons (2½ sticks) butter,
melted

⅓ cup freshly grated Parmesan
cheese

Combine the mayonnaise, scallions, lemon juice, garlic, and tarragon to make a sauce. Lightly sprinkle the chicken pieces with salt and pepper.

Unroll the phyllo; cover with waxed paper and then with a damp kitchen towel to keep it from drying out. Place a sheet of phyllo on a flat surface. Quickly brush with melted butter (about 2 teaspoons). Place a second sheet on top of the first. Brush with melted butter. Spread about 1½ tablespoons of sauce on each side of a chicken breast (3 tablespoons in all). Place the breast on one end of the buttered phyllo sheets. Fold the corner over the breast, then fold the sides over and roll the breast up in the sheets to form a package. Place in an ungreased baking dish. Repeat with the remaining breasts and phyllo sheets, keeping the unused phyllo covered until ready to use it.

Brush the packets with the rest of the melted butter and sprinkle with Parmesan cheese. At this point, the dish may be tightly sealed and frozen. Thaw completely before baking. Bake at 375 degrees for 20 to 25 minutes, or until golden. Serve hot.

SERVES 12   *Private Collection 2,* Palo Alto, CA

CHICKEN WITH PROSCIUTTO AND CHEESE

4 boned and skinned chicken breast
halves

Salt and ground black pepper

Flour for dredging

3 tablespoons butter

2 tablespoons vegetable oil

8 thin slices prosciutto

8 thin slice Bell Paese cheese

4 teaspoons grated Parmesan cheese

2 tablespoons chicken stock

Preheat the oven to 350 degrees. Lightly oil a shallow baking dish large enough to hold the chicken pieces in one layer.

Place one of the chicken breast halves on a work surface and hold it flat with the palm of one hand while slicing it in two horizontally. Repeat with the remaining chicken breasts, to make a total of 8 fillets. Put a fillet between 2 sheets of waxed paper and pound lightly. Season with salt and pepper; dip in flour, shaking off excess, and brown lightly in butter and oil. Remove to the prepared baking dish. Repeat with the remaining fillets. Put a slice of prosciutto and one of cheese on each fillet. Sprinkle with grated Parmesan and pour stock over into the pan. Bake just until the cheese is melted. Do not overcook. Serve at once.

SERVES 4   *Culinary Creations,* Kingston, NY

APRICOT CHICKEN EN PAPILLOTE

4 tablespoons (½ stick) butter,
    melted

4 chicken breast halves, boned and
    skinned

8 fresh apricots, halved (or 8 dried
    apricots soaked in water or wine
    for 30 minutes)

4 ounces prosciutto, finely diced

4 sprigs fresh rosemary or 1
    teaspoon dried

½ teaspoon dried sage

2 garlic cloves, minced

Salt and freshly ground black pepper
    to taste

Juice of 1 lemon

4 tablespoons (½ stick) butter,
    softened

Preheat the oven to 350 degrees. Cut 4 large sheets of cooking parchment into 18-inch circles. Brush one half of each sheet with butter. Lay a chicken breast half in the middle of each buttered circle. Slice the apricots thin. Arrange them on the chicken with the prosciutto. Sprinkle each breast evenly with the seasonings and lemon juice and dot with butter. Fold the remaining half of the parchment over each breast and crimp the edges to seal. Place on a baking sheet and bake for 45 minutes. Break open the top of each packet and serve immediately, or allow the diners to break open their own packets at the table. N O T E : For this dish you will need cooking parchment, available in gourmet cooking shops and some mail order houses.

S E R V E S 4   *Without Reservations,* Pittsburgh, PA

FORBIDDEN CITY CHICKEN

¾ cup soy sauce

2 tablespoons butter, melted

1 tablespoon curry powder

1 teaspoon ground cinnamon

1 teaspoon ground ginger

1 garlic clove, crushed

2 dashes Tabasco

2 small broiler chickens, split

Sesame seeds

Arrange the chicken halves skin side up in one layer in a baking pan. In a bowl mix together the soy sauce, melted butter, curry powder, cinnamon, ginger, garlic, and Tabasco. Spread the mixture over the chicken and chill for 1 hour.

Preheat the oven to 325 degrees. Sprinkle sesame seeds over the chicken and bake uncovered for about 1 hour, until the chicken is golden.

S E R V E S 4   *One Magnificent Cookbook,* Chicago, Ill

BALSAMIC CHICKEN BREASTS

4 boneless chicken breasts, split

Salt and freshly ground pepper

2 tablespoons flour

2 tablespoons olive oil, or 1
    tablespoon olive oil and 1
    tablespoon unsalted butter

3 cloves garlic, minced

8 ounces porcini mushrooms, sliced

¼ cup balsamic vinegar

¾ cup chicken broth

3 tablespoons white wine

Rinse the chicken and pat dry. Sprinkle with salt and pepper. Dredge the chicken in a mixture of flour, salt, and pepper; shake off any excess flour. Cook the fillets in the olive oil in a sauté pan over medium-high heat for 3 minutes on one side or until brown. Add the garlic. Turn the chicken over; sprinkle with the mushrooms. Cook for 3 minutes, shaking the sauté pan to redistribute the mushrooms so they will cook evenly. Stir in the balsamic vinegar, chicken broth, and wine. Cook, covered, over medium-low heat for 10 minutes, turning the chicken occasionally.

S E R V E S 4   *I'll Taste Manhattan,* New York, NY

PERFECT PICNIC CHICKEN IN A BASKET

½ cup all-purpose flour
1½ tablespoons sesame seeds
1½ teaspoons dried thyme
¾ teaspoon dried tarragon
1½ teaspoons poppy seeds
1 teaspoon salt
1 teaspoon ground black pepper
8 chicken thighs
2 egg whites, lightly beaten
2 tablespoons butter
2 tablespoons vegetable oil
1 round fresh sourdough bread,
  unsliced
Herb and Seeds Butter Sauce (see
  below)

HERB AND SEEDS BUTTER SAUCE
4 tablespoons (½ stick) butter
3 tablespoons sesame seeds
1 tablespoon dried thyme
1½ teaspoons dried tarragon
1 tablespoon poppy seeds

Preheat the oven to 350 degrees. In a small mixing bowl combine the flour, sesame seeds, thyme, tarragon, poppy seeds, salt, and pepper. Dip the chicken thighs in the beaten egg white and then coat each piece thoroughly in the flour mixture. Melt the butter and oil in a large skillet. Brown the chicken thoroughly, about 7 minutes per side, over medium heat. Put the chicken in one layer in a baking pan, cover, and bake 40 minutes.

To prepare the basket, slice off a large top in the bread round. Scoop out the inside of the loaf, leaving about ¾ inch of bread all the way around the edge. With a pastry brush, spread Herb and Seeds Butter Sauce over the entire inside of the loaf and the inside of the top. Place the loaf and top butter side up on a cookie sheet.

Put the chicken in the basket and return the chicken, basket, and top to the oven on the cookie sheet to bake for an additional 20 minutes, uncovered. Remove from the oven, put the top on, and wrap the basket in several layers of foil, surrounded by several layers of newspaper. It will remain very warm for several hours this way.

To prepare the sauce, melt the butter in a small saucepan and add the sesame seeds, thyme, tarragon, and poppy seeds. Use as a sauce for Picnic in a Basket or for a delicious herb spread to brush over slices of hot French or Italian bread.

SERVES 4–6   *The California Heritage Cookbook,* Pasadena, CA

POULET AU CITRON

2 tablespoons grated lemon peel
½ cup fresh lemon juice
2 cloves garlic, crushed
2 teaspoons dried thyme
1 shallot, chopped fine
1½ teaspoons salt
1 teaspoon ground black pepper
2 fryers (2½ to 3 pounds each),
  quartered
8 tablespoons (1 stick) butter,
  melted
2 lemons, sliced thin
½ cup finely chopped fresh parsley

Combine the lemon peel, lemon juice, garlic, thyme, shallot, salt, and pepper in a mixing bowl. Place the chicken pieces in a single layer in a shallow baking dish and cover with the lemon marinade. Turn the chicken until it is thoroughly coated. Refrigerate covered in the marinade for 3 to 4 hours, turning the chicken several times.

Preheat the oven to 425 degrees. Lift the chicken from the marinade and drain well on paper towels, reserving the marinade. Place the chicken pieces in a single layer in a shallow quart baking dish and brush with the melted butter.

Bake the chicken uncovered for 25 minutes. Brush with the reserved marinade, lower the heat to 325 degrees, and bake for an additional 30 to 35 minutes until the chicken is browned and thoroughly cooked.

Remove the chicken from the oven and strain off as much grease as possible. Arrange the pieces on a serving platter. Surround with the lemon slices and sprinkle with the chopped parsley.

SERVES 6–8   *The California Heritage Cookbook,* Pasadena, CA

FRIED CHICKEN WITH CREAM GRAVY

Just like mother and grandmother make!

1 (3-pound) broiler-fryer chicken,
    cut up
1 cup self-rising flour (see Note)
1½ teaspoons salt
¼ teaspoon freshly ground black
    pepper
⅛ teaspoon paprika
1 egg, slightly beaten
Vegetable oil for frying
¼ cup all-purpose flour
1½ cups milk
Salt and pepper to taste

Remove and discard the skin from the chicken. Wash and pat the chicken pieces dry. Put the self-rising flour, salt, pepper, and paprika in a plastic bag. Combine the egg and 2 tablespoons of water in a pie plate. Dip one piece of chicken at a time into the egg mixture, then place in the flour bag, shaking to coat.

In a large skillet over medium-high heat, heat ¾ inch of oil until the oil begins to look as if it's "cracking," or the temperature reaches 350 degrees on a deep-fat thermometer. Place the chicken pieces in the hot oil. Fry until browned, turning once, then reduce heat to medium. Continue frying, frequently turning the pieces in the pan. Total cooking time should be about 25 minutes.

Remove the chicken pieces; drain on paper towels. Keep warm. Carefully pour off the fat from the skillet, leaving the brown crusty particles in the pan. Measure 3 to 4 tablespoons of the cooking fat and return to the skillet. Blend in the all-purpose flour. Cook over low heat, stirring constantly until the mixture is bubbly, making sure to stir in the crusty bits from the bottom of the pan.

Combine the milk with 1½ cups of water. Add all at once to the mixture in the skillet; blend well. Cook over medium heat, stirring constantly with a wooden spoon in a figure eight motion, until the mixture is thickened and bubbly and has a smooth and velvety consistency. Add salt and pepper to taste.

NOTE: For 1 cup of self-rising flour you may substitute 1 cup all-purpose flour mixed with 1¼ teaspoons of baking powder and a pinch of salt.

SERVES 4   *Peachtree Bouquet,* DeKalb County, GA

AUNT KAY'S SESAME CHICKEN

Very tasty.

5 chicken breast halves, boned,
    skinned, and cut into bite-size
    pieces
¼ cup all-purpose flour
Salt and ground black pepper
½ cup peanut oil
¼ cup sugar
¼ cup soy sauce (preferably
    Japanese style)
2 tablespoons sesame seeds
¼ cup chopped scallions

Dredge the chicken pieces in flour seasoned with salt and pepper. In a large frying pan heat the oil and cook the chicken chunks 3 to 4 minutes or until done. Work in batches if necessary to avoid crowding the pan. Drain the chicken on paper towels and set aside, covered to keep warm.

Combine the sugar and soy sauce in a saucepan and heat until the sugar dissolves. Add the chicken chunks. Toss the chicken in the sauce with the sesame seeds and scallions. Serve at once.

NOTE: Be careful not to overcook the chicken pieces; this will make them tough.

SERVES 4   *Utah Dining Car,* Ogden, UT

JALAPEÑO SOUTHERN FRIED CHICKEN

The best fried chicken ever! The sauce turns this into dinner party fare.

5 cups buttermilk
2 large cloves garlic, minced
2 medium jalapeño peppers, seeded and minced
5 to 6 pounds chicken breast halves
1½ cups self-rising flour (see Note)
2 teaspoons finely shredded orange peel
1 teaspoon salt
½ teaspoon dried basil, crushed
¼ teaspoon ground red pepper (cayenne)
8 tablespoons (1 stick) butter
½ cup honey
Vegetable oil for frying
Jalapeño pepper slices for garnish

Combine the buttermilk, garlic, and half the minced jalapeño pepper. Place the chicken pieces in a large bowl; pour the buttermilk mixture over. Cover and chill for 1½ to 2 hours.

In a medium bowl, combine the flour, orange peel, salt, basil, and red pepper. Drain the chicken. Coat the chicken in the flour mixture, shaking off excess flour. Place the coated chicken pieces on waxed paper; let stand at room temperature 20 minutes.

For the sauce, in a heavy 1½-quart saucepan, melt the butter over low heat. Add the remaining minced jalapeño pepper. Cook and stir for 1 minute. Stir in the honey. Bring to boiling; reduce the heat. Simmer for 15 minutes. Remove from the heat, cover, and keep warm.

Meanwhile, in a heavy 12-inch skillet, heat ½ to ¼ inch of cooking oil to 375 degrees. Add the chicken in batches (do not crowd) and fry for 5 to 7 minutes per side or until crisp and golden brown. Drain on paper towels. Transfer to a platter. Garnish with jalapeño slices and pass the honey-jalapeño sauce.

NOTE: For self-rising flour you may substitute 1½ cups of all-purpose flour mixed with 2 teaspoons of baking powder and ⅛ teaspoon of salt.

SERVES 10–12

Heart & Soul, Memphis, TN

PANKO-CRUSTED SESAME CHICKEN

Perfect picnic fare. The panko, special Japanese coarse bread crumbs, make a crunchy topping that stays crisp for hours after cooking.

3½ pounds chicken, cut in serving pieces
½ cup cornstarch
¼ cup all-purpose flour
¼ cup sugar
2 teaspoons salt
2 eggs, lightly beaten
5 tablespoons soy sauce
¼ cup sliced scallions, including 3 inches of the green part
2 cloves garlic, minced
¼ cup toasted white sesame seeds
¼ cup safflower oil
2½ cups panko (Japanese bread crumbs)
Peanut oil for frying

Wash the chicken and pat dry. In a small mixing bowl, combine the cornstarch, flour, sugar, and 1½ teaspoons of the salt. In a large mixing bowl, whisk together the eggs, soy sauce, scallions, garlic, sesame seeds, and safflower oil. Whisk in the cornstarch mixture.

Place the chicken pieces in a zipper-lock plastic bag. Pour in the batter and turn to coat. Marinate in the refrigerator for at least 2 hours or as long as overnight, turning the bag occasionally to keep the marinade combined. Overnight marinating enhances the flavor of the chicken.

Season the panko with the remaining ½ teaspoon of salt and spread on a work surface. Remove the pieces of chicken from the bag, allowing the excess marinade to drip back into the bag. Roll the chicken in the panko, making certain that each piece is well coated.

In a 12- to 14-inch skillet, heat 1 cup of peanut oil to 350 degrees. Fry the chicken for 25 minutes or until golden brown, turning frequently. The chicken is done when the thickest part of the thigh is pierced with a fork and the juices run clear. Drain on paper towels. Serve warm or at room temperature.

VARIATION: Try this also with boned breasts. Slice in strips before serving.

SERVES 6

California Heritage Continues, Pasadena, CA

CHICKEN VEGETABLE LINGUINE

2 skinless boneless chicken breasts
2 carrots, sliced thin
2 unpeeled zucchini, sliced
1 cup sliced fresh mushrooms
2 medium tomatoes, cut into
    wedges
1 (8-ounce) package linguine
4 tablespoons (½ stick) butter
¾ cup grated Parmesan cheese
1 egg, slightly beaten
8 ounces Monterey Jack cheese,
    grated

Poach the chicken breasts: Place the chicken breasts in a saucepan and add cold water to cover. Bring slowly to a simmer and cook gently for 8 to 10 minutes, or until they are no longer pink in the center. Do not overcook. When the poached chicken is cool enough to handle, cut into julienne strips. Set aside.

Arrange the carrots in a vegetable steamer over 1 inch boiling water; put zucchini on top of carrots, then layer the mushrooms and tomatoes. Steam for 5 to 7 minutes, until vegetables are tender-crisp.

Cook the linguine according to package directions. Drain well. Toss with the butter. Blend the Parmesan cheese and egg; gently toss with the linguine. Spread the linguine in a buttered 2-quart casserole. Make a layer of steamed vegetables and then one of chicken over the linguine. Top with the grated Monterey Jack cheese. Bake uncovered in a preheated 350 degree oven until the cheese is melted and bubbly.

SERVES 4–6   *Palm Country Cuisine*, Greater Lakeland, FL

CHICKEN FRICASSEE

1 large broiler-fryer, cut up
Salt
Ground black pepper
4 tablespoons vegetable oil
4 tablespoons all-purpose flour
2 medium onions, chopped
1 bunch scallions, chopped
3 cloves garlic, chopped
Ground red pepper (cayenne)
4-5 sprigs parsley, chopped
3 cups hot cooked rice

Season the chicken with salt and pepper. Heat the oil in an iron pot, then add the chicken pieces and brown on all sides slowly. Remove the chicken. On a low flame, gradually add flour to make a roux, stirring constantly with a wooden spoon. When the mixture turns a dark mahogany color (in about 35 minutes), add 4 cups of water. Raise the heat until the mixture boils and add the onions, scallions, and garlic. Lower the heat, cover, and cook for 45 minutes. Add the chicken and season to taste with salt, black pepper, and red pepper. Cook covered until the chicken is tender, approximately 1 hour. During the last 15 minutes add a small amount of chopped parsley. Serve over cooked rice.

SERVES 8   *Tell Me More*, Lafayette, LA

COMITE INTERNACIONAL PRO-CIEGOS
JUNIOR LEAGUE OF MEXICO CITY, MEXICO

The Comite Internacional Pro-Ciegos (International Committee for the Blind) is a project of the Junior League of Mexico City, Mexico, working to rehabilitate adults who are blind or nearly blind, giving them confidence and preparing them to lead independent lives. The project offers library services, vocational instruction, recreation, and classes in Braille. This program began in 1937 and continues today, training the blind and providing them with a multitude of services.

JAVA CHICKEN CURRY

5 medium onions, peeled
5 small dried hot red chili peppers,
    seeds removed
1 tablespoon chopped fresh
    gingerroot
10 cloves garlic, peeled
1½ teaspoons salt
½ teaspoon turmeric
1 (3-4 pound) chicken, cut up
¼ cup vegetable oil
1 (16-ounce) can whole tomatoes,
    undrained
1 tablespoon soy sauce
1 teaspoon grated lemon zest
1 tablespoon curry powder
1-2 tablespoons brown sugar

Slice 3 of the onions and set aside. Cut the remaining 2 onions in chunks. In a food processor, using the metal blade, process the 2 onions, the chili peppers, ginger, and garlic until puréed.

Mix together the salt and turmeric and rub onto the chicken pieces. Heat the oil in a large frying pan over medium-high heat; add the chicken, and cook, turning once, until browned (about 10 minutes). Remove the chicken and add the sliced onions and puréed onion mixture to the pan. Cook, stirring occasionally, for 5 minutes or until the sliced onion is very limp.

Process the tomatoes and their liquid until smooth; add to the onions along with ⅓ cup of water, the soy sauce, lemon zest, curry powder, and brown sugar. Return the chicken to the pan, cover, and simmer for 45 minutes.

With a slotted spoon, remove the chicken pieces to a serving platter and keep warm. Boil the sauce, uncovered, stirring constantly, until reduced to about 3 cups. Skim off fat and spoon the sauce over the chicken.

SERVES 4–6   *The Seattle Classic,* Seattle, WA

ORANGE TARRAGON CHICKEN BREASTS

2 cups freshly squeezed orange juice
1 cup chicken stock or canned
    chicken broth
2 teaspoons chopped fresh tarragon
    or 1 teaspoon dried
2 whole chicken breasts, split,
    skinned, boned, and pounded thin
Salt and freshly ground pepper to
    taste
2 tablespoons unsalted butter
Orange sections for garnish

In a large skillet bring the orange juice, chicken broth, and tarragon to a boil. Season the chicken breasts with salt and pepper and add to the skillet. Cook the chicken for 2 minutes per side over medium-high heat. Remove the chicken from the pan and set aside.

Reduce the orange juice and chicken broth mixture over high heat to approximately 4 tablespoons of liquid, about 5 to 10 minutes. Remove the pan from the heat and stir in the butter until melted. Return the chicken to the pan and heat 1 minute on each side.

Remove the chicken from the pan with a slotted spoon and arrange on a heated serving platter. Spoon sauce over chicken and serve immediately. Garnish with small orange sections.

SERVES 4   *More Than a Tea Party,* Boston, MA

PARMESAN CHICKEN

6 chicken breast halves, skinned and
  boned
6 slices Monterey Jack cheese, ¼
  inch thick
10 tablespoons (1 stick plus 2
  tablespoons) butter
2 tablespoons Dijon mustard
1 cup fine dry bread crumbs
1 cup freshly grated Parmesan
  cheese
¼ cup minced fresh parsley
½ cup all-purpose flour
Salt and ground black pepper

Preheat the oven to 350 degrees. With a sharp knife, cut a pocket lengthwise in each chicken breast and insert a piece of Monterey Jack cheese.

In a small saucepan melt 1 stick of butter and stir in the mustard. In a separate bowl combine the bread crumbs, Parmesan, and parsley. Dust the chicken with flour and dip in the melted butter, turning to coat. Roll in the bread crumb mixture.

In a large skillet heat the remaining 2 tablespoons of butter and brown the chicken lightly on all sides. Place the chicken in an oven-proof casserole. Season with salt and pepper to taste. Bake uncovered for 30 minutes.

SERVES 6   *Winning at the Table*, Las Vegas, NV

CHICKEN BREASTS PORTOFINO

1 cup buttermilk
Salt and freshly ground pepper
4 chicken breast halves, skinned and
  boned
Flour
5 tablespoons olive oil
¼ pound fresh mushrooms, wiped,
  trimmed, and sliced
1 garlic clove, minced
2 tablespoons pine nuts
¼ cup dry white wine
¼ cup chicken broth
Chopped parsley

Season the buttermilk with salt and pepper. Place the chicken breasts in the seasoned milk and refrigerate for at least 2 hours, turning occasionally. When ready to cook, drain the chicken and dust with flour.

In a skillet over medium heat, sauté the breasts in 4 tablespoons of the olive oil for 5 minutes per side. Remove from the heat. In another skillet over medium heat, sauté the mushrooms and garlic in the remaining 1 tablespoon of olive oil for 2 minutes. Add the pine nuts, wine, and chicken broth. Stir well and continue to cook until the sauce has been reduced slightly. Add the sautéed chicken, cover, and simmer over low heat for 5-8 minutes or until the chicken is done. Sprinkle with fresh parsley and serve.

SERVES 2–4   *Winning at the Table*, Las Vegas, NV

KANSAS ACTION FOR CHILDREN, INC.
JUNIOR LEAGUE OF WICHITA, KANSAS

Kansas Action for Children, Inc., is a statewide advocacy agency that began as a collaboration between Kansas Children's Service League and the Junior Leagues of Wichita, Topeka, and Kansas City, Kansas. The mission of Kansas Action for Children is to give a voice to the children of Kansas by informing public officials and citizens about the extent of children's problems in each county of Kansas, from juvenile crime to lack of health care to the far-reaching implications of teen pregnancy and child abuse and neglect.

CHICKEN AND CHAMPAGNE

Wonderful taste!

1 frying chicken (or breasts and thighs), cut into pieces, boned, and skinned

Salt and freshly ground pepper to taste

3 ounces (6 tablespoons) clarified butter

2 ounces (¼ cup) brandy

1 tablespoon chopped parsley

2 or 3 shallots, chopped

4 or 5 truffles, sliced

½ cup Champagne or dry white wine

¾ cup heavy cream

Season the chicken with salt and pepper; brown in the butter in a large skillet. Heat the brandy, pour over the chicken in the pan, and ignite. Shake until the flame is out. Add the parsley, shallots, truffles, and Champagne and blend well. Cover the skillet and cook slowly until tender, 30 to 40 minutes.

Remove the chicken to a hot platter. Add the cream to the liquid remaining in the pan and blend well. Correct the seasoning, and reduce the sauce over high heat until fairly thick. Pour over chicken to serve. (Two truffles may be sliced and sprinkled over the top of the chicken instead of in the sauce.)

SERVES 4–6   *Epicure,* Orange County, CA

TOMATO-MUSTARD CHICKEN

1 tablespoon butter

1 tablespoon vegetable oil

4 skinless boneless chicken breast halves, sliced crosswise into thin strips

1 onion, chopped

½ teaspoon dried thyme

½ teaspoon dried tarragon

¼ cup dry white wine

1 cup chicken broth

2 cups seeded chopped tomatoes

1½ tablespoon tomato paste

1 clove garlic, minced

1 tablespoon Dijon mustard

3 tablespoons minced parsley

Heat the butter and oil in a skillet or wok over medium heat. Sauté the chicken slices, stirring constantly, for 3 to 4 minutes. Remove from the pan. Add the onion and herbs. Cook 5 minutes. Add the wine, broth, tomatoes, tomato paste, and garlic. Simmer, stirring occasionally, 10 minutes. Increase the heat to high. Cook 3 minutes. Stir in the mustard and chicken. Cook 2 minutes. Sprinkle with parsley.

Serve with pasta or noodles if desired.

SERVES 4   *Gatherings,* Milwaukee, WI

LEMON CHICKEN BREASTS

1 cup sliced mushrooms
1 clove garlic, minced
1 tablespoon olive oil
2 whole chicken breasts, skinned
and boned
2 tablespoons flour
½ teaspoon dried rosemary
¼ cup lemon juice
¼ cup chicken broth
2 tablespoons chopped parsley

In a frying pan over medium heat, sauté the mushrooms and garlic in the oil for 3 to 5 minutes. Remove from the pan. Sprinkle the chicken with flour and rosemary and brown on both sides. Add the lemon juice and chicken broth to the pan and scrape up the browned bits from the bottom.

Return the mushrooms to the pan. Lower the heat to a simmer, cover the pan, and cook for 15 minutes. Sprinkle with parsley.

Serve over brown rice or fettuccine noodles if desired.

SERVES 2-4   *Savor the Flavor of Oregon,* Eugene, OR

STIR-FRY SESAME CHICKEN

1 pound skinless boneless chicken
breasts
1 tablespoon sesame seeds
2 tablespoons soy sauce
¼ teaspoon ground black pepper
3 teaspoons vegetable oil
1 cup thinly sliced carrots
½ cup snow peas
1 to 1½ cups sliced mushrooms
1 tablespoon cornstarch

Place the chicken breasts in 1 layer in the freezer for about ½ hour. Slice the chicken while partially frozen (across the grain, in thin strips). Toss with the sesame seeds, soy sauce, pepper, and 2 teaspoons of the oil in a small bowl. Let stand at least 5 and up to 25 minutes.

Parboil the carrots for 3 to 4 minutes until slightly tender. Drain. Heat a wok over moderately high heat. When hot, add the chicken mixture and stir constantly for 5 to 7 minutes, until the chicken is lightly cooked. Remove to a bowl. Put the remaining teaspoon of oil in the wok. Add the carrots, broccoli, snow peas, and mushrooms and stir-fry for 2 or 3 minutes. Reduce the heat, add the broth, cover and simmer 3 minutes, until the vegetables are tender but still crisp. Stir in the cornstarch mixed with ½ cup of cold water; stir until boiling. Add the chicken. Cover and simmer 2 minutes.

SERVES 4-5   *Treasures of the Smokies,* Johnson City, TN

SPINACH FETTUCCINE WITH CHICKEN AND PESTO

1 cup heavy cream
2 sticks (½ pound) unsalted butter,
cut into pieces
¾ cup freshly grated Parmesan
cheese
2 to 3 tablespoons vegetable oil
4 skinless boneless chicken breast
halves, cut into bite-sized pieces
4 tablespoons pesto (see page 16)
¾ pound spinach fettuccine, cooked
according to package directions
Salt and pepper to taste

Heat the cream in a small heavy saucepan over medium heat. Add the butter and stir until melted. Gradually add the Parmesan cheese and stir until melted. Reduce the heat to low and keep the sauce warm.

Heat the oil in a skillet or wok over medium heat. Add the chicken and stir until opaque, approximately 3 minutes. Transfer to a bowl with a slotted spoon. Mix in 1 tablespoon of the pesto and cover to keep warm.

Toss the cooked fettuccine with the remaining pesto and the cheese sauce. Arrange the pasta on a platter. Spoon the chicken over and season with salt and pepper. Serve immediately. Pass additional grated Parmesan cheese.

SERVES 6   *Above and Beyond Parsley,* Kansas City, MO

CHICKEN SAUTÉED WITH BALSAMIC VINEGAR

¾ pound mushrooms, wiped and trimmed

3 medium zucchini

2 medium onions

4 tablespoons olive oil

4 boneless chicken breast halves

2 tablespoons flour

1 (16-ounce) can tomatoes, undrained

3 tablespoons balsamic or red wine vinegar

½ teaspoon salt

Thickly slice the mushrooms and zucchini; chop the onion. In a large heavy skillet over medium-high heat, in 1 tablespoon of hot olive oil, cook the zucchini until tender-crisp and lightly browned about 2 minutes; remove to a plate. In the same skillet, in 1 more tablespoon of hot oil, cook the mushrooms 2 minutes, until browned; remove to a bowl.

Coat the chicken with the flour. In the same skillet, in 2 tablespoons of hot oil, cook chicken until lightly browned and the juices run clear when pierced, about 10 minutes. Remove to the bowl with the mushrooms. In the pan drippings over medium heat, cook the onion until tender and browned, 5 to 6 minutes. Stir in ½ cup of water. Return the chicken and mushrooms to the skillet, add the tomatoes, vinegar, and salt; heat to boiling. Reduce the heat to low, simmer, uncovered, 5 minutes. Add the zucchini, heat, and serve.

SERVES 4 — *A Slice of Paradise,* West Palm Beach, FL

CHICKEN PETALUMA

2 whole chicken breasts, split, skinned, and boned

Salt and freshly ground pepper

Flour

4 tablespoons (½ stick) butter

½ cup white wine

¾ cup heavy cream or crème fraîche

1 (10-ounce) package frozen artichoke hearts, thawed and drained

1 cup pitted black olives, halved

Lemon wedges

Pound the breasts between sheets of waxed paper to ¼ inch thickness. Cut each breast into 3 pieces. Sprinkle with salt and pepper. Coat lightly with flour. Heat the butter in a large skillet over medium-high heat and sauté the chicken turning once, until golden brown, about 3 minutes on each side. Remove to a heated platter and keep warm.

Pour off the butter remaining in the skillet. Pour in the wine and bring to a boil. Cook for a few minutes and add the cream. Simmer over moderate heat until the sauce thickens. Stir in the artichokes and olives.

Place 3 chicken slices on each plate. Spoon some of the sauce over each fillet. Garnish with lemon wedges to squeeze over each serving.

SERVES 3-4 — *San Francisco Encore,* San Francisco, CA

HABITAT FOR HUMANITY—ALL WOMEN-BUILT HOUSE
JUNIOR LEAGUE OF DALLAS

In 1994, the Junior League of Dallas sponsored a Habitat for Humanity house, which was built entirely by women. Both volunteers and paid workers were women. Women acted as project managers, electricians, drywallers, painters, plumbers and roofers, and all of the Junior League volunteers attended special training classes to learn building techniques and safety prior to each building stage. This was the fourth Habitat house sponsored by the Junior League of Dallas, but was the first "all women built house" in Dallas.

TARRAGON CHICKEN WITH ANGEL HAIR PASTA

6 boneless chicken breast halves
3 tablespoons butter
2 cloves garlic, minced
1 teaspoon dried whole tarragon, crumbled
1 cup heavy cream
¾ cup grated Parmesan cheese
¼ teaspoon salt
½ cup dry white wine
¼ teaspoon ground red pepper (cayenne)
1 pound angel hair pasta, cooked

Lightly pound the chicken between pieces of waxed paper to ¼ inch thickness. Sauté in the butter over medium-high heat for about 1 minute on each side. Add the garlic, tarragon, cream, Parmesan cheese, salt, wine, and cayenne pepper. Stir until blended; cook over medium heat until the chicken is done and the sauce is slightly reduced, about 15 minutes. Serve over angel hair pasta.

SERVES 6   *Peachtree Bouquet,* DeKalb County, GA

CHICKEN CACCIATORE

2 (3-pound) chickens, cut into serving pieces
1 cup all-purpose flour seasoned with salt and pepper
6 tablespoons olive oil
2 onions, chopped fine
2 or 3 cloves garlic, crushed
8 ripe tomatoes, peeled, or 2 (1-pound) cans tomatoes, seeded and chopped
4 green bell peppers, chopped
4 bay leaves
1 cup white wine
1 pound mushrooms, wiped, trimmed, and sliced
2 (4-ounce) jars pimientos, drained and sliced
2 tablespoons cornstarch dissolved in ¼ cup cold water
Parsley for garnish

Dry the chicken well and dip the pieces in the seasoned flour, shaking off the excess. In a large skillet, sauté the chicken in hot olive oil until well browned, working in batches if necessary to avoid crowding the pan. As the chicken browns, remove the pieces to a plate. In the same oil, sauté the onion and garlic until golden. Return the chicken to the pan and add the tomatoes, peppers, bay leaves, and wine. Cover the skillet and simmer for 30 minutes or until the chicken is tender. Add the mushrooms and pimientos and cook for 10 minutes. Stir in the cornstarch paste and cook for 1 to 2 minutes, until the sauce is thickened. Garnish with parsley.

SERVES 8   *The Dallas Junior League Cookbook,* Dallas TX

PRETTY LAKE VACATION CAMP
JUNIOR LEAGUE OF
KALAMAZOO, MICHIGAN

Pretty Lake Vacation Camp was founded in 1916 with the specific mission to provide a cost-free camping experience to children in need. In 1930, the Junior League of Kalamazoo, Michigan, joined forces with the Kiwanis Club to sponsor the camp. Together these groups raise funds, collect clothes, clean the camp each spring, paint, put in the dock and handle child selection. Over 40,000 Kalamazoo County youth have been served, and last year approximately 93 percent of the campers were from families below the U.S. poverty level.

CHICKEN DIJONNAISE

CRÈME FRAÎCHE
¼ cup heavy cream
¼ cup sour cream

½ cup Dijon mustard
½ cup Pommery-style mustard
2½ to 3 pounds chicken breasts, skinned, boned, and halved
1 tablespoon plus 1½ teaspoons minced fresh tarragon
⅓ cup dry white wine
Chopped fresh parsley

Prepare the crème fraîche: Whisk the creams together in a bowl. Cover loosely with plastic wrap and let stand in warm kitchen overnight or until thickened. Cover and refrigerate at least 4 hours so that the mixture is quite thick.

Meanwhile, mix the mustards with 1 tablespoon of tarragon. Spread on both sides of the chicken. Place the chicken in a 13 × 9-inch glass baking dish, cover, and marinate for 2 hours at room temperature or overnight in the refrigerator.

When ready to cook, preheat the oven to 350 degrees. Pour the wine over the chicken and place the baking dish on the center rack. Bake uncovered for 40 to 45 minutes, basting occasionally. Remove the dish from the oven and scrape the mustard off the chicken and into a saucepan. Set the chicken breasts aside and keep warm. Add the juices from the dish to the mustard in the saucepan, making no more than ⅓ cup. Bring the mustard and juices to a boil over medium heat. Add the remaining 1½ teaspoons of tarragon and the crème fraîche. Reduce the heat to low and simmer for 5 to 10 minutes or until reduced by a third. Spoon the sauce over the chicken and top with parsley.

SERVES 3–4

With Great Gusto, Youngstown, OH

CHICKEN VÉRONIQUE

Lovely to look at with green and orange accents.

2 tablespoons flour
½ teaspoon salt
½ teaspoon ground black pepper
1 broiler-fryer, 3 to 4 pounds, cut into serving pieces
¼ cup peanut oil
½ cup dry white wine
⅓ cup orange juice
2 tablespoons honey
1 tablespoon snipped parsley
2 tablespoons slivered orange peel
1 cup seedless white grapes, halved
Garnish: grapes and orange sections

Combine the flour, salt, and ¼ teaspoon of the pepper. Lightly dust the chicken. In a large skillet, brown the chicken in the oil. Add the wine, juice, honey, parsley, and remaining pepper. Simmer covered over low heat for 30 minutes, turning the chicken pieces occasionally. Add the orange peel. Continue cooking until tender, about 15 minutes.

Remove the chicken to a serving platter. Add the grapes to the pan juices. Cook and stir 2 minutes. Pour over the chicken and garnish with whole grapes and orange sections.

SERVES 4–6

Tea-Time at the Masters, Augusta, GA

PASTA WITH CHICKEN

Different and very easy.

1 pound green spinach noodles
¼ cup olive oil
8 tablespoons (1 stick) butter
1 cup finely chopped onion
1 teaspoon minced garlic
4 skinless boneless chicken breast
   halves, cubed
½ pound zucchini, cubed
4 cups cherry tomatoes
2 teaspoons salt
Few grindings black pepper
1 teaspoon dried basil
1 teaspoon dried oregano
2 cups shredded Swiss cheese

Cook the noodles according to package directions until tender but still firm. While the pasta is cooking, heat the oil and 4 tablespoons of the butter in a skillet over high heat. Add the onion and garlic and cook until the onion is golden. Turn down the heat and add the cubed chicken. Stir-fry until the chicken is white, about 5 minutes. Add the zucchini, tomatoes, salt, pepper, basil, and oregano.

Mix the hot drained pasta with the remaining 4 tablespoons of butter. Add the chicken mixture and toss gently. Sprinkle with cheese and serve.

SERVES 6

Soupçon I, Chicago, IL

HURON VALLEY CHICKEN

This is a winner.

7 tablespoons butter
1 large Granny Smith apple, peeled,
   cored, and chopped
1 teaspoon honey
1 teaspoon lemon juice
½ cup all-purpose flour
Salt and ground black pepper to
   taste
4 skinned and boned chicken breast
   halves
1 cup chicken broth
1 cup apple juice
½ cup cranberry juice
¼ cup applejack or brandy
1-inch piece cinnamon stick
Snipped fresh chives

Melt 2 tablespoons of the butter in a small heavy skillet over medium heat. Add apple, honey, and lemon juice. Sauté until just tender and golden, about 4 minutes. Set aside.

Place the flour in bowl. Season with salt and pepper. Dredge the chicken in the flour, shaking off excess.

Melt 2 tablespoons of the butter in a large heavy skillet over medium heat. Add the chicken and cook until golden on both sides. Transfer to a serving plate and keep warm. Add the broth, apple and cranberry juices, applejack, and cinnamon stick to the skillet and bring to a boil, scraping up the browned bits. Boil until reduced to ⅔ cup, about 15 minutes. Stir in the apple mixture and 3 tablespoons of butter, along with salt and pepper to taste. Discard the cinnamon stick.

To serve ladle the sauce over the chicken and sprinkle with chives.

SERVES 4

The Bountiful Arbor, Ann Arbor, MI

MEXICAN CHICKEN LASAGNE

1 (16-ounce) jar mild salsa

1 (16-ounce) jar medium salsa

½ teaspoon ground black pepper

2 tablespoons chili powder

1 teaspoon ground cumin

2 cloves garlic, minced

1 (10-ounce) package dry lasagne noodles

2 cups nonfat cottage cheese

2 eggs

⅓ cup chopped fresh parsley

1 (4-ounce) can diced green chiles

4 cups diced cooked chicken

1 cup shredded sharp Cheddar cheese

1 cup shredded Monterey Jack cheese

Pour both jars of salsa into a large nonaluminum saucepan. Add the pepper, chili powder, cumin, and garlic. Bring to a boil; reduce the heat and simmer uncovered, stirring often, until the sauce is reduced to 4 cups, about 10 minutes.

Meanwhile, cook the lasagne noodles according to package directions and drain well. Preheat the oven to 375 degrees. Lightly coat a 13 × 9-inch baking dish with vegetable oil cooking spray. Combine the cottage cheese, eggs, parsley, and chiles; mix well and set aside.

Arrange half the cooled lasagne noodles in the bottom of the prepared baking dish. Spread half the cottage cheese mixture over the pasta, then half the cooked chicken, then half the salsa mixture. Sprinkle half the shredded cheeses on top. Repeat the layering steps, ending with the shredded cheeses. Bake, covered, until bubbly and heated thorough, about 45 to 50 minutes. Let stand uncovered for 10 minutes before cutting.

SERVES 8–12   *Making Waves in the Kitchen,* Indian River, FL

LIGHT CHICKEN ENCHILADAS

1 (16-ounce) can no-salt-added stewed tomatoes

1½ cups picante sauce

3 cups shredded or diced cooked chicken

1 red bell pepper, chopped

¼ cup coarsely chopped slivered toasted almonds

¼ teaspoon ground cinnamon

1 clove garlic, minced

12 (7-8-inch) flour tortillas

½ cup shredded Monterey Jack cheese

½ cup shredded part-skim-milk mozzarella cheese

Lettuce, ripe olive slices, chopped tomatoes, nonfat yogurt, or reduced fat sour cream for garnish (optional)

Heat the oven to 350 degrees. Spray a 13 × 9 × 2-inch baking dish with vegetable oil cooking spray.

Combine the tomatoes, ¾ cup of the picante sauce, the chicken, red pepper, almonds, cinnamon, and garlic in a large nonreactive skillet. Bring to a boil, reduce the heat, and simmer uncovered for 10 minutes or until most of liquid is absorbed.

Spoon ⅓ cup of the chicken mixture down the center of each tortilla. Roll up; place seam side down in the prepared baking dish. Spoon the remaining ¾ cup of picante sauce evenly over the tortillas. Cover with foil. Bake for 20 minutes or until heated through. Sprinkle with the shredded cheeses; let stand for 5 minutes. Garnish if desired and serve with additional picante sauce.

SERVES 6   *River Road Recipes,* Baton Rouge, LA

GREEN ENCHILADA CASSEROLE

3 large onions, chopped
1 large clove garlic, minced
3 tablespoons olive oil
3 pounds fresh tomatillos verdes
   (Mexican green tomatoes), husked
   and washed
1 tablespoon snipped fresh cilantro
1 teaspoon salt
2 (4-ounce) cans mild green chiles,
   drained and chopped
2 dozen corn tortillas, cut into
   pieces
3 cups diced cooked chicken
1 pound mozzarella cheese, grated
Sour cream
Picante sauce to taste

Sauté 1 chopped onion and the garlic in the olive oil for 3 to 5 minutes, until wilted but not brown. Add the tomatillos, cover, and simmer 5 to 10 minutes, until soft. Add the cilantro, salt, and chiles. Purée in a blender. This sauce may be prepared and frozen ahead of time.

Preheat the oven to 325 degrees. Grease a casserole with olive oil. Layer half the tortillas, half the chicken, half the remaining onion, half the cheese, and half the sauce. Repeat layers, ending with sauce and cheese.

Bake uncovered for 1 hour or until the cheese is melted and the casserole is bubbly. Serve with sour cream and picante sauce.

VARIATION: This recipe may be translated to true green enchiladas by softening each whole tortilla in hot oil, dipping into the sauce, filling with chicken, onion, cheese, and a little sour cream, covering with the remaining sauce, and baking for 15 to 20 minutes. Top with sour cream, broil, and serve with picante sauce.

SERVES 12   *Flavors,* San Antonio, TX

CHICKEN ENCHILADAS IN RED SAUCE

32 corn tortillas
1¼ pounds ripe tomatoes, peeled
   and seeded
1 small onion
1 clove garlic, minced
4 to 6 serrano chiles or other small
   fresh green chiles, seeded and
   deveined (use more or less, to
   taste)
½ cup vegetable oil
Salt to taste
3 chicken breast halves, cooked and
   shredded
1 cup heavy cream, heated
Onion rings and grated cheese for
   garnish

Heat the oven to 350 degrees. Lightly oil a 13 × 9-inch baking dish.

Purée the tomatoes, onion, garlic, and chiles in a blender. Heat ¼ cup of the oil in a saucepan and cook the tomato mixture over medium heat for 8 to 10 minutes, until thickened. Season with salt.

Heat the remaining ¼ cup of oil in a small frying pan. Fry the tortillas one at a time, turning once, for several seconds or until softened. Stack them one atop the other and keep warm.

Dip a tortilla in the sauce to coat lightly, place some of the chicken down the middle, and roll up. Place seam side down in the prepared baking dish. Repeat with the remaining tortillas, sauce, and chicken. Pour a little of the sauce between the layers of enchiladas; top with the remaining sauce.

Cover the dish tightly with foil and place in the oven for about 20 to 30 minutes, until heated through. Remove the foil, pour the heated cream around the edge of the dish, and top the enchiladas with the onions and grated cheese. Serve hot.

SERVES 8   *Buen Provecho,* Mexico City

PON-PON CHICKEN

This dish can be served as a first course or as a light luncheon entree.

1 frying chicken, about 2½ pounds, or 2 whole chicken breasts
1½ tablespoons sesame seed paste
1 tablespoon soy sauce
1 teaspoon chili oil
1 teaspoon sugar
1 teaspoon sesame oil
1 teaspoon rice vinegar
1 teaspoon Asian bean sauce
1 teaspoon minced scallion
1 teaspoon minced fresh gingerroot
½ teaspoon minced garlic
⅛ teaspoon crushed red pepper flakes
4 ounces water chestnuts, sliced
Lettuce leaves
Fresh cilantro sprigs

Steam the chicken or chicken breasts until tender, about 20 to 30 minutes. Remove from the heat and let stand until cool. Combine the sesame paste, soy sauce, chili oil, and seasonings. Mix well and refrigerate until ready to use.

Remove the meat from the chicken and cut into strips. Mix the sauce thoroughly again and pour over the shredded chicken and the water chestnuts. Toss until evenly coated with the sauce. Cover the bottom of a serving platter with lettuce leaves. Arrange chicken strips on top of the lettuce. Garnish with cilantro sprigs, if desired.

SERVES 4-6   *San Francisco Encore,* San Francisco, CA

SPICY EGGPLANT WITH CHICKEN

An interesting combination of Asian flavors.

1 teaspoon fresh gingerroot, minced
3 tablespoons soy sauce
1 tablespoon white wine vinegar
2 or 3 cloves garlic
1 tablespoon sugar
2 or 3 fresh Hawaiian red chili peppers, minced with seeds
1 teaspoon cornstarch
½ to ¾ pound long eggplant, sliced diagonally ½ inch-thick
¾ pound ground chicken or turkey
2 tablespoons vegetable oil, or as needed
Chopped fresh cilantro for garnish

Mix the ginger, soy sauce, vinegar, garlic, sugar, chili peppers, and cornstarch. Set aside.

Sauté the eggplant in the oil in a large skillet until the slices are slightly browned. Set aside. Sauté the chicken in the same pan until browned. Return the eggplant to the skillet and add the sauce. Cook until thoroughly heated. Garnish with cilantro.

SERVES 4   *Another Taste of Aloha,* Honolulu, HI

CHICKEN TETRAZZINI

3 (2-pound) chickens, cut up
1½ cups chopped celery tops
¼ cup chopped fresh parsley
1 medium onion, sliced
2½ teaspoons salt
5 tablespoons butter
8 ounces mushrooms, wiped, trimmed, and sliced
¼ cup all-purpose flour
¼ teaspoon ground black pepper
1 cup heavy cream
2½ tablespoons dry sherry
3 to 4 tablespoons sliced blanched almonds
1 (8-ounce) box egg noodles, boiled and drained
¾ cup fine dry bread crumbs
5 tablespoons grated Parmesan cheese

Place the chicken pieces in a large saucepan with the celery, parsley, onion, 2 teaspoons of salt, and 3½ cups of water. Bring to a boil, cover, reduce the heat, and simmer until tender. Remove the skin and bones from the chicken and cut the meat into bite-size chunks. Strain and reserve the broth.

Melt the butter in a large saucepan. When hot, add the mushrooms and sauté for 2 minutes. Stir in the flour, remaining ½ teaspoon of salt, and the pepper. Gradually stir in 2 cups of the reserved broth along with the cream and cook, stirring constantly, until thickened. Add the chicken and sherry to the sauce. Add the almonds.

Place the noodles in a greased shallow baking dish. Top with the chicken mixture. Sprinkle with bread crumbs and cheese. Brown under the broiler.

SERVES 6–8 *300 Years of Carolina Cooking,* Greenville, SC

CHICKEN AND SAUSAGE JAMBALAYA

1 small fryer
1 rib celery with leaves
1 onion, halved
3 cloves garlic
2 cups converted long grain rice
1 pound smoked sausage, sliced ½ inch thick
1 pound ham, cubed
4 tablespoons (½ stick) butter
1 cup chopped yellow onion
¾ cup chopped scallions
¼ cup chopped fresh parsley
1 (6-ounce) can tomato paste
1 large bay leaf
¼ teaspoon dried thyme
2 teaspoons salt
½ teaspoon ground black pepper
¼ teaspoon Tabasco

In a large pot, cover the chicken with water; add the halved celery, onion, and 1 clove of garlic. Bring to a boil, lower the heat, cover, and simmer until tender, about 1 hour. Strain and reserve the stock. Remove the meat from the bones.

In 5 cups of the stock, cook the rice until all liquid is absorbed, about 25 minutes. Set aside. In a Dutch oven, fry the sausage and ham until lightly browned, about 3 to 5 minutes. Remove the meat. Add the butter to the pan and sauté the chopped onion, scallions, and parsley until limp, about 3 minutes. Add the chicken, sausage, and ham. Mince the remaining 2 cloves of garlic and add, along with the tomato paste, bay leaf, thyme, salt, pepper, and Tabasco. Add the rice and mix thoroughly. Cook over low heat 15 minutes, stirring frequently. Remove the bay leaf and serve.

SERVES 8–10 *Jambalaya,* New Orleans, LA

LIGHTER LASAGNE

A healthy alternative that doesn't sacrifice flavor.

1 pound ground turkey
½ pound turkey sausage
1 clove garlic, minced
1 tablespoon dried basil
1½ teaspoons salt
1 (16-ounce) can tomatoes, cut up
1 (6-ounce) can tomato paste
1 (12-ounce) container low-fat cottage cheese
2 eggs, beaten
1 teaspoon salt
½ teaspoon ground black pepper
2 tablespoons dried parsley flakes or ¼ cup chopped fresh parsley
½ cup grated Parmesan cheese
8 wide lasagne noodles, cooked to package directions
1 pound low-fat mozzarella, shredded

Preheat the oven to 350 degrees. Brown the turkey and sausage in a heavy pan, stirring to break up lumps. Drain off any fat. When the meat is browned, add the garlic, basil, salt, tomatoes, and tomato paste. Simmer uncovered until the sauce is thick, about 30 minutes.

While the sauce is thickening, combine the cottage cheese, eggs, salt, pepper, parsley, and Parmesan cheese. Arrange 4 noodles without overlapping in a 13 × 9-inch baking dish. Spread half the cheese mixture over the noodles and sprinkle half the mozzarella over the top. Cover with half the meat sauce. Repeat, ending with the meat. Bake for 40 minutes. Let stand for 10 minutes before cutting into serving pieces.

SERVES 6–8   *California Sizzles,* Pasadena, CA

SAVORY SMOKED TURKEY BREAST

1 boneless turkey breast, 5 to 6 pounds
3 tablespoons butter, melted
1 tablespoon seasoned salt
2 teaspoons dried whole basil leaves
1 teaspoon dried whole oregano leaves
1 teaspoon dried thyme leaves
¾ teaspoon paprika

Rinse the turkey breast with cold water; pat dry. Tuck loose ends under the thickest part of the breast. Secure the meat at 2-inch intervals, using heavy string. Brush with melted butter.

Combine the seasoned salt, basil, oregano, thyme, and paprika. Sprinkle over the turkey. Prepare a charcoal fire in one end of the grill; let it burn for 15 to 20 minutes. Soak hickory chips in water at least 15 minutes; place hickory chips on the coals.

Place the turkey breast on the grill opposite the hot coals; close the grill hood. Cook 2½ to 3 hours or until a meat thermometer reaches 170 degrees when inserted into the thickest part of the breast. Remove string before serving.

SERVES 12   *Very Virginia,* Hampton Roads, VA

SMOKED JALAPEÑO GAME HENS

4 fresh Cornish game hens
8 tablespoons (1 stick) butter
1 (8- or 10-ounce) jar hot jalapeño
    pepper jelly

Rinse the game hens and pat dry. Using poultry shears or kitchen scissors, cut along both sides of the backbone of each bird to remove the backbone completely. Flatten the game hen by pressing it with the hands to break the breastbone.

Light the barbecue. Soak 2 or 3 handfuls of wood chips, such as hickory or mesquite, in water for 20 minutes. Melt the butter and pepper jelly together. When the charcoal is hot, distribute the soaked wood chips over the coals. Immediately place the game hens over the grill, bone side down, and cover. After 15 minutes of cooking, turn the hens and begin basting with the butter/jelly mixture. Baste often. Cook until the juices run clear when a thigh is pierced with a fork, approximately 35 to 45 minutes. Reheat the butter/jelly mixture if it becomes too thick to baste with. The game hens should be a rich mahogany color from the smoking process and shiny and moist from the jalapeño glaze. Although hot pepper jelly is used, the taste is savory but not spicy.

SERVE 4–6   *Feast of Eden,* Monterey, CA

GAME HENS WITH WILD RICE AND ORANGE SAUCE

4 fresh Rock Cornish game hens
13 tablespoons (1½ sticks plus 1
    tablespoon) butter, softened
Salt and pepper
3 oranges
¼ cup Grand Marnier or other
    orange-flavored liqueur
1 cup chicken broth
1 tablespoon flour
2 cups wild rice, cooked according
    to package directions and kept hot
½ cup chopped walnuts

Preheat the oven to 350 degrees. Rinse and dry the hens, spread each one with 2 tablespoons of softened butter, and sprinkle with salt and pepper. Arrange in a shallow roasting pan and bake for 50 to 60 minutes, turning the birds and basting them frequently with the pan juices. Remove the birds to a warm serving platter and keep warm.

Remove the thin orange rind from 1 orange with a vegetable peeler and cut the rind into very fine shreds. Cover the orange shreds with water, bring to a boil, and simmer for 10 minutes. Drain. With a sharp knife, peel the other 2 oranges, removing all the rind and every trace of the bitter white covering. Cut the oranges into sections, free of connecting membranes, and add to the shredded rind.

Pour off the fat from the roasting pan. Add the Grand Marnier to the pan and ignite. When the flame burns out, stir in the chicken broth and cook, stirring in all the brown glaze from the bottom of the pan. Stir in the flour mixed to a paste with 1 tablespoon of softened butter. Cook, stirring, until the sauce is slightly thickened. Add the shredded orange rind and orange sections and simmer for 2 minutes.

Toss the cooked rice with the walnuts, the remaining 4 tablespoons of butter, and salt and pepper to taste. Serve the hens with the rice and the orange sauce.

SERVES 4   *The Dallas Junior League Cookbook,* Dallas, TX

CORNISH HENS WITH GRAPE COGNAC SAUCE

8 fresh Cornish game hens
Salt
Ground black pepper
Baking soda
8 tablespoons (1 stick) butter,
    softened
½ cup finely chopped ham
1 cup finely chopped celery
½ pound mushrooms, wiped,
    trimmed, and sliced
3 cups soft white bread crumbs
1 cup finely chopped parsley
1 teaspoon ground white pepper
½ cup Cognac

SAUCE
2 pounds seedless grapes, halved
1 cup consommé
2 tablespoons butter
½ cup Cognac
Salt and ground black pepper to
    taste

Preheat the oven to 350 degrees. Rinse and dry the hens; rub the cavities with equal parts of salt, pepper, and soda.

In a heavy skillet, melt 2 tablespoon of butter and sauté the ham for 3 to 4 minutes. Remove ham and set aside. Heat 3 tablespoons of butter in the pan and sauté the onion with the celery for 10 minutes. Add the mushrooms and sauté for 2 minutes. Remove from the heat and mix in the bread crumbs, ham, parsley, and white pepper. Stuff the birds, coat with the remaining 4 tablespoons of softened butter, salt and pepper lightly, and place in a shallow roasting pan. Sprinkle the hens with ¼ cup of Cognac and bake uncovered for 50 to 60 minutes, basting with the remaining Cognac. Transfer hens, halved if desired, to a heated serving dish and keep warm while preparing the sauce.

To the pan drippings, add the grapes, consommé, butter, Cognac, salt, and pepper. Simmer until thoroughly heated. Serve over the hens or in a separate sauceboat.

SERVES 8   *The Plantation Cookbook,* New Orleans, LA

BURGUNDY GAME BIRDS

4 pounds pheasant, quail, duck
    breast, or doves
Salt and freshly ground pepper
1 cup all-purpose flour
8 tablespoons (1 stick) butter
¼ cup finely chopped shallots
1 cup finely chopped mushrooms
2 cups finely chopped cooked ham
2 cups dry red wine
2 tablespoons brandy
½ teaspoon dried thyme
⅛ teaspoon dried tarragon
½ small bay leaf
Pinch of grated nutmeg
2 tablespoons finely chopped parsley

Wash the birds and pat dry with paper towels. Season with salt and pepper and roll in flour, shaking each bird to remove excess flour. In a large heavy skillet, melt 4 tablespoons of butter over moderate heat. When the foam subsides, add the birds, turning frequently to brown on all sides. Remove the birds from the skillet and set aside.

Melt 2 tablespoons of butter in the same skillet. Add 3 tablespoons of the shallots and cook for 4 to 5 minutes over moderate heat, stirring frequently. Add the mushrooms and ham. Cook, stirring occasionally, for 4 minutes. Transfer the mixture to a bowl and set aside.

Melt the remaining tablespoon of butter in the skillet and cook the remaining tablespoon of shallots for 2 to 3 minutes, until soft and lightly colored. Add the wine and brandy and bring to a boil over high heat, scraping up any pan drippings. Add the thyme, tarragon, bay leaf, nutmeg, and salt and pepper to taste. Return all the birds to the skillet and baste. Reduce the heat to low, cover, and simmer for 20 to 30 minutes or until the birds are tender. Remove the bay leaf and serve the birds with the sauce.

SERVES 4   *Thymes Remembered,* Tallahassee, FL

SMOTHERED QUAIL

½ cup chopped bacon
8 quail
¼ teaspoon salt
⅛ teaspoon ground black pepper
2 scallions with tops, minced
1 tablespoon minced celery leaves
6 tablespoons all-purpose flour
Pinch of dried thyme
½ bay leaf
1 tablespoon chopped parsley
3 cups chicken broth, or as needed

In a large heavy skillet, cook the bacon, while stirring, until browned. Remove with a slotted spoon and reserve.

Rinse the quail, pat dry with paper towels, and sprinkle with the salt and pepper. Brown the birds on all sides in the drippings; remove to a plate. Cook the scallions and celery for 1 to 2 minutes and stir in the flour, along with the thyme, bay leaf, and parsley. Gradually stir in the 3 cups of chicken broth and cook over medium heat until the sauce is thickened.

Return the bacon and quail to the skillet. Cover, lower the heat, and simmer 30 minutes, turning occasionally, until done. Add more chicken broth if necessary.

SERVES 4

Savannah Style, Savannah, GA

WILD DUCK WITH LEMON SAUCE

2 mallard or wood ducks, cleaned
   and dressed
½ apple per bird, peeled, cored, and
   chopped coarse
½ orange per bird, peeled,
   sectioned, and chopped coarse
2 stalks celery per bird, chopped
   coarse
Salt and pepper to taste
½ teaspoon grated orange rind
1 cup orange juice or water
¼ to ½ cup lemon juice
2 sticks (½ pound) butter
¼ to ½ cup chopped parsley
¼ cup chopped scallions
1 tablespoons Worcestershire sauce
2 to 3 teaspoons Dijon mustard

Preheat the oven to 300 degrees. Sprinkle the ducks inside and out with salt and pepper. Stuff the cavities loosely with apple, orange, and celery. Place the birds in a roasting pan and add rind and juice to cover the bottom of the pan. Bake for 2 to 3 hours or until very tender. Remove the ducks from the pan, degreasing and reserving juices. Discard the stuffing. Skin and bone the ducks; chop or slice the meat and set aside.

To make the sauce, in a saucepan combine the lemon juice, butter, parsley, scallions, Worcestershire, mustard, and the duck juices; cook for about 5 minutes. Place half the duck meat in a casserole and top with half the sauce. Repeat the layers. Cover and set aside for 2 to 3 hours at room temperature, or store overnight in the refrigerator. Reheat in a preheated 300 degree oven for 30 minutes or until hot and bubbly. Serve with wild rice.

SERVES 6

Atlanta Cooknotes, Atlanta, GA

MIDNIGHT BASKETBALL
JUNIOR LEAGUE OF EL PASO, TEXAS

In conjunction with the City of El Paso Parks and Recreation Department and the El Paso Police Department, the Junior League of El Paso formed a program which offers organized team sports at high crime hours. Basketball games are played on Friday and Saturday nights from 11 p.m. to 3 a.m. In addition, a mandatory educational workshop is held weekly for all Midnight Basketball players, who range in age from 15 to 20.

GLAZED WILD DUCK

2 tablespoons butter
2 tablespoons solid vegetable
  shortening
¾ cup all-purpose flour, or as
  needed
Salt and pepper to taste
1 wild duck, cleaned and dressed
½ orange
4 dried apricots
2 strips bacon
2 tablespoons frozen concentrated
  orange juice
1 cup orange wine
1 cup chopped onion
½ cup chopped celery
¼ cup chopped parsley

Heat the butter with the vegetable shortening in a Dutch oven. Combine the flour, salt, and pepper in a deep dish; roll the duck in the seasoned flour, shaking off the excess. Fry the duck in the hot fat for about 15 minutes, until brown all over. Remove the duck to a plate. Pour off all but ¼ cup of the fat remaining in the Dutch oven and stir in ¼ cup of the seasoned flour. When the mixture is bubbly and golden brown, gradually stir in 1½ cups of water and simmer until the gravy is thickened and smooth.

Heat the oven to 300 degrees. Stuff the cavity of the duck with the orange half and place the duck in the pan of gravy. Arrange the 4 apricots over the duck's breast. Cover with 2 strips of bacon and the frozen concentrated orange juice. Add the orange wine or just any wine you might have on hand. Sprinkle with the chopped onion, chopped celery, and parsley. Cover and bake for 2 to 3 hours until tender. Baste every 40 minutes. When a leg tests tender, your duck is just right.

SERVES 2   *The Cotton Country Collection,* Monroe, LA

HOLLY LAWRENCE'S WILD DUCK

The gravy is as good as the duck. Serve it over wild rice.

4 wild ducks, cleaned and dressed
1 cup all-purpose flour
1 cup vegetable oil
4 garlic cloves, peeled
½ to 1 teaspoon crushed red pepper
  flakes per duck
2 teaspoons celery seed per duck
2 teaspoons chili powder per duck
2 teaspoons salt per duck

Heat the oil in a deep heavy kettle until very hot. Add the flour gradually, ⅓ cup at a time, stirring constantly with a long-handled spoon or whisk. Continue to cook and stir until the roux turns a very dark brown—be careful not to let it burn. Remove from the heat and continue to stir until the mixture has cooled slightly, to prevent scorching. When the mixture has cooled, return to the heat and add 4 cups of cold water. Stir until completely blended, then add the garlic.

Preheat the oven to 325 degrees. Rub the inside of each duck with red pepper, celery seed, chili powder, and salt. Submerge the ducks in the roux, cover, and bake about 3 hours, until tender.

NOTE: If ducks are large, increase the amount of roux so that the ducks will be submerged while cooking.

SERVES 4   *The Bounty of East Texas,* Longview, TX

BAKED WILD DUCK WITH SWEET POTATOES

Salt
Ground red pepper (cayenne)
Ground black pepper
6 wild ducks, cleaned and dressed
2 onions, cut into chunks
4 tablespoons (½ stick) butter
2 sweet potatoes
2 apples
1 cup dry red wine
1 large can mushrooms

Season the ducks inside and out with salt, red pepper, and black pepper. Sauté the onions in 1 tablespoon of the butter for 5 minutes. Parboil the potatoes until partially cooked but still firm. Peel and dice the potatoes and apples and mix with the onions. Stuff the ducks loosely.

Place the ducks in a heavy baking pan with a tight lid. Bake in a 325 degree oven for 2 hours. Melt the rest of the butter and add the wine. Baste the ducks with this mixture until all is used, then continue basting with the pan juices. About 15 minutes before the ducks are done, raise the oven heat to 450 degrees, add the mushrooms, uncover the pan, and brown the ducks. Be sure to baste often during browning period.

SERVES 6

Talk About Good I, Lafayette, LA

ROAST WILD GOOSE

1 young wild goose (8 pounds or less)
1 apple, quartered
1 onion, quartered
2 stalks celery
3 tablespoons currant jelly
1½ tablespoons butter
½ tablespoon dried rosemary
1½ teaspoons salt
1½ teaspoons ground black pepper
Onion salt to taste
Garlic salt to taste
½ teaspoon oregano
½ teaspoon thyme
1 cup red wine (optional)

Eviscerate the goose, saving the liver and heart for pâté. Hang by the feet in a cool, dry, well-ventilated place for at least 24 hours—2 or 3 days longer if a gamy flavor is preferred. (The bird can hang as long as 3 weeks if the temperature is below 45 degrees.)

Dry-pluck the feathers, and remove the down by dipping the bird into a bath of hot water and melted paraffin, allowing to cool, and peeling off the hardened paraffin.

Remove the feet, wings, head, and neck and reserve for making stock. Stuff the cavity with the apple, onion, and celery.

In a saucepan, combine the remaining ingredients except the wine and simmer for 10 minutes. Let cool while placing the goose in roasting pan and preheating the oven to 500 degrees. Cover the bottom of the pan with red wine mixed with 1 cup of water. Spoon the sauce over the breast of the goose. Cook, basting often, 30 minutes for rare or 1 hour for well done.

SERVES 4

Hunt to Harbor—An Epicurean Tour, Baltimore, MD

PARENTING GUIDANCE CENTER
JUNIOR LEAGUE OF FORT WORTH, TEXAS

The Junior League of Fort Worth, Texas, created the Parenting Guidance Center in 1975, and its mission remains the same: the prevention of child abuse and neglect and the promotion of positive parenting. At its founding, Parenting Guidance Center was the first in the United States to provide both counseling and education from a professional staff augmented by highly trained volunteers working in both the remedial and preventive/education programs, and the center has become a nationwide model.

A CELEBRATION OF THE PRESENT

As we sit on the edge of the twenty-first century, at no other time in our history have we needed a greater willingness to embrace change—to reinvent ourselves, to look at how we do business, to examine how we interact on the community level. Are we doing all we can do? Can we do better?

Throughout society, there is a questioning of our institutions and a feeling that they are failing us. For many there is distrust and apathy. Some question whether institutions like the Junior League that were created a hundred years ago can endure the kinds of changes and transitions that will be demanded of them if they are to be effective in the future.

This is the reality that Junior Leagues are confronting as they look at the increasing opportunities available to women other than traditional women's organizations and the limited time that women have to give to volunteer efforts. Junior League members are keenly aware that today's pressures require a reflection and a discipline in order to make a successful transition to the next stage of our organizational being.

Throughout their history, the Junior Leagues have provided society with a unique laboratory. In the crucibles of their communities, Leagues take risks and experiment with new concepts, generating a unique and valuable database of what works and

League members set up a booth and offer service to the community at the Third Avenue Fair, 1984.

what doesn't. Today is no exception, with Leagues testing out new priorities and new organizational thinking.

To achieve greater impact in their communities, many Leagues are evaluating how they utilize their resources, both human and financial, and are embracing a goal-centered approach to strategic planning. They are recognizing that they need increased buy-in from their members and are involving as many members as possible in focus groups and neighborhood meetings to discuss their vision for the community and where they think their League should concentrate its efforts. By planning with their total memberships, Leagues are finding that their members feel more connected to what they are doing and feel pride in the impact their League is making in the community. Leagues are becoming increasingly multicultural in their memberships and are developing far-reaching collaborations that involve partners from every segment of the community.

Perhaps most importantly, the Junior League believes that the key to unlocking the door to a second hundred years of successful history lies in having a clear vision. We don't know what the answers are, but we are certain that "since we can't predict the future, we must invent it." We celebrate the journey.

BREADS &
BREAKFASTS

BREADS

ZUCCHINI BREAD

1 whole egg plus 2 egg whites
1½ cups sugar
⅓ cup vegetable oil
⅔ cup nonfat plain yogurt
1 teaspoon vanilla extract
2 cups all-purpose flour
1 teaspoon ground cinnamon
2 teaspoons baking soda
¾ teaspoon salt
½ teaspoon baking powder
2 cups grated zucchini
⅓ cup chopped walnuts

Preheat the oven to 350 degrees. Grease and flour two 8-inch loaf pans.

In a large bowl, beat together the eggs, sugar, oil, yogurt, and vanilla. In a separate bowl, mix the flour, cinnamon, soda, salt and baking powder. Add to the first mixture and stir until blended. Fold in the zucchini and walnuts. Pour into the prepared pans and bake for 45 minutes, or until the loaves shrink slightly from the sides of the pans. Cook in the pans for 10 minutes, then turn out onto a rack.

VARIATION: For 1 cup zucchini, substitute ½ cup grated carrot, 1 large apple, finely chopped, and 1 tablespoon fresh orange zest.

MAKES 2 LOAVES

River Road Recipes: A Healthy Collection, Baton Rouge, LA

HONEY BREAD

3½ cups all-purpose flour
1¼ cups firmly packed brown sugar
1 tablespoon baking powder
1 teaspoon baking soda
1 teaspoon salt
2 teaspoons ground cinnamon
1 teaspoon ground allspice
1 teaspoon ground cloves
½ teaspoon grated nutmeg
4 eggs
1½ cups honey
4 tablespoons (½ stick) butter, melted
1 cup black coffee
1 cup chopped pecans
1 cup raisins

Preheat the oven to 350 degrees. Grease and flour two 9-inch loaf pans.

In a large bowl combine the flour, brown sugar, baking powder, soda, salt, cinnamon, allspice, cloves, and nutmeg. Stir with a whisk until well combined.

In a separate bowl, beat together the eggs, honey, butter, and coffee. Blend the wet ingredients into the dry, stirring just until mixed. Fold in the nuts and raisins.

Pour the batter into the prepared pans and bake 1 hour. Cool in the pans for 10 to 15 minutes, then turn out onto a rack.

MAKES 2 LOAVES

Celebrate Miami! Holiday Recipes for Children from Miami's Melting Pot, Miami, FL

POPPY SEED BREAD

3 cups all-purpose flour
1½ teaspoons salt
1½ teaspoons baking powder
3 eggs
1½ cups milk
1 cup plus 2 tablespoons vegetable
    oil
2½ cups sugar
2 tablespoons poppy seeds
1½ teaspoons vanilla extract
1½ teaspoons almond extract
½ teaspoons butter flavoring

GLAZE
½ teaspoon butter flavoring
½ teaspoon almond extract
½ teaspoon vanilla extract
¾ cup sugar
¼ cup orange juice

Preheat the oven to 350 degrees. Grease and flour two 9-inch loaf pans.

Whisk together the flour, salt, and baking powder; set aside. Beat the eggs in a large bowl and stir in the milk, oil, and sugar. Add the poppy seeds, vanilla, almond extract, and butter flavoring. Mix in the dry ingredients until the batter is smooth. Pour the batter into the prepared pans. Bake for 1 to 1¼ hours. Remove loaves from pans and place on a rack to cool.

Mix together glaze ingredients in a small bowl. Spoon glaze over warm loaves.

MAKES 2 LOAVES   *Honest to Goodness,* Springfield, IL

PEANUT LOAF

5 tablespoons butter, softened
¼ cup packed brown sugar
1 cup shelled peanuts, chopped
2 cups all-purpose flour
½ teaspoon baking soda
1 teaspoon baking powder
⅓ teaspoon salt
2 tablespoons peanut butter
1 egg
1 cup packed brown sugar
1 cup buttermilk or sour milk

Preheat the oven to 350 degrees. Grease a 9-inch loaf pan. Spread 3 tablespoons of the butter over the bottom of the pan; cover with brown sugar and chopped peanuts.

Whisk the flour, soda, baking powder, and salt together. Melt the remaining 2 tablespoons of butter with the peanut butter. Beat the egg until frothy and beat in the brown sugar gradually. Stir in the peanut butter mixture and the buttermilk. Mix this liquid mixture with the dry ingredients but do not beat. Pour the batter over the brown sugar topping and bake 1 hour. Cool in the pan for 10 minutes, then invert on a rack.

MAKES 1 LOAF   *Soup & Bread,* Butte, MO

RHUBARB BREAD

1½ cups packed brown sugar
⅔ cups vegetable oil
1 egg
1 teaspoon vanilla extract
1 teaspoon salt
1 teaspoon baking soda
1 cup sour milk or buttermilk
2½ cups all-purpose flour
1½ cups sliced rhubarb
½ cup chopped nuts
½ cup granulated sugar
1 tablespoon butter, softened

Preheat the oven to 325 degrees. Grease and flour two 8-inch loaf pans.

In a large bowl, beat together the brown sugar, oil, and egg. Add the vanilla and salt. Mix the soda with the sour milk and add to the egg mixture.

Stir the flour into the wet ingredients just until combined. Fold in the rhubarb and nuts. Pour the batter into the prepared pans. Mix the granulated sugar and butter together and sprinkle over the loaves. Bake for 1 hour, or until a toothpick inserted near the center comes out clean. Allow to cool in the pans for 10 minutes, then turn the loaves out onto a rack.

MAKES 2 LOAVES   *Posh Pantry,* Kankakee, IL

STRAWBERRY NUT BREAD

A delicious accompaniment to fresh fruit, this bread can be served cold with a flavored butter or with a dollop of whipped cream topped with lemon zest.

3 cups all-purpose flour
1 teaspoon baking soda
1 tablespoon ground cinnamon
2 cups sugar
3 eggs, well beaten
1½ teaspoons vanilla extract
1 cup vegetable oil
Grated rind of 1 lemon
3 cups chopped strawberries
¾ cup chopped pecans

Preheat the oven to 350 degrees. Grease and flour two 9-inch loaf pans.

In a large bowl, combine the flour and baking soda and stir until the soda is well distributed. Add the cinnamon and sugar. Mix well. In a separate bowl, combine the eggs, vanilla, oil, and lemon rind. Spoon the strawberries into the liquid ingredients and stir gently to coat them. Add this mixture in batches to the dry ingredients, incorporating by hand. Fold in the nuts. Pour the batter into the prepared pans and bake 1 hour, or until a wooden pick inserted near the center comes out clean. Allow loaves to cool in the pan for 5 minutes, then turn out onto a rack. Do not slice until ready to serve.

MAKES 2 LOAVES   *Delicious Decisions,* San Diego, CA

FRESH AUTUMN PEAR BREAD

8 tablespoons (1 stick) unsalted
   butter, softened
1 cup sugar
2 eggs, slightly beaten
1 teaspoon vanilla extract
2 cups all-purpose flour
½ teaspoon salt
1 teaspoon baking powder
½ teaspoon baking soda
⅛ teaspoon grated nutmeg
¼ cup buttermilk or yogurt
1 cup coarsely chopped fresh ripe
   pears, skin left on

Preheat the oven to 350 degrees. Butter a 9-inch loaf pan.

In a large bowl, using an electric mixer, cream the butter and sugar together until light and fluffy. Add the eggs and vanilla. In a separate bowl, combine the flour, salt, baking powder, baking soda, and nutmeg. Add the four mixture to the butter mixture alternately with the buttermilk, mixing gently but thoroughly. Gently stir in the pears. Transfer the dough to the prepared pan. Bake for 1 hour, or until a cake tester inserted near the center comes out clean.

MAKES 1 LOAF   *More Than a Tea Party,* Boston, MA

APRICOT WALNUT TEA BREAD

1 cup dried apricots
1½ cups boiling water
2½ cups all-purpose flour
1 tablespoon baking powder
½ teaspoon salt
1 egg
1 teaspoon vanilla extract
1 cup sugar
½ cup vegetable oil
1 cup coarsely chopped walnuts

Preheat the oven to 350 degrees. Grease a 9-inch loaf pan.

Cut the apricots into small pieces and place in a bowl. Add the boiling water; set aside to cool. Sift the flour, baking powder, and salt and set aside. In a large bowl, combine the egg, vanilla, sugar, and oil; beat until blended. Gradually add the apricot mixture, beating constantly. Add the flour mixture and beat until smooth. Stir in the nuts. Scrape the dough into the prepared pan.

Bake for 1 hour. Let the bread cool in the pan for 10 minutes, then loosen with spatulas and transfer to a rack. Cool. Wrap in foil and store in the refrigerator at least 12 hours before serving.

MAKES 1 LOAF   *A Bountiful Arbor,* Ann Arbor, MI

ORANGE BREAD

Juice and rind of 1 orange
5 ounces pitted dates
½ cup pecans
3 tablespoons unsalted butter,
   softened
½ cup sugar
1 egg, lightly beaten
1 teaspoon vanilla extract
1 cup unbleached all-purpose flour
1 cup whole wheat flour
1 teaspoon baking soda
1 teaspoon baking powder
1 teaspoon salt

Preheat the oven to 350 degrees. Grease and flour a 9-inch loaf pan.

Squeeze the orange juice into a measuring cup and add enough boiling water to make 1 cup. In a food processor using steel blade, finely chop the orange rind. Add the dates and chop; add the pecans and chop. Combine the juice, butter, sugar, egg, and vanilla in a large bowl. Add the chopped date mixture and mix well.

Whisk together the all-purpose and whole wheat flours, soda, baking powder, and salt. Combine with the orange-date mixture and stir just enough to moisten. Pour and scrape into the prepared loaf pan and bake for 50 to 60 minutes, until a wooden pick inserted near the center of the loaf comes out clean. Cool in the pan for 10 minutes, then turn out onto a rack.

MAKES 1 LOAF   *Fare by the Sea,* Sarasota, FL

CRANBERRY ORANGE BREAD

1 orange
1 egg, beaten
1 cup sugar
2 tablespoons butter
¼ teaspoon salt
2 cups all-purpose flour
1½ teaspoons baking powder
1 cup cranberries, chopped coarse
1 cup pecans, chopped

Preheat the oven to 325 degrees. Butter and flour a 9-inch loaf pan.

Squeeze the juice from the orange and grate the rind. Add enough boiling water to the juice and rind to make ¾ cup of liquid. Combine the egg, sugar, and butter and beat well. Mix together the flour, salt, and baking power and add to the egg mixture alternately with the liquid. Mix well. Fold in the cranberries and pecans. Spoon the batter into the prepared pan. Bake for 45 to 60 minutes, until a cake tester inserted near the center of the loaf comes out clean. Cool in the pan before removing.

MAKES 1 LOAF   *Aw Shucks,* Fort Wayne, IN

CRANBERRY BANANA BREAD

4 tablespoons (½ stick) butter, softened
1 cup sugar
1 egg
2 cups all-purpose flour
1 tablespoon baking powder
½ teaspoon ground cinnamon
½ teaspoon salt
1 cup mashed banana
½ cup milk
1 teaspoon grated orange rind
1 cup fresh cranberries, chopped coarse
½ cup chopped walnuts

Preheat the oven to 350 degrees. Grease a 9-inch loaf pan.

In a large bowl, cream the butter and sugar, add the egg and beat well. Stir together the flour, baking powder, cinnamon, and salt. In a small bowl, combine the banana, milk, and orange rind. Add the dry ingredients and banana mixture alternately to the creamed mixture, stirring well after each addition. Fold in the cranberries and walnuts. Pour and scrape into the prepared pan. Bake for 1 hour or until a cake tester inserted near the center comes out clean.

MAKES 1 LOAF   *More Than a Tea Party,* Boston, MA

SOUR CREAM BANANA BREAD

8 tablespoons (1 stick) butter, softened
1 cup sugar
2 eggs, beaten
1½ cups all-purpose flour
1 teaspoon baking soda
½ teaspoon salt
1 cup mashed bananas (about 3 bananas)
½ cup sour cream
1 teaspoon vanilla extract
½ cup chopped pecans

Preheat the oven to 350 degrees. Grease and flour one 9-inch loaf pan or several smaller pans.

In a large bowl, cream the butter with the sugar until light and fluffy. Add the eggs and mix well. Whisk together the flour, baking soda, and salt; combine with the butter mixture. Add the bananas, sour cream, and vanilla; stir well. Fold in the nuts. Pour into the prepared pan and bake for 1 hour, or until a wooden pick inserted near the center of the loaf comes out clean. Cool in the pan for 10 minutes, then turn out onto a rack.

MAKES 1 LOAF   *Celebrations on the Bayou,* Monroe, LA

BEST BANANA BREAD

What takes this banana bread out of the realm of the traditional is the addition of flaked coconut and raisins to the batter.

2 cups all-purpose flour

1 cup sugar

2 teaspoons ground cinnamon

2 teaspoons baking soda

1 teaspoon salt

1 cup vegetable oil

2 cups mashed ripe bananas

½ cup raisins

½ cup flaked coconut

3 eggs, beaten

Preheat the oven to 350 degrees. Grease two 8-inch loaf pans.

In a large bowl stir together the flour, sugar, cinnamon, baking soda, and salt. Add the oil, bananas, raisins, coconut, and eggs. Mix well. Pour into the prepared pans and let stand 20 minutes.

Bake for 1 hour, or until a toothpick inserted near the center comes out clean. Allow the loaves to cool in the pans for 10 minutes, then turn out onto a rack.

MAKES 2 LOAVES   *Winning at the Table,* Las Vegas, NV

FAVORITE BANANA BREAD

3 ripe or overripe bananas, mashed

1 cup sugar

1 egg

4 tablespoons (½ stick) butter, melted

1 teaspoon vanilla extract

1½ cups all-purpose flour

1 teaspoon baking soda

½ teaspoon salt

Preheat the oven to 325 degrees. Grease and flour an 8-inch loaf pan.

In a large bowl, combine the mashed bananas, sugar, egg, melted butter, and vanilla. Beat until thoroughly mixed. In a separate bowl, whisk together the flour, baking soda, and salt. Stir the flour mixture into the banana mixture just until blended. Pour and scrape the batter into the prepared pan. Bake for 1 hour, or until a wooden pick inserted near the center of the loaf comes out clean. Allow the bread to cool in the pan for 10 minutes, then turn out onto a rack.

MAKES 1 LOAF   *Amarillo Junior League Cookbook,* Amarillo, TX

FRESH APPLE BREAD

2 cups all-purpose flour

2 teaspoons baking powder

1 teaspoon salt

½ teaspoon ground cinnamon

¼ teaspoon grated nutmeg

8 tablespoons (1 stick) butter, softened

1¼ cups sugar

2 eggs

1½ cups finely grated peeled apple

½ cup chopped pecans or walnuts

Preheat the oven to 350 degrees. Butter and four a 9-inch loaf pan.

Mix the dry ingredients together and set aside. Cream the butter and sugar together in a large bowl until fluffy. Beat in the eggs one at a time. Stir in the dry ingredients, then add the apple and pecans. Bake for 1 hour or until a wooden pick inserted near the center comes out clean. Cool in the pan for 10 minutes, then turn out on a rack. Cool before slicing.

MAKES 1 LOAF   *Culinary Creations,* Kingston, NY

WENATCHEE APPLE BREAD

2 cups all-purpose flour
½ teaspoon baking soda
1 teaspoon baking powder
1 teaspoon salt
½ teaspoon ground allspice
½ teaspoon grated nutmeg
1 teaspoon ground cinnamon
12 tablespoons (1½ sticks) butter,
　 melted
⅔ cup sugar
3 eggs, beaten
¼ cup applesauce
1 cup peeled and diced apples
⅓ cup sour cream
¼ cup chopped walnuts
⅓ cup raisins

TOPPING
¼ cup applesauce
¼ cup firmly packed brown sugar
¼ teaspoon ground cinnamon

Preheat the oven to 375 degrees. Butter and flour a 9-inch loaf pan.

Whisk the dry ingredients together and set aside. Combine the butter and sugar and stir until well blended. Stir in the eggs a little at a time, and add the applesauce, diced apples, sour cream, nuts, and raisins. Stir in the flour mixture, mix well, and pour into the prepared pan.

Mix the ingredients in a small bowl and spread on top of the batter. Bake the bread for 50 minutes, or until a tester inserted near the center of the loaf comes out clean. Cool in the pan for 10 minutes, then turn out on a wire rack.

MAKES 1 LOAF　　　　*The Seattle Classic,* Seattle, WA

APPLELICIOUS BREAD

4 cups baking apples, peeled and
　 diced
1 cup finely chopped pecans
2 cups sugar
3 cups all-purpose flour
2 teaspoons baking soda
¼ teaspoon salt
¼ teaspoon ground allspice
¼ teaspoon ground cinnamon
2 sticks (½ pound) butter, melted
2 eggs, slightly beaten
2 teaspoons vanilla extract

Preheat the oven to 325 degrees. Butter and flour two 9-inch loaf pans.

In a large bowl, combine the apples, pecans, and sugar and stir well. Mix the flour with the soda, salt, spices, and butter; add to the apple mixture. Combine the eggs and vanilla and add to the batter. Mix well. Pour into the prepared pans. Bake for 1 hour, or until a wooden pick inserted near the center of the loaf comes out clean. Cool in the pans 10 minutes; then turn out onto a rack.

MAKES 2 LOAVES　　　　*Celebrations on the Bayou,* Monroe, LA

PUMPKIN SPICE BREAD

This is great served warm with whipped cream.

8 tablespoons (1 stick) butter, softened
1¼ cups sugar
2 eggs
1⅔ cups all-purpose flour
¼ teaspoon baking powder
1 teaspoon baking soda
1 teaspoon ground cinnamon
1¾ teaspoons ground ginger
½ teaspoon grated nutmeg
½ teaspoon ground cloves
½ teaspoon salt
1 cup canned pumpkin purée
½ cup finely chopped walnuts or pecans (optional)

Preheat the oven to 350 degrees. Butter and flour a 9-inch loaf pan.

Cream the butter and sugar in a large mixing bowl until light and fluffy. Beat in the eggs one at a time. Mix together the flour, baking powder, baking soda, cinnamon, ginger, nutmeg, cloves, and salt. Add to the creamed mixture alternately with ½ cup of water, mixing well after each addition. Beat in the pumpkin; stir in walnuts. Spoon into the prepared pan. Bake for 1 hour. Cool in pan for 10 minutes; remove to a wire rack to cool completely

MAKES 1 LOAF   *The Best of Wheeling,* Wheeling, WV

HARVEST LOAF BREAD

A delightful sweet bread.

2 cups canned pumpkin purée
4 eggs, beaten
1 cup vegetable oil
⅔ cup cold water
3⅓ cups all-purpose flour
2 teaspoons baking soda
3 cups sugar
2 teaspoons pumpkin pie spice
Dash of grated nutmeg
Dash of ground cinnamon
1 teaspoon salt
1 cup chopped walnuts
2 cups chocolate chips

Preheat the oven to 350 degrees. Grease and flour three 8-inch loaf pans.

Combine the pumpkin, eggs, oil, and water in a large bowl. Mix the flour with the baking soda, sugar, spices, and salt. Add to the first mixture; stir well. Fold in the nuts and chocolate chips. Turn into the prepared pans and bake for 50 to 60 minutes or until a cake tester inserted near the center of a loaf comes out clean. Cool in the pans for 10 minutes, then remove to a wire rack.

MAKES 3 LOAVES   *America Discovers Columbus,* Columbus, OH

SUN-DRIED TOMATO BREAD

2 cloves garlic
⅓ cup oil-packed sun-dried
  tomatoes
1 bunch scallions
2½ cups all-purpose flour
2 teaspoons baking powder
1¼ teaspoons salt
½ teaspoon baking soda
5 ounces provolone cheese, grated
¾ teaspoon dried rosemary
¾ teaspoon ground black pepper
⅓ cup pine nuts, lightly toasted
2 tablespoons solid vegetable
  shortening at room temperature
2 tablespoons sugar
2 large eggs
1¼ cups buttermilk

Preheat the oven to 350 degrees. Grease one 9-inch loaf pan or three 5 × 3 × 2-inch pans.

In a small saucepan, cook the garlic in boiling water to cover for 15 minutes. Meanwhile, drain and chop the tomatoes, reserving 2 tablespoons of the oil. Slice the scallions thin, and include 1 inch of the green part. In a large bowl, stir together the flour, baking powder, salt, and baking soda. Add the cheese, scallions, rosemary, pepper, sun-dried tomatoes, and pine nuts. Toss the mixture until combined. In a small bowl, whisk together the shortening, reserved oil, and sugar until the mixture is smooth.

When the garlic has finished cooking, drain, peel, and mash it with a fork. Add to the shortening mixture along with the eggs and butter-milk. Add the shortening mixture to the flour mixture and blend until well combined. Pour the batter into the prepared pan. Bake in the middle of the oven until a cake tester comes out clean, 25 to 30 minutes for the small loaves, 45 to 50 minutes for the large loaf. Cool the bread in the pan on a wire rack for 5 minutes. Turn onto the rack and cool completely. The bread keeps, wrapped tightly in foil and refrigerated, for up to 4 days.

MAKES 1 LARGE LOAF OR 3 MINI LOAVES

Maine Ingredients, Portland, ME

NEW YORK CHEDDAR CHEESE BREAD

All you need is soup to make this hearty bread into a delectable meal on a winter's night.

2 cups all-purpose flour
2 teaspoons baking powder
1 tablespoon sugar
½ teaspoon salt
8 tablespoons (1 stick) butter
1 cup grated sharp Cheddar cheese
1 tablespoon grated onion
1½ teaspoons dried dill weed
¾ cup milk
1 egg, lightly beaten

Preheat the oven to 350 degrees. Grease a 9-inch loaf pan.

In a large bowl, mix the flour with the baking powder, sugar, and salt. Using 2 knives or a pastry blender, cut in the butter until the mixture resembles coarse crumbs. Stir in the cheese, onion, and dill; mix well. Combine the milk and egg; pour into the flour mixture. Stir just until moistened. Turn in the prepared pan. Bake for 40 to 50 minutes or until the top is golden brown and the loaf shrinks slightly from the sides of the pan. Let cool 10 minutes before removing from the pan. Serve slightly warm.

MAKES 1 LOAF

Family & Company, Binghamton, NY

CALIFORNIA CALZONE

Inside these uniquely shaped crusty pizza sandwiches, you will find the distinctive flavor of tangy goat cheese.

1 recipe pizza dough (page 40)
Olive oil
4 ripe tomatoes, peeled, seeded, and
  sliced
4 ounces prosciutto, chopped
10 ounces chèvre cheese, crumbled
8 ounces Monterey Jack cheese,
  grated
¼ cup chopped fresh parsley
4 cloves garlic, minced
1 teaspoon dried thyme

Preheat the oven to 450 degrees. Divide the dough into 8 pieces. Roll out on a floured board into ¼-inch circles. Brush each circle lightly with olive oil. Arrange tomato slices on half a dough circle. Sprinkle with some of the prosciutto, cheeses, parsley, garlic, and thyme, leaving a ½-inch border. Fold the other half of the dough over, pressing the edges together with the tines of a fork to seal. Brush with olive oil and cut two small slits on top. Place on a cookie sheet. Repeat with the remaining dough circles. Bake for 20 to 30 minutes or until puffed and nicely browned.

SERVES 8   *San Francisco Encore,* San Francisco, CA

SOFT PRETZELS

1 package active dry yeast
1 scant tablespoon sugar
¾ cup warm water
½ teaspoon salt
2 cups all-purpose flour, or as
  needed
¼ cup baking soda
Coarse salt

Dissolve the yeast with the sugar in the warm water until bubbly; mix in the salt and enough flour to make a soft dough. Knead until the dough becomes smooth. In a 9- to 10-inch skillet, dissolve the baking soda in 4 cups of water. Heat slowly until the water is simmering.

Preheat the oven to 425 degrees. Separate the dough into 6 sections. Roll each piece into a long rope about ½ to 1 inch thick. Twist into pretzel shape. Using a slotted spoon, gently submerge 3 or 4 pretzels in simmering water for about 30 seconds. Remove with a slotted spoon and place the pretzels on a well-greased baking sheet that has been sprinkled with coarse salt. Sprinkle the tops of the pretzels with salt. Bake for 15 minutes or until golden brown.

NOTE: The recipe may be doubled.

MAKES 6 PRETZELS   *Settings,* Philadelphia, PA

PLAYGROUND FOR ALL CHILDREN
JUNIOR LEAGUE OF BILLINGS, MONTANA

The Junior League of Billings, Montana, working in cooperation with the City of Billings, sponsored the construction of the Playground for All Children, a barrier-free, all-accessible play area for disabled children. While especially designed for physically and mentally challenged children, the Playground provides an opportunity for children of all abilities to play together. This project is the first all-accessible public playground in the state of Montana, and one of only several in the Rocky Mountain region.

MEXICAN CORN BRUNCH BREAD

2 sticks (½ pound) butter
1 cup sugar
4 eggs
1 (4-ounce) can green chiles, seeded and chopped
1 (1-pound) can cream-style corn
½ cup shredded Monterey Jack cheese
½ cup mild Cheddar cheese
1 cup all-purpose flour
1 cup yellow cornmeal
4 teaspoons baking powder
¼ teaspoon salt

Preheat the oven to 350 degrees. Grease and flour a 13 × 9-inch baking dish.

In a mixing bowl, cream the butter and sugar until light and fluffy. Add the eggs one at a time, beating well. Add the chiles, corn, and cheeses; mix well. Stir together the flour, cornmeal, baking powder, and salt. Add to the corn mixture. Pour and scrape into the prepared pan. Put in the oven, reduce the heat to 300 degrees, and bake 1 hour. Serve warm.

SERVES 10   *Epicure,* Orange County, CA

BUTTERMILK CORNBREAD

Nothing takes the place of real iron skillets in real Southern cooking.

1 cup yellow cornmeal, coarse grind
¼ teaspoon baking powder
½ teaspoon salt
½ teaspoon baking soda
3 tablespoons solid vegetable shortening
1 cup buttermilk
1 egg, slightly beaten

Preheat the oven to 425 degrees. Stir the dry ingredients together in a large bowl. Place the shortening in an 8-inch cast-iron skillet and heat. Add the buttermilk and egg to the dry ingredients and mix well. Pour into the hot skillet. Bake for 25 minutes.

NOTE: May be frozen at completion. This is good when used for making cornbread dressing.

SERVES 6   *Junior League of Albany Cookbook,* Albany, NY

WEST TEXAS CORNBREAD

2 eggs
½ cup vegetable oil
1 cup sour cream
1 cup cream-style corn
1 cup yellow cornmeal
1 tablespoon baking powder
1 cup shredded Cheddar cheese
1 (4-ounce) can chopped jalapeño peppers

Preheat the oven to 400 degrees. Thoroughly grease a Bundt cake pan or a medium-size cast-iron skillet.

In a mixing bowl, beat the eggs; add the oil, sour cream, and corn and beat until combined. Mix the cornmeal with the baking powder and stir into the wet ingredients. Fold in the cheese and peppers.

Turn the batter into the prepared pan and bake for 30 to 40 minutes, until golden brown.

MAKES 1 CORNBREAD   *Seasoned with Sun,* El Paso, TX

SAVORY HERB BREAD

1 package active dry yeast
1½ cups warm water
2 tablespoons solid vegetable
   shortening
2 teaspoons salt
2 tablespoons sugar
1 teaspoon caraway seeds
½ teaspoon grated nutmeg
1 teaspoon ground sage
3 cups all-purpose flour
1 teaspoon butter

In a large mixing bowl, dissolve the yeast in the warm water. Add the shortening, salt, sugar, caraway seeds, nutmeg, sage, and half the flour. Beat at medium speed, scraping the sides of the bowl frequently. Add the remaining flour and blend until smooth. Scrape the sides of the bowl well, cover the bowl with a kitchen towel, and let rise in a warm place for 30 minutes. Beat the batter about 25 strokes. Spread evenly in a greased 8-inch loaf pan. Smooth the top and pat into shape. Cover and let rise about 40 minutes. Meanwhile, preheat the oven to 375 degrees. Bake the bread for 45 to 50 minutes. Remove from the pan and brush the top with butter. Cool on a rack.

MAKES 1 LOAF   *Very Virginia,* Hampton Roads, VA

DILL BREAD

1 package active dry yeast
¼ cup warm water (110–115
   degrees)
2 tablespoons plus ½ teaspoon sugar
1 cup sour cream, at room
   temperature
1 beaten egg plus 1 egg yolk
1 tablespoon butter, softened
1 scallion with top, chopped fine, or
   1 teaspoon onion flakes
1 tablespoon dried dill seed
1 tablespoon dried dill weed
1 teaspoon salt
2¾ cups bread flour or as needed

In a large bowl, sprinkle the yeast over the warm water and stir in ½ teaspoon of sugar. Let stand until foamy. Stir in the sour cream, egg, butter, scallion, 2 tablespoons sugar, the dill seed, dill weed, salt, and 1 cup of flour. Beat with a wooden spoon or mixer until well blended. Stir in as much of the remaining flour as possible with a spoon, then turn the dough out onto a floured surface. Knead in enough additional flour to make a moderately stiff dough. Continue kneading until the dough is smooth and elastic, about 8 minutes. Place in greased bowl; turn the dough to coat with oil. Cover with a kitchen towel and let rise until doubled, about 1¼ to 1½ hours. Punch dough down.

For braid: Divide the dough into 3 pieces. Roll each piece into an 18-inch rope and braid the 3 pieces together. Place on an ungreased baking sheet. Cover and let rise until doubled.

For rolls: Turn the dough out onto a lightly floured surface and roll to 1½-inch thickness. Cut with a biscuit cutter. Place on greased baking sheets. Cover and let rise until doubled, 30 to 60 minutes.

Beat the egg yolk with 2 tablespoons of water. Brush on rolls or loaf. Bake in a preheated oven at 350 degrees: 25 minutes for the loaf and 15 to 20 minutes for rolls.

MAKES 1 LOAF OR 24 TO 30 ROLLS

Even More Special, Durham, NC

BUTTERMILK RAISIN BREAD

1 cup raisins
1½ cups buttermilk
1 package active dry yeast
¼ cup sugar
2 eggs
8 tablespoons (1 stick) butter,
  melted
5 to 5½ cups all-purpose flour
1½ teaspoons salt
½ teaspoon baking soda

Add the raisins to the buttermilk in a saucepan and heat until warm. Cool to lukewarm. Add the yeast and sugar; let stand 5 minutes or until the yeast is dissolved.

Slightly beat the eggs in a large bowl. Add the cooled butter and stir in the buttermilk-yeast mixture. Stir together the flour, salt, and soda; add by thirds to the yeast-egg mixture, beating well after each addition. Turn out onto a well-floured board and knead the dough for 8 to 10 minutes. Place in an oiled bowl, brush with oil, cover with a kitchen towel, and let rise 1 hour or more, until doubled in bulk. Divide the dough in half and let it rest 15 to 20 minutes before shaping into 2 loaves. Place in well-greased 8-inch loaf pans. Cover and let rise until doubled (about 1 hour). Bake in a preheated 400 degree oven for 25 to 30 minutes, until the loaves are golden brown and sound hollow when thumped. Cool on a rack.

MAKES 2 LOAVES   *Clusters of Culinary Creations*, Kankakee, IL

SESAME BREAD

1 cup milk
2 teaspoons sugar
2 teaspoons salt
4 tablespoons (½ stick) unsalted
  butter
1 cup warm water (110–115 degrees)
2 tablespoons or 2 packages active
  dry yeast
7 to 8 cups unbleached all-purpose
  or bread flour
2 eggs, beaten
1 egg white
Sesame seeds

In a small saucepan, scald the milk. Add the sugar, salt, and butter. Stir well. Set aside to cool. Pour the warm water into a large mixing bowl. Add the yeast and stir until dissolved. To the yeast mixture, add the cooled milk and 3½ cups of flour. Beat until smooth with a wooden spoon or an electric mixer. Add the beaten eggs. Beat well. Gradually add enough of the remaining flour to make a soft dough that can be handled easily. Turn the dough out onto a floured surface and knead for 10 minutes or until smooth and elastic. Place in large greased bowl. Cover with a kitchen towel and let rise in a warm place until doubled in bulk, about 1½ hours.

Punch down the dough and divide it into thirds. Divide each third into 3 pieces and roll the 3 pieces into a rope about 15 inches long. Pinch the tops of the rope together and braid. Pinch the ends together and tuck under the braided loaf. Repeat with the remaining dough. Place each braid in a greased 9-inch loaf pan or place on a greased baking sheet. Cover and let rise until doubled in bulk.

Meanwhile, preheat the oven to 425 degrees. Beat the remaining egg white with 1 tablespoon of water. Brush on the loaves. Sprinkle generously with sesame seeds and brush again with egg white. Bake for 10 minutes at 425 degrees. Reduce the oven temperature to 375 degrees and continue baking until golden, 10 to 15 minutes. Remove from the oven. Remove from the pans to wire racks to cool completely before storing airtight or freezing.

MAKES 3 LOAVES   *Even More Special*, Durham, NC

GRANDMOTHER'S SWEDISH RYE BREAD

When Grandmother Johnson boarded the ship to emigrate from Sweden, this was one recipe she made certain was packed with her.

1 medium potato, peeled and cut up
2 packages active dry yeast
3 cups all-purpose flour, plus
    additional as needed
4 cups rye flour
3 cups lukewarm water
1 cup sugar
2 tablespoons salt
½ cup solid vegetable shortening
½ cup dark molasses
2 teaspoons sugar

Make potato water: Simmer the cut-up potato in 3 to 4 cups of water for half an hour. Remove potato (reserve for another use) and cool the water to lukewarm. Dissolve yeast in 2 cups of this water. Beat in the all-purpose flour. Cover the sponge and let it rise until doubled.

In a large bowl, sift the 4 cups of rye flour. Pour the 3 cups of lukewarm water over this flour to make a paste. Add the yeast sponge, the sugar, salt, shortening, and molasses. Mix in enough additional white flour to form a stiff dough. Turn out onto a floured surface and knead for 10 minutes or until the dough is smooth and elastic. Transfer the dough to a large well-greased bowl, grease the top, cover with a towel, and let rise in a warm place until doubled, about 2 hours. Punch the dough down and let rise again until doubled. Punch down and turn out onto a lightly floured surface. Divide the dough into 6 equal pieces and form into 6 round loaves. Grease 2 baking sheets and sprinkle with cornmeal. Arrange 3 loaves well apart on each sheet. Cover and let rise about 1½ hours, until nearly doubled.

Preheat the oven to 350 degrees. Bake the loaves for 1 hour. While the bread is still hot, dissolve 2 teaspoons of sugar in a little hot water and brush over the tops of the loaves to make a glaze.

MAKES 6 LOAVES   *Thyme for All Seasons,* Duluth, MN

BUNDT BREAD

This makes a beautiful loaf that easily pulls apart.

1 cup solid vegetable shortening
1½ teaspoons salt
¾ cup plus 1 tablespoon sugar
1 cup boiling water
2 packages active dry yeast
1 cup warm water
5½ to 6 cups all-purpose flour
2 eggs, well beaten
8 tablespoons (1 stick) butter

Combine the shortening, salt, and ¾ cup of sugar in a large mixing bowl. Add the boiling water and stir to dissolve the sugar and melt the shortening. In a small bowl, sprinkle the yeast over the warm water; add the remaining tablespoon of sugar and let stand until creamy, about 10 minutes.

Add 2 cups of flour to the shortening mixture and beat in the eggs. Add the dissolved yeast and gradually add enough of the remaining flour to form a soft dough. Cover with a kitchen towel and allow to rise in a warm place for 45 minutes or until the dough has doubled in size. Punch down. (At this point the dough may be refrigerated, covered tightly with plastic wrap, for 1 to 2 days.)

Melt 4 tablespoons of the butter. Grease two Bundt pans. Divide the dough in half and roll out on a floured surface ¼ to ½ inch thick. Cut into rounds with a biscuit cutter. Dip each round into the melted butter and stand the rounds up in one of the prepared pans, very close to each other, making a full circle. Repeat with the remaining dough and butter. Cover with a towel and let rise until very light—up to 3 hours if the dough has been chilled.

Preheat the oven to 350 degrees. Bake the loaves for 30 to 35 minutes, until they are golden brown and shrink slightly from the sides of the pan. Transfer to a rack to cool.

MAKES 2 LOAVES   *Encore! Nashville,* Nashville, TN

FRENCH BREAD

2 cups warm water
2 packages active dry yeast
1 tablespoon sugar
1 teaspoon salt
3 tablespoons vegetable oil
5 to 6 cups all-purpose flour, or as
    needed
2 tablespoons cornmeal

In large bowl, combine the warm water, yeast, and sugar. Let stand until creamy, about 10 minutes. Add the salt and 2 tablespoons of the oil. Stir in 4 cups of the flour. When it becomes difficult to stir, put some of the remaining flour on a flat surface, turn the dough out, and knead 10 to 12 minutes or until smooth and pliable, adding more flour if needed. Grease a large bowl with the remaining tablespoon of oil and place the dough in it, turning once to grease the top. Cover the bowl with a damp cloth and let rise in a warm place until doubled, about 1 hour.

Turn the dough out onto a floured surface and divide into fourths. Roll each section into a rectangle about 6 × 12 inches. Roll up like a jelly roll, starting with a long end, keeping it as tight as possible. Pinch the seams shut and shape the ends. Grease two baking sheets and sprinkle with cornmeal. Place the loaves seam side down on the sheets, positioning them well apart and stretching if necessary to make each loaf 15 inches long. Brush the tops with water; make a ¼-inch-deep slash down the length of each loaf. Allow to rise uncovered until doubled, about 1 hour.

Preheat the oven to 400 degrees. Place a pan of hot water on the floor of the oven. Brush the loaves with water, bake 10 minutes, brush with water again and bake 20 minutes longer. Bread should be a deep golden brown on top; it is done if it sounds hollow when thumped.

To freeze: Wrap cooled loaves tightly in plastic. Reheat bare loaves in a 400 degree oven for 10 to 15 minutes to restore crispness.

MAKES 4 LOAVES
Jambalaya, New Orleans, LA

YOUTH CHALLENGES
JUNIOR LEAGUE OF TYLER, TEXAS

The Youth Challenges program is a cooperative effort by the Junior League of Tyler, Texas, and the Tyler Independent School District to combat the problems of teen pregnancy, sexually transmitted diseases, and AIDS. The program, initiated in 1988 by the League, attempts to make middle and high school youth aware of the problems and responsibilities associated with teen sexuality, and gives them reasons and tools to say "no." Volunteers serve as facilitators in the classroom and as parent educators through curriculum review.

ORANGE-HONEY MUFFINS

1½ cups sifted all-purpose flour
½ cup sugar
2 teaspoons baking powder
½ teaspoon salt
¼ cup solid vegetable shortening
½ cup milk
2 eggs, beaten
1 thinly sliced orange with rind
Honey

Preheat the oven to 400 degrees. Sift together the dry ingredients and blend in the shortening. Add the milk and eggs together and stir until all ingredients are blended. Place in each well-greased muffin cup one slice of orange and one teaspoon honey. Top with batter, filling the cups ⅔ full, and bake 20 minutes. Turn out upside down.

MAKES 18 MUFFINS   *Recipe Jubilee,* Mobile, AL

CRANBERRY ISLAND MUFFINS

2 cups all-purpose flour
½ cup firmly packed brown sugar
½ cup toasted wheat germ
2 teaspoons baking powder
1 teaspoon baking soda
1 cup coarsely chopped fresh
  cranberries or frozen, thawed and
  drained
⅓ cup granulated sugar
¾ cup orange juice
⅓ cup vegetable oil
1 egg, slightly beaten
1½ teaspoons grated orange peel
1 teaspoon vanilla extract
½ cup chopped pecans

Preheat the oven to 400 degrees. Grease 12 muffin cups. In a large bowl, stir together the flour, brown sugar, wheat germ, baking powder, and baking soda. In a small bowl, stir the cranberries and sugar together. In a medium bowl, stir together the orange juice, oil, egg, orange peel, and vanilla until blended.

Make a well in the center of the dry ingredients; add the cranberry mixture and orange juice mixture and stir just to combine. Do not overmix. Fold in the pecans. Spoon batter into muffin cups, filling them ⅔ full. Bake 15 to 20 minutes or until a cake tester inserted in center of a muffin comes out clean. Cool 5 minutes on a wire rack before removing from muffin cups.

MAKES 12 MUFFINS   *Maine Ingredients,* Portland, ME

BEST EVER BLUEBERRY MUFFINS

6 tablespoons butter, softened
1¼ cups plus 2 teaspoons sugar
2 large eggs
2 cups all-purpose flour
½ teaspoon salt
2 teaspoons baking powder
½ cup milk
1 pint blueberries, washed and
  drained

Preheat the oven to 375 degrees. Cream the butter with 1¼ cups of sugar. Add the eggs, one at a time, and beat well. Whisk together the flour, salt, and baking powder and add to the egg mixture alternately with the milk.

Reserve ½ cup of blueberries; dry the remaining berries very well with paper towels. Crush the ½ cup of blueberries with a fork and mix them into the batter by hand. Fold in the remaining berries. Grease the flat tops of two 8-cup muffin pans and place paper cups in each well. Fill ⅞ full. Sprinkle with 2 teaspoons sugar. Bake for 30 minutes or until nicely browned. Cool for 30 minutes before removing from pan. Store uncovered or they will be too moist the second day.

MAKES 16 MUFFINS   *Clock Wise Cuisine,* Detroit, MI

BLUEBERRY MUFFIN CAKES

½ cup solid vegetable shortening
1½ cups sugar
2 eggs
2⅓ cups all-purpose flour
½ teaspoon salt
2½ teaspoons baking powder
½ teaspoon grated nutmeg
¾ cup milk
1½ cups fresh blueberries, rinsed
and dried
8 tablespoons (1 stick) butter,
melted
¼ teaspoon ground cinnamon

Preheat the oven to 350 degrees. Cream the shortening until light and fluffy. Gradually beat in ¾ cup of the sugar. Beat in the eggs one at a time. Mix the flour with the salt, baking powder, and nutmeg. Alternately add the dry ingredients and milk to the egg mixture, beginning and ending with the dry ingredients. Fold in the berries.

Spoon the batter into greased muffin cups, filling them ¾ full. Bake for 20 to 25 minutes. Remove the muffins from the pans and cool slightly. Meanwhile, mix the cinnamon with the remaining ¾ cup of sugar. Roll the muffins in melted butter, then in the cinnamon sugar.

MAKES 18 MUFFINS   *Tested, Tried and True*, Flint, MI

LEMON-DIPPED BLUEBERRY MUFFINS

Not too tart, not too sweet, just right.

1¾ cups all-purpose flour
1 cup sugar, or as needed
2½ teaspoons baking powder
¼ teaspoon salt
1 egg, well beaten
⅓ cup vegetable oil
¾ cup milk
1 cup fresh blueberries, washed and
dried
2 teaspoons grated lemon rind
2 tablespoons butter, melted
¼ teaspoon lemon juice

Preheat the oven to 400 degrees. In a large bowl, mix the flour with ½ cup of sugar, the baking powder, and salt. Make a well in the center. Combine the egg, oil, and milk. Add to the dry ingredients, stirring just until moistened. Toss the blueberries with 2 tablespoons of sugar and the lemon rind. Fold into the batter. Fill muffin papers or greased muffin pans ⅔ full. Bake for 20 minutes or until golden brown.

While the muffins bake, prepare the topping by mixing the melted butter and lemon juice. Dip the warm muffins in the butter mixture, then in sugar.

NOTE: The batter will keep if refrigerated overnight in paper-lined muffin pans covered with plastic wrap. Just bake, dip, and serve.

MAKES 14 MUFFINS   *To Market, to Market*, Owensboro, KY

L.I.N.K. CLINIC (LET'S INVEST NOW IN KIDS) JUNIOR LEAGUE OF SPRINGFIELD, MISSOURI

In 1992, the Junior League of Springfield, Missouri, joined forces with Advocates for a Healthy Community to start the L.I.N.K. (Let's Invest Now in Kids) Clinic. L.I.N.K. is the major source of preventive health care and the only consistently available health care for medically needy children. In addition, the clinic provides health education services to maximize primary prevention and to further educate families as healthcare consumers.

GRAHAM MUFFINS

1½ cups all-purpose flour
1½ cups graham flour
1 teaspoon salt
1 teaspoon baking soda
2 teaspoons baking powder
1 egg
½ cup sugar
½ cup molasses
2 tablespoons vegetable oil
1 cup buttermilk
½ cup California raisins (optional)

Preheat the oven to 350 degrees. Stir together the all-purpose flour, graham flour, salt, baking soda, and baking powder. Set aside. In a large bowl, beat the egg and sugar together. Add the molasses, oil, and buttermilk; mix. Add the dry ingredients and mix just until moistened. Fold in the raisins. Divide the batter among 18 greased and floured muffin cups and bake for 20 minutes.

MAKES 18 MUFFINS   *California Treasures,* Fresno, CA

MUNCHO MUFFINS

The batter, if well covered, can be kept in the refrigerator up to nine weeks.

1 quart buttermilk
1 (15-ounce) box raisin bran cereal
2 cups sugar
5 cups all-purpose flour
2 teaspoons salt
4 teaspoons baking soda
4 eggs, slightly beaten
2 sticks (½ pound) butter, melted

Put the buttermilk and raisin bran in a bowl and let stand while sifting the sugar, flour, salt, and soda together in a very large bowl. Add the eggs, melted butter, and buttermilk-bran mixture. Stir well. Fill well-greased muffin tins ⅔ full; bake at 400 degrees for 20 minutes.

BLUEBERRY MUFFINS: Use 3 cups of sugar and substitute bran flakes for raisin bran. Fold in 1 (8-ounce) can of blueberries, drained.

MAKES ABOUT 6 DOZEN MUFFINS

Home Cookin', Wichita Falls, TX

CHEESE MUFFINS

2 cups all-purpose flour
1 teaspoon salt
4 level teaspoons baking powder
2 tablespoons butter
1 cup grated cheese
1 cup milk

Preheat the oven to 425 degrees. Mix together the flour, salt, and baking powder in a large bowl. Cut in the butter with a pastry blender or two knives until the mixture resembles coarse crumbs. Stir in the grated cheese.

Add the milk all at once and stir quickly with a fork or whisk for 20 seconds. The batter should be lumpy; do not overmix. Divide the mixture among 12 greased muffin cups, filling them ⅔ full. Bake for 15 to 20 minutes, until lightly browned.

MAKES 12 MUFFINS   *Junior League of Dallas Cookbook (1920),* Dallas, TX

KITTY'S BISCUITS

2 cups self-rising flour
1 teaspoon sugar
½ cup plus 1 rounded tablespoon
  solid vegetable shortening
¾ cup very cold milk (buttermilk
  may be substituted, adding ⅛
  teaspoon baking soda)

Preheat the oven to 450 degrees. Mix the flour and sugar in a bowl and work the shortening into the flour until it resembles coarse crumbs. Pour enough milk into the mixture to make a soft dough. Handle lightly, using upward motions instead of pressing down. Toss onto a floured board and lightly roll out with a floured rolling pin to about ½ inch thickness for fluffy biscuits, ¼ inch for crispy biscuits.

Cut out with small biscuit cutter. Dip the cutter in flour often for easy cutting. Place on greased cookie sheet and bake on the top rack of the oven for 5 to 7 minutes, until golden brown.

To freeze, place a pan of unbaked biscuits in the freezer until firm, then package in plastic bags. They will keep as long as two weeks. Take out as many as needed, place on a greased pan, and thaw. Follow the same baking instructions.

MAKES 1½ DOZEN   *Gator Country Cooks*, Gainesville, FL

BUTTERY BISCUIT ROLLS

Delicious and simple to prepare. They may be prepared ahead and frozen.

2 sticks (½ pound) butter (do not
  substitute)
1 (8-ounce) carton sour cream
2 cups self-rising flour, unsifted

Preheat the oven to 350 degrees. Melt the butter in a large saucepan and remove from the heat. Add the sour cream and flour to the butter and mix thoroughly. Drop the batter into ungreased miniature muffin tins, filling them to the top. Bake for 25 minutes.

MAKES 2 DOZEN ROLLS   *Magic*, Birmingham, AL

QUICK SALLY LUNN

This version of an old Southern favorite is leavened with baking powder instead of yeast. Try it with Brunswick stew and salad.

2 eggs, separated
½ cup plus ¼ cup sugar
2 cups all-purpose flour
1 tablespoon baking powder
½ teaspoon salt
¾ cup milk
2 tablespoons butter, melted

Preheat the oven to 350 degrees. Beat the eggs yolks with ½ cup of sugar. Mix the flour, baking powder, and salt. Add the dry ingredients to the sugar mixture alternately with the milk. Stir in the melted butter. Beat the egg whites until stiff and fold into the batter. Pour into a greased loaf pan and sprinkle ¼ cup of sugar on top. Bake 40 to 45 minutes.

MAKES 1 LOAF   *Virginia Hospitality*, Newport, Hampton, and
Williamsburg, VA

TEA SCONES

2 cups all-purpose flour
½ cup sugar
2 teaspoons cream of tartar
1 teaspoon baking soda
¾ teaspoon salt
½ cup solid vegetable shortening
½ cup raisins, currants, snipped figs,
   or chopped prunes
2 eggs, slightly beaten
¼ cup milk

Preheat the oven to 400 degrees. Stir together the flour, sugar, cream of tartar, soda, and salt. Blend in the shortening with a pastry blender until the mixture resembles fine bread crumbs. Add remaining ingredients. Mix with a fork until just combined. Divide into two parts and turn each part out onto a floured board. Do not handle excessively. Flatten with a rolling pin into circles ½ inch or more thick. Cut into triangles (optional) and place on a greased and floured baking sheet. Bake for 15 minutes, or until golden brown. Serve warm and lightly buttered.

MAKES 1 ½ DOZEN   *Thru the Grapevine*, Elmira-Corning, NY

CREAM CHEESE BRAID

1 cup sour cream
½ cup sugar
1 teaspoon salt
8 tablespoons (1 stick) butter, melted
2 packages active dry yeast
½ cup warm water
2 eggs, beaten
4 cups all-purpose flour, or as
   needed
Cream cheese filling (below)
Glaze (below)

CREAM CHEESE FILLING
1 (8-ounce) package cream cheese,
   softened
¾ cup sugar
1 egg, beaten
⅛ teaspoon salt
2 teaspoons vanilla extract

GLAZE
2 cups confectioners' sugar
¼ cup milk
2 teaspoons vanilla extract

Put the sour cream in a small saucepan and place over low heat until it is warm. Stir in the sugar, salt, and butter; cool to lukewarm. In a large bowl, sprinkle the yeast over the warm water and let stand for 5 minutes or until it dissolves. Add the sour cream mixture, eggs, and enough flour to form a firm dough; mix well. Cover tightly with plastic wrap and refrigerate overnight.

The next day divide the dough into 4 parts. Roll out each part on a floured board into a 12 × 8-inch rectangle. Spread ¼ of the cream cheese filling on each. Roll up jelly roll fashion beginning with a long end. Pinch the edges together and fold the ends under slightly. Place the rolls seam side down on greased baking sheets. Make V-shaped slits at 1-inch intervals ⅔ of the way through the dough. Cover with a kitchen towel and let rise in a warm place for 1 hour or until doubled. Bake at 375 degrees for 12 to 15 minutes. Spread with glaze while warm.

For the cream cheese filling: Thoroughly combine all ingredients and use as directed.

For the glaze: Combine all ingredients and use as directed.

MAKES 4 BRAIDS   *Tennessee Tables*, Knoxville, TN

LIGHT-AS-A-FEATHER REFRIGERATOR ROLLS

1 cup solid vegetable shortening
1 cup sugar
2 teaspoons salt
1 cup boiling water
2 eggs, lightly beaten
2 packages active dry yeast
1 cup lukewarm water
6 cups all-purpose flour
4 tablespoons (½ stick) butter, melted

Place the shortening, sugar, and salt in a large mixing bowl. Add the boiling water. Beat with an electric mixer until the shortening is melted and the mixture has cooled slightly. Add the eggs; continue beating.

Dissolve the yeast in the lukewarm water. Add to the shortening mixture, beating well. Add flour gradually, continuing to beat until a soft dough forms. If dough becomes too stiff for electric mixer to handle, add remaining flour by hand. Cover tightly; store in the refrigerator up to 10 days.

When ready to bake, remove the desired portion to a floured surface. Roll out to less than ¼ inch thickness. Cut with a biscuit cutter. Brush the surface with butter; fold over, pinching edges together slightly. Place on lightly greased baking sheet. Cover; let rise until doubled in bulk, 1½ to 2 hours. Bake 450 degrees for 10 to 15 minutes. Brush tops with butter.

MAKES ABOUT 4 DOZEN ROLLS   *Perennials*, Gainesville, GA

THE DEMPSTER ROLLS

1 cup lukewarm unseasoned mashed potatoes
1 package active dry yeast or 1 (½-ounce) cake compressed yeast
½ cup lukewarm potato water, left over from boiling potatoes
⅔ cup solid vegetable shortening
⅔ cup sugar
1 cup milk, scalded
2 eggs, well beaten
2 teaspoons salt
6-8 cups all-purpose flour

Dissolve the yeast in the lukewarm potato water. Add the shortening, sugar, salt, and mashed potato to the scalded milk. When cool, add the yeast mixture. Blend well with the eggs and beat in enough flour to make a dough stiff enough to form a ball. Cover tightly and place in a well-greased bowl. Refrigerate overnight. After removing from the refrigerator, knead the dough thoroughly. Shape into ½-inch rolls and place ½ inch apart in well-greased cake pans. Cover with kitchen towels and let rise until doubled in size, about 2 hours. Bake in a preheated 450 degree oven for 12 to 15 minutes or until lightly browned.

BROWN AND SERVE ROLLS: Bake at 275 degrees for 20 to 25 minutes, until the rolls are set but not brown. Cool and freeze. To serve, bring to room temperature and bake at 400 degrees for 6-7 minutes, until browned.

MAKES ABOUT 5 DOZEN ROLLS

The Pear Tree, Knoxville, TN

BRAN REFRIGERATOR ROLLS

1 cup solid vegetable shortening
¾ cup sugar
1½ teaspoons salt
1 cup bran
1 cup boiling water
2 eggs, beaten
2 (½-ounce) cakes compressed yeast
    or 2 envelopes active dry yeast
1 cup lukewarm water
5 ½ to 6 cups all-purpose flour

Put the shortening, sugar, salt, and bran in a mixing bowl and add the boiling water. Stir until the shortening melts. Let cool to lukewarm. Add the eggs, then the yeast softened in the lukewarm water. Thoroughly blend in enough flour to make a soft dough. Place the dough in a clean well-greased bowl; turn to grease the top. Cover the bowl tightly with plastic wrap and refrigerate overnight, or until about 2 hours before baking.

Punch the dough down and turn out onto a floured surface. Use a sharp knife to cut off pieces of equal size. Shape into 1½-inch balls and arrange 2 inches apart on greased baking sheets (or for pan rolls, place the rolls just touching in greased 8- or 9-inch round cake pans). Cover lightly with a dry towel and let rise until doubled, about 2 hours.

Preheat the oven to 375 degrees. Bake the rolls 25 to 30 minutes, or until light brown.

MAKES ABOUT 3 ½ DOZEN

Huntsville Heritage, Huntsville, AL

LETA'S SOUR CREAM ROLLS

These are superb! Don't fail to try them.

2 sticks (½ pound) butter
3½ cups all-purpose flour
1 package active dry yeast
¼ cup warm water
1 egg plus 2 eggs yolks, beaten well
¾ cup sour cream
½ cup sugar

In a mixing bowl, cut the butter into the flour with a pastry blender or two knives. Add the yeast which has been dissolved in ¼ cup of warm water, the beaten eggs, and the sour cream. Mix well. Cover the bowl with a damp cloth and place in the refrigerator for at least 2 hours or overnight if possible.

On a well-floured board, roll the dough into an oblong approximately ¼ inch thick. Sprinkle with half the sugar. Fold one side ¾ of the way over, then fold the other side over. Roll out to the original size. Sprinkle with the remaining sugar and repeat the folding process. Again roll into an oblong. Cut the dough into strips ½ inch wide and about 5 inches long. Twist into small rods. The shape is up to you; either figure eights (tucking ends under so they won't separate during baking), small loops, or even knots. Place 1 inch apart on a greased baking sheet. Bake immediately in a 350 degree oven about 12 to 15 minutes.

NOTE: These rolls are sweet flaky dreams. They are simple to make, there is no kneading required, and they do not have to rise before cooking. This is an excellent party recipe. Shape the rolls and refrigerate on a baking sheet until time to bake.

MAKES ABOUT 3 DOZEN SMALL ROLLS

Cotton Country Cooking, Morgan County, AL

POTATO ICEBOX ROLLS

1½ cups milk, scalded and cooled to lukewarm (see recipe above)
½ cup lukewarm unseasoned mashed potato
½ cup water from cooking potato
½ cup sugar
8 tablespoons (1 stick) butter, softened
1 package active dry yeast
2 teaspoons salt
6-7 cups all-purpose flour, or as needed

Combine the milk, mashed potato and potato water, sugar, butter, yeast, and salt in the large bowl of an electric mixer. Add 3 cups of flour; beat well and allow to rest 15 minutes. Add the remaining 3-4 cups flour gradually to make a stiff but sticky dough. Attach a dough hook to the mixer and process, adding a little flour if necessary, for 5 minutes. (If not using a dough hook, turn the dough out onto a lightly floured surface and knead 10 minutes, until smooth and elastic.) Transfer to a greased bowl; cover tightly and refrigerate. Punch the dough down every hour for 3 or 4 hours or until dough is completely chilled. Use immediately or refrigerate up to 5 days.

For dinner rolls: Roll out the dough to ½ inch thickness on a lightly floured surface; cut into desired shapes. Place on a greased cookie sheet; cover loosely with a kitchen towel. Let rise in a warm place 1 to 1½ hours. Preheat the oven to 400 degrees. Bake 20 minutes.

NOTE: Or substitute ½ cup nonfat dry milk dissolved in 1½ cups of warm water.

MAKES 5–6 DOZEN DINNER ROLLS

The Carolina Collection, Fayetteville, NC

STICKY BUNS

Potato icebox roll dough (see recipe above)
Butter, softened
Cinnamon
Granulated sugar
Heavy cream or evaporated milk
Brown sugar
Chopped pecans

Using the desired amount of dough, roll it out on a lightly floured surface into a rectangle ¼ inch thick. Spread generously with butter, sprinkle with cinnamon and granulated sugar. Roll as for jelly roll, starting with a long end. Cut into 1-inch pieces. Choose a baking pan with 2-inch sides. Cover the bottom of the pan with a thin layer of brown sugar. Pour in cream or milk to ¼ inch depth. Sprinkle heavily with chopped pecans. Place the rolls, cut side up, ½ inch apart in the prepared pan. Cover; let rise in a warm place for 1 to 1½ hours. Preheat the oven to 400 degrees. Bake the buns 20 minutes. While hot, invert the pan onto a serving plate. Serve warm.

MAKES 5–6 DOZEN   *The Carolina Collection,* Fayetteville, NC

ORANGE ROLLS

Terrific flavor and color.

1 package active dry yeast
¼ cup warm water
1 cup sugar
1 teaspoon salt
2 eggs
½ cup sour cream
8 tablespoons (1 stick) butter, melted
2¾ to 3 cups all-purpose flour
2 tablespoons grated orange rind

Dissolve the yeast in the warm water in a small bowl. In the large bowl of an electric mixer combine ¼ cup of the sugar, the salt, eggs, sour cream, and 6 tablespoons of the melted butter. Gradually add 2 cups of flour, beating until smooth. Work in enough of the remaining flour to form a soft dough. Let rise in a warm place, covered with a towel, until doubled, about 2 hours.

Turn the dough out onto a well-floured surface and knead 15 times. Roll half the dough into a 12-inch circle. Combine the remaining ¾ cup of sugar and the grated orange rind. Brush the dough circle with 1 tablespoon of melted butter and sprinkle with half the orange-sugar mixture. Cut into 12 wedges. Roll up, starting with the wide end. Repeat with the remaining dough. Place point side down in three rows in a greased nonstick 13 × 9-inch pan. Cover with a towel and let rise in warm place about an hour.

Meanwhile, preheat the oven to 350 degrees. Bake the rolls for 20 to 30 minutes, until golden. Top with glaze.

GLAZE
¾ cup sugar
½ cup heavy cream
2 tablespoons orange juice
4 tablespoons (½ stick) butter

Combine the sugar, cream, orange juice, and butter in a saucepan and boil for 3 minutes, stirring constantly. Pour over the rolls when removed from oven.

SERVES 10–12   *Sunflower Sampler,* Wichita, KS

CINNAMON ROLLS

2½ cups sifted cake flour
1½ teaspoons baking powder
½ teaspoon salt
3 tablespoons solid vegetable shortening
¾ cup milk
12 tablespoons (1½ sticks) butter
⅔ cup plus ½ cup firmly packed brown sugar
1 teaspoon ground cinnamon
1 cup raisins

Preheat the oven to 425 degrees. Sift the flour, baking powder, and salt together. Cut in the shortening with a pastry blender or two knives. Add the milk all at once and stir well. Turn out onto a slightly floured board and knead for 30 seconds. Roll out ¼ inch thick into a rectangle 15 inches long.

Cream 4 tablespoons of the butter and ⅔ cup of brown sugar together with the cinnamon. Spread evenly on the dough. Sprinkle with raisins. Roll up as for a jelly roll, starting with a long end, and cut into 1¼-inch slices.

Melt the remaining 8 tablespoons of butter with the remaining ½ cup of brown sugar in an 8 × 8-inch baking pan. Place the dough slices in the syrup, cut side down. Bake at 425 degrees for 15 minutes. Reduce the heat to 350 degrees and bake 15 to 20 minutes longer.

MAKES 12 LARGE ROLLS

Junior League of Dallas Cookbook, Dallas, TX

GOOEY BUNS

DOUGH
1 package active dry yeast
¼ cup plus 2 tablespoons sugar
¼ cup warm water (105–110 degrees)
1 tablespoon salt
2 cups hot water
⅓ cup solid vegetable shortening
1 egg, lightly beaten
5½ to 6 cups all-purpose flour

SYRUP
12 tablespoons (1½ sticks) butter
1¾ cups firmly packed brown sugar
3 tablespoons half-and-half
1¾ cups chopped pecans

FILLING
12 tablespoons (1½ sticks) butter, melted
½ cup granulated sugar
¼ cup ground cinnamon

Dissolve the yeast and 2 tablespoons of the sugar in the warm water. Allow to stand for 5 minutes. Meanwhile, dissolve the salt and ¼ cup sugar in the hot water. Add the shortening and mix until the shortening is melted. Add the egg, 2 cups of flour, and the yeast mixture. Beat until smooth. Add 2 more cups of flour, working the dough until moistened. Add the remaining 1½ to 2 cups of flour and work the dough until smooth. Place the dough in a greased bowl, turning to coat all sides. Cover tightly with plastic wrap and let rise in the refrigerator overnight.

In a large saucepan, melt the butter. Add the brown sugar and half-and-half; bring to a simmer. Cover the surface of two 9 × 13-inch pans with this syrup. Sprinkle evenly with pecans. Remove the dough from the refrigerator; divide in half. On a floured surface, roll each dough half into a 12 × 8-inch rectangle.

Spread the dough with the melted butter. Combine the granulated sugar and cinnamon; sprinkle over the dough. Starting from a long side, roll each rectangle jelly roll style. Pinch the outside edge to the main body of the dough. Slice into 1-inch pieces. Place the slices cut side down in the prepared pans, leaving space between for expansion. Cover with a kitchen towel and let rise until doubled in size, 1 hour or longer. Bake in a preheated 350 degree oven for 20 to 25 minutes. While the buns are still hot, loosen the edges with a knife and invert each pan over a serving platter. Allow the pan to stay in place for a minute or two before removing.

MAKES 24 BUNS *A Cleveland Collection*, Cleveland, OH

TARGETED INTERVENTION PROGRAM (TIP)
JUNIOR LEAGUE OF NORMAN, OKLAHOMA

The Targeted Intervention Program (TIP) is a dropout prevention program that works with seventh and eighth grade students who have been identified as "at risk" of dropping out of school. The Junior League of Norman, Oklahoma, works with the Norman Public School System to provide volunteers and funds for the program. League members volunteer as tutors, mentors, resource coordinators, advisors and chaperones, and emphasis is one-on-one contact with the students.

CHOCOLATE CHIP BOURBON PECAN LOAF

This wonderfully rich bread may be served as a dessert. It is best served the day after it is made.

2 cups all-purpose flour
1 teaspoon baking powder
¾ teaspoon baking soda
½ teaspoon salt
2 eggs
8 tablespoons (1 stick) butter, softened
½ cup pure maple syrup
⅓ cup packed dark brown sugar
½ cup buttermilk
½ cup chocolate chips
1 cup coarsely chopped pecans
5 tablespoons Bourbon whiskey

Preheat the oven to 350 degrees. Oil a 9-inch loaf pan.

In a medium bowl, stir together the flour, baking powder, baking soda, and salt. Set aside. Beat the eggs, butter, syrup, and sugar together with an electric mixer at medium speed until light and fluffy. Reduce the speed to low. Add the flour mixture and buttermilk alternately to the egg mixture, beating well after each addition. Stir in the chocolate chips, pecans, and Bourbon. Pour into the prepared pan, smoothing the top. Bake for 50 minutes to 1 hour or until a tester inserted near the center comes out clean.

Allow the loaf to cool in the pan for 10 minutes. Remove the loaf from the pan and cool completely on a wire rack. Store in a sealed plastic bag or airtight container.

MAKES 1 LOAF   *Gourmet L.A.*, Los Angeles, CA

CRANBERRY CRUNCH CAKE

TOPPING
¾ cup chopped almonds, pecans, or walnuts
4 teaspoons sugar
½ teaspoon ground cinnamon

BATTER
8 tablespoons (1 stick) butter, softened
1 cup sugar
2 eggs
2 cups all-purpose flour
1 teaspoon baking powder
1 teaspoon baking soda
½ teaspoon salt
1½ teaspoons almond extract
1 cup sour cream
1 (16-ounce) can whole-berry cranberry sauce

Preheat the oven to 350 degrees. Grease a 10-inch tube pan and spread the combined topping ingredients on the bottom. Set aside.

In a large bowl, cream the butter and sugar until fluffy. Add the eggs one at a time, beating well. Mix the flour, baking powder, baking soda, and salt together. Stir the almond extract into the sour cream. Mix the flour mixture and the sour cream alternately into the butter mixture. Pour half the batter into the prepared pan. Carefully spread cranberry sauce over batter. Pour the remaining batter over the cranberry sauce. Bake 55 minutes. Cool 5 minutes in inverted pan. Serve warm.

MAKES 1 CAKE   *Sassafras! The Ozarks Cookbook*, Springfield, MO

BLUEBERRY BUCKLE

4 tablespoons (½ stick) butter,
    softened
¾ cup sugar
1 egg
1 ½ cups all-purpose flour
2 teaspoons baking powder
½ cup milk
2 cups fresh blueberries (frozen
    berries, thawed and drained, may
    be substituted)

CRUMB TOPPING
½ cup sugar
⅓ cup all-purpose flour
½ teaspoon ground cinnamon
4 tablespoons (½ stick) butter, cut
    up

Preheat the oven to 375 degrees. Grease and flour an 8-inch square pan.

In a large bowl, cream together the butter and sugar until fluffy. Blend the egg into the creamed mixture. In another bowl, whisk together the flour, baking powder, and salt. Add the flour mixture alternately with milk to the creamed mixture, beating after each addition. Gently fold the blueberries into the batter.

Pour the batter into the prepared pan. Sprinkle evenly with crumb topping (see below). Bake for 40 to 45 minutes, or until a toothpick inserted near the center comes out clean. Place on a rack to cool. Cut into squares and serve warm as a coffee cake or cooled, topped with whipped cream, for dessert.

To prepare the topping: in a small bowl, mix together the sugar, flour, and cinnamon. With 2 knives or a pastry blender cut the butter into the sugar mixture until the mixture resembles coarse meal.

SERVES 8   *The California Heritage Cookbook,* Pasadena, CA

TOFFEE NUT PEAR COFFEE CAKE

2 cups all-purpose flour
½ teaspoon salt
1 teaspoon ground cinnamon
½ teaspoon grated nutmeg
2 cups packed brown sugar (no
    lumps)
8 tablespoons (1 stick) butter
2 large Bartlett pears, peeled, cored,
    and cut into eighths
1 teaspoon baking soda
¾ cup sour cream
1 egg, lightly beaten
½ cup chopped walnuts

Preheat the oven to 350 degrees. Butter a 9-inch square baking pan.

In a large bowl, whisk together the flour, salt, cinnamon, and nutmeg. Mix in the brown sugar. Cut in the butter with a pastry blender or two knives. Spoon half the butter-flour mixture evenly into the prepared pan. Top with pears. Stir the baking soda into the sour cream and add the egg. Mix into the remaining flour mixture. Spoon over the pears and sprinkle with walnuts. Bake for 40 to 50 minutes, or until a wooden pick inserted near the center comes out clean. Serve warm.

MAKES 1 COFFEE CAKE   *Without Reservations,* Pittsburgh, PA

RASPBERRY CREAM CHEESE COFFEE CAKE

CAKE
2½ cups all-purpose flour
¾ cup sugar
12 tablespoons (1½ sticks) butter
½ teaspoon baking powder
½ teaspoon baking soda
¼ teaspoon salt
¾ cup sour cream
1 egg, lightly beaten
1 teaspoon almond extract

Preheat the oven to 350 degrees. Grease and flour a 9-inch springform pan.

In a large bowl, combine the flour and sugar; cut in the butter, using a pastry blender or two knives, until the mixture resembles coarse crumbs. Remove 1 cup of crumbs for the topping. To the remaining crumb mixture, add the baking powder, soda, salt, sour cream, egg, and almond extract; blend well. Spread the dough over the bottom and 2 inches up the side of the prepared springform pan. The dough should be ¼ inch thick on all sides.

FILLING
1 (8-ounce) package cream cheese, softened
¼ cup sugar
1 egg
½ cup raspberry jam

In a small bowl, combine the cream cheese, sugar, and egg; blend well. Pour over the dough in the pan. Carefully spoon jam evenly over the cheese filling.

TOPPING
½ cup sliced almonds

In a small bowl, combine the 1 cup reserved crumb mixture and the almonds; sprinkle over the top. Bake for 50 to 60 minutes, or until the cream cheese filling is set and the crust is a deep golden brown. Cool in the pan for 15 minutes. Remove the sides of the pan. Serve warm or cool. Cover and refrigerate leftovers.

MAKES 1 COFFEE CAKE *A River Runs Backward,* Jacksonville, FL

SAN ANTONIO ZOO EDUCATION PROGRAMS—DOCENT PROGRAM, SUMMER ZOO CAMP, EDUCATION CENTER
JUNIOR LEAGUE OF SAN ANTONIO, TEXAS

The San Antonio Zoo's education programs were started by the Junior League of San Antonio working in collaboration with the Zoo staff and the San Antonio Zoological Society in 1969. Junior League volunteers started the docent program with League volunteers in 1969, and today the program includes 156 volunteers from the community at large. The League started the Zoo Camp program for elementary age children and created and funded the educational facility at the Zoo, as well.

COWBOY COFFEE CAKE

2½ cups all-purpose flour

1½ cups firmly packed light brown sugar

½ cup plus 2 tablespoons granulated sugar

½ teaspoon salt

1½ teaspoons ground cinnamon

12 tablespoons (1½ sticks) butter, softened

1 cup coarsely chopped walnuts or pecans

¼ heaping teaspoon grated nutmeg

1 teaspoon baking soda

1 egg

1 cup buttermilk

Preheat the oven to 350 degrees. Butter and flour a 13 × 9 × 2-inch pan.

Combine the flour, brown sugar, ½ cup of the granulated sugar, the salt, and 1 teaspoon of the cinnamon in a mixing bowl. With the mixer on low speed, blend in the butter until the mixture is crumbly. Remove 1½ cups of the crumb mixture and mix with the nuts. Press 1¼ cups of the nut mixture onto the bottom of pan.

Take ¼ cup of the nut mixture and add the remaining ½ teaspoon cinnamon, the nutmeg, and the 2 tablespoons of sugar. Set aside for topping. Mix the remaining cup of the nut mixture into the remaining crumb mixture and add the baking soda, egg, and buttermilk. Mix at medium speed for ½ minute. Pour this batter over the crumb mixture in the pan. Sprinkle with reserved topping. Bake for 40 to 45 minutes. Serve warm or at room temperature.

MAKES 1 COFFEE CAKE

The Star of Texas Cookbook, Houston, TX

ST. TIMOTHY'S COFFEE CAKE

Named for St. Timothy's church and a great favorite of Winston-Salem.

2 sticks (½ pound) butter, softened

2 cups sugar

½ teaspoon vanilla extract

2 eggs

2 cups all-purpose flour

1 teaspoon baking powder

¼ teaspoon salt

1 teaspoon ground cinnamon

1 cup chopped nuts

½ cup golden raisins

1 cup sour cream

Cinnamon sugar to sprinkle

Preheat the oven to 350 degrees. Grease and flour a Bundt pan.

Cream the butter until light and fluffy; add the sugar gradually and continue to beat. Blend in the vanilla. Add the eggs, one at a time, beating well after each addition. Whisk together the flour, baking powder, salt and cinnamon; add the nuts and raisins and stir to coat well. Add the dry ingredients to the creamed mixture alternately with the sour cream. Blend well (the batter looks like whipped cream tinged with honey).

Turn the batter into the prepared pan. Sprinkle with cinnamon sugar. Bake for 1 hour or until the cake tests done. Leave in the pan for at least 1 hour before turning out. Turn out and sprinkle with more cinnamon sugar.

MAKES 1 COFFEE CAKE

Heritage of Hospitality, Winston-Salem, NC

BREAKFASTS

CHEESE BLINTZES

CREPES
2 eggs
½ teaspoon salt
1 cup all-purpose flour, sifted
1 cup water
Melted butter

Combine the eggs and salt. Beat until lemon-colored. Alternately add flour and water, beating until smooth. The mixture should be the consistency of cream. Add more water if it is too thick.

Butter a 6-inch skillet or crepe pan and heat on medium heat. Pour 2 tablespoons of batter onto the skillet to make a very thin pancake, tilting the skillet from side to side to cover the bottom. Cook about 30 seconds, on one side only. Cool on paper toweling, cooked side up, stacking the crepes as they are made. Regrease the skillet as necessary. Continue until all the batter is used.

FILLING
1 (8-ounce) package cream cheese, softened
1 pound farmer cheese
1 egg, beaten
Sugar
¼ teaspoon salt

Unsalted butter, for frying
Sour cream

Combine the cheeses in a mixing bowl. Add the egg and stir until smooth. Add 1 tablespoon of sugar and the salt; stir to mix well. Place a rounded tablespoon of filling on the cooked side of each crepe and fold over all sides into an envelope shape. As the blintzes are made, place them on a platter, folded side down, and refrigerate until ready to serve. Or they may be wrapped in foil and frozen at this point.

To fry the blintzes, melt 2 to 3 tablespoons of butter in a skillet over moderate heat. Add the blintzes and cook until golden brown on one side; turn and brown the other side. The blintzes should be crisp and the filling warmed through. Serve hot, accompanied by a bowl of beaten sour cream to be spooned on at the table.

MAKES 12 TO 14; SERVES 4   *Jacksonville County Cookbook,*
Jacksonville, FL

COUCHE-COUCHE

Couche-couche has long been a Cajun breakfast favorite. It is simply cornmeal, water, and salt cooked in a well-greased iron skillet and served with caillet (clabber) and syrup. There was a time when this simple breakfast was a matter of economic necessity. Today, many people consider it a real treat.

¼ cup vegetable oil
2 cups cornmeal
¾ teaspoon baking powder
1 teaspoon salt
½ cup milk

Heat the oil in a 10-inch black iron pot. Mix the cornmeal, baking powder, and salt. Add the milk and 1 cup of water, making sure it is not too dry. The mixture will be thick. Spoon into the hot oil: cover to steam and form a crust, about 10 minutes. Uncover and stir. Break into small pieces. Lower the heat; stir frequently while cooking for the next 15 minutes. Serve as a cereal with cold milk or yogurt.

SERVES 4   *Tell Me More,* Lafayette, LA

OVERNIGHT CHILE EGGS

8 eggs

6 slices bread, crusts removed, cut into ½-inch squares

4 tablespoons (½ stick) butter, cut into ¼-inch squares

2 cups milk

2 cups green chiles, chopped

1½ cups grated Monterey Jack cheese, or a mixture of your choice

Salt and pepper to taste

In a large bowl, beat the eggs slightly and add the bread, butter, milk, chiles, grated cheese, salt, and pepper. Mix together and pour into a large rectangular baking pan that has been well greased. Refrigerate, covered, at least 1 hour or overnight. Bake uncovered in a 300 degree oven for 1 hour, until puffed and golden brown.

SERVES 6–8   *La Piñata,* McAllen, TX

SOUR CREAM PANCAKES

2½ cups all-purpose flour

1 tablespoon baking powder

2 teaspoons baking soda

1 teaspoon salt

1 tablespoon sugar

3 eggs

2 cups buttermilk

1 cup sour cream

2 tablespoons melted butter

Preheat a griddle over moderate heat while you mix the batter.

Whisk together the flour, baking powder, baking soda, salt and sugar into a wide-mouthed pitcher or a bowl. In a separate bowl, beat the eggs; blend in the buttermilk, sour cream, and melted butter. Slowly stir the egg mixture into the dry ingredients, mixing only until dampened. The batter should be lumpy.

When the griddle is hot enough so that a drop of cold water will dance on it, pour about 3 tablespoons of batter for each pancake, spacing the cakes well apart. Bake until the surface is covered with bubbles; turn and bake the flip side until brown. As the pancakes are baked, stack them on a heated plate and serve at once.

SERVES 8   *Home Cookin',* Wichita Falls, TX

PUMPKIN PUFF PANCAKES

1 cup all-purpose flour

2 teaspoons baking powder

½ teaspoon baking soda

¼ teaspoon salt

⅛ teaspoon grated nutmeg

2 large eggs

2 tablespoons butter, melted

1 cup canned pumpkin purée

½ cup unflavored yogurt

2 tablespoons sugar

2 teaspoons lemon juice

1 teaspoon vanilla extract

Warmed maple syrup

In a small bowl, whisk the flour, baking powder, baking soda, salt, and nutmeg together. Set aside. In a large bowl, whisk together the eggs and melted butter. Add the pumpkin, yogurt, sugar, lemon juice, and vanilla. Blend in the dry ingredients and mix gently until just evenly moistened. Drop by heaping tablespoonful into a hot greased griddle. When firm and lightly browned, flip and cook other side. Serve immediately with warmed maple syrup.

SERVES 4   *Simply Classic,* Seattle, WA

APPLE PUFFED PANCAKE WITH ORANGE SYRUP

Mom has made this for fifty years.

PANCAKE
6 eggs
1½ cups milk
1 cup all-purpose flour
3 tablespoons granulated sugar
1 teaspoon vanilla extract
½ teaspoon salt
¼ teaspoon ground cinnamon
8 tablespoons (1 stick) butter
2 apples, peeled and sliced thin
2 tablespoons brown sugar

Preheat the oven to 425 degrees. Combine the eggs, milk, flour, granulated sugar, vanilla, salt, and cinnamon in a mixer bowl, blender, or food processor. Blend and set aside. Melt the butter in a 9 × 13-inch glass baking dish. Layer the apples in the melted butter and return to the oven until the butter sizzles. Do not let the butter brown. Remove the pan from the oven; immediately pour the batter over the apples and sprinkle with brown sugar. Bake for 20 minutes or until puffed and golden. Serve immediately with syrup.

ORANGE SYRUP
1 cup firmly packed brown sugar
½ cup orange juice
2 tablespoons grated orange peel

Combine all ingredients in a small saucepan while the pancake is baking. Simmer over low heat for 5 minutes. Pass the syrup with the pancake.

SERVES 6

The Bountiful Arbor, Ann Arbor, MI

APPLE FLENSJES (DUTCH APPLE PANCAKES)

1 cup all-purpose flour
1 cup dark beer
2 eggs, separated
4 to 6 tablespoons granulated sugar, depending on desired sweetness
1 teaspoon ground cinnamon
4 tablespoons (½ stick) butter, or as needed
4 tart apples (McIntosh are good), cored and sliced into 4 or 5 rings
Dark brown or confectioners' sugar, sweetened whipped cream or vanilla ice cream

Mix the flour and beer in a large bowl and beat in the egg yolks and sugar thoroughly. Beat the egg whites until stiff and add to the flour-beer mixture spoonful by spoonful, stirring well after each addition. Add the cinnamon.

Melt 4 tablespoons of butter in large heavy skillet and sauté the apple slices for 2 to 3 minutes on each side, until they are tender but not too soft. Remove to a plate. This may be done in advance. Butter the skillet, arrange a few apple slices in it about 2 inches apart, and ladle some of the batter over each apple slice to make a pancake. Cook about 2 to 3 minutes, turn and cook another 2 to 3 minutes until the pancake in done. Sprinkle generously with brown or confectioners' sugar or serve with sweetened whipped cream or vanilla ice cream. If brown sugar is used, the pancakes may be put under the broiler quickly, about 2 minutes, to melt sugar. Serve immediately.

SERVES 6–8

New York Entertains, New York, NY

GINGERBREAD PANCAKES

Serve with maple syrup or melted butter with honey.

2¼ cups all-purpose flour
½ teaspoon salt
1 teaspoon ground cinnamon
1 teaspoon grated nutmeg
1 teaspoon ground ginger
½ teaspoon ground cloves
1½ teaspoons baking powder
1½ teaspoons baking soda
1 tablespoon instant coffee granules
1 egg
4 tablespoons (½ stick) butter,
    melted
¼ cup packed brown sugar
¾ cup buttermilk

In a wide-mouth pitcher or large mixing bowl, whisk together the flour, salt, spices, baking powder, baking soda, and coffee granules. In a small bowl, beat the egg and blend in the butter, brown sugar, buttermilk, and ¾ cup of water. Stir into the dry ingredients, mixing only until dampened. The batter will be lumpy.

Pour about ¼ cup of batter per pancake onto a preheated nonstick griddle. Bake until covered with bubbles; turn and brown the other side. Serve hot.

SERVES 8   *Hearts and Flours,* Waco, TX

STEVE'S FAVORITE WAFFLES

2 eggs separated
2 cups all-purpose flour
4 teaspoons baking powder
½ teaspoon salt
2 tablespoons sugar
1¾ cups milk
8 tablespoons (1 stick) butter,
    melted

Preheat a waffle iron. Beat the egg whites until stiff and set aside. Whisk together the flour, baking powder, salt, and sugar in a large bowl. Gradually add the milk, beaten egg yolks, and butter. Stir well. Fold in the egg whites. Pour into waffle iron following the manufacturer's directions and bake until the steaming stops and the waffles are golden brown.

MAKES 6 TO 8   *Hearts and Flours,* Waco, TX

FABULOUS FRENCH TOAST

1 loaf unsliced white or French
    bread
1 cup milk
¼ cup granulated sugar
4 eggs, beaten
1 teaspoon vanilla extract
¼ teaspoon salt
¼ cup bacon grease or vegetable oil
Confectioners' sugar for garnish
Maple syrup

Cut the bread into ¾-inch-thick slices. Heat the milk in a saucepan; add the sugar, stirring to dissolve. Remove from the heat; cool slightly. Add the eggs, vanilla, and salt; mix well. Dip each slice of bread into the milk mixture until well coated. Place in a flat baking dish and pour the remaining liquid over the bread. Refrigerate, covered, overnight.

In a heavy skillet, fry the bread in very hot bacon grease until golden on both sides. Sprinkle with confectioners' sugar. Serve hot with maple syrup.

VARIATION: Add 2 tablespoons of Grand Marnier to the milk; decrease the sugar to 1 tablespoon and the vanilla to ½ teaspoon.

SERVES 4   *Peachtree Bouquet,* Dekalb County, GA

PAIN PERDU

An elegant French toast with a touch of lemon, for a company brunch. This is also a family favorite.

2 eggs
½ cup granulated sugar
1 cup milk
1 teaspoon vanilla extract
1 teaspoon grated lemon peel
8 slices day-old French bread, ½ inch thick
4 tablespoons (½ stick) butter, or as needed
Confectioners' sugar
Grated nutmeg

In a small bowl, beat the eggs and granulated sugar until thick. Stir in the milk, vanilla, and lemon peel. Arrange the bread in a single layer in a shallow dish; pour the egg mixture over the slices and let stand for 30 minutes. Heat the butter in a large skillet; sauté the bread until golden brown, about 6 minutes on each side. Arrange on warm platter; sprinkle with confectioners' sugar and grated nutmeg. Nice with syrup.

SERVES 4

Epicure, Orange County, CA

CHEESE STRATA

Prepare on Christmas Eve to help relieve Christmas morning bedlam.

10 slices white bread
8 ounces sliced cheese (American or cheddar)
4 ounces diced ham
6 eggs
3 cups milk
Salt to taste
8 tablespoons (1 stick) butter, melted
1 teaspoon prepared mustard
2 to 4 tablespoons finely chopped onion

Oil a 13 × 9-inch casserole or baking dish. Using a biscuit cutter, cut circles out of the bread slices. Set the circles aside for the top of the casserole and fit the scraps of bread into the prepared dish. Cover the bread scraps with cheese slices and sprinkle with the ham. Arrange the bread circles on top.

Beat the eggs in a mixing bowl. Whisk in the milk, salt, butter, mustard, and onion. Pour over the casserole, cover with plastic wrap, and refrigerate overnight.

Remove the dish from the refrigerator and preheat the oven to 350 degrees. Bake uncovered for 1 hour, until puffed and golden. Allow to rest for 5 minutes before cutting.

SERVES 6

America Discovers Columbus, Columbus, OH

HALE KIPA "THE HOUSE OF FRIENDLINESS" JUNIOR LEAGUE OF HONOLULU

Hale Kipa "The House of Friendliness" began in 1970 as a response from the community to address the plight of runaway and homeless girls and abused wives. The Junior League of Honolulu provided the initial seed money and the first volunteers, and in the early days, provided staying power, strength and continuity through some rough spots in its launch. Today Hale Kipa offers preventative services to youth awaiting permanent placement, independent living programs for older teens, and youth outreach for the community.

A Celebration of the Future

We know that to be successful in the future we cannot live in the past. While it is affirming to approach our hundred-year mark as a community-serving organization by celebrating the path we've been on and where that journey has brought us, we know we cannot move forward unless our gaze is fixed firmly on the challenges ahead.

In 1943, in the midst of the most devastating war the world has known, poet Archibald MacLeish wrote: "We have, and we know we have, the abundant means to bring our boldest dreams to pass— to create for ourselves whatever world we have the courage to desire." It may take no special courage to desire, as the Junior League does today, communities that embrace diverse perspectives, build partnerships and inspire shared solutions," but it will require a great deal of courage to build that world.

In this era of rapid and unsettling change, community problems seem increasingly complex and so deep and systemic that no one group can solve them alone. The Junior League is convinced that the next major step in our own and in the world's history lies in encouraging much broader participation in community problem solving. We believe it lies in listening with understanding and appreciation to new voices in our communities and to those who

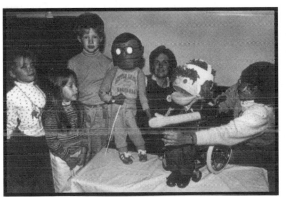

Members bring the Kids on the Block puppets to school children— a favorite educational project among the Leagues.

have been excluded from decision making in the past, making sure that all partners are included and valued at the community-building table.

The Junior League believes that communities can no longer do business as usual. We believe that all of us— volunteers, community organizations, any individual who's interested in making the world a better place— need to hear new voices, entertain new ideas. Through outreach and dialogue, we need to seek better ways to bring groups together to draft blueprints that are truly empowering of all in the community—because all share a stake in the issues and in their solutions. We hold that being resolutely open to a journey of discovery is the only way to create strong and healthy communities.

It is only by working together, discarding the systems and attitudes that have kept us separate, that we can untangle the complexities, ambiguities, and contradictions that riddle our changing communities. The Junior League steps out onto this path, bolstered by the knowledge that we are marking nearly hundred years of community service, mindful of our past shortcomings as well as our strengths, and determined to approach the beckoning century with a boldness of mind and spirit that will enable us to welcome the new adventures, whatever they may be, that will surely come our way in the next hundred years.

DESSERTS

COOKIES

CHOCOLATE CHOCOLATE CHIP COOKIES

What would a cookbook be without a chocolate chip cookie recipe? We think this one is a winner.

1¾ cups all-purpose flour
¼ teaspoon baking soda
2 sticks (½ pound) butter, softened
1 teaspoon vanilla extract
1 cup granulated sugar
½ cup packed dark brown sugar
1 egg
⅓ cup unsweetened cocoa powder
2 tablespoons milk
1 cup chopped pecans or walnuts
6 ounces semisweet chocolate chips

Preheat the oven to 350 degrees. In a small bowl, whisk together the flour and baking soda. Set aside. Using an electric mixer, cream the butter. Add the vanilla and sugars and beat until fluffy. Beat in the egg. At low speed, beat in the cocoa, then the milk. With a wooden spoon mix in the flour just until blended. Stir in the nuts and chocolate chips.

Drop the dough by rounded teaspoonfuls onto nonstick or foil-lined cookie sheets. Bake for 12 to 13 minutes. Remove from the oven and cool slightly before removing from the cookie sheets. Cool on a rack.

MAKES ABOUT 3 DOZEN   *Winning at the Table,* Las Vegas, NV

OATMEAL LACE COOKIES

2 sticks (½ pound) butter
2 tablespoons pure maple syrup (no substitutes)
1 cup all-purpose flour
½ teaspoon baking soda
1 teaspoon baking powder
2½ cups quick oats
1 cup granulated sugar

Melt the butter with 2 tablespoons of water in a small saucepan. Add the syrup. Whisk together the flour, baking soda, baking powder, oats, and 1 cup of the sugar. Add the melted butter and blend well. Chill 1 hour.

Preheat the oven to 350 degrees. Put the remaining ½ cup of sugar into a saucer. Remove the dough from the refrigerator and form into 1-inch balls. Roll in sugar and place the balls on an ungreased baking sheet, spacing them 3 inches apart. Flatten slightly. Bake for 12 to 15 minutes. Remove from the pan immediately and cool on a rack.

MAKES ABOUT 4 DOZEN   *Mountain Measures—A Second Serving,* Charleston, WV

AMISH COOKIES

5 cups sugar
2½ cups solid vegetable shortening
3 eggs
½ cup molasses
1 tablespoon vanilla extract
7 cups all-purpose flour
2 tablespoons baking soda
2 tablespoons baking powder
1½ teaspoons grated nutmeg
1 tablespoon ground cinnamon
1 tablespoon salt
6 cups oats
1 cup buttermilk or sour milk
1 cup raisins
1 cup peanuts, chopped
1 egg white, beaten
⅛ teaspoon cinnamon mixed with 2
    tablespoons sugar

In a very large mixing bowl, combine the sugar and shortening. Mix thoroughly. Add the eggs, molasses, and vanilla. Mix well. In a large bowl, whisk together the flour, baking soda, baking powder, nutmeg, cinnamon, and salt. Add the oats to the dry ingredients and mix. Add the flour mixture gradually to the creamed mixture, alternating with the buttermilk. Fold in the raisins and nuts. Chill 2-3 hours or overnight.

Preheat the oven to 375 degrees. Using an ice cream scoop, form the dough into large balls. Place 4 inches apart on lightly greased cookie sheets. Flatten with the fingers. Brush each cookie with beaten egg white and sprinkle with cinnamon sugar. Bake 12 to 15 minutes.

MAKES ABOUT 5 DOZEN LARGE COOKIES

Great Beginnings, Grand Finales, South Bend, IN

IMPERIAL COOKIES

2 sticks (½ pound) unsalted butter,
    softened
¼ cup sugar
½ teaspoon baking soda
½ teaspoon vinegar
½ teaspoon vanilla extract
1½ cups all-purpose flour
½ cup chopped nuts

Preheat the oven to 300 degrees. Beat together the butter, sugar, soda, vinegar, and vanilla with an electric mixer on high speed for 15 minutes. Fold in the flour and nuts. Drop the dough by the teaspoonful onto ungreased cookie sheets and bake 20 to 25 minutes.

MAKES ABOUT 3 DOZEN   *Delicious Decisions,* San Diego, CA

COWBOY COOKIES

1 cup vegetable oil
1 cup granulated sugar
1 cup packed brown sugar
2 eggs
2 cups all-purpose flour
1 teaspoon baking soda
½ teaspoon baking powder
½ teaspoon salt
12 ounces semisweet chocolate chips
2 cups oats

Preheat the oven to 350 degrees. In a large mixing bowl, beat the oil and sugars together; add the eggs and beat well. Whisk the flour with the soda, baking powder, and salt and add to the egg mixture. Stir in the chocolate chips and oats. Drop by teaspoonfuls onto nonstick cookie sheets and bake for 15 minutes. These do not get very brown, so don't attempt to brown them or they will dry out.

VARIATION: May substitute ½ cup of wheat germ for ½ cup of flour.

MAKES ABOUT 9 DOZEN   *Epicure,* Orange County, CA

SESAME-ANISE MELT COOKIES

2 cups all-purpose flour

¼ teaspoon baking soda

12 tablespoons (1½ sticks) unsalted
butter, softened

¾ cup sugar

1 tablespoon anise seed, crushed

¼ teaspoon salt

1 egg

¾ cup sesame seeds, toasted

Preheat the oven to 400 degrees. Grease four large baking sheets. In a medium bowl, whisk together the flour and baking soda. Set aside. In a large mixing bowl, beat the butter with the sugar, anise seed, and salt until light and fluffy. Beat in the egg. Stir in the flour mixture ½ cup at a time, blending well after each addition.

Place the sesame seeds in a bowl. With well-floured hands, roll heaping teaspoons of dough into 1-inch balls. Roll the balls in the sesame seeds. Place on a baking sheet and flatten to ¼-inch thickness with the bottom of glass. Bake 6-9 minutes, until lightly browned on the edges. Cool on racks.

MAKES ABOUT 3 ½ DOZEN   *Maine Ingredients,* Portland, ME

MRS. REESE'S SUGAR COOKIES

For roll-and-cut-out cookies, prepare the dough a day ahead.

8 tablespoons (1 stick) butter,
softened

8 tablespoons (1 stick) margarine

1 cup sugar

1 egg

1 teaspoon vanilla extract

3 cups all-purpose flour

1 teaspoon baking powder

⅛ teaspoon salt

Combine the butter, margarine, and sugar in a mixing bowl. Beat with an electric mixer until fluffy (at least 5 minutes). Add the egg and vanilla. Beat well. Put the flour, baking powder, and salt into a sifter and sift into the butter mixture. Beat well.

These can be rolled out, used with a cookie press, or dropped and garnished with a nut on top. If rolled out, put the dough in the refrigerator overnight. Take out a little at a time and roll on a pastry cloth. If used with a cookie press or dropped, *do not* put in the refrigerator. Bake at 350 to 375 degrees until light brown, about 10 minutes. Decorate as desired.

MAKES ABOUT 75 COOKIES   *Magic,* Birmingham, AL

GINGERBREAD MEN

2 cups sugar

½ cup solid vegetable shortening

8 tablespoons (1 stick) butter, softened

2 eggs

½ cup dark molasses

4 cups all-purpose flour

2 teaspoons ground cinnamon

1 teaspoon ground ginger

1 teaspoon ground cloves

1 teaspoon grated nutmeg

1 teaspoon baking soda

¼ teaspoon salt

Raisins for decorating (optional)

In a large bowl, beat together the sugar, shortening, and butter until light and fluffy. Stir in the eggs, one at a time. Stir in the molasses. Whisk together the flour, spices, baking soda, and salt. Stir into the egg mixture; mix until well blended. Roll into a ball in wax paper. Refrigerate for 3 hours.

Preheat the oven to 325 degrees. Grease one or more cookie sheets. Roll out the dough on a floured surface to ⅛ to ¼ inch thick. Cut out men using a cookie cutter. If decorating with raisins, add them now. Place the cookies on the prepared sheets. Bake 10 to 12 minutes. Remove from the pan and cool. Decorate with frosting, colored sugars, and candies.

MAKES 2-3 DOZEN   *Celebrate Miami!,* Miami, FL

KIEFLIES

A Hungarian cookie that is well worth the effort.

COOKIES

6 cups all-purpose flour
1½ teaspoons salt
4 sticks (1 pound) butter
12 egg yolks, whites reserved
1 cup sour cream
1 teaspoon vanilla extract

FILLING

12 egg whites
3½ cups (1 pound) confectioners'
sugar, plus additional for
sprinkling
6 cups (1½ pounds) chopped nuts

For cookies: Mix the flour and salt together. Cut the butter into the flour mixture with a pastry blender or two knives until completely blended. In a separate bowl, mix the egg yolks, sour cream, and vanilla. Add to the flour and butter mixture. Blend and knead until the mixture is the consistency of pie dough. Form into small walnut-size balls. Refrigerate.

For filling: Beat the egg whites until stiff. Add the sugar and beat well. Stir in the nuts. Refrigerate.

To assemble: Take a few of the cookie balls from the refrigerator. Roll each ball into a thin circle on a well-floured surface. Place a heaping teaspoon of filling on each circle. Fold into a crescent shape and pinch the seams closed. Arrange on lightly greased cookie sheets and bake in a preheated 350 degree oven for 12 minutes. Cool and sprinkle with confectioners' sugar.

MAKES ABOUT 6 DOZEN *Nutbread and Nostalgia,* South Bend, IN

BEV'S CREAMY CHOCOLATE WAFERS

Wickedly rich and delicious!

BROWNIE LAYER

4 ounces (4 squares) unsweetened
chocolate
2 sticks (½ pound) butter
4 eggs
2 cups granulated sugar
1 cup all-purpose flour

VANILLA BUTTERCREAM LAYER

8 tablespoons (1 stick) butter,
softened
3½ cups (1 pound) confectioners'
sugar
¼ cup cream
1 teaspoon vanilla extract

CHOCOLATE GLAZE

4 ounces semisweet chocolate
4 tablespoons (½ stick) butter

For brownie layer: Preheat the oven to 350 degrees. Grease and flour a 15½ × 10½-inch jelly roll pan. Melt the chocolate and butter over hot water in the top of a double boiler. Cool slightly. In a separate bowl, beat the eggs until light and lemon-colored. Gradually add sugar to the egg mixture. Add the butter and chocolate; stir in the flour. Pour into the prepared pan. Bake for 15 to 20 minutes or until a toothpick poked in the center comes out clean. Cool and chill in the refrigerator.

For vanilla buttercream layer: Cream the butter thoroughly with an electric mixer. Gradually add the confectioners' sugar alternately with the cream. Add the vanilla and beat until very light and fluffy. Spread evenly over the cooled brownie layer. Chill in the refrigerator at least 10 minutes.

For chocolate glaze: Melt the chocolate and butter together in top of double boiler over hot water. Beat well. Drizzle over the chilled buttercream in a lacy pattern. Chill 1 hour or longer. Cut into squares and serve.

MAKES 2 DOZEN *Nutbread and Nostalgia,* South Bend, IN

MERRY MERINGUE CHRISTMAS COOKIES

As pretty as they sound.

2 egg whites, at room temperature
⅛ teaspoon salt
⅛ teaspoon cream of tartar
¾ cup sugar
½ teaspoon vanilla extract
1 cup semisweet chocolate chips
1 cup chopped nuts
3 tablespoons crushed peppermint
   candy

Preheat the oven to 250 degrees. Lightly grease two or more baking sheets. Using an electric mixer, beat the egg whites in a medium bowl until foamy. Add the salt and cream of tartar and continue beating until soft peaks form. Add the sugar, 1 tablespoon at a time, beating well after each addition. Continue beating until the meringue is stiff. Fold in the vanilla, chocolate chips, nuts and candy.

Drop by teaspoonfuls, ½ inch apart, onto the prepared baking sheets. Bake for 40 minutes. Remove to cake racks to cool. May be prepared ahead and frozen.

MAKES ABOUT 5 DOZEN   *Plain & Fancy,* Richardson, TX

DOUBLE-FROSTED BOURBON BROWNIES

BROWNIES
¾ cup sifted all-purpose flour
¼ teaspoon baking soda
¼ teaspoon salt
½ cup sugar
⅓ cup solid vegetable shortening
1 (6-ounce) package semisweet
   chocolate chips
1 teaspoon vanilla extract
2 eggs
1½ cups chopped walnuts
4 tablespoons Bourbon whiskey

WHITE ICING
8 tablespoons (1 stick) butter,
   softened
1 teaspoon vanilla extract
2 cups confectioners' sugar

CHOCOLATE GLAZE
1 tablespoon solid vegetable
   shortening
1 (6-ounce) package semisweet
   chocolate chips

Brownies: Preheat the oven to 325 degrees. Grease a 9-inch square baking pan.

Sift together the flour, soda, and salt. Set aside. Combine the sugar and shortening with 2 tablespoons of water in a saucepan. Bring just to a boil, stirring constantly. Remove from the heat. Stir in the chocolate chips and vanilla, stirring until smooth. Beat in the eggs one at a time. Add the flour mixture and the nuts and mix well. Turn into the prepared pan and bake for 30 minutes. Remove from the oven and sprinkle with Bourbon. Cool.

White icing: Combine the butter and vanilla, beating until creamy. Gradually add the confectioners' sugar, beating until smooth. Spread over the cooled brownies.

Chocolate glaze: Melt together the shortening and chocolate in a double boiler over hot water. Spread over the iced brownies. When the glaze has set, cut into squares and serve.

MAKES 16 BROWNIES   *To Market, to Market,* Owensboro, KY

PEANUT BUTTER BROWNIES

2 sticks (½ pound) butter
⅓ cup cocoa powder
2 cups granulated sugar
4 eggs
1½ cups all-purpose flour
½ teaspoon salt
1 teaspoon vanilla extract
1 cup crunchy peanut butter

FROSTING
8 tablespoons (1 stick) butter
¼ cup cocoa powder
⅓ cup milk
8 large marshmallows
¼ teaspoon salt
1 teaspoon vanilla extract
3½ cups (1 pound) confectioners'
  sugar, sifted

Preheat the oven to 350 degrees. Grease a 13 × 9 × 2-inch baking pan. Melt the butter with the cocoa in a double boiler over hot water. Cool. Blend in the sugar, eggs, and vanilla. Combine the flour and salt; add to the first mixture. Bake in the prepared pan for 25 to 30 minutes. Remove from the oven, spoon the peanut butter over the hot cake, and spread as it melts.

Melt together ½ cup butter, cocoa, milk, marshmallows, salt, and vanilla. Beat in the confectioners' sugar until smooth. Spread over the cooled peanut butter.

MAKES 4 DOZEN 1 ½-INCH SQUARES

Some Like It South, Pensacola, FL

RICH MINT BROWNIES

BROWNIES
4 eggs
1 cup granulated sugar
8 tablespoons (1 stick) butter,
  melted
16 ounces chocolate syrup
1 cup all-purpose flour

MINT FROSTING
8 tablespoons (1 stick) butter,
  softened
3½ cups (1 pound) confectioners'
  sugar
¼ cup milk
2 teaspoons peppermint extract
10 drops green food coloring

CHOCOLATE GLAZE
8 tablespoons (1 stick) butter
12 ounces semisweet chocolate chips

Preheat the oven to 350 degrees. Grease a 16 × 11-inch jelly roll pan or baking pan, dust it with flour, and invert to shake out excess flour.

In a large bowl, beat the eggs and gradually beat in the sugar. Add the butter and chocolate syrup, blend, and stir in the flour. Turn the batter into the prepared pan and bake for 20 minutes. Cool in the pan while you prepare the frosting.

Mint frosting: Beat the butter, sugar, and milk together until fluffy. Stir in the peppermint extract and food coloring; mix thoroughly. Spread the mixture over the brownies after they have cooled completely. Refrigerate for at least 20 minutes.

Chocolate glaze: Melt the butter and chocolate chips together over very low heat. Spread on top of the mint frosting. Refrigerate until firm. Cut into small squares with a small sharp knife, wiping the knife blade clean after each cut.

MAKES 8 DOZEN

Honest to Goodness, Springfield, IL

OATMEAL BROWNIES

OATMEAL LAYER
½ cup all-purpose flour
¼ teaspoon salt
1 cup quick oats
½ cup packed brown sugar
8 tablespoons (1 stick) butter,
  melted

BROWNIE LAYER
6⅔ tablespoons butter
2 ounces (2 squares) unsweetened
  chocolate
2 eggs
1 cup granulated sugar
½ teaspoon salt
1 teaspoon vanilla extract
¾ cup all-purpose flour
½ cup chopped nuts (optional)

ICING
1¾ cups confectioners' sugar
4 tablespoons (½ stick) butter,
  softened
2 tablespoons milk
1 teaspoon vanilla extract

Preheat the oven to 350 degrees. Grease a 9-inch square baking pan. Combine the flour, salt, oats, and brown sugar. Mix in the butter until blended. Spread evenly in the prepared pan and bake for 10 minutes. Meanwhile, prepare the brownie layer.

Melt the butter and chocolate together over low heat or in a microwave and cool. Beat the eggs in a mixing bowl and stir in the sugar, salt, and vanilla. Add the chocolate mixture, the flour, and the nuts. Spread brownie mixture over the baked oatmeal layer and bake for 25 minutes. Remove from the oven and cool in the pan.

Combine the sugar, butter, milk, and vanilla and beat until smooth and creamy. Ice the brownies after they have cooled.
VARIATION: For chocolate icing, add ¼ cup cocoa. To make it even richer, use ⅓ cup butter and use cream instead of milk.
MAKES 2 DOZEN   *Encore! Nashville*, Nashville, TN

WHITE CHOCOLATE BROWNIES

8 tablespoons (1 stick) unsalted
  butter
8 ounces white chocolate chips or
  coarsely chopped white chocolate
2 large eggs
Salt
½ cup sugar
½ teaspoon vanilla extract
1 cup all-purpose flour
8 ounces semisweet chocolate chips

Preheat the oven to 350 degrees. Lightly grease an 8-inch square pan. Line the bottom with foil and lightly grease the foil.

Melt the butter in a heavy saucepan over low heat. Remove the pan from the heat. Add half the white chocolate; do not stir. Using an electric mixer, beat the eggs with a pinch of salt in a large bowl until frothy. Gradually add the sugar and beat until the mixture is pale yellow and a slowly dissolving ribbon forms when the beaters are lifted. Add the butter-chocolate mixture, the vanilla, and ½ teaspoon salt. Stir in the flour and mix until just combined. Fold in the semisweet chips and remaining 4 ounces of white chocolate. Spoon the mixture into the prepared pan; smooth the top with a spatula. Bake 30 minutes. Cool. Cut into 16 squares. Can be made a day ahead.
MAKES 16   *Very Virginia*, Hampton Roads, VA

MRS. NIGEL'S CHOCOLATE PEPPERMINT BROWNIES

These are rich and wonderful.

BROWNIES

2 ounces (2 squares) unsweetened
  chocolate
8 tablespoons (1 stick) butter
2 eggs
1 cup granulated sugar
½ cup all-purpose flour
Pinch of salt
¼ teaspoon peppermint extract
½ cup chopped pecans

FROSTING

1 cup confectioners' sugar
2 tablespoons butter, softened
1 tablespoon evaporated milk
½ teaspoon peppermint extract
1 to 2 drops green food coloring

GLAZE

2 squares unsweetened chocolate
2 tablespoons butter

Preheat the oven to 350 degrees. Butter an 8- or 9-inch square baking pan.

Brownies: In a large saucepan over low heat, melt the chocolate and butter together. Remove from the heat and let cool for 5 minutes. Beat in the sugar, then beat in the eggs one at a time. Stir in the flour, salt, and peppermint; fold in the nuts. Turn into the prepared pan and bake for 15 minutes. Remove from the oven and cool in the pan.

Frosting: Mix the confectioners' sugar, butter, and evaporated milk until smooth. Stir in the peppermint extract and food coloring until thoroughly blended. Spread on the brownies and chill in the refrigerator.

Glaze: Melt the chocolate and butter together over low heat. Let stand until cool. Spread over the frosting on the brownies and refrigerate until the chocolate is firm. Cut into squares and store in a covered container in the refrigerator.

N O T E : This recipe can be easily doubled, in which case the amount of frosting should be tripled.

M A K E S   1 6   *American Discovers Columbus,* Columbus, OH

BEST GOOEY BROWNIES

1 (12-ounce) package semisweet
  chocolate chips
1 can sweetened condensed milk
  (not evaporated milk)
½ pound (2 sticks) plus 2
  tablespoons butter
1 pound (2¼ cups packed) brown
  sugar
2 eggs
1 teaspoon vanilla extract
2 cups all-purpose flour
1 teaspoon salt
¾ cup pecans or walnuts, chopped

Preheat the oven to 350 degrees. Lightly oil a 13 × 9 × 2-inch baking pan.

In a large saucepan over low heat, melt the chocolate chips with the condensed milk and 2 tablespoons of butter while stirring slowly. Remove from the heat and cool slightly. Melt the remaining ½ pound of butter, stir in the sugar, and add to the chocolate mixture. Beat in the eggs one at a time. Stir in the vanilla, flour, and salt; fold in the nuts.

Turn the mixture into the prepared pan and bake for 30 to 35 minutes. Do not overbake—this is best if still gooey in the center. Cut while warm. These are divine if cut into larger squares and served with ice cream as a dessert.

M A K E S   2 4   L A R G E   B R O W N I E S

Treat Yourself to the Best, Wheeling, WV

KAHLÚA AND PRALINE BROWNIES

PRALINE CRUST
⅓ cup firmly packed light brown
    sugar
5⅓ tablespoons butter
⅔ cup all-purpose flour
½ cup finely chopped pecans

Make the praline crust: Mix together the brown sugar, butter, flour, and pecans. Pat evenly over the bottom of a 9-inch square baking pan and set aside.

BROWNIE FILLING
2 ounces (2 squares) unsweetened
    chocolate
¼ cup solid vegetable shortening
4 tablespoons (½ stick) butter
¼ cup granulated sugar
½ cup firmly packed light brown
    sugar
1 teaspoon vanilla extract
2 large eggs
¼ cup Kahlúa liqueur
½ cup all-purpose flour
¼ teaspoon salt
½ cup chopped pecans

Preheat the oven to 350 degrees. In a large saucepan, melt the chocolate with the shortening and butter over low heat. Remove from the heat and cool for 5 minutes. Beat in the sugars and vanilla; add the eggs one at a time while beating. Stir in the Kahlúa. Add the flour and salt, mixing to a smooth batter. Fold in the pecans. Pour into the pan lined with praline crust and bake for 25 minutes, being careful not to overbake. Let cool in the pan.

KAHLÚA BUTTER CREAM FROSTING
2 tablespoons butter, softened
2 cups sifted confectioners' sugar
1 tablespoon Kahlúa liqueur
1 tablespoon cream

Make the frosting: Beat all the ingredients until smooth and creamy. If necessary, beat in additional Kahlúa for a good spreading consistency. Spread frosting over the top of the brownies; place in the refrigerator ½ hour to set before cutting into.

MAKES 3 DOZEN   *Some Like It Hot,* McAllen, TX

LEMON BARS DELUXE

2¼ cups all-purpose flour
½ cup confectioners' sugar, plus
    additional for sprinkling
2 sticks (½ pound) butter
4 beaten eggs
2 cups granulated sugar
⅓ cup fresh lemon juice
½ teaspoon baking powder

Preheat the oven to 350 degrees. Whisk together 2 cups of the flour and the confectioners' sugar. Cut in the butter until the mixture clings together. Press the dough into a 13 × 9 × 2-inch baking dish. Bake for 20 to 25 minutes or until lightly browned.

Meanwhile, beat together the eggs, granulated sugar, and lemon juice. Mix the remaining ¼ cup flour with the baking powder; stir into the egg mixture and pour over the hot baked crust. Bake for 25 minutes longer. Remove from the oven and sprinkle with confectioners' sugar. Cool. Cut into 1½-inch bars.

MAKES 30 BARS   *Mountain Measures,* Charleston, WV

CHOCOLATE SHERRY BARS

1ST LAYER

4 ounces (4 squares) unsweetened
  baking chocolate
2 sticks (½ pound) butter
4 eggs
2 cups granulated sugar
1 cup all-purpose flour
½ teaspoon salt
1 teaspoon vanilla extract

2ND LAYER

8 tablespoons (1 stick) butter,
  softened
3½ cups (1 pound) confectioners'
  sugar
¼ cup sherry
1 cup pecans, chopped fine

3RD LAYER

3 ounces semisweet chocolate chips
1½ tablespoons water
2 tablespoons butter, softened

To prepare the first layer: Preheat the oven to 325 degrees. Grease a 14 × 10-inch glass baking dish, dust with flour, and invert to shake out excess flour. In a double boiler; melt the chocolate and butter over hot water. Cool. In a large bowl, beat the eggs and gradually add the sugar. Stir in the chocolate mixture, flour, salt, and vanilla. Beat for 1 minute. Pour into the prepared baking dish. Bake 25 minutes. Cool in the pan.

To prepare second layer: Combine the butter, sugar, and sherry. Stir until smooth; fold in the nuts. Spread over the first layer. Chill.

To prepare third layer: In a double boiler melt the chocolate with the water and butter. Stir to combine. Drizzle over the layers. Freeze. Before serving, slice into 2-inch bars.

MAKES 3 DOZEN   *South of the Fork,* Dallas, TX

TOFFEE COOKIE DIAMONDS

2 sticks (½ pound) butter, softened
1 cup packed brown sugar
1 egg yolk
1 cup all-purpose flour
6 (1½-ounce) chocolate bars (white
  chocolate may be used)
⅔ cup chopped pecans

Preheat the oven to 350 degrees. Line a 15 × 10-inch jelly roll pan with foil; grease the foil.

Cream together the butter, brown sugar, and egg yolk. Add the flour and stir until mixed. Spread the mixture in the prepared pan. Bake 20 minutes or until brown. Immediately top with the candy bars. When melted, spread the bars with a spatula and top with pecans. Cut on the diagonal into diamond shapes.

MAKES 2 DOZEN   *Beyond Parsley,* Kansas City, MO

Toffee Bars

These freeze well.

2 cups all-purpose flour
1¾ cups packed light brown sugar
3 sticks (¾ pound) butter (no substitutes)
1 cup pecans, chopped
1 (6-ounce) package semisweet chocolate chips

Preheat the oven to 350 degrees. Mix the flour and 1 cup of the brown sugar; cut in 1 stick of the butter until the mixture resembles fine crumbs. Press into the bottom of a 13 × 9-inch ungreased baking pan. Sprinkle with the pecans.

Bring to a boil the remaining 2 sticks of butter and ¾ cup of brown sugar. Boil exactly 1 minute, stirring constantly. Pour over the pressed mixture and bake exactly 20 minutes. Let sit 1 minute; then sprinkle with chocolate chips. When completely softened, spread the chocolate with a spatula. Chill thoroughly; return to room temperature before cutting.

MAKES 3 DOZEN *Georgia on My Menu,* Cobb-Marietta, GA

Lemon Mardi Gras Squares

1½ cups all-purpose flour
½ teaspoon salt
¼ teaspoon baking powder
3 eggs, separated
1 cup confectioners' sugar
8 tablespoons (1 stick) butter, softened
1 cup granulated sugar
⅓ cup lemon juice
2 tablespoons grated lemon rind

FROSTING
1 cup confectioners' sugar
1 tablespoon cream
2 tablespoons butter, softened
Chopped nuts

Preheat the oven to 350 degrees. Grease and flour a 13 × 9 × 2-inch baking pan. Whisk together the flour, salt, and baking powder. In a mixing bowl, beat the egg whites until soft mounds begin to form. Add the confectioners' sugar gradually, beating after addition. Continue beating until stiff, straight peaks are formed.

In a large bowl, beat the butter; gradually add the granulated sugar, beating until light and fluffy. Add the egg yolks one at a time. Beat for one minute. Add the lemon juice alternately with the flour mixture. Blend thoroughly. Add the grated lemon rind. Fold in the beaten egg whites gently but thoroughly. Pour into the prepared pan. Bake for 25 to 30 minutes.

Meanwhile, make the frosting: Mix the confectioners' sugar, cream, and butter together until smooth. Remove the cake from the oven and frost in the pan while still warm. Sprinkle with chopped nuts. When cool, cut into squares.

MAKES 2 DOZEN *River Road Recipes,* Baton Rouge, LA

Apricot Bars

1⅔ cups quick oats
1⅔ cups all-purpose flour
1 scant teaspoon baking soda
¼ teaspoon salt
1 cup packed light brown sugar
8 tablespoons (1 stick) butter, melted
1 (10-ounce) jar apricot preserves

Preheat the oven to 350 degrees. Grease a 15 × 10 × 1-inch jelly roll pan. In a mixing bowl, combine the oats, flour, baking soda, salt, and brown sugar. Add the butter and mix until crumbly. Pack half the mixture firmly into the prepared pan. Spread apricot preserves evenly over the mixture. Sprinkle the remaining mixture evenly over the preserves and pat down gently. Bake for 30 minutes or until lightly browned.

MAKES ABOUT 80 SMALL SQUARES

Gator Country Cooks, Gainesville, FL

RASPBERRY BARS

12 tablespoons (1½ sticks) unsalted
    butter, softened
1½ cups sugar
2 eggs
1½ cups all-purpose flour
1 cup raspberry preserves
½ cup shredded coconut
1 cup chopped pecans or almond
    slices

Preheat the oven to 350 degrees. In an electric mixer, beat the butter and 1 cup of the sugar until light and fluffy. Beat in the egg yolks and gradually add the flour. Spread into an ungreased 13 × 9 × 2-inch pan. Bake for 25 minutes. Cool slightly and spread with raspberry preserves; sprinkle with coconut.

Beat the egg whites until stiff. Gradually beat in the remaining ½ cup sugar until soft peaks form. Gently fold in the nuts. Spread the mixture over the baked layer and bake again at 350 degrees for 12 minutes or until golden brown. Cool and cut into bars.

MAKES 24–36 BARS   *Above and Beyond Parsley*, Kansas City, MO

KEY LIME BARS

1 cup plus 2 tablespoons all-purpose
    flour
¼ cup confectioners' sugar, plus
    additional for sprinkling
8 tablespoons (1 stick) butter,
    softened
2 eggs
1 cup plus 2 tablespoons granulated
    sugar
⅓ cup Key lime juice (see Note)

Preheat the oven to 350 degrees. Grease an 8-inch square baking pan. In a medium bowl, mix 1 cup of the flour with the confectioners' sugar. Add the butter and work with the hands to form a dough. (This all may be done in a food processor.) With lightly floured fingertips, pat the dough firmly and evenly into the bottom of the prepared pan. Bake for 15 to 20 minutes.

Meanwhile, in a small bowl, beat the eggs slightly. Stir in 1 cup of the granulated sugar; add the remaining 2 tablespoons of flour and stir until blended. Add the lime juice. (This may also be done in a food processor.) Pour onto the warm crust. Bake for 20 to 25 minutes. Place on a rack to cool. Before slicing and serving, sprinkle the top with 2 tablespoons or more sifted confectioners' sugar.

NOTE: If Key lime juice is unavailable, regular lime juice may be substituted.

MAKES 12 LARGE OR 24 SMALL BARS

Sunny Side Up, Fort Lauderdale, FL

CARMELITAS

1 cup plus 3 tablespoons all-purpose
    flour
1 cup quick-cooking oats
¾ cup packed brown sugar
12 tablespoons (1½ sticks) butter,
    melted
½ teaspoon salt
½ teaspoon baking soda
6 ounces semisweet chocolate chips
½ cup chopped nuts
¾ cup butterscotch topping

Preheat the oven to 350 degrees. Mix together 1 cup of the flour, the oats, sugar, butter, salt and baking soda. Pat half of this mixture into a 9 × 12-inch baking pan. Bake for 10 minutes. Remove from the oven. Sprinkle with the chocolate chips and nuts. Mix the butterscotch topping with the remaining 3 tablespoons of flour and warm slightly in a small pan. Drizzle over the nuts and chocolate chips. Cover with the remaining oat/sugar mixture. Bake for 20 more minutes. Cool and cut into bars.

MAKES 48   *Celebrate!*, Sacramento, CA

STRAWBERRY SQUARES WITH CLARET SAUCE

CRUST
1 cup all-purpose flour
¼ cup packed brown sugar
½ cup chopped pecans
8 tablespoons (1 stick) butter, melted

Preheat the oven to 350 degrees. In a small bowl, stir the flour and brown sugar together; add the pecans and butter. Spread evenly in a shallow pan. Toast the crumbs for 20 minutes, stirring occasionally while baking. Sprinkle ⅔ of the crumbs evenly in a 13 × 9 × 2-inch pan; press crumbs against the bottom of the pan to form a crust. Reserve the remaining crumbs.

FILLING
2 egg whites
⅔ cup granulated sugar if using frozen berries, or 1 cup sugar if using fresh
2 tablespoons lemon juice
2 cups sliced fresh strawberries, or 1 (10-ounce) package frozen strawberries, mostly thawed
½ pint heavy cream, whipped

Combine the egg whites, sugar, lemon juice, and berries. Beat at high speed with an electric mixer until high peaks form—about 10 minutes. Fold in the whipped cream. Spoon over the crust in the pan. Sprinkle evenly with the remaining crumbs. Freeze 6 hours or overnight.

SAUCE
1 cup sugar
¼ cup claret or other dry red wine

Combine the sugar and ¼ cup of water. Bring to a boil, lower the heat, and simmer for 8 minutes. Add the claret.

To serve, cut into squares, put a spoonful of sauce on each square, then pass more sauce.

MAKES 12–16 SQUARES   *Little Rock Cooks,* Little Rock, AR

NANAIMO BARS

12 tablespoons (1½ sticks) plus 1 tablespoon butter
¼ cup granulated sugar
¼ cup cocoa powder
1 egg
1 teaspoon vanilla extract
1½ cups graham cracker crumbs
½ cup coconut flakes
½ cup chopped walnuts
2 cups confectioners' sugar
2 tablespoons vanilla pudding powder
2 tablespoons milk
1 tablespoon white rum
2 ounces (2 squares) semisweet chocolate
2 ounces (2 squares) unsweetened chocolate
1 tablespoon butter

In the top of a double boiler combine 1 stick of butter, the granulated sugar, cocoa, egg, and vanilla. Heat and stir over hot water until the butter has melted. Remove from the heat and add the crumbs, coconut and walnuts. Spread the mixture into an ungreased 9-inch square pan and set aside.

Soften ½ stick of the butter and mix with the confectioners' sugar. Combine the pudding mix, milk, and rum and beat into the butter mixture. Pour over the prepared crust and refrigerate until the pudding has set. Melt the chocolate with the butter over low heat, carefully pour over the custard, and refrigerate until the icing is firm. Cut into squares.

MAKES 9 SQUARES   *A League of Cooks,* Vancouver, BC

WALNUT SLICES

BOTTOM LAYER
8 tablespoons (1 stick) butter, softened
1 cup all-purpose flour

TOP LAYER
1½ cups packed brown sugar
2 tablespoons all-purpose flour
¼ teaspoon baking powder
½ teaspoon salt
2 eggs, slightly beaten
1½ teaspoons vanilla extract
1 cup walnuts, chopped
½ cup coconut flakes

ORANGE FROSTING
1½ cups confectioners' sugar
2 tablespoons butter, melted
2 teaspoons lemon juice
2 tablespoons orange juice

Preheat the oven to 350 degrees. To make the bottom layer, blend the butter and flour. Press into a greased 9-inch square pan. Bake for about 15 minutes.

To make the top layer, combine the brown sugar, flour, baking powder, and salt. Add the eggs, vanilla, nuts, and coconut flakes; blend well. Spread evenly over the warm bottom layer. Bake for 25 minutes. Cool in the pan.

To make the frosting, blend the sugar, butter, lemon and orange juices. Spread over the cooled top layer. Cut into slices.

MAKES 32 · *Scarsdale Entertains,* Central Westchester, NY

MOTHER'S GLAZED ORANGE GEMS

1¼ cups sifted cake flour
¼ teaspoon salt
1 tablespoon baking powder
¼ teaspoon baking soda
3 tablespoons butter, softened
½ cup sugar
1 egg
1 tablespoon grated orange rind
½ cup chopped pecans
½ cup orange juice

Preheat the oven to 375 degrees. Sift together the flour, salt, baking powder, and baking soda. Cream the butter. Gradually add the sugar. Blend well. Beat in the egg. Stir in the orange rind and pecans. Add the dry ingredients alternately with the orange juice, mixing well but very quickly. Fill greased 2-inch muffin pans two thirds full. Bake for 15 minutes. Remove from the pan. Cool. Insert a fork into each cupcake and dip in orange syrup. Strike the fork against the edge of the pan to allow excess syrup to drop off. Place on a rack to cool.

ORANGE SYRUP
½ cup orange juice
1 cup sugar
1 teaspoon grated orange rind

Mix the orange juice, sugar, and orange rind well and stir over low heat until the sugar is dissolved. Increase the heat and boil rapidly for 5 minutes or until a candy thermometer registers 230 degrees.

MAKES ABOUT 22 MINIATURE CUPCAKES

From Market to Mealtime, Fayetteville, NC

TEA-TIME TASSIES

1 (3-ounce) package cream cheese
8 tablespoons (1 stick) butter
1 cup all-purpose flour

Let the cream cheese and butter soften at room temperature. Blend. Stir in the flour. Chill the dough about 1 hour. Shape into 2 dozen 1-inch balls; place in ungreased 1¾-inch muffin tins. Press the dough on the bottoms and sides of cups.

PECAN FILLING
1 egg
¾ cup packed brown sugar
1 tablespoon butter, softened
1 teaspoon vanilla extract
Dash of salt
⅔ cup pecans, chopped

Preheat the oven to 325 degrees. Beat together the egg, brown sugar, butter, vanilla, and salt until smooth. Divide half the pecans among the pastry-lined cups; add the egg mixture and top with the remaining pecans. Bake for 25 minutes or until the filling sets. Cool before removing from pan.

MAKES 2 DOZEN MINIATURE PASTRIES

Virginia Hospitality, Newport News, Hampton and Williamsburg, VA

WALL STREET KISSES

Bulls and bears will delight!

2 sticks (½ pound) unsalted butter, softened
½ cup confectioners' sugar, plus additional for dusting
1 teaspoon vanilla extract
2 cups all-purpose flour
1 cup finely chopped walnuts
1 (6-ounce) package milk chocolate kisses

Preheat the oven to 375 degrees. Cream the butter, confectioners' sugar, and vanilla in a bowl with an electric mixer until light and fluffy. Add the flour and walnuts. Beat at low speed until combined. Shape a small amount of the dough around each chocolate kiss, forming a sphere. Place on an ungreased cookie sheet. Bake for 12 minutes, or until the cookies are set but not brown. Roll the warm cookies in additional confectioners' sugar. Cool on a wire rack.

MAKES ABOUT 36 KISSES *I'll Taste Manhattan,* New York, NY

OATMEAL PECAN REFRIGERATOR COOKIES

2 sticks (½ pound) butter, softened
1 cup packed grown sugar
1 cup granulated sugar
2 eggs, well beaten
1 teaspoon vanilla extract
1½ cups all-purpose flour
1 teaspoon baking soda
1 teaspoon salt
1½ cups chopped pecans
2 cups oats

Preheat the oven to 325 degrees. Cream the butter and sugars together in mixing bowl. Add the eggs and vanilla extract. Stir the flour, soda, and salt together. Add the sugar-egg mixture. Stir in the pecans and oats. Form the dough into 1½-inch logs; wrap in plastic wrap. Chill for 1 hour or longer.

Slice ¼ inch thick and arrange 2 inches apart on an ungreased baking sheet. Bake for 10 minutes. Turn oven off and let cookies crisp for a few minutes.

MAKES ABOUT 4 DOZEN   *Quail Country,* Albany, GA

LES OREILLES DE COCHON

2 cups all-purpose flour
½ teaspoon baking powder
4 tablespoons (½ stick) butter,
    softened
2 eggs
1 teaspoon vinegar
Lard or vegetable shortening for
    deep frying
1½ cups cane syrup or light corn
    syrup
½ cup sugar

Mix the flour, baking powder, and ½ teaspoon of salt; rub in the butter until the mixture resembles coarse crumbs. Beat the eggs with the vinegar and mix into the flour; add a teaspoon or two of water if necessary to form a dough. Knead briefly until smooth. Wrap in waxed paper and chill for ½ hour. Divide the dough into 12 pieces.

Roll out each piece of dough on a floured surface into a 5-inch square; cut the squares in half on the diagonal. In a heavy skillet, heat about ½ inch of fat to 360 degrees. Fry the dough pieces a few at a time until golden brown, turning once. Bend one end of the pastry with tongs as it cooks. Drain on paper towels.

Meantime, combine the syrup, sugar, and a pinch of salt in a small saucepan and cook to the soft crack stage, about 275 degrees. Pour 1 tablespoon of this mixture over each pig ear. Serve at once.

MAKES 2 DOZEN   *Talk About Good I,* Lafayette, LA

MELTING MOMENTS

COOKIES
2 sticks (½ pound) butter, softened
⅓ cup confectioners' sugar
⅔ cup cornstarch
1 cup all-purpose flour

FROSTING
4 tablespoons (½ stick) butter,
    softened
2 cups confectioners' sugar
2 tablespoons lemon juice
Grated rind of 1 lemon

Cookies: Preheat the oven to 325 degrees. Cream the butter and sugar together until light. Whisk together the cornstarch and flour; add to the butter mixture and blend thoroughly. Drop by teaspoonfuls onto ungreased cookie sheets and bake for 15 to 20 minutes. Cool and frost.

Frosting: Cream the butter. Beat in the sugar alternately with the lemon juice and rind, beginning and ending with sugar.

MAKES ABOUT 5 DOZEN   *Superlatives,* Oklahoma City, OK

RONALD McDONALD HOUSE OF COLORADO SPRINGS
JUNIOR LEAGUE OF COLORADO SPRINGS, COLORADO

The Ronald McDonald House of Colorado Springs, a project of the Junior League of Colorado Springs, serves as a temporary lodging facility for families with critically ill children in the intensive care nurseries and pediatric units of area hospitals. From its opening in 1987, until September of 1994, the RMH has served 2,465 families. Sixty-five trained volunteers assist the House Manager with the daily operations of the house and provide a caring environment for the guests.

CAKES AND PIES

SUNSHINE CAKE

This cake is good whether it's filled, iced, glazed, served with ice cream and chocolate syrup, or just plain.

6 eggs, separated
1 cup sugar
2 teaspoons vanilla
⅔ cup all-purpose flour
⅔ teaspoon cream of tartar
¼ teaspoon salt

Preheat the oven to 350 degrees. Beat the egg whites until frothy. Add the sugar gradually and beat until stiff and glossy. Fold in the beaten egg yolks and vanilla. Stir the dry ingredients together and fold into the batter lightly. Bake in an ungreased tube pan for 40 to 45 minutes. Remove from the pan when cool.
SERVES 12

Company's Coming: Food for Entertaining, Kansas City, MO

ITALIAN CREAM CAKE

8 tablespoons (1 stick) butter, softened
½ cup solid vegetable shortening
2 cups granulated sugar
5 eggs, separated
1 teaspoon baking soda
1 cup buttermilk
2 cups all-purpose flour
1 teaspoon vanilla extract
1 small can coconut flakes
¾ cup pecans, chopped fine

Preheat the oven to 350 degrees. Grease and flour three 9-inch cake pans.

Cream the butter, shortening and sugar together until fluffy. Add the egg yolks; mix well. Stir the soda into the buttermilk. Add flour to the butter mixture alternately with buttermilk, beginning and ending with flour, and mixing well after each addition. Stir in the vanilla, coconut, and pecans. Fold in the stiffly beaten egg whites. Turn into the prepared pans and bake for 25 minutes.

Cool in the pans on a rack for 10 minutes. Then remove from pans, invert on a rack, and turn right side up to cool thoroughly before frosting.

CREAM CHEESE FROSTING
1 (8-ounce) package cream cheese, softened
8 tablespoons (1 stick) butter, softened
1 box (1 pound) confectioners' sugar
1 teaspoon vanilla extract
2 tablespoons frozen orange juice concentrate

Cream the cheese and butter together until thoroughly mixed. Gradually beat in the remaining ingredients. Spread between the layers of the cooled cake, then frost the top and sides.
MAKES ONE 3-LAYER CAKE

The Blue Denim Gourmet, Odessa, TX

THREE-FLAVOR POUND CAKE

This is a delicious, moist cake that can be prepared ahead and frozen.

½ cup solid vegetable shortening
2 sticks (½ pound) butter, softened
3½ cups sugar
5 eggs
3½ cups all-purpose flour
½ teaspoon baking powder
1 cup milk
1 teaspoon rum flavoring
1 teaspoon coconut flavoring

GLAZE
¼ cup plus 1 tablespoon water
1 cup sugar
½ teaspoon almond extract

Preheat the oven to 300 degrees. Grease and flour a Bundt pan.

Cream together the shortening, butter, and sugar. Add the eggs one at a time, beating well after each addition. Whisk together the flour and baking powder. Add the dry ingredients to the shortening mixture alternately with the milk, beginning and ending with flour. Beat in the rum and coconut flavoring. Pour into the prepared pan and bake 1½ to 1¾ hours. Do not open the oven door.

Shortly before the cake is removed from the oven, make the glaze: Bring the water and sugar to a rolling boil. Remove from the heat and add almond flavoring. Pour the hot mixture over the hot cake and let stand until cool. Remove from pan.

SERVES 16–18   *Necessities and Temptations,* Austin, TX

NO-FAULT SOUR CREAM POUND CAKE

2 sticks (½ pound) butter, softened
3 cups sugar
6 eggs
3 cups cake flour
¼ teaspoon baking powder
1 cup sour cream
1 teaspoon almond extract
1 teaspoon vanilla extract

Preheat the oven to 300 degrees. Grease and flour a 9-inch tube or Bundt pan.

Cream the butter and sugar together until light and fluffy. Add the eggs, two at a time, beating thoroughly after each addition. Sift together the cake flour and baking powder; add to the butter mixture alternately with the sour cream beginning and ending with flour. Blend in the almond and vanilla. Bake 1¼ to 1½ hours, until the cake shrinks slightly from the sides of the pan.

Cool in the pan 10 minutes, then invert on a rack, turn upright, and allow to cool completely.

MAKES 1 TUBE CAKE   *Sunsational,* Greater Orlando, FL

BONE MARROW DONOR PROGRAM
JUNIOR LEAGUE OF MORRISTOWN, NEW JERSEY

The Junior League of Morristown, New Jersey, through its Bone Marrow Donor Program, is becoming a leader in educating the public about the necessity of registering potential bone marrow donors. The project's purpose is to increase the number of people registered on the National Bone Marrow Registry. In collaboration with HLA Registry Foundation, Inc., the League has been educating the community, approaching corporations for funding and sponsorship, and organizing and conducting typing drives.

FRESH GINGER CAKE

2 tablespoons butter, softened

2 tablespoons granulated sugar

1 large egg

⅓ cup honey

2 tablespoons grated fresh ginger

1 teaspoon grated lemon rind

1 teaspoon vanilla extract

1½ cups all-purpose flour

1 teaspoon baking soda

¾ teaspoon baking powder

½ teaspoon ground coriander

½ teaspoon ground cinnamon

½ teaspoon grated nutmeg

⅛ teaspoon salt

2 tablespoons finely chopped crystallized ginger

½ cup buttermilk

2 teaspoons confectioners' sugar

Preheat the oven to 350 degrees. Grease and flour the bottom and sides of an 8-inch round cake pan. Set aside.

In a large bowl, beat the butter and granulated sugar until light and fluffy. Beat in the egg, honey, fresh ginger, lemon rind, and vanilla. The mixture will curdle slightly. Whisk together the flour, baking soda, baking powder, coriander, cinnamon, nutmeg, and salt.

In a small bowl, toss the crystallized ginger with ½ teaspoon of the dry ingredients. Add the dry ingredients and the buttermilk alternately to the butter mixture, beating well after each addition. Stir in the crystallized ginger. Pour the batter into the prepared pan. Bake for 30 minutes, until a cake tester inserted in center comes out clean.

Place on a rack and cool in the pan 10 minutes. Run a knife around the edge of the cake and turn it out of the pan. Place right side up on the rack and let cool completely. Sift confectioners' sugar over the top just before serving.

NOTE: Sift confectioners' sugar over a paper doily placed on top of the cake for a special but effortless decoration.

SERVES 8   *Simply Classic*, Seattle, WA

PUMPKIN–CREAM CHEESE ROLL

3 eggs

1 cup sugar

⅔ cup pumpkin purée

1 teaspoon lemon juice

¾ cup all-purpose flour

1 teaspoon baking soda

½ teaspoon salt

1 teaspoon grated nutmeg

1 teaspoon ground ginger

1 teaspoon ground cloves

1 cup chopped walnuts

1 cup confectioners' sugar, plus additional for sprinkling

1 (8-ounce) package cream cheese, softened

4 tablespoons (½ stick) butter, softened

½ teaspoon vanilla extract

Preheat the oven to 375 degrees. Line a 15 × 10 × 1-inch jelly roll pan with waxed paper.

In a large mixing bowl, beat the eggs at high speed for 5 minutes while slowly beating in the sugar. Stir in the pumpkin and lemon juice. In a small bowl, whisk together the flour, baking soda, salt, cinnamon, nutmeg, ginger, and cloves. Add to the pumpkin mixture and stir to combine.

Spoon the batter evenly into the prepared pan. Sprinkle with the chopped nuts and bake for 15 minutes, until springy to the touch. Loosen the edges with a knife and turn out onto a clean kitchen towel that has been lightly sprinkled with confectioners' sugar. Peel off the paper. Roll up the cake with the towel, starting with a short side. Allow to cool on a rack.

Meanwhile, beat the cream cheese, butter, and vanilla together with 1 cup of confectioners' sugar until smooth. Unroll the cake and remove the towel. Spread the cream cheese filling on the cake to about ½ inch from the edges. Roll back up, put on a plate seam side down, and refrigerate until set. Slice and serve. This freezes well for up to 2 months.

MAKES 12 SERVINGS   *Amber Waves*, Omaha, NE

COCONUT POUND CAKE

2 sticks (½ pound) butter, softened
½ cup solid vegetable shortening
3 cups sugar
6 eggs
3 cups all-purpose flour
1 cup milk
1 teaspoon vanilla extract
1 teaspoon lemon extract
1 tablespoon coconut flavoring
1 teaspoon almond extract
1 (3½-ounce) can flaked coconut

Preheat the oven to 325 degrees. Grease and flour a 9-inch tube pan. In a large mixing bowl, cream the butter and shortening with the sugar until light and fluffy. Add the eggs two at a time, beating well after each addition. Combine the milk and flavorings. Beat in the flour alternately with the liquid ingredients, beginning and ending with flour. Fold in the coconut. Turn the mixture into the prepared pan. Bake 1½ hours, or until the cake shrinks slightly from the sides of the pan. Cool in the pan for 10 minutes, then invert onto a rack, turn right side up, and allow to cool completely.

SERVES 10–12   *Palm Beach Entertains,* West Palm, FL

FOURTEEN KARAT CAKE

"This book is about real food. The fabulous Fourteen Karat Cake recipe alone is worth double the price!"—Charles Kuralt, CBS News

2 cups all-purpose flour
2 teaspoons baking powder
1½ teaspoons baking soda
1 teaspoon salt
2 teaspoons ground cinnamon
4 eggs
2 cups sugar
1½ cups vegetable oil
2 cups grated raw carrots
1 (8½-ounce) can crushed pineapple, drained
½ cup chopped nuts
Vanilla cream cheese frosting (below)

Preheat the oven to 350 degrees. Grease and flour three 9-inch cake pans.

Sift together the flour, baking powder, baking soda, salt, and cinnamon. In a large bowl, beat the eggs with a wire whisk. Add the sugar and oil and beat until combined. Stir in the flour; fold in the carrots, pineapple, and nuts. Mix well. Turn into the prepared pans. Bake 35 to 40 minutes, until the cakes shrink slightly from the sides of the pans. Cool in the pans for 10 minutes. Invert onto racks to cool completely. Spread vanilla cream cheese frosting between the layers and on the top and sides of the cake.

VANILLA CREAM CHEESE FROSTING

8 tablespoons (1 stick) butter, softened
1 (8-ounce) package cream cheese, softened
1 teaspoon vanilla extract
1 (1-pound) box confectioners' sugar

Combine the butter, cream cheese, and vanilla in a mixing bowl and blend until smooth. Add the sugar gradually, beating until well incorporated.

MAKES 12 SERVINGS   *Stirring Performances,* Winston-Salem, NC

CARROT CAKE WITH LEMON CREAM CHEESE FROSTING

1¼ cups vegetable oil

1 cup packed light brown sugar

1 cup granulated sugar

4 large eggs

1 cup all-purpose flour

1 cup less 2 tablespoons, whole wheat flour

1 teaspoon salt

2 teaspoons baking soda

2 teaspoons baking powder

2 teaspoons ground cinnamon

3 cups (packed) finely shredded raw carrots

1 (8½-ounce) can crushed pineapple, drained

Lemon cream cheese frosting (below)

½ cup chopped nuts

Preheat the oven to 350 degrees. Grease and flour two 9-inch round cake pans. In a large bowl, blend together the oil and sugars. Add the eggs one at a time, beating after each addition until blended. In a separate bowl, sift together the flours, salt, soda, baking powder, and cinnamon. Add the flour mixture, ⅓ at a time, to the oil mixture, beating just enough to blend. Fold in the carrots and pineapple and stir in the nuts.

Pour the batter into the prepared pans. Bake 35 to 40 minutes or until a toothpick inserted near the center comes out clean. Cool the cakes in the pans for 10 minutes, then turn out onto a rack to cool completely. Spread lemon cream cheese frosting over the first cake layer. Top with the second layer and spread frosting over the top of the cake. Allow to rest one day for best flavor. Refrigerate up to a week or freeze without frosting.

LEMON CREAM CHEESE FROSTING

1 (8-ounce) package cream cheese, softened

4 tablespoons (½ stick) unsalted butter, softened

2 cups confectioners' sugar

1½ teaspoons vanilla extract

1 tablespoon grated lemon peel

Cream together the cream cheese and butter until fluffy. Add the confectioners' sugar and beat until well blended. Beat in the vanilla and lemon peel.

NOTE: The whole wheat flour in this recipe adds a new dimension to the taste and texture of carrot cake, and it gets even better after a mellowing period.

SERVES 12–15

Come on In!, Jackson, MS

THE EMILY ANDERSON FAMILY LEARNING CENTER AT PHOENIX CHILDREN'S HOSPITAL
JUNIOR LEAGUE OF PHOENIX, ARIZONA

The Emily Anderson Family Learning Center at Phoenix Children's Hospital was adopted as a project by the Junior League of Phoenix, Arizona, while still in its conceptual form. The League shepherded the idea into reality, as a medical library and resource center for the families and friends of children with special health care needs. Open to the public, the library contains adult and children's books, pamphlets, and video tapes on a wide range of topics relating to children's chronic, serious, and terminal illnesses, as well as training for families who must learn special care of ill children.

APPLE CAKE WITH HOT CARAMEL RUM SAUCE

CARAMEL RUM SAUCE
½ cup granulated sugar
½ cup packed brown sugar
½ cup heavy cream
8 tablespoons (1 stick) butter
¼ cup dark rum

2 sticks (½ pound) butter, softened
1 cup granulated sugar
2 eggs, well beaten
1½ teaspoons vanilla extract
1½ cups all-purpose flour
1 teaspoon ground cinnamon
1 teaspoon grated nutmeg
1 teaspoon baking soda
½ teaspoon salt
3 medium apples, peeled, cored,
    and chopped
¾ cup coarsely chopped pecans

Make the caramel rum sauce: Combine the sugars and cream in the top part of a double boiler and cook over simmering water, stirring occasionally, for 1½ hours. Add the butter and cook another 30 minutes. (The mixture may look curdled but will smooth out when beaten.) Remove from the heat, add the rum, and beat until smooth.

Make the cake: Preheat the oven to 350 degrees. Grease a 10-inch pie plate or 9-inch square baking pan. Cream the butter and sugar together until light and fluffy; beat in the eggs and vanilla until well mixed. Whisk together the flour, cinnamon, nutmeg, soda, and salt; blend into the butter mixture. Stir in the apples and pecans. Spoon the batter evenly into the prepared pan and bake about 45 minutes or until golden brown. Serve with the warm sauce.

SERVES 8–10

Superlatives, Oklahoma City, OK

ELEGANT LAYERED APPLE CAKE

This triple-layer apple cake makes a very professional-looking birthday cake.

3 cups all-purpose flour
1½ teaspoons baking soda
½ teaspoon salt
3 cups grated pared tart apples
½ cup chopped walnuts
1 teaspoon grated lemon rind
2 cups granulated sugar
1½ cups vegetable oil
2 eggs

FROSTING
1 (8-ounce) package cream cheese,
    softened
8 tablespoons (1 stick) butter,
    softened
1 box (1 pound) confectioners' sugar
1 teaspoon vanilla extract
1 cup finely chopped walnuts

Grease well and flour three 9-inch cake pans. Preheat the oven to 350 degrees.

Whisk together the flour, baking soda, and salt; set aside. In a small bowl, combine the grated apples, nuts and lemon rind. In a large bowl, combine the granulated sugar, oil, and eggs; mix well with a wooden spoon. Add the dry ingredients, mixing until smooth. Incorporate the apple mixture; stir until well combined. Spread evenly into the prepared pans. Bake for 30 to 40 minutes or until the surface springs back when pressed lightly. Cool the cake in the pans for 10 minutes. Remove from the pans and cool thoroughly on wire racks.

Prepare the frosting: Cream the cheese and butter together and beat in the sugar and vanilla until smooth. Spread between layers, on sides and top. Press nuts around sides of the cake. Refrigerate until serving time.

SERVES 10–12

Pinch of Salt Lake, Salt Lake City, UT

APPLE CAKE

4 large apples
2 teaspoons ground cinnamon
2 cups plus 5 tablespoons sugar
3 cups all-purpose flour
1 tablespoon baking powder
¼ teaspoon salt
4 eggs
1 cup vegetable oil
¼ cup orange juice
2½ teaspoons vanilla extract

Preheat the oven to 350 degrees. Grease a Bundt pan.

Peel and slice the apples. Mix the cinnamon and 5 tablespoons of sugar. Set aside. In a medium bowl, whisk together the flour, baking powder, and salt. In a large bowl with an electric mixer, beat the eggs; add the oil, 2 cups of sugar, the orange juice and vanilla. Add the flour mixture and beat at low speed just until mixed. Spoon one third of the batter into the prepared pan. Top with half the apples and half the cinnamon sugar. Cover with another third of the batter. Add the rest of the apples and cinnamon sugar. Top with the remaining batter.

Bake for 1¼ hours or until the cake shrinks slightly from the sides of the pan. Remove from the pan and cool on a rack.

MAKES 1 BUNDT CAKE   *Culinary Creations,* Kingston, NY

NEBRASKA CITY CAKE

CAKE
½ cup solid vegetable shortening
2 cups granulated sugar
2 eggs
2 cups all-purpose flour
2 teaspoons baking soda
1 teaspoon salt
2 teaspoons ground cinnamon
1 teaspoon grated nutmeg
4 cups diced apples (about 6 apples)
1 cup chopped nuts

Preheat the oven to 350 degrees. Grease a 13 × 9-inch baking pan.

Cream together the shortening and sugar. Add the eggs. Mix well. Add the flour mixed with the soda, salt, cinnamon, and nutmeg; mix. Stir in the apples and nuts. The mixture will be dry. Pour into the prepared pan and bake for 50 to 60 minutes, until the mixture shrinks slightly from the sides of the pan. Remove from the oven and cool in the pan on a rack. To serve, cut into squares and top with warm butterscotch sauce.

BUTTERSCOTCH SAUCE
8 tablespoons (1 stick) butter
2 tablespoons flour
½ cup granulated sugar
½ cup packed brown sugar
½ cup half-and-half

Over low heat, melt the butter. Gradually stir in the flour and sugars. Stir in the cream. Cook, stirring constantly, until thickened. Serve warm over the cake.

MAKES 24 SERVINGS   *Amber Waves,* Omaha, NE

DRIED APPLE CAKE

3 cups dried apples, chopped
3 cups sugar
2 sticks (½ pound) butter, softened
2 eggs
3 cups all-purpose flour
2 teaspoons baking soda
½ teaspoon salt
1 teaspoon ground allspice
1 teaspoon ground cloves
1 teaspoon grated nutmeg
1 teaspoon ground cinnamon
1 cup sour milk or buttermilk (see Note)
1 teaspoon lemon extract
1 teaspoon vanilla extract
1 cup chopped nuts
1 cup raisins, plumped (see Note)

Cover the apples with water and soak 5 to 6 hours or overnight. Wring out excess moisture and run through a food mill. Measure 2 to 3 cups of apple purée and mix in a saucepan with 2 cups of sugar; cook until thick. Cool.

Preheat the oven to 300 degrees. Grease and flour two 9-inch loaf pans or a 10-inch Bundt pan. In a very large bowl, cream the butter and 1 cup of sugar; beat in the eggs. Combine the flour, baking soda, salt, and spices. Alternately add the flour mixture and the sour milk to the creamed mixture, beginning and ending with flour. After the batter is well mixed, add the lemon and vanilla extracts. Add the chopped nuts, raisins, and apple mixture to the batter. Pour into the prepared pans. Bake the Bundt pan for 1½ hours, the loaves 50 to 60 minutes, or until a toothpick inserted in the center comes out clean. Cool in the pans 10 to 15 minutes; unmold and let cool completed on a rack.

This cake keeps very well if it is tightly wrapped; it actually becomes more moist after a day or two. If the cake dries out, pierce the top with a fork, drizzle apple juice or apple brandy over the top, and seal in plastic wrap for a day or two.

NOTE: To make sour milk, add 1 tablespoon lemon juice or 1 tablespoon vinegar to 1 cup of milk. To plump raisins, cover with boiling water and let stand for 5 minutes. Drain well.

MAKES 1 BUNDT CAKE OR 2 LOAVES

Treasures of the Smokies, Johnson City, TN

APRICOT BRANDY POUND CAKE

2 sticks (½ pound) butter, softened
3 cups granulated sugar
6 eggs
3 cups all-purpose flour
½ teaspoon salt
¼ teaspoon baking soda
1 cup sour cream
1 teaspoon orange extract
1 teaspoon vanilla extract
½ teaspoon lemon extract
½ teaspoon rum extract
¼ teaspoon almond extract
½ cup apricot brandy
Confectioners' sugar

Preheat the oven to 325 degrees. Grease and flour a 10-inch tube pan. Cream the butter and sugar. Add the eggs one at a time, beating well after each addition. Whisk together the flour, salt, and soda. Combine the sour cream, flavorings, and brandy. Alternately add the flour and sour cream to the butter mixture, beginning and ending with flour. Blend well. Pour into the prepared pan. Bake for 80 to 90 minutes, until the cake pulls slightly from the sides of the pan. Cool in the pan for 30 minutes. Carefully invert on a rack, turn right side up, and allow to cool completely before slicing. Dust the cooled cake with confectioners' sugar.

NOTE: The cake is even better after 3 or 4 days.

SERVES 15–20

Tidewater on the Halfshell, Norfolk–Virginia Beach, VA

APRICOT CRUMB CAKE

This rich and delicious treat may be served as a dessert or a coffee cake.

2¼ cups all-purpose flour

1½ cups sugar

1 tablespoon cinnamon

10 tablespoons butter, softened

1 (8-ounce) package cream cheese, softened

1 teaspoon vanilla extract

2 eggs

1 teaspoon baking powder

½ teaspoon baking soda

¼ teaspoon salt

½ cup milk

1 (12-ounce) jar apricot preserves

Grease a 9-inch Bundt pan. Preheat the oven to 350 degrees. Mix ¼ cup of the flour, ¼ cup of sugar, and the cinnamon. Rub in 2 tablespoons of butter until the mixture is crumbly; spread on the bottom of the pan.

Beat the remaining 8 tablespoons of butter with the cream cheese and 1¼ cups of sugar until fluffy. Beat in the vanilla and eggs. Mix the remaining 2 cups of flour with the baking powder, soda, and salt. Add the flour mixture to the butter mixture alternately with the milk, beginning and ending with the flour. Beat until smooth. Pour half the batter into the pan. Spread the preserves on the batter. Top with the remaining batter. Bake for 50 to 60 minutes. Cool in the pan for 30 minutes. Loosen the edges and invert onto a cake plate.

SERVES 12

Posh Pantry, Kankakee, IL

STRAWBERRY BLITZ TORTE

TORTE

1 cup sifted cake flour

1 teaspoon baking powder

¼ teaspoon salt

½ cup solid vegetable shortening

½ cup granulated sugar

4 egg yolks

3 tablespoons milk

1 teaspoon vanilla extract

MERINGUE

4 egg whites

½ teaspoon salt

½ teaspoon cream of tartar

1 cup granulated sugar

½ teaspoon vanilla extract

STRAWBERRY FILLING

½ cup heavy cream

2 tablespoons confectioners' sugar

1 cup sliced strawberries

Preheat the oven to 350 degrees. Grease two 8-inch layer cake pans.

Torte: Sift the flour, baking powder, and salt 3 times. Set aside. Cream the shortening; add sugar and beat until fluffy. Beat the egg yolks until thick and add to the creamed mixture. Stir in the milk and vanilla. Add the dry ingredients and beat until the batter is smooth. Spread into the prepared pans.

Meringue: Beat the egg whites, salt, and cream of tartar until soft peaks form. Add the sugar, 2 tablespoons at a time, beating well after each addition. Add the vanilla. Carefully pour half the meringue mixture over the batter in each pan. Bake for about 35 minutes. Remove from the oven, loosen the sides of the tortes from the pans, and remove them to wire racks, keeping the meringue side up. When cool spread strawberry filling between the layers.

Strawberry filling: Combine the cream and confectioners' sugar; whip until stiff. Fold in the sliced strawberries; spread between layers of the torte.

SERVES 8–10

Cookbook, Grand Rapids, MI

FRESH FLORIDA ORANGE CAKE

CAKE

8 tablespoons (1 stick) butter, softened
¼ cup solid vegetable shortening
1½ cups granulated sugar
3 eggs
2¾ cups all-purpose flour
1½ teaspoons baking soda
¾ teaspoon salt
1½ cups buttermilk
1½ teaspoons orange extract
1 cup chopped dates
½ cup chopped pecans
1 tablespoon grated orange rind

FROSTING

6 tablespoons butter, softened
6 cups sifted confectioners' sugar
¼ cup plus 2 tablespoons fresh orange juice
1 teaspoon orange extract
1 teaspoon grated orange rind
Orange segments, grated orange rind, orange rind strips, mint leaves for garnish (optional)

Preheat the oven to 350 degrees. Grease and flour three 9-inch round cake pans. To prepare the cake, cream the butter and shortening. Gradually add the sugar, beating well at medium speed. Add the eggs one at a time, beating well after each addition. Combine the flour, soda, and salt. Add to the creamed mixture alternately with the buttermilk, beginning and ending with the flour mixture. Beat with an electric mixer at high speed for 3 minutes. Stir in the orange extract, dates, nuts, and orange rind. Pour the batter into the prepared pans. Bake for 30 minutes or until a wooden toothpick inserted in the center of the cake comes out clean. Cool in the pan 10 minutes. Remove the layers from the pans to a rack and let cool completely.

To prepare the frosting, cream the butter. Add the confectioners' sugar alternately with the orange juice. Stir in the orange extract and orange rind and beat until smooth. Add more juice if needed to reach the desired spreading consistency. Add red and yellow food coloring, if desired. Spread the orange frosting between the layers and on the top and sides of the cake. Garnish the frosted cake with orange segments, grated orange rind, orange rind stripe, and mint leaves.

SERVES 16   *Thymes Remembered,* Tallahassee, FL

DENTAL HEALTH FOR ARLINGTON, INC.
JUNIOR LEAGUE OF ARLINGTON, TEXAS

At Dental Health for Arlington, Inc., a project of the Junior League of Arlington, Texas, the goal is to improve the oral health of economically disadvantaged children and adults in the community. DHA operates a low-cost dental clinic and a public schools preventive education program. A dental health clinic is open two days a week, and a staff of dental professionals and trained volunteers travels to public schools presenting educational programs, on-site oral health screenings, and the application of dental sealants.

JACK'S FAVORITE CAKE

This rich moist cake is a special nine-teenth-hole treat for golfer Jack Nicklaus.

2 cups all-purpose flour
1½ cups sugar
1 teaspoon baking soda
1 teaspoon salt
1 teaspoon ground cinnamon
1 teaspoon ground nutmeg
1 cup vegetable oil
½ cup buttermilk
3 eggs, lightly beaten
1 cup stewed pitted prunes, chopped
1 cup chopped pecans
1 teaspoon vanilla extract

SAUCE
1 cup sugar
8 tablespoons (1 stick) butter
½ cup buttermilk
1 teaspoon baking soda

Preheat the oven to 350 degrees. Grease and flour a 13 × 9-inch baking pan. In a large mixing bowl, whisk together the flour, sugar, soda, salt, cinnamon, and nutmeg. Add the oil, buttermilk, and eggs and mix well. Stir in the prunes, nuts, and vanilla. Pour the mixture into the prepared pan. Bake 35 to 40 minutes.

To prepare the sauce, combine the sugar, butter, buttermilk, and baking soda in a saucepan and bring to a boil, stirring constantly. While the cake is still hot, prick the top in several places with a fork. Pour the warm sauce over the warm cake. Cool and cut in the pan.

MAKES ABOUT 18 SQUARES

Palm Beach Entertains, West Palm Beach, FL

CONFETTI CHRISTMAS CAKE

A gorgeous holiday dessert. Nice for a buffet or a large family dinner and light enough to follow a big meal perfectly.

2 envelopes unflavored gelatin
½ cup cold water
1 cup hot water
1 cup sugar
½ teaspoon salt
1 cup orange juice concentrate
2 cups heavy cream
1½ cups golden raisins, plumped (see Note)
⅔ cup candied fruit (mixture of red and green cherries and pineapple)
½ cup chopped pecans
1 or 2 packages split ladyfingers

Soften the gelatin in ½ cup of the cold water; add 1 cup of hot water, stirring to dissolve. Stir in the sugar, salt, and orange juice concentrate; blend thoroughly. Chill until thick. Whip the cream until it forms soft peaks. Fold the whipped cream into the orange mixture along with the raisins, candied fruit, and pecans. Line the bottom and sides of a 10-inch springform pan with ladyfingers. (Ladyfingers may need to be trimmed to fit the pan.) Carefully spoon the fruit mixture over the ladyfinger lining. Refrigerate until congealed. Keeps well for several days.

NOTE: To plump the raisins, cover with boiling water and let stand for 5 to 10 minutes. Drain well.

SERVES 12–16

Perennials—A Southern Celebration of Foods and Flavors, Hall County, GA

ALMOND CRUNCH CAKE

CAKE

1½ cups all-purpose flour
1½ cups sugar
8 eggs, separated
¼ cup cold water
1 tablespoon lemon juice
1 teaspoon vanilla extract
1 teaspoon cream of tartar
1 teaspoon salt

ALMOND-BRITTLE TOPPING

1½ cups plus 2 tablespoons sugar
¼ teaspoon instant coffee granules
¼ cup light corn syrup
¼ cup hot water
¼ teaspoon baking soda
2 to 2½ cups heavy cream
2 teaspoons vanilla extract
Almonds, blanched, halved, and
    toasted

Cake: Preheat the oven to 350 degrees. Whisk together the flour and ¾ cup of the sugar in a mixing bowl. Make a well in the center, add the egg yolks, water, lemon juice, and vanilla and beat until smooth. In a separate bowl, beat the egg whites, cream of tartar, and salt just until soft peaks form. Add the remaining ¾ cup of sugar, 2 tablespoons at a time, continuing to beat until stiff. Fold the flour mixture gently into the egg white. Pour the batter into a 10-inch tube pan or two 2-quart baking pans. Do not grease the pans. Cut carefully through the batter, going around the tube five or six times with a knife to break up air bubbles. Bake for 50 to 55 minutes or until the top of the cake springs back when lightly touched. Invert the pan for 1 hour or until cool. Remove the cake and split into 4 equal layers if using a tube pan. Make the cake with 2 or 4 layers if using baking pans.

Almond-brittle topping: Combine 1½ cups of the sugar, the coffee, corn syrup and water in a saucepan, stirring well. Boil to 300 degrees, or until a little syrup dropped in cold water turns brittle. Remove from heat. Add the soda. Stir vigorously until the mixture blends and pulls away from the sides of the pan. Quickly pour onto a shallow baking sheet. Do not grease the sheet. Let the brittle stand until cool. Knock out of the pan and crush the candy into small chunks with a rolling pin.

Whip the cream and fold in the sugar and vanilla. Spread half the cream between the cake layers and the remainder over the top and sides. Cover the tops and sides with the candy, pressing it into the cream. Decorate with almonds. Do not press the candy and almonds into the cream more than 6 hours before serving. Refrigerate.

MAKES ONE 4-LAYER CAKE   *Flavors,* San Antonio, TX

ANTI-DRUG PUPPET TEAM
JUNIOR LEAGUE OF McALLEN, TEXAS

The Junior League of McAllen, Texas, began the Anti-Drug Puppet Team in 1978, and each year gives over forty performances at area public and private schools. The presentation is twenty minutes long with a follow-up of questions and answers for the students. The team is accompanied by a McAllen police officer who follows the puppet show with a talk to the students covering eight ways to say "no," a discussion on peer pressure, and role playing by the students.

ALMOND CREAM MERINGUE

This is well worth the rather lengthy preparation.

MERINGUE
4 egg whites, at room temperature
½ teaspoon cream of tartar
1 cup sugar

Preheat the oven to 250 degrees. Trace four 9-inch circles on waxed paper and place on foil-covered baking sheets. Beat the egg whites with the cream of tartar until soft peaks form, then add ⅔ cup of sugar very gradually, a tablespoon at a time. When the egg whites are stiff, gently fold in the remaining ⅓ cup of sugar. Drop by heaping spoonfuls on the 9-inch circles and smooth with a spatula (see Note). Bake for 1 to 1½ hours, until firm and creamy white. Turn off the oven and leave the meringue in the oven at least 3 hours without opening the oven door. Gently peel off the paper.

ALMOND BUTTER CREAM FILLING
½ cup heavy cream
4 to 5 tablespoons butter, softened
¾ cup sugar
1 teaspoon almond extract
4 egg yolks (optional; see Note)
1½ cups sliced blanched almonds

Whip the cream until it forms soft peaks. In a separate bowl, cream the butter and sugar and add the almond extract. Beat in the egg yolks one at a time. Fold the mixture into the whipped cream. Fold in the almonds, saving some for garnish on top.

AMARETTO CREAM FILLING
2 cups heavy cream
¼ cup powdered sugar
2 to 3 tablespoons amaretto liqueur

Whip the cream until it forms soft peaks, then beat in the sugar. Fold in the liqueur.

To assemble: Place 1 meringue on a serving platter. Spread ¼ of the almond butter filling evenly over the first meringue. Then spread ¼ of the amaretto filling over it. Top with the next meringue layer and repeat the process for each of the remaining layers. When assembled, a springform may be placed around it. Cover tightly with plastic wrap and place in the freezer for at least 18 hours. Remove from the freezer 20 minutes before serving and garnish with almonds and flowers or fruit. Cut into wedges for serving.

NOTE: Make meringues as flat as possible without any swirls and they will layer better. The egg yolks remain uncooked; omit them if you prefer.

SERVES 12   *Cornsilk,* Sioux City, IA

APPLE BROWNIE CAKE

A delightful combination that is easy to make.

8 tablespoons (1 stick) butter, softened
⅓ cup granulated sugar
2 eggs
1 teaspoon vanilla extract
1 cup instant cocoa powder
1 cup all-purpose flour
1 teaspoon baking soda
Pinch of salt
½ teaspoon ground cinnamon
2 cups chopped peeled apples

CINNAMON FROSTING
4 tablespoons (½ stick) butter, softened
1½ cups confectioners' sugar
Pinch of salt
2 tablespoons milk
½ teaspoon vanilla extract
1 teaspoon ground cinnamon

Preheat the oven to 325 degrees. Grease a 9-inch square baking pan. Cream the butter and sugar. Beat in the eggs and vanilla. Whisk together the cocoa powder, flour, soda, salt, and cinnamon and beat into the butter mixture until combined. Stir in the apples. Pour into the prepared pan and bake for 40 to 45 minutes. Cool in the pan.

To make the frosting, cream the butter and sugar; beat in the remaining ingredients. Spread on the cooled cake.

MAKES 1 CAKE   *Sunny Side Up,* Fort Lauderdale, FL

SNOW WHITE CHOCOLATE ROLL

6 tablespoons cake flour
6 tablespoons unsweetened cocoa powder
½ teaspoon baking powder
¼ teaspoon salt
¾ cup granulated sugar
4 egg whites, stiffly beaten
4 egg yolks, beaten until thick
1 teaspoon vanilla extract
Sifted confectioners' sugar

FILLING
1 cup heavy cream, whipped
1 (3½-ounce) can coconut flakes
½ teaspoon almond extract

Preheat the oven to 400 degrees. Grease a 15 × 10 × 1-inch jelly roll pan and line it with waxed paper.

Sift the flour, cocoa, baking powder, and salt together three times. Beat the sugar gradually into the egg whites. Beat in the egg yolks and vanilla. Fold in the flour gradually. Spoon evenly into the prepared pan and bake for 13 to 15 minutes. Meanwhile, mix together the filling ingredients.

After baking, turn the cake out onto a cloth covered with sifted confectioners' sugar. Peel off the paper and quickly remove the crisp edges of the cake with a sharp knife. Spread with the filling and roll immediately, beginning at a narrow side. Wrap in cloth and cool. Place in refrigerator until serving time.

SERVES 12   *Cotton Country Cooking,*
                          Morgan County, AL

PETITE FUDGE CAKES

5 squares (5 ounces) semisweet
    chocolate or white chocolate
2 sticks (½ pound) butter
1 cup chopped pecans (optional)
1¾ cups granulated sugar
1 cup all-purpose flour
4 large eggs, unbeaten
1 teaspoon vanilla extract
Confectioners' sugar

Preheat the oven to 325 degrees. Butter miniature or regular-sized muffin tins or line them with paper cupcake liners.

Melt the chocolate and butter together in the top of a double boiler over simmering water. Add the pecans, if desired, and stir until well coated. Remove from the heat and set aside to cool. In another bowl, combine the sugar, flour, and eggs. Add the chocolate mixture; stir until just mixed. Add the vanilla. Spoon the batter into the prepared tins. Bake for 12 to 15 minutes for small cakes, 30 minutes for larger ones. Be careful not to overbake. They should be gooey. Cool and dust with confectioners' sugar.

NOTE: For fancy cakes, use gold or silver cupcake liners and add a dot of whipped cream to each cake. Sprinkle with silver shot.

MAKES ABOUT 68 SMALL OR 24 REGULAR CUPCAKES

Beyond Parsley, Kansas City, MO

KILLER CUPCAKES

Loved by all children from ages four to forty-four. The moist, fudgy cupcake holds a creamy cheesecake surprise.

CUPCAKES

4 squares (4 ounces) semisweet
    chocolate
1 teaspoon vanilla extract
2 sticks (½ pound) butter
4 eggs
1½ cups sugar
1 cup all-purpose flour

Preheat the oven to 350 degrees. Line standard muffin tins with paper cupcake liners. In the top part of a double boiler over simmering water, melt the chocolate with the vanilla and butter. In a large bowl, beat the eggs until thick and add the sugar. Beat in the flour. Fold in the butter-chocolate mixture. Spoon into the prepared tins, filling the cups ⅔ full.

FILLING

8 ounces cream cheese, softened
¼ cup sugar
1 egg, beaten
Dash of salt
¾ cup semisweet chocolate chips

Mix the cream cheese, sugar, egg, and salt until just blended. Stir in the chocolate chips. Drop a rounded teaspoon of filling onto the top of each cupcake. Bake for 30 minutes.

MAKES 20–22 CUPCAKES

San Francisco Encore, San Francisco, CA

CHOCOLATE POUND CAKE

1 cup unsweetened cocoa
2 cups all-purpose flour, sifted
½ teaspoon baking powder
1 teaspoon salt
2 tablespoons instant coffee granules
3 sticks (¾ pound) unsalted butter, softened
3 cups granulated sugar
2 teaspoons vanilla extract
5 eggs
1 cup buttermilk

Preheat the oven to 325 degrees. Butter and flour a 10-inch tube pan.

Whisk together the cocoa, flour, baking powder, salt, and coffee granules. Set aside. In a large bowl, cream the butter with an electric mixer until light and fluffy. While beating, add the sugar in a slow stream, beating for 5 minutes on high speed. Turn the mixer to low speed and add the vanilla. Add the eggs one at a time, beating briefly after each addition. Mix the buttermilk with ¼ cup of the water. Beat the dry ingredients and buttermilk alternately into the butter mixture, beginning and ending with dry ingredients.

Pour the well-blended mixture into the prepared pan and bake in the upper third of the oven for 1 hour and 20 minutes or until a tester inserted in the center comes out clean. Let the cake rest in the pan for 20 minutes before removing. Cool completely on a rack before serving.

SERVES 10

More Than a Tea Party, Boston, MA

CHOCOLATE PECAN UPSIDE-DOWN CAKE

PECAN TOPPING
4 tablespoons (½ stick) unsalted butter, melted
½ cup packed brown sugar
½ cup light corn syrup
1½ cups coarsely chopped pecans

CAKE
2 cups all-purpose flour
1 teaspoon baking powder
½ teaspoon salt
8 tablespoons (1 stick) butter, softened
1½ cups sugar
3 eggs
3 squares (3 ounces) unsweetened chocolate, melted
¾ cup sour cream
1 teaspoon vanilla extract

To make the topping: In a small bowl, combine the butter, brown sugar, and syrup. Pour into a greased 8 × 12-inch baking pan. Scatter pecans evenly on top and set aside.

To make the cake: Preheat the oven to 350 degrees. Whisk together the flour, baking powder, and salt and set aside. Cream the butter; gradually add the sugar. Beat until light and fluffy. Beat in the eggs one at a time. Stir in the melted chocolate. Combine the sour cream and vanilla. Add to the batter alternately with the dry ingredients. Pour over the topping in the pan. Bake for 45 minutes or until a tester inserted in the center of the cake comes out clean. Loosen the edges with a sharp knife. Invert onto a cake plate immediately. Serve with whipped cream or vanilla ice cream.

SERVES 8 TO 12

Scarsdale Entertains: Appetizers and Desserts, Central Westchester, NY

NASHVILLE'S ONE-PAN FUDGE CAKE

8 tablespoons (1 stick) butter

1¼ squares (1¼ ounces) bittersweet chocolate

1 cup sugar

2 eggs

½ cup all-purpose flour

¼ teaspoon baking powder

⅛ teaspoon salt

1 teaspoon vanilla extract

1 cup nuts, chopped coarse

Preheat the oven to 325 degrees. Thoroughly grease an 8-inch square baking pan.

In a medium saucepan over very low heat, melt the butter with the chocolate. Remove from the heat and stir in the sugar. Beat in the eggs. Mix the flour, baking powder, and salt in a measuring cup and stir into the chocolate mixture along with the vanilla. Fold in the nuts. Turn into the prepared pan and bake for 35 minutes. Cut into squares while hot, but do not remove from the pan until cooled.

SERVES 12   *Nashville Seasons,* Nashville, TN

CHOCOLATE CAKE WITH RUM BUTTER SAUCE

2 squares (2 ounces) unsweetened chocolate

8 tablespoons (1 stick) butter

2 eggs

1 cup granulated sugar

1 teaspoon vanilla extract

¼ teaspoon salt

½ cup all-purpose flour

RUM BUTTER SAUCE

1 cup heavy cream

¾ cup packed light brown sugar

8 tablespoons (1 stick) butter

3 tablespoons dark rum

½ teaspoon vanilla extract

Preheat the oven to 325 degrees. Butter a 9-inch springform pan.

For the cake: In a double boiler, melt the chocolate and butter over hot, not boiling, water, stirring occasionally until smooth. Remove from the heat and cool to room temperature. With an electric mixer, beat the eggs at high speed for 3 to 4 minutes. Gradually beat in the sugar and continue to beat until very thick, about 5 minutes. Beat in the vanilla, salt, and cooled chocolate mixture. On low speed, blend in the flour. Pour into the prepared pan. Bake 30 to 35 minutes or until a toothpick inserted in the center comes out clean. Cool completely in the pan on a wire rack.

To prepare the sauce: Combine the cream, brown sugar, and butter in a saucepan. Cook over low heat, stirring frequently, until the mixture boils. Boil 5 minutes, stirring occasionally. Remove from the heat. Stir in the rum and vanilla. To serve, spoon a moderate amount of warm sauce on a rimmed dessert plate. Top with a wedge of cake.

SERVES 12   *California Fresh,* Lafayette, CA

IMMUNIZATION PROJECT
JUNIOR LEAGUE OF OGDEN, UTAH

The Junior League of Ogden, Utah, initiated a three-county coalition to address the low rate of children fully immunized in those counties. The League realized the problem was statewide, and proceeded to form a statewide coalition. Public Service Announcements were developed, a mobile immunization van runs each summer, and since the program, there has been a statewide increase of fully immunized children of over 30 percent.

DARK CHOCOLATE CAKE WITH WHITE CHOCOLATE BUTTERCREAM FROSTING

2 cups all-purpose flour

¼ teaspoon salt

¼ teaspoon freshly grated nutmeg

1½ teaspoons baking soda

4 squares (4 ounces) unsweetened chocolate

2 sticks (½ pound) unsalted butter, softened

1¾ cups sugar

4 eggs

1⅓ cups buttermilk

1 teaspoon vanilla extract

White chocolate buttercream frosting (below)

Preheat the oven to 325 degrees with the shelf positioned in the lower third of the oven. Line two 9-inch round cake pans with circles of baking parchments.

Whisk together the flour, salt, nutmeg, and baking soda and set aside. Melt the chocolate in the top of a double boiler over hot, but not boiling, water. Remove chocolate from the heat and stir until smooth. Let cool. Cream the butter and sugar until light and fluffy, stopping the mixer to scrape the bowl and beaters several times. Add the eggs one at a time, beating after each addition. Add the flour mixture and buttermilk alternately to the batter, beginning and ending with flour mixture and mixing well after each addition. Stir in the vanilla and cooled chocolate, blending until the color is even.

Pour the batter into the prepared pans. Smooth the batter level, then spread it slightly from the center toward the edges of the pan so that the cake will rise evenly. Bake for 35 to 45 minutes or until the top is lightly springy to the touch and a cake tester inserted in the center comes out clean. Remove the layers from the pan and cool completely on wire racks. Prepare the frosting. Center one of the cake layers on a serving plate and cover with frosting. Place the second layer on top and frost the top and sides of the cake with the remaining frosting.

WHITE CHOCOLATE BUTTERCREAM FROSTING

6 tablespoons heavy cream

4 ounces white chocolate, chopped fine

¼ cup crème de cacao

2 sticks (½ pound) unsalted butter, softened

4 cups (1 box) confectioners' sugar

Bring the cream to a boil in a small saucepan. Pour the hot cream over the chopped white chocolate and stir until completely smooth. Stir crème de cacao into the white chocolate mixture. Cool, stirring occasionally. Cream the butter in a large bowl. Add the confectioners' sugar and beat for 5 minutes, until light and fluffy. Add the white chocolate mixture to the butter mixture gradually, beating at low speed until the desired consistency is reached.

N O T E : This cake is beautiful decorated with dark chocolate rosettes or shavings.

S E R V E S   1 2   *Savor the Brandywine Valley,* Wilmington, DE

BEST-EVER CHEESECAKE

CRUST
1 cup all-purpose flour
¼ cup sugar
1 teaspoon grated lemon peel
8 tablespoons (1 stick) butter
1 egg yolk, slightly beaten
¼ teaspoon vanilla extract

CHEESE FILLING
5 (8-ounce) packages cream cheese, softened
1¾ cups sugar
3 tablespoons all-purpose flour
¾ teaspoon grated lemon peel
¼ teaspoon salt
¼ teaspoon vanilla extract
5 eggs (1 cup)
2 egg yolks
¼ cup heavy cream

Preheat the oven to 400 degrees. Combine the flour, sugar, and lemon peel. Cut in butter with a pastry blender until the mixture is crumbly. Add the egg yolk and vanilla; blend well. Pat ⅓ of the dough on the bottom of a 9-inch springform pan (sides removed). Bake about 6 minutes, or until golden; cool. Butter the sides of the pan; attach to the bottom. Pat the remaining dough evenly on the sides to a height of 2 inches.

Heat the oven to 500 degrees. Put the cream cheese in a mixing bowl and beat until fluffy. In a separate bowl, combine the sugar, flour, lemon peel, salt, and vanilla. Gradually blend into the cheese. Add the eggs and yolks, one at a time; beat well after each addition. Gently stir in the cream. Turn into the crust-lined pan. Bake at 500 degrees for 5 to 8 minutes, or until the top of the crust is golden. Reduce the heat to 200 degrees; bake 1 hour longer. Remove from the oven; cool in the pan for 3 hours. Remove the sides of the pan. Chill 6 hours or overnight. Cut into small slices to serve.

SERVES 20   *One of a Kind,* Mobile, AL

PRIZE-WINNING PUMPKIN CHEESECAKE

This recipe won a prize in Creative Cooking's cheesecake contest. It's best when prepared two days in advance of serving.

3 cups finely ground gingersnaps
½ cup confectioners' sugar
12 tablespoons (1½ sticks) butter, melted
2 (8-ounce) packages cream cheese, softened
5 eggs
¾ cup packed light brown sugar
1 (16-ounce) can solid-pack pumpkin
1½ teaspoons ground cinnamon
¼ teaspoon ground cloves
¼ teaspoon ground ginger
¼ teaspoon ground mace
¼ teaspoon vanilla extract
½ cup brandy
2 cups sour cream
¼ cup granulated sugar

Preheat the oven to 350 degrees. Combine the gingersnap crumbs, confectioners' sugar, and melted butter in a bowl and mix thoroughly. Press the crumb mixture onto the bottom and up the sides of an ungreased 9-inch springform pan.

Beat the cream cheese with an electric mixer on medium speed. Add the eggs, one at a time, the brown sugar, pumpkin, spices, vanilla, and ¼ cup of the brandy to the cream cheese and mix until smooth. Pour the pumpkin mixture into the prepared pan and bake for 40 minutes or until the edge of the cheesecake begins to pull away from side of pan.

Remove the cheesecake from the oven and reset the temperature to 400 degrees. Whisk together the sour cream, sugar, and remaining ¼ cup of brandy in a small bowl. Spread the sour cream mixture over the hot cheesecake, return to the oven, and bake for 10 minutes more. Cool to room temperature, cover, and refrigerate in the pan overnight or up to 4 days. Remove the sides of the pan before serving.

SERVES 12   *Savor the Brandywine Valley,* Wilmington, DE

CHEESECAKE PAR EXCELLENCE

1 cup graham cracker crumbs
¼ cup firmly packed brown sugar
6 tablespoons unsalted butter
2 cups creamy peanut butter
2 cups sugar
2 (8-ounce) packages cream cheese,
    softened
2 teaspoons vanilla extract
1½ cups heavy cream, whipped
1 cup chopped unsalted dry-roasted
    peanuts
4 squares (4 ounces) semisweet
    chocolate
3 tablespoons plus 2 teaspoons hot
    brewed coffee

In a medium bowl combine the crumbs, brown sugar, and 4 tablespoons of the melted butter. Press onto the bottom and up the sides of a 9-inch springform pan.

In a large bowl, combine the peanut butter, sugar, cream cheese, remaining 2 tablespoons of butter, and the vanilla. Beat until smooth and creamy. Fold in the whipped cream and peanuts. Spoon the filling into the crust. Refrigerate for 6 hours.

In a double boiler over hot water, melt the chocolate and coffee together. Spread over the filling. Refrigerate until firm. Remove the sides of the springform before serving.

SERVES 16   *For Goodness Taste*, Rochester, NY

PRALINE CHEESECAKE WITH PECAN SAUCE

CRUST
1¼ cups graham cracker crumbs
¼ cup granulated sugar
¼ cup pecans, chopped and toasted
4 tablespoons (½ stick) butter,
    melted

Preheat the oven to 350 degrees. Combine the crumbs, sugar, and pecans in a bowl. Add the melted butter and mix well. Press the crumb mixture over the bottom and 1½ inches up the sides of a 9-inch springform pan. Bake for 10 minutes.

FILLING
3 (8-ounce) packages cream cheese,
    softened
1 cup packed brown sugar
⅔ cup evaporated milk
2 tablespoons flour
1½ teaspoons vanilla extract
3 eggs
1 cup pecan halves, toasted

Beat together the cream cheese, brown sugar, evaporated milk, flour, and vanilla. Add the eggs and beat just until blended. Pour into the hot baked crust. Bake for 50 to 55 minutes. Cool in the pan 30 minutes, loosen the sides of the springform, and remove the rim. Cool completely. Arrange the pecan halves on top of cheesecake.

PECAN SAUCE
1 cup dark brown sugar, packed
2 tablespoons cornstarch
2 tablespoons butter
½ cup broken pecan pieces

In a saucepan, mix the brown sugar and cornstarch. Add 1½ cups of water. Bring to a boil and stir over medium heat until thickened and bubbly, about 5 minutes. Stir in the butter and add the pecans. Serve the sauce over the cheesecake or pass in a sauceboat.

SERVES 12   *Without Reservations*, Pittsburgh, PA

FRESH BANANA CHEESECAKE

CRUST
1½ cups quick-cooking oats
½ cup pecans, finely chopped
½ cup packed brown sugar
5 tablespoons butter, melted

Preheat the oven to 350 degrees. Stir together the oats, pecans, brown sugar, and butter until well combined. Press firmly into the bottom and up the sides of a 9-inch springform pan. Bake for 18 minutes or until golden brown. Cool.

FILLING
2 (8-ounce) packages cream cheese, softened
1 cup mashed ripe bananas
¾ cup granulated sugar
2 teaspoons lemon juice
4 eggs

TOPPING
1 cup sour cream
2 tablespoons granulated sugar
1 teaspoon vanilla extract
Banana slices for garnish

Preheat the oven to 350 degrees. Beat together the cream cheese, bananas, ¾ cup sugar, and lemon juice until well blended. Add the eggs one at a time, beating well after each addition. Pour into the crust. Bake for 40 minutes. While the cake is baking, prepare sour cream topping by mixing together the sour cream, 2 tablespoons sugar, and vanilla until well blended. Remove the cheesecake from the oven and top with the sour cream mixture. Return to the oven and bake for 10 minutes more. Cool slightly. Loosen the cake from the sides of the pan and remove the springform. Cool the cake to room temperature. Refrigerate, covered, overnight. Garnish with banana slices before serving.

SERVES 12 TO 16 — *Another Taste of Aloha*, Honolulu, HI

PASKHA

This Russian Easter dessert must be prepared 24 hours in advance

4 (8-ounce) packages cream cheese
8 tablespoons (1 stick) butter, softened
1 (1-pound) package confectioners' sugar
7 egg yolks (see Note)
Grated rind of 1 lemon
1 teaspoon vanilla extract
1 (5-ounce) can toasted unsalted almonds, slivered
¼ cup chopped citron candies
¼ cup chopped candied orange peel
¼ cup chopped candied lemon peel

Thoroughly scrub a new clay flowerpot measuring 6 inches across at the top. Line with a double thickness of dampened cheesecloth. (Or oil a 4-sided pyramid-shaped paskha mold.)

In a mixing bowl, cream together the cream cheese and butter. Beat in the sugar; when well mixed, add the egg yolks, lemon rind, and vanilla. Beat until thoroughly combined. Fold in the almonds, citron, and orange and lemon peel.

Pour the mixture into the prepared container. Cover and freeze for 24 hours. Thaw before serving. (The paskha will keep in the freezer for at least a month.) Unmold on a platter and serve with sesame crackers and fresh strawberries or pineapple spears.

NOTE: The egg yolks remain uncooked in this recipe. Omit them if you wish.

SERVES 20–24 — *The Bounty of East Texas*, Longview, TX

CHOCOLATE AMARETTO CHEESECAKE

CRUST

1½ cups finely chopped blanched
   almonds

2 tablespoons sugar

3 tablespoons butter, melted

FILLING

5 ounces milk chocolate chips

5 ounces semisweet chocolate chips

2 tablespoons butter

⅓ cup amaretto liqueur

2 (8-ounce) packages cream cheese,
   softened

⅓ cup sugar

2 eggs

1 cup sour cream, at room
   temperature

Preheat the oven to 350 degrees. Combine the almonds, sugar, and butter in a mixing bowl, mixing well. Press onto the bottom and ⅓ of the way up the sides of a 9-inch springform pan. Bake for 15 to 20 minutes or until lightly browned. Reduce the oven heat to 325 degrees.

Melt the chocolate chips and butter with the amaretto in a double boiler, stirring until smooth. In a mixing bowl, beat the cream cheese and sugar together. Add the eggs and sour cream, mixing well. Pour in the chocolate mixture and blend. Pour into the prepared crust and bake for 45 minutes. Cool to room temperature and remove the sides of the pan. Chill before serving.

SERVES 8   *Hearts and Flours,* Waco, TX

CHOCOHOLIC CHEESECAKE

A chocolate lover's delight.

CRUST

1 cup chocolate wafer crumbs

4 tablespoons (½ stick) butter, melted

½ cup pecans or macadamia nuts,
   chopped fine

FILLING

3 (8-ounce) packages cream cheese,
   softened

1 cup sugar

4 eggs

8 ounces semisweet chocolate,
   melted and cooled

2 tablespoons unsweetened cocoa
   powder

2 teaspoons vanilla extract

2 cups sour cream

8 tablespoons (1 stick) butter,
   melted

Whipped cream for garnish
   (optional)

Combine the wafer crumbs, butter, and nuts until well blended. Press evenly onto the bottom and partially up the sides of a 10-inch springform pan. Cover the outside of the pan with foil to prevent leakage. Chill.

Preheat the oven to 350 degrees. Beat the cream cheese until fluffy in a large mixing bowl. Gradually add the sugar. Beat in the eggs one at a time, beating until well blended after each addition. Stir in the chocolate, cocoa, and vanilla; mix well. Fold in the sour cream and butter. Pour into the prepared pan. Bake for 50 to 55 minutes or until the edges are set. Remove from the oven and cool. Refrigerate overnight. Serve in small slices, garnished with whipped cream if desired.

SERVES 16   *I've Got a Cook in Kalamazoo,* Kalamazoo, MI

CHOCOLATE ZEBRA CHEESECAKE

1½ cups chocolate wafer crumbs
(about 30 wafers)

3 tablespoons butter, melted

½ (6-ounce) package semisweet
chocolate pieces (½ cup)

4 (8-ounce) packages cream cheese,
softened

1¼ cups sugar

3 tablespoons cornstarch

¼ teaspoon salt

5 large eggs

1 (8-ounce) container sour cream

2 teaspoons vanilla extract

1½ cups heavy cream

12 ounces (12 squares) semisweet
chocolate

8 ounces white chocolate

Sweetened whipped cream,
maraschino cherries, and mint
leaves for garnish

Preheat the oven to 350 degrees. Grease a 9-inch springform pan. In a bowl, mix the crumbs and butter; press firmly onto the bottom of the pan. Bake the crust for 12 to 15 minutes. Remove from the oven; sprinkle with chocolate pieces. Let stand several minutes until the chocolate pieces soften, then spread the softened chocolate evenly over the crust. Refrigerate while preparing the filling.

In a large bowl, with an electric mixer at medium speed, beat the cream cheese until light and fluffy. In a small bowl, mix the sugar, cornstarch, and salt and gradually beat this mixture into the cream cheese until blended. With the mixer on low speed, beat in the eggs one at a time. Add the sour cream, vanilla, and 1 cup of the heavy cream, continuing to beat until blended and smooth.

Divide the batter evenly between two large measuring cups or other containers with pouring spouts. In a small saucepan over low heat, melt 8 squares of the semisweet chocolate. In another small saucepan over low heat, melt the white chocolate. Stir the white chocolate into the batter in one cup and stir the melted semisweet chocolate into the batter in the second measuring cup.

To create a zebra design, pour half the dark batter into springform pan. Holding the white batter about two feet above the pan, pour about half the batter directly into the center of the dark batter. Pouring from this height will cause the batter in the center of the cake to be pushed toward the edge of the pan, forming a bull's-eye or zebra design. Repeat this procedure three times, decreasing the amount of batter each time and pouring from high above the pan only into the center, ending with the white batter. The top of the cake should look like a series of concentric circles.

Bake the cheesecake 30 minutes. Lower the oven heat to 225 degrees and bake 1¾ hours or longer, until the center is set. Turn off the oven; let the cheesecake remain in the oven 1 hour. Remove from the oven, and run a thin-bladed spatula or knife around the edges of the cheesecake to loosen it from the sides of the pan. Cook the cake in the pan on a wire rack. Refrigerate at least 6 hours or until well chilled.

About 1 hour before serving, prepare a glaze by heating the remaining ½ cup of heavy cream in a saucepan over medium heat until small bubbles form around the edge of pan. Remove the saucepan from the heat. Stir in the remaining 4 squares of semisweet chocolate until melted and smooth. Cool the glaze 10 minutes. Meanwhile, carefully remove the cake from the springform to a cake plate; with a spatula spread the glaze over the top and sides. Refrigerate 30 to 45 minutes, until the glaze is set. If you like, garnish with whipped cream, maraschino cherries, and mint.

SERVES 20   *A River Runs Backward,* Jacksonville, FL

GLAZED CHOCOLATE CHIP CHEESECAKE

1¼ cups chocolate wafer crumbs
5 tablespoons butter, melted
3 (8-ounce) packages cream cheese, softened
¾ cup sugar
3 eggs
1 cup semisweet chocolate chips, coarsely chopped in a blender or food processor
1 teaspoon vanilla extract

GLAZE
½ cup unsweetened cocoa powder
½ cup sugar
½ cup heavy cream
4 tablespoons (½ stick) unsalted butter, cut into pieces
Chocolate leaves or other garnish

Preheat the oven to 450 degrees. Mix the crumbs and melted butter. Press onto the bottom and ⅓ of the way up the sides of an 8- or 9-inch springform pan. Set aside.

Beat the cream cheese and sugar in an electric mixer at medium speed until blended. Add the eggs one at at time, beating well after each addition. Add the chocolate chips and vanilla. Pour into the prepared pan. Bake 10 minutes. Reduce the heat to 250 degrees. Continue baking for 35 minutes. Loosen the cake from the edges of pan. Cool before removing the sides. Chill.

Combine the glaze ingredients in the top of a double boiler over simmering water. Stir until smooth and shiny, about 5 minutes. Pour over the chilled and unmolded cake, tilting to cover evenly. Use a spatula to spread over the top and sides. Refrigerate several hours. Decorate with chocolate leaves.

SERVES 12   *Gatherings*, Milwaukee, WI

WHITE CHOCOLATE MOUSSE

The texture of velvet, the sheen of satin, the taste of heaven.

WHITE CHOCOLATE MOUSSE
9 ounces imported white chocolate, chopped
3 large egg yolks
⅓ cup confectioners' sugar
1¼ cups chilled heavy cream

RASPBERRY SAUCE
1 (10-ounce) package frozen raspberries, defrosted and drained
¼ cup superfine sugar
2 tablespoons Grand Marnier (orange liqueur)
Candied violet blossoms for garnish

Mousse: Melt the white chocolate in the top of a double boiler over barely simmering water. Stir occasionally with a wooden spoon. Remove from the heat. In a bowl set over a saucepan of simmering water, whisk together the egg yolks and sugar until well combined. Remove the bowl from the saucepan and beat in ¼ cup of the cream. Slowly stir in the melted chocolate until well combined. Whip the remaining 1 cup of cream until stiff peaks form. Gently fold together the whipped cream and white chocolate mixture. Spoon into wine goblets and refrigerate until ready to serve.

Sauce: Put the raspberries, sugar, and Grand Marnier in a blender or food processor and purée. Do not strain, as the seeds enhance the texture. To serve, top each goblet of white chocolate mousse with raspberry sauce and garnish with a candied violet.

SERVES 6   *A Matter of Taste*, Morristown, NJ

SLICES OF SIN

A fantastically rich dessert that improves with age.

8 ounces semisweet chocolate
½ cup strong brewed coffee
2 sticks (½ pound) butter
1 cup sugar
4 eggs, beaten
1 cup heavy cream
2 to 3 teaspoons brandy

Preheat the oven to 350 degrees. Line a glass loaf pan with foil; butter the foil. In the top part of a double boiler, melt the chocolate in the coffee. Add the butter and sugar, stirring until the butter is melted. Cool the mixture for 10 minutes. Beat in the eggs one at a time. Pour the mixture into the prepared loaf pan. Bake until a crust forms on top, approximately 35 to 45 minutes. Set the loaf pan in enough cool water to come halfway up the pan. The dessert will rise and fall as it cools. When cool, wrap the pan well and refrigerate for at least 2 days or up to 2 weeks. When ready to serve, beat the cream until stiff. Stir in the brandy. Unmold the loaf and slice into individual servings. Garnish with dollops of cream.

SERVES 10–12   *Capital Classics,* Washington, D.C.

CHOCOLATE ICEBOX CAKE

2 (4-ounce) cakes German sweet
   chocolate
3 tablespoons boiling water
2 teaspoons confectioners' sugar
4 egg yolks
1 teaspoon vanilla extract
4 egg whites, beaten stiff
18 ladyfingers
Whipped cream for garnish

Melt the chocolate in the top of a double boiler. Mix in the water and sugar. Remove from the heat and let cool slightly. Add the egg yolks one at a time, beating well after each addition. Stir in the vanilla, then fold in the egg whites. Split the ladyfingers in half and line a mold with them. Pour in some of the chocolate mixture. Cover with a layer of ladyfingers. Repeat until all ingredients are used, ending with a layer of ladyfingers. Chill in the refrigerator overnight. Unmold and serve with whipped cream.

SERVES 8   *Junior League of Dallas Cookbook,* Dallas, TX

CHOCOLATE ALMOND TERRINE WITH RASPBERRY PURÉE

3 egg yolks, slightly beaten
2 cups heavy cream
16 ounces (16 squares) semisweet
   chocolate
¾ cup light corn syrup
8 tablespoons (1 stick) butter
½ cup confectioners' sugar
1 teaspoon vanilla extract
¼ teaspoon almond extract
1 (10-ounce) package frozen red
   raspberries, thawed
1 to 2 tablespoons raspberry liqueur
   or almond liqueur
Fresh red raspberries and mint
   leaves for garnish

Line an 8-inch loaf pan with plastic wrap. In a small bowl, mix the egg yolks and ½ cup of the cream. In a 3-quart saucepan, combine the chocolate, ½ cup of the corn syrup, and the butter. Cook and stir over medium heat until the chocolate and butter are melted. Blend a little of the hot mixture into the yolks, add the yolks to the pan, and cook for 3 minutes, stirring constantly. Cool to room temperature.

In a small bowl, beat the remaining 1½ cups cream, the confectioners' sugar, vanilla, and almond extract with an electric mixer until soft peaks form. Fold into the chocolate mixture until no streaks remain. Pour into the prepared loaf pan. Cover and chill overnight.

For the purée, in a blender container or food processor, purée the raspberries; press through a sieve to remove the seeds. Stir in the remaining ¼ cup of corn syrup and the liqueur.

To serve, invert the pan and cut the loaf into ⅝-inch slices. Pool some of the purée onto each dessert plate. Place a slice of terrine over the purée. Garnish with fresh raspberries and mint leaves.

SERVES 12   *Heart and Soul,* Memphis, TN

CHOCOLATE PÂTÉ WITH CRÈME ANGLAISE AND RASPBERRY COULIS

PÂTÉ

1 pound bittersweet chocolate
1 cup heavy cream
4 tablespoons (½ stick) unsalted butter, cut into slices
4 egg yolks, slightly beaten
1 cup confectioners' sugar
¼ cup eau-de-vei (kirsch or framboise)
¼ cup sliced almonds
½ pint raspberries, for garnish

In the top part of a double boiler over simmering water, partially melt the chocolate. Add the cream and butter and place the pan directly over low heat, whisking frequently until the chocolate is fully melted and the mixture is smooth. Blend a little of the hot mixture into the yolks. Add the yolks to the pan and gradually mix in the sugar and liqueur. Remove from the heat. Line a loaf pan with waxed paper, using enough to extend up and over the sides. Pour the mixture into the pan and let cool.

Toast the almonds slices in a low oven until golden. Sprinkle the almonds on top of the chocolate mixture, pressing down slightly so that portions stick in the chocolate. Cover and refrigerate overnight or a minimum of 6 hours. Invert the pâté onto a platter and peel off the waxed paper. Keep refrigerated until serving time.

CRÈME ANGLAISE

3 egg yolks
¼ cup granulated sugar
⅛ teaspoon salt
1 cup heavy cream
1 vanilla bean
2 tablespoons amaretto
½ teaspoon vanilla extract

Whisk the yolks, sugar, and salt together in a bowl until light and thick. In a heavy saucepan, combine the cream and the vanilla bean and bring to a boil. Remove from the heat and allow the mixture to cool slightly, about 5 minutes. Add the cream mixture to the egg mixture, whisking constantly. Pour the combined cream and egg mixtures into the saucepan and cook over low heat until thick enough to coat the back of a spoon. Do not allow the mixture to boil or it will curdle. Remove the pan from the heat and stir in the amaretto and vanilla extract. Remove the vanilla bean. Strain the sauce through a sieve if desired. May be refrigerated up to 3 days.

COULIS

1½ cups raspberries
¼ cup confectioners' sugar
¼ cup framboise

Blend or process the ingredients together and strain. Keep refrigerated until serving time.

To serve, cut the pâté into ½-inch slices with a knife dipped in cold water. Pool 2 tablespoons of crème anglaise on the left side of a dessert plate and 2 tablespoons of raspberry coulis on the right. Place a few raspberries along the outer edges of the sauces and place pâté in the center.

SERVES 12–16   *Above and Beyond Parsley*, Kansas City, MO

FLOURLESS GRAND MARNIER CAKE WITH RASPBERRY GINGER SAUCE

CAKE

1½ cups granulated sugar

7 tablespoons water

3 tablespoons Grand Marnier (orange liqueur)

8 ounces (8 squares) unsweetened chocolate, chopped fine

4 ounces (2 squares) semisweet chocolate, chopped fine

2 sticks (½ pound) unsalted butter, softened

5 large eggs, room temperature

Confectioners' sugar

SAUCE

1 pint fresh raspberries

3 pieces candied ginger, chopped

¼ cup grenadine syrup

¼ cup framboise (raspberry liqueur)

The cake: Preheat the oven to 350 degrees. Line a 9-inch round baking pan with waxed paper; grease the waxed paper. In a heavy saucepan, combine 1 cup of the granulated sugar, the water, and the Grand Marnier; bring to a boil. Remove from the heat. Add 4 ounces of unsweetened chocolate and 2 ounces of semisweet chocolate; stir until smooth. Whisk in the remaining chocolate and the butter until smooth; set aside. In a large mixing bowl, beat the eggs with ½ cup of sugar until they are pale yellow and ribbons form when the beaters are lifted. Beat in the chocolate mixture until well blended. Pour the batter into the prepared pan. Place the cake pan in a large baking pan. Add enough boiling water to the larger pan to come halfway up the sides. Bake for 30 minutes, or until the cake remains firm in the center when shaken gently. The cake will be slightly wet in the center. Remove the cake from the water bath; cool 10 minutes. Unmold the cake onto a serving plate; cool completely. Sift confectioners' sugar over the top of the cake. Store loosely wrapped at room temperature.

The sauce: In a food processor, purée the raspberries and ginger. Add the grenadine and framboise and process until smooth. Pour and press through a strainer. Serve at room temperature. To serve, pool a spoonful of sauce onto a dessert plate and place a cake wedge on top of the sauce

SERVES 10 TO 12   *A Cleveland Collection,* Cleveland, OH

APPLE HUCKLEBERRY PIE WITH FRENCH CRUMB TOPPING

Pastry for 9-inch pie crust (page 338)

FILLING

5 cups pared and thinly sliced tart apples

1 cup huckleberries (blueberries can be substituted)

¾ cup granulated sugar

¼ cup all-purpose flour

½ teaspoon grated nutmeg

½ teaspoon ground cinnamon

TOPPING

8 tablespoons (1 stick) firm butter

1 cup all-purpose flour

½ cup packed brown sugar

Preheat the oven to 375 degrees. Fit the pastry into a 9-inch pie plate and flute the edges. Combine the filling ingredients and spoon into the pie shell. To make the topping, cut the butter into the flour with a pasty blender until crumbly. Toss with the brown sugar. Sprinkle the topping over the pie filling. Bake for 50 minutes. Cover with aluminum foil the last 10 minutes if the top browns too quickly.

SERVES 8   *Gold'n Delicious,* Spokane, WA

BAVARIAN APPLE TORTE

CRUST

8 tablespoons (1 stick) butter, softened

⅓ cup sugar

¼ teaspoon vanilla extract

1 cup all-purpose flour

FILLING

1 (8-ounce) package cream cheese, softened

¼ cup sugar

1 egg

½ teaspoon vanilla extract

TOPPING

½ teaspoon ground cinnamon

⅓ cup sugar

4 cups peeled, cored, sliced apples

Preheat the oven to 450 degrees.

To make the crust, cream the butter and sugar. Stir in the vanilla. Add the flour and mix well. Press onto the bottom and 2 inches up the sides of a greased 9-inch springform pan.

For the filling, combine the softened cream cheese and sugar. Add the egg and vanilla, mixing well. Spread evenly over the pastry.

Make the topping: In a large mixing bowl, sprinkle the sugar and cinnamon over the apples. Toss well. Spoon the apples over the filling. Bake at 450 degrees for 10 minutes. Reduce the temperature to 400 degrees and bake the torte 25 minutes longer. Cool before removing from pan.

SERVES 8–10   *Even More Special,* Durham and Orange County, NC

FRESH BERRY SHORTBREAD TART

SHORTBREAD

8 tablespoons (1 stick) butter, softened

3 tablespoons sugar

1⅓ cups all-purpose flour

½ teaspoon salt

1 teaspoon vanilla extract

1 egg yolk

CUSTARD

3 tablespoons all-purpose flour

¼ cup sugar

1 egg yolk

½ cup milk

2 teaspoons orange liqueur

BERRIES

1½ pints strawberries, sliced lengthwise

1 cup blueberries or blackberries

⅓ cup seedless raspberry jelly

1 teaspoon orange liqueur

Shortbread: Preheat the oven to 375 degrees. Cream the butter and sugar together until light and fluffy. Beat in the flour and add the remaining ingredients. Form into a ball and chill 30 minutes. Roll out the dough and press into the bottom of a 9-inch tart pan with a removable bottom. Prick all over with a fork. Chill 30 minutes. Cover with foil and bake at 375 degrees for 15 minutes. Remove the foil and bake 10 to 15 minutes more until light brown. Cool in the pan.

Custard: Combine the flour and sugar in a saucepan. Beat in the egg yolk. Stir in the milk. Cook over low heat, stirring, until it boils and thickens. Boil 2 minutes while stirring. Strain through a sieve and add the liqueur. Cool in the refrigerator. Spread over the cooked tart shell.

Berries: Spread strawberries around the outer edge of the tart in concentric circles. Place blueberries in the center. Melt the jelly with the liqueur. Brush over the berries. Chill and serve.

SERVES 8   *Feast of Eden,* Monterey, CA

SOUR-CREAM APPLE PIE

1 egg
1 cup sour cream
1 teaspoon vanilla extract
¾ cup granulated sugar
¼ teaspoon salt
2 tablespoons all-purpose flour
3 cups peeled and diced tart
  Michigan apples
1 (9-inch) unbaked pie shell

TOPPING
½ cup packed brown sugar
⅓ cup all-purpose flour
4 tablespoons (½ stick) butter,
  softened

Preheat the oven to 400 degrees. In a mixing bowl, beat the egg and stir in the sour cream and vanilla. Add the sugar, salt, and flour and beat until combined. Stir in the apples. Pour the mixture into the pie shell and bake for 25 minutes.

Meanwhile, make the topping: Combine the brown sugar and flour and work in the butter with the fingers until the mixture resembles coarse crumbs. Sprinkle on top of the hot apple pie and bake 20 minutes longer. Cool at least 10 minutes before cutting. Serve hot or cold.

SERVES 6–8   *Tested, Tried & True,* Flint, MI

STEVE OWENS' FAVORITE APPLE PIE

DOUBLE-CRUST PASTRY
2 cups all-purpose flour
½ teaspoon salt
⅔ cup solid vegetable shortening
5 to 6 tablespoons cold water

APPLE PIE FILLING
6 cups sliced peeled apples
1 cup sugar
½ teaspoon ground cinnamon
¼ teaspoon salt
2 tablespoons all-purpose flour
2 tablespoons butter
½ teaspoon lemon juice

Pastry: Put the flour and salt in a shallow bowl and cut in the shortening with a pastry blender or two knives until the mixture resembles coarse meal. Sprinkle with water, a tablespoon at a time, while tossing with a fork; stir lightly until the pastry holds together. Gather the dough into two balls; flatten into circles 1 inch thick. Roll out on a floured surface, using a lightly floured stockinette-covered rolling pin, into a 12-inch circle for the bottom crust. Fit into an 8- or 9-inch pie pan. Roll out the top crust in the same fashion and make a few slashes in the center to allow steam to escape.

Pie: Arrange apples in layers on the bottom crust. Mix the sugar, cinnamon, salt, and flour and sprinkle over the apples. Dot with butter. Pour lemon juice over this. Place the top crust over the filling. Seal the top and bottom crust together and crimp the edges. Bake in a preheated 375 degree oven for 50 minutes. Serve with French vanilla ice cream.

SERVES 6–8   *Sooner Sampler,* Norman, OK

MOONLIT BLUEBERRY PIE WITH ALMOND CRÈME CHANTILLY

PIE
4 cups fresh blueberries, washed (see Note)
¾ cup sugar
2 tablespoons cornstarch dissolved in 2 tablespoons water
1 tablespoon butter
1 tablespoon Cointreau or other orange liqueur
¼ cup slivered almonds, toasted
1 9-inch baked pie shell

CRÈME CHANTILLY
1 cup heavy cream
2 tablespoons sugar
¼ teaspoon almond extract

For pie: Combine 1 cup of the blueberries, the sugar, and ½ cup of water in a blender and purée until smooth. Pour the mixture into a medium saucepan and add the dissolved cornstarch. Heat until thickened, stirring frequently. Stir in the butter and Cointreau. Add almonds and remaining blueberries, stirring gently to combine. Pour into baked pie shell and chill.

For crème Chantilly: Combine the cream, sugar, and almond extract in a chilled small bowl and whip until stiff peaks form. Just before serving, spread on top of the chilled pie.

NOTE: It is best not to wash the blueberries until just before you are ready to use them.

SERVES 8

Dining by Fireflies: Unexpected Pleasures of the New South, Charlotte, NC

FRESH BLUEBERRY CINNAMON PIE

2⅓ cups all-purpose flour
1½ teaspoons salt
⅔ cup plus 2 tablespoons solid vegetable shortening
5 tablespoons cold water
4 cups fresh blueberries, washed
½ cup sugar
½ teaspoon ground cinnamon
1 tablespoon lemon juice
2 tablespoons butter

Preheat the oven to 425 degrees. Combine the 2 cups of flour and the salt. Cut in the shortening with a pastry blender or two knives. Sprinkle in water until all the flour is moistened and the dough comes away from the sides of bowl. Divide the dough into two balls. Roll one ball into a 12-inch circle and fit into a 9-inch pie pan. Trim the edges so there is a 1-inch extension beyond the rim.

Stir the blueberries, sugar, the remaining ⅓ cup of flour, the cinnamon, and lemon juice together. Spoon the blueberry filling into the pie shell. Dot with butter. Roll out the second ball of dough into a circle; cut vents for steam to escape. Place the rolled crust over the filling. Trim the upper crust to 1 inch beyond the rim, turn under the bottom crust, seal, and flute the edges. Place a 2- to 3-inch-wide foil strip around the rim to prevent excessive browning. Bake 35-45 minutes, until the crust is lightly browned. Remove the foil for the last 15 minutes of baking.

SERVES 8

Aw Shucks: Another Junior League Cookbook, Fort Wayne, IN

RASPBERRY-RHUBARB PIE

Pastry for a 9-inch pie (page 338)
1⅓ cups sugar, plus additional for sprinkling
3 tablespoons cornstarch
½ teaspoon grated orange rind
2 cups fresh rhubarb, cut into ½-inch pieces
2 cups fresh or unthawed frozen raspberries
2 tablespoons butter

Preheat the oven to 425 degrees. Line a pie plate with pastry. In a small bowl, combine the sugar, cornstarch, and orange rind. Set aside. In a separate bowl, combine the rhubarb and raspberries. Turn half the fruit into the pastry-lined pie plate and sprinkle with half the sugar mixture. Repeat with the remaining fruit and sugar and dot with butter.

Cover with the top crust, seal, and flute the edges. Cut slits in the top crust and sprinkle with sugar. Cover the edge with strips of aluminum foil to prevent overbrowning. Bake for 30 minutes. Remove the foil and bake about 15 minutes longer or until crust is light brown and juices bubble through the slits.

SERVES 8   *From Portland's Palate,* Portland, OR

FRUIT PIZZA

CRUST
8 tablespoons (1 stick) butter
¾ cup granulated sugar
1 egg
½ teaspoon vanilla extract
1 tablespoon milk
1¼ cups all-purpose flour
½ teaspoon baking powder

GLAZE
3 tablespoons cornstarch
3 tablespoons strawberry-flavored gelatin mix
1 cup granulated sugar

CREAM LAYER
1 cup confectioners' sugar
1 (8-ounce) package cream cheese, softened

TOPPINGS
2 bananas, sliced
1 (8-ounce) can mandarin orange sections, drained
1 (8-ounce) can crushed pineapple, drained
8 to 10 fresh strawberries, sliced
2 kiwifruit, sliced
1 cup blueberries

To make the crust, preheat the oven to 350 degrees. Cream together the butter and sugar. Add the egg, vanilla, and milk. Beat thoroughly. Combine the flour and baking powder. Add the dry ingredients to the butter mixture; blend well. Pat into a 14-inch pizza pan. Bake for 8 to 10 minutes.

Combine the glaze ingredients with 1 cup of water in a saucepan. Boil until thickened. Refrigerate until cool. Whip together the confectioners' sugar and cream cheese to form a cream layer. Spread over the baked crust.

Place sliced bananas atop the cream layer. Cover completely with the cooled glaze to prevent the bananas from turning brown. Scatter the remaining fruit over glaze, pizza-style.

SERVES 6-8   *Family & Company,* Binghamton, NY

STRAWBERRY MERINGUE TORTE

This delightful creation must be made the day before you serve it.

MERINGUE

4 egg whites, at room temperature
Pinch of salt
¼ teaspoon cream of tartar
1 teaspoon cider vinegar
1 teaspoon vanilla extract
1 cup granulated sugar

FILLING

1 (6-ounce) package semisweet
   chocolate chips
4 cups heavy cream
¼ cup confectioners' sugar
1 tablespoon vanilla extract
2 quarts fresh strawberries, washed
   and hulled (reserve several whole
   berries for garnish)

Meringue: Preheat the oven to 275 degrees. Beat the egg white, salt, cream of tartar, vinegar, and vanilla until soft peaks form. Gradually beat in the sugar, 1 tablespoon at a time, beating until stiff and glossy.

Line cookie sheets with baking parchment, foil, or waxed paper. Trace three 8-inch circles. Spread the meringue evenly over the circles. Bake for 1 hour, until meringues are creamy white and firm. Turn off the oven and let the meringue dry without opening the oven door for 15 minutes more. Remove from the oven, peel the meringues from the paper, and put on racks.

Filling: Melt the chocolate chips with 3 tablespoons of water in a double boiler over hot water. When smooth, remove from heat; stir occasionally to keep it soft. Whip the cream until very stiff, gradually adding the confectioners' sugar and vanilla. Slice the strawberries lengthwise and drain on paper towels.

Assembly: Place a meringue layer on a serving platter, flat side down. Spread a thin layer of chocolate over the meringue. Top with a layer of whipped cream and a layer of strawberries. Place a second layer of meringue over the strawberries and repeat the layers. Top with third layer of meringue. Cover the entire torte (top and sides) with the remaining whipped cream. Refrigerate at least 6 hours or overnight. If desired, decorate the top with whole strawberries.

VARIATION: Extra strawberries may be sliced and sugared to top each slice when served.

SERVES 10   *Clock Wise Cuisine*, Detroit, MI

CALAMONDIN PIE

1 (14-ounce) can sweetened
   condensed milk (*not* evaporated
   milk)
⅓ cup calamondin juice (see Note)
1 cup heavy cream, whipped
1 baked 9-inch graham cracker crust
   (see page 342)

Combine the milk and juice. Add to the whipped cream and mix thoroughly. Pour into the pie shell and refrigerate overnight.

NOTE: You may substitute a mixture of half orange juice and half lime juice.

SERVES 6 TO 8   *Heart of the Palms,* West Palm Beach, FL

VALLEY GRAPE PIE

GRAHAM CRACKER CRUST
1½ cups graham cracker crumbs
3 tablespoons sugar
5 tablespoons butter, melted

FILLING
3 tablespoons cornstarch
⅔ cup plus 1 tablespoon sugar
1 quart stemmed California
    Thompson seedless grapes
1 tablespoon fresh lemon juice
1 cup sour cream
1 teaspoon vanilla extract

Preheat the oven to 350 degrees. Combine the crumbs with the sugar and melted butter; toss with a fork until well blended. Reserve ¼ cup of the crumb mixture. Press the rest evenly onto the bottom and sides of a buttered 9-inch pie pan. Bake for about 8 minutes. Cool.

In a saucepan, dissolve the cornstarch in ¼ cup of cold water; stir in ⅔ cup of sugar and, when dissolved, add the grapes. Bring to a boil, stirring carefully, then reduce the heat and simmer about 5 minutes. Remove from the heat, stir in the lemon juice, and cool. To serve, turn the cooled grape filling into the pie shell; blend the sour cream with the remaining 1 tablespoon of sugar and vanilla and spread evenly over top. Sprinkle with the reserved crumbs.

SERVES 6

California Treasure, Fresno, CA

WILD BERRY TART

CRUST
1⅓ cups all-purpose flour
2 tablespoons sugar
8 tablespoons (1 stick) butter
1 egg yolk
2 to 4 tablespoons ice water

FILLING
2 tablespoons cornstarch, dissolved
    in orange juice
¼ cup sugar, plus additional for
    sprinkling
2 cups blueberries
1 cup raspberries
1 cup blackberries
1 egg yolk, lightly beaten
Whipped cream (optional)

To prepare the crust, mix the flour and sugar in a medium bowl. Cut the butter into pieces and add to the flour. Mix with the fingers or a pastry blender until the butter is evenly distributed and the mixture resembles coarse meal. Blend in the yolk. Sprinkle with water while mixing lightly with a fork until the mixture can form a ball. Shape the dough into a disk, wrap in waxed paper, and refrigerate until ready to use.

To prepare the filling, cook the cornstarch, sugar, and blueberries in a saucepan over medium heat until the mixture starts to thicken. Add ½ cup of raspberries and ½ cup of blackberries and continue to cook until fully thickened. Remove from the heat and cool completely.

Preheat the oven to 400 degrees. Bring the dough to room temperature. Place it between two sheets of waxed paper and roll out to ¼ inch thickness. Peel off the waxed paper and place the dough on a 12- to 14-inch tart pan or round flat pan. Spread the filling evenly over the center of the pastry, leaving 1 inch at edges. Fold the edges of the pastry up over the filling, allowing the pastry to overlap. Brush with egg yolk and sprinkle with sugar.

Bake the tart 20 to 25 minutes, until golden brown. Remove from the oven and cool. Top with whipped cream if desired and decorate with the remaining berries.

SERVES 6

Maine Ingredients, Portland, ME

NECTARINE TART

CRUST
1 cup all-purpose flour
¼ cup confectioners' sugar
8 tablespoons (1 stick) butter

GLAZE
½ cup (5 ounces) red currant jelly
2 tablespoons cornstarch
2 tablespoons granulated sugar
¼ teaspoon ground mace
⅛ teaspoon grated nutmeg
⅔ cup strained fresh orange juice
Grated rind of 1 orange

FILLING
4 to 6 ripe nectarines
Juice of ½ lemon
Granulated sugar for sprinkling

TOPPING
1 cup heavy cream
2 tablespoons confectioners' sugar
1 teaspoon grated nutmeg

Preheat the oven to 350 degrees. To prepare the crust, combine the flour and sugar. Cut in the butter with a pasty blender or two knives until crumbly. Press the mixture onto the bottom and up the sides of a 9- to 10-inch fluted tart pan with a removable bottom. Bake 15 minutes, or until lightly browned. Cool.

To prepare the glaze: In a small saucepan, combine the jelly, cornstarch, sugar, mace, and nutmeg. Stir thoroughly to blend. Add the orange juice and rind. Cook over medium heat, stirring constantly, until the mixture just comes to a boil and is thick and clear. Set aside.

To prepare the filling: Slice the unpeeled nectarines into thin slivers. Toss with lemon juice to prevent discoloring. Arrange in overlapping concentric circles in the cooled tart shell. Sprinkle with sugar, if desired, to sweeten the nectarines.

Pour the glaze over the fruit, spreading so that all the slices are coated. Refrigerate until serving time. To prepare the topping, combine the cream, 2 tablespoons of confectioners' sugar, and nutmeg. Whip until the cream holds its shape. To serve, remove the fluted metal ring, slice the tart into wedges, and pass the topping separately.

SERVES 8   *California Fresh*, Oakland–East Bay, CA

DIVINE LIME PIE

MERINGUE SHELL
4 egg whites
¼ teaspoon cream of tartar
1 cup sugar

FILLING
4 egg yolks
¼ teaspoon salt
½ cup sugar
⅓ cup fresh lime juice (2 to 3 limes)
1 cup heavy cream, chilled
1 tablespoon grated lime peel
Whipped cream and lime peel for
  garnish

Meringue: Preheat the oven to 275 degrees. Generously butter a 9-inch pie plate. In a mixing bowl, beat the egg whites and cream of tartar until foamy. Beat in the sugar very slowly, 1 tablespoon at a time, until stiff and glossy, about 10 minutes. Pile into the pie pan, pushing up around the sides. Bake for 1 hour, until firm and creamy white. Turn off the oven, leaving the meringue in the oven with the door closed for 1 hour. Remove from the oven and place on a rack.

Filling: Beat the egg yolks until light and lemon-colored. Stir in the salt, sugar, and lime juice. Cook over medium heat, stirring constantly, until the mixture thickens, about 5 minutes. Cool completely. In a chilled bowl, beat the cream until stiff. Fold in the filling mixture and the grated peel. Pile into the meringue shell and chill at least 4 hours. Garnish with whipped cream and lime peel twists.

SERVES 8   *The Star of Texas Cookbook*, Houston, TX

MARGARITA PIE

1 envelope unflavored gelatin
1 cup sugar
¼ teaspoon salt
4 eggs, separated
½ cup fresh lime juice
1 teaspoon grated lime peel
¼ cup tequila
2 teaspoons Triple Sec or other
  orange liqueur (optional)
Baked 9-inch pie shell
Whipped cream and thinly sliced
  lime for garnish

Combine the gelatin, ½ cup of the sugar, and the salt in a saucepan. Beat the egg yolks and lime juice together and add to the gelatin. Cook over medium heat for 5 to 7 minutes, until the gelatin dissolves. Remove from the heat. Stir in the lime peel, tequila, and liqueur. Chill in the refrigerator until the mixture thickens like pudding.

Beat the egg whites with the remaining ½ cup sugar until stiff. Fold into the tequila mixture. Spoon the filling into the pie shell. Garnish with whipped cream and lime slices.

SERVES 6–8   *Seasoned with Salt,* El Paso, TX

SOUR CREAM LEMON PIE

The best ever lemon pie!

1 baked 9-inch pie shell

FILLING
1 cup sugar
3 tablespoons cornstarch
1 tablespoon all-purpose flour
1 tablespoon grated lemon rind
⅓ cup fresh lemon juice
1 cup light cream
4 tablespoons (½ stick) butter
1 cup sour cream

TOPPING
1 cup heavy cream
2 tablespoons confectioners' sugar
½ cup sour cream
½ teaspoon almond extract
Grated lemon rind
Lemon slices for garnish

Filling: In a saucepan, over medium heat, combine the sugar, cornstarch, flour, lemon rind and juice, and light cream. Bring slowly to a boil, stirring constantly. Add the butter and cook until thick and smooth. Remove from the heat and cool. Stir in the sour cream and pour filling into the pie shell. Refrigerate until ready to serve.

Topping: Whip the cream and fold in the confectioners' sugar, sour cream, and almond extract. Spoon over the lemon pie filling. Sprinkle with grated lemon rind and decorate with lemon slices.

SERVES 6–8   *Jubilation,* Toronto, ON

PRALINE PUMPKIN PIE

⅓ cup chopped pecans
1 cup packed brown sugar
2 tablespoons butter, softened
1 unbaked 9-inch pie shell
2 eggs, beaten
1 cup canned pumpkin purée
1 tablespoon all-purpose flour
½ teaspoon salt
½ teaspoon ground cinnamon
½ teaspoon ground ginger
½ teaspoon ground cloves
⅛ teaspoon ground mace
1 cup evaporated milk

Preheat the oven to 450 degrees. Combine the pecans, ⅓ cup of the brown sugar, and the butter. Press into the bottom of the pie shell. Bake for 10 minutes.

Meanwhile, combine the eggs and pumpkin. Add ⅔ cup of brown sugar, the flour, salt, spices, and milk. Beat until smooth and creamy. Pour into the partially baked pie shell. Lower the oven heat to 325 degrees and bake 45 minutes.

SERVES 8   *Necessities and Temptations,* Austin, TX

ICE CREAM PUMPKIN PIE

A change for the holidays.

1 (9-inch) pie crust
1 pint vanilla ice cream
1 cup heavy cream
½ teaspoon vanilla extract
1 cup canned pumpkin purée
¾ cup sugar
¼ teaspoon grated nutmeg
½ teaspoon ground ginger
½ teaspoon ground cinnamon
½ teaspoon salt

Bake and cool the pie crust. Soften and spread the ice cream on the bottom of the pie crust. Place in the freezer for 15 minutes. Whip the cream until it forms soft peaks; add the vanilla. Mix the pumpkin with the sugar, spices, and salt; stir until thoroughly blended. Fold in the whipped cream. Pour the filling over the layer of ice cream and smooth the top. Place in the freezer for at least 6 hours. Cut into wedges 10 to 15 minutes before serving.

SERVES 6-8   *Epicure,* Orange County, CA

CHICAGO PEANUT BUTTER PIE

8 to 10 ounces fudge cookies,
    ground fine
⅓ cup sugar
8 tablespoons (1 stick) butter,
    softened
1 (8-ounce) package cream cheese,
    softened
1 cup chunky peanut butter
1 cup confectioners' sugar
1 cup heavy cream, whipped

Preheat the oven to 350 degrees. Combine the cookie crumbs, sugar, and butter until well blended. Press the mixture onto the bottom and up the sides of a 9-inch plate and bake for 15 minutes. Cool.

In a food processor, combine the cream cheese, peanut butter, and confectioners' sugar. Process until almost smooth. Gently stir in the whipped cream and pour into the pie shell. Chill.

SERVES 8   *One Magnificent Cookbook,* Chicago, IL

COCONUT CREAM PIE WITH ALMOND CRUMB CRUST

ALMOND CRUMB CRUST

1½ cups vanilla wafer crumbs

½ cup finely ground blanched almonds

¼ cup packed brown sugar

¼ teaspoon grated nutmeg

5 tablespoons butter, melted

¼ teaspoon almond extract

Combine all the ingredients and pat the mixture evenly onto the bottom and up the sides of a greased 9-inch pie plate. Bake at 400 degrees for 8 minutes or until lightly browned. Cool.

FILLING

2 cups milk

½ cup sugar

¼ cup plus 1 tablespoon cornstarch

½ teaspoon salt

2 egg yolks, beaten

1 tablespoon vanilla extract

1 tablespoon butter

1 cup shredded or flaked coconut

Scald the milk in a large saucepan. Mix together the sugar, cornstarch, and salt in a small bowl. Slowly add the dry ingredients to the heated milk. Cook over low heat just until thickened, stirring constantly. Remove from the heat. Add a little of the hot mixture to the egg yolks and stir to combine. Return to the saucepan along with the vanilla, butter, and coconut. Cook over medium heat for 3 to 4 minutes, stirring.

Remove from the heat; cover the mixture with a sheet of waxed paper or plastic wrap placed directly on the surface so the filling will not form a skin. Cool, then chill for 2 hours or more. Pour the filling into the pie shell.

TOPPING

2 cups heavy cream

1 teaspoon vanilla extract

1 teaspoon sugar

Combine the cream, vanilla, and sugar. Whip until the mixture forms soft peaks. Spread over the filling.

SERVES 6 TO 8   *Heart of the Palms,* West Palm Beach, FL

SOUTHERN PECAN PIE

Even though it's the recipe on the Karo label, it's a classic.

4 tablespoons (½ stick) butter, softened

½ cup sugar

3 eggs, beaten

1 teaspoon vanilla extract

1 cup light corn syrup

1 cup pecan halves

Unbaked 9-inch pastry shell

Preheat the oven to 350 degrees. Cream the butter and sugar together. Add the eggs, vanilla, and corn syrup. Mix well. Arrange the nuts over the bottom of the pastry. Pour the filling over the pecans. Bake 50 to 60 minutes, until the crust is golden and the filling is puffy.

SERVES 6 TO 8   *Holiday Flavors and Favors,* Greensboro, NC

FROZEN PRALINE PIE

4 egg whites
½ teaspoon cream of tartar
1 cup sugar
2 quarts vanilla ice cream, softened
Butterscotch sauce (recipe follows)
1 cup pecan halves
1 cup chopped pecans

BUTTERSCOTCH SAUCE
2 cups light corn syrup
3¾ cups sugar
12 tablespoons (1½ sticks) butter
2 cups heavy cream
1 teaspoon vanilla extract

Preheat the oven to 325 degrees. Grease a 10-inch springform pan. Beat the egg whites until frothy; add the cream of tartar. Beat until stiff. Add the sugar slowly, beating until smooth and glossy. Line the pan with the meringue and mound meringue up around the sides. Bake 1 hour. Turn off the oven and let the meringue cool without opening the oven door for about 1 hour.

Spoon 1 quart of ice cream over the meringue shell, pour over a layer of butterscotch sauce, and cover with pecan halves. Freeze until firm. Spread the remaining ice cream on top of the sauce. Freeze until firm. Top with a thick layer of sauce and cover entirely with chopped pecans. Cover with foil and freeze. Serve in wedges, pouring more sauce over the top.

In a deep heavy saucepan over low heat, combine the corn syrup, sugar, butter, and 1 cup of cream. Cook to the soft ball stage (236 degrees on a candy thermometer). Add the remaining cup of cream to the sauce and cook to 218 degrees. Cool; add vanilla.

SERVES 8   *Tennessee Tables*, Knoxville, TN

HAZELNUT TARTS

PASTRY
2 cups all-purpose flour
1 teaspoon salt
¾ cup solid vegetable shortening
¼ cup cold water

FILLING
8 tablespoons (1 stick) butter
1 cup packed light brown sugar
2 eggs
2 teaspoons grated orange or lemon
 rind
½ cup half-and-half
1 cup chopped hazelnuts
1 cup (8 ounces) dried figs, chopped
½ cup raisins
1 teaspoon vanilla extract

For the pastry: Combine the flour and salt in a bowl. Cut in the shortening with a pastry blender or two knives until the mixture resembles coarse meal. Sprinkle with water, a tablespoon at a time, mixing lightly with a fork, until a dough forms. Divide into 12 parts. On a lightly floured surface, roll one part into a 5-inch circle. Fit the circle into a 3½-inch tart pan and trim the edges. Repeat until 12 tart shells are made.

For the filling: Preheat the oven to 425 degrees. Cream the butter and sugar. Add the eggs one at a time, mixing well after each addition. Stir in the orange rind, half-and-half, chopped nuts, figs, raisins, and vanilla. Fill the tart shells ¾ of the way full. Bake at 425 degrees for 10 minutes, reduce the heat to 350 degrees, and bake for an additional 30 minutes, or until firm. Cool the tarts on a wire rack. Remove from pans and serve.

SERVES 12   *Savor the Flavor of Oregon*, Eugene, OR

PAPA'S FAVORITE TORTE

"It became increasingly difficult to find an appropriate gift for Papa, so one holiday I treated him to this wonderful almond torte. It's been his special Christmas present ever since."

PASTRY SHELL
1½ cups all-purpose flour
5 tablespoons sugar
8 tablespoons (1 stick) butter, softened
1 egg yolk, lightly beaten

Preheat the oven to 325 degrees. In a medium-sized bowl, combine the flour and sugar. Using a pastry blender or two table knives, cut in the butter until the mixture resembles coarse meal. Stir in the egg yolk. (Do not be concerned about crumbly appearance.) Using your fingers, press the pastry mixture into a fluted 10-inch tart pan with a removable bottom, working it evenly over the bottom and up the sides.

FILLING
8 ounces almond paste, crumbled
2 tablespoons sugar
2 tablespoons flour
2 eggs
1 egg white
½ teaspoon almond extract

Combine and blend the almond paste, sugar, flour, and 2 eggs in an electric blender or food processor. Add the egg white and almond extract. Blend again, then pour into the pastry shell. Bake 1 hour or until the top is a rich golden brown. Cool 10 minutes before glazing.

GLAZE
½ cup sliced almonds
1 cup confectioners' sugar
2 tablespoons milk

While the torte is cooling, spread the almonds out on an ungreased cookie sheet and toast in the oven at 325 degrees for 10 minutes, until lightly browned. Combine the confectioners' sugar and milk and spread over the top of the torte. Sprinkle with the almonds. When cool, remove from the pan and serve in small slices.

SERVES 12   *Private Collection 2,* Palo Alto, CA

CHOCOLATE BOURBON PIE

Wow your last-minute company with this!

2 eggs
1 cup sugar
8 tablespoons (1 stick) butter, melted
¼ cup Bourbon whiskey
¼ cup cornstarch
1 cup pecans, chopped
1 cup semisweet chocolate chips
1 (9-inch) pie shell
1 cup heavy cream, whipped

Preheat the oven to 350 degrees. In a mixing bowl, beat the eggs and gradually add the sugar. Add the melted butter and Bourbon; blend in the cornstarch. Stir in the pecans and chocolate bits. Pour into the pie shell and bake for 45 minutes. Serve slightly warm with whipped cream.

SERVES 6–8   *Mountain Elegance,* Asheville, NC

COFFEE TOFFEE PIE

PASTRY

1½ cups all-purpose flour
6 tablespoons butter, softened
¼ cup packed brown sugar
¾ cup finely chopped pecans
1 ounce (1 square) unsweetened
  chocolate, grated
1 teaspoon vanilla extract

FILLING

12 tablespoons (1½ sticks) butter,
  softened
1 cup granulated sugar
1½ ounces (1½ squares)
  unsweetened chocolate
1 tablespoon instant coffee granules
3 eggs (see Note)

COFFEE TOPPING

2 cups heavy cream
½ cup confectioners' sugar
2 tablespoons instant coffee granules
2 tablespoons Kahlúa or other coffee
  liqueur
Chocolate curls for garnish

For the pastry: Preheat the oven to 350 degrees. Combine the flour, butter, brown sugar, pecans, and grated chocolate. Mix the vanilla with 1 tablespoon of water, stir in, and blend well. Butter a 10-inch pie plate and turn the mixture into the plate, pressing onto the bottom and up the sides with the back of a spoon. Bake for 15 minutes. Cool.

For the filling: Beat the butter until creamy. Gradually add the sugar, beating until light and fluffy. Melt the chocolate over hot water, cool slightly, and add to the butter mixture. Stir in the coffee granules. Add the eggs one at a time, beating well after each addition. Pour the filling into the cooled pie shell and refrigerate, covered, overnight.

For the topping: Beat the cream until stiff, then beat in the confectioners' sugar, coffee granules, and liqueur. Spread over the filling and garnish with chocolate curls. Refrigerate for at least 2 hours before serving.

NOTE: The eggs are not cooked in this filling. You may substitute an equal volume of pasteurized liquid whole eggs.

SERVES 10   *San Francisco à la Carte,* San Francisco, CA

OLD-FASHIONED CHOCOLATE MERINGUE PIE

1¼ cups plus 6 tablespoons sugar
½ cup cocoa powder
⅓ cup cornstarch
¼ teaspoon salt
3 cups milk
3 eggs, separated
3 tablespoons butter
1½ teaspoons vanilla extract
1 baked 9-inch pastry shell
¼ teaspoon cream of tartar

Combine 1¼ cups of sugar into the cocoa powder, cornstarch, and salt in a heavy saucepan. Whisk to remove any lumps. Gradually whisk in the milk. Cook over medium heat, stirring constantly, until the mixture thickens and comes to a boil. Boil 1 minute; remove from the heat. Beat the egg yolks until thick and lemon colored. Stir ¼ of the hot mixture into the yolks; add the yolks to the remaining hot mixture, stirring constantly. Cook over medium heat for 2 minutes. Remove from the heat and stir in the butter and vanilla. Pour into the pastry shell.

Preheat the oven to 400 degrees. Combine the egg whites and cream of tartar. Beat until foamy. Gradually add the remaining 6 tablespoons of sugar, 1 tablespoon at a time, beating until stiff peaks form. Spread over the filling, sealing to the edge of the pastry. Bake for 8 minutes or until lightly browned. Cool before serving.

SERVES 6 TO 8   *The Wild, Wild West,* Odessa, TX

MOCHA CHIFFON PIE IN PRALINE PIE SHELL

1 tablespoon unflavored gelatin
¼ cup cold water
⅓ cup cocoa powder
¾ cup granulated sugar
½ teaspoon salt
4 eggs, separated
1 cup strong brewed coffee
Praline pie shell (below)
Whipped cream (optional)
Chocolate shavings (optional)

Soften the gelatin in the cold water. In the top of a double boiler, combine the cocoa powder, ¼ cup of the sugar, and the salt. Beat the egg yolks well. Stir the yolks and the coffee into the cocoa mixture. Set the pan over hot water and cook the custard, stirring constantly, until it coats the spoon. Add the softened gelatin to the hot custard. Pour the mixture into a cold bowl to cool, stirring from time to time to prevent a crust from forming.

In a separate bowl beat the egg whites with the remaining ½ cup sugar until very stiff and glossy. Fold the meringue into the mocha custard. Pour the filling into the cooled pie shell. Chill the pie until ready to serve. Garnish with lightly sweetened whipped cream and shaved chocolate if desired.

PRALINE PIE SHELL
9-inch pie shell
5 tablespoons butter
⅓ cup packed brown sugar
½ cup chopped pecans

To prepare the shell, follow the directions for double-crust pastry on page 338, halving the recipe; bake at 400 degrees for only 5 to 7 minutes. Combine the butter and brown sugar in a small saucepan. Cook and stir until the sugar melts and the mixture bubbles vigorously. Remove the mixture from the heat, stir in the pecans, and spread the praline over the bottom of the lightly baked pie shell. Bake in a preheated 425 degree oven for 5 minutes, or until bubbly. Remove from the oven and cool thoroughly before filling.

SERVES 8   *The California Heritage Cookbook,* Pasadena, CA

WHITE CHOCOLATE MOUSSE PIE

CRUST
2 cups chocolate wafers, crushed
1 tablespoon sugar
8 tablespoons (1 stick) butter,
 melted

FILLING
12 ounces white chocolate baking
 bars
¼ cup milk
1 teaspoon vanilla extract
3 egg whites (see Note)
¼ teaspoon salt
2 cups heavy cream
Sugar for whipping cream (optional)

Crust: In a medium bowl, combine the wafers, sugar, and butter. Mix thoroughly. Press onto the bottom and up the sides of a 10-inch springform pan. Chill while making filling.

Filling: In a metal mixing bowl over hot (not boiling) water, combine the white chocolate and milk. Stir until the chocolate is melted and smooth. Whisk in the vanilla. Transfer to a large bowl and set aside for 15 minutes. In a medium bowl, beat the egg whites and salt until stiff peaks form. Gently fold the egg whites into the chocolate mixture. In a medium bowl, whip the cream with a dash of sugar until stiff peaks form. Gently fold half the cream into the chocolate mixture. Spread the mixture into the pie shell. Decorate the top of the pie with the remaining cream.

NOTE: This filling contains uncooked egg whites. Use another filling if you are concerned about possible salmonella contamination.

SERVES 8   *From Portland's Palate,* Portland, OR

LAYERED LEMON PIE

A different and delicious combination.

CRUST
20 chocolate wafers
4 tablespoons (½ stick) butter,
  melted

FILLING
4 tablespoons (½ stick) butter
⅓ cup lemon juice
¾ cup sugar
Dash of salt
3 eggs, slightly beaten
1 pint vanilla ice cream

To make the crust, preheat the oven to 350 degrees. Crumble the chocolate wafers or pulverize in a blender. Mix with the melted butter and pat into a 9-inch pie pan. Bake 8 minutes.

For the filling, melt the butter in a saucepan and stir in the lemon juice, sugar, and salt. Stir over low heat until the sugar is dissolved. Pour half the hot mixture into the slightly beaten eggs. Return this mixture to the saucepan and cook over medium heat until thickened. Cool and chill.

Divide the ice cream in half. Spread half onto the cookie crust. (You can put this in the microwave to soften, then spread around and return to freezer to reharden.) Pour half the lemon filling over the ice cream. Freeze. Repeat the layers. Freeze. Garnish with cookie crumbs or chocolate curls. Let stand 10 minutes at room temperature before serving.

SERVES 8 *America Discovers Columbus*, Columbus, OH

PEANUT BUTTER PIE WITH PRETZEL CRUST

This must be done ahead . . . but you'll have rave reviews.

PRETZEL CRUST
¾ cup finely crushed pretzels
3 tablespoons granulated sugar
6 tablespoons butter, melted

Combine the pretzels, sugar, and melted butter, mixing well. Press firmly onto the bottom and up the sides of a 9-inch pie pan. Bake at 350 degrees for 10 minutes. Cool on a rack.

FILLING
1 (8-ounce) package cream cheese
1 cup confectioners' sugar
½ cup peanut butter
1 large container Cool Whip

Mix the cream cheese, sugar, and peanut butter together in food processor. Fold in the Cool Whip. Pour into the cooled pretzel crust and chill 2 to 3 hours.

SERVES 6 *Desserts,* Reading, PA

OTHER DESSERTS

MARINATED BERRIES

We have chosen three berry types for this recipe, but any number of fresh varieties can be combined successfully.

½ cup sugar
½ cup good-quality Burgundy
½ teaspoon ground cinnamon
1 tablespoon lemon juice
1 pint fresh raspberries
1 pint fresh blueberries
1 pint fresh blackberries

Bring the sugar and ½ cup of water to a boil, reduce the heat, and stir until the sugar is dissolved. Remove from the heat and add the wine, cinnamon, and lemon juice. Cool.

Wash the berries and drain thoroughly. Pour the liquid over the berries and marinate at least two hours. Chill slightly before serving in parfait glasses or stemmed dessert goblets.

SERVES 8–10   *Delicious Decisions,* San Diego, CA

SUN RAY COMPOTE

This was a specialty of Mar-a-Lago. Mrs. Marjorie Merriwether Post often served it as a salad.

1 cup watermelon balls
8 slices cantaloupe
8 slices Crenshaw melon
8 grapefruit sections
16 orange sections

Mound watermelon balls in the center of a serving platter. Arrange the remaining fruit around the center like rays of the sun. Serve with banana dressing.

BANANA DRESSING
2 ripe bananas
2 tablespoons lemon juice
¼ cup packed brown sugar
¼ cup honey
1 cup heavy cream, whipped

Using a blender, combine the bananas, lemon juice, brown sugar, and honey and purée until smooth. Fold in the whipped cream.

SERVES 6–8   *Palm Beach Entertains,* West Palm Beach, FL

SHERMAN STRIKES AGAIN

4 large peaches, peeled and sliced
½ cup white wine
2 ounces peach or apricot brandy
1 quart peach ice cream

Put the peaches in a pan, add the wine; heat just before serving. Add the brandy and heat. Ignite and serve flaming over ice cream.

SERVES 4   *Puttin' On the Peachtree,* DeKalb County, GA

NECTARINES WITH SPICED CARAMEL

A union of summer's bounty and fall flowers.

3 tablespoons unsalted butter
3 tablespoons packed dark brown
   sugar
¼ teaspoon ground cinnamon
¼ teaspoon ground ginger
⅛ teaspoon ground allspice
3 tablespoons Grand Marnier
2 tablespoons fresh lemon juice
2 nectarines, sliced

Melt the butter in a small sauté pan over low heat. Add the brown sugar, cinnamon, ginger, allspice, Grand Marnier, and lemon juice; mix well. Add the nectarines. Boil for 30 seconds, stirring constantly. Serve in stemmed goblets.

SERVES 2   *I'll Taste Manhattan,* New York, NY

FRESH BERRIES WITH ORANGE CREAM

*A simple but most pleasing summer treat.
Do notice the nice variations.*

1 pint strawberries
½ cup plus 1 tablespoon sugar
2 teaspoons grated orange rind
½ cup orange juice
1 cup heavy cream

Wash and hull the berries, cutting in half or leaving whole. Combine them with 1 tablespoon sugar in a small bowl. Combine the ½ cup sugar, orange rind, and orange juice in a small saucepan. Bring to a boil, stirring only until the sugar dissolves. Simmer 10 minutes without stirring. Cool completely. Whip the cream until soft peaks form. Gently fold in the orange syrup. Serve over the berries.

VARIATION: Substitute fresh blueberries or raspberries and, instead of orange, use lemon juice and rind the same quantities.

SERVES 4   *Private Collection I,* Palo Alto, CA

SHERRIED BANANAS IN WINE SAUCE

6 bananas
Juice of 1 or more lemons
2 eggs, separated
¼ cup sugar
½ cup sherry
Grated rind of 2 lemons
Few grains of freshly grated nutmeg
Dash of salt
¾ cup heavy cream, whipped

SAUCE
8 tablespoons (1 stick) unsalted
   butter, softened
½ cup confectioners' sugar
Dash of salt
3 tablespoons sherry

Cut the bananas diagonally in ½-inch slices and arrange in an attractive pattern in a shallow serving casserole. Squeeze a generous amount of lemon juice over them and let stand for 30 minutes.

Preheat the oven to 325 degrees. Beat the egg yolks thoroughly, adding sugar and sherry. When quite smooth, add the grated rind and nutmeg. Fold in the egg whites, which have been beaten with the salt until stiff but not dry. Fold in the whipped cream and pile the mixture on top of the bananas. Bake for 30 minutes. Serve from the casserole, topped with sauce and sprinkled with nutmeg.

Cream the butter, sugar, and salt until fluffy; add the sherry and mix until smooth.

SERVES 6   *The Gasparilla Cookbook,* Tampa, FL

WORLD'S FASTEST STRAWBERRY MOUSSE

1 (10-ounce) package frozen
    sweetened strawberries
½ cup sour cream
½ cup sugar
1 teaspoon vanilla extract

Mix all ingredients in the blender and freeze. Serve in sherbet glasses.
SERVES 4–6

River Road Recipes: A Second Helping, Baton Rouge, LA

WAR EAGLE BAKED APPLES

The cream sauce makes this dish.

½ cup sugar
¼ teaspoon ground cinnamon
Dash of freshly grated nutmeg
2 cups apple juice
6 large Rome apples
¼ cup coarsely chopped walnuts
¼ cup cake crumbs (yellow, white,
    spice) or cookie crumbs
    (gingersnaps, vanilla wafers)
¼ cup chopped dates or currants or
    raisins
½ cup heavy cream

Preheat the oven to 400 degrees. Combine the sugar, cinnamon, nutmeg, and apple juice in a saucepan. Bring to a boil, lower the heat, and simmer only until the sugar dissolves. Starting at the stem end, peel ⅓ of each apple. Carefully core to within ½ inch of the blossom end. Mix the nuts, crumbs, and dates; stuff into the apples.

Arrange the apples in a shallow 8 × 11-inch baking dish and pour the hot apple syrup over the top. Bake, basting often with the pan juices, 45 minutes or until the apples are shiny, sticky, and soft. Transfer to dessert dishes. Strain the baking juices into a saucepan. If necessary, boil over high heat until the liquid is reduced to about ½ cup, but do not allow juices to caramelize. Stir in the cream and pass separately as a sauce.

SERVES 6   *Sassafras! The Ozarks Cookbook,* Springfield, MO

CHILLED ZABAGLIONE WITH RASPBERRY PURÉE

A wonderful way to end a meal on a hot summer night.

1 package unflavored gelatin
2 cups milk
1 tablespoon cornstarch
Sugar
6 large egg yolks
¾ cup Marsala wine
1½ to 3 cups fresh raspberries

Place ¼ cup of cold water in a small bowl and sprinkle with the gelatin. Pour the milk into a small heavy saucepan, bring just to a boil and remove immediately from the heat. Add the softened gelatin. In a medium bowl, combine the cornstarch, and ⅓ cup of sugar, then whisk in the egg yolks until the mixture is smooth. Slowly pour half the hot milk into the egg mixture, whisking constantly. Pour the egg-milk mixture slowly back into the milk remaining in the saucepan and stir over medium heat until the custard thickens. Pour the custard into a mixing bowl and let cool for 5 minutes. Stir in the Marsala. Divide the mixture among 8 individual ramekins or pour it into a single 1-quart bowl or mold. Chill in the refrigerator until set, about 1½ hours for ramekins or 2½ hours for a 1-quart mold.

Purée the raspberries in a blender or food processor. Pass the purée through a sieve to remove the seeds. Add sugar to taste and stir until the sugar dissolves. To serve, gently turn the custards out into individual dessert plates or a single serving dish. Spoon a little of the raspberry purée over the custards and serve the remaining purée separately in a bowl or pitcher.

SERVES 8   *The Bountiful Arbor,* Ann Arbor, MI

HOT FRUIT COMPOTE

1 pound dried apricots
⅔ cup sugar
¼ teaspoon salt
Juice and rind of 1 lemon and 1
  orange
2 cups dry white wine
1½ cups pitted halved prunes
1 cup diced pineapple and its juice
1 can white peaches, drained
½ cup slivered almonds
2 tablespoons grated candied ginger
½ cup Grand Marnier
1 to 2 cups seedless white grapes
  (optional)
1 to 2 cups sliced strawberries
  (optional)

Simmer the apricots with the sugar, salt, lemon and orange juice and rind, and white wine until the apricots are tender. Add the prunes and cook until prunes are tender. Remove the lemon and orange rinds and add the remaining ingredients. Serve warm to accompany roasts, game, or fowl, or at a brunch. Serve with cold ice cream or a little whipped cream for dessert.

SERVES 6–8   *Cincinnati Celebrates,* Cincinnati, OH

PAVLOVA

A dramatic finale.

4 egg whites, room temperature
1 cup sugar
1 teaspoon white wine vinegar
½ teaspoon vanilla extract
1 tablespoon cornstarch

TOPPING
1 cup heavy cream
⅓ cup confectioners' sugar
2 cups sliced or chopped fresh fruit

Preheat the oven to 400 degrees. Line a baking sheet with aluminum foil. Lightly butter the foil. In a bowl, beat the egg whites until stiff but not dry. Add the sugar gradually, beating constantly. Add the vinegar and vanilla; beat for 5 minutes. Add the cornstarch; beat for 1 minute. Mound the meringue onto the prepared baking sheet into a disk about 2 inches high. Imprint the edge of the disk with the back of a spoon with an upward motion. Place in the oven; reduce the heat to 250 degrees. Bake for 1½ hours, remove from the oven, and cool.

Beat the cream until soft peaks form. Gradually add the sugar, beating until stiff peaks are formed. Fold in the fruit. Mound the fruited cream in the center of the pavlova. Cut into wedges and serve.

SERVES 10   *Nuggets: Recipes Good as Gold,* Colorado Springs, CO

PEAR DUMPLINGS WITH CREAM CUSTARD

1½ cups all-purpose flour

8 tablespoons (1 stick) butter, softened

4 ounces cream cheese, softened

½ teaspoon ground cinnamon

¼ cup plus 1½ teaspoon sugar

3 ripe Bartlett pears, peeled, halved, and cored

1 egg, separated

2 cups heavy cream

4 teaspoons cornstarch

½ teaspoon salt

½ teaspoon vanilla extract

6 mint leaves

Preheat the oven to 375 degrees. In a medium mixing bowl, combine the flour, butter, and cream cheese. Knead by hand until blended. On a lightly floured surface, roll half the pastry to ⅛ inch thickness, using a floured rolling pin. Cut six 7-inch circles (a salad plate may be used as a pattern) from the rolled-out pastry.

Mix the cinnamon with 1½ teaspoons of sugar in a small bowl and sprinkle evenly over the pastry circles. Place a pear half, cut side up, in the middle of each pastry circle. Fold the pastry around the pears, brush the pastry with egg white, and place seam side down on an ungreased cookie sheet. Bake the dumplings 30 minutes or until golden. Remove from the oven and cool slightly on a wire rack.

To prepare the custard, combine the cream, cornstarch, salt, egg yolk, and ¼ cup of sugar. Cook over medium heat, stirring constantly, until the custard coats the back of a spoon. Remove from the heat, add the vanilla, and allow to cool. When ready to serve, pool some custard on a dessert plate and place a pear dumpling on top. Garnish the dumpling with mint to resemble a pear leaf. Dumplings and custard may be made ahead of time and refrigerated, separately, to be served chilled later.

SERVES 6

Rouge River Rendezvous, Jackson County, OR

CRANBERRY APPLE CRISP

3 cups peeled and chopped apples

2 cups fresh cranberries

½ cup plus 2 tablespoons all-purpose flour

1 cup granulated sugar

3 packages instant oatmeal with cinnamon and spice

¾ cup pecans, chopped

½ cup firmly packed brown sugar

8 tablespoons (1 stick) butter, melted

Pecan halves and fresh cranberries for garnish

Preheat the oven to 350 degrees. Combine the apples, cranberries, and 2 tablespoons of the flour; toss to coat. Add the granulated sugar and mix well. Place in a 2-quart casserole. Combine the oatmeal, pecans, ½ cup flour, and the brown sugar. Add the butter and stir well. Spoon over the fruit mixture and bake uncovered for 45 minutes. Garnish with pecan halves and cranberries. Serve with ice cream.

SERVES 8

Sensational Seasonings: A Taste & Tour of Arkansas, Fort Smith, AR

RASPBERRY PEACH COBBLER

1 cup fresh raspberries
6-8 fresh peaches, peeled and sliced
2 cups all-purpose flour
2 cups sugar
2 teaspoons baking powder
2 eggs
2 tablespoons butter, melted

Preheat the oven to 350 degrees. Place the raspberries in a buttered 13 × 9-inch baking dish. Top with the peaches. Combine the flour, sugar, and baking powder. Add the eggs and blend (the mixture will be dry). Drop the topping by rough tablespoonfuls over the fruit. Drizzle melted butter over the top. Bake uncovered for 1 hour. Cool to room temperature before serving.

NOTE: This is a light buttery dessert that is best served in a bowl topped with heavy cream, ice cream, or whipped cream.

SERVES 4-6   *Gourmet L.A.*, Los Angeles, CA

WONDERFUL PEACH COBBLER

The almond flavoring makes this special.

8 cups sliced fresh peaches (4 to 5 pounds)
2 cups sugar
3 tablespoons all-purpose flour
½ teaspoon grated nutmeg
1¼ teaspoons almond extract
5⅓ tablespoons butter
Pastry for double crust pie (page 338)

Combine peaches, sugar, flour, and nutmeg in large saucepan. Let stand 20 minutes until syrup forms. Bring peach mixture to a boil, reduce heat, and cook 10 minutes. Remove from heat; blend in almond extract and butter, stirring so that the butter melts.

Preheat the oven to 475 degrees. Butter an 8 × 12-inch baking dish. Roll out half the pastry on a floured surface into an 8 × 12-inch rectangle. Spoon half the peach mixture into the buttered dish; top with the pastry rectangle. Bake for 12 minutes. Spoon the remaining peaches over the baked pastry. Roll out the remaining pastry and cut into ½-inch wide strips. Arrange over the peaches in a lattice design. Return to the oven and bake for 10 to 15 minutes, until lightly browned.

SERVES 8   *Peachtree Bouquet*, DeKalb County, GA

HELP OF SOUTHERN NEVADA
JUNIOR LEAGUE OF LAS VEGAS, NEVADA

HELP of Southern Nevada was started 25 years ago by the Junior League of Las Vegas. It was created to be a central location for volunteers in the community to be matched up with nonprofits who needed their services. Since its founding, HELP has grown to encompass four major programs, two smaller programs, an annual budget of over $1.2 million, and a staff of 22. HELP's mission is to promote self-sufficiency in all clients served by the program, and all the six projects work toward that goal.

RASPBERRY SQUARES

BOTTOM LAYER
1 cup all-purpose flour
1 teaspoon baking powder
8 tablespoons (1 stick) butter, softened
1 tablespoon milk
½ cup raspberry jam

Preheat the oven to 375 degrees. Whisk the flour and baking powder together. Cut in the butter with a pastry blender or two knives until the mixture resembles coarse meal. Add the milk and toss to combine. Spread the mixture in an ungreased 8 × 8-inch pan. Cover with raspberry jam.

TOP LAYER
1 egg
4 tablespoons (½ stick) butter, melted
1 cup sugar
2 cups coconut flakes
1 teaspoon vanilla extract

Beat the egg with the melted butter. Mix in the sugar, coconut, and vanilla. Spread the mixture over the jam. Bake for 30 minutes or until the top is golden brown. Cool at least 1 hour. Cut into squares.
MAKES 16 SQUARES

The Stenciled Strawberry Cookbook, Albany, NY

GRAPEFRUIT SORBET

Refreshing.

¾ cup sugar
2¼ cups grapefruit sections (about 3 large grapefruit)
1 cup fresh grapefruit juice
2 tablespoons kirsch (optional)
1 egg white

Place the sugar in a food processor or blender and run on high for 30 seconds; remove and set aside. Purée the grapefruit sections in the processor or blender; remove and set aside. In a medium saucepan, combine the sugar, juice, and kirsch; bring to a boil, stirring until the sugar is dissolved. Reduce the heat and simmer 5 minutes. Cool. Blend in the grapefruit purée. Pour into a shallow baking dish and freeze until solid.

Remove from the freezer and let stand until slightly softened. Spoon into a processor or blender and mix until smooth. Add the egg white and mix until satiny. Pour into a bowl or individual serving dishes and return to the freezer until firm, at least 3 hours. Soften several minutes prior to serving. The sorbet will keep 2 weeks in the freezer if covered tightly with plastic.
VARIATION: Substitute pink grapefruit and add a dash of grenadine.
SERVES 6

Gulfshore Delights, Fort Meyers, FL

MINT SHERBET

Monroe's famous sherbet.

6 tablespoons mint leaves
Juice of 6 oranges
Juice of 2 lemons
Grated rind of 1 lemon
2 cups sugar
Green food coloring (optional)
1 stiffly beaten egg white
½ pint heavy cream

Chop the mint leaves and soak in the orange and lemon juices along with the grated lemon rind for at least 30 minutes. Boil the sugar and 2 cups of water for 5 minutes, without stirring. Pour the hot mixture into the fruit juices. When cold, strain. Add a few drops of food coloring if desired. Stir in the egg white and cream. Freeze in an electric or hand freezer.

SERVES 6-8 — *The Cotton Country Collection*, Monroe, LA

SINFULLY SCRUMPTIOUS ICE CREAM

4 cups plus ¾ cup heavy cream
¾ cup milk
1½ cups sugar
½ teaspoon salt
8 egg yolks, well beaten
5 cups mashed peaches or strawberries

Scald the ¾ cup cream with the milk in the top of a double boiler over direct heat. Add the sugar and salt. Pour a small mount of the milk mixture into the beaten egg yolks. Add the yolks to the milk mixture, and over simmering water cook until thickened to a custard consistency (coating the back of a spoon). Remove from the heat and cool. Mix the mashed fruit with the remaining 4 cups of cream. Blend with the cooled custard.

If using a manual freezer, fill the container ¾ full. Pack ice and rock salt around the edges, using 3 parts ice to 1 part salt. When the crank gets too hard to turn and the ingredients have solidified to a soft ice cream stage, remove the dasher and pack down the ice cream. Repack fresh ice and salt around the sides, wrap in burlap or newspaper, and let stand 1 hour. Freeze in paper cartons. For an electric ice cream freezer, follow the directions of the manufacturer.

SERVES 12 — *Rare Collection*, Galveston, TX

PEACH ICE CREAM

1 quart peeled and mashed peaches
2 cups sugar
1 quart half-and-half
3 drops almond extract

Mix the peaches with 1 cup of the sugar and chill. Add the remaining cup of sugar to the half-and-half and chill. Place the cream mixture in an ice cream freezer, add flavoring, and freeze until semi-stiff. Add peaches and finish freezing.

MAKES 16 TO 20 SERVINGS

The Southern Collection, Columbus, GA

FRESH FIG ICE CREAM

8 eggs
2 cups sugar
1 quart homogenized milk
1 quart cream or half-and-half
2 teaspoons vanilla extract
½ teaspoon salt
1 quart peeled fresh figs

Beat the eggs in a blender until thick and lemon colored. Blend in the sugar. Combine with the milk and cream in a large double boiler and cook over simmering water until the custard is thick, stirring all the while it is being cooked. Remove from the heat, add the vanilla and salt, and fold in 1 quart of slightly mashed figs. Process in an electric ice cream freezer. This keeps almost indefinitely in the freezer.

SERVES 15   *Talk About Good II,* Lafayette, LA

LEMON PUDDING

4½ tablespoons butter
1½ cups sugar
3 eggs, separated
4½ tablespoons flour
1½ cups milk
Grated rind and juice of 2 lemons
    (use more lemon juice if you like
    it tart)
Whipped cream (optional)

Preheat the oven to 350 degrees. Butter an oblong glass baking dish.

Cream the butter and 1 cup of the sugar together until fluffy. Beat the egg yolks and add to the creamed mixture, stirring until well combined. Beat in the flour. Add the milk, lemon rind, and lemon juice; stir to mix. Beat the egg whites with the remaining ½ cup of sugar until soft peaks form; fold into the creamed mixture.

Pour into the prepared baking dish. Set the dish in a shallow pan and pour hot water into the pan to a depth of 1 inch. Bake uncovered for 1 hour. Remove from the oven and from the water bath. Cool and chill. Serve with or without whipped cream.

SERVES 6   *Furniture City Feasts,* High Point, NC

UPSIDE DOWN LEMON CUPS

1 cup sugar
3 tablespoons flour
Pinch of salt
Juice and grated rind of 1 large
    lemon
1 tablespoon melted butter
2 egg yolks, slightly beaten
1 cup milk
2 egg whites, beaten stiff

Preheat the oven to 350 degrees. In a mixing bowl, combine the sugar, flour, salt, lemon juice and rind, melted butter, egg yolks, and milk. Fold in the egg whites. Divide the mixture among 6 greased custard cups and set them in a pan of hot water. Bake for 30 to 35 minutes. Cool and chill. Remove the custards from the cups to serve, turning them upside down.

SERVES 6   *Junior League of Dallas Cookbook,* Dallas, TX

SAN FRANCISCO BREAD PUDDING

5 ounces stale French bread, broken into small pieces
1 cup milk
1 cup heavy cream
1 cup sugar
4 tablespoons (½ stick) unsalted butter, melted
1 whole egg plus 1 egg yolk, beaten
½ cup raisins
½ cup shredded coconut
½ cup chopped pecans
1 tablespoon vanilla extract
½ teaspoon ground cinnamon
¼ teaspoon grated nutmeg
Lemon rum sauce (below)

Preheat the oven to 350 degrees. In a large bowl, combine all the ingredients except the sauce; blend well. The mixture should be very moist. Pour into a buttered 11 × 7-inch baking dish. Bake uncovered for 45 minutes or until set. Serve warm with lemon rum sauce.

LEMON RUM SAUCE
6 tablespoons unsalted butter
3 tablespoons sugar
¼ cup lemon juice
Grated rind of 1 large lemon
2 egg yolks, beaten
3 to 6 tablespoons rum

In a saucepan, combine the butter and sugar. Cook over low heat until well blended. Stir in the lemon juice and rind. Pour some of the butter mixture into the yolks and whisk to blend. Pour this mixture back into the pan. Whisk over low heat until slightly thickened. Stir in rum to taste.

SERVES 6–8   *San Francisco Encore,* San Francisco, CA

BREAD PUDDING WITH COGNAC SAUCE

2 cups milk
4 tablespoons (½ stick) butter
½ cup sugar
4 cups stale French bread cubes
½ cup raisins
2 eggs, beaten
⅛ teaspoon salt
½ teaspoon grated nutmeg
1 teaspoon vanilla extract
¼ cup shredded coconut (optional)
Cognac sauce (below)

Preheat the oven to 350 degrees. Scald the milk. Melt the butter in the hot milk and stir in the sugar. Pour over the bread and raisins in a mixing bowl and let stand for 15 minutes. Add the beaten eggs, salt, nutmeg, vanilla, and coconut. Bake uncovered in a well-greased 1½-quart dish for 35 to 45 minutes. Serve warm, topped with Cognac sauce.

COGNAC SAUCE
8 tablespoons (1 stick) butter
2 cups confectioners' sugar
¼ cup Cognac

Cream butter and sugar together until fluffy and gradually add the Cognac. Mix until well blended.

SERVES 8   *The Plantation Cookbook,* New Orleans, LA

COLD LEMON CUSTARD SOUFFLÉS

1 cup sugar
¼ cup all-purpose flour
⅛ teaspoon salt
2 tablespoons butter, melted
5 tablespoons lemon juice
Grated rind of 1 lemon
3 egg yolks, well beaten
1½ cups milk, scalded
3 egg whites

Preheat the oven to 325 degrees. Generously butter 8 custard cups.

Combine the sugar, flour, salt, and butter. Stir in the lemon juice and rind. Whisk a little of the hot milk into the beaten yolks; whisk all the yolks back into the milk. Stir the yolk mixture into the lemon mixture until well blended. Beat the egg whites until firm but not dry. Fold the lemon mixture into the egg whites. Spoon into the prepared custard cups. Place the filled cups in a baking pan. Pour enough hot water into the baking pan to come halfway up the sides of the cups. Bake for 45 minutes. Cool to room temperature. Refrigerate until chilled, about 4 hours. Serve cold.

SERVES 8   *San Francisco Encore,* San Francisco, CA

ORANGE CUSTARD

3 cups fresh orange juice
¾ cup sugar
12 eggs, well beaten
¾ cup dark rum
1½ cups heavy cream, whipped
2 tablespoons grated orange rind

Preheat the oven to 350 degrees. Mix the orange juice and sugar and stir until the sugar is dissolved. Blend in the eggs and rum. Pour into a 2-quart soufflé dish or 8 ovenproof custard cups and put in a shallow pan of hot water. Bake the custard for 50 to 60 minutes (the large custard will take about 10 minutes longer than the small). Test by inserting a knife in the center. If the knife comes out clean, the custard is cooked. Chill several hours. Serve with whipped cream and grated orange rind.

SERVES 8   *New York Entertains,* New York, NY

MEXICAN PINE NUT AND ALMOND DESSERT

8 cups milk
1½ cups sugar
8 egg yolks
1 cinnamon stick
¼ cup blanched almonds
¼ cup pine nuts
2½ tablespoons butter
Toasted pine nuts and almonds for
  garnish

In a large, deep saucepan, combine the milk, sugar, egg yolks and cinnamon stick. Bring to a boil over medium heat, then boil rapidly until thickened, stirring occasionally. In a blender, blend the almonds and pine nuts with a small amount of milk. Add the blended mixture to the thickened milk mixture. Continue stirring and simmer 30 minutes or longer, until the mixture becomes like caramel. Remove from the heat, add the butter, and allow to cool. Pour into a serving bowl and garnish with pine nuts and almonds.

SERVES 12   *Buen Provecho,* Mexico City, Mexico

TRES LECHES (THREE MILK CAKE)

This is a typical Nicaraguan and Cuban dessert.

3 eggs
1 cup sugar
1½ cups all-purpose flour
2 teaspoons baking powder
½ cup milk
1 teaspoon vanilla extract
1 (14-ounce) can sweetened
   condensed milk
1 (12-ounce) can evaporated milk
1 cup heavy cream

TOPPING
3 egg whites
1 cup sugar
1 teaspoon vanilla extract

Preheat the oven to 350 degrees. Beat the eggs until foamy. Gradually add the sugar. Add the flour mixed with baking powder, the milk and vanilla. Pour into an ungreased 13 × 9-inch pan. Bake for 20 to 25 minutes. Cool the cake and then poke holes with a fork all over the cake. Mix the condensed milk, evaporated milk, and cream. Pour the mixture slowly over the cake until absorbed.

To make the topping, beat the egg whites, sugar, and vanilla until foamy. Spread over the cake. Refrigerate until serving time.

SERVES 6–8   *Celebrate Miami!,* Miami, FL

SPANISH CUSTARD (FLAN DE LECHE)

3 cups sugar
6 eggs
1 teaspoon vanilla extract
Scant ¼ teaspoon anisette
Pinch of salt
2 cups boiling milk

Preheat the oven to 350 degrees. Boil 1 cup of sugar and ½ cup of water together until the mixture turns dark brown, then pour the caramel into 6 custard cups. Beat the eggs, add the remaining 2 cups of sugar, the vanilla, anisette, and salt and beat again. Add the boiling milk little by little, then strain through cheesecloth or a fine sieve. Pour the mixture into the custard cups. Put cups in a large shallow pan and add hot water to the pan to a depth of 1 inch. Bake for 30 minutes. Don't let the water boil or the custard will be full of holes. Cool in the refrigerator. When ready to serve, press the edges of the custard with a spoon to break away from the mold, then turn upside down onto a dessert plate. The caramel then tops the custard.

SERVES 6   *The Gasparilla Cookbook,* Tampa, FL

MOCHA POT DE CREME

½ cup sugar
1½ teaspoons instant coffee granules
1 (6-ounce) package semisweet chocolate chips
2 eggs
1½ cups heavy cream (no substitute)
1 to 2 pints fresh strawberries for garnish

Combine the sugar and instant coffee with ½ cup of water in a saucepan and bring to a boil. Boil 3 minutes, stirring constantly. Place the chocolate chips in a blender or food processor fitted with a steel blade. Add the hot sugar syrup and blend for 6 seconds. Add the eggs and blend for 1 minute.

Whip the cream until soft peaks form. Fold into the chocolate mixture. Pour into 1½-quart soufflé dish or, if desired, a 9-inch square glass pan. Cover and refrigerate at least 8 hours. To serve, scoop into small balls from the soufflé dish or cut into squares from the pan. Garnish with fresh strawberries.

SERVES 10 *Even More Special,* Durham, NC

CREAMY PRALINES

1 cup packed brown sugar
2 cups granulated sugar
3 tablespoons light corn syrup
1 cup milk, whole or evaporated (the latter makes richer pralines)
4 tablespoons (½ stick) butter
2 to 3 cups pecan halves
2 teaspoons vanilla extract

In a heavy pot, combine the sugars, corn syrup, and milk. Cook slowly, stirring constantly, over moderately high heat. Add half the butter when the candy first comes to a boil, then continue to cook until it reaches 236 degrees (soft ball stage). Remove from the heat, add the remaining butter, and beat, using about 150 vigorous strokes. Add the vanilla and pecans and continue beating until the candy becomes slightly lighter in color and is more creamy. This is the most important step. While the candy is still hot, drop onto buttered waxed paper so that it will form smooth creamy pieces about 2 inches in diameter. Allow to harden before serving.

MAKES ABOUT 18 PRALINES *A Cook's Tour,* Shreveport, LA

APRICOT ALMOND BALLS

Excellent for Christmas

1¾ cups vanilla wafer crumbs
1 cup toasted almonds chopped
⅔ cup confectioners' sugar
½ cup dried apricots, chopped fine
¼ cup light corn syrup
2 tablespoons apricot brandy

In a large bowl, mix the wafer crumbs, almonds, ½ cup of the sugar, and the apricots. Stir in the corn syrup and brandy until well blended. Knead with the hands until well mixed. Shape into 1-inch balls. Roll in the remaining ¼ cup confectioners' sugar. Store in a tightly covered container.

MAKES ABOUT 4 DOZEN *Fare by the Sea,* Sarasota, FL

CHOCOLATE NUT TOFFEE

1 cup chopped pecans or walnuts
8 tablespoons (1 stick) butter
¾ cup packed brown sugar
1 (6-ounce) package semisweet
    chocolate chips

Spread the nuts in the bottom of a well-greased 8-inch baking pan. Melt the butter in a heavy saucepan, add the sugar, and boil the mixture for 7 minutes, stirring constantly. Pour immediately over the nuts; let stand a few minutes. Spread chocolate chips on top. Cover with a bread board to keep in heat. When the chocolate has softened, spread evenly. Refrigerate. When cool, break into pieces.

MAKES 12–15 PIECES   *Huntsville Heritage,* Huntsville, AL

CHOCOLATE RASPBERRY TRUFFLES

The League members request this recipe.

1⅓ cups plus 1½ cups semisweet
    chocolate chips
2 tablespoons heavy cream
1 tablespoon butter
2 tablespoons seedless raspberry jam
Confectioners' sugar to taste

Combine 1⅓ cups of the chocolate chips with the cream and butter in the top part of a double boiler. Cook over hot water until smooth, stirring constantly. Stir in the jam. Allow the mixture to cool, then freeze, covered with plastic wrap, for 20 minutes. Shape into balls. Place on a cookie sheet. Freeze until firm. Melt the remaining 1½ cups of chocolate chips in a double boiler over hot water, stirring occasionally. Using a wooden pick, dip the candy balls one at a time into the chocolate. Place on a cookie sheet. Chill until set. Dust with confectioners' sugar.

The Best of Wheeling, Wheeling, WV

AIDS COMMUNITY EDUCATION OUTREACH PROJECT
JUNIOR LEAGUE OF LOS ANGELES

AIDS Community Outreach Project, co-sponsored by the Junior League of Los Angeles and by AIDS Project Los Angeles, staffed a hotline and speaker's bureau providing information to the community. This led to Caring for Babies with AIDS, the first hospice for HIV positive children west of the Mississippi. In addition, the Ask Us About AIDS Project is a peer counseling program that targets high-risk adolescents, including urban youth, preteens, and teens. The Los Angeles League's involvement in AIDS projects is nationally recognized and accepted as progressive and cutting-edge volunteer work.

A CELEBRATION OF PARTNERSHIP

Creating shared solutions is the cornerstone of the Junior League's vision. In our collaborations, we believe that organizational boundaries must become increasingly flexible and fluid, allowing for the constant forming and reforming of alliances as changing circumstances require. We are convinced that we must partner in everything we do to create the new vision and the solutions that will build strong communities in the future. The Junior League's hope is to bring to the future facilitative skill and a genuine desire to bring people together.

It would take volumes to thank everyone with whom we have worked, so with apologies for this limitation, we set forth below a partial list of our more recent partners:

Association Partners and Supporters

Advocacy Institute
Aetna Foundation Inc.
Alliance for American Renewal
Allstate Insurance Company
American Academy of Pediatrics
American Association of Retired Persons
American Association of School Administrators
American Public Welfare Association
Angotti, Thomas, Hedge Inc.
Association for Volunteer Administration
Benton Foundation
BMW of North America, Inc.
The California Wellness Foundation
Capital Cities/ABC Inc.
Carnegie Corporation of New York
Children's Defense Fund
Coalition for Goals 200
The Commonwealth Fund
Corporation for National Service
Corporation for Public Broadcasting
Council of Jewish Federations
Danforth Foundation
Edna McConnell Clark Foundation
Emergency Medical Services for Children

The Equitable Companies
Every Child By Two
Exxon Company, U.S.A.
Family Service America
First Book
Foundation for Child Development
Generations United
Girls Inc.
Girl Scouts of the U.S.A.
The Luke B. Hancock Foundation
Healthy Mothers/Healthy Babies
William Randolph Hearst Foundation
Immunization Education and Action Committee
Independent Sector
Institute for Women's Policy Research
The James Irvine Foundation
The Johnson Foundation
Kiwanis International
Leadership Conference on Civil Rights
Library of Congress—Center for the Book
March of Dimes
Maternal and Child Health Coalition
Merrill Lynch & Co. Foundation
Mothers and Others for a Livable Planet
Charles Stewart Mott Foundation

National Assembly
National Association for Non-Violent Programming
National Association of Child Advocates
National Association of Children's Hospitals and Related Institutions
National Black Child Development Institute
National CASA Association
National Center for Children in Poverty
National Child Abuse Coalition
National Citizens Commission on Alcoholism
National Civic League
National Collaboration for Youth
National Council on Alcoholism and Drug Dependence
National Council on the Aging
National Council of Jewish Women
National Council of La Raza
National Council of Negro Women
National Education Association
National Federation for Non-Profits
National Issues Forum
National Middle School Association
National PTA
National School Health Education Coalition

National Women's Law Center
Points of Light Foundation
The Quaker Oats Foundation Inc.
Quest International
The Stuart Foundations
United Methodist Church, Women's
  Division
U.S. Centers for Disease Control
United Way of America
Weingart Foundation YMCA
Women's Legal Defense Fund
YWCA of the U.S.A.

Canada
Canadian Advisory Council on the
  Status of Women
Canadian Centre for Philanthropy
Girl Guides of Canada

National Council of Women of
  Canada
The Coalition of National Voluntary
  Organizations
YWCA of Canada

Mexico
American Express Co., S.A. de C.V.
American Foundation for Overseas
  Blind
Asociacion Mexicana de Distribuid-
  ores Ford, A.C.
D.H.L. International de Mexico, S.A.
  de C.V.
Ford Motor Company de Mexico
Fundacion W.K. Foundation
Junta de Asistencia Privada
Lumen Papelerias

Rockefeller Committee for Inter-
  American Affairs

Great Britain
The British Dyslexia Association
The Disabled Living Foundation
Ellesmere House
Fulham Parents and Children
The Kensington Housing Trust
Monroe Young Family Centre
National Children's Home
Notting Hill Housing Trust
The Royal Academy of Arts
The Royal Borough of Kensington
  and Chelsea
Tavistock Clinic
The Westminster Volunteer Bureau

JUNIOR LEAGUE
PROGRAMS OF DISTINCTION

Akron, Ohio
Akron Child Guidance Center
Free Shots for Kids
Safe Landing Youth Shelter

Albany, New York
Design for Healing
Food Shuttle

Annapolis, Maryland
Done in a Day
Kids on the Block

Arlington, Texas
Alpha Foundation
Community Service Outreach & Training Project
Dental Health for Arlington, Inc.

Asheville, North Carolina
Park Place, Arts and Science Center
W.N.C. Nature Center
Youth Enrichment Services, Y.E.S.

Austin, Texas
Center for Battered Women, Inc.
Hispanic Mother Daughter Program
The People's Community Clinic

Baltimore, Maryland
Baltimore Baseball League
New Start Furnishings
Second Chance

Billings, Montana
Playground for All Children
Tumbleweed Runaway Program
Youth Court Conference Committee

Birmingham, Alabama
Backyard Wildlife Habitat
M.O.R.E. Literacy Program
Youth Violence Prevention

Canton, Ohio
Playright

Central Westchester, New York
Child Safety Awareness Day
Spring Harvest

Charleston, West Virginia
Patchwork of Daymark, Inc.
Vandalia Terrace Housing Project

Cincinnati, Ohio
Fernside Center for Grieving Children

Clearwater-Dunedin, Florida
Gateway Children's Shelter

Colorado Springs, Colorado
C.A.S.A. of Colorado Springs, Inc.
Parks Project

Columbus, Ohio
Join the PARTY: Participate in Reading
Kelton House Museum & Garden

Dallas, Texas
Camp John Marc Myers—Special Camps for Special Kids
Dallas Museum of Art—Gateway Gallery
Habitat for Humanity—All Women Built House

Dayton, Ohio
C.A.S.A. (Court Appointed Special Avocate)
Exhibits-to-Go
Nurturing Plants & People

Daytona Beach, Florida
Easter Seal Center

DeKalb County, Georgia
DeKalb Rape Crisis Center
Mini-Grants for Elementary School Teachers

Denver, Colorado
Child Support Enforcement
Curtis Park Community Center
Mile High Transplant Bank

Duluth, Minnesota
Depot Square
First Witness: Child Abuse Resource Center
Together We Build Playground Park on the Bay

Eastern Fairfield County, Connecticut
Crippled Children's Workshop
Wonder Workshop
Youth Opportunities Unlimited

Edmonton, Alberta, Canada
Canadian Native Friendship Centre
Central Volunteer Bureau
Kids in the "No"

El Paso, Texas
The Learning Trolly
Los Murales
Midnight Basketball

Fayetteville, North Carolina
Holly Home
Puppets
Tots of Teens

Fort Myers, Florida
Calusa Nature Center ad Planetarium, Inc.
Community Harvest
Volunteer Center of Lee County

Fort Wayne, Indiana
Displaced Homemakers
Matthew 25 "Preventive Health Education"
Project LEAD

Fort Worth, Texas
Parenting Guidance Center
Tarrant County Youth Collaboration
Van Cliburn International Piano Competition

Fresno, California
Break the Barriers, Inc.
Fresno Children's Home
Impact Fresno

Galveston County, Texas
The Centre on the Stand
L.E.A.P.: Literacy, Education and
Parenting
Ronald McDonald House

Grand Rapids, Michigan
Hippy: Home Instruction Program
Kent County Adolescent Pregnancy
Child Watch
Very Special Arts

Great Falls, Montana
Charles M. Russell Art Museum—Art-
ist's Cabin Studio
Child Evaluation Center

Greater Elmira Corning, New York
C.A.S.A. of Chemung County
Clemens Center
Southern Tier Hospice, Inc.

Greater Fort Lauderdale, Florida
Museum of Discovery and Science
SOS Children's Village of Florida, Inc.
South Florida Women's Business
Conference

Greater Orlando, Florida
The Crisis Nursery
Partners in Education

Greater Vancouver, British Columbia,
Canada
Science World
"One on One:" A Child's Literacy
Program

High Point, North Carolina
Childwatch
Therapeutic Respite Center
Women's Shelter

Honolulu, Hawaii
AIDS Education Comic Book
Hale Kipa—"The House of
Friendliness"
Iolani Palace

Jacksonville, Florida
Family Visitation Center

Kalamazoo, Michigan
Hospital Hospitality House of South-
western Michigan
Pretty Lake Vacation Camp

Kankakee, Illinois
Pledge for Life
Project Cornerstone

Kingsport, Tennessee
The Children's Advocacy Center of Sul-
livan County
Rascals Teen Center, Inc.

Knoxville, Tennessee
Big Brothers/Big Sisters
C.A.S.A.—Court Appointed Special
Advocates
The Gift of Life—Pass It On

Lafayette, Louisiana
The Family Tree

Lake Charles, Louisiana
Children's Museum of Lake Charles
The Literacy Council of Southwest
Louisiana, Inc.

Las Vegas, Nevada
Community Alternative Sentencing
HELP of Southern Nevada
The Sustainer's Adopt-a-Bear Christmas
Project

Little Rock, Arkansas
The Parent Center

Long Beach, California
HOPE
Woman to Woman

Los Angeles, California
Adolescent Pregnancy ChildWatch
Program
AIDS Community Education Outreach
Project
The Los Angeles Women's Appoint-
ment Collaboration

Lynchburg, Virginia
Adult Day Care
Day in the Park
Lynchburg Sheltered Industries

McAllen, Texas
Anti-Drug Puppet Committee

Memphis, Tennessee
The Memphis Speech and Hearing
Center
The Volunteer Center of Memphis
WKNO Educational Television Station

Mexico City, Mexico
Pro-Ciegos

Minneapolis, Minnesota
CARE—Children's Cancer Assistance
Resource and Encouragement
Violence Against Women Coalition
Success by 6 Partners Project

Monroe, Louisiana
Star Lab Planetariums
Teen Court
Youth House

Monterey County, California
Monterey County Youth Museum

Morgan County, Alabama
HANDS—Helping Adolescents Need-
ing Direction & Supervision
PACT—Parents and Children Together

Morristown, New Jersey
Bone Marrow Donor Program
Born to Read

Nashville, Tennessee
Our Kids
Kare for Kids

New Orleans, Louisiana
CADA/SAENO
The Parenting Center

New York, New York
The Early Childhood Development
Center
NYJL Hospital Volunteers
Pelham Fritz Apartments—NYJL's Re-
sponse to Homelessness

Norfolk-Virginia Beach, Virginia
Growing Up Great

Norman, Oklahoma
Baby Steps Day Care and Parenting
Center
Elderly Day Out
Targeted Intervention Program

Oakland-East Bay, California
Battered Women's Alternative
Disabled Children's Computer Group
Family House

Odessa, Texas
Child's Play
Hospice of the Southwest
Odessa Teen Court

Ogden, Utah
Guardian Ad Litem
Immunization Project
Ogden Nature Center

Oklahoma City, Oklahoma
Courtwatch
Harvest II
Passageway/Positive Tomorrows

Palo Alto•Mid Peninsula, California
Christmas in April—Mid Peninsula
Court Designated Child Advocates
Daybreak Program for Homeless Youth

Pasadena, California
Huntington Art Gallery Docents
Kidspace
Parent Resource Center

Pensacola, Florida
Awareness Team
Grants for Excellence
Speak Up! Say No!

Peoria, Illinois
AWAKE
Family House
Women's Heath Awareness Project

Philadelphia, Pennsylvania
College Access Committee's video,
"College, Get Busy!"
Restoration of the Fairmount
Waterworks
Wheels Medical Transportation

Phoenix, Arizona
Emily Anderson Family Learning Center/Phoenix Children's Hospital
The Orpheum Theatre
YWCA Women in Transition

Pittsburgh, Pennsylvania
Pittsburgh Children's Museum
Transplant Recipients International
Organization
Vintage, Inc.

Portland, Maine
WasteCap Portland

Saint Louis, Missouri
St. Louis Family Theatre Series
TOTAL—Teen Opportunities to
Achieve in Life

Saint Paul, Minnesota
Awareness, Advice & Advocacy: The
Child Abuse Project

San Angelo, Texas
Christmas in April
Hospice of San Angelo
Volunteers in Public Schools

San Antonio, Texas
MATCH—Mothers and Their Children
San Antonio Zoo Education Programs

San Diego, California
CanCare
Kids on the Block
St. Vincent de Paul Enrichment
Program

Sarasota, Florida
Co-Ed: Community Outreach—Emotionally Disturbed
Kids Can Cop
Teen Court

Savannah, Georgia
Coastal Children's Advocacy Center

Shreveport, Louisiana
The Lighthouse
Red River Revel
Sci-Port

Sioux City, Iowa
Fairview Pioneer Schoolhouse
Hands-On-Gallery
Kids on the Block

South Bend, Indiana
Central Blood Bank
Kidsfirst Anniversary Project
Michiana Arts and Sciences Council

Springfield, Illinois
The Mini O'Beirne Crisis Nursery
Sojourn Women's Center
Student Mother Child Care Program

Springfield, Missouri
American Red Cross Self-Contained
Unit
Public Television—Channel 21
LINK Clinic—Let's Invest Now in
Kids

Tampa, Florida
Child Abuse Council
MacDonald Training Center
Parenting Power

Topeka, Kansas
ERC Resource & Referral
Topeka Community Foundation

Toronto, Ontario, Canada
Eating Disorders Video
New Directions
Toronto with Ease

Tyler, Texas
St. Louis Special Education School
Stewart Regional Blood Center
Youth Challenges

Washington, DC
Bright Beginnings

Wichita, Kansas
Accent on Kids, Inc.
Better Beginnings
Kansas Action for Children, Inc.

Winston-Salem, North Carolina
Cancer Patient Support Program
Horizons Residential Care Center
Welcome Baby

JUNIOR LEAGUE
VOLUNTEERS OF DISTINCTION

The following women were selected by their individual Junior Leagues as Volunteers of Distinction. To illustrate the variety and scope of the volunteer experience, additional information follows on 100 of these volunteers, as denoted by the asterick (*).

Lidalyn Bennett Adams, Dallas, Texas
* H. Terri Adelman, Barrington, Rhode Island
Carolyn Radcliff Akers, Mobile, Alabama
Louise Gray Altick, Monroe, Louisiana
* Martha B. Alexander, Charlotte, North Carolina
Jane Stewart Altmeyer, Wheeling, West Virginia
Ruth Collins Sharp Altshuler, Dallas, Texas
* Gigi Armbrecht, Mobile, Alabama
* Donna Anderson, Minneapolis, Minnesota
Susan Shelly Anthony, Cincinnati, Ohio
Chris Kazen Attal, Austin, Texas
Debra Baron, Kankakee, Illinois
* Daryl Cameron Barrett, Salt Lake City, Utah
Joan Ragsdale Baskin, Midland, Texas
Mildred Jordan Bausher, Reading, Pennsylvania
Terry Best, Peoria, Illinois
Sally B. Bierman, North Harris County, Texas
Elaine Ewing Born, Baltimore, Maryland
Charlotte Stump Benjamin, Northern Virginia, Virginia
* Roseann Bentley, Springfield, Missouri
* Ronni W. Bermont, Coral Gables, Florida
Mary Pat Berry, Madison, Wisconsin
Carrie-Mae MacNair Blount, Albuquerque, New Mexico
Claire Whalen Bogaard, Pasadena, California
Mary McGee Boggs, Shreveport, Louisiana
* Donna Pace Bonner, Harlingen, Texas
Sharon K. Bourgeois, Lafayette, Louisiana

Breda Bova, Albuquerque, New Mexico
Marian Hornsby Bowditch, Hampton Roads, Virginia
* Elisabeth "Betty" Edson Bowers, Topeka, Kansas
* Marjorie Montgomery Bowker, Edmonton, Alberta, Canada
Virginia McCormick Brackett, Lubbock, Texas
* Elizabeth C. "Betsy" Brady, Toledo, Ohio
Bonnie T. Drannon, Asheville, North Carolina
Barbara Brink, Greater Vancouver, British Columbia, Canada
* Deborah Brittain, Alexandria, Virginia
Sheri M. Broudy, Butte, Montana
Jennifer Logan Brown, Knoxville, Tennessee
Ruth Buck, Cedar Falls, Iowa
* Rosemarie "Rosie" Gibson Bullard, Fayetteville, North Carolina
* Dorothy Stimson Bullitt, Seattle, Washington
Deborah Burnight, Sioux City, Iowa
Beth Burns, Gwinnett & North Fulton County, Georgia
* Barbara G. Bush, New Orleans, Louisiana
* Lee Byron, Sarasota, Florida
Barb Carlson, Rockford, Illinois
Beth Cartwright, North Little Rock, Arkansas
* Mary Florence "Muffi" Chanfrau, Daytona Beach, Florida
* Linda W. Chapin, Greater Orlando, Florida
Linda Townsend Christ, Racine, Wisconsin
Kathy Cigala, Indian River, Florida

Margo Coleman, Toronto, Ontario, Canada
Shirley B. Conner, Oakland-East Bay, California
* Nancy C. Connolly, Augusta, Georgia
Stephanie Connor, Eugene, Oregon
* Glorida Houston Cook, Daytona Beach, Florida
* Betty Cotton, Central Westchester, New York
* Ruth Ulfelder Covo, Mexico City, Mexico
Sue Ann Cowgill, Lexington, Kentucky
Jan Charbonnet Crocker, Fort Lauderdale, Florida
Norma Sims Crooke, Pensacola, Florida
Eva Riis Culver, Hamilton-Burlington, Ontario, Canada
* Alice D. Cutler, Morristown, New Jersey
* Linda Suzann Dase Daily, Central Westchester, New York
* Elizabeth "Betsy" T. Dalrymple, Greater Elmira-Corning, New York
Julia Daniels, Raleigh, North Carolina
Sandra S. Dawson, Akron, Ohio
* Jan S. Deering, Wichita, Kansas
Debra Deur, M.D., Arlington, Texas
Geraldine Devers, New Britain, Connecticut
Frances B. "Fran" Dietz, Sarasota, Florida
Mary O'Connor Donohue, Troy, New York
* Loretta Jablonski Donovan, Central Westchester, New York
Mary Frey Eaton, Baton Rouge, Louisiana
Susan Shirley Eckel, Galveston County, Texas
* Sally Kahn Efremoff, Canton, Ohio

Maribeth Amrhein Eiken, Dayton, Ohio

Ann C. Ellis, Brooklyn, New York

* Cheryl Elliott, Ann Arbor, Michigan

Cynthia Weber Farah, El Paos, Texas

Gerry MacPherson Fleuriet, Harlingen, Texas

* Susan Flowers, Akron, Ohio

Marsha Fish, Pensacola, Florida

Janice M. Flanagan, Kansas City, Missouri

Luceille Fleming, Harrisburg, Pennsylvania

Nancy Torbett Ford, Tampa, Florida

* Judith C. Frick, Wichita, Kansas

Carolyn Booth Fritz, Tuscaloosa, Alabama

Joan Smith Gehrke, Detroit, Michigan

Elizabeth "Pudd" Gingrich, Tacoma, Washington

Eileen Goodwin, San Jose, California

Sylvia Paige Klumok Goodman, Shreveport, Louisiana

* The Reverend Margaret M. Graham, Washington, DC

* Shirley Grant, Washington, DC

Susan Ray Graves, Oklahoma City, Oklahoma

Suzanne Gray, McAllen, Texas

Kay Green, Kankakee, Illinois

* Judie B. Greenman, Fort Worth, Texas

Pam Griffith-Nock, Youngstown, Ohio

Sue Grinnell, Rochester, New York

Phyllis W. Gustafson, Eastern Fairfield County, Connecticut

Jane Doyle Guthrie, Kansas City, Missouri

Margaret Hance, Phoenix, Arizona

Patricia I. Hannan, Jacksonville, Florida

Emily Symington Harkins, Norfolk-Virginia Beach, Virginia

Mary Harriman, New York, New York

Vickie Griffith Hawver, Topeka, Kansas

Holly Hartman Henriod, Salt Lake City, Utah

Harriet Daniel Herd, Midland, Texas

* Elizabeth Jane Hewes, Edmonton, Alberta, Canada

* Marjorie McCullough Hiatt, Cincinnati, Ohio

Elaine Ewing Holden, Lancaster, Pennsylvania

* Josephine "Jiggie" Jones Holt, Lynchburg, Virginia

* Glenda Evans Hood, Greater Orlando, Florida

* Anne B. Hoover, Fort Wayne, Indiana

Lorraine Hovis, York, Pennsylvania

Holley Evans Howard, Tyler, Texas

Ann Rosteet Hurley, Lake Charles, Louisiana

Gail Preston Hurst, Decatur, Alabama

Carol A. Ingarra, Kingston, New York

Cherry Harris Jacobus, Grand Rapids, Michigan

* Bonnie Borden Jamesson, Oakland-East Bay, California

* Lila Skonovd Johnson, Honolulu, Hawaii

* Marjorie Johnston, Winnipeg, Manitoba, Canada

* Gail Kaess, Detroit, Michigan

* Bobbie Kahler, Clearwater-Dunedin, Florida

Shirley Wright Keeney, Summit, New Jersey

Marjorie Runge Kelso, Galveston County, Texas

* Deborah C. Kennedy, Baltimore, Maryland

* Ann Kenworthy-Pillar, Des Moines, Iowa

Harriet Balzer Kenworthy, Flint, Michigan

Peggy Kirby, Sioux Falls, South Dakota

Walker Dillard Kirby, Morristown, New Jersey

E. Ruth Kitchen, Toronto, Ontario, Canada

Virginia Constance Knecht, Youngstown, Ohio

* Shell H. Knox, Augusta, Georgia

Sandra Kontra, Racine, Wisconsin

Terry Korpela, Great Falls, Montana

* Genevieve Ramsey Koschak, San Angelo, Texas

Sidney McIlvain Kutz, Reading, Pennsylvania

Bobbie Lam, Kalamazoo, Michigan

* Judith T. Lau, Fresno, California

* Emily "Sissy" Dunlap Lawson, Gainesville, Georgia

Martha V. "Marty" Leonard, Fort Worth, Texas

Sharon Levy, Fresno, California

Mary Mooris Leighton, South Bend, Indiana

Hilda Lewin, McAllen, Texas

Diana M. Lewis, New Orleans, Louisiana

Cindy Long, Indian River, Florida

* Arva Moore Parks McCabe, Miami, Florida

Susan H. McClinton, Asheville, North Carolina

Claudia McCoy, Rochester, New York

Evelyn McCoy, Little Rock, Arkansas

Anne McCurdy, Norman, Oklahoma

Faith Bannister McDonald, Anderson, South Carolina

* Virginia Holt McFarland, Houston, Texas

Holley Phelps McGehee, Memphis, Tennessee

Deloris Madison McMullen, Tuscaloosa, Alabama

* Carol H. McNamee, Honolulu, Hawaii

* Susan Gilmore McSwain, Manatee County, Florida

Wendy Fox Macala, Canton, Ohio

Deborah "Debbie" Ritchey Mahony, Lafayette, Louisiana

Eleanor Malkin, Greater Vancouver, British Columbia, Canada

Patty Mallicote, Gwinnett & North Fulton County, Georgia

* Libby Snyder Malone, Austin, Texas

Mary Lee Mann, Fort Myers, Florida

* Cynthia Blythe Marshall, Charlotte, North Carolina

Linda Martens, North Harris County, Texas

Denise J. Martin, Portland, Maine

Marianna E. Martin, Poughkeepsie, New York

* Susan L. Martin, Toledo, Ohio

* Tracie J. Martin, Fort Wayne, Indiana

* Elizabeth Upjohn Mason, Kalamazoo, Michigan

Cathy O'Kelley, Eugene, Oregon

* Doris Okada Matsui, Sacramento, California

Sue Ellen Owens Mears, DeKalb County, Georgia

* Mary Kay Meek, Springfield, Missouri

Judith P. Mendenhall, High Point, North Carolina

Rexanne Davis Metzger, Norfolk-Virginia Beach, Virginia

Linda Miller, Norman, Oklahoma

Sharon P. Miller, Fort Lauderdale, Florida

Kathryn Davis Milliken, Greater Elmira-Corning, New York

* Ellen Foley Mullaney, Minneapolis, Minnesota

* Ann L. Murphey, Tampa, Florida

* Rosemary Denmark Murphy, Grand Rapids, Michigan
Judy Nadler, San Jose, California
Jacquelyn D. Nance, Knoxville, Tennessee
Carolyn Neal, Lubbock, Texas
Margaret Hirst Nelson, Poughkeepsie, New York
Sharon Nelson, Rockford, Illinois
Margaret S. "Tog" Newman, Winston-Salem, North Carolina
Caroline Noojin, Huntsville, Alabama
* Margaret Nuzum, Brooklyn, New York
* Sandra Day O'Connor, Phoenix, Arizona
Beverly L. O'Neill, Long Beach, California
Beth O'Shea, Nashville, Tennessee
Barbara Hesse Odum, San Angelo, Texas
Carolyn Oxtoby, Springfield, Illinois
Sally Page, Peoria, Illinois
* Jane Webster Paine, St. Louis, Missouri
* Vilma Kennedy Pallette, Los Angeles, California
Constance N. Parker, Wilmington, North Carolina
Catherine "Kitty" Butts Pattison, Cumberland, Rhode Island
* Joan M. Pendexter, Portland, Maine
Jean Peterson, Butte, Montana
Sisty Phillips, Memphis, Tennessee
Mary Sue Polleys, Columbus, Georgia
Lou Turner Pontius, Fort Myers, Florida
Doris Swords Poppler, Billings, Montana
Barbara A. Prendergast, York, Pennsylvania
Emily Preyer, Greensboro, North Carolina
Amy T. Pride, Decatur, Alabama
Hazel Quinton, Winnipeg, Manitoba, Canada

* Ernestine Morris Raclin, South Bend, Indiana
* Carol Hampton Rasco, Little Rock, Arkansas
Becky Ray, Fayetteville, North Carolina
Mary Anne Reed, Ottawa, Ontario, Canada
Georgeanne Reuter, Columbus, Ohio
Alice Derrick Reynolds, Montgomery, Alabama
* Ann C. Ring, Winston-Salem, North Carolina
* Mary R. Ripley, Los Angeles, California
* Dorothy "Bill" Robertson, Yakima, Washington
Emily Roberts Robinson, Baton Rouge, Louisiana
Nancy Rogers, New Britain, Connecticut
* Juliet Rowland, Harrisburgh, Pennsylvania
* Virginia H. "Gina" Rugeley, Charleston, West Virginia
Cynthia M. Rogerson, Madison, Wisconsin
Elsie Sadler, Pasadena, California
Pamela Powell Sanderson, Billings, Montana
* Kathy Sawyer, Montgomery, Alabama
* Audrey Lincourt Schiebler, Gainesville, Florida
* Minor Mickel Shaw, Greenville, South Carolina
* Beth Shortt, Oklahoma City, Oklahoma
Ann Bennet Simpson, Honolulu, Hawaii
Patricia K. Smith, Anniston-Calhoun, Alabama
Connie M. Snowden, Arlington, Texas
Jocelyn L. Staus, San Antonio, Texas
Nancy M. Stephenson, Great Falls, Montana

Marjorie Quarles Stinson, Hampton Roads, Virginia
* Lisa Wald Stone, Springfield, Illinois
Georgia H. Street, Monroe, Louisiana
Margaret A. Talburtt, Ann Arbor, Michigan
Della "Dudie" Krause Thielen, Lake Charles, Louisiana
* Betsy Triplett-Hurt, Odessa, Texas
* Martha S. Vanderroort, Anniston-Calhoun, Alabama
Elizabeth Moody Wagner, Lexington, Kentucky
Kate B. Webster, Seattle, Washington
* Carol Welsh, Palo Alto•Mid Peninsula, California
Ruth Anderson Wheeler, Tacoma, Washington
Ann Douglas White, Savannah, Georgia
Dela W. White, San Antonio, Texas
Martha Whitehead, Longview, Texas
Janet L. Whitman, Summit, New Jersey
Mary Hart Keys Wilheit, Gainesville, Georgia
Betty Jo "B. J." Williams, San Diego, California
* Elizabeth Ira Williams, Jacksonville, Florida
* Gayle Edlund Wilson, San Diego, California
* Janice Woods Windle, El Paso, Texas
Getrude Buckley Windsor, Tyler, Texas
* Katrina Moulton Wollenberg, Palo Alto•Mid-Pennisula, California
* Mary Brent Wright, Raleigh, North Carolina
* Lynn Hardy Yeakel, Philadelphia, Pennsylvania
* Joyce Young, Dayton, Ohio

H. TERRI ADELMAN

Not many women can say they built an agency from scratch; H. Terri Adelman can. The Barrington, Rhode Island, mother of three parlayed her school volunteering and her Junior League placements into her job as executive director of the agency she founded—the Adolescent Child Watch. In that time she served on the state's 21st Century Education Committee.

This winner of the Junior League's President's Award for Volunteering donates her time to the League of Women Voters, Providence Public Schools, Healthy Mothers/Healthy Babies, and the Advisory Commission on Women, and is lucky to be able to say that her vocation is also her avocation.

MARTHA BEDELL ALEXANDER

Martha Bedell Alexander lists "legislator" as her profession, but it was in fact a change of professions in 1992, after a distinguished career in the field of treatment of alcohol and substance abuse. After serving as president of the Junior League of Charlotte, North Carolina, she went back to college to earn her master's degree then went from chaplain's assistant at Presbyterian Hospital to executive director of the Charlotte Council on Alcoholism and Chemical Dependency. She left that post to serve in the North Carolina House of Representatives, where she was named Legislator of the Year by the North Carolina Alliance for the Mentally Ill and was judged as one of the "most effective" freshman legislators.

DONNA ANDERSON

Donna Anderson chaired the VIE project for the Junior League of Minneapolis. From that jumping-off point, she provided the leadership, direction, and vision that developed this project into a national nonprofit organization. She is president and founder of the National Retiree Volunteer Coalition, the leader in bringing together retirees, their former employers, and community agencies to produce a dynamic product—the Corporate Retiree Volunteer Program.

Anderson is a member of the Board of Advisors of the National Council on Aging's Institute on Age, Work and Retirement, serves as vice president of City Innovation, as well as on the Advisory Boards of the International Executive Service Corps and Life Course Institute of Cornell University.

GIGI ARMBRECHT

"I am often asked to speak to our League's provisionals about how to translate volunteer work into paid employment. I am fortunate that my paid job calls upon many of the social and communication skills I learned in the Junior League of Mobile, Alabama," says Gigi Armbrecht, who parlayed her work with the JLM into a job as the executive director of Mobile United, an organization committed to bringing leaders of all races to the table to discuss issues of concerns to all Mobilians.

Armbrecht has served on sixteen nonprofit boards of directors since 1978, including the American Red Cross, United Way, the YMCA, the Mobile Mental Health Center, and Mobile 2000, and has served in leadership positions on thirteen of those.

DARYL CAMERON BARRETT

Daryl Cameron Barrett, a member of the Junior League of Salt Lake City, has dedicated herself to the prevention of child abuse and neglect. This involvement had its roots in her League work where, as co-chair of the Child Advocacy Committee, she helped develop and staff the first Family Support Center (crisis nursery) in Utah.

Barrett provided leadership to found the Utah chapter of the National Committee for Prevention of Child Abuse, created the Child Abuse Prevention Plan for Utah, help develop and organized regional multidisciplinary child abuse prevention teams, and helped develop the Children's Trust Fund, a legislative permanent funding mechanism for prevention programs. She looks out for the welfare of children further through her election to the Utah State Board of Education, where she serves as vice chair.

ROSEANN BENTLEY

The majority of Roseann Bentley's community service—volunteer and elected—has been directed toward education. From the Springfield, Missouri, school board and its presidency, she advanced to the position of president of the Missouri State Board of Education. From there she was elected president of the National Association of State Boards of Education by her colleagues from across the United States.

She was the first president of the Junior League of Springfield after their Community Service League was accepted into the Association of Junior Leagues International.

For her, that involvement extended to founding the public television station for Springfield and the Ozarks. Bentley has been given the Mary Harriman Award by AJLI and the Women Who Make a Difference Award by the Chamber of Commerce.

RONNI W. BERMONT

Ronnie W. Bermont passed away on March 18, 1995, from ovarian cancer. It was as a role model for both diversification and for women with cancer that she pointed to with most pride. "My efforts in diversification have been most meaningful to me," she said. "As the first Jewish president of the Junior League of Miami, I knew I was in a unique position. As I served on different community boards, I always felt that one needed to include all segments of the population. During the past two years I have been battling ovarian cancer and I have heard from so many people how I helped to mentor them and inspire them over the years. The tributes have been so meaningful. Not everyone is fortunate to have a negative experience become a positive one."

The list of her community involvement was seemingly endless. She was president of the Junior League of Miami, chair of the board of Trustees of the Historical Museum of South Florida, member of the Community Relations Board of Dade County, past chair of the Citizens' Coalitions for Public Schools, and member of the Temple Israel of Greater Miami Board of Trustees.

MARY PAT BERRY

A deeply committed child advocate, Mary Pat Berry is the founder as well as a past president of the Junior League of Madison, Wisconsin.

Berry learned much about child advocacy through her earlier involvement with the Junior League of Milwaukee. There she founded a citizen review board system to review the case plans for children in foster care in Milwaukee County. "For three years I was totally consumed with the development and implementation of Review Board System," she says. "The work highlights included loads of research, developing a steering committee representative of the community, facing several hundred very angry social workers to tell them citizens would be reviewing their case plans, writing a manual, fighting the battle on confidentiality, developing training, and convincing the judges of the value of the system.

DONNA PACE BONNER

Donna Pace Bonner has always jumped into challenges. She and her husband took on raising his two half-brothers (ages nine and ten) when Donna was pregnant with

the first of their own four children. She was president of the Junior League of Harlingen, Texas; owned and operated her own retail business, a women's shoe store; was selected the first woman City Council member in her community, served three terms, then retired voluntarily.

This outstanding woman credits the League for much of her life's work. "It was through my work with the League's Crippled Children's Cottage that I became a lifelong activist against bureaucratic stagnation. It was the knowledge of basic bookkeeping, which I gained through the League, that gave me the confidence to pursue successful business opportunities. Most important, it was through my League experience that I gained new respect for the ability of women to get a job done regardless of who took credit."

ELISABETH "BETTY" EDISON BOWERS

Some contemporary members of the Junior League think that "training" is a relatively new addition to the volunteer culture. Don't try to tell that to Elisabeth "Betty" Edison Bowers, a founder of the Junior League of Topeka, Kansas. At age ninety-six she lists as her most meaningful Junior League experience "the training provided by the League. It helped me to help my community as an effective volunteer." In the 1930s, when the Topeka League was formed, the Menninger Foundation, Topeka's renowned psychiatric hospital and research center, provided training in understanding human behavior to the members of the young Junior Charity League.

Betty Bowers went on to serve as the League's executive secretary, and was given the first Gold Rose Award, honoring a sustainer for outstanding service to the League and the community. Today she still volunteers.

MAJORIE MONTGOMERY BOWKER

Marjorie Montgomery Bowker joined the Junior League of Edmonton, Alberta, Canada, in 1946, before its affiliation with the

Association of Junior Leagues International in 1959. Her League placements mostly dealt with child safety, family violence, youth concerns, and legal matters. This is most appropriate, since she is a lawyer who became a judge in the Family and Juvenile Courts of Alberta and served in this capacity for seventeen years.

In 1983, she won the Award of Merit from the American Association of Conciliation Courts for establishing the first-in-Canada, court-centered Marriage Conciliation Service aimed at preventing divorce, reducing divorce, and conciliating differences created by divorce.

BREDA BOVA

Breda Bova's fame in her community rests perhaps on her constant and successful efforts to bring about diversity awareness and practices in both her professional and volunteer lives. As an associate professor at the University of New Mexico, she is the first female to direct the campus's Multicultural Center. As the president of the Junior League of Albuquerque, she served as a delegate to Membership Practices II Network to assist with the diversity effort in her League. She later became a member of the Diversity Support Team that went on site to work with Leagues across the country, and that led to her chairing the Diversity Committee for the AJLI Board.

Bova has served on the boards of directors of United Way, the New Mexico Zoological Society, and the American Cancer Society.

ELIZABETH C. "BETSY" BRADY

When asked to list some of the skills she learned as a Junior League of Toledo volunteer, Elizabeth C. "Betsy" Brady mentions "organization, teamwork, motivation, creativity, problem identification, pulling resources together." As volunteer development chairman, community vice president, and—ultimately—as president of the Toledo League, she undoubtedly made good use of those talents. And she was recognized for her leadership outside of the

League by winning the Outstanding Volunteer Award for Toledo in 1991, nominated jointly by some of the other organizations with which she has shared her volunteer talents—United Way, Planned Parenthood, the Toledo Hospital, and the Corporation for Effective Government.

DEBORAH C. BRITTAIN

Just reading Deborah C. Brittain's volunteer history is exhausting; she is one of those women who seem to be able to "do it all." As if it were not enough to have held positions in the Junior League of Northern Virginia, such as chairman of the Court Appointed Special Advocates (CASA) project, community, vice president, personnel committee chairman, program development chairman and president, she has held leadership positions with many other organizations, including LINKS, Inc., the Coalition of 100 Black Women, and Alpha Kappa Alpha Sorority, Inc. She is on the board of directors of the Association of Junior Leagues International, Inc., was co-chairman of the Strategic Planning Task Force for Alexandria City Public Schools, and is a member of the Arlington Housing Corporation Board of Directors.

ROSEMARIE "ROSIE" GIBSON BULLARD

Rosemarie "Rosie" Gibson Bullard's Junior League of Fayetteville, North Carolina, career has been dedicated to children, with some of her placements including Child Advocacy, Kids Count, Adolescent Pregnancy Watch, and the Middle Grades Improvement.

Bullard, who is executive director of Cumberland County Partnership for Children, Inc., has also been instrumental in creating two other child-serving projects. "I worked with collaborative partners," she says, "to create a Family Resource Center (Bridges) in a troubled neighborhood. Also as a volunteer, Bullard wrote the country's Smart Start application. "Smart Start," she says, "brings together families, educators, nonprofits, churches, businesses, and local

government to focus on the needs of young children."

DOROTHY STIMSON BULLITT

The late Dorothy Stimson Bullitt of Seattle, Washington, had one of those success-story lives movies are made of. Born in 1892, in an age when women stayed at home, she married an attorney who became a leader in Democratic politics. He died in 1932, and that year she took his place at the Democratic National Convention to place Franklin D. Roosevelt's name in nomination for President. In the depth of the Depression, Mrs. Bullitt found herself a widow with three young children and no job skills. She took responsibility for her family's Stimson Realty Company, and rebuilt it into a thriving business. In 1947, with the purchase of a struggling radio station, she embarked upon a "new adventure"—broadcasting—and in 1949 acquired the first television station in the Northwest. Her King Broadcasting conglomerate was worth $400 million soon after her death in 1989.

But she was not just a smart businesswoman. Mrs. Bullitt was a community treasure. She was a charter member of the Junior League of Seattle; she was a trustee of Children's Hospital and Medical Center for 35 years; she was appointed to the University of Washington Board of Regents, and later became president; she was the first woman vestry member of the Episcopal Cathedral of St. Mark; she founded the Bullitt Foundation, one of the largest private foundations in the nation.

BARBARA G. BUSH

Barbara G. Bush has had to spend a lot of time—most of it humorously—explaining to people that she is not Barbara Bush, wife of the former president of the United States, but is Barbara Bush, former president of the Junior League of New Orleans, community volunteer par excellence. A board member of the Association of Junior Leagues International, she says she has "turned a sense of community into a commitment." By being involved in all aspects

of project development, fundraising, and financial management in the League, she has learned to handle delicate issues and been able to make a difference in New Orleans and in the lives of those who live there.

Some of the organizations which are beneficiaries of her voluntarism include United Way, Audubon Park Commission, and the Tulane Center for Cardiovascular Health Advisory Board.

LEE BYRON

From joining the Junior League as a Boston debutante at age seventeen to being elected to the Sarasota School Board as a member with a reputation for toughness, Lee Byron has come a long way. As a member of the Junior League of Sarasota, Florida, Byron has worked tirelessly for children's issues. The Teen Court Board of Directors, the Consortium for Children and Youth Board of Directors (president), the Sarasota Compass Education Committee, and the Florida School Board Association are but a few of the memberships she holds.

MARY FLORENCE "MUFFI" CHANFRAU

Mary Florence "Muffi" Chanfrau, has turned many concepts into reality in her life. She shepherded the Daytona Junior Service League into affiliation with the Association of Junior Leagues International, serving as president during this difficult but rewarding time.

In 1989, she created Teen Task Force, a nonprofit organization and prevention program to organize drug- and alcohol-free activities for teenagers.

In addition, Chanfrau has served as PTA president four times, has organized the first Students Against Substance Abuse at a middle school and Students Against Drunk Driving at a high school, has created Project Graduation (an all-night drug- and alcohol-free party for graduating seniors), set up a procedure to register eighteen-year-old high school students to vote, and was a member of a team that created a trade apprentice program for high school students who would not be going to college.

LINDA W. CHAPIN

Linda W. Chapin, a former president of the Junior League of Greater Orlando, is serving her second term as Orange County Chairman, which is the chief executive officer position for Orange County, Florida.

Chapin has taken the lead role in many issues of community concern, including affordable housing, water conservation, and juvenile justice. She was the founder of the Orange County Citizens Commission for Children, and led the effort to create the Juvenile Assessment Center. Her twenty-year record of public service includes two terms as chairman of the Greater Orlando Aviation Authority, present of the League of Women Voters, the State of Florida's Taxation and Budget Reform Commission, the Metropolitan Orlando Urban League, and the Florida center for Children and Youth.

NANCY C. CONNOLLY

"Being President of the Junior League of Augusta, Georgia, put into focus the full scope and mission of the Junior League," says Nancy Cumming Connolly.

Connolly went on to become a prolific community volunteer in Augusta, holding membership on and chairing numerous boards and commissions.

Among the organizations that have benefited from her leadership as a member of their governing bodies are, community-wide, the Augusta Richmond county museum, Historic Augusta Inc., the mayor's committee on the restoration of the Old Government House, Augusta Symphony Guild, Scared Heart Cultural Center, Sand Hills Garden Club, the National Society of the Colonial Dames of America in the state of Georgia; and state-wide, Georgia Public Telecommunications Commission and the Georgia Trust for Historical Preservation.

GLORIA HOUSTON COOK

Through her experience with the Junior League of Daytona Beach, Gloria Houston Cook found the volunteer area that was most meaningful to her. At the Orthopedic Center she began working as a physical and occupational therapy aide. This sparked a lifelong commitment to the Easter Seals Society, including a stint as president and chief executive officer of the National Easter Seal Society, the country's second largest charitable health organization, and an appointment by the Secretary of the U.S. Department of Health and Human Services to the National Advisory Child Health and Human Development Council of the National Institutes of Health.

BETTY COTTON

From PTA president to Junior League of Central Westchester (New York) president to a member of the Scarsdale Citizens Non-Partisan School Board Nominating Committee, Betty Cotton has done it all when it comes to advocating for children in her community. Her Junior League life began by chairing the Public Affairs Committee as a first-year active, and her other volunteer efforts include serving on the boards of the Juvenile Law Education Project and the Scarsdale Child Care Association, as well as being appointed to the Scarsdale Advisory Council on Youth.

Cotton works as executive director for the Westchester Holocaust Commission, and considers it one of her greatest personal achievements to have brought the "Anne Frank in the World" traveling pictorial exhibit to Westchester County.

RUTH ULFELDER COVO

After working in "almost all League projects" since being admitted in 1936, Ruth Ulfelder Covo became president of the Junior League of Mexico City, Mexico.

It is for her work with the blind that she is probably best known. Her greatest achievement in this area is her writing and copyrighting two Braille/print manuals for the teaching of reading and writing of Braille. Her interest in the blind started when she chaired a Junior League project for the blind, becoming Printshop Chairman and Braille Library Chairman. She founded the Comité Internacional pro Ciegos as an agency to take over the Junior League Project for the Blind. She then served as President of the CIPC board. Covo was the Mexican representative on UNESCO for the World Congress for the Blind.

EVA RIIS CULVER

The legacies of most volunteers are intangible. Eva Riis Culver of the Junior League of Hamilton-Burlington, Ontario, Canada, will be able to point to something that is almost literally bricks and mortar. Culver developed the Junior League's Enviro-House project, overcoming school board barriers, developing a collaborative team, acquiring funding, and watching her project come to fruition. The Enviro-House is a portable scale model of an environmentally sound home which teaches wise uses of resources to fourth, fifth and sixth graders, through hands-on activities and experiments. Some of her other achievements include serving as president of the Hamilton Council of Home and School Association, and being awarded the Hamilton Volunteer of the Year Award for community leadership in education.

ALICE D. CUTLER

Alice Darlington Cutler approaches all areas in her life head-on. When she left the high-powered life as an assistant vice president at Drexel Burnham Lambert in New York for the full-time life of a volunteer and housewife in Morristown, New Jersey, she approached her new career in an equally high-powered style. She was elected at age 33 one of the youngest presidents of the Junior League of Morristown, and has since gone on to represent her League on the Executive Committee of the board of United Way of Morris County.

Cutler's volunteer history includes positions as a trustee of the Macculloch Hall Historical Museum, the Northwood School, and the Trustees of the Green.

LINDA SUZANN DASE DAILY

One of the crowning achievements of a Junior League volunteer, and one that exemplifies the way the League operates, is identifying a community need, starting a program to address that need, nurturing the program until it is strong, and then turning it over to others in the community. That is precisely what Linda Suzann Dase Daily did in the Junior League of Central Westchester (New York) when she initiated the Spring Harvest Food Drive, building a county-wide partnership of Junior Leagues, schools, Scouts, businesses, and the Coalition of Food Pantries

A past president of the JLCW, Daily is now the executive director of the nonprofit agency FIRST (Family Information and Referral Service Teams), where she developed a new service for the agency.

ELIZABETH "BETSY" T. DALRYMPLE

This former president of the Junior League of Greater Elmira–Corning and AJLI board member, combines a career as a trust officer with the Chemung Canal Trust Company, family life with a husband and two teenagers, and volunteer service that has included presidencies of the boards of the United Way, Glove House, an elementary school PTO, and the Community Foundation of the Elmira–Corning Area.

Her crowning achievement, however, has been her key role in starting the community foundation in her area. Dalrymple shepherded the idea into reality, developing a project proposal that resulted in the Junior League granting $5,000 in start-up expenses. She has watched her "baby" grow from that initial $5,000 into a foundation with over $2 million in permanent endowment funds that awards over $100,000 in grants annually.

JAN S. DEERING

Jan S. Deering helped establish two Ronald McDonald Houses in Wichita, Kansas, making Wichita the first community in the world to have two such facilities. She now works as the executive director, and under her leadership these houses have provided temporary lodging and emotional support

for over ten thousand families of critically ill children.

Her term as president of the Junior League of Wichita gave her an interest in the Junior League organization nationwide and encouraged her to go on to chair her Area IV Council, and later to become an AJLI board member. Those positions led to what she considers her most meaningful Junior League experiences: lobbying and testifying before various Senate and House committees in behalf of a foster care bill and the Medical Leave Act.

LORETTA JABLONSKI DONOVAN

Loretta Jablonski Donovan did what every Junior League hopes its members will do— she took her League training and used it in her life and in her community at large. As a member of the Junior League of Central Westchester (New York), Donovan founded the antiques show and the community newsletter, won the President's Award, and as community vice president encouraged a committee to run with an Arts in Education project, culminating with the founding of the Science Port museum.

The League, she says, introduced her to her current profession, as national director of training for the March of Dimes Birth Defects Foundation. "I then moved to higher education as director of continuing education at Marymount College, where my focus continues to be the education of adults—especially women."

CHERYL ELLIOTT

Cheryl Elliott's professional life began as a secondary public school teacher. Her love of helping teenagers never wanted, during her ten years out of the paid employment world. She tended to choose placements for the Junior League of Ann Arbor, Michigan, that benefited young people. After serving as the president of the League, she brushed up her résumé, using the AJLI Volunteer Skills Portfolio, and landed the job of program director of the Ann Arbor Area Community Foundation.

Winner of a JLAA Annual Recognition Award and the JLAA President's Award for

Distinguished Service, Elliott supports agencies in Ann Arbor as diverse as the United Way, the Ann Arbor Symphony Orchestra, and Soundings: A Center For Women.

SALLY KAHN EFREMOFF

When she first moved to Canton, Ohio, attorney Sally Kahn Efremoff joined the Junior League. Efremoff took those opportunities and ran with them, participating in everything from Leadership Canton and the Chamber of Commerce to the Canton Ballet and the Cultural Center for the Arts. She is particularly proud of her role in helping to create the Hospice of Stark County, and her honors include Woman of the Year for the Junior League of Canton and Volunteer of the Year for Avondale School.

The Junior League enhanced her boardsmanship and training ability, qualities which no doubt have proven valuable as she has served Canton as an elected member of the Plain Local School Board since 1980.

EMILY SYMINGTON HARKINS FILER

It is possible for benefit and good to come from sadness and tragedy. Emily Symington Harkins Filer, CVA, a former president of the Junior League of Norfolk–Virginia Beach, proved that to be true after the tragic death from Hodgkins disease of her daughter, Lee Harkins. Taking the leadership and management skills she learned from the League, Filer formed Lee's Friends, a unique volunteer support program for cancer patients of all ages and stages, and their families. The agency has received numerous awards, including the President's Volunteer Action Award, the Governor's Gold Medal Award, the J. C. Penney Golden Rule Award, and the Distinguished Merit Award from the National Conference of Christians and Jews. Having grown from nine volunteers to over three hundred and fifty, and having helped thousands of patients and trained over six hundred staff and volunteers, Lee's Friends is a national model.

SUSAN FLOWERS

To say that Susan Flowers embraces life is an understatement. She beat an advanced case of breast cancer in 1986 and has responded by giving her all-out efforts to others affected by the disease. She's a Reach-to-Recovery counselor (for which she has been named Outstanding Volunteer in 1990); a public speaker on behalf of the University Ireland Cancer Center in Cleveland, a worker and speaker for the Susan Koemen Foundation on Race for the Cure; and a tireless fundraiser, throwing her own fundraising party—Still Kickin'—to celebrate her fifth year cancer-free.

Flowers has held many leadership positions in the Junior League of Akron, and is known for her creative presentations.

She was a writer for a program called "Remember the Children—Guiding Parents Through Divorce" for the Child Guidance Center Women's Board, and has seen it mandated by the courts for all divorcing parents in Akron.

JUDITH C. FRICK

Judith C. Frick's placements for the Junior League of Wichita, Kansas, include chair of the following: Child Advocacy, Kansas Action for Children, and Child Watch. A crowning achievement of Frick's League years was her three-year presidency of the Kansas Action for Children, a statewide child advocacy organization of the three Junior Leagues in Kansas. Outside of the League, she has worked for CASA, the Wichita Youth Home Board, Wichita Commission on the Status of Children and Youth, Comprehensive Services for Children and Families in Crisis, and the Sedgwick County Adolescent Pregnancy Network. She's been appointed to the U.S. Advisory Board on Child Abuse and Neglect and the Governor's Commission on Children and Families.

Currently the executive director of the Wichita/Sedgwick County Cities in Schools program, Frick likes the continuity and overlap in her volunteer and professional lives.

THE REVEREND MARGARET M. GRAHAM

The Reverend Margaret M. Graham, an Episcopal priest and a past president of the Association of Junior Leagues International, Inc., lists her three greatest achievements in life: (1) finding God; (2) celebrating thirty-two years of marriage; (3) three glorious daughters. A sustainer with the Junior League of the City of Washington, D.C., she has dedicated her life to the service of others, through the church as well as through a number of agencies, including the National Committee to Prevent Child Abuse, the National Alliance to Find Homelessness, the Children's Defense Fund, and the Bright Beginnings Developmental Daycare for Homeless Children. Her impact is best felt, she says, through her "powerful, prominent focus on the issues of women and children."

SHIRLEY GRANT

Shirley Grant probably didn't know it then, but her life's path was unalterably influenced by a little girl she met while doing junior high school summer volunteer work for the Red Cross. Adrienne had hydrocephaly, or water on the brain, and Grant was deeply touched by her experience with the child and the moments of happiness she was able to bring to her. Shirley Grant went on to become a family physician, and a Junior League of Washington, D.C., member who has devoted her rich volunteer life to the welfare of children.

For the League, she wrote and chaired the Boarder Baby Project at D.C. General Hospital.

In addition, Grant works for Healthcare for the Homeless, the Mayor's Committee on Infant Mortality, her children's schools' PTAs, and the Coalition of 100 Black Women as well as Delln Research and Education Foundation.

JUDIE B. GREENMAN

After being president of the Junior League of Fort Worth, Texas, a member of the board of Association of Junior Leagues International, and a stellar member of a huge number of community boards, Judie B. Greenman took her volunteer experience and became the managing partner of Training Unlimited, a training and consulting firm specializing in organizational development strategies and human resource development. A sampling of her other community involvement includes the Funding Information Center, the United Way of Tarrant County, Planned Parenthood, the American Red Cross, Fort Worth Children's Medical Center, the Alliance for Children, the Adolescent Pregnancy Prevention Board, and the National Council of Jewish Women.

ELIZABETH JANE "BETTIE" HEWES

Elizabeth Jane "Bettie" Hewes, a former president of the Junior League of Edmonton, Alberta, Canada, lists as one of her finest achievements in life "encouraging women to use their whole selves, particularly in public life." She has practiced what she preached, as she has made an impact on a national scope, having served as chairman of Canadian National Railways, as a City of Edmonton Alderman for ten years, and currently, as a Member of the Provincial Legislature of the Province of Alberta in her third term.

She worked for seven years on the Edmonton Social Planning Council as a planner and acting director. Among her many awards are the Canadian Mental Health Award, the Province of Alberta Achievement Award for Community Service, and Edmonton Big Sisters Society Award.

MARJORIE McCULLOUGH HIATT

It would have been easy for Marjorie McCullough Hiatt to rest on her laurels after serving as president of the Association of Junior Leagues from 1960–62. Instead, she has gone on to the presidency of another national organization—the Girl Scouts of the U.S.A.—and continues as a volunteer dynamo in her hometown of Cincinnati.

With the Junior League of Cincinnati, she helped start the Children's Theatre, founded a nursery school for the hearing impaired at the Speech and Hearing Center, staffed a clinic at the General Hospital, and chaired League fundraisers. A premier fundraiser much in demand, Hiatt currently is working on eleven fundraising campaigns, and loves every minute.

JOSEPHINE JONES "JIGGIE" HOLT

Josephine Jones "Jiggie" Holt began her service with the Junior League of Lynchburg, Virginia, in 1941, when there was no talk of "networking," "leadership tracks," or "skills training," but rather, simply, "doing your part."

For the Junior League, she worked on the Preschool program, the Prenatal and Birth Clinic, the Department of Physical Therapy, the Children's Clinic, and the Children's Theatre and Children's Radio programs.

She still balances volunteer leadership roles (on the boards of the Interfaith Outreach Association and Adult Care center and as chair of United Way Planned Giving Committee) with hands-on volunteering (tutoring young students after school, driving blind and cancer patients to their doctors' appointments, providing lunch for Habitat for Humanity workers).

GLENDA EVANS HOOD

Glenda Evans Hood's first placement (age twenty-three) for the Junior League of Greater Orlando was teaching English as a second language to Spanish-speaking children. "This gave me the opportunity to have a profound influence on the lives of these individuals and their future in our country and community," she says. She went on—after serving as president of the League—to become the first woman and youngest person ever to be elected mayor of Orlando.

Prior to being elected mayor, she owned her own public relations, consulting business, had served as an Orlando City Commissioner for ten years, and traveled around

the country for the Association of Junior Leagues International as a diversity consultant. Like other League-trained elected officials, Hood lists many skills she learned through her League work—strategic planning, consensus building, professionalism, and selflessness.

ANNE B. HOOVER

Former Junior League of Fort Wayne, Indiana, president and former Association of Junior Leagues president Anne B. Hoover says that her Junior League work led her to her mission in life: empowering youth to service. "This mission," she says, "is the mission of the nonprofit which I direct [Community Partnerships with Youth, Inc.] and I see it as an opportunity to build citizens with a strong belief and value system demonstrated through service to the community."

Aside from her Junior League work, Hoover has served on a plethora of boards—local, state, and national—and won the Sagamore of the Wabash Award, which is the highest award given by the Governor of Indiana for work on behalf of the youth of Indiana.

BONNIE BORDEN JAMESON

Ask a group of Junior League women what the most important part of their League experience was and a significant portion will say, "Training." Bonnie Borden Jameson, a sustainer in the Junior League of Oakland/East Bay, California, has devoted her life to training, first as a volunteer, and now professionally as a Designer/Trainer/Facilitator for Human Resource Development.

For the past fifteen years Jameson has designed and presented Training for Trainers workshops for thousands of nonprofit staff people. She has served on a number of community boards, including the Marcus A. Foster Educational Institute, the Oakland Youth Works, and the Oakland Athletics Baseball Company's Community Advisory Board. She is also the recipient of the Junior League of Oakland/East Bay's Sustainer of the Year award.

LILA SKONOVD JOHNSON

After serving the Junior League of Honolulu as President, Lila Skonovd Johnson went on to join the Area VI Council and then the Association of Junior Leagues International Board. Along the way, she narrowed her volunteer focus. She went back to graduate school and earned a master's degree in public health, complementing her undergraduate nursing degree, and then launched a full-scale attack against breast cancer and for tobacco control.

She has an appreciation for the parliamentary skills she learned in the League. She continues to teach, and she is the Parliamentarian for the National Board of Directors of the American Cancer Society. In 1992, Johnson was presented the National Volunteer Leadership Award.

MARJORIE JOHNSTON

"Everything I learned and used in community work I learned while a member of the League," says Marjorie Johnston, a former president of the Junior League of Winnipeg, which she joined in 1941.

Marjorie's most memorable League project was Age and Opportunity of which she served as president. Age and Opportunity, which was the first group in Winnipeg to work on behalf of senior citizens, advocated for senior housing, set up counseling services, started a job bureau, developed recreation programs and retirement planning. As a direct result of this League effort, Winnipeg now has many senior centers across the city.

GAIL KAESS

Gail Kaess, former president of the Junior League of Detroit, tells of her experience chairing the first Junior League joint public/private project with the city of Detroit. She was elected to the Gross Point Farms City Council, and has served four consecutive terms. She has since been awarded the Taubman Foundation fellowship to attend the John F. Kennedy School of Government at Harvard.

Kaess has won the State Board of Education Parent of the Year Award, the United Way Heart of Gold Volunteer Award, the Outstanding Community Service Award from the Racial Justice Center, and the Michigan Municipal League Life Member Award.

BOBBIE KAHLER

After hearing a speech to the Junior League about needs of children and children's issues, Bobbie Kahler of the Junior League of Clearwater-Dunedin. and several others asked to form a task force to research children's needs in their county. They determined that there was a great need for day care for homeless preschoolers residing in shelters with their parents. They created such a facility from scratch. "It took three years of hard work, but the Gateway Children's Shelter became a reality."

Kahler spearheaded the project for the League, and when Gateway was completed in December of 1991, it had two infant nurseries, four preschool classrooms and one pre-kindergarten classroom, two nicely equipped playgrounds, two offices, a reception area, and a full-service kitchen serving two hot meals daily and nutritious snacks for 96 children.

DEBORAH C. KENNEDY

"I grew up in a large ethnic blue-collar family," says Deborah C. Kennedy, past president of the Junior League of Baltimore. "My dad worked in a steel mill and my mom waited tables. But they always inspired me to feel as if I could do anything." After working hard on full scholarship at the Church Hospital School of Nursing, she earned her nursing degree and received the Citizenship Award for outstanding service to the school, hospital, and community. She later earned both a BSN and MS in nursing from the University of Maryland.

That college-era community service foreshadowed her intense devotion to volunteer work in her adult life, and aside from a full slate of Junior League jobs, she serves on the boards of Maryland Friends

Foster Care, Ronald McDonald House, and the Babe Ruth Museum.

ANN KENWORTHY-PILLAR

After serving as president of the Junior League of Des Moines, Iowa, Ann Kenworthy-Pillar was nominated by her League to serve on the board of directors of United Way of Central Iowa. She served on that board in a number of capacities until she was elected chairman of the board, the first woman to ever serve in that position.

After living in several cities throughout her adult life, Kenworthy-Pillar knew the importance of setting down "volunteer roots," and she envisioned a center of volunteerism where all residents could see listings of volunteer opportunities and receive direction to the various agencies and their volunteer needs. She established the volunteer Bureau of Central Iowa, known as one of the finest volunteer clearinghouses in the nation.

CAROL HARRISON KLEINER

Colorado Springs, Colorado, has a superlative advocate for children in Carol Kleiner. A former Junior League of Colorado Springs president as well as a member of the Association of Junior Leagues International Board of Directors, she has directed her recent efforts toward the public schools in her hometown.

Elected to two terms on the Board of Education, Kleiner is a strategic planner for the school system. "The multicultural journey," she explains, "has given me strength to stand up to prejudice in the public school environment." She has the creativity and vision to help solve problems and create systems for the improvement of public schools and is the founder and first chairman of a community collaboration supporting public education. She mentions, "This group led to a Public School Foundation and the inclusion of patrons in public education decision-making."

SHELL HARDMAN KNOX

Shell Hardman Knox has taken her experience as president of the Junior League of

Augusta, Georgia, and proceeded to hold a multitude of other volunteer leadership positions, including those of statewide magnitude. Past president of the Greater Augusta Arts Council and the Augusta Ballet; a former chairperson of the Southeastern Regional Ballet Festival; a board member of the Augusta Symphony Guild, the Sacred Heart Cultural Center Guild, Historic Augusta, and the Morris Museum of Art, Knox has focused the majority of her energies toward the arts in Georgia. The culmination of this involvement came when she was named chair of the Georgia Council for the Arts.

GENEVIEVE RAMSEY KOSCHAK

Many volunteers win awards. Genevieve Ramsey Koschak has one named for her. The annual Genevieve Koschak Award in the Volunteers in Public Schools (VIPS) program in San Angelo, Texas, was established in 1984 to recognize outstanding service to the VIPS program. The Junior League of San Angelo began the VIPS program, with League member Koschak as the first director. From its beginning with 103 volunteers in 1981, the program has grown to 4,000 volunteers annually, serving all students in the San Angelo school district.

Koschak worked with others to guide their service league into acceptance by the Association of Junior Leagues International, and served as its first president in 1957–1958. During her tenure as president, the Baby Clinic, an important commitment of the League, was turned over to the City-County Welfare Department.

JUDITH T. LAU

"It was in the Junior League," says Judith T. Lau of the Junior League of Fresno, California, "that for the first time in my life I lost the feeling of being an outsider. I had always felt like a stranger in many strange lands during my youth, as we lived in seven countries and fourteen cities over twenty-one years while my father was a Nationalist Chinese diplomat. Though I was not even a U.S. citizen when I first joined the

League, and I was the first Asian member of the JLF, as well as the first Junior League president of Chinese extraction on the U.S. mainland, I never felt I was a foreigner."

"It has been said that 'America is a willingness of the heart,'" says Lau. "Each time I have spoken on voluntarism, the response from the audience has been tremendous. It takes an 'outsider' to remind Americans that the immense vitality and diversity of opportunities in our country is due in no small part to our voluntary sector."

EMILY "SISSY" DUNLAP LAWSON

"I entered the Junior League at the age of twenty-three as a young wife and mother whose life was filled with self and family. My League experience led me on a course of voluntarism and compassion which positively altered the direction of my life." So says Emily "Sissy" Dunlap Lawson, who served as president of the Junior League of Gainesville–Hall County, Georgia, before being elected to the Gainesville City Council in 1985, becoming the first female elected official. Subsequently, she was chosen mayor by her fellow Council members; as mayor she was the catalyst in forming the City of Gainesville Summer Games Committee, which ultimately attracted to Gainesville the competitions in rowing, canoeing, and kayaking for the 1996 Olympic Games.

ELIZABETH "LIBBY" SNYDER MALONE

"As the president of the Junior league of Austin, Texas, I was the acting CEO of a 'small business' with a 1,200-member work force, a million-dollar operating budget, and a shopping center with nine retail tenants as an unrelated business activity," says Elizabeth "Libby" Snyder Malone. She is a Texas Tornado, doing a myriad volunteer jobs and collecting accolades along the way. She's received the Legacy Award from the Brackenridge Foundation, was one of six Women of the Year for the Women's Symphony League, was Volunteer Extraordinaire for the Junior League of Austin, was the High School Volunteer of the Year for the Austin Independent School District, and won the Getting Better All the Time award from the Women's Fund.

CYNTHIA BLYTHE MARSHALL

Cynthia Blythe Marshall jumped directly from president of the Junior League of Charlotte, North Carolina, into the position of founding executive director of the Charlotte Cities in Schools.

For the League, she became the first child advocacy chair, spearheading a committee which studied child abuse and neglect, child care, and learning disabilities. From these studies, the Junior League assisted in the creation of three new agencies—the Council for Children, the Family Support Center, and Child Care Resources.

As the organizing executive director for Cities in Schools, she credits her advocacy skills of assessment and planning, lobbying for change, negotiation, and monitoring results with her agency's success in Charlotte. The Cities in Schools program was one of President George Bush's Points of Light in 1990.

SUSAN L. MARTIN

In 1984, after twenty years of marriage and motherhood and no paid employment, Susan L. Martin found herself divorced and looking for a job. Not to worry. She was just finishing her term as president of the Junior League of Toledo, and she parlayed her Junior League and other volunteer experiences into a terrific job as executive director of the Toledo Bar Association. "Being League president launched me into a career and paid employment," she says. In addition to her local League service, Martin served for two years on the Association of Junior Leagues International pilot project on Diversity.

TRACIE J. MARTIN

Tracie J. Martin served the Junior League of Fort Wayne, Indiana, in a number of capacities, but her true legacy is Erin's House for Grieving Children. "Erin's House is named after a six-year-old friend of mine who died," Martin says. She is now president of the board of Erin's House, and has served on the boards of the Historical Society, Family and Children's Services.

She explains the Erin's House for Grieving Children project: "Truancy, alcoholism, drug abuse, depression, violent behavior, suicidal tendencies, and the inability to form a significant relationship later in life can all be traced to a child's inability to cope with the death of a loved one. Erin's House is a 'nip in the bud' program, which gets at potential problems, allowing children to grow and go on living and loving after the death of an important person in their lives."

ELIZABETH UPJOHN MASON

Elizabeth Upjohn Mason has been able to lead her life in several sequenced stages. After graduating from the Medill School of Journalism at Northwestern University, she was the woman's editor of the Kalamazoo, Michigan, *Gazette*. After joining the Junior League of Kalamazoo, Michigan, she threw herself into that life and ultimately became its president. Now she is involved in wide-ranging community service in Kalamazoo, where her focus leans toward fundraising and teaching others the "power of philanthropy and the joy of giving."

Some of the recipients of her time, talent, and treasure include the Kalamazoo Foundation, the Kalamazoo Symphony Orchestra, the Kalamazoo Institute of Arts, the Child Guidance Clinic Foundation, the Michigan Council of the Arts and Cultural Affairs, the United Way, and Kalamazoo College.

DORIS OKADA MATSUI

As a member of the Junior League of Sacramento, California, Doris Okada Matsui chaired the Education, Provisional, and Placement committees, and served on the Board of Directors and the Nominating Committee. After a move to Washington, D.C., which was necessitated by her husband's election as a U.S. Congressman, she affiliated with the Junior League of Washington, D.C..

She was president of the Congressional Club, a bipartisan group of spouses of Members of Congress, the Cabinet and the Supreme Court Justices. She was on the Steering Committee for Congressional Families for Drug-Free Youth, the Steering Committee of Peace Links, on the National Board of the Christmas in April Foundation, and on the Governing Board of the House of Representatives Child Care Center.

Currently, she holds the position of Deputy Assistant to the President at the White House, Deputy Director of Public Liaison.

ARVA MOORE PARKS McCABE

Arva Moore Parks McCabe has spent the majority of her volunteer and professional life bettering her community. With over two dozen community service involvements and over twenty awards and honors to her credit she says that skills she learned as a Junior League volunteer are the basis for her success.

McCabe joined the Junior League of Miami and immediately plunged into a League placement producing films for public television. She turned her thesis on the history of Coconut Grove into a thirty-minute film, and went on to write and produce *Ours Is a Tropic Land* for the same placement. This second film won six awards, including the Emmy from the Florida Academy of Television Arts and Sciences.

McCabe has worked diligently to improve race relations in Miami. "In 1970," she recalls, "when the federal court ordered the pairing of three formerly all-white Coral Gables schools with an all-black Coconut Grove School, I—along with a close Junior League friend—initiated an interracial summertime program at our church. Today, this school is still considered one of the most successful schools in the county and continues to draw an interracial student population."

VIRGINIA HOLT McFARLAND

"I'm not through learning and growing," says Virginia Holt McFarland. "There is much yet to do!" this comes from a woman who joined the Junior League of Houston in 1958.

She was Texas Children's Hospital Outpatient Clinic Chairman, Advisory Clinic Chairman, and a member of the Study of Learning Differences in the Children of Houston and Harris County Committee during her active Junior League years. She's been a Texas Children's Hospital Trustee since 1972, is an honorary lifetime trustee of the National Association of Children's Hospitals and Related Institutions, Inc., and speaks on their behalf in Washington, D.C. She is a founding board member of Initiatives for Children, Inc., which does child care programs and advocacy.

CAROL H. McNAMEE

After her stint as president of the Junior League of Honolulu, Carol H. McNamee took on a project that has been her "consuming involvement" for over ten years. McNamee founded the Honolulu chapter of Mothers Against Drunk Driving and has continued to work fervently for the organization. "MADD has a clear mission which is not duplicated by other groups," she says.

Through this association with MADD, McNamee has won the National Highway Traffic Safety Administration Award for Service in the Field of Alcohol Countermeasures, the national MADD President's Golden Achievement Award, the Junior League of Honolulu Sustainer of the year Award, and has been selected by the Honolulu *Star Bulletin* as one of "Ten Who Made a Difference" in 1991.

SUSAN GILMORE McSWAIN

As chairman of the Hope Project for the Junior League of Manatee County, Florida, Susan Gilmore McSwain oversaw a vision become not only reality but an award-winning model project for the Association of Junior Leagues International. The Hope Project, a coalition of twelve organizations spearheaded by the Junior League of Manatee County, completely renovated the shelter for battered women and their children. "Through the coalition," McSwain says, "with only $15,000 in League money, we were able to provide over $75,000 in improvements to the shelter in goods and services. In addition, we built bridges to other community organizations—including an African-American sorority—that have continued over time."

MARY KAY MEEK

Mary Kay Meek has experienced success in all areas of her life: as a wife and mother who had "created balance" in her life; as a property manager and developer; and as a community volunteer. She credits the Junior League of Springfield, Missouri, with giving her the leadership skills she's used in all areas of life. She's been president of: her League, the United Way of the Ozarks, the Community Foundation of the Ozarks, the Springfield Little Theatre, the Springfield Catholic Schools, and the Greene County Board for the Developmentally Disabled. She has served on the Area IV Council for the AJLI and as a member of the Missouri Humanities Council.

She is the only woman to have been named Springfieldian of the Year, and along with her husband was named Philanthropist of the Year by the National Society of Fundraising Executives.

ANN LOWRY MURPHEY

Ann L. Murphey's fame lies in her work for children. This former president of the Junior League of Tampa started the Children's Board to fund childen's services which now has a staff of 29 and the 1995 annual budget is over $13 million.

Murphey's work at the Children's Home, a residential treatment center for emotionally disturbed children, is the stuff of volunteer legend. Becoming president of the board in 1979, she inherited a desperate situation: finances were in a shambles, the executive director had agreed to leave, the existing program was totally inadequate.

After her term as president expired, the Children's Home had turned around and she remained as an unsalaried development director. Within a few years the annual budget included over $1 million in contributions, and Murphey became the associate director of the agency.

ROSEMARY DENMARK MURPHY

Some volunteers choose one area of interest and concentrate their efforts there. Rosemary Denmark Murphy of the Junior League of Grand Rapids, Michigan, chose three areas—health care, children's services, and criminal justice—and excelled in effecting change in all of them. Along with serving on the Association of Junior Leagues International Board, she holds membership on thirteen other boards and lists twelve other volunteer positions on her résumé as well. For the State of Michigan, she served on the Commission on Aging, the Child Care Services Committee, the Untied Way of Michigan, the Michigan Advisory Unit to the U.S. Civil Rights Commission, and the Michigan Council of Voluntary Action.

ELLEN FOLEY MULLANEY

Ellen Foley Mullaney of the Junior League of Minneapolis, took the devastating event of her sister's murder and created the Violence Against Women Coalition as a League project. "Founding and nurturing the Violence Against Women Coalition," she says, "stretched my own leadership skills while creating an important awareness of sexual violence in the community and giving JLM and JL–St. Paul a higher profile in our state."

"After Mary's murder, JLM became an important support group and a network that helped me and many in our community channel our outrage and grief about sexual violence into proactive solutions." Mullaney was the executive director of this coalition of thirty-five community groups that created public awareness and action to stop the rising incidence of rape and domestic battering.

MARGARET NUZUM

Margaret Nuzum of the Junior League of Brooklyn is an educator, teaching at Teachers College; an entrepreneur, owning Empire Education; and a community volunteer, serving as the elected president of her local school board.

Early in her life, she says, "It became crystal clear that if there were ever to be equal opportunity, equity in education must be available to all children." Nuzum left a career in banking and made a lifelong commitment to education. She served on the New York City Chancellor's Task Force on Middle School Education, and as president of her local school board has spearheaded the restructuring of the middle schools. For the Junior League, for more than ten years, Nuzum has been a representative to the Education Priorities Panel, a coalition of twenty-six civic, advocacy, and parent groups that work together to monitor the New York City Board of Education.

SANDRA DAY O'CONNOR

It is quite telling that Sandra Day O'Connor, when asked to list her profession, writes simply, "attorney/judge." Most Americans know her as the first female Associate Justice of the United States Supreme Court. The League knew her when she was president of the Junior League of Phoenix at the same time she was the Assistant Attorney General of Arizona and before she was an Arizona state senator or a member of the Arizona Court of Appeals. Of her Junior League experience, O'Connor says, "It helped me mature and become active in my community. The experience of learning how to work from within a committee structure and the experience of learning leadership techniques were among the most meaningful Junior League experiences.

"It is voluntarism," she says, "that sets our nation apart and that fosters a community spirit in those who participate."

JANE KRAUSE PAINE

By combining her professional experience with her volunteer work through the Ju-

nior League of St. Louis, Jane Krause Paine has been able to serve the greater community in focusing on the needs of children and families. In 1964 she helped initiate the Junior Kindergarten Program, a partnership between the JLSL and the Page Park YMCA. Her interest in parent/child education led to the development of the National Parents as Teachers Program. The first early childhood–parent education legislation to be introduced in Missouri followed a 1976 Governors' Conference which Pine helped to initiate. Paine was also responsible for helping to develop many other programs, including Teen Outreach and Caring Communities.

VILMA KENNEDY PALLETTE

If there are two things a Junior Leaguer knows—especially if she's been placement chair and president of her League—they are the value of trained volunteers and how to gather, organize, and train those volunteers. Vilma Kennedy Pallette, former president of the Junior League of Los Angeles, has put this knowledge into play in a scope most volunteers would only dream of (or have nightmares about). First, Pallette initiated and developed a volunteer corps which trained guides to state and city historic downtown Los Angeles landmarks.

That success begat another volunteer job. Pallette was the Manager of Volunteer Services for the Los Angeles Olympic Organizing Committee for the 1984 Olympic games in L.A. This effort expanded to include some 32,000 volunteers through the Volunteer Services Department. "It was the first time that the concept of unpaid staff had been introduced to the international Olympic movement," she says.

JOAN M. PENDEXTER

Joan M. Pendexter is a case study in the melding of professional and volunteer worlds. As a pediatric nurse practitioner, she is vitally interested in the safety of children. As a Junior League of Portland, Maine, volunteer, she learned skills that trained her for a political life. As a Maine state senator, she has used her political clout to help realize some of her nurse practitioner goals. For example, she is chairman of the Maine Highway Safety Commission, and was responsible for passing safety belt legislation in both the Senate and House in 1993.

"I owe everything I know to my Junior League experience!" she asserts. "Fundraising, organizational, strategic planning, and volunteer management skills are all invaluable in a political campaign, and are all skills readily acquired through Junior League membership, Pendexter says.

ERNESTINE MORRIS RACLIN

Ernestine Morris Raclin tells of attending a Junior League conference in Canada where the Ambassador to the United Nations gave the keynote address. "After the death of her husband the Prime Minister asked her to be Canada's representative to the UN," recounts Raclin. "She was surprised and told the PM she had no experience. Whereupon he told her, 'Your volunteer work has given you more than enough experience to fill these shoes!' Had I not heard this speaker, I do not know if I would have had the courage to take on the leadership role I did upon the death of my own husband." But courage Raclin had, and she subsequently assumed the leadership of the 1st Source Corporation and 1st Source Bank of South Bend, Indiana, which now have assets of over $1.57 billion.

Her leadership has extended deep into the community, from her volunteer roots in the Junior League of South Bend. She founded the North Central Indiana Planned Parenthood, she's been on the United Way of America and United Way International Boards, and she's been a trustee for seven academic institutions, including the University of Notre Dame (where she co-chaired the $150 million fund drive).

CAROL HAMPTON RASCO

Junior League members throughout the country are constantly looking for ways to influence public policy. Carol Hampton Rasco, member of the Junior league of Lit-

tle Rock, Arkansas, has found the best way imaginable. She is Assistant to the President for Domestic Policy.

Starting as an elementary school teacher, she rose to become the Liaison to Human Services and Health Agencies in Arkansas for Governor Bill Clinton, and then became his Executive Assistant for Governmental Operations. The rest, as they say, is history, and when Clinton moved to the White House, so did Rasco.

A good bit of her volunteer work—not surprisingly—is in the area of advocacy. She served on the Little Rock Public School Special Education Advisory Committee, and the Arkansas Coalition for the Handicapped, and she organized the Little Rock Municipal Court's Volunteers in Probation.

ANN C. RING

Ann C. Ring has a truly extensive volunteer history. From a host of chairmanships in the Junior League of Winston-Salem, North Carolina, including service as its president, to almost every imaginable job at her United Methodist Church, with a comprehensive roster of board and committee positions in between, she has served her community ably. There are, however, several areas in which she shines.

Ring was the first woman given the privilege in Winston-Salem of chairing the United Way; she also chaired a capital campaign to build the Horizons Residential Care Facility, a long-term-care facility housing profoundly and multi-handicapped children.

As chair of the board of trustees of Old Salem, Inc., she had the opportunity to help develop African-American history as it relates to Old Salem and the Moravians who settled it. Ring is leading the effort to restore one of the oldest existing black churches in America.

MARY R. RIPLEY

Mary R. Ripley has been a "professional volunteer" all her life, and has managed to expand upon her local volunteer jobs (including the presidency of the Junior League

of Los Angeles) into national and even global positions. She is a founder and first president of International Association for Volunteer Effort, which began in 1970 with 10 countries and 120 representatives, and in 1994 had 63 countries and 700 representatives at its international conference in Tokyo. She was the first nonprofessional woman president of the National Conference of Social Welfare, and the only woman serving on the Executive Committee of the Independent Sector.

Among the more than fifty volunteer positions she has held, Planned Parenthood is one of her primary interests; not only has she served as president of the Los Angeles affiliate, she has traveled extensively for the organization, observing family planning efforts worldwide.

DOROTHY "BILL" ROBERTSON

Dorothy "Bill" Robertson, a 92-year-old founder and past president of the Junior League of Yakima, Washington, is one of those legendary characters who are famous in volunteer lore.

A noted philanthropist, Robertson has spent a large part of her life underwriting fundraisers in Yakima, including the Yakima Valley Memorial Hospital Follies, the Rotary International's Polio Plus project for 7,000 immunizations, the Memorial Hospital Tiny Tim Fund, and Heritage College.

It is her public presence for which she is best known. The public television station always made more money on pledge nights if Robertson was the spokesperson. She was always onstage in community theater productions, and she crowned her performing career in 1992 at age 89. In the finale for the *Hospital Follies* (which she underwrote), she descended from a height of forty feet on a swing from the rafters of the Italianate Capitol Theatre, bringing the crowd of 1,600 to its feet.

JULIET C. ROWLAND

As the Association of Junior Leagues board vice chairman, Juliet C. Rowland (of the

Junior League of Harrisburg, Pennsylvania) was responsible for national program development, public policy activities, and membership development. Some of the programs that grew up under her tenure include Project LEAD, a national model of youth leadership, and the Teen Outreach Program (TOP), which increases self-esteem of high school students.

Under her direction, AJL collaborated with other national organizations such as the Children's Defense Fund to advance understanding of children's issues.

Rowland testified before several Congressional committees on issues affecting women and children; she assisted in preparing organizations in the United States and England to become new Junior Leagues; and she conducted membership diversity workshops for Leagues across the country.

VIRGINIA H. "GINA" RUGELEY

After a year as president of the Junior League of Charleston, West Virginia, and another year as an Association of Junior Leagues Area II Council member, Virginia H. "Gina" Rugeley created the position of training chairman for her League and launched herself into a career. Along with a League friend, she created "Training Dynamics," marketing training classes to volunteer and nonprofit organizations as well as small businesses.

She has been responsible for leading board retreats, teaching workshops for staff and volunteers, taking agencies through the long-range planning process, helping non-profits to restructure, as well as writing and revising by-laws for a wide range of non-profit organizations.

KATHY SAWYER

Kathy Sawyer remembers her introduction to the Junior League of Montgomery, Alabama. "I was the first African-American member," she says, "and the reception presenting our provisional group was quite interesting and funny, as many members appeared startled and disbelieving." She went on to become one of the most valued

members, chairing the Future Planning committee and assisting in the reestablishment of Camp Sunshine which serves hundreds of children living in public housing communities by providing year-round programs.

A social worker and Director of Advocacy Services for the Alabama Department of Mental Health and Mental Retardation, Sawyer was named Social Worker of the year for the Montgomery chapter in 1993.

AUDREY LINCOURT SCHIEBLER

In 1975, Audrey Schiebler, a past president of the Junior League of Gainesville, Florida, was one of those chosen to conduct the Association of Junior Leagues Child Advocacy Survey. She was assigned to the area of child abuse and neglect, which so captured her that it became the focus of all her subsequent voluntary efforts. "It was through the education and training in the area of child abuse," she recounts, "that I was capable of taking a leadership role in the development of many programs for children. I was fortunate to be part of the team that developed the first statewide Guardian ad litem program in the country."

Most of her recent volunteer efforts reflect this focus on children such as membership on the boards of the National Committee for the Prevention of Child Abuse, the National Association of Council for Children, and the Ronald McDonald House.

MINOR MICKEL SHAW

As president of the Junior League of Greenville, South Carolina, Minor Mickel Shaw saw her position as giving her the opportunity to influence both League members and the community.

Shaw has gone on to make an impact in several important areas in Greenville. She was the founding chairman of the Roper Mountain Science Center Association, helping develop the Science Center as a valuable resource for the Greenville community.

Just a few of her varied volunteer positions are: chair of the United Way of

Greenville, trustee of the South Carolina Governor's School for the Arts, trustee of Wofford College, trustee of the Daniel-Mickel Foundation, and chair-elect of the Independent Colleges and Universities of South Carolina.

CHARLENE SHELTON

A keen interest in the welfare of teenagers is Charlene Shelton's hallmark. Professionally, she is a teaching assistant at Dobbyns-Bennett Alternative School for at-risk high school students in Kingsport, Tennessee. As past president of the Girls Incorporated Board of Directors, she has been given the Girls Incorporated Outstanding Service Award, the Girls Incorporated Region IV Volunteer of the Year Award, and the Woman of Excellence Girls Incorporated Award.

Her biggest project began when she took on the chairmanship of a task force for the Junior League of Kingsport. There was interest in a teen center, and Shelton's League task force studied the feasibility of such a center; it became a board-based community coalition, and ultimately Shelton found herself as president of the Board of Directors of Rascals Teen Center, Inc.

BETH SHORTT

It was an almost logical jump for Beth Shortt from president of the Junior League of Oklahoma City to the board of directors of the Association of Junior Leagues International to the executive director of Leadership Oklahoma City. Her Junior League skills have served her well. "I would not be the executive director for Leadership Oklahoma City if I had not been President of the Junior League of Oklahoma City."

She notes with affection the essence of the League: "Women do change the world through the Junior League," she says. "Sometimes the world of a lonely child in pain, sometimes the world of the juvenile court system, sometimes the world of the inadequately immunized children throughout the U.S. Women in the Junior League improve their own lives while improving the lives of others."

LISA WALD STONE

Lisa Wald Stone tells this story about her experience in helping start chapter of Habitat for Humanity in Springfield, Illinois, and it carries over to her experiences while serving as president of the Junior League of Springfield, or working for the Sojourn Women's Center, or any of the numerous community efforts she's spearheaded. "As one of a few Jews on a board of Christians," she recounts, "I enabled the board of Habitat for Humanity to think ecumentically in all its publicity, prayers, fundraising. I taught these friends about the Jewish value of 'Tikkun Olam,' repairing God's world as God's partner, which was my ra tionale for my involvement. By the same token, I learned a great deal from my close association with Christians who spoke at every board meeting from their personal mission to help the poor because of Christ's example and call to them."

MARGARET A. TALBURTT

Margaret A. Talburtt's dissertation for her Ph.D. in 1976 was entitled "Promoting Creative Risk-Taking in Women." It's not at all surprising, therefore, that she would go on to join the Junior Service League, shepherd her group into affiliation with the Association of Junior Leagues International as the Junior League of Ann Arbor, Michigan, and go on to lead the League as president. She has a career as an educator, teaching at the University of Michigan, but she also pursues her career as a community volunteer, devoting time to the Affordable Housing Network, the Ann Arbor Area Community Foundation, Ann Arbor area 2000, the Museum of Art at the University of Michigan, and the Wild Swan Theater.

BETSY TRIPLETT-HURT

A former television news reporter and news director, Betsy Triplett-Hurt has used all her journalism and public relations skills in her work in the Junior League of Odessa, Texas, and in statewide volunteer work. For the League, she chaired the Community Research and Public Affairs commit-tees, was the community vice president, and was the co-chair to write the new League cookbook.

In 1993, Governor Ann Richards appointed Triplett-Hurt to the Texas Board of Health. This six-member board oversees the Texas Department of Health and its 4,500 employees, 90 programs, and $7 billion budget.

She is also a member of the Texas Lyceum Association, a statewide think tank of 96 men and women who meet quarterly to discuss issues facing Texas. She just completed her term as president of the Odessa Chamber of Commerce, the first female president in the Chamber's 56-year history.

MARTHA S. VANDERVOORT

Martha S. Vandervoort was responsible for the application and assisted in the ultimate acceptance of her area's service organization into the Association of Junior Leagues International. Her efforts, along with many other women's, brought about the Junior League of Anniston/Calhoun, Alabama. She has served as the League's first president.

A counselor by profession, Vandervoort's choice of volunteer jobs displays her compassion and concern for her community. These include: the Soup Bowl, Meals on Wheels, the Community Enabler, and the Interfaith Counseling Center. But it is Habitat for Humanity which has captured her heart and she marks as one of her greatest achievements helping to bring Habitat to Calhoun County.

KATE B. WEBSTER

A former president of the Junior League of Seattle, Kate B. Webster has a talent for putting together corporate/nonprofit partnerships, and for bringing complementary agencies together.

"As chairman of Seattle's Children's Hospital and Medical Center Board," she says, "I was a leader in developing the 1974 affiliation between Children's Hospital and the University of Washington School of Medicine." She's been on numerous boards and has won a number of awards, including the Matrix Award from Women in Com-munications, the Paul Harris Rotary recognition, the Smith College Medal, and the Junior League of Seattle Dorothy Stimson Bullitt Community Service Award.

CAROL WELSH

As chair of the Junior League of Palo Alto's Homeless Task Force, Carol Welsh helped to launch one of the JLPA's most ambitious projects, Day Break, a shelter for homeless teenagers. When created, Day Break Shelter was the only homeless youth shelter in a suburban setting in the United States. Welsh was instrumental in designing the program structure, meeting with community agencies to enlist their support, and obtaining funding for the shelter. She successfully developed resources and marketed the issues of homeless youth and youth in crisis in many important ways. She convinced California Junior Leagues to support a statewide Runaway Hotline and facilitated a statewide roundtable on youth violence prevention. As a volunteer member of the California Child Youth and Family Coalition Board, she has gained access to state legislators for the purpose of advocating for youth-related issues.

RUTH ANDERSON WHEELER

One of the charter members and the second president of the Junior League of Tacoma, Washington, the late Ruth Anderson Wheeler left her indelible mark upon the community's volunteer sector. One of the League's highest awards is the Ruth Wheeler Annual Sustainer of the Year Award, and current League members speak to the foundations she directed, community boards she chaired, and service organizations she guided.

Some friends in Tacoma had these comments about her rich volunteer life: "There is no woman in our community today, or even in the past, who was more committed and dedicated to the principles and purpose of the Junior League of Tacoma."

"Ruth Wheeler was steadfast in her convictions and unrelenting in her devotion to a cause."

ELIZABETH IRA WILLIAMS

"The best description of what I have learned from the Junior League of Jacksonville," says Elizabeth Ira Williams, "came to me when I was asked to be the keynote speaker for the Health and Rehabilitative Services Volunteer Appreciation Ceremony. I explained that right out of college, my résumé was one and one-half pages of education and employment experience and about five lines of volunteer experience. When I decided to enter the job market again over ten years later, my résumé was quite different. There were approximately ten lines of education and work experience, and one and one-half pages of volunteer experience." That second résumé helped her snag a job as the county coordinator for Guardian Ad Litem.

Her crowning achievement was the implementation of Quigley House, a shelter for battered women and their children.

GAYLE EDLUND WILSON

"As the First Lady of California, I am a full-time volunteer," says Gayle Edlund Wilson, a former president of the Junior League of San Diego. "I've devoted my energies primarily to ensuring that the children of California have the best possible start in life. I am the State's spokesperson for BabyCal, which encourages prenatal care and a healthy lifestyle for pregnant women. Also through Healthy Star, I work with prevention and early intervention programs for children and families in California. I have found that by my focusing on these issues, the level of visibility has been raised, funding has been put into these programs, and lives have been changed because of it."

Wilson credits her fifteen years in the Junior League with giving her important skills she uses now.

JANICE WOODS WINDLE

Janice Woods Windle found her main career through her League newsletter. "I read about a project of the Junior League of El Paso to form a community founda- tion, and at first I just wanted to find out more about it," she says. "Then I applied to be president of the new organization." She got that job in 1977, and she has led the El Paso Community Foundation as it has grown into a philanthropy backed by a permanent endowment of $45 million. Her peers recognized her accomplishments when they recently elected her vice chairman of the Council on Foundations, the international association of 3,000 grant-making institutions.

KATRINA MOULTON WOLLENBERG

Katrina Moulton Wollenberg, former president of the Junior League of Palo Alto•Mid-Peninsula, launched Christmas in April in her area with the support of the Junior League of Palo Alto•Mid-Peninsula. "Christmas in April," she says, "is the only organization to offer home rehabilitation services to low-income families at no charge so that they may live in warmth, safety and independence. Since 1990, more than 8,800 volunteers have renovated 215 homes and 25 community facilities in our community. The program beneficiaries have reported that 40 percent of their neighbors have begun to fix up their homes."

In February of 1995, Wollenberg became chairman of the Board of Christmas in April USA, the national organization with 152 affiliates in 44 states. Public speaking, financial planning, volunteer management, board development, facilitating and strategic planning have been the Junior League skills she points to as laying the foundation for her national volunteer work.

MARY BRENT WRIGHT

Mary Brent Wright is probably the resident expert on fundraising events in Raleigh, North Carolina. When she was president of the Junior League of Raleigh, the League held three major fundraisers within a ten-week period which also included the holiday season. "We are the only League in the world," she explains, "to sponsor a governor's Inaugural Ball." Once the election was over in November, the League sprang into action to organize the January ball. The stress was worth it, with the Ju- nior League raising $300,000 for community projects.

Wright has been a member of the Area III Council of the Junior League, and has also served as an Association of Junior Leagues International Director.

LYNN HARDY YEAKEL

Outraged at the treatment Anita Hill received at the 1991 Judiciary Committee session in the U.S. Senate, Lynn Hardy Yeakel decided to convert her anger to action and, without any previous campaign experience, announced her decision to run for the U.S. Senate. She went on to win a landslide upset victory over the party-endorsed candidate in the primary, and then lost narrowly in the general election to powerful incumbent Arlen Specter, a 25-year political figure who outspent her two to one.

That theme had appeared years before, when Yeakel was president of the Junior League of Philadelphia. "I led Junior League members into a wide range of community groups and activities," she says, "always working to improve the lives of others and to change things that need changing."

Currently, Yeakel serves as regional director of the U.S. Department of Health and Human Services.

JOYCE YOUNG

Joyce Young was admitted to the Junior League of Dayton, Ohio, in 1959. She was the chair of several committees, was chair of the Ohio State Public Affairs Committee, and then was president of the Dayton League. Instead of settling down after her presidency, her life picked up momentum and strength.

She received her B.A. degree from Wright State University in 1975, the year in which she was awarded the National Association of Social Workers Award for outstanding service in the area of human services.

Young has the distinction of being founding president of the board of Miami Valley Child Development Centers, Inc., the first Head Start agency in Montgomery County.

INDEX

Caribe, 157
dill, 159
Poulet au citron, 236
Pound cake
apricot brandy, 317
chocolate, 325
coconut, 313
sour cream, no-fault, 311
three-flavor, 311
Praline(s)
cheesecake with pecan sauce, 329
creamy, 364
and Kahlúa brownies, 302
pie, frozen, 347
pie shell, mocha chiffon pie in, 350
pumpkin pie, 345
Prawns, dilled grilled, 25
Prawns, seasoned, 43
Pretty green salad, a, 58
Pretzels, soft, 268
Prize-winning pumpkin cheesecake, 328
Prosciutto
asparagus wrapped in, 5
chicken with cheese and, 234
pinwheels, puff pastry, 32
Provolone spinach soup, 100
Pudding
bread, with Cognac sauce, 361
lemon, 360
spinach, St. Anthony Hotel's famous, 132
Puff pastry, tomato dill soup in, 101
Puff pastry prosciutto pinwheels, 32
Puffs, four-cheese, 18
Pumpkin
bread, harvest loaf, 266
bread, spice, 266
cheesecake, prize-winning, 328
-cream cheese roll, 312
pie, ice cream, 345
pie, praline, 345
puff pancakes, 289
soup
Bayou bisque, 95
cold purée of, 95
wild rice, 95
Punch
champagne, 53
hot spiced percolator, 50
milk, Al's holiday, 54
Orchid Island sea-breeze, 54
party, watermelon, 50

Quail, Burgundy, 254
Quail, smothered, 255
Quiche, Savannah, 35

Quiche, smoked salmon, 204
Quick Sally Lunn, 277

Raisin bread, buttermilk, 271
Raisins, golden, wild rice medley with toasted pine nuts, dried apricots, and, 147
Raspberry
bars, 305
chocolate truffles, 365
coulis, chocolate pâté with crème anglaise and, 335
cream cheese coffee cake, 286
ginger sauce, flourless Grand Marnier cake with, 336
peach cobbler, 357
purée, chilled zabaglione with, 354
purée, chocolate almond terrine with, 334
-rhubarb pie, 340
squares, 358
Rave review baked beans, 140
Real Cajun red beans and rice, 139
Red beans
and rice, 182
Louisiana, 116
real Cajun, 139
South Louisiana, 139
Red bell pepper purée, vegetable timbales with, 126
Red bell pepper shrimp, 226
Red bell pepper soup, 99
Redfish special, 196
Red sauce, chicken enchiladas in, 249
Red snapper. See also Snapper
seviche, 41
and toasted pecan butter, 195
Veracruz, 194
Red wine. See Wine, red
Refried beans, in mucho gusto dip, 3
Refrigerator cookies, oatmeal pecan, 308
Refrigerator rolls, bran, 280
Refrigerator rolls, light-as-a-feather, 279
Rhubarb bread, 261
Rhubarb-raspberry pie, 340
Rice
brown, and black-eyed pea salad, spicy, 75
dirty, 147
Indienne, 146
nutty, 145
pilaf, pecan, 145
pilaf with minced vegetables, 146
red, Savannah, 147
red beans and, 182

Louisiana, 116
real Cajun, 139
risotto, morel and asparagus, 39
salad, Indonesian, 76
Rich mint brownies, 299
Risotto, morel and asparagus, 39
Roast barbecue, 157
Roast beef salad with pesto vinaigrette, 90
Roast lamb with two sauces, 166
Roast veal Dijon, 186
Roast wild goose, 257
Roll, chocolate, Snow White, 323
Roll, pumpkin-cream cheese, 312
Rolls. See also Buns
buttery biscuit, 277
cinnamon, 282
the Dempster, 279
icebox, potato, 281
orange, 282
refrigerator, bran, 280
refrigerator, light-as-a-feather, 279
sausage, 32
sour cream, Leta's, 280
Romaine and orange toss, 59
Romaine toss, crunchy, 60
Rosemary, lamb noisettes with, 166
Rum butter sauce, chocolate cake with, 326
Rum caramel sauce, hot, apple cake with, 315
Rye bread, grandmother's Swedish, 272

Saffron shrimp, 220
Saffron vinaigrette, warm scallop salad with, 81
St. Anthony Hotel's famous spinach pudding, 132
St. Timothy's coffee cake, 287
Salad(s), 57–90
Salad
asparagus, marinated, 68
asparagus with pecans, cold, 67
beef
cold, 88
roast, with pesto vinaigrette, 90
steak supper, 89
wild rice and, Minnesota, 90
beet, zesty, 68
berry summer, 80
broccoli, I, 69
broccoli, II, 69
celery root, 66
center stage, 61
"Charlie the tuna," 81
chicken